Sociology of Law

Sociology of Law

FOURTH EDITION

Dragan Milovanovic

Professor Emeritus, Justice Studies

Northeastern Illinois University

Carolina Academic Press

Durham, North Carolina

Library of Congress Cataloging-in-Publication Data

Names: Milovanovic, Dragan, 1948- author. | Milovanovic, Dragan, 1948-
Primer in the sociology of law.
Title: Sociology of law / Dragan Milovanovic.
Description: Fourth edition. | Durham, North Carolina : Carolina Academic
Press, LLC, [2022] | Includes bibliographical references.
Identifiers: LCCN 2022003851 (print) | LCCN 2022003852 (ebook) | ISBN
9781611638820 (paperback) | ISBN 9781531000080 (ebook)
Subjects: LCSH: Sociological jurisprudence.
Classification: LCC K370 .M55 2022 (print) | LCC K370 (ebook) | DDC
340/.115--dc23/eng/20220429
LC record available at https://lccn.loc.gov/2022003851
LC ebook record available at https://lccn.loc.gov/2022003852

Carolina Academic Press
700 Kent Street
Durham, North Carolina 27701
(919) 489-7486
www.cap-press.com

Printed in the United States of America

Contents

Preface to the Fourth Edition

The fourth edition of *Sociology of Law* has been greatly revised. Many new developments in the field have necessitated a wider framework and significant updating. I have benefited from teaching a similarly titled course at least a dozen times since the third edition in 2003. Student feedback has been useful in revising the present edition. The outside reviewers of the book proposal were also quite helpful in rethinking content for inclusion. The book has been expanded significantly, without loosing the overall intent of introducing students to sociology of law. Researchers can also use it for reference material. General interest readers will find it illuminating reading. It can also be adopted for law school courses seeking to provide a more sociological understanding of law. The field continues to grow and is witnessing an increasingly greater readership. The book makes no claims to be exhaustive. It offers some basic understandings in the field, orientations, and tools for more critical inquiry. The earlier chapters in Part 1, "Orientations and Classical Foundations for Sociology of Law" (Chapters 1–5), orient the reader to the field. They are meant to be read sequentially, building a base from which to engage the second part of the book. Part 2, "Perspective in the Sociology of Law," has greatly expanded from four chapters to seven. Many topics are provocative. They are meant for engagement, for constructive critical reading. Review questions have been added to each chapter to provide a review and an opportunity for application of the material covered. Sociology of law is a multidisciplinary field that necessitates discussion at multiple, interconnected levels. The approach distinguishes itself from law school education in that law school is more singular preparing the student to practice law. Sociology of law looks at the historical development of particular forms of law, their functions, their origination, forms of reasoning, their inclusions and exclusions in a political economy. It offers tools and concepts with which to rethink law, how it can be otherwise, how it can be more inclusive, how it can be more just.

Dragan Milovanovic
April 10, 2022

Acknowledgments

Books don't materialize out of a vacuum. Many people are involved in their inspiration and production. I owe many thanks and gratitude to Joyce Kelly who has always been supportive and encouraging, often with critically constructive thoughts. Her assistance in preparation of the manuscript and suggestions were invaluable. To the staff at Carolina Academic Press, I am greatly appreciative for making the book an actuality. Beth Hall, editor at Carolina Academic Press, was always unwavering in her support for the project. Beth is always a pleasure to work with and more than an author could possibly ask for as the editor of a book. Thanks also to Kathleen Soriano-Taylor, book designer at Carolina Academic Press, for her meticulous and expeditious work on this project. Graeme Newman, my dissertation chairperson for the Ph.D. at SUNY, Albany, was the inspiration for doing the original book and procuring the initial book contract. The fourth edition has grown significantly from its inception. Thanks also to Bruce Arrigo, Stuart Henry, Richard Quinney, and Herman ("Hi") Schwendinger, and, in remembrance, Julia Schwendinger. I have always drawn much inspiration from the early to current dialogs with them, and their support. And this book acknowledges those in struggle, in trying to re-make the world for all in which to live peacefully, supportively, collectively, and not in stasis, but a continuous becoming where differences and commonalities can co-exist. Their struggles for justice and a responsive, more inclusive law continue to make a difference.

Sociology of Law

Introduction

To study law is to study the evolving structures of society in a developing political economy. In addressing the question, "What is law?", one responds to the question of how society is organized. In this introductory text, our goal is to introduce the reader to some of the dominant thought in Western Society on the subject of the sociology of law. This is not to downplay the significance of non-Western Society, but more a concern with not trying to do too much in too little space. A comparative sociology of law certainly is important. Ours is an introductory text. The focus is to acquaint the reader with some key themes in the literature, the basis of which may stimulate the reader for more specialized follow-up research. It provides overviews of some of the most compelling theoretical works on the subject. And, as an introduction, it presents the contours of the discipline. Our goal in our exposition is to be primarily descriptive and expository in focus. Critical comparisons will only be done in passing and they are therefore of secondary concern. This would certainly be the next stage after the student has acquainted themself somewhat with the literature.

The theorists and perspectives that have been chosen are based on their centrality in current trends in the sociology of law. Because this is an introductory text, many less central theories relating to the diverse facets of law have been necessarily excluded. Nor have we embarked on a lengthy history of the sociology of law. Empirical studies have also been avoided in favor of concentrating on the key thoughts in a discipline that is still in its infancy. One of the key issues is to establish what falls within the sociology of law, and what does not.

Accordingly, we will clarify the difference between the traditional legal science ("jurisprudence") and a sociology of law. Legal science, taught in law school, and practiced in the courts is a dogmatic approach that mostly remains within laws that are pregiven (internal critique). Sociology of law extends analysis to an outsider critique, (external critique), stressing the historical, political, ideological, and economic factors that are involved in law, both in its formulation and in its practice. As we will see, there are diverse orientations in doing a sociology of laws.

The structure of the book is in two parts. Part 1, "Orientations and Classical Foundations for a Sociology of Law," is a general introduction to key concepts in the discipline as well as founding sociologists of law. Part 2, "Perspectives in the Sociology of Law," includes key perspectives in the sociology of law.

Part 1, "Orientations and Classical Foundations for a Sociology of Law", includes five chapters. The first two chapters acquaint the reader with the field of sociology of law. They introduce key concepts, definitions, and approaches in more sociologically-centered studies of law. The next three chapters introduce the work of Emile Durkheim, Max Weber, and Karl Marx, who are generally recognized as founding contributors to a sociology of law. Most subsequent work in the field engages these works, be it in a critically constructive manner. Their views, particularly being key formative thinkers in the field of sociology, are examined for their contributions to law. We will be particularly concerned with their views concerning the development of society, the form of law and legal thought, the juridic subject (the so-called "reasonable man in law"), the contract, the idea of private property rights, and the various functions of law. Each theorist presents a different explanation for how distinct forms of law and contracts develop. What is the driving force for the development of particular forms of law? Are social developments directly associated with particular forms of law? Is law equivalent to justice? What functions beyond facilitative are operative? Is law simply reflections of powerful groups?

Much comparison amongst the three scholars can and should be undertaken. Even though their work appeared over 100 years ago, this body of knowledge remains most relevant in sensitizing the interested researcher to key parameters and for stimulating further investigation, including case studies of particular societies. An understanding of the classical theorists provides us foundations for understanding emerging perspectives in the sociology of law. Let us provide more details for each chapter.

Chapter 1, "The Discipline of Sociology of Law," prepares the reader for more substantive discussions that follow. Entering the study of sociology of law means familiarizing oneself with the contours of the field. We review the early contributions to the developing field. Our work focuses on Western forms of law that is often characterized as formal rational, or liberal legalism. We present various other legal systems (Islamic, Socialist, Customary, Slavery and Colonizers law). A distinction between jurisprudence (legal science) and sociology of law is offered. In later chapters we also recognize an "in-betweener," sociological jurisprudence. Defining law is presented, noting various views. The difference between consensus and conflict perspectives is developed, noting how each competes with the other in the study of law. The relationship between law and justice is discussed. We note they are not necessarily the same thing. We conclude with clarification of often-used concepts in law.

Chapter 2, "Law in Action," looks at law's development and how law is activated, how it is practiced. This chapter introduces the functions of law (facilitative, ideological, repressive, constitutive), noting how they often appear in combination with perhaps one salient. We find that law is a complex term in its functioning. We present a model for the relationship between law and the fulfillment of social values. It locates "ideal types" of legal systems and how they function. It is merely a simplified model to sensitize us to how law enhances or diminishes the realization of social values. We include a summary of law and the rise of the legal profession, noting the early development of lawyers in ancient times through the middle-ages, to the present, and particularly addressing what interests they serve. Relatedly, we discuss the rise of law schools and their possible connection with well-to-do interest groups. We conclude the chapter with discussion concerning the relationship between law, social movements and social change, examining how social movements impact the formation of law and how law in turn impacts the movements. Does social change cause change in law? Or, does law affect social change? Or, does the arrow go both ways?

Chapter 3, "Durkheim: Toward a Systematic Sociology of Law," begins our investigation into the three key founding figures of a sociology of law. We begin with Emile Durkheim. Durkheim's work covers the spontaneous evolution of society and the nature of solidarity that appears with it. He includes the "abnormal forms" of the evolution of society. He follows with what type of laws, contracts, and legal thought are associated with each form of society. He notes how "external" inequalities affect the spontaneous development of society, especially played out in forms and substance of contracts. He offers the conditions for a just contract that revolves on the exchange of social value. His work underscores the importance of examining law in social development.

Chapter 4, "Max Weber: Law in Economy and Society," concerns the systematic work of Max Weber in developing a sociology of law. Though his work is often contrasted to the work of Karl Marx, we note some convergences. He investigates the relationship of capitalism to forms of law, noting that the economy by itself is not an exclusive cause in the rise of a form of law, but that a number of factors in combination must be investigated in determining the cause. With the emergence of capitalism, the juridic subject appeared, the abstract bearer of rights. He provides a model of different forms of law and their connectedness to legal thought. Capitalism, he informs us, is associated with formal rational law. Formalism, as it is often called, is about the abstract system of laws providing a complete mechanism for facilitating transactions, and within which conflicts can be resolved. A particular way of reasoning, deductive logic and syllogistic reasoning, is at center of appropriate decision-making in formal rationality. Weber also notes other form of law, such as substantive rationality, where external principles seek to enter the dominant system of law. Those in struggle in overcoming forms of oppression seek to introduce their principles of justice into law. An "insoluble conflict" persists between these two forms of law. Weber, like Durkheim, addresses the wherewithal of the contract. He notes, apart from the facilitative functions of law, repressive and ideological functions can exist. Weber points out how inequalities in property produce imbalances in contractual relations.

Chapter 5, "Karl Marx: Law in Socio-Political Economy," concerns the critical work of Karl Marx as it relates to law. Unlike Weber and Durkheim, Marx did not provide us with a systematic statement on law. Rather, interested readers have had to mine his work for various passages that address law. Accordingly, we witness various Marxist perspectives. The most noted difference pointed out is the difference between instrumental Marxism and structural Marxism. He provides us with a model of how to study society and law, the base-superstructure metaphor. There are various "modes of production" that are identified, each connected with a particular form of society and associated with a system of laws and rights. Law, in Marxism, has repressive and ideological functions, since it is associated with capital logic where inequalities and acute competition drives economic development. The "motor" for social change is dialectical materialism, the development of contradictory forces and their resolutions. In late capitalism, Marx argues, the contradictions will reach the most acute form leading to a revolutionary change to "the higher forms" where law and the state apparatus will "wither away." Pashukanis has been a key interpreter of Marxist law. His work indicating the similar development of commodity fetishism and legal fetishism is pivotal in understanding the contract, as well as the development of a legal subject endowed with abstract rights. Formal equality, he tells us, is often a myth, a legitimizing principle, disguising substantive inequalities.

Part 2, "Perspectives in the Sociology of Law," examines some contemporary perspectives in the development of a sociology of law. We include seven chapters. They offer a diverse range of topics. We first review traditional legal science (jurisprudence) as taught in law schools and practiced. Dean Langdell, we shall see, provided a model of education in the late 1800s that remains a key orientation in learning law. Law can be studied, he tells us, like other "hard" sciences, in the laboratories; here, the student of law studies case law in the law library The early 1900s to 1940s witnessed alternative, more critical and pragmatic orientations to the study of law. Sociological jurisprudence and legal realists, spearheaded by such figures as Rosco Pound introduced sociological principles in investigating law-in-action. In the 1970s, after a lull from the 1940s on, this initial momentum was resurrected and generated the critical legal studies movement (CLS). This movement questioned many of the assumptions of legal science, pointing out repressive functions that follow system-generated inequalities and differentials in power. Many offsprings, we shall see, emerged, and continue to emerge, such as critical race theory and critical feminist law as well as approaches that were focused on Latinx, queer theory, and aboriginal studies. We also witness the development of a structural functionalist perspective that argues for the interconnectedness of law and society, with law being primarily a facilitator. Since narratives, story-telling, is much a part of law, we include two chapters, one on semiotics and law and the other on a socio-legal semiotics as foci in a sociology of law. Our last two chapters offer suggestions for a paradigm change in law, the first to a postmodern law, the second to a post postmodern law. Let us provide a bit more detail for each of the seven chapters included in Part 2.

Chapter 6, "Sociological Jurisprudence and Critical Legal Studies: The First Wave," moves away from legal science conceptualized most forcefully in the later 1800s by Dean Christopher Langdell, toward a sociological jurisprudence orientation. Roscoe Pound, Karl Llewellyn, Jerome Frank, Oliver Wendell Holmes and Benjamin Cardozo questioned the established study and practice of law. They question how rules are invoked and applied, and how facts were established in law. The chapter focuses on: sociological jurisprudence (1900–1920), developed as a more sociological orientation within the legal profession itself; legal realism (1920–1940), which studied law in action indicating how what is on the books often differs in practice; and the critical legal studies (CLS) movement, that emerged in the 1970s and 1980s, which brought more critical examination of law, the legal profession, and law schools. Many adherents were based at prestigious law schools such as Harvard University Law School. The chapter provides some examples of substantive issues addressed by the CLS movement, including: law school as preparation for hierarchy; labor relations law; anti-discrimination law; contract law; criminal law; tort law; and woman's subordination. CLS addressed the ideological and repressive functions of law. The chapter closes by presenting the strategy of deconstruction in law as well as strategies for reconstruction. The CLS was not without its critics. We list some more notable ones. The chapter highlights the movement from a more dogmatic legal science to an approach incorporating sociological principles in the study of law. There is no systematic attempt, however, in developing a unitary sociology of law. Although Marx was often invoked, the approach drew from various critical writers. This body of literature was to be inspirational for the second wave of the mid-1980s onward.

In Chapter 7, "Critical Approaches in Law: Spawnings, The Second Wave," we include some of the offsprings of CLS: feminist jurisprudence (fem-crits), critical race theory (CRT); Latinx theory (Lat-Crits); Queer theory; LGBTQA, sometimes LGBTQIA; Asian-American Crits; and Tribal-Crits. Sometimes these critical thinkers were collectively referred to as "crits." The approaches in Chapter 7 are in-betweeners, between legal science and sociology of law. The chapter includes discussion of intersectionality, how gender, sexual orientation, race, ethnicity and class intersect in producing vulnerabilities in law. Included is an application of intersectionality in admissions programs, noting the conflicts that are emerging among the different identity groups. We also address intersectionalities and commonalities. Formal equality before the law and its denial is often a central concern. Other concepts discussed are racialization, microaggressions, rule- and fact-skepticism, counter storytelling, standpoint epistemology and interest convergence. We note how the movement in law from sociological jurisprudence, to legal realist, to critical legal studies has provided the basis for much further differentiated and focused inquiry in the sociology of law. Many scholars in this tradition are based in law schools. As with approaches discussed in Chapter 6, these approaches do not seek to develop a full-fledged sociology of law. They are in-betweeners, between legal science and a sociology of law. They are much more concerned, however, with the inclusion of sociological principles than only dogmatic legal science.

Chapter 8, "Structural Functionalism, Autopoiesis and the Behavior of Law," includes approaches that are more fully focused on a sociology of law. We examine the structural functionalism of Talcott Parsons, Adam Podgorecki, and Niklas Luhmann which conceive sociological studies in terms of the inter-relatedness of institutions. Law was seen as mostly facilitative. It functions to provide a framework where people and firms can accurately plan their activities. We include autopoiesis and law, focusing on two key exponents, Guenther Teubner and Niklas Luhmann, an approach that draws an analogy with biological systems noting how all things recursively develop. The notion of structural coupling is explicated noting the interconnections of law with external factors and how the latter undergo translation into legal categories. The "behavior of law" thesis by Donald Black is developed. He presents specific propositions of how law "behaves." It is said to behave in predictable, patterned ways, and in the process, defining law breakers, the definition of crime, the severity of crime, identity of the deviant, social reality and generating statistics that are its support. Related to this, we explicate Black's the "sociology of the case," where he demonstrates how his thesis can be applied to the practice of law ("sociological litigation").

Chapter 9, "Semiotics and Law," addresses how law-in-action is based on storytelling, narratives and speech acts. Words employed (signifiers) take on specific meaning in law. Consider such concepts as "person," "life," "liberty," "property," "duress," "intent," "willingly," "insanity," "entrapment," etc. Accordingly, this chapter reviews several prominent semioticians for their contributions. We include the works of C.S. Peirce, Ferdinand de Saussure, Algiradas Greimas, and Louis Hjelmslev. John Austin's work on a performative semiotics follows. His work demonstrates that saying is often doing. This is associated with speech-act theory that focuses on pragmatic encounters in law and how realities are constructed. In legal science, these theorists often remain implicit in legal commentaries. Legal semiotics as a focus in law took on development with the work of Roberta Kevelson (C.S. Peirce) and Bernard Jackson (building on Algiradas Greimas). The use of legal language, we will see, structures what can be said and how realities can be constructed. We note, too, that power differentials exist in acceptable story forms rendering some without a full voice. The second part of the chapter focuses on some expressive forms of legal semiotics, particularly visual, rhetoric, and audial. We are also acquainted with a musical semiosis in law in its developmental stage, e.g., "acoustic jurisprudence", particularly concerned with identity and social construction in law. Semiotics, in other words, can take on forms of expression beyond the written. Cases being litigated increasingly witness multi-expressive forms being employed. Examples of applications of legal semiotics will be included.

Chapter 10, "Socio-Legal Semiotics in Sociology of Law," turns to a more explicit sociological application of semiotic to law. It focuses on legal discourse (language) and its relationship to capabilities of expression, either enhancing or limiting forms. It studies the connectedness of a particular form of language to socio-economic, political structure. Users of legal language use semiotic resources (written, visual, verbal, auditory) in particular contexts which shape meaning construction. We review various forms of socio-legal semiotics, including critical discourse studies and critical socio-legal semiotics, both of which highlight power, domination, ideology and inequalities and their shaping effects in the construction of reality. The chapter studies the resurgence of a materialist Marxist semiotics in the first two decades of the 21st century. This was a response to its earlier subordination in studies of language as an independent force, separate from materialist underpinnings. We include proposals for and commentaries on critical methodologies in socio-legal semiotics. A hypothetical example in the application of a critical methodology is provided. In our final section of the chapter, we turn to a variant of a Marxist material socio-legal semiotics and provide specific examples of its application: how higher courts in their use of "interest-balancing" shape language that then becomes the basis of understanding, including in social movements; how jailhouse lawyers (inmate who have taught themselves law while incarcerated) in constructing realities permissible in court must subordinate genuine issues in order to develop stories that have legal standing; how inmates at parole hearings must struggle in situating themselves in an official language to provide stories that enhance the possibilities of their release; and how activist lawyers before the law find themselves in a dilemma in representing the genuine issues of their clients before the law. For activists as well as jailhouse lawyers the dilemma is whether to argue for a technical defense and further legitimize the law the very structure claimed to be oppressive, or try and stay true to the political agenda and face the sanctioning forces of the judge. We are left with outstanding questions: Are we prisoners of language? Are we constrained in our constructions of reality because of the very legal language we employ? How can dispossessed, disenfranchised people speak in law? How do we produce alternative languages in law? Does the law school educational system cool out would-be activists and reformers? Are they, as Duncan Kennedy has argued, preparing the student for hierarchy?

Chapter 11, "Postmodern Contributions to Sociology of Law," argues that dominant thinking in the sociology law is rooted in "modernism," a development of the Enlightenment. And it is marked by key assumptions as to the nature of agency, society, cause, and change. Postmodern thought fundamentally challenges this tradition in rethinking ontology (what we take as givens). We include the work of Jacques Lacan, a revisionist Freudian, who had much to say about how semiosis exists within the working of the unconscious, the unconscious structured like a language. Jacques Lacan's psychoanalytic semiotics is a key entry point to those wishing to do postmodern analysis in law. Lacan's four discourses indicate how thought and reality construction in law are structured. Lacanian feminist postmodern law is explicated. We summarize key early work of developers. We review postmodernist evolution and its key developers. They include: Friedrich Nietzsche, Michel Foucault, Jacques Derrida, Jean-Francois Lyotard, Richard Rorty, Gilles Deleuze, and Felix Guattari. We also summarize key concepts of complexity (chaos) theory and constitutive theory and show how their work contributes to the development of a sociology of law. Work by Drucilla Cornell and Judith Butler begins to more directly apply this body of work to law. Next, we show the applicability of complexity theory (chaos theory) to law. Our last section of the chapter introduces constitutive law, how agency, structure and law are co-constructed.

Chapter 12, "Post Postmodernist Perspectives," focuses on developments in the early 2000s. This body of knowledge has questioned some of the key points of postmodernists. Many, however, retain selected concepts from postmodern analysis. Both perspectives challenge the central concepts inherited from the Enlightenment period, the basis of classical contemporary thought in the social sciences and in law. These concepts were incorporated and internalized as unexamined assumptions that are the basis of disciplinary developments including law. We witness a number of emerging perspectives: posthumanism, new materialism, sociomateriality, digi-modernism, eco-feminism, and more recently, quantum- and quantum holographic-informed views. Legal materiality is a central concern, which brings material back in, arguing that representational theories (those based on discourse theory), alone, do not suffice. Posthumanist feminists have been especially outspoken against Eurocentric narratives in law. New forms of agency have been theorized, including work concerning non-human forms and nature (green jurisprudence). Do rivers, trees, rain forests, animals, even plants have rights? What are rights? Post postmodernist, however, were quick to jettison a model of the human psychic apparatus. We introduce one possible model, Schema QD. The new sciences (quantum mechanics, quantum holography) are mined for their possible contributions to a sociology of law. The notion of quantum decision-making in law is addressed. The work of Karan Barad and Edwina Taborsky are developed for their contributions to a material-discursive semiotics of law. Our final section of the chapter concerns the development of quantum holographic semiotics of law. It highlights studying and applying the new sciences to how information is encoded, accessed, and decoded. We provide a discussion of the relevance of integrating the notion of "legal assemblage" (the "law machine," Deleuze), semiotics, quantum holography, and agency in furthering a sociology of law, a direction that is in its incipient stages of development.

The organization of the book addresses both the general readers as well as students taking a course in the subject area. The book is self-enclosed and does not depend on an extensive background in sociology. The book is organized to follow a regular in-class semester schedule, with one chapter per week. With twelve substantive chapters, one could be assigned for each week. It is also organized for online courses. Law schools, too, can find this book a useful supplement or as a central text to a seminar course in the sociology of law. At the end of each chapter there are 8–10 review questions. They can also be employed as "discussion questions" for online courses. They are meant for review by engagement with the topics of the respective chapters. Included questions range from analytical to more application, researching, and for class discussions. As an interdisciplinary approach, there are many disciplines from which a sociology of law draws. This book introduces these developments. It is often provocative, encouraging further thought on the subject. Let's begin the exciting journey!

PART 1

Orientations and Classical Foundations for Sociology of Law

1

The Discipline of Sociology of Law

Introduction

There are various orientations in the study of law. Various contributions to the formation of a sociology of law can be offered, even as we limit ourselves primarily to Western law. Numerous questions arise. What is the domain of inquiry? What are the parameters for a disciplinary study in the sociology of law? How does sociology of law differ from legal practitioner's understanding? Does law school training prepare for sociological understandings? What in fact is law? How do we define it? What is the difference between the consensus and conflict approach in law? Why is it even important to distinguish? Is there a difference between law and justice? How are they interconnected? These are central questions in what follows.

We will, accordingly, define contributions to a sociology of law, the parameters of the domain of inquiry, diverse definitions of law, perspective or paradigms employed, difference between law and justice, and forms of law.

Contributions to the Sociology of Law

We pick up the study of the sociology of law beginning with the Enlightenment, and particularly with the rise of the industrial revolution in the West. Certainly, other comprehensive book-length works need to be done or have been done. Other forms of law exist such as Islamic, Socialist, and customary laws. Conspicuously absent in the literature, however, has been a Slavery and Colonizers Law that cuts across various areas of study, the contemporary after-effects of which still remain in effect. This certainly would benefit from a detailed historical analysis, and offer students of sociology of law an opportunity to contribute to an understanding to the contemporary condition.

Islamic Law, or *Shariah* are practiced in the Middle East, Northern Africa, and some areas of Asia. India represents a mixture of approaches, one of which includes Shariah (Baxi, 1986). Much of this law is derived from the *Koran*. The *Shariah* includes specific rules for both private and public life. State and religion are intimately connected, not like the U.S. where a fundamental split exists.

Socialist law has its major contribution from Marx and Lenin. Considerably influential has been the work of post-revolutionary Russian scholar Pashukanis (Milovanovic, 2011). China, Russia, Vietnam, and Cuba are key countries where versions exist. Sometimes Socialist law is incorrectly referenced as "communist law," since the Marx-Lenin predictions argue that in communism, the "higher forms," the State and laws "wither away." Socialist law, on the other hand, can accommodate capital logic without necessarily seeing its demise. Socialist laws place restrictions on private property. The last two decades, however, have witnessed considerable movement in socialist law countries toward some form of capitalism and recognizing some individual ownership of property.

"Democratic socialism" draws from some ideals expressed in socialism and capitalism, but subject to democratic control rather than top-down authority. Here a decentralized, socially owned market economy is subject to democratic principles and participatory decision-making at workplaces and other spheres (see, for example, Hardt and Negri's *Commonwealth*, 2011; see also Holland's *Nomad Citizenship*, 2011, for how an alternative political economy could vibrantly flourish).

We also have customary or indigenous law, most often unwritten rules and customs and orally practiced and transmitted, and experiencing a history of repression by colonial powers (see for example experiences in America, Africa, Australia, New Zealand, and Canada; *Indigenous Law Resources*, 2021). *Status* plays an important role rather than achieved accomplishments. Again, each approach (Islamic, Socialist, customary) requires extensive examination in their own right.

Slavery and colonizer's law most often reflected the colonizer's imposition of their respective form of law on existing customary law. Along with the North American experience, we witnessed colonizer's law imposed in the South: Africa, South America, Australia and other countries. With independence, vestiges of the previous laws remain, with often concessions for the traditional customary ways. South Africa, for example, remains a *common law* country: established rules undergo modification with judge's interpretations, the notion of *stare decisis* (*see* Milner, 1967; Joireman, 2001). In Brazil, we see the influence of Portugal's *civil law* (codified laws and statutes, where judge's interpretation are not the basis of *stare decisis*). Under slavery laws, people were characteristically seen as property (chattel), in earlier forms articulated as "slave codes" (Gilmartin, 2019). It was stipulated, at core, in terms of master-slave relationships. Colonizers often employed the concept of *Terra Nulius*, empty land, to justify their occupation of indigenous lands, and even when occupied, argued they were characterized as uncivilized and their oral tradition transmitting customary laws irrelevant. The legacy and imagery has remained to the present, sometimes operative in an unconscious fashion, sometimes in conscious fashion as in advocates of white supremacy (white racists), more understood as systemic (contrary to the attempts by U.S. President Trump to rewrite it otherwise). European colonizers of Africa, included Britain, Belgium, France, Germany, Italy, Portugal, and Spain (for an overview, see *Encyclopedia Britannica*, "Law and Slavery."). We will have occasion throughout this introductory book to consider some applications in the sociology of law. Colonization in the West, of course, has a long history back to the Phoenicians,

Greeks, Romans, and the Ottoman Empire. The rise of capitalism has generally been connected with expansion in colonization and in demands for exploitable slave labor (Gilmartin, 2019: 115–116). Much of the source for slavery law arises, ironically, from biblical sources: Hebrew, Christian, and Islamic (ibid., "Slave Code"). We will address the American early experience below.

There are even differences in how to study law in society. In England, for example, it often falls under "socio-legal studies," with diverse perspectives based on Marxism, symbolic interactionism, postmodernism, and more eclectic approaches practiced by the Oxford Centre for Socio-Legal Studies in Great Britain. In the U.S., sociology of law is offered in sociology, criminology, criminal justice, and justice studies departments usually as sociology of law, or law and society.

And we have the difference between the study of *abstract law*, the interpretation of law bounded by mechanistic study of the meaning of the "*letter of the law*," precedents and emphasized in law schools in the West, versus "*law in practice*," more focused on how law is being constantly re-interpreted and what forces are at play for change. This book is more about the latter. And as we shall see below, the parameters for a sociology of law as a discipline are still being formulated.

Many scholars have contributed to the movement of the sociology of law as a discipline. Early contributors to some aspects of the discipline, without providing a comprehensive sociology of law, include Cesare Beccaria (1738–1794), Herbert Spencer (1820–1903), William Graham Sumner (1840–1910), and Baron de Montesquieu (1689–1755). Sir Henry Maine (1822–1888), in his *Ancient Law* (1861), perhaps provided a disciplinary approach with key momentum. He studied law from its ancient origins in Roman law to its modern forms. His most famous conclusion on the development of law is that it evolved from "status to contract," in other words from tradition where one's status was determining of rights in law, to the centrality of autonomous individuals engaging in contractual freedoms. Along with Maine, Eugen Ehrlich (1862–1922), particularly his *Fundamental Principles of the Sociology of Law* (translated in 1936, originally published in1913), is a key pioneer that is often cited in the scholarship. His primary contribution explained how "living law," more customary, is often more important than laws on the books, and this living law can be understood more sociologically.

Within legal circles, jurists who contributed to a sociology of law, a sociological jurisprudence, include Roscoe Pound (1870–1964), Oliver Wendell Holmes (1841–1935), and Karl Llewellyn (1893–1962). They studied law from "inside" as well as "outside" (sociologically) the legal profession (we will return to this in Chapter 6). Influential "Eastern-European pioneers" include, along with Eugen Ehrlich, Georges Gurvitch (1894–1965), Nicholas S. Timasheff (1886–1970), and Leon Petrazycki (1867–1931) (Trevino, 2011: 151). They were more explicitly interested in developing a comprehensive sociology of law. Here, we do not provide a full examination of each's contribution; to do justice to this would require volumes; much already appears in the literature in more comprehensive form. But considerably more awaits to be done with comparing, contrasting, critiquing, integrating and synthesizing their respective works.

What we find, however, by the 1950s, sociologists began to be more extensively engaged with this emerging discipline. Perhaps the spark was the publication translated into English of Max Weber's *Law and Economy in Society* (1954) (see Chapter 4 below). Philip Selznick (1959) provided three stages for the developing sociology of law: a more "primitive" stage where offered were disparate perspectives in the sociology of law, apparently traced to those listed above; a more developmental stage where research in sociology became more focused and applied to real legal issues; and a third stage where the goal was to "explore the meaning of legality itself, to assess its moral authority, and to clarify the role of social science in creating a society based on justice" (ibid., 124; see also Trevino, 2009: 8–9; we shall have more to say about law and social change at the end of this chapter). The 1960s and 1970s were to witness the emergence of law associations, conferences, and publications specifically on sociology of law. From the late 1980s to the current era, we add, the influence of critical legal studies and its many off springs that continue to emerge as central players (we shall have more to say in Chapters 6, 7). We also note the prevalence of college and university courses such as Law and Society, Legal Studies, or the Sociology of Law in both sociology departments at universities, as well as in criminal justice and criminology departments, law schools, and within the many new departments doing social justice studies.

However, it was Emile Durkheim, Max Weber and Karl Marx—who had and still have a major impact not only in sociology but in the discipline of sociology of law—who established many of the parameters for the study of the sociology of law, as we will explain in the following chapters (3–5). Unlike jurists (traditional legal scholars, jurisprudes, employed as professors in law schools), these sociologists studied law *outside* of the profession. However, early developers of the sociology of law, and especially advocates of Critical legal studies and their off springs, we shall see, often employed inside the profession (law schools), frequently move from inside to an outside critique.

Defining the Domain of Inquiry

An initial question concerns defining the field of inquiry. We can contrast jurisprudence with a sociology of law model. Jurisprudence is often viewed as the "science of law," legal formalism, analytic, natural, legal positivism, or doctrinal analysis techniques of which are learned in law schools. It comes from the Latin, *juris prudentia*, the science of law. Sociology of law, on the other hand, has its emphasis on the social sciences and sociology. Let us provide some contrasts.

Jurisprudence includes but is not limited to the study of:

(1) the existing system of written rules, established in codified form by the state (statutory and case law);

(2) their ongoing systematization into a body of relevant law by some coordinating principle of justification;

(3) the application of doctrinal legal discourse that is structured by a relevant morphological structure (word meanings) and syntactical structure (linear

constructions of narratives and texts) in doing "correct" reasoning in legal decision-making;

(4) the formal, logical application of abstract and general legal propositions and doctrines by the use of doctrinal legal discourse to "factual" situations by a specialized staff which provides a high degree of probability of resolution of the issue(s) in controversy (i.e., by the use of syllogistic reasoning, deductive logic);

(5) and the analysis of how all conflicts can be inevitably subsumable (self-referencing) to some absolute postulates, which provide the body of core premises and criteria for the correct resolution of differences in a self-regulating (homeostatic) formal system.

Let's examine these propositions. Members of the legal profession, be they practitioners or law professors, due to their educational experience provided in law schools and the continuous affirmation in everyday practice, internalize this emphasis in law. (We should add, too, that many legislators are legally trained.) It becomes the focal point of their practice. Rules promulgated by the legislative branch are taken as a given. Abstract legal propositions are applied to "factual" situations (the "what happened?") in an attempt to resolve different conflicts (e.g., one learns how to apply an "equal protection" or a "due process" analysis that is rooted in the Fourteenth Amendment to the U.S. Constitution). Precedents, or *stare decisis*, provides a background that constrains decision-making processes. A specialized staff—lawyers, trained in a specific discourse—apply their learned skills to points of controversy. The doctrinal legal discourse in use is structured by two axes: the morphological structure and the syntactical structure.

The morphological structure is the repository of correct legal meanings of words (e.g., words such as intent, duress, reckless, person, etc., have legally established meanings). The syntactical structure provides the correct method of linear construction of these words in narratives and text. In other words, within legal practice there is a particular way of constructing narratives: for example, in cross-examination there are particular methods of not leading witnesses, of correctly introducing evidence, etc. (see Tiersma, 1999). In formal rational logical form of law, as espoused in the U.S., the use of syllogistic reasoning and deductive logic is the main formula in arriving at legal decisions.

Any situation is said to be resolvable in law. One only needs to find the appropriate rule and premise(s), and by the use of formal logic, specifically, syllogistic reasoning and deductive logic, to proceed step by step toward the correct conclusion. "Truth" is said to exist independently of discourse, politics, and subjective evaluations. It can be discovered by the correct legal reasoning. Students in law school use the *case method* to learn the techniques of law (formal rationality). They prepare "briefs" that follow the logic of cases summarized by judges in law books stacked in law libraries. They read a legal case and study its decision-making. First, is the summary of the facts, or the "what happened?" Next is clearly articulating the issue involved (i.e., one of the Constitutional Amendments). Thus, for example, it could be stated as an "equal protection" clause that is at issue (5th or 14th Amendment), a "due process" issue (5th or 14th Amendment), an "unreasonable search and seizure" (4th Amendment), or a freedom of expression issue" (1st Amendment). Then, the student, following the judge's decision-making, applies it to the factual situation, tracing the linear logic that leads from the facts, to the issue, to the logic employed, to a decision. This is deductive logic or syllogistic reasoning. Often different cases are examined on how they handled a similar case. In class, the Socratic method of questioning and answering is said to instill the correct skills for the budding lawyer.

In more adversarial systems of criminal justice, "truth" can be objectively obtained, it is argued, by the clash of two opposing sides, the prosecutor and the defense in criminal cases, or the plaintiff and the defense in civil cases. The legal system is seen as a potentially self-regulating (homeostatic) formal system, providing internal criteria and premises for resolving disputes. That is, the legal system not only deals with all points of controversy, but also is said to be adaptable as it grows (legal precedents).

Practitioners of law and law professors who do attempt to go beyond mere doctrinal legal analysis most often find the basis of their philosophical inquiry in the works of such exemplary theoreticians as Hart (1958, 1961, 1983) and Kelsen (1970), with their conceptualizations of law as a system of rules positively developed (legal positivism); Finnis (1980, 1983), with his reliance on "natural law" based on some deep structures of human nature and moral thought and the ultimate necessity of coercion in law; Austin, 1995; originally, 1832), whose published lectures advocated logical fundamentals of law, irrespective of the content's moral virtues; or in Dworkin (1978, 1985, 1986), with his liberal conception of rights and interpretive theory of reading the legal text (hermeneutics). Arguably, Dworkin is at the borders of doing jurisprudence and has one foot in a sociology of law.

Within jurisprudence, therefore, several schools of thought exist including legal positivism, classical natural law theory, and rights theory. There has been, however, a movement away from strict jurisprudence toward inclusion of sociology and the social sciences as found in sociological jurisprudence, realist theory, critical legal studies, critical feminist analysis, critical race theory and various persuasions of legal semiotics. Key initiators in this move are Rosco Pound, Oliver Wendell Holmes, and Karl Llewellyn. As cases in point, we shall develop some of these in Part 2, Chapter 6. In Chapters 9 and 10 we will present two representative examples from the legal semiotics perspective.

Langdell (1826–1906), as we shall see below and in Chapter 6, was a key developer of how law should be taught from a jurisprudence perspective. He was Dean at the Harvard Law School (1870–1895). He articulated the *case method* which emphasized legal cases studies. His was a "science" much like the natural sciences and laboratory studies. He advocated the Socratic method of questioning and answering as the best teaching method of law. Law students would spend long hours in the law library deciphering cases, pulling out inconsistencies, tracing the syllogistic reasoning and deductive logic that was employed, comparing case material on similar issues, drawing correct logical conclusions. In class, students would be quizzed about the facts, how the decision was derived, the logic employed, and comparisons with other case material. His Socratic method was to become a dominant form of pedagogy for law school throughout the U.S.

Academic jurisprudes who focus on doctrinal legal analysis find their main conduit for dissemination in law school classes and university law journals. Most law schools of repute support or subsidize a university law journal. Within these journals one finds critique, comparison, and comment on how cases could have been decided otherwise, alternative ways of constructing the issues and "facts," an examination of the consistency or inconsistency of a decided case, etc. It is this body of material, as well as published case material (summaries of decisions by judges at various levels — district/local, appeal, Supreme Court) that is the focal point of study for the law student. The neophyte jurisprude is likely to receive a very limited introduction to the classic, progressive philosophers and sociologists. Consequently, those within the jurisprudence school of thought are more likely to continue to do doctrinal legal analysis, to be more technicians than theoreticians. Sociologist of law in critique would argue that some internalized but yet uncritically examined theory of society, social order, and the human being (referred to as a meta-narrative) is the underlying basis of much of jurisprude's analysis and critique of law which is avoided in their formal legal training and subsequent practices.

Sociology of law, on the other hand, includes but is not limited to the study of:

(1) the evolution, stabilization, function, dysfunction, and justification of forms of social control, and underlying core assumptions of society and personhood;

(2) the form of law, legal thought, and reasoning as they relate to a particular political economic order;

(3) the legitimation principles and the effects that evolve with them;

(4) the "causes" of the development of the form of social control and staff of specialists that are its promoters;

(5) the transmission of "correct" methods of legal reasoning;

(6) the creation of the juridic subject with formal, abstract and universal rights;

(7) the evolution of the juridico-linguistic coordinate system (legal discourse) in use and its nexus with the political economic sphere;

(8) the degree of freedom and coercion existing in the form of law, its enhancement or diminishment of capabilities;

(9) the formal body of law, the difference between abstract law and law-in-action, possible inherent biases and discriminatory effects, and law's ability to actualize social value;

(10) and, the possibility for alternative forms of law.

Rather than taking rules, forms of law, rights and abstract notions of the legal subject (juridic subject) as a given, this approach examines the evolution of these forms and how they become the dominant factors in legal thinking and in the resolution of conflicts in society. The emphasis is on specifying the causes of law, legitimation principles, the specific legal discourse and forms of legal reasoning that arise, the development of a specialized staff to use it, the evolution of the so-called juridic subject (the "reasonable man" in law), the degree of coercion and freedom that exist in law, its functions and disfunctions, and the relationship of law to realization of justice. This approach is often multi-disciplinary. Finally, this approach examines the connection (nexus) between the form of law and the political, economic and social spheres.

Sociologists of law would generally argue that jurisprudes—as well as scholars like Finnis, Hart and Dworkin—operate within a horizon of thought that has been preconstituted (Poulantzas, 1973: 207; Kerruish; 1991: 147, 157–160). See "constitutive law," Chapter 11, which is especially focused on this issue. In other words, contra jurisprudes, the form of law, the basis of rights, and the nature of the legal subject in law (the juridic subject) are said to be, in the first instance, connected to and generated by socio-economic relations, "behind people's backs" as Karl Marx would tell us (Pashukanis, 1980, 2002; Beirne, 1979b; Beirne and Quinney, 1982; Beirne and Sharlet, 1980; Kerruish, 1991; Milovanovic, 1981, 1987, 1997). Thus, sociologists of law would criticize jurisprudes for uncritically accepting categories generated from historically-specific socio-economic relations. Jurisprudes would respond by saying that "[t]he appearance ... *is* the reality of rights and law" (Kerruish, 1991: 158; my emphasis). In other words, that law can be analyzed on its own terms and not as a reflection of other societal institutions. And herein lies the core difference between jurisprudes and sociologists of law.

In the United States, those doing sociology of law are more likely to find themselves in criminology, sociology, legal studies, political science, and criminal justice departments within colleges and universities rather than law schools. Although they occasionally have their work published in university law journals, more often their work appears in social science journals, the dominant ones being, *Law and Society Review*, *Law and Social Inquiry*, and *Law and Policy*. They are also active in presenting their analysis in various social science conferences. The American Sociological Association also has a sociology of law sub-division. In the United Kingdom, the Socio-Legal Studies Association (SLSA) is a prominent organization.[1] A key journal in the UK is the *British Journal of Law and Society*. There are also other more critical legal theory journals, one being *Law and Critique*, established in 1990, the other, the journal of *Social and Legal Studies*, in 1992. Machura's (2020) review of the literature suggests that in contemporary teaching at law schools in the UK, black letter law is no longer the primary focus, with more weight placed on scrutinizing contexts. Socio-legal studies has become a dominant approach (Foster and Osborn, 2016; Crownie and Bradney, 2018; Sugarman, 2011; Creutzfeld, 2019). Most of the SLSA membership is from law schools (Machura, ibid.; Bradney, 2007). In the US, there still remains a strong adherence to "black letter law" (legal science, jurisprudence). In many Eastern European countries, any semblance of sociology of law, along with criminology, falls within the law departments.

Since the 1980s a new dimension in the study of law, legal semiotics, has emerged. In some forms it is well appropriated in jurisprudence as legal language; in other forms, it decisively moves beyond mere analysis of legal language. Whether legal semiotics can be seen as a standalone subsuming legal studies is problematic; however, for some theorists, we can do so by incorporating the conceptual tools offered in legal semiotics and in semiotics (see Chapters 9 and 10). A semiotic perspective has been neglected for far too long in the literature.

Be that as it may, in this book we are more interested in introducing some recent works in the sociology of law tradition, in which semiotics is one of the key elements. Thus, for example, we will include a Marxist view that makes heavy use of a linguistic determinism (Chapter 10). An alternative Marxist view argues for co-construction in the relationship of law to the political economy. We will also include postmodern views and how they have incorporated a perspective on semiotics derived from Jacques Lacan (see Chapter 11). We include two of the most dominant legal semiotics approaches that have developed, one Peircian, the other Greimasian (see Chapter 9). And more recently, we trace the outlines of a possible post postmodern view, a quantum holographic semiotics in law (Chapter 12).

Several approaches in a critically grounded sociology of law, we shall see, make extensive use of semiotic analysis: postmodernist, feminist, Marxist (of the structural interpellation variety), and the constitutive approach.

Sociological jurisprudence and legal realism that emerged in the early 1900s to 1940s, practiced primarily within law schools, was to go beyond merely jurisprudential analysis in drawing from sociology. Key developers were Roscoe Pound (1870–1964) and Eugen Ehrlich (1862–1922). Ehrlich's *Fundamental Principles of the Sociology of Law* (1936, originally, 1913) was to make a fundamental contribution. Roscoe Pound was to publish extensively on the importance of sociology and advocated not limiting the study of law to the laboratory (law libraries) of law schools (see Chapter 6).

But since the turn of the 20th century, even with some impact by sociological jurisprudence, the jurisprudence school of thought has dominated the analysis of law. Members of the legal profession have continued to operate within its more narrowly construed domain (legal formalism). Thus, within law schools, but also within liberal arts programs of universities that offer law courses, the emphasis in the study of law has been predominantly legal science (jurisprudence), except in Sociology departments. Not so in the UK as we previously indicated (Machuro, 2020). Since the middle 1970s, it has been marked, however, by an increased emphasis on sociologically informed examination of law. Many critical scholars have returned to the classical theorists—Durkheim, Weber and Marx—in order to develop more sociologically oriented approaches. Law is increasingly seen as intimately connected with the internal dynamics of a political economic order. It is toward the second approach that this book is dedicated.

Definition of Law

Definitions of law vary widely. It is a concept that has no consensus in the field. The *Merriam-Webster On-Line Dictionary* provides a primary definition as "a binding custom or practice of a community: a rule of conduct or action prescribed ... or formally recognized as binding or enforced by a controlling authority." We find complexities within this definition. At one end of the continuum is the classic statement of Rousseau in the *Social Contract* (1954) that law is but the reflection of the will of all derived by a mythically established contract by members in a social body to end the "war of all against all" (that which Hobbes, in *Leviathan* [1946, originally 1651], posits as the "state of nature"). At the other end of this spectrum stands one variant of the Marxist's perspective, which states that law is class rule, or bourgeois law (Quinney, 1974). We shall develop this in Chapter 5. Between these extremes many alternative definitions arise. Take, for example Hoebel, an anthropologist who, in *The Law of Primitive Man* (1974) offered the following: "A social norm is legal if its neglect or infraction is regularly met, in threat or in fact, by the application of physical force by an individual or group possessing the socially recognized privilege of so acting."

The key elements of his definition are: "social norm," by which is meant regularity in behavior; "regularly met," by which we mean with a high degree of probability; "application of physical force," which means that some external body will administer force against identified lawbreakers; and "an individual or group possessing the socially recognized privilege of so acting," which implies that a particular individual or staff is in the legitimate position of administering punishment. The enforcer, too, can assume, can expect as a right, no legal retaliation. This definition, then, would exclude such behavior as the Bible's *lex talionis*—an eye for an eye, a tooth for a tooth. But issues with this line of thought emerge where there is some support for the wrongdoer. Consider, for example, Bernhard Goetz, who in 1984 shot four black youths in a New York City subway, arguing that it was a preventive strike given the highly violent experiences often incurred in subways of NYC (one wonders, however, what would have happened if it was the other way around, an African-American shooting four whites using the same logic). It would also have problems with the Red Brigade (revolutionaries in the 1970s and late 1980s operating in Italy who kidnapped members of the upper class and subjected them to a "people's trial" and then, upon conviction, inflicted punishment). Of course, the question of whether they are more correctly identified as revolutionary or terrorist is not withstanding). Other problem areas would include "bandits" (the Robin Hood types) that Hobsbawm (1969) has studied. Clearly, the question of "possessing the socially recognized privilege of so acting [application of physical force]," runs into a problem here, particularly because of substantial open or tacit support by some segments of the population in these situations, not least of which is racist support being the motivation.

Let's take a more classic definition. Weber has attempted to clarify the difference between mere customary behavior and law. Here, Weber introduces the notion of an "order." He begins with a more general definition. "An order will be called ... convention so far as its validity is externally guaranteed by the probability that deviation from it within a given social group will result in a relatively general and practically significant reaction of disapproval" (Weber, 1978: 34). Notice that within this broad definition no externally defined specialized group is given the power to enforce deviation from an order. An "order" he defines as a regular orientation to rules of conduct ("maxims") (Weber, 1978: 31).

On the other hand, "an order will be called ... *law* if it is externally guaranteed by the probability that physical or psychological coercion will be applied by a staff of people in order to bring about compliance or avenge violation" (Weber, 1978: 34, emphasis in the original). Note the emphasis on a "staff" of people given the responsibility of assuring compliance or for avenging violations. Notice, too, that psychological coercion is included. Weber's definition, then, would seem to include "laws" of bodies such as the American Bar Association, the American Medical Association, etc., in that they, too, have codes of ethics and disciplinary procedures enforced by a staff to bring about compliance. The coercion and probabilistic elements have also been included by others: Consider a definition of law by Justice Benjamin Cardozo: "a principle or rule of conduct so established as to justify a prediction with reasonable certainty that it will be enforced by the courts if its authority is challenged" (1924: 52). In this direction, also consider the Durkheim-influenced anthropologist Alfred Reginald Radcliffe-Brown, "law is the maintenance or establishment of social order ... by the exercise of coercive authority through the use, or possibility of use, of physical force" (cited in Schur 1968: 74–75).

Yet others have argued against the reliance on "coercion" in a definition of law. Barkan (2018: 25–27), for example, notes the strong prohibition to violate law may come about because of its perception as morally wrong, a sense of obligation, concerns about informal reprimands, that the contemplated violation might lead to personal harm, and by pure habit. And others have argued that because of rationalization or neutralization of the binds of the law, its significance disappears. See for example the classic statement on the "techniques of neutralization" by Sykes and Matza (1964) who applied it to understanding juvenile delinquency. Cressey (1956) has also applied rationalizations in explaining embezzlement. In other words, the moral binds of the law are rendered non-binding releasing its articulator to possibly violate the law. Recently, these neutralizations and extensions have been adapted by many explaining cybercrime. An objection could be quickly raised to law disappearing in its effects: that in responding to something by using rationalizations or neutralizations we are assuming something's existence; ergo, law *does* exist. And after all, law exists in written form. However, a counter which a constitutive approach would make (see below and Chapter 2, constitutive function) and also more recently made by using an emerging quantum paradigm (Chapter 12), argues that law exists only in potential, a possibility, an abstraction, a virtual reality until it is brought into existence (enacted), through performative discursive action in particular contexts.[2]

Other theorists have offered a behavioral definition of law. Black, for example, defines law as "governmental social control" (1976, 1989). For Black, in explaining such things as crime, one need not get into the question of the motivation of the deviant. Law behaves in patterned ways that can be identified in propositions. Law, as a quantitative variable (it varies in time and space) and as a qualitative variable (different styles of law can be applied, even to the same situation) can be fruitfully investigated in terms of the mobilization of law. In other words, the more law that is mobilized, the more serious is the perceived event. The seriousness of the offense, the definition of crime, who the offenders are, and official crime statistics can all be explained by how much law is mobilized. We shall return to Black in Chapter 8.

Malinowski, an anthropologist, has noted that laws are not necessarily written (1976). The Trobriander of Melanesia, for example, found themselves in a web of continuous relationships. The subjects depended on each other and found themselves in reciprocal relationships. There existed an intricate network of privileges, duties and benefits within which identity was centered. The bond of reciprocity and the felt obligations were so strong that for all intents and purposes these intricate relationships also constituted the law. This is the realm of customary law.

Anarchists would take Malinowski's analysis one step further. For them, stateless societies have been shown to successfully exist, and can thus be duplicated in a society of the future. Kropotkin (1902, 1913) has argued that a society can function perfectly well guided by the principle of "mutual aid" and shared responsibility. In his words, the principle of mutual aid "grants the best chance of survival to those who best support each other in the struggle for life" (ibid., 115; see also Morland, 1997). It is unclear, however, if stateless societies have no "law." For Black (1976), by definition, a stateless society has no law ("law is governmental social control"). For others, such as Luhmann (1985), law exists in every society (it is a generalization of expectations, see Chapter 8). Thus, anarchists may argue, on the one hand, that without a state, no law exists, but on the other, they can equally argue, by the definition given, that law in fact exists (for example, Weber's general definition of "order" mentioned above, more informal than formal laws). (For additional information on stateless societies, see, Michalowski, 1985: 45–68; Black, 1976: 123–137; Kennedy, 1976; Tift and Sullivan, 1980; Ferrell, 1999; Williams and Arrigo, 2001).

As Maine has noted, in ancient society, when an individual sins, the punishment extends to his children, his kinfolk, his tribesmen — and even as a substitute for him, in his absence (1861: 75). Thus, for the ancient, collective responsibility and liability existed. Law, then, was directed to the family as a unit, rather than to an individual. "Primitive societies," usually referencing societies with fewer formal organizations and greater use of customary law, were characterized by membership in some group. "Primitive," however, has a pejorative sense in traditionally vernacular; others have used customary societies; Durkheim has offered the notion of less differentiation and specialization. We shall see that Durkheim (Chapter 3) and Weber (Chapter 4) will have more to say about this. It was within the group that rights, privileges and duties were defined. Individuality as we know it today was totally out of accord with the organizational structure of primitive society. Property, too, belonged to the family. The father was the supreme authority (*patria pesetas*). Even his spouse was treated more as a daughter, not as an equal in law (1861: 91). However, the literature indicates the historical existence of matriarchal societies (Madams, 2019; in Iroquois society, for example, many critical decisions were made by women).).

Commentators such as Gibbs (1967) have noted that many definitions of law assume a coercive form. Gibbs offers a "composite" definition of law, which is a grand synthesis of all the coercive forms. The elements include:

(1) an evaluation of conduct held by at least one person in a social unit; and

(2) a high probability that, on their own initiative or at the request of others, persons in a special status will attempt by coercive or non-coercive means to revenge, rectify, or prevent behavior that is contrary to the evaluation; with

(3) a low probability of retaliation by persons other than the individual or individuals at whom the reaction is directed (Gibbs, 1967: 431).

In his composite definition, rather than using such words as norm or order, he substitutes "evaluation" of conduct, which is not necessarily collective. "Special status," rather than necessarily implying an official, court, or state, implies that someone must occupy a status, which is universally accepted. And finally, his definition relies on the idea that this enforcing party is immune from retaliation ("when a perpetrator can rely on other parties to rally to his cause ... law does not exist," Gibbs, 1967: 433).

The autopoeitic (Luhmann, 1992; Teubner, 1993; and Chapter 8 of this book) as well as the constitutive perspective (Henry and Milovanovic, 1996, 1999, 2020) view the emergence of a particular definition of law more in terms of a relatively stabilized manifestation at historical junctures of otherwise more hidden complex, inter-related elements at work. It is not just the economic that is determinative, nor just the ideological sphere. Thus, law is not simply class rule, nor the product of enlightened, rational thought. Law is both constituted by and constitutive of socially constructed reality. Law appears in a trial court setting, legislative discussion, police encounter, and so forth, as well as in individual dealings with everyday conflict situation. The "micro" exists in the "macro" and the "macro" exists in the "micro."

At this point in our introduction to the sociology of law we merely wish to indicate the varying positions on the definition of law. This is not merely an academic exercise. Take for example, the instrumental Marxists. They argue that even under the "first phase of communism," that is, socialism, law will still be dictatorial, or class rule, be it in the form of proletarian law. For Marxists, it is only in the "higher phases" that the state and law will "wither away" (see Chapter 5). Here, by definition, absent a state and a staff, no law exists. Clearly the accepted definition of law dictates the scope of the analysis of law. It also defines, or even "creates" crime (see Black, 1976; see the various discussions in Henry and Lanier, 2015).

Conflict v. Consensus Approaches in Law and Beyond

Apart from the differences between a jurisprudence orientation and a sociology of law, we have a more fundamental difference in background assumptions that are often remain as unanalyzed assumptions. That is, they are taken for granted. These perspectives are often conceptualized as the conflict and consensus paradigms. These are often unverbalized expression of fundamental relationships.

Those from the consensus paradigm assume an orderly, harmonious, predictable world of agreements on basic core values in society. Society is conceived as one whole melting pot where socialization acclimates people to the core values. Law is a neutral framework responding to any differences that emerge. In itself, it is not biased. It is integral and functional for a social system to operate smoothly. It contributes to stability and harmony. Jean-Jacques Rousseau, in *The Social Contract* (1762) best expresses how a social contract emerged in society to overcome Hobbesian "war of all against all." The latter, in *Leviathan* (1651), spelled out how life is short and brutish given the variability of human desires. Rousseau's social contract was a response to this state of nature. Human beings form a compact. They give away some of their unrestrained pursuits in exchange for a peaceful state, a contract. Law is a symbol of this collective understanding. Thus, a consensus is said to exist for this desireable social compact, and all accept law as expressing this concern. Those that go outside of the social contract are law breakers. Within law, one of the most prominent exponents has been Roscoe Pound (1943). He argued, even with consensus in core values people pursue social interests that might come at odds with one another and hence these must be reconciled for social integration and harmony to prevail with the maximum realization of social values. Talcott Parsons (1962), a noted sociologist from the structural-functionalist perspective to which we will return later, has advocated for law's contribution to maintaining a well-integrated system.

Conflict analysis sees things differently. Traced to the work of Georg Simmel (1969) and his followers (Lewis Coser, Ralph Dahrendorf, George Vold, and Austin Turk, to name a few more dominant names).[3] Conflict is seen as ubiquitous. Liberal pluralism embraces this notion of humans attempting to maximize rewards and thus are subject to going beyond the boundaries of acceptability. Law is seen as resulting from diverse groups in conflict attempting to introduce their respective interests. Some, too, attain greater power and disproportionally exercise their influence on conflict resolutions through law. As Austin Turk (1976) explains, law becomes a weapon in social conflicts. Thus, conflict, coercion, and dissensus must be considered as central forces in law in practice. Conflict, too, has positive functions, such as defining boundaries of acceptability, the basis of social change, and the source for innovation.

Offshoots of conflict analysis were to emerge in the 1960s and 1970s, particularly in criminology and sociology. The Marxist perspective assumes rather than merely diverse agents in conflict, there is a fundamental conflict between capitalists (owners of the means of production), and proletariat (workers). Law reflects the interest of the capitalist class (Quinney, 1974; Chambliss and Seidman, 1982).

In the 1970s a sharper distinction was made between various Marxist perspectives. The fundamental split was between those advocating an instrumental Marxism and those a structuralist Marxist (we will return to this in later chapters for more fuller development). The instrumental Marxist argue that a homogeneous ruling class governs, and law simply reflects their interests. The structuralist Marxists, on the other hand, argue that it is the very fundamental structural of a capitalist mode of production and its inherent capital logic that drives interests, coalitions, and the formation of law. For the structuralist, struggle (unionization, strikes, demonstrations) does lead to some piecemeal change but the structure itself remains. Law, for the structuralists, follows a more complicated pathway whereby conflicts within the ruling elite (between say, the military, banking, auto, and oil interests) lead to coalitions within the ruling elite and these coalitions formulate law reflecting their interest. Different coalitions, however, lead to different laws.

These paradigm differences were expressed in the work of sociological jurisprudence and critical legal studies. Critical legal studies (CLS) emerging in the mid- to late-1970s drew more from various forms of conflict analysis. Early CLS was to become more differentiated with focused attention to critical analysis by African Americans, feminists (Fem-Crits), Lat-Crits, Asian-American Crits, Queer-Crits, etc. This field is still differentiating. We will return to this in Part Two.

To reiterate. These paradigms are often not formally expressed, often remaining implicit and somewhat at a subconscious level as background assumptions. Lawyers and sociologists of law draw from these background assumptions. Practicing lawyers, judges, police, correction officers, and others from the criminal justice system, given their everyday demands, often find little time to indulge in sustained engagement with critical examination of paradigms, most often referring to the Rousseau-Hobbes mythical debate whereby the desirability of a social contract overcomes the war of all against all. Expressed, sometimes in self-justifying rhetoric (ideology) as "the thin blue line," as advocating order rather than an inevitable disorder without law. Operatives in the legal order often dismiss lengthy critical analysis on the subject of law, relegating it to "ivory tower" musings, nothing to do with reality.

More recent examination of paradigms includes a focus on the difference between modernists and postmodernist. The modernist perspective builds on the key insights from the Enlightenment period, embracing free will, rationality, the majesty of science, and language as merely an instrument for dialogue. The postmodernists challenge (Chapter 11) each of these assumptions. Forms of law predicated on the one or the other perspective can lead to very different results. And even this has been eclipsed by referencing post-postmodernism, or didgimodernism, the world of the internet, virtual realities, and new forms of understanding materialism (Chapter 12). For the latter, one expression is the sociomateriality perspective, much of the basis of which is traced to Karan Barad's (2007) quantum-driven analysis, which is a key challenge to earlier models. A semiotic sociology of law is especially cognizant of these developments in providing new ways of conceptualizing law. We will return to these developments in a final section of the book focused on emergent approaches in sociology of law.

Law and Justice

We often assume law and justice are the same thing. Although they are connected, we see instances where law is not necessarily justice. Consider, for example, the following U.S. Supreme Court decisions: *Dred Scott v. Sandford* (1857), denying African-

American claims to citizenship protected by the Constitution; *Plessy v. Ferguson* (1899), establishing the concept "separate but equal," justifying segregation; and *Korematsu v. United States* (1944) stating the internment of 120,000 Japanese Americans was constitutional. We have witnessed a long history of slave laws in the South in America. The 13th Amendment to the U.S. Constitution (1865) formally abolished slavery. But we witnessed the development of Jim Crow Laws, Black codes (Urofsky, 2021) that perpetuated racial segregation in public spaces, limiting for example, jobs, education and voting, vestiges of which still remain in the "new Jim Crow Laws" (Alexander, 2010), mass incarceration, and school-to-prison pipelines, disproportionally affecting African-Americans (Wacquant, 2002). And colonial law is replete with repression in law directed against indigenous populations.

Laws are established through a legislative process. It is ostensibly based on some underlying conception of justice. Law is said to have primarily facilitative functions that assure predictability and order. We shall see in the next chapter, however, that other functions of law also exist (ideological, repressive, constitutive). Justice principles are focused on notions of fairness. They are more abstract and philosophical. We find competing definitions (see Capeheart and Milovanovic, 2020; see also the classic early statement by jurist Roscoe Pound, 1914); e.g., just deserts, equality, needs, mutual aid, etc. Laws are perceived as just if they are derived from democratic processes and rationally and logically applied. Max Weber explains, for example, that in legal domination, and by domination he simply means an orientation to some order, legitimation rests with rationally enacted and logically applied principles of law. He, like Emile Durkheim and Karl Marx also note (see Chapters 3, 4, 5) the potentially repressive functions of law. We note in the next chapter, that in "repressive formalism" the most rational and logically applied laws, even within a legal system seen as independent from power elites, can still, in formally equal applications, be repressive.

Practitioners in law resign themselves to applying rational logic principles in arriving at a legal decision, without, ostensibly, concern with the innate justice. Justice is seen as already embodied in the prevailing law and the legal practitioner merely applies legal principles and logic to factual situations in arriving at the correct decision in law. Rulings that follow deductive logic and syllogistic reasoning in formal rational law leading to a decision are seen in themselves as an application of justice. Barkan (2018: 12) argues "whether a legal ruling is just or unjust or fair or unfair for any party in a case is irrelevant in legal scholarship [jurisprudence]. If a ruling is logically defensible, then it is a 'right' ruling, regardless of its possible unfairness or unjustness." Similarly, Chaplin (2019) notes that legal positivism [jurisprudence, legal science taught in law schools] "advances the view that while law may in fact be placed in service of substantive moral or social objectives like justice—and legal positivists argues that it's the task of democratic politics to make those decisions—an adequate account of law can still be given without mentioning any of them. In essence, law is a morally neutral instrument of social control."

Discussions of the philosophy of justice, for practitioners of law, is punted to sociologists and philosophers. Thus, those from a jurisprudence background more often do *internal* critiques of the mechanics of law, fine-tuning the machinery to better serve or actualize a particular conception of justice already incorporated in law. This exercise appears in law journals where application and use of deductive logic in case material is scrutinized. Theirs is a pragmatic exercise. Philosophical debates about justice are seen as esoteric; rather, mechanical application is the norm. Whereas sociologists of law are more likely to do *external* critiques, studying for example, what principle(s) of justice are being embodied in law, how they have been done so, what interests they may serve, what alternatives could have been, or could be implemented, and what limitations and/or opportunities exist in political economy.

Others argue more forcefully that law can only be understood by engagement with principles of justice (McIlroy, 2019; see also Gould, 2020; Chaplin, 2021). Thus, any discussion of law and order builds on a more fundamental discussion about law and justice. Thus "shallow justice" is when decisions follow strictly formal rationality; justice is equated with law. "Deep justice" is what is behind the law (ibid., 23, 32); it is the deeper basis for law's existence and thus the standard for critiquing law. Justice "is the ultimate purpose of law; it is the goal (telos) towards which law aims" (ibid., 2). For McIlroy, "law is not merely a practice of issuing rules backed by force; it is a practice of issuing rules that carry with them reasoning explaining their justification ... rules that claim to be just" (ibid., 15). Thus, this underscores the idea that often legal practitioners limit themselves in believing they are only engaged in legal practice excluding advocating any particular conception of justice not already embodied in existing law.

Yet others, we shall see in following chapters make yet further distinctions between law and justice. Jacques Derrida (1992), for example, in a much-cited and celebrated article, "The Force of Law," argues that law exists in the rationally calculable and predictable domain of economics, whereas justice is more like a gift, an inherent interconnectedness with the Other and unmeasurable reciprocal duties owed. Sometimes, we also witness external principles of justice being advocated in decision making at the formal level, but quickly dismissed by authoritative judges as non-justiciable issues having no legal "standing" in court. These "substantive rational" principles are always present as a destabilizing force, and a force for social change toward a more just society. Social struggles and social movements respond to this need.

Forms of Law

Some confusion exists when law concepts are invoked, particularly the differences between substantive and procedural law; civil and criminal law; statutory and case law; public and private law; natural and positive law. Let's briefly provide some differences. We shall not be exhaustive; much has been written on each. We merely want to sensitize the reader to various concepts that do exist when talking about law. Nevertheless, many shall be referenced throughout the book.

Substantive law concerns particular rights, duties, and proscriptions; procedural law has to do with how these are formally adjudicated. Civil law concerns relations and transactions between people, sometimes also referred to as private law, violations of which are called "torts"; criminal law, on the other hand, concerns state defined crimes, and generally, after conviction, some form of deprivation of liberty is involved. The latter has been characterized in earlier times as infringing on the King's Peace, and hence a public act deserving the attention of the State for prosecution. The concept civil law has also been used in another way.

The distinction between civil and common law is that civil law is traced to Roman origins in terms of specific written laws promulgated by State organs (i.e., parliaments). The emphasis is on codified law and their enforcement as specified by legislative acts. Common law is usually defined as "case law" and usually builds on precedents as judges interpret State law. Common law as practiced in the U.S. concerns interpretation of statutes and reasoning based on precedents, most often aided by syllogistic reasoning and deductive logic.

Common law countries include the U.S., Great Britain, Canada, India, New Zealand, and Australia. Civil law countries include Germany, Spain, France, Greece, Italy, Japan, Mexico, Russia and China. Some countries, such as South Africa use a combination of both civil and common law. There are certainly marked differences even within countries with a particular orientation.

Relatedly is the difference between statutory and case law. Statutory law has to do with the laws on the books. For example, in criminal law in the U.S., each act defined as criminal must be clearly specified with clear procedures for conviction. Case law concerns interpretation by judges establishing new laws that become the basis for subsequent consideration (*stare decisis*). In the U.S., case law can concern State and/or Federal levels; thus, we have State courts which begin at the trial level, then State appeals courts, and the highest court, the State Supreme court; Federal courts have the same three levels culminating in the U.S. Supreme court as the highest court of the land that makes final determination of laws in controversy. To add to the differences, there is a distinction between public and private law. Public law concerns what the government codifies as rules, procedures, and structures. Criminal law is one example. Private law is often used in the context of civil law which deals with transactions and relations, both between people and organizations.

There is also the distinction between "natural law" and "positive law," traced to Aristotle's separation, where the former legal principles are traced to nature itself as universal truths, and the latter, human made and thus always subject to human interpretation and biases.

Summary

We have begun our journey to understanding a sociology of law. We concentrate on Western forms of law. We note many contributors to the formation of law, and that its contours are still emerging. There is, we argued, a distinction between jurisprudence and a sociology of law, where the former is mechanistic and taught in law school in preparation for practice, the latter, on the other hand, is generally interdisciplinary and generally is offered in sociology, criminology, criminal justice and law and society departments. Next, we engaged the question of what is law? We noted there are a number of definitions. Max Weber's is one of the most prominent in the literature. We visited the notion of paradigms in law and noted how background assumptions often are productive of different understandings and forms of law. The difference between law and justice was introduced. We concluded with some clarifications of concepts in law.

Review Questions

1. This is a field exercise. Ask five people the question, "What is law?" Summarize these responses and bring to class. Discuss in class. Then, see if the answers could be grouped in terms of commonalities and differences. Place on board. Discuss them.

2. In trying to resolve cases of discrimination, should lawyers and judges be better trained in the sociology of law? Or would it hinder their ability to clearly arrive at "objective" decisions. Explain.

3. Under the *Terra Nullius,* the ideology of colonizers, indigenous lands and ways of life were denied and replaced by the colonizer's law. If lands were returned in Australia, Canada and the U.S. how would customary law conflict *or* augment the use of Western Law focused on purely jurisprudence. Should we rely only on jurisprudes? What would those in the sociology of law bring to the table?

4. You may have the occasion, or will have the occasion to talk with a law student, graduate or practitioner about a particular controversial subject. After reading this chapter, you notice that lawyer's reasoning is quite different from yours, and quickly you fall into accepting the "higher" logic of the lawyer, especially as they seduce you into yes-no answers, building to a conclusion (via deductive logic, syllogistic reasoning). How would you introduce a more sociology of law argument to gain some footing in the discussion? (Some argue, for starters, not getting seduced by simply responding in yes-no format.)

5. Defining law, we have seen, witnesses many scholarly positions. Some argue that law can disappear in the use of rationalizations or neutralizations. How is this so? Can rationalizations and neutralization not be so, but accurate reflection of reality? Who determines this? Does this make a difference? For whom? How?

6. Usually, lawyers attend legal conferences, whereas sociologists of law attend sociology, criminal justice, criminology, and law and society conferences. Similarly for publications in legal journal published by law schools or social science journals. How could this be a hinderance to better development of law and justice?

7. Class exercise for Professor. Divide your class into those who wish to advocate for the logical form of reasoning done by lawyers, those who advocate more sociological form of thinking, and those who cross boundaries applying both. In class, discuss advantages and disadvantages of each.

8. Some practicing lawyers would argue that truth and justice is strictly an outcome of what can be resolved in law. What are your thoughts on this?

Endnotes

1. For a comparison of socio-legal studies in United Kingdom compared to Germany, see Hendry *et al.* (2020) and Machura (2020). For developments in Germany, see Machura (2012) and Raiser (2010).

2. Relatedly in criminology, the 1960s witnessed the labeling perspective where crime was an emergent, an outcome of the interaction between some audience observing and someone engaged in problematic behavior. Depending on the outcome of the definitional process specific consequences follow, i.e., stigmatization with a criminal label, an official statistic, or, alternatively a disavowing of deviance and no label. So, the same acts can be defined differently depending on the societal reaction dynamics.

3. One of the clearest critiques of the consensus paradigm was launched by Ralph Dahrendorf (1958a, 1958b, 1959). He especially targeted Talcott Parson and his downplaying conflict, coercion and dissensus.

2

Law in Action

Introduction

The question of law in action can be addressed, in part, by clarifying the functions of law, the relationship of law to the fulfilment of social values, law and the rise of the legal profession, and the relationship of law to social change. With these, we continue to introduce key concepts and conceptualizations employed by those doing a sociology of law. Our introductory text provides a necessary background for doing more specific and particular analysis. Here, we engage law in action rather than just limiting ourselves to law on the books, the latter a centerpiece of a more dogmatic jurisprudence.

Functions of Law

Let us now turn to the functions of law. Put simply: what does law do? How does it function? What are its doings and functionings? From these questions and their answers we can derive the concept, law. Law has repressive, facilitative, ideological, and constitutive dimensions. Any given system of laws will probably have aspects of all four within them. However, one may be dominant.

The *repressive function* of law addresses the question of coercion in law. Thus, legal repression is variable. Law can be more or less coercive. By repressive functions we mean the degree of mobilization of physical force in the service of social control. There are some theorists who rest their argument on the necessity of repression on particular ontological assumptions (the philosophy of essential being). For example, there are those from a Freudian or Hobbesian perspective (acknowledged or not), who assume that because of strong hedonistic, self-centered (egoistic) or biological impulses, a person left to themselves in a state of nature would act out their impulses without regard or respect for others if it was not for an external force, law. It is argued that a person's appetite has to be controlled. Durkheim has even argued that absent an external force, a person left to themselves would not develop their two sides (duality) — egoism and altruism — in a balanced way. That is, they would not regulate their conduct, or synchronize it with social requirements. In this frame work, whether we talk about a "superego," "leviathan," or the "collective conscience," an external force is needed to coerce individuals to abide by the law.

There are those who argue that some coercion is necessary, but beyond this, "surplus repression" exists (Marcuse, 1962: 32–34, 80). The latter arises because of the existence of political elites and their interest in dominating and maintaining their ruling position. An excess amount of force is generated to maintain a political economic system advantageous to them. A full blown version of this idea is the instrumental Marxist position (Quinney, 1974, 2002). These theorists argue that an illegitimate ruling group dominates at the expense of the laboring classes. Weber, too, argues that even though we have formal equality in law, because of vast economic differences of exchangers (contractors) entering a contract, coercion can still exists. That is, the propertied class can simply use its leverage to maintain control (i.e., dictating the terms of the contract), while giving the formal appearance that the worker, for example, is free to enter the contract or not. Thus, the form can appear as assuring liberties, whereas the content may produce domination.

Certain questions still remain. Pure coercive definitions of law do not adequately answer the questions of: (1) why people conform to legal norms outside of the particular threats of punishment; (2) the significance of the prevailing belief in the "correctness" or "legitimacy" of law and how it correlates with actual behavior (i.e., belief in legitimacy and the actual behavior do not necessarily correlate: an individual might see law as generally "just" but still violate it: yet law may be seen as "unjust" but the individual might still conform); (3) what other functions are served by law; (4) the ideological dimension of law, that is, how the "rule of law" ideology is constructed and maintained and what purpose is served by it; and (5) the constitutive function addressing how law and the legal agent are co-constructed at each moment of practice and articulation. In sum, the issue of the repressive functions of law cannot be entirely separated from the issue of its facilitative, ideological, and constitutive functions.

The *facilitative function* in law can be defined as the degree to which law aids in assuring predictability and certainty in behavioral expectations. Whether we read Durkheim, Weber, Marx, Maine, Unger, or Selznick, we find the notion presented that there has been an evolution of law from status to contract. Durkheim (Chapter 3), for example, shows that a less differentiated, specialized and decentralized society—we use this instead of "primitive" (some use "customary") society—is marked by "mechanical" bonds of solidarity (attraction based on similarity, sameness). Thus, similar encounters among the members of a society and the consequently similarly developed lifestyles and outlooks lead to a highly predictable order. The evolution to a more complex, differentiated type of society, however, produces bonds of solidarity he calls "organic" (the bond being attraction of opposites). In modern societies, involvements are more diverse and more transitory. But the range of behaviors existing, both normal and "pathological," have increased tremendously. As a consequence, less predictability and certainty in everyday behavior is the norm. Satisfaction of needs cannot be assured by interacting within small circles. The contract, for Durkheim, resolves some of the dilemmas: it assures certainty in behavior (see further, Chapter 3), or, at least, a high degree of predictability.

Weber's notion of the "rationalization" of society (see Chapter 4 below) also states that society evolved from the primitive status contract (agreements made affected the whole personality of the transactor and their standing in the community) to the purposive contract (characterized by temporary relationships in which agreements were freely made). This coincided with the coming of commerce and the competitive marketplace marked by money transactions. Here the contract, reflecting mutually and freely agreed upon terms, assured subjects in the social formation that their expectation of results would be supported by an external force, the State and its laws. Hence, economic calculation could now be made more predictable because the many variables in society could now be quantified. Profit motives, then, can find expression in a stable framework in which expectations and obligations are more calculable.

Marx (Chapter 5), too, argued that the breakup of feudalism, as a mode of production (a specific means of producing and distributing goods in a society), and its replacement by capitalism, entailed a movement away from barter (exchange for direct personal use) to commodity-exchange (exchange for profit) in the competitive marketplace and money economy. But in the capitalist mode of production, Marx argued, predictability and certainty in transactions needed to be assured if capitalism was to continue. What was needed, then, was a centralized State with machinery of enforcement to facilitate egocentrically-driven subjects pursuing profits.

A contemporary writer who has stated the facilitative functions of law quite precisely is Luhmann (1985). In this view, law is the "generalization of expectations" and is not primarily repressive (1985: 78). His rather cumbersome definition of law is that it is a "structure of a social system which depends upon the congruent generalization of normative behavioral expectations" (1985: 82). Put simply, Luhmann argues that within changing societies people need some reference point that becomes the basis of structuring expectations and obligations; absent this, people will witness endless disappointments and hardships. Law acts as that reference point. We shall have more to say about his approach in Chapter 8, but here we merely wish to stress that for Luhmann law reflects the requirement that participants in a social formation need to be able to structure their expectations — or, said in another way, to be able to orient their behavior towards predictable responses and expectations.

Law, in its facilitative function allows coordination, planning, and the expectation that certain behaviors will normally follow other behaviors. So long as there is congruency between us concerning our expectations, we both can plan, participate, respond and carry projects forward with a minimum of difficulty. Luhmann argues that as society evolves to greater complexity, however, there is even a greater necessity for structuring expectations of expectations. Law is said to respond to this necessity. To this degree, Luhmann argues, law must always exist in every society (1985: 83).

Many dilemmas exist when interactions cannot be planned nor outcomes predicted. Consider, for example, Laing's point of two people in interaction who cannot draw from a common background understanding or reference point (1970: 22). Jill: "You think I am stupid." Jack: "I don't think you're stupid." Jill: "I must be stupid to think you think I'm stupid if you don't ..." This guessing what the other is thinking, can go on to no end (infinite regress). If the other party is also trying to anticipate what I am thinking, then establishing meaning or coming up with a common understanding can be rather a precarious situation. At a minimum, many disappointments will occur and much remedial work would need to be done (see, especially, Goffman, 1971: 95–187).

The contract is the instrument that is the purest expression of the need to assure predictability and fulfillment of obligations. Maine (1861), Renner (1949), Selznick (1969), Klare (1979) and Weber (1978) have all argued that a movement from status to contract has characterized society's progress. In brief, they argue that in less differentiated society with customary law most often practiced, one's status in the community (who you are, what position you occupy in the society, what specific role you play) is central in determining rights, obligations and duties. One's identity is intimately connected to a web of social relationships. This "web," in itself, assures that the contracting parties abide by their agreements. In more "advanced societies", this state of affairs is replaced by the contract, which assumes free agreements of individuals. Each contractor is assumed to be capable of freely exchanging what they possess. And each is assumed to be able to meet the other on an equal footing, with equal rights. It is but a temporary bond touching on a very small part of the whole identity of the interacting parties. Here, fulfillment of the contract terms is assured by the State. The contract, as well as the notions of individual responsibility and liability, private property rights, the juridic subject and the state are recent inventions. We need not go far back in history for their origins. We will have more to say about this throughout the book. In sum, the facilitative function of law concerns the question of how certain legal instruments — the contract for example — develop, why they do so, and how they answer the call for predictability and certainty in economic transactions and social interactions.

The third function of law is *ideological.* Ideology as a belief system is always present in law. In other words, law systematically embodies the values of some people, but disregards some values of others. Accordingly, the question of gender, race, ethnicity, class, sexual preference, intersectionality, etc., becomes a central issue in discussions of ideology (for an illuminating critical analysis of ideology in law, see Kerruish, 1991). A particular form of discourse transmits ideology, what we will refer to as a linguistic coordinate system (Chapters 9 and 10). Words attain their legal meaning only by way of struggle in which one definition comes to prevail (Milovanovic, 1987, 2002). For example, consider the Fourteenth Amendment to the U.S. Constitution, which reads, in part, "no person shall be deprived of life, liberty or property without due process of law." The words "person," "life," "liberty," "property," and the notion "due process" have been the subject of much litigation. It has been given meaning by court rulings, the ultimate authority in the U.S. being the U.S. Supreme Court.

Ideological and repressive functions in law often appear together, with the former often disguising the latter. For example, for over 200 years in Australian law the notion of *terra nullius* prevailed. This doctrine had it that Australia, when first "discovered" by Britain, was "uninhabited" and was thus settled as a colony. This doctrine denied the indigenous peoples the lands they had traditionally held for over 40,000 years. In 1992, the High Court of Australia in *Eddie Mabo and Others v. The State of Queensland* overturned this doctrine, recognizing "native title." Currently, much internal resistance exists within different sectors of Australia as to transforming "native title" into government practice.

Several critical concepts are central when examining the ideological function of law: domination, legitimation, hegemony, and reification. We shall have more to say about each throughout the book. As to the issue of *domination*, Max Weber has informed us that subjects in a social formation orient their behavior to an order. But why do they do so? When they do, do they in fact accept it as just? This question of *legitimation* is central. Weber, for example, has shown three forms of domination: charismatic, traditional and legal (see Chapter 4). Subjects predictably abide by the order because it is seen as right, or just. The question of why they do see it as so will be examined in subsequent sections of this book.

Subjects, too, advertently and inadvertently contribute to the maintenance of the socio-political-legal and ideological order, be it one that is more democratic or, ironically as it may sound, one that is totalitarian. Would-be revolutionaries or reformers often, inadvertently, reconstruct the dominant legal order (and its ideologies) by making use of the categories, procedures, and language that are part of the dominant order in their very efforts to redress their grievances (see, for example, the case of jailhouse lawyers in Thomas and Milovanovic, 1999). This is the idea of *hegemony*. Said in yet another way, it is the active participation by subjects in the mechanism of their own oppression. Oppositional groups will often find themselves faced with the dialectics of struggle: struggles, on the one hand, can contribute to emancipatory practices, but on the other, also contribute, be it inadvertently, to the establishment of new forms of hierarchy and repression (see, for example, Cornell, 1998).

The continuous process of reconstructing structures that attain a relatively independent existence is known as *reification*. In other words, subjects collectively construct a social order, and this order comes to take on an "objective" appearance, now dominating subjects.

The flip side of the notion of hegemony is the question of legitimation. Why and how, it might be asked, do subjects inadvertently and advertently participate in the mechanism of their own oppression? Marxist analysis of law places this question in the center of its investigation of law (see Chapter 5). The ideological role of law, then, is said by some, particularly Marxists, to help "persuade the dominated elements in American society that their domination is justified—or that their material conditions of existence are justified or, equivalently, that they are not dominated at all" (Tushnet, 1977: 100). This legitimating function addresses the question of why subjects may follow the law, seeing it as just, where in fact the very distribution of resources might be highly skewed.

> People believe that a practice which is legal is, by that fact alone, a practice which is just. Thus, if one criticizes the distribution of wealth in the society, the ideology of the legal order answers that the distribution is just simply because it arose from transactions that were legal; property, that is, is not

theft because the acquisition of property does not meet the legal definition of theft (Tushnet, ibid.).

In other words, the power bloc's position requires that it articulate justifications for its privileged status (see for example Chapter 4); otherwise, subjects may question the gross disparity in wealth and privilege. Looking toward the law, subjects will see what appears as an autonomous legal system that rests on such principles as formal "equality before the law." The citizen perceives the existence of a democratic society governed by the "rule of law." Hence, the perception created is that it is not the law that aids in maintaining inequality; rather, the discrepancy must be found in the lack of initiative, lack of hard work and so forth. The ideological function of law, then, includes the idea that law may legitimize domination by the power bloc.

In the later pages we shall also focus on the specialized discourse in use by the staff of enforcers (Tiersma, 1999). Whether one uses the oath or the invocation of a divine being as the guarantor of the promise made, or whether as in contemporary society one makes use of trained specialists (lawyers), a particular specialized discourse is used in resolving conflicts (see Chapters 9 and 10). Law-finding—by which we mean the application of specific rules of evidence and reasoning to "factual" situations in order to construct "what happened"—entails the use of a specific linguistic coordinate system (discourse). One must situate oneself in the appropriate linguistic coordinate system in order to be able to do the "correct" reasoning to attain a legal result. Thus, in doing law in the existing form under contemporary capitalism, lawyers bring with them linguistic skills that are obtained by training in law school. The discourse available for use in decision making, in constructing "what happened," is not random; rather a particular method of legal thought must be brought to bear on the "facts" for a legal resolution (see Chapters 6, 7). Durkheim, Weber and Marx all suggest that the members of a staff that engages in law-finding situate themselves within this legal discourse, which often has a sacred character to it. Only the staff knows of its complex use; the layman, the common citizen, is said to be incapable of mastering it. Consider, for example, my recent encounter with a real estate lawyer. Faced with my continuous critical questions, he finally emphatically and authoritatively blurted: "give me your thoughts and I'll find the legal words." In sum, the ideological function of law focuses on how certain ideals are systematized in law and how these ideals are conveyed by the rule of law.

A fourth function of law is *constitutive*. Doing law, legal praxis (theory and action), constitutes phenomena in legal categories and creates reality and agents that do not pre-exist its functioning, its doing. Invoking law, performing law, enacts boundaries, categories, identities, institutional frameworks, focal point, and capabilities. Law is co-constitutively and performatively enacted where that which is created creates the agents (juridic subjects) it needs for its very functioning. The agent as a legal subject emerges in this process. Enacted law establishes the context that provides phenomena legal standing for further litigation. Lawyering brings into being the reality it stipulates (see also Cabantous and Gond, 2011: 578; Gond *et al.*, 2016: 447). Thus, lawyering constitutes a legal reality. Premises of law become legal reality. Consider, for example, how accumulated effects of deprivation and discrimination in hierarchical, unequal society produce a variety of possible grievances, some more amorphous, and how both victim and grievances undergo transformation in legal discursive practices. Consider how the rational agent in law is performatively enacted by material discursive practice. Law and agents (juridic subjects) are co-constructed events performatively enacted in contextualized material discursive practices (e.g., in the context of legal language, texts, identities, architectural arrangements). (We shall have more to say about the mechanisms at play in Chapter 11, "constitutive law.") The constitutive function in law highlights the co-constitutive, performative processes underlying legal realities. Doing law enacts its categories and a legal image of social reality. It brings law into being.

The constitutive function reverses the linear, unidirectional cause-effect relation: rather than, for example, studying race as an independent variable that predicts legal outcomes one of which dichotomizes race as either Black or White. Critical theorists often argue it is law that is the independent variable that explains race (Gomez, 2012). A constitutive function can be seen in "the role played by law in constructing racial identities and categories, as well as compared to how law has shaped the experiences of different racial groups in the U.S." (ibid., 47). This cause-effect is bidirectional: "law not only construct race, but race constructs law" (ibid.). Further, a constitutive function sees this bi-directionality in dialectical terms. The end result both "reproduces and transforms racial inequality" (ibid., 48, 57). Consider the constitutive function in studying culture. Contrary to what traditional historical analysis assumes, it is not culture that only effects law, but law constitutes culture. It "views law as participating in the constitution of culture and thereby in the constitution of people's minds, practices, and social relations" (Mautner, 2011: 841.). Consider, too, the relation between religion and law. Law and courts "constitute political struggle over religion ..." This approach ... helps to uncover the various ways that law and courts catalyze ideological contestations" (Moustafa, 2018: 13–14). Doing law, in short, enables, constitutes, the very categories and identities it seeks to explore.

All four functions of law — repressive, facilitative, ideological, and constitutive — become central in the sociology of law. They often operate, to a degree, together in complex relations, and some are more prominent than others. We have, to many degrees, oversimplified by separating the four into neat categories for pedagogical purposes. Some theorists, we will note in subsequent chapters, focus more on one dimension than another.

We could also speak of the dysfunctions of law. Vago (2012: 20–21), for example, lists at least four: (1) legal systems perpetuate the status quo, (2) often rigidity in application of rules, (3) overregulation, and (4) discriminatory aspects inhering in law itself. To which we could add Barkan's (2018: 6–7) contributions: (5) may "create and perpetuate inequality," (6) may "reflect the moral values of influential social groups," and (7) may "complicate matters more than eases them." Other dysfunctions of note include the narrowness of legal education, archaic language, law and justice at a price (ibid). Nevertheless, both the functions and dysfunctions of law must be included in critical examinations in the sociology of law.

Law and Fulfillment of Social Values

A final core issue needs to be addressed. In studying law, we need to ask: What is the relationship of law and a legal order to the fulfillment of social values (see Trubek, 1977: 545–555)? After all, law and its contributions must be judged by some standard. Law's legitimacy rests, according to many theorists, on the promise that law promotes certain values in a social formation. The first step in this examination then entails "understanding the nature of social ideals which law is thought to foster.... [and in examining] ... empirically and theoretically, the purported relationship between legal institutions and these ideals" (Trubek, 1977: 546). To this end, Trubek has given us a conceptual model in examining the relationship of a legal order to the fulfillment of social values (see Figure 1). Moving beyond Trubek, we also need to respond to the question of the "withering away of law" and capitalism, as some have advocated (Figure 2).

Figure 1. Legal Order and Fulfillment of Social Values under Western Capitalism

Legal order: autonomy and generality		Fulfillment of social values: low	Fulfillment of social values: high
	high	Repressive Formalism	Liberal legalist (formal rationality, rule of law)
	low	Instrumental Marxism	Informalism

Fulfillment of social values
(Adapted from Trubek, 1977: 551)

This model includes two dimensions: the degree of autonomy and generality of the legal order, and the degree to which the legal order contributes to the realization of certain social values. This figure helps us pinpoint *ideal types*, or conceptually pure models. It is a heuristic model in the sense that it gives us a snapshot view of complex, ongoing dynamic systems. It provides us with a beginning point in further critical analysis. Here, in Figure 1, two degrees of freedom are incorporated. Of course, we could develop more complicated models with more than two dimensions, or degrees of freedom. And the two concepts may not even go together on some occasion. For example, autonomy and generality may on occasion be mutually exclusive concepts; that is, they may not be positively correlated. Here there is a tradeoff; simplifying a model gives us a quick starting point for further refined analysis but at a cost of over simplification; a more complex model incorporating more degrees of freedom would provide us with increasingly more accurate models but at the cost of easy and useful initial understanding that sensitize us to the issues. We add that Figure 1 offers not only a descriptive snapshot of a legal order but can also provide a prescriptive dimension, offering suggestions for social change.

Let's examine the first dimension. A legal order can be operationally defined by its "autonomy" (the degree of independence of a legal order from any particular person or interest group) and by its "generality" (the degree to which decisions and rules are made according to previous rules, and applied similarly to all without favorable treatment to any). We can specify a range or scale, from highly autonomous/general to low. A legal order that is "low" on the autonomy dimension would be one where some powerful group or person controls the legal apparatus and law is discriminatorily applied reflecting their interest(s). "High" on this dimension is where the State and law are independent, where no particular power group monopolizes law developments. "High" represents universal standards such as in the U.S. law in its use of the "reasonable man in law," conceptualized as a juridic subject with abstract and universal rights (formal equality). "Low" on generality is where more substantive principles are involved; that is, each person is treated uniquely, and no universal standard is applied.

The second dimension, "social values," Trubek identifies as incorporating *equality* (equal treatment by the State), *individuality* (degree of self-actualization that is realizable), and *community* (degree to which participating and sharing in a greater group is possible). Instead of "individuality" which is already a biased view of the nature of human beings suggesting a self-determining, self-aware, and fully in control agent, we employ "agency," defined as having the ability or capability to affect and be affected which is contextual, historically specific, and evolving in networks of interacting humans. Here we are concerned with human agency (there also exists diverse forms of non-human agency). Social values can be operationally defined in terms of these three. All three will be collapsed so that we can speak of this dimension as ranging from "high" to "low" on our "fulfilment of social values" scale in Figure 1. Thus, some legal systems may contribute more, some less to the realization of social values. (With some reflection on this collapsing operation we could point out that some contradictions may appear—the inherent dangers of over simplification!).

Contemporary perspectives in the sociology of law can be placed at the intersections of these two dimensions. In other words, as we begin to examine different approaches in the sociology of law, we need to be able to make use of some type of organizing framework, which sensitizes us to key issues. Fruitful investigation of the relationship between law and the fulfillment of social values can then take place. It is but the starting point for more refined scholarly analysis. We merely offer this conceptual model as a way of putting in perspective the many examinations of law, which follow. We shall identify four models as examples.

The upper right-hand corner represents the orientation referred to as *liberal legalism*. It is also called formalism, legal formalism, formal rationality or logical formal rationality; at other times, it is simply referred to as the "rule of law." This orientation in the sociology of law states that the legal order is highly autonomous and general; that is, it is independent from the influence of any particular power bloc or person, and it is also seen as offering, at the same time, the potential for maximal fulfillment of social values. Law, it is argued, deals with conflicts in a neutral, value-free manner so that maximal realization of social values is achieved or potentially achievable. In other words, the rule of law is said to allow maximal freedom and minimal coercion in law.

The assumption in this perspective is that an ideal order identified as legal formalism provides the best solution to the question of how to handle ongoing conflicting interests and values for the good of all. Law schools and their curricula teach the fundamentals of correct legal reasoning (precedence, syllogistic reasoning, deductive logic) in preparation for carrying out this ideal legal system. Assumed, too, in this model is that if we fine-tuned the machinery of legal formalism, eradicating extra-legal factors that may come into play such as race, class, gender, and intersectional biases in decision-making, replacing them by adherence to the formal rules, logic and rationality, society would be the better for it, since maximal realization of values would be attained or potentially attainable. The rule of law is said to be the ideal toward which we should strive. Such a principle as the "equal protection clause" incorporated in the Fourteenth Amendment to the U.S. Constitution, a central element of the rule of law, expresses it best: equally situated should be equally treated.

Let us provide an example in the use of this model as it deals with liberal legalism's solution to racism or sexism in the legal order. We begin by identifying biases of the legal order against certain segments of the population. The realization of social values for this segment is shown to be significantly less than others similarly situated. Here we have a legal order that is not highly autonomous or general (some segment of the population is subject to discrimination), and as a consequence this group is denied the fulfilment of social values. In this hypothetical, law students are taught to apply an "equal protection" argument in order to move the functioning of the legal order toward the upper right-hand corner as an ideal, hence eradicating biases and prejudices and also providing the way for the greater opportunity for the realization of social values. However, the critique of the wherewithal of the "equal protection clause" does not exist; the clause is taken as a given and applied to problematic situations. Thus, we can appropriately identify this legal work as primarily mechanical in nature. To be successful in law school and subsequent law work, students in law school must show their mastery of the process for correct legal decision-making (syllogistic reasoning, deductive logic).

Liberal legalism has most often been the focal point of those in the *jurisprudential* tradition rather than the sociology of law tradition. Members of the practicing legal profession as well as academic law professors most often work within the logic of jurisprudence. Sociologists of law, on the other hand, most often focus on trying to also understand the other three ideal types in Figure 1. Hence, what we find is that different questions and solutions are offered because of these particular foci. For example, questions might focus on: what were the backgrounds of the "founding fathers" who established core principles (axioms in law)?; what interests did they advocate?; from where did the "equal protection clause" spring?; and what other forms of decision-making may be viable?

"Instrumental Marxism" appears in Figure 1 at the intersection of low autonomy and generality and low fulfillment of social values. Law is seen as being dependent on some dominant group or person (i.e., the ruling class). Here the majority of the population, in Marxist's view the proletariat, the "working classes," is seen as being denied genuine opportunity in the fulfillment of social value. The ruling class is said to use the system of law and legal order as an instrument (hence "instrumental Marxism") to maximize its own interest in making profits ("surplus value"), repressing opposition, and subjugating dissidents to the legal apparatus it controls.

Exploitation of the worker, alienation, fragmentation, excessive competition, racism, sexism, class exploitation, the rewarding of egoistic behavior at the expense of altruism—all, according to the instrumental Marxist position, are part and parcel of the workings of the capitalist mode of production (capital logic). Law, then, is primarily repressive, favoring the powerful group in control. The less powerful are held in check by the legal order (for a precise statement, see Quinney, 1974, 2002). The instrumental Marxists would argue that the very ideology that develops—advocating the necessity of coercive law because of the existence of predatory individuals—is convoluted, mystifying and self-serving. The system, it is said, produces these individuals ("crippled monstrosities") in the first instance and then creates an ideology for the necessity of controlling this end product. Lawyers who uncritically follow the *Lawyers Code of Ethics* are sometimes seen as lackeys of the dominant, exploitive order.

"Repressive formalism" (top left, "high" in autonomy/generality and "low" in fulfilment of social values) is an orientation that poses a paradox. The legal order can be highly autonomous and general, but, at the same time, this situation may: (1) still further the interests of the capitalist "class" as a whole; and (2) contribute very little to the overall realization of social values. In other words, this orientation has it that the legal order, on a formal level, may indeed advocate for the ideals of autonomy and generality, and the ideals specified, for example, in the Bill of Rights. It will *not* be under the direct control of the capitalist "class," and will render the principle of formal equality a central valued place in society. Yet, genuine fulfillment of social values will be denied. As Trubek has argued (1977: 553), "the capitalist mode of production leads to increasing inequality of income and power, to domination and destruction of genuine individuality, and to the rupture of communal ties and thus alienation." But these effects, according to those within this tradition, are obscured and mystified by a legal order that, on its face, appears as autonomous and general. Capitalists as well as workers, in other words, are both subject to the legal system and receive formal equal treatment before the law; but what is overlooked by the operations of the legal system is the vast economic disparities and how these are transformed into privileges for the powerful. It has often been referred to as "repression by formal rationality." Some would argue that within this model, lawyers rationally and logically applying principles of law are inadvertently re-constituting powers of domination.

For example, consider the formal application of the "equal protection clause" of the U.S. 14th Amendment to the Constitution. Consider Anatole France's much-cited quip that the rich and poor are equally prohibited from sleeping under the bridges of the Seine in France. Both are being treated (formally) on an equal footing. However, with a little reflection it becomes quite apparent that formal equality may hide and perpetuate substantive inequality. Consider the situation of two individuals, one making $100,000 the other $10,000 per year. They both are given tickets for driving 15 miles per hour over the speed limit (thus they are equally situated vis-a-vis the infraction). Assume they both get equivalent legal services (equally treated). And they both are fined $50 dollars per person (again, equally treated). Conclusion: since equally situated were equally treated, this is constitutionally permissible (e.g., is in accordance with the 14th Amendment "equal protection" clause); in this case it is the ideal. We have formal equality in law. Those from the liberal legalist position focus on identifying the circumstances in which and by which equally situated are not equally treated (i.e., biases due to racism, sexism, intersectionality etc.), and attempt to fine-tune the machinery in order that formal equality reigns, overlooking the substantive nature of differences in income levels, for example in a hierarchical society. A close examination of this example leads us to question whether substantive justice results in light of the initial difference in wealth. Surely a $50 fine has a different significance for a person making $10,000 per year than it does for a person making $100,000 per year.

In sum, this orientation indicates that the legal ideals generated, formulated and institutionalized after the demise of feudalism and with the development of capitalism, are both an affirmation and a negation, a dialectic (see also Balbus, 1977a; we will also return to this in the chapters on Karl Marx and Max Weber). Proclaimed ideals such as "equality for all" may, at a deeper level of analysis, indicate hidden repressive dimensions. Ironically and inadvertently, then, activists might at times be unintentionally reinforcing a more hidden form of repression. This brings out the various forms of hegemony (domination) that we shall return to on several occasions throughout this book. It is also the basis of the dialectics of struggle whereby disenfranchised groups, for example, do in fact benefit from "rights discourse"; they do receive some alleviation from discrimination and suffering, but, inadvertently, their efforts contribute to the legitimation of the rule-of-law ideology. See, for example, the ambiguous relationship people of color and women have with this: on the one hand, they are provided with a voice in law, but, on the other, by this very practice, inadvertently or not, furthers the legitimacy of the rule of law.

Of course, the example provided above can lead to many intriguing questions and analyses. It offers, in a snapshot form, the tension between formal principles in law (i.e., the equal protection clause: equally situated should be equally treated) and substantive principles in law (i.e., Marx's notion: "from each according to his [her] abilities, to each according to his [her] needs"). Marxists, therefore, would argue for *different* treatment for *different* people (a principle of inequality?): the person who makes $100,000 per year in our example above would need to pay a fine that is proportionally greater, here ten times, than that of a person who makes $10,000 per year, or $500. Consider, for a moment, the ramifications of this example for an entire legal order! Some European countries already try to work these possible outcomes into their legal system by the use of "day fines" whereby a convicted speeder, for example, is levied a two-day penalty based on their income level. Hence, if a well-to-do makes, say $1,000 per day we multiply by two in arriving at penalty, contrasted to a person who makes $50 per day ($2,000 versus $100 fine).

The final orientation, "informalism," indicates a legal order that is "low" on generality and autonomy but "high" on the realization of social values (see lower right-hand corner of Figure 1). Thus, "low" on generality due to each person being treated uniquely (substantive law); and low on autonomy due to dependence of the legal order on some authority, be it a group or person/agent. We offer, as examples, two variants. A benevolent dictatorship is where the leader has primal power, but yet rules to the benefit of all societal members. To those who need the most, so they shall receive. A formal system of law would not necessarily be in existence but where it is, rules and policies would reflect the leader's desire for enhancing more equitable justice. (Village or tribal elders or chief, in less differentiated, specialized and formally structured societies regulated by customary law, played this role). The benevolent dictator would be guided by an acute sense of justice. It is often seen as a transitional state to more equitable law and justice. Some historical examples have been offered: Mustafa Kemal Ataturk (Turkey, 1923–1938); Josip Tito (Yugoslavia, 1953–1980); Lee Kuan Yew (Singapore, 1959–1990); Abd al-Karim Quasim (Iraq, 1958–1963); and France-Albert René (Seychelles, 1977–2004) (see Wikipedia, *Benevolent Dictatorship*). Arguably, perhaps a more recent case-in-point can be made for the rise of Singapore from an early form of benevolent dictatorship particularly under Lee Kuan Yew to its current ruling "People's Action Party." It has often been cited for ushering in exceptional gains in transportation, housing, private property ownership, life expectancy (85), as well as universal health care, efficiency of health care, and climate change, although income disparities have been on the rise. Benevolent dictatorships, however, are subject to much critique. Historically, benevolent dictatorships can transition either way, liberation, to permanent dictatorship and forms of instrumental Marxism where the latter only being undone by revolutionary action.

A second variant of informalism is the "dictatorship of the proletariat" (will reappear in Figure 2). It is assumed by Marxists to take place after the overthrow of the capitalist mode of production and is assumed to be a "transitional state." Here there is "low" autonomy since the proletariat now in power are assumed to unilaterally rule. This variant is also "low" on generality, since all will be treated differently (substantive justice), with more harshness directed towards those wishing to resurrect the previous exploitive order. It can also be, in critique, the occasion for a system-wide political correctness ideology. In this variant, it is predicted that greater fulfilment of social values follows than that found in the previous order overthrown.

Figure 2. Legal Order and Fulfillment of Social Values in Transitional ("withering away") Capitalism

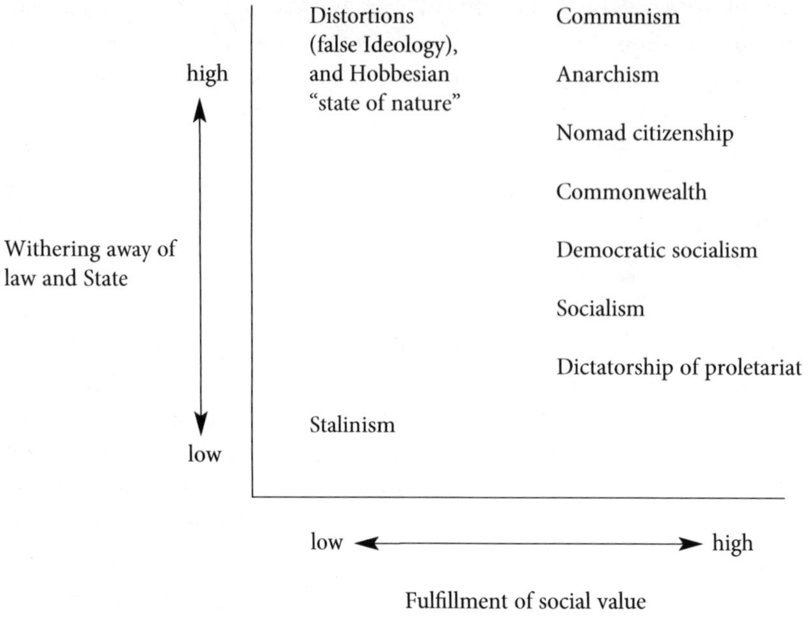

Let us move on to Figure 2 which focuses on transitional capitalism and the relationship of the legal order to the fulfilment of social values. It is a pedagogical exercise in stimulating imaginative thought, a provocation, a push for thinking alternatively.

Figure 2 responds to those critics of what is perceived as excessively competitive, exploitive, and monopolistic capitalism, one with a package of evils: hierarchical power differential arranged in class distinctions; degradation of the environment under the name of "progress"; generation of categories that discriminate (i.e., race, gender, class, intersectional); othering practices that distance and reduce the Other (i.e., seeing the Other as an "it" rather than a "you"); alienation of workers; health and education based on monetary standing; reduction of things' worth to the monetary; not fully compensating workers for their labors (surplus value is extracted from workers and disproportionally given to the "bourgeoisie"); decision-making based on differential power; little genuine participatory democracy, etc. Here, critics search for alternative forms law. In some scenario, these critics argue, capitalism disappear altogether with a return to substantive law/justice and mutual aid as the guiding principle; in other scenarios, capitalism remains but is more regulated for community as well as people's development. Marx, for example, did say with the emergence of capitalism we were released from the shackles of feudalism, religions, superstition, customary practices. Possibilities for development and released energies for alternatives, as a consequence, were now considerably opened.

There are other possibilities in developing pedagogical models; each model can provide provocative tools for further critical inquiry. In our model, there are two main variables: first, the degree of "withering away" of law and State, and second, degree of fulfilment of social values (each ranged from low to high). Let's look at the right hand column for examples. Here we include a range from: the "dictatorship of the proletariat" to communism. The question of "autonomy" of law begins to lose its significance as we move to the "high" position since the State and law, following Marx and Lenin's thesis (Chapter 5), are predicted to wither away. The question of "generality" is, here, inverse to that in Figure 1; that is, as we move to the "high" position there is little generality since each person is treated differently in their uniqueness ("from each according to his [their] abilities, to each according to his [their] needs"—responding to different needs and abilities), more substantive law and justice. A key distinguishing factor is that all the listed examples leading to the final one espouses, to various degrees, a high value on transition to a more humanistic society. Whether an order is indeed "transitional" or not remains; we only provide a starting point for further critically informed historical examination.

Let's examine some of the examples. In the "dictatorship of the proletariat," according to Karl Marx, a successful proletarian-led revolution temporary establishes a unilateral legal system instilling proletarian values. Here the State and law would still exist, but now authoritatively instilling proletariat ideology. It is more top down, since the leadership is generally recognized as having exceptional leadership qualities reflecting principles of a more humanistic society which they seek to effectuate; however, in the extreme negative form, we have the authoritarian dictatorship of the Stalin era (1928–1953), listed in the lower left corner of Figure 2. History is replete with examples. It should be noted, many States that are often perceived as "communist" are more democratic socialism. "Communism," to be clear, following Marx and Lenin would be a stateless society, with no central powers, law, police, prisons, etc.

In socialism we often see two variants. For Marx, socialism, a transitional period, is still top down but insisting on more genuine equality and reward principles. In democratic socialism unrestrained capitalism is questioned replaced with the ideal of a socialist market economy which State power pursues with the promise of actualizing humanistic ideals. This includes substantive law such as day fines and income-ratio regulation, along with varying forms of participatory democratic decision-making.

The notion of the "commonwealth" is offered by Hardt and Negri (2011). It is a continuous replacement of exploitive forms of capitalism with the rational that since all contribute in society all should reap full benefits from their work rather than having it forcefully extracted in wage labor. Instead of the rule by some homogeneous proletariat, they advocate the "multitude," a shifting cross section and alliances, a "rainbow coalition" of differences.

Another example, affirmative nomad citizenship (Holland, 2011), argues for a free-market communism, one grounded in freeing labor from capitalist exploitation (surplus value), breaking the State's monopolistic powers, making use, instead, of a self-organizing model based on improvisational jazz, and following a strategy for getting there, a "slow motion strikes" (gradually de-committing to capital logic). Here, organizations are leaderless, and are more dissipative structural in form; meaning, they undergo continuous change, ever sensitive to even the smallest input defying the rigidity of structures such as bureaucracies and formal logical rationality (see also chaos theory, Chapter 11). Formal, universal, abstract "rights," for this line of thought, as Gilles Deleuze (Boutang, 1989; Lefebvre, 2008) has argued are too rigid. And the dogmatic tendency of "subsumption" (in resolving cases, lawyers and judges search for the "correct" acceptable legal concepts under which to subsume it and then do linear deductive logic to arrive at a "correct" decision) are too reactive to be the basis of law. Rather, each case is seen as unique in and off itself and legal decision-making must follow this logic, a form of case law. The use of deductive *and* inductive reasoning, sometimes referred to as "abduction," will lead to more genuine decision-making.

Next, anarchist would seek a stateless society guided by mutual support and care. The salient point is mutual aid, solidarity and reciprocity. This assures the maximal realization of social values, with minimal law and no dependency on a State.

We return to communism as Marx envisions it. In Marx's view (see Chapter 5) of the "withering away of law," socialist law and the "dictatorship of the proletariat" would undergo transformation in light of Marx and Lenin's prediction of the emergence of the "higher forms" of modes of production. Here, the prediction is that socialism, said to be an outcome of irreparable contradictions of the capitalism mode of production, would transform into communism where law withers away replaced by indigenous community organizations. Anarchists share this view to various degrees. The governing needs/abilities principle would be "from each according to his [their] abilities, to each according to his [their] needs"). Law would be substantive, treating each unique person according to their respective needs and abilities. Community justice centers, as a formal authority, would be more dissipative structures in form, highly sensitive and responsive to community needs. Examples offered in incipient form would be: "village committees" (China), worker self-management (former Yugoslavia), and other informal tribunals and justice centers. Only with the removal of the capitalist mode of production, it is argued, will the state, law, lawyers, and the "juridic subject" (abstract bearer of rights) disappear. In their place, informal community "moots" and tribunals would develop in the "higher forms" of communism. The first line of defense against the development of troublesome behavior is, however, the establishment of a society focused on altruism, cooperation, collective development, mutual aid, and the social ideal of the Renaissance person.

In the upper left-hand corner of Figure 2, we conceptualize more distorted forms. Even while advocating the withering away of law and the potential for a liberated society based on fulfillment of social values, it is belied by what is actually afoot perpetuated by a false ideology (ideological function). More Stalinism in sheep's clothing. Some critics, too, would argue that the "withering away of law" potentially returns us to the Hobbesian state of "war of all against all."

In sum, Trubek's conceptual model (Figure 1) with modifications allows for much fruitful conceptualization of the relationship of laws to the fulfillment of social values. It is a convenient tool in the sociology of law. It can be read descriptively as a convenient, summary snapshot of a legal order; pedagogically, as a basis of focusing critical research efforts; and prescriptively, as a tool for envisioning social change. We will return to it several times throughout this book as a guide to our presentations and analyses. Figure 2, offers some conceptualizations of possible less exploitive forms of organization and the promise for the fulfillment of social values. It too provides a basis for expanding the imagination toward the possible. Not a blueprint, but more an exercise of disrupting conventional thinking in the sociology of law in the hopes of generating affirmative visions toward more fulfilling societies.

Law and the Rise of the Legal Profession

The rise of the legal profession has witnessed stages in development (Vago, 2012: 344–353; Barkan, 2018: 241–245).[1] In "primitive," or better customary and/or pre-literate societies characterized as less differentiated and specialized, and more decentralized, identified traditionally as hunters and gathers, customary law prevailed. No need for specialists, nor for formal written laws (Schwartz and Miller, 1964). All practiced an informal law, all thoroughly knew the correct ways (see Durkheim, Chapter 3). The beginnings of lawyering can be traced to ancient Greece and Rome where "orators" prevailed (Bonner, 1969 [1927]; Crook, 1967; Schultz, 1946; Brundage, 2010; see also Barkan, 2018: 241–242; for a noted jurist's view who was influential in developing a sociological jurisprudence, see Pound, 1944). These were people who could speak on behalf of someone, and who were trained in rhetoric, public speaking, the art of persuasion and oratory, and normally did not take a fee. In Rome, during the time of Marcus Cicero (106–43 BC), who wrote extensively on rhetoric, politics and philosophy, orators, now called *juris prudentes*, rhetoric began to be more extensively incorporated as prominent elements in law-in-practice. Practitioners would render advice, but still remained part-time advocates (Vago, 2012: 344). During the Imperial Period (27 BC–476 AD), where law in the Roman Empire became more detailed, this class began to be more dedicated to the study and practice of law. Under Roman Emperor Tiberius Claudius (41 AD–54 AD), legal practices were legalized, although rhetoric was still the tool, and practitioners did not apply any systematic formal principles of law. Fees were allowed, but with ceilings (Crook, ibid). However, a new group was to emerge, *jurisconsultus*, or jurists. Jurisconsults (*juris consulti*) were usually well-to-do (Crook, 87–90).

Things changed by the Middle Ages (5th to the 15th century, including feudalism, beginning circa 8th century, and the "dark ages," 500 AD–1,000 AD; some debate exists about the precise cut-off points). With the breakup of Rome's Empire in Western

Europe, the church became more dominant as the purveyor of law (Brundage, 2010). During feudalism, land ownership determined basic serf-nobleman relations (status), privileging the latter.

Even so, law and the legal profession was still taking some form, be it in a hindered way, especially during the 12th and 13th Century (mid 1100s to 1200s; Brundage, 2010). In England, the *barrister* (legal advocate) had to have permission by the King to appear to represent someone (see also Abel, 1988); in France (1356) there were *legisters*, or men of law, who represented clients in court (Vago, 2012, 345 citing Jacoby, 1973: 14). In the English experience the Norman Conquest (1066) initiated greater use of common law. Power was centralized by monarchies, each proclaiming that disturbances in the social order is an attack on "the King's Peace" and hence will be dealt with by the State. Under the reign of Henry 11 (1154–89) we witnessed consolidation and centralization of the judiciary with dignitaries visiting areas inquiring about the delivery of justice. There was now a marked division between the delivery of law between the Church and State (Glendon *et al.,* 2020). Under the reign of Edward 1 (1272–1307) systematized civil law followed, away from merely applying snippets of Roman law (a form of civil law). The judge now became a full-time position. The legal credentials of those who wished to practice laws were formalized, now dependent on legal training.

Legal guilds initially provided some avenue for learning the common law, which were the forerunners to the Inns of Court. The Inns of Court, four in total, offered a social club for well-to-do, lodging, and training in law for apprentices by more experienced barristers; an early form of law school. Initially barristers were called "storytellers" (Vago, 2012: 347). Also, a legal status, the "solicitors" was created: people who prepared cases and provided advice, but did not practice law in the courtroom. All barristers (those who actually participated in actual litigation in courts), had to belong to one of the Inns of Court. Lectures and attendance at Court proceedings were part of the education. Students took notes summarizing the logic of decision-making employed in court trials, and these in 1280 were summarized in annual *Year Book.* These were the forerunners of annual printed law books, stored in law libraries, reflecting legal decisions at various levels: in the U.S., State and Federal Courts—trial, appeals, Supreme Court. The emergence and the importance of case law and the continuation and dominance of common law was now solidified (Glendon, *et al.,* ibid). Formalization had found a most importance take-off point. And by 1758, Sir William Blackstone, writer of *Commentaries on the Law of England,* consisting of four books (1765–1769), now professor at Cambridge University, formalized legal education in Universities (Glendon *et al.,* ibid.). The legal profession had now been well established.

It was with the more formal development of capitalism (17th Century)[2] that greater momentum once again was created for the development of lawyers and law (see Max Weber, Chapter 4; Karl Marx, Chapter 5). The notion of the "juridic subject," an abstract bearer of rights and subject to the formal logical rational principles in law (in the U.S., the "reasonable man in law") was to emerge, away from *status.* A distinct legal discourse was to become further solidified, a language often sprinkled in Latin terms, increasingly obscure and inaccessible for common folk to comprehend (see Chapter 9). The question of law's causal evolution (does the economy cause the development of formal law?) will have important explanations by Emile Durkheim (Darwinian), Max Weber (multi-causal), and Karl Marx (unicausal in the instrumental form, but reciprocal in the structural version of Marxism; see next three chapters).

The rise of the legal profession in the U.S. starts with the pre-revolutionary experiences of the colonists. The colonists drew much early inspiration from the legal developments in England (common law). Its practitioners were more well-to-do. Evidence indicates early practitioners of law-for-a-fee was frowned upon, as a source of disruptions of harmony, and against their church (Protestant), particularly the Puritan ideals. There was noted animosity toward lawyers (see for example, Pound, 1944). Those who did practice it, similar to experiences in England, learned their trade through apprenticeship practices which most often privileged the well-to-do, white male. But perhaps an indicator of their growing influence and power, twenty-five of fifty-six men who signed the U.S. Declaration of Independence (1776) had training in law. Post-revolutionary times, particularly from late 1700s–1870 saw movement toward more formal training, especially noted with the law school founded in Litchfield, Connecticut in 1784. Harvard and Yale Universities were to establish university training in early 1800s, even as William and Mary did so in the late 1793. But standards and curricula were loose. Neither a college education nor formal legal training was required for legal practice with apprenticeships still the dominant form.

It is of note, that the first slave codes appeared in the colonies between 1691–1730, often traced to the Barabados' model (1661) (Rugemer, 2013; Olsen: 1944; Finkelman, 2014, 2019). Slaves had few legal rights, could not own property or make contracts, could not assemble nor vote, had restrictions on movement and marriage, could not testify against whites, and were not allowed to learn to read and write ("Slave Code," *Encyclopedia Britannica*). Few incentives existed for lawyers to represent the slave. The U.S. Constitutional Convention witnessed 25 of the 55 delegates as slave owning, and for the Declaration of Independence, 41 of 56 signers. The U.S. Constitution (1787) remained protective of slavery (Finkelman, 2014). By early 1850s, over 40% of the population in the South were slaves, working primarily on cotton farms, generating substantial profits for white landowners. So, for some in the population, there was reason for optimism in legal developments; for African-Americans, rights were substantially restricted, until the signing of the 13th Amendment to the U.S. Constitution outlawing slavery, but it then continued, as history has shown, in different forms, systematic and often more unconscious as well as conscious. The legacy continuous regardless of any talk of a "post-colonial" society.

To return to further developments of the legal profession. From 1870s onward we witness a shift to greater professionalization, on the one hand, and domination on the other. A significant development took place at Harvard Law School under Christopher Langdell's Deanship (Kimball, 1999, 2006, 2009; Wells, 2010; see also Chapter 6). He introduced the Socratic method, case studies, syllogistic reasoning, and generally argued for law training as a science much like the natural sciences. He also lengthened the degree requirement to three years of education and introduced more stringent standards. His model became the standard for law schools throughout the land which still remain in the U.S. In 1878 the American Bar Association (ABA) was established. On the one hand, professionalization and higher standards were instituted, but on the other, note critics, it was a monopolistic institution of exclusion (excluding, quite openly, African Americans, women and other non-whites; Friedman, 1984, 1998, 2005; Abel, 1986). And by limiting the number of lawyers, it assured higher fees and income. As Friedman (1984: 245–246) argued, its early form was a "club for white males," "white shoe firms" (shoes made of white buckskin). Its exclusionary practices continued into the twentieth century, well up to the 1950s. Developing law firms also continued these exclusionary practices through the 1950s; white Anglo-Saxon Protestants remained dominant employees. The 1960s and 1970s, however, witnessed the beginning of greater access.

Large corporate law firms began to appear in late 1880s, whereas prior to this period, particularly before the Civil War, small offices were concerned with land, trade, and commercial transactions. The building of railroads placed higher demands for lawyers as controversies emerged, and so did the growing banking industries. New partnerships emerged. Corporate law became most esteemed and rewarding (Vago, 2012, 352, referencing Auerbach, 1976). Nevertheless, exclusionary practices often prevailed similar to the early ABA and law schools well into the 1950s.

Things did not progress so linearly, however. From 1900 to 1940 the legal realists, inspired by Oliver Wendell Holmes (key exponents, Jerome Frank, Karl Llewellyn) and sociological jurisprudence (key exponent, Rosco Pound) critiqued the law respectively from *inside* (law in action versus law on the books) and *outside* (drawing more from sociology). After a gap from 1940 to mid-1970s, things began to change internally in law schools with the development in the mid to late-1970s of the critical legal studies movement (see Chapters 6, 7). Ironically, its base was Harvard Law School where a small group of "crits" were very vocal and articulate and attracted many students including the press. The battles between the classical law professors and the new Turks spilled over to the media. By the 1980s, critical legal studies increasingly challenged the application of law, its perpetuated ideology, and its alignment with those in power, and argued law school was a "preparedness for hierarchy." The ideals perpetuated by the ABA and law schools were a focus of critical examination; often challenged was their complicity, be it inadvertent or advertent (i.e., dialectics of struggle), with maintaining the dominant order. Critical legal studies spawned offspring's in the 1990s to the present: critical race theory (CRT), critical feminist (Fem Crits), Queer Crits, Lat Crits, Asian-American Crits, etc. as well as intersectional studies (see Chapter 7; see also Capeheart and Milovanovic, 2020: 239–265). Law, the courts, and lawyers, more and more, were being critically studied in terms of ideological, constitutive, and repressive functions along with their formally announced facilitative functions. For "cause lawyers," realized more and more was the "dialectics of struggle." For many activist lawyers, however, law offered a weapon for social change and overcoming system-wide discriminatory barriers, be they conscious or unconscious. For many activists and others, law was seen as a "necessary evil" (Friedman, 1985: 96).

Law, Social Movements, and Social Change

The relationship of law to social change is a complex one. Does law produce social change? Or does social change produce law? Or, is there a co-constitutive relationship where the causal arrow works both ways (see Vago, 2004: 389–392; 308–311; Dror, 1969)?[3] Thus:

social change → law?

law → social change?

social change ↔ law?

Sociology of law, in examining the first, social change → law, often begins with the return to the classic writings of Emile Durkheim (evolution and continuous differentiation of society to ever more complexity demanding new responsive law), Max Weber (the rise of capitalism necessitating a new form of law, formal rationality, that was in accord with capital logic), and Karl Marx (in the instrumental Marxist approach, economic power translating into political power with the ability of controlling the development of law) (Chapters 3–5). Law, in other words, is said to be shaped by developments in society. More recently, we must consider developments in postmodern analysis and post postmodern analysis along with digimodernism (Chapters 11, 12), a society of rapid technological advancements, the continued evolution of the internet and internet commerce (transactions, protections, cybercrimes, etc.), growing importance on the reliance of information particularly the digital, expansion of virtual dealings, plethora of risks and uncertainties (environmental, terrorist, international conflicts, employment, new diseases, catastrophes, etc.), and evolving diverse and complex identities.

Criticism of the social change → law causal direction includes: law is often slow to respond to changing social conditions, law sometimes blunts and translates social developments into system supporting ways, it may "cool out the mark" stymying dissent by providing limited concessions, sometimes has unintended consequences, and law often raises a myriad of obstacles to activism advocating for real responsive changes.

In the second variant, law → social change, studies attempt to show how changes in law itself produce significant social changes. Take, for example, the U.S. Supreme Court decision, *Brown v. Board of Education* (1954) that called for desegregation. It led to many lower court decisions more directly responding to confronting racism in society. Let us, however, not underestimate struggles and advocacy. The NAACP Legal Defense and Educational Fund predated the decision, along, with the thoughts from some that the returning African-American soldier from the Korean War was not going to "sit at the back of the bus," and looming was the potential recruitment, some have argued by the active Communist Party at the time. Similarly, the Civil Rights Act (1964) and Voting Rights Act (1965), in the activist climate of the 1960s, provided new momentum for desegregation (Barkum, 2018: 191). Other cases such as *Roe v. Wade* (1973) (abortion rights, right to privacy) and *Miranda v. Arizona* (1966) (right to remain silent, right to lawyer), and *Obergefell v. Hodges* (2015) (legalizing same sex marriage) had clear effects in social policy at various levels.

A key question has to do with the effectiveness of law in social change. Effectiveness must also consider direct and indirect effects. Direct effects are where law produces immediate changes to behavior; indirect is where law works its way through an "intervening variable" and then has its effects (i.e., law may change some organization or institution and that in turn affects behavior and/or attitudes) (see Dror, 1969; Barkun, 2018: 193; Vago, 2012: 316–318). Consider the question of racial desegregation through law. Historically, we have witnessed the initial approach by *Brown* and legal cases through the 1960s citing contributing "conditions." This was dramatically altered by the late 1970s to focus on "bad apples" where the *intent* to discriminate must be proven, focusing on individual agents rather than statistical evidence of patterns to discriminate connected to detrimental social conditions. This had its most clear expression in the ruling by the U.S. Supreme Court in *McCleskey v. Kemp* (1987), where, despite clear sophisticated use of social science methodology and data (Baldus Report) showing clear patterns in capital punishment sentences, clearly discriminating against African-Americans, nevertheless fell back to the "bad apple" requirement leaving contributing conditions unexamined and as they are. We also recall, the horrendous decision by the U.S. Supreme Court in *Dred Scott v. Sanford* (1857), and latter, allowing continuing discrimination, in *Plessy v. Ferguson* (1896), with the "separate but equal doctrine" that was to justify segregation and racism for the next 50 years. Recently (2020), with particularly the activism by the Black Lives Matter and other movement groups, there is a growing public perception that "systematic racism" exists, and that it can be of the conscious or unconscious variety, a return to the much more compelling notions of "conditions" and contexts that are conducive to racisms, as well as holding individual perpetrators accountable.

It has often been noted that lawyers, because of their traditional legal training in law school, are often ill-equipped to adequately engage in social movement struggles (Lopez, 1992; Kennedy, 1992; Freeman and Freeman, 2016). However, lawyers are important allies for social movements and where enlisted, there is an on-going call for their reorientation and sensitization to the movement's goals. Thus, the "goal for lawyers working in solidarity with oppressed communities should be for each of the strategies and tactics we employ to result in those communities acquiring more political, communication/media, grassroots, or legal influence relative to their opponents" (Freeman and Freeman, ibid., 147).[4]

Environmental movements in struggles for eco-justice, too, have found that the use of law is a tool, but in its use, can be co-opted, shaped along capital logic terms, and can limit activism and more genuine structural reform (see Capeheart and Milovanovic, 2020: 144–177). There has been ongoing evidence that more genuine and permanent changes may occur through legislative policy changes than through legal action. On the other hand, some note the dramatic changes toward modernization brought about by a top-down form of law in China, Russia, and Eastern Europe, notwithstanding questions of authoritarian rule. From the material that exists, social activists can conclude that law can work both ways; nevertheless, in fighting for rights, it remains a tool for change, a "necessary evil."

The third relation, social change ↔ law, argues that there is a co-constitutive or reciprocal relationship. Social change can lead to new law, but the new law in turn shapes the nature and form of social change (Chapter 11, "constitutive law"; see also Vago, 2012: 308–309). Consider the U.S. "plain view doctrine" established by the U.S. Supreme Court responding to the Fourth Amendment requirement against "unreasonable searches and seizures." It allows for any contraband in plain view to be further investigated, and if illegal, confiscated with an arrest, without first procuring a required search or arrest warrant signed by a judge. Working the other way around (reciprocal, co-constitutive), at times, police officers may illegally search and later for the court record and admissibility requirements, state that it was in plain view. Therefore, social change can induce changes in law, but law, in turn can shape the very form of expression of the social change that social agents seek. Thus, everyday discourse, including the language of social movement adherents, is replete with legal expressions as well as the sentiments of real people going about their everyday business. Consider, too, how the First Amendment to the U.S. Constitution stipulating freedom of expression, has been interpreted by the highest court to mean expression can be regulated in terms of time, place, manner. Hence, social change agents and social movements often find that the new language of the courts becomes incorporated and imbedded in their everyday discussions, constructions of the problem at hand, and strategizing. This also brings out the work of the constitutive law approach (Chapter 9) and the constitutive function of law previously described. The relationship is "intra-active," agency and legal structure each informs the other and co-determinately, and in performative actions produce the reality we perceive.

A fourth relation has been advocated in the literature (Freeman and Freeman, 2016):

Social movements → litigation, lawsuits → social change (e.g., policy change).

Thus, the mobilization of power activates more willing submissions and receptivity of law suits which leads to social change. Freeman and Freeman (ibid., 164) argue, for example, "most of the influential lawsuits or administrative complaints are best understood as effects or byproducts of this social movement, rather than causes of significant contributors to its creation or development." Thus, power drives policy (ibid.) and the example they provide (mobilization to abate the "school-to-prison pipeline" brought about by get-tough and zero-tolerance rhetoric[5] which reached a crescendo by 2006) "generated enough power [over the next decade] to force policymakers to respect its arguments in conventional legal processes to support its priorities" (ibid.). The Black Lives Matter movement brought to a crescendo with disproportional killings of disarmed African-Americans is also a case in point.

Related to our first relation above, that social change effects law, is the question of social movements and their effects. Social movements are more conscious efforts by organizations with degree of structure and varying degrees of longevity, and more often directed at changing an oppressive law or policy, modifying it, or advocating a replacement (i.e., Black Lives Matter, Rainbow Coalition, Environmental Justice Movements, Occupy Wall Street, etc.; see also, Freeman and Freeman, 2016; Freeman, 2015; Cummings, 2016, 2018). Other societal-wide forms seek state recognition (i.e., Palestinians in the Middle East, Basque in Spain, Scotland in Great Britain). We also have "cause lawyering" (Sarat and Scheingold, 2006), or public interest law, usually practiced by individuals or firms, sometime *pro bono*, and often single issue (i.e., "lemon" laws). But we also witness more regressive practices such as hate groups, those advocating white supremacy in the U.S., and neo-Nazism in Europe. In extreme form, social movements may lead to transitions to a new political order (i.e., Arab Spring, early 2010s).

Social movements generally are more decentralized, although charismatic leaders such as Martin Luther King Jr. and Malcolm X certainly galvanize organizations. They have a particular operative ideology defining the opposition and providing an explanation for their struggles in a common discourse (i.e., labor, civil rights, feminist, women's suffrage, eco-justice, animal rights, etc.). Successful social movements, often from the ground-up, witness specific changes in law and social policy. They then may disband, but often transform to confronting other social injustices.

The use of legal mobilization, has, however, a number of impediments (Barkan, 2018: 200–202): unsympathetic courts, lack of financial resources, procedural obstacles in the courts, resistance by targeted group, channeling of activist's energy into formal legalism with only minor possibilities of change (i.e., "cooling out the mark"), and the eventual purely symbolic victory devoid of substance. We also witness law used against social movements: agent provocateurs, infiltrations, police/FBI surveillance, harassment, arrests, overcharging, counter suits for libel and slander (ibid., 204). In addition, a number of other sources of resistance to change come into play at different levels and in combination: social factors, psychological, cultural, and economic (Vago, 2012: 330–337).

Jim Freeman, a long-time activist and founder of Grassroots Action Support Team, an organization that advocates for low-income African-Americans countering system-wide injustice and desiring social change at the systems level, has provided useful suggestions ("five essential elements") for social movement lawyers (2015; see also Freeman and Freeman, 2016; Cummings, 2016, 2018):

1. Dedication to building the capacity and power of oppressed communities;
2. Willingness to address the root causes of structural disempowerment and oppression;
3. Use of knowledge, skills, and connections to support community organizing and movement-building;
4. Commitment to meeting the full array of on-the-ground advocacy needs; and
5. Professional humility.

The Systemic Justice Project at Harvard Law School (initiated in 2014) and with Howard University School of Law is a forerunner in sensitizing law students and others in the system-wide nature of racism, and seeks to foster creative solutions for social change. Their operative philosophy states (*The Systemic Justice Project*, p. 1):

> The Justice Initiative is a community of social justice-oriented law students, lawyers, law-school faculty, legal organizations, organizers, and activists devoted to thinking creatively about the role lawyers can play in reimagining, dismantling, and remaking unjust systems, working to repair longstanding injustices, assisting law students hoping to pursue justice-oriented careers, and providing opportunities for further study, engagement, advising, organizing, and collaboration among its members.

Summary

Sociology of law is a wide field of study that is continuously in search of disciplinary boundaries. It is however, a vibrant study, multi-level, both system and agent focused, particularly in their co-constitution, and distinguishable from rigid jurisprudential analysis still prominent at law schools. We focused on law-in-action. We saw that law not only has a facilitative function but appears with ideological, repressive and constitutive dimensions. To study law, one must ask which, in the singular or, more likely, combination, are at play. We then looked at law in relationship to the realization of social values (Figure 1); and the relationship between the notion of withering away of law and realization of social values (Figure 2). They were offered for pedagogical and heuristic purposes, meant more for sensitizing, organizing, provoking, and imagining alternative possibilities rather than for advocating a particular position. We followed by tracing the rise of law and the legal profession and extended this to early forms in America. The rise of lawyers, their various organizations, and law school were all seen as responding to social and economic factors, undergoing developments from the very informal to the formal apparatus we have today. We noted some of the biases and exclusionary practices favoring the well-to-do. Here we return to the four functions of law for further insights. We closed with the relationship of law to social change. It is problematic in which direction the causal arrow flows. A co-constitutive model argues it goes both ways. We noted the significance of social movements for changing law, even as the changed law, in turn affected social movements (their organization, form of expression, etc.). Some suggestions for the useful role for lawyers in social movements were included.

Review Questions

1. Find a U.S. legal case on something to do with racism or sexism. Summarize it and the dissenting views. Then, explain how functions and dysfunctions of law are applicable.

2. Rights activists engaged in demonstrations sometimes find themselves recipient of law enforcement. Explain how their lawyer might offer them a technical defense, but in the process further legitimize the "rule of law," the very thing activists say is system supporting.

3. Environmental law allows for the selling by otherwise polluting companies "pollution credits." Is this system change, or does it further support the political economic system, now with law's blessing?

4. This is a class exercise. The professor will choose a recent U.S. Supreme court case on university entrance policies dealing with affirmative action. The class will have some students assigned to reading, summarizing and doing a more sociology of law critique of the majority opinion. The other half of the class will be assigned a dissenting view. In class be prepared to argue for arguing whether and to what degree the majority or dissent is engaging some sociology of law, or are totally jurisprudence in orientation.

5. Abbie Hoffman, an activist of the 60s, once argued that revolutions take place in the street, not in the hallowed halls of Ivory Tower. Explain how each of the four functions might be at work in law passed to regulate the streets (surveillance cameras, traffic lights, parking regulations, traffic rules, etc.), especially what effects they might have on the form and expression of the demonstrators.

6. Take the "withering away of law" thesis in Figure 2, and argue for how legal rights would appear in two of the examples in the right-hand column.

7. There is a difference between formal and substantive equality. Work with two other students from the class in explaining the difference. Then provide two examples to be presented in class.

8. Reality court TV often witnesses the judge trying to construct a linear story from the contrasting differences of the antagonists. Watch an episode and try and show how deductive logic was employed by the judge in creating a coherent story of "what happened."

9. The rise of the legal profession was seen as offering a needed service in resolving disputes in increasing commercial society, enhancing empowerment, but at the same time, excluding and disenfranchising many voices. Would insisting on some classes in a sociology of law while formally studying law in law school help to make things better? Explain why or why not.

10. Take Freeman's five suggestions for social movement lawyers. Do some research for each proposition. Bring to class your further analysis of each of the suggestion for class discussion. Place summaries on board for class discussion. Or post online for further discussion.

Endnotes

1. Much has been written on the rise of the legal profession; however, for an introductory text in the sociology of law, we can only provide a condensed summary, particularly drawing from Vago (2012), Barkan (2018), and Glendon *et al*'s (2020) compilation.

2. Capitalism already had early development several centuries prior to the 17th Century; we under score, however, how more formal developments began to emerge. The industrial revolution that emerged in the 18th century along with the need to exploit labor and resources gave further impetus.

3. For a useful general introduction to social change, see Harper and Leicht (2018). For a much earlier, but still useful text, see Noble (2000). His is a useful introduction to social change since included are Durkheim, Weber, Marx, structural functionalists, and postmodernists, each topic of which is covered later in the book but with the connection to law.

4. Lopez (1992) explains how, by the use of Paulo Freire's (1973) dialogical pedagogy, a "conscientization" can develop, a counter to the pure worship of formal rationality in law and "objective" detachments.

5. For example, wide use of suspensions, more stringent discipline, transfers to alternative schools, school arrests, and referrals to the juvenile justice system (Freeman and Freeman, ibid., 161)—all culminating in a path toward criminalization, a school-to-prison pipeline. This encouraged the development of more creative and sensitive methods in responding to youth's conflicts and deviations.

3

Emile Durkheim

Toward a Systematic Sociology of Law

Introduction

Emile Durkheim (1858–1917) was born in Epinal near Strasbourg, France. His early interest was in philosophy, but he always had a strong sociological focus. He graduated from École Normale Supérieure (1882). His first academic positions were minor appointments in provincial high schools. In 1885–1886, he took a year's leave of absence to study in Germany. He subsequently completed his doctoral dissertation, the *Division of Labor* (1886), and published in 1893. In 1887 he married Louise Dreyfus and went on to have two children. In 1887, he received a professorship of sociology and education at Bordeaux. It was there that Durkheim wrote three of his four most influential books: *The Division of Labor in Society* (1893), *Rules of Sociological Method* (1895), and *Suicide* (1897). He founded (1896) an influential journal, *L'année sociologique.* Later, in 1902 he attained the distinction of being appointed to the prestigious Sorbonne in Paris, France. There was a gap of 15 years before he wrote *Elementary Forms of the Religious Life* (1912). His son, André-Armand, died in battle in 1915 (learned in February, 1916) and Durkheim never recovered grieving. His health declined, already being experienced before his son's death. His scholarly production dropped. In 1917, he passed away at the age of 59.[1]

There were a number of influences on Durkheim including the classic ancient Greek philosophers, as well as Auguste Comte (applying scientific method in the social sciences, positivism), Herbert Spencer (evolutionary theory), Wilhelm Wundt (study psychology as a science), Jean-Jacques Rousseau (social contract), and Emmanuel Kant (epistemology, ethics). He lived through the early 1870s which were tumulus times around him (war with Germany, left wing uprising) to be followed by a general stability with the "Third Republic." He lived through a time period of industrial advancements. He was somewhat supportive of socialism, was acquainted with the work of Karl Marx, but was critical of the literature and saw sociology as a source for political change, not revolution. And he witnessed WW1. (For a more detailed biography, see Lukes, 1975; Fournier, 2012.)

Durkheim's main concern throughout his writings related to the question of social solidarity, social integration and what held society together.[2] His approach was against focusing on the individual, suggesting that pure psychological explanations of social phenomena were sure to be incorrect (1964a: 104). Pure sociology was his main concern. Take for example his classic statements: "Man is man only because he lives in society," and "collective life is not born from individual life, but it is, on the contrary, the second which is born of the first" (1958: 60; 1964b: 279). His was a functionalist approach focusing on the question of social integration and social stability in evolving society toward increasing differentiation and complexity. Many of his subsequent critics have said that this obsession for purely social or interpersonal factors led him to overlook political and economic determinants of social phenomena.

He insisted on the possibility of studying society scientifically. His very first rule was to "consider social facts as things" (1964a: 14). Social facts can be characterized by their ability to resist change. They have a coercive quality, and their violation is met with some type of sanction, or at least some resistance. Law is the exemplary "social fact." But, to Durkheim, law is also a "visible symbol," an "external" index that reflects the nature of social solidarity. Since many sociological phenomena and a person's state of mind are inaccessible to an outsider, the best way to study society, and particularly social solidarity, according to Durkheim, is by studying existing law, which is the "objective" indicator of solidarity.

Much debate exists as to the importance of law in Durkheim's writing. There are those who argue that it was "indirect," "tangential," or a secondary concern (Hunt, 1978: 65). To this extent, it might be argued that he did not really develop, nor was he interested in developing a sociology of law. He did not, for example, try to develop an overall framework or a particular methodology for a sociology of law. Others have argued that law indeed was his main concern (Lukes and Scull, 1983: 1–2). For he has said "instead of treating sociology in *genere* ... we have always been occupied only with legal or moral rules, studied in terms of their genesis and development" (Durkheim, cited in Lukes and Scull, 1983: 2). The form of law, then, was an indicator of the form of solidarity in existence. A careful reading of Durkheim indicates that he was always preoccupied with the development of rules. It is a moot point whether in fact he actually wanted to develop a sociology of law. The evidence clearly indicates that in many of his writings he connected law to the whole ensemble of social existence.

Evolution of Society and Social Solidarity

The question of the evolution of society from the "simple" to the "more complex" forms played an important part in Durkheim's first major work, *The Division of Labor in Society* (1964b). By "simple" and "primitive" (société inférieur) he is not employing it in the pejorative sense, but a society marked by little division of labor, that is with little differentiation and specialization; by "complex," or "more advanced," he meant a society characterized by an extensive division of labor. Vago (2011) retains "primitive societies," Trevino (2009) introduces "pre-industrial," and Barkum (2018), "traditional." The use of "ancient" and "pre-modern" does not help clarify. Nor pre-modern and modern, since they are rigid dichotomies overlooking the continuum in existence. We will employ "traditional" throughout the chapter; meaning, less differentiated, specialized, more homogeneous, and most often bound by customary law consistent with Durkheim's intent.

He sets out to analyze the different forms of solidarity, or the bonds, within these two types of societies. Bonds based on sameness reflected the idea that similar experiences and outlooks (i.e., beliefs, habits, values, thoughts, and attitudes) would find a natural attraction. "Difference," he tells us, "as likeness, can [also] be a cause of mutual attraction" (ibid., 55). The basis of this attraction through difference rests on the idea that because of some incompleteness, the other who fulfills this lack, or who provides some resources, which make for more completeness, provides in the process a strong bonding force, an interdependence. Durkheim is quite direct here: "Only certain kinds of differences attract each other. They are those which, instead of opposing and excluding, complement each other" (ibid., 55). It is in this book, too, that he advances the idea that society produces two forms of solidarity, "mechanical" and "organic." In fact, he argues that society develops from a traditional (mechanical) form to a higher (organic) form, the latter characterized by an extensive division of labor. Even with more contemporary highly differentiated society, each form exists within it; but Durkheim's theses is about the most prevalent form.

Mechanical solidarity was seen as the normal type of social bonds in traditional societies, where very little division of labor existed. The "glue" or the bond was sameness or similarity between members of society (homogeneity). Uniformity was central in this type of society. In other words, the range of personality types was not extensive. All were said to participate intimately in each other's lives. Standing above all the members of this type of society was the *conscience collective* (nowadays usually referred to as the collective conscience, or collective consciousness). It represents the collective identities, sentiments, and thoughts of the group. Its source was the same conditions and adaptations that all were said to share. All individual experiences, impressions and beliefs, then, were similar. The *conscience collective* was beyond the ability of the individual to change. It was a social fact. It was internalized by each member of society and became the background standard by which the person would judge themselves and others. It was a conservative force in so much as those who dared to test its borders were subject to harsh reactions by the rest of the community. Individualism was almost nonexistent. It could not be tolerated because it implied that the person strayed some distance from the common bond. The morally good person was the one who participated entirely within the terms of the *conscience collective*.

Accordingly, deviance is defined as anything that goes against the collective conscience; hence, deviance will always exist since there are always, he argues, those that fall outside of the boundaries of the acceptable. We can also speak about the functions of deviance,[3] since it clarifies the boundaries of a group, and in exercising collective displeasure, reinforces the conscience collective in existence.[4]

Organic solidarity, on the other hand, exists in advanced, differentiated societies (heterogeneity). In other words, it is prevalent in a society that has an extensive division of labor. In this highly specialized society, with an abundance of specialized functions and roles, mutual dependence is the glue. Organic solidarity is, Durkheim argued, much more binding than mechanical solidarity since it is based on people's need for each other because each complements the other for their inadequacies. In this society the *conscience collective* weakens. It does not have the same force. Collectivism is now replaced by individualism.

Durkheim argues that societies evolve from the condition of mechanical solidarity to organic solidarity. The decisive factor, the determinate cause, is *social density.* Durkheim drew from Darwinism and Social Darwinism of Herbert Spencer as the catalyst for explaining the evolution of society. With greater social density—that is, the higher concentration of the population, the formation of cities, and in the increasing development of transportation and communication—a greater division of labor is needed. The "struggle for existence is more acute" (Durkheim, 1964b: 266). The result is a more extensive division of labor. With this increasing differentiation, the *conscience collective* loses its control. It too becomes more differentiated. And this leads to further differentiation because people are released from the bonds of a common morality.

But, Durkheim asks, how could all this be measured? How can we examine these phenomena scientifically? The answer for Durkheim was to look at the nature of the most prevalent type of law in existence. Knowing what type of law is most prevalent would then tell us something about the kinds of bonds of solidarity in existence. "[W]herever social solidarity exists, it resides not in a state of pure potentiality, but manifests its presence by sensible indices" (1964b: 64).

The question, then, must be asked: what form of law would indicate one type of solidarity as opposed to the other? What were these "sensible indices?" Durkheim specifies the procedure to be followed. "Since law reproduces the principal forms of social solidarity, we have only to classify the different types of law to find therefrom the different types of social solidarity which correspond to it" (1964b: 68). To this end, he identifies two types of sanctions or laws. One he calls "repressive," the other "restitutive."

Repressive law is characterized by punishment, by suffering, by some loss applied to the individual. This loss could include liberty, life, honor or fortune. Penal laws are its most clear type. This type of reaction arises spontaneously when acts go against the *conscience collective.* Crime, then, can be defined as acts that shock the common, or collective sentiments prevalent in most people's consciences. In traditional societies, it is the collective that reacts to acts that go against the common sentiment. Because of this, it is not necessary to have written obligatory rules. The rule is well understood by all. Punishment then is retributive. The offended collective sentiments that reside within all cannot accept contradictions or challenges. It cannot remain in this state.

To allow such challenges is to have the very fabric of society undermined. It must be corrected. The existence of crime can then be traced to the existence of strong collective reactions by the community.

Restitutive law can be characterized as *"the return of things as they were,* in the re-establishment of troubled relations to their normal state ..." (1964b: 69; emphasis in the original). He gives the example of civil laws, commercial law, administrative and constitutional law and, all types of procedural laws.[5] The system of restitutive law has a non-punitive emphasis. The goal is simply to return relations to their previous state, particularly with intervention by some "organs" of the State. For repressive laws, it is not necessary, on a theoretical level, to have a central enforcement machinery since all participate in enforcement. Examples in contemporary society of restitutive law include the use of conflict resolution such as found in restorative justice and other avenues such as civil court which provide compensation and restoration.

For restitutive laws, special "organs" were required. Durkheim cites examples of administrative tribunals, councils of arbitration, and industrial tribunals. These, he argues, become increasingly specialized. Legislators, in codifying restitutive laws, must be especially concerned with specifying with great clarity what the obligations and the appropriate reaction to their infractions entail. Magistrates and lawyers, because of their special skills in interpreting and applying law, become necessary in resolving conflicts (law-finding). Thus, implied with restitutive laws is the need for a central State and the formal machinery for law-making and law enforcement.[6]

Where restitutive laws are highly developed an "occupational morality" develops with it (1964b: 227). That is, within fields of specialization a certain obedience to norms and rules of behavior are required. For example, the American Bar Association and the American Medical Association have codes of ethics. To go against these norms is to invoke censure or reprimand. These associations, then, because they have more permanence than transactions with transient clients, also develop a particular common ideological outlook. The *conscience collective* of traditional societies is now increasingly replaced by a multiplicity of smaller *conscience collectives.* Each of these binds its members.

Restitutive laws, then, are not rooted in the *conscience collective,* and thus are not marked by strong punitive reactions. Rather, they focus on re-establishing relations that have gone wrong.

A little more than seven years after the publication of *Division of Labor in Society,* Durkheim expanded his analysis in an article entitled "Two Laws of Penal Evolution" (1901; see 1983c). (Actually, the title could be clearer if we were to use "principles" rather than "laws.") Here he spelled out in greater detail the evolution of society, the forms of solidarity, and the form of punishment for law violation. He offers two principles of development, one "quantitative," the other "qualitative."

The first principle, the "quantitative" law, states that "the intensity of punishment is the greater the more closely societies approximate to a less developed type—and the more the central power assumes an absolute character" (Durkheim, 1983c: 102).

In traditional societies, he argues, punishments were severe. In explaining this he first notes, "it is in the evolution of crime that one must seek the cause determining the evolution of punishment" (ibid., 121). He already noted that traditional societies are characterized by a strong *conscience collective*. Acts going against the *conscience collective* arouse similar and focused energies. The evolution of the type of punishment, then, simply follows the evolution of the type of society. In complex societies marked by an extensive division of labor, the *conscience collective* loses its hold, and becomes more differentiated, allowing even further differentiation. Here the form of punishment is restitutive, revolving around the need to mend relations that have gone wrong. Harsh sanctions here are not necessary.[7]

His second principle, "qualitative" law, states that "deprivation of liberty, and of liberty alone, varying in time according to the seriousness of the crime, tends to become more and more the normal means of social control" (1983c: 114). In traditional societies, he argues, imprisonment serves no need. Here responsibility is collective. All take part in inflicting the punishment. In many ways, all are police, prosecutors, judges, jurors and punishers. If the violator absconds, a kinsman can be substituted. After all, it has been the collective sentiment that has been violated and the aroused sentiment must be relieved.

In traditional societies the conditions do not exist for the notion of a prison. These societies did not need separate buildings to punish, since the whole group participated in punishing any wayward group member. In traditional societies houses are built exclusively for private purposes. With the development of "city states," he notes, special houses were built to serve particular functions. Temples, for example, appear at a relatively late period. The subsequent specialization of buildings led to the logic of buildings that function as prisons. The early prisons had a philosophy of punishment consistent with repressive law. But this gradually gave way to the present-day form where deprivation of liberty itself was seen as punishment (i.e., a convicted offender is sentenced to a particular length of confinement commensurate to the gravity of the crime). As individualism developed in more complex societies, it was only natural that the liberty associated with it was now to be the focus of its withdrawal for violators. This, too, necessitated the use of prison to assure that the violator did not try to prematurely regain their liberty against the wishes of the State.

Durkheim's thesis has been the subject to much debate over the years, and nevertheless endures as a vibrant, stimulating reading generating ever new scholarly investigations of social solidarity and its relation to law.[8]

In sum, for Durkheim, to understand crime, punishment and the nature of social solidarity, one should analyze an external index which is its expression. The most prevalent form of law in existence, then, tells us much about the nature of society.

The Abnormal Forms

Durkheim spends most of his analysis in the *Division of Labor in Society* on the normal, spontaneous forms of societal development. He spells out the ideal progression or evolution of a society. In the last short three chapters, however, he presents the "abnormal forms," of which there are three types.

Durkheim assumes that society, left to itself, will evolve from the traditional to the complex form. The key is spontaneous development. As society evolves, all parts and all subjects, adjust themselves to the overall structure of society. To this extent, society runs smoothly. It is in a state of "equilibrium." It is only through exploring, testing, experimenting and consequent mutual adjustments that the elements of society become adjusted. However, there are also instances (the "abnormal forms") where these adjustments do not take place, producing a state Durkheim referred to as "anomie."

People's desire and needs, for Durkheim, have diverse sources; they require some satisfaction, but yet also some externally imposed limitation.[9] As Durkheim (1961: 39–40) says: "A need, a desire, freed of all restraints, and all rules, no longer geared to some determinate objective, and through this some connection, limited and contained, can be nothing but a source of constant anguish, for the person experiencing it." Sometimes regulation or adjustment is not brought about. The elements (the "organs") have not adjusted themselves in a rapidly advancing society. Such societies experience a state of *anomie* (Durkheim, 1964b: 368). This is one of the abnormal forms. Commentators have often translated "anomie" as a state of normlessness, at other times as a state of deregulation. Many criminologists imbed or assume this thesis in their explanation of crime (see especially strain and social disorganization theory).

The second abnormal form focuses on the rules themselves as the cause of evil. This is the "forced" division of labor. According to Durkheim, "for the division of labor to produce solidarity, it is not sufficient ... that each have his task; it is still necessary that this task be fitting to him" (1964b: 375).[10] If some "external force" coerces subjects, or constrains them in a function or a role, then a gap remains between "individual natures and social functions" (ibid., 376). "Happiness" is realized when a person's "needs are in relation to his means" (ibid.). Said in another way, equilibrium exists when a person's "nature" is in accord with the social function they perform. A spontaneous division of labor is where "natural" inequalities (i.e., in abilities, temperament, dexterity, and so forth) are exactly reflected or expressed in the relations that have evolved. Those, for example, who have excelled by their own talent, should be rewarded in kind. But in the forced division of labor, relations are being held together by force and constraint: individual nature and social function are not in accord. Thus it may very well be the case that on a formal level, two individuals "freely" consent to a contract; that is, there is a verbal or a written agreement. But the objective consequences may favor one over the other because one may have entered the terms with more resources at their disposal. The other contractor may simply have accepted what was offered.

The third abnormal form is where different functions of members of society are distributed in such a way that people are deprived of fulfilling activity (1964b: 389). This lack of coordination produces waste. "Where functions languish," Durkheim tells us, "they are not well specialized, they are badly coordinated, and incompletely feel their mutual dependence" (ibid., 390). An example here could be a rigidly bureaucratized society where functions of members no longer are in accord with changes in society, but nevertheless the person carries them out routinely and monotonously.

In sum, the abnormal forms of division of labor are pathological cases. That is, they go against the movement toward cooperation, mutual fulfillment and happiness that inheres in the spontaneous forms. If there were any convergence among the three classic thinkers in sociology—Durkheim, Weber, and Marx—one of its closest examples would be with the questioning of the "free" contract. We now turn to its examination by Durkheim.

Form of Law, Contract and Legal Thought

Given a form of law, the questions to be asked are: What is the appropriate form of legal thought to be used to arrive at agreements? To assure promises made are met? And if they are not, what remedies or means of enforcement can be mobilized?

Contracts, in the majority of cases, imply reciprocal obligation. Two people, in other words, orient their behavior to each other, regardless of how brief, in order to exchange something. Some agreement is reached in the process. For Durkheim, the contract "is, *par excellence,* the juridical expression of co-operation" (1964b: 123, emphasis in the original). Thus "the contract is the symbol of exchange" (ibid., 125). We may safely say, with Durkheim, that the form of contract, therefore, can again be seen as an index of the type of solidarity in existence. He returns to the whole question later in his career in the form of lecture notes, which were subsequently published after his death in *Professional Ethics and Civic Morals.*

The development of the contract is connected with the development of the division of labor. Here he develops a similar notion as Maine (1861) in *Ancient Law.* Maine argued that the progression of law could be characterized by its movement from *status* to *contract.* Durkheim notes a similar development.

Durkheim's analysis once again begins with traditional societies. True contracts, he argued, did not appear until a late age. Traditional societies depended on various forms to assure that agreements were fulfilled. So, for example, the *blood covenant* was such that if people needed to create ties outside of the immediate family, the form used duplicated what they knew well. They shared blood in some manner (i.e., each placed a few drops into a container and both dipped their hands into it and hence created blood ties), they duplicated the primary bond of kinship, namely the blood ties of the family. Similarly, one could also share common food, or drink from the same cup. Symbolically, then, these served the same function. Trevino (2009: 249) offers the example of the induction ceremony of Mafia members. The would-be member had his finger pricked and with the appearance of blood the Mafia boss would pronounce "This blood means that we are now one family" (ibid., citing Mass, 1968: 98). Another example is the Christian communion.

Real contracts are those where one thing is immediately exchanged for another. Here the relation ends. One product is exchanged directly for another and each person goes their separate way.

Then, Durkheim argued, there is a form of exchange and the bond, however temporary, that goes with it, in which some declaration is made in words coupled with invoking a deity (Durkheim, 1983b: 199). This he called the *solemn contract.* The oath or the invocation of a divine being is an integral part of the bond, which created a third party to the contract. This third party, a divine being or deity, became the guarantor of the declaration made. "Each contracting party," Durkheim continued, "pronounces some phrase that binds him and a formula by which he calls down upon his head certain divine curses if he should fail in his undertaking" (ibid., 199). Thus, one exchanger could pronounce: "I promise you the delivery of 20 lbs. of tomatoes in two weeks, and let God be my witness." Sometimes this was even followed by sacrifices and magical rites. That is, the words themselves in the promise made became sacred. They no longer belonged to the individual transactor alone (even to this day we have such expressions as "you have my word on it"). Words became things that could be possessed. But these words had to be uttered in a precise way. There was a particular formula for their use and only this assured fulfillment of promise. Here "if the solemn ritual is lacking, there is no contract" (ibid., 200). If one does not fulfill the promise made they have offended the divine authority, the third party. They would be exposed to vengeance by the Gods or deities. The words uttered, then, could not be changed. They were no longer theirs to change. They could only be carried out. The solemn ritual committed the two parties to the contract. Unlike the blood covenant, it could be used for many everyday transactions.

This type of contract was to give way to a modern type, the *consensual contract.* The causes of this change were numerous. An extensive increase in trade made solemn contracts hindering formalities. The need for flexibility, particularly in a vastly increased pace of life, too, made the old types obsolete. And generally, the demands of the new economic order were too much to allow the more traditional form of contract to exist. Exchanges and transfers of property were all too frequent. But here Durkheim cautions us: just because there is a need for a particular institution does not mean that it will materialize by itself out of a vacuum. The way the new form, the consensual contract, came into being was as follows. The previous solemn contract had two major elements: promises expressed in words and guaranteed by divine authority, and promises expressed to others in words that they now possessed as a thing. Thus, breaking a promise now means offending the Gods as well as the other. The bond was two-fold: to the Gods and to the other. It is the second that eventually detached itself from the first and became the consensual contract

(Durkheim, 1983b: 210). Divine authority, too, in an advancing society, was becoming generally weaker. And this, in combination with the needs generated by a complex, busier life, further necessitated this split. For Durkheim, the contract based on solemn ritual was, however, the stronger bond. And to this day the more important transactions often have some characteristics of the earlier forms. Think, for example, the various "swearing in" ceremonies during trial court proceedings and in the appointment of high government officials (e.g., raising a hand and uttering "In God we trust").

The consensual contract, or the "contract by mutual consent" (1983b: 212), was for Durkheim "a revolutionary innovation in the law" (ibid., 219). Its most important feature was that it invoked the will. Only if I willingly enter into an agreement can you demand that I fulfill the promise. If the agreement was imposed on me, if my will was not responsible for the promise, the contract is not binding (ibid., 221).

This led Durkheim to offer his ideal contract, the highest form, the *just contract,* or the *contract of equity.* For Durkheim,

> the coming on the scene of the contract by mutual consent, together with an increase in human sympathies, inclined the minds of men to the idea that the contract was only moral and only to be recognized and given sanction by society, provided it was not merely a means of exploiting one of the contracting parties, in a word, provided it was just (1983b: 223).

Here Durkheim recognized that a "freely" entered contract, in itself, does not necessarily mean that the contract is "just." Put in another way, consensual contracts, by focusing on a subjective dimension (free will) do not assure objective consequences that are fair and just. There are times, Durkheim argued, where the individual was compelled to "yield what he did not wish to, and it takes from him by force something that he owned ... a case of extortion" (1983b: 225). Thus, fairness of the contract should not only turn on the question of consent.

"Equality in the external conditions of conflict" is necessary to assure that: (1) functions are linked to one another spontaneously; and (2) that individuals will attach themselves to their functions (Durkheim, 1964b: 381). Inheritance makes the "external" conditions unbalanced and hence the contract can favor one over the other. In the forced division of labor this imbalance is at its maximum.[11]

The key elements in defining fairness, or what constitutes *being just,* for Durkheim, are "social value" and "useful labor." He argues that objects of exchange can be measured by the amount of useful labor which they embody (1964b: 382). Useful labor is associated with "useful social effects" (ibid., 383). Three elements (or what social scientists refer to as variables), according to Durkheim, define social value: (1) "the sum of efforts necessary to produce the object"; (2) "the intensity of the needs which it satisfies"; and (3) "the extent of the satisfaction it brings" (ibid., brackets added). Notice that a range exists for each of the elements. In the chapter below on Karl Marx we shall see that certain useful comparisons can be made with the idea of "use value."

Genuine consent, for Durkheim, occurs only where "the services exchanged have an equivalent social value" (1964b: 383). If, for example, we take two exchangers, A and B, and look at the three elements defining social value, giving each element, for the more quantitative inclined reader, a range from 1–10, and note that if person A and B each receives a combined score of say 24 after the transaction, then the exchange or contract is "just." We are of course assuming for the sake of this example that we could provide quantitative scores reflecting these three aspects rather accurately. And the question of the appropriate cut-off point for being "just" is problematic. This notwithstanding, if person A receives a 24, person B a 12, there would be a basis to conclude that the exchange may, perhaps, have been agreed to (as in the consensual contract), but remains unjust (we shall see that there is much here that can be usefully compared with Marx's idea of the appropriation of "surplus value"[12]).

In other words, contracts are balanced and fair (an "equilibrium of wills") if inherent inequalities ("internal inequalities," ibid., 384) are the sole bases of exchange. "Internal inequalities" may reflect natural differences in, say, muscular dexterity, thereby allowing person A to pick one bushel of apples in two hours; with person B it may take two and a half hours. However, one person may receive an additional advantage, say, by way of inheritance, but that does not reflect inherent difference (i.e., different abilities, hereditary constraints and so forth), or differences arrived at by way of self-development. "Mere verbal consent," for Durkheim, is not the determinant of a fair contract (ibid., 383). Here, one contractor is forced to accept the terms of the contract. In other words, the latter may have to accept any price for their service. This, for Durkheim, produces a disequilibrium in the conditions of exchange. Durkheim is quite direct:

> If one class of society is obliged, in order to live, to take any price for its services, while another can abstain from such action thanks to resources at its disposal which, however, are not necessarily due to any social superiority, the second has an unjust advantage over the first at law (1964b: 384).
>
> And: "... that which one individual exercises over another because he is stronger or richer, above all if this wealth does not express his social worth, is abnormal and can only be maintained by violence" (ibid., 123).

Both Max Weber and Karl Marx, we shall show below, also describe the often hidden repressive dimensions of the contract.

For Durkheim, the contract, in the normal division of labor, is a temporary "truce" in the competition among individuals. People in a complex society seek things that they need, that fulfill them. Ideally, for a just contract to exist, each should give free consent. The contract made should not have forced one or the other to unwillingly agree to the terms. And this coercive consent arises where some external factor (i.e., inheritance) has placed one in a more advantageous position. An imbalance has been created.

Thus, Durkheim's prediction states that the just contract arises because of an enlightened public wishing to weigh the objective outcomes of the contract in terms of fairness or equity. Society, then, intervenes to assure that the objective consequences are just. We have this in present law in such stipulations as "good faith dealings." The nemesis of the just contract, for Durkheim, again, is inheritance.

Inheritance creates inequality directly from birth. This received wealth is unrelated to a person's merits. "There cannot be rich and poor at birth," he tells us, "without there being unjust contracts" (1964b: 384). Thus, to ensure a just contract, the available resources of each must be equal. Only then will things be exchanged fairly; that is, according to their true value. Indeed, for Durkheim, inheritance goes against the whole spirit of individualism that inheres in a society marked by an extensive division of labor. It was Marx and Weber, we shall see in the following chapters, who extended this notion of external inequality when analyzing the vast differences in wealth induced by capitalism.

Property

Where did private property rights come from? How has the right to private property been established? In answering these questions Durkheim turns to religious beliefs. "The origins of property are to be found in the nature of certain religious beliefs" (1983a: 165).

The right to property, according to Durkheim, can be characterized by its "right of exclusion." I can use a particular thing from which I can exclude others. To understand how this right of exclusion came about one must look at how, the world over, the sacred exists separately and distinctly from the profane. Sacred entities can only be touched by priests or others who have a sacred character. In other words, they are removed from general circulation. And everything that touches the sacred also becomes sacred. Special individuals, priests, have the power to make objects they touch sacred.

Durkheim, examining traditional property markers of land by clans or families, notes that they too were permeated with the sacred. Subjects who were not members of the family or the clan were excluded from this landed property's use. Boundaries to cultivated fields were surrounded by marker stones. These stones represented the sacred. Customs assured that they would be respected. Thus, the fields had sacred qualities. Elaborate rituals established these grounds as sacred. These rituals, often combined with a sacrifice, established a moral bond between the clan or family members and the gods. Henceforth, "the land has ... become attached to men by a sacred bond" (1983a: 179). Thus, the right to property had its origins here: "Man's right of property is only a substitute for the right of property of the gods" (ibid.). The respect we have for property, then, is respect that we once had for the sacred now transferred to property. The rights of gods now are the rights of people. Disrespect for property became equated with disrespect for the sacred. Both brought the wrath of god.

Initially, the clan owned the sacred land in common. The fishing and hunting grounds, too, were sacred and collectively owned. But how did individual ownership come about? How did the individual come to develop private property rights?

Durkheim offers two "causes." First, a member of the family is elevated in status "in some way—by a chain of circumstances" (1983a: 186). This person becomes endowed with prestige beyond the rest of the group. Now the things that were bound to the group are directly connected to this superior individual. Since the person was invested with this status, property belonging to the group now belongs more so to this person. With the coming of patriarchal and paternal power this process was complete (ibid.). Authority now rested with the head of the family. He became the supreme owner of property. The sacred character of the land was now invested in the head of the family.

The second cause, which "ran parallel" and "reinforced" the first, was the development of movable property. In pre-industrial societies, primarily agricultural societies, property was land, which had a sacred character and was owned by the community. All property was characterized by its immovable nature. Hence, all things of the clan were connected within this narrow sphere. But with the development of industry and trade, property became movable. The individual could now dispose of things outside of real estate more freely. Property had loosened itself from the moral and sacred binds of the community. Once cast adrift, nothing made them immovable. This property now depended only on the person who had acquired it. As opposed to landed property, this property had a much freer quality about it. The individual who possessed it had flexibility in its use. Henceforth, according to Durkheim,

> [I]t is man who stands above *things,* and it is a certain individual in particular who occupies this position, that is, who owns or possesses. Whole categories of profane things take shape independently of the family estate, free themselves of it and thus become the subject of the new right of property, one that is in its essence individual (1983a: 189; emphasis in the original).

Property, originally communal and sacred, thus becomes divided into the landed and movable forms. Different kinds of law develop to stipulate the use of each. Movable property is the more flexible and freer. And the communal property is increasingly replaced by rights of private property. The weakening of the *conscience collective* finds its counterpart in the ascendance of individual rights to private property. This is in combination with the diminution of the sacred. The individual is released from the bonds of the collectivity and absorbs the divine qualities originally attached to communal property in the form of private property.

Summary

Law, Durkheim showed us, was intimately connected with the nature of solidarity. Knowing the most prevalent form of law would tell us much about the nature of society. Law was an external indicator of social bonds. In traditional society, the *conscience collective* was supreme. The bonds of solidarity were mechanical. What held society together, the attractive force, the "glue," was the sameness of its individual members. Those who went against the collective sentiments would be met with a uniform hostile reaction. Crime, then, could be defined as an act that offended the *conscience collective.* The stronger the collective reaction, the more serious was the crime. Laws were repressive. They were characterized by their punitiveness. Since the whole community was offended, no need existed for a professional staff of enforcers. All were police, prosecutors, judges, jurors and punishers.

As society evolved and as it became more complex, more differentiated, a new bond appeared. This bond's characteristic was the attraction of opposites. A society marked by an extensive division of labor—that is, with many specializations that were interdependent—demanded restitutive laws. It was no longer punishment that was the most prevalent form of reaction, but rather the emphasis was to reestablish an equilibrium. The *conscience collective,* too, became weaker, allowing subjects to further differentiate. The individual was born.

Whereas in traditional societies, *status*—one's overall standing in the community (the clan, the family)—was intimately implicated in transactions, in the more differentiated societies the exemplary instrument, the form for exchange, was the *contract.* The State with its functionaries and machinery now assured the fulfillment of the contract. It established the external conditions for its use. A special class arose to litigate. Lawyers, with their special training and skills, were now needed to handle the numerous and complex contracts that were negotiated.

Law, in a society with an extensive division of labor (spontaneously divided), was not primarily repressive. It was primarily facilitative. In fact, in these societies the division of labor served the function that was previously fulfilled by the *conscience collective.* In the abnormal forms, however, undue constraint produced unjust contracts. Even where an agreement has been signed, where each consented to the terms of the contract "willingly," coercion could still underlie the contract. Here, repressive formalism militated against individuals realizing their full value of services or commodities in exchange. The ideal for Durkheim was that all external forces be equal. Social inequalities should match *natural* inequalities. This is the state of a spontaneously divided labor. The ideal is not anarchy, but rather a carefully regulated society where each specialized role is intimately connected in the spirit of cooperation with a multitude of others. The clearest expression of these cooperative relationships is the *just contract* where things or services exchanged realize their exact social value.

Thus, his evolutionary schema for the spontaneous division of labor can be summarized. Each proposition has and continues to be the basis of a researchable hypothesis subject to further scholarly investigation for support, refutation, qualification, revision, and substitution. The investigations have been wide and robust with conclusions often at odds with each other. The interested reader is encouraged to do further studies.

For the spontaneous division of labor:

- Homogeneity → heterogeneity
- *Conscience collective* → differentiated forms

- Collective (sameness) → individual (complexity)
- Mechanical solidarity → organic solidarity
- Collective responsibility → individual responsibility
- Repressive law → restitutive law
- Status (solemn contract) → consensual contract (just contract, the highest form)

For the abnormal forms:

- Disassociation (needs, desires, and possibilities for actualization) → anomic, forced, unfulfilling states

In sum, law in a spontaneous division of labor is autonomous and general. In its pure form of development, absent "external forces," it does not reflect the interests of a particular class. At the same time liberty is found *in* law. The formally just contract, by controlling external force, assured the maximum fulfillment of social values—liberty, equality and community (cooperative development).

Review Questions

1. Provide an example of similarities and one for dissimilarities being an attraction. Explain, according to Durkheim, how each can be a source of attraction (bond). Why is Durkheim saying the second is the stronger bond?

2. Why is the use of "primitive" pejorative in describing traditional societies? Are they more complex and differentiated than often depicted? Explain.

3. How is the law in existence reflective of the kind of solidarity in existence? Explain.

4. Field exercise. Describe two crimes to an acquaintance, one a "typical" crime of the streets, the other, crime of the suites. Ask the person whether (1) penal punishment should follow, or (2) some restitution and compensation should be employed in each case. Summarize the response(s) and bring to class for discussion without mentioning any people's names or relationship. Be sure to get their permission.

5. Choose one of the "abnormal forms" in non-spontaneous division of labor and explain possible outcomes.

6. Think of an economic encounter you may have had and you felt even though completing it, it was not just (not a "just contract"). Explain.

7. Bring to class a recent use of the "solemn" contract in some public ceremony of induction, selection, or promotion. Explain how Durkheim's description is applicable.

8. "Moveable" property is often seen as the grounds for celebration and liberation, rather than landed and community-based property. Should the former be celebrated? Explain the positive and negative consequences.

Endnotes

1. For an informative and general background about Durkheim, see Parsons (1974). A number of works by Durkheim have been collected and published posthumously: in 1924, *Sociology and Philosophy* (1974); in 1925, *Moral Education: A Study in the Theory and Application of the Sociology of Education* (1961); in 1928, *Socialism* (1962); in 1937, *Montesquieu and Rousseau: Forerunners of Sociology* (1960); in 1938, *The Evolution of Educational Thought* (1977); in 1950, the *Professional Ethics and Civic Morals* (1958); in 1955, *Pragmatism and Sociology* (1983d).

2. We will not attempt to do critiques and response in this introduction, as will also be the case in the next two chapters, for our intent is to only introduce key concepts of the founding figures of sociology. Interested students will find much lively discussion in the literature on each of the three figures. For some beginning orientation to critiques, responses, and integrations see Lukes and Scull (2013), Pearce (2001) and end note 8.

3. See Collins, 2004; Harlow, 2004; Hawdon *et al.*, 2010. Hawdon *et al.* (ibid.), for example, show how solidarity increases significantly after an especially horrendous crime, remained strong for about six months, and then started to subside. It has also been shown to be so after extensive natural disasters and other tragedies. Specific conditions are often necessary for the solidarity response: (1) the extensiveness of the tragedy, and (2) framing by "key opinion makers" that portray crime as effecting the whole community (Hawdon *et al.*, ibid.; Collins, 2004; Ryan and Hawdon, 2008).

4. Other functions of deviance include stimulating change. In post-industrial societies, it also provides jobs. Barkan (2018: 43) summarizes: "Deviance creates jobs ... especially, for the segments of society—police, prisons, criminology professors, etc ... If deviance and crime did not exist, hundreds of thousands of law-abiding people in the United States would be out of work!" To this list we can add racialized boundaries. Wacquant (2002), in discussing African-Americans in U.S. prisons, points out that racial biases create categories of attention for the police-prison industrial complex providing a population for extensive policing, perpetuating a ghetto-to-prison cycle, and for the inflictors, opportunities for venting insecurities, anxieties, prejudices, hate.

5. Criminal law, the repressive form, can be distinguished from procedural criminal law. The question for the latter concerns fair play, fundamental fairness in dealings, a fair process to be used in arriving at a decision.

6. Durkheim makes a further distinction. Restitutive law can be separated into two types (1964b: 115–122). Relations that he calls *negative* revolve around the relationship between the individual and things. Property and tort law are primary examples. These simply dictate that the subject not harm another. On the other hand, *positive* relations are rooted in cooperation itself, which develops out of the division of labor. Here we find contract law, constitutional law, and, generally, procedural law.

7. It could be argued that this is belied by the movement to mass incarceration in contemporary non-traditional Western societies. However, a Durkheimian response would begin to point out that his principles are at work when no external force is at play; the latter releasing, for example, greed, egoism, unrestrained appetites, and generating increasing alienation, poverty, vast income disparities—together, factors for increasing street and suite crimes, the latter of which, nevertheless, remain less policed and less punitively punished. In contemporary society, we witness more "abnormal forms" (see below) that go against natural developments. Thus, for instance, if we could overcome methodological criticism of Durkheim's developmental principles (see Note 8), and if the projected linear progression does not develop, then, perhaps the result can be seen as an indicator, in the spirit of Durkheim, for one or more of the "abnormal forms" and the associated institutions (e.g., mass incarceration and more punitive criminal justice systems as a response to "anomic" conditions).

8. For early (1970s) fruitful discussions of Durkheim's evolutionary theory relating the division of labor to developing forms of law see Hunt (1978), Clark (1976), Cartwright and Schwartz (1973), Cotterrell (1977, 1984, 1991, 1999, 2010), and Wimberley (1973). Useful debates also took place: see often-cited Schwartz and Miller (1964), response by Baxi (1974), and counter by Schwartz (1974), and Turkel's (1979) further contribution to the debate. See also Spitzer's (1979) critique and Turkel's (1979) response. Stedman (2001) has reconsidered Durkheim's theses. Pearce's (1989) critique includes a Marxist synthesis. More recent insightful analysis is by Greenhouse (2011), Johnson *et al.* (2017) and Trevino (2009: 264–274). Most compelling have been methodological issues that have been raised

in trying to study Durkheim's thesis empirically (Turkel, ibid.; Trevino, reviewing, ibid., 271, Sanders, 1990). Sander's critique concerns longitudinal studies that are said to be weak due their vagueness and validity, and suggests, going beyond Durkheim, studies should attempt analysis at two levels, the macro- and micro-level. Turkel (ibid.) has been most forceful and remains relevant today. He questioned how Durkheim's concepts have been operationalized, the inability of empirical tests to relate particular hypotheses to the underlying theory, the limitations due to the researcher's assumptions stemming from a paradigm assumed, the omission of a holistic perspective, the limitation to abbreviated or neglected aspects of Durkheim's overall model, that samples often used are not representable of those in the world, simplifications that distort main variables, use of rigid dichotomies, and generalizations that overlook the particularities of a society's development. Although Johnson *et al.* (2017) do not engage Turkel's methodological critique, they do bring out the complexities involved in the relationship of societal development and legal outcomes. Greenhouse's (2011) encourages scholars to continue to apply Durkheim's theory as relevant in contemporary society (see for example, Peng, 2020, applying Durkheim to Chinese society; Lukes and Scull, 2013). So, as we can see, Durkheim evolutionary theory is still alive and subject to lively debate, spawning many insights in the field.

9. Pearce (1989: 87) has argued that Durkheim and Jacques Lacan's notion of desire "complement each other." He also notes that Lacan's notion of "the name of the father" resonates with Durkheim's emphasis on some form of constraint needed. Indeed, Lacan in 1950 (co-authored with Michel Cenac) presented a paper, entitled "A Theoretical Introduction to the Functions of Psychoanalysis in Criminology," that very much echoes Durkheimian themes (Lacan, 1996; see also my comments on this article, Milovanovic, 1997).

10. We shall see that there is some similarity with Marx's "needs"/"abilities" principle; here, in part, "from each according to his [their] abilities ..."

11. See Herzog (2018: 113–116, 119–122) interpreting Durkheim as arguing that it is "high inequality" particularly produced in class structures that undermines substantive justice. Citing Durkheim (1984: 384), "there cannot be rich and poor at birth without there being unjust contracts" (Herzog, ibid., 116; see also Cotterrell, 2010b).

12. In capitalism, Marx argues, "the sum of efforts necessary to produce the object" is not fully rewarded. The owners of factories and businesses appropriate a significant portion.

4

Max Weber

Law in Economy and Society

Introduction

Max Weber, with little dispute, stands out as one of the foremost scholars in the sociological tradition. Even one of his staunchest critics has said "one could describe [his work] ... as almost superhuman: it is astonishing that anyone could know so much about so many legal systems" (Andreski, 1984: 86). Only recently have scholars turned to his thoughts on law.

Weber was born in 1864 in an upper middle-class family in Erfurt, Germany. He had said, "I am a member of the bourgeois classes, I feel myself as such and I am educated in its views and ideals" (cited in Hunt, 1978: 94). After serving military service, he studied law with an interest in Roman law at University of Heidelberg and then Berlin. He passed the equivalent of the bar exam in the U.S., called a "Referendar." His doctoral dissertation of 1889 was entitled "A Contribution to the History of Medieval Business Organizations." Here his studies of the early beginnings of capitalism signaled his later concerns with the rise of capitalism. While training to become a member of the legal bar in 1891, he wrote "Roman Agrarian History and Its Significance in Public and Private Law." This allowed him to become an instructor in law at the University of Berlin in 1893. In this treatise, he wrote about the early legal institutions of Roman agriculture. At the University of Berlin he taught commercial law and legal history. He married Marianne Schnitger, a committed Calvinist, an accomplished sociologist, author and an earlier contributor to feminist sociology, who also became Weber's biographer and editor of his late works after his death. In 1894, he accepted a chair in economics at the University of Freiburg. He then attained a position at Heidelberg. A short time after his father's death in 1897, his health deteriorated, and Weber was to suffer a major nervous breakdown which incapacitated him from mid-1998 to 1903. For over four and a half years he published not a word.

When he recovered (late 1902 and early 1903) he began to write at an incredible rate. Three major essays came forth in 1903 alone. He had an insatiable desire to explain as many phenomena as he could. A short time later he wrote the classic, *The Protestant Ethic and the Spirit of Capitalism* (1904–1905). Weber examined the relatively independent influence of ideas on the development of capitalism. Here his "debate with the ghost of Marx" was at full throttle. He rejected the idea that the materialist, economic factor alone, was the cause of social phenomena.

It was in his two-volume monumental work, *Economy and Society,* first published in 1921 after his death, that we find Weber's fully developed sociology of law. The scope of the subject material, covered in incredible detail, is breathtaking. His work can truly be called encyclopedic. Marianne Weber noted in her biography of Max Weber that the book unintentionally grew into his major work. During 1918 and 1920, Weber concentrated on fine-tuning definitions and concepts, especially in Part One of his work. He spent much time with the categories that he had developed, trying to clarify each. He died a short time later, in 1920, from pneumonia at the age of 56, his work incomplete. His two-volume work was, at best, his first draft.

Parsons has stated that "the core of Weber's substantive sociology lies neither in his treatment of economic and political problems nor in his sociology of religion, but in his sociology of law" (cited in Hunt, 1978: 102). Ironically, it is only recently that much of his analysis has been subject to careful examination.[1]

Defining Law

Part One of his *Economy and Society*, as we noted, was heavily oriented to definitions and concepts. Here he offers us a formal definition of law:

> an order will be called *law* if it is externally guaranteed by the probability that coercion (physical or psychological), to bring about conformity or avenge violation, will be applied by a *staff* of people holding themselves specially ready for that purpose (1978: 34, emphasis in the original).

One can immediately note that on the surface of it, the critical element in his definition is the existence of some staff ready to apply coercion for enforcement. But further reading of Weber indicates that he had an even deeper meaning. Law was really a subcategory of his notion of legitimate order (Trubek, 1972: 726). An "order" for Weber existed when "conduct is, approximately or on the average, oriented toward determinable 'maxims"' (1978: 31). By "maxims," he means rules of conduct. In other words, Weber tells us that people consciously or unconsciously take into consideration some stable set of commonly accepted assumptions and rules of behavior (that is, they orient themselves to an order). Consider, for example, why mass collisions don't occur on a busy sidewalk or at a major street intersection. Furthermore, an order is *valid* (i.e., legitimate) if members not only orient their behavior to this normative order but also see it as obligatory, as binding. Externally measured, an order can be defined as valid to the degree that action has a high probability of being oriented to it.

But law was just one form of a legitimate order. He also identified other orientations: "affectual," where subjects surrender themselves emotionally to an order; "value-rational," where subjects comply because they see the order as a statement of "ultimate" values such as an ethical type; or "religious," where orientation to the order is due to the belief that salvation will occur if the order is obeyed (1978: 33).

Hence, Weber's definition of law more accurately includes coercion as an *added* element. Subjects may, for example, orient their behavior to an order because of coercive sanctions. They may also do so because they feel the law is legitimate; that is, it is seen as being right. In this case, then, coercion is not necessary. The whole question of law turns on why subjects orient themselves to law.

Capitalism and Law

One of Weber's primary concerns was the rise of capitalism. He wanted to know what forces had allowed its development (Weber, 1958). He was also interested in explaining how, with the rise of capitalism, certain institutions developed. The central issues revolved around cause, the form of law and legal thought, rationality, domination, and the development of the contract and the legal subject in law (the juridic subject). Why is it, he would often ask, that subjects orient their behavior to some order? And, did the development of the contract necessarily assure greater freedom *in* law?

The question of cause, for Weber, was critical. He rejected, in contrast to some variants of Marxism, the view that economic factors were necessarily the prime cause in the development of law. Consider his classic statement:

> I would like to protest the statement ... that some one factor, be it technology or economy, can be the 'ultimate' or 'true' cause of another. If we look at the causal lines, we see them run, at one time, from technical to economic and political matters, at another from political to religious and economic ones, etc ... [T]he view ... that the economic is in some sense the ultimate point in the chain of causes is completely finished as a scientific proposition (cited in Bendix and Roth, 1971: 242–243).

Weber argues that the economy is one factor, but that many factors are simultaneously at work in producing social phenomena. In this multi-causal approach, the researcher must examine many factors and determine how much weight is to be placed on each *cause*. Weber was more concerned with constellations, or the interplay of several forces together exerting an influence. For Weber, looking for a unique (singular) cause was naive and counterproductive.

The method of the social scientist should be as follows. First, the social scientist must choose a particular topic, which already reflects their value preference. Second, they must select specific possible "causes" out of a whole constellation of factors on the basis of the question they are addressing. Third they must abstract possible "causal" chains (i.e., in the form of "if X then Y," "if A then B," etc.; for example, if poverty then crime). Fourth, they must then eliminate one or more of these causal chains, one by one, and see if the effect (the result) is in the predicted direction. If, for example, eliminating one of the factors indicates that the result will still be the same, then this factor would not be seen as contributory and would be removed as a possible causal factor. If, on the other hand, the result would be different, then we have identified one factor in the causal chain. Finally, the researcher will determine which factors are of importance in producing a particular social phenomenon. That is, they can now identify the decisive factor(s) that are at work (Weber, 1949: 173, 182–183; Parsons, 1968: 610–611; Hekman, 1979: 71–74).

According to Weber, law, once developed, can have an influence on the economic sphere. This is a "recursive" model, meaning that the economic may be one of the important factors in the development of law, but law, once established, may then have an effect on the economic sphere of society (Weber, 1978: 667). In the social sciences, some argue that this way of reasoning is sound and provides an accurate picture of reality. Others, in criticism, argue that it can lead to circular reasoning or, in other words, tautological reasoning.

Why, Weber asks, is the form of law that develops under capitalism quite in accord with it? That is, why has a form of law developed that is closely related to the internal dynamics of capitalism? For example, the dynamics of formal rational law are said to be in close accord with capitalistic dynamics, e.g., as reflected in utilitarianism, profit maximization, the ethic of individual responsibility, etc. The connection may seem self-evident, but Weber wanted to know how it came to be. The key, for Weber, lies with the needs of a capitalist economic system. For Weber, "the modern capitalist enterprise rests primarily on *calculation* and presupposes a legal and administrative system, whose functioning can be rationally predicted ... by virtue of its fixed general norms, just like the expected performance of a machine" (1978: 1394, emphasis in the original). In other words, this economic system needs a stable framework within which firms, as well as individuals, can calculate appropriate means to attain specific ends and within which to predict possible results with a fair amount of precision.

Actions must be predictable, at least within a knowable and calculable range, for effective planning to occur. In the rational calculation of costs and benefits, for example, one must be assured that the many variables can be quantified to be weighed logically and rationally for maximum return. Some predictability must exist. Some certainty that, given act A, act B will follow, must be assured. Stability must exist so that a subject may not only know what to expect of the other, but also what the other expects of them. Finally, some method for enforcement must be in place to assure that agreements are kept. And if broken, remedies must be readily available.

But just because an economic system needs a particular legal system does not in itself assure that it will be discovered. How then, asks Weber, has this discovery come about? And how is it that subjects now willingly orient themselves to this order, to this stable environment?

To this end, we first examine his forms of law and legal thought. In other words, we can identify particular types of law and particular ways of legal reasoning. We then turn to the question of how "domination" is sustained (in the West, the word domination is used more often in its pejorative sense, unlike the sense that Weber implied). Then, we address the connection between domination and forms of legal thought. We will summarize his ideas concerning the development of capitalism in connection with the emergence of bureaucracy, rationalism, and the present-day form of law, "formal rationality." Finally, we turn to his explanation of the exemplary form of exchange, the contract, where he discusses the notion of freedom and coercion *in* law. We turn first to his typology of forms of law and legal thought.

Forms of Law and Legal Thought

In order to examine social phenomena, Weber constructed what he called "ideal types." These were simply theoretical constructions that aided research. They did not necessarily reflect reality. Rather, they helped the researcher in their investigation to illuminate and clarify existing complex phenomena. They were, in other words, "heuristic" tools. Unlike the "hard" sciences where much technology can be applied in the investigation of physical interactions, the social scientist works with conceptual tools, which offer varying degrees of access to and understanding of complex and dynamic phenomena. Weber was a pioneer in developing these heuristic tools in the sociology of law, particularly in using them to clarify the forms of law and legal thought.

The critical question for Weber was: What are the underlying processes in law-making (formulating laws) and law-finding (applying rules and reaching decisions) at particular historical periods? Are there regularities that exist? If there are, how are they structured? And how are they connected to the needs of other institutions in society?

To this end, Weber constructed a typology, a summary diagram of types of legal systems and legal thought (see Figure 1).[2] What this typology does is to capture different ideal types; it gives us a beginning understanding of complex legal systems. It sensitizes the researcher to important aspects of a legal system and its form of reasoning used in arriving at legal decisions. In reality, of course, we are unlikely to find these clear-cut ideal types. In the real world, we probably see mixtures. However, in examining legal system historically, we can distinguish some that resemble more one type rather than another.

Weber's typology of forms of law and legal thought can be constructed by the use of two dimensions: the degree of rationality and the degree of formality. Each dimension (or variable) can be ranged from "high" to "low"; in other words, a legal order can be placed within a continuum on each dimension. For simplification purposes, however, it can be collapsed into two categories for each variable (or to use sociological jargon, we can dichotomize the variables). And since we have two possible categories on the rationality dimension (high, low), and two possible categories on the formality dimension (high, low), we have a two-by-two diagram providing four possible ideal types. In other words, we can construct four possible pure models of forms of law and legal thought. More complex ideal types could be constructed. For

Figure 1. Typology, Forms of Law and Legal Thought

Formality	Rationality: High	Rationality: Low
High	Formal rationality e.g., syllogism, deductive logic, purposive contract, due process model	Formal irrationality e.g., magic, oracle, revelation, ordeal
Low	Substantive rationality e.g., affirmative action, necessity defense, just contract	Substantive irrationality e.g., jury decisions, khadi justice, crime control model; jury nullification

(Modified from Trubek, 1972: 729)

example, we could construct a three-by-three, a four by-four, etc. But notice the trade-offs: a two-by-two schema provides us with a heuristic tool with a degree of simplicity and a starting point in examining complex phenomena.

However, as we add categories a very complex schema with a multitude of intersecting points would emerge that may indeed approximate actual phenomena, but would also bring the attendant loss of a "handle," a beginning point in examining complex phenomena. The dimension referred to as "formality" stands for the employment of criteria, standards, principles and logic that are internal, that are intrinsic to the legal system. In other words, formality stands for the application by lawmakers and law-finders of rules and procedures that are totally internal to a given legal system. Put in yet another way, the decision maker is bound by some general body of laws and a procedure for its application. They do not have to go outside of this. Decision making takes place entirely within this framework. "Law ... is 'formal' to the extent that, in both substantive and procedural matters, only unambiguous general characteristics of the facts of the case are taken into account" (Weber, 1978: 656–657).

Opposing a formal system is a "substantive" system (or one with a "low" degree of "formality"). Here, decision making takes place by the use of rules and procedures that are outside of the formal system. In other words, decision making employs external criteria. Thus, some ethical, ideological and political criteria or standards may be applied. For example, some "political prisoners" in U.S. prisons may attempt to introduce United Nations' standards of human rights into U.S. court proceedings. Prosecutors, however, will insist that arguments remain within the formal framework of law, and all else is non-justiciable, it does not have "legal standing."

Thus, along this first dimension, legal systems can be seen as more formal or more substantive in orientation. In Figure 1, we have specified the degree of formality as being either "high" (more formal) or "low" (more substantive).

The second dimension, "rationality," means "following some criteria of decision which is applicable to all like cases." In other words, it stands for generality; it means dealing with all similarly situated subjects in a similar way. In Weber's words, it is characterized by "the reduction of the reasons relevant in the decision of concrete individual cases to one or more 'principles,' i.e., legal propositions" (ibid., 655). On the other hand, irrationality (or low rationality) means that similar cases are dealt with differently. The same case, then, can have different outcomes. Little, if any predictability exists as to how a case will be decided. In Figure 1, we have specified the degree of rationality as being either "high" (more rational) or "low" (less rational, or, better, irrational).

From Weber's analysis (1978; see also Hunt, 1978; Trubek, 1972) we can identify four ideal types of forms of law and legal thought. Let's pause for a moment and reflect on this construction and the magnitude of Weber's assertion. Weber is claiming that if we take a particular form of law and legal thought, past or present, we can locate it at some point of intersection of these two dimensions. Let's examine each.

Formally Irrational Law

This form of law, sometimes also referred to as formal irrationality, as an ideal type, occurs where decision making rests on magic, the oracle, or revelation. It employs "means which cannot be controlled by the intellect" (Weber, 1978: 656). It is formal to the extent that rules, technically, do exist concerning appropriate procedures to be applied. "Forfeiture of the relevant legal remedy, and potentially of the whole procedure," Weber tells us, "results from the slightest error by any of the parties in their enunciation of the ceremonial formula which constitutes each procedural act" (ibid.). Thus, "even the slightest deviation from the magically effective formula renders the whole [procedure] void" (ibid., 761). But the authority or decision maker alone is the knower of these rules and formula. And no reasons are provided for the justification of the decision. This system is "irrational" to the extent that the decision itself is not predictable, since even where some hidden rule supposedly does exist, it is applied differently to different people. Consider, too, the relationship of law to magic (Corcos, 2010; Crane, 1915), shamanism (Walker, 2015; Taussig, 1987), sorcery (Herriman, 2013; Rio, 2010), and witchcraft (Mills, 2013). Even though the standard for decision making is intrinsic to the system (i.e., some oracle), there is no way an outsider can understand how decisions are made. As a result, similarly situated persons will receive vastly different treatment.

Substantively Irrational Law

This occurs when each concrete situation determines the decision. It is substantive to the extent that any one of a number of external (extra-legal) ethical, political, ideological, moral, emotional, etc., criteria is used. No *general* norm, in other words, is being applied to the situation. Rather, a number of possible standards could be chosen for application. It is irrational to the extent that even similarly situated individuals with the same standard applied against them will be treated differently. Weber has called this "Khadi justice" (sometimes spelled Cadi, or Kadi). The authority, in other words, is not bound by any particular system of rules. They may decide a case by an idiosyncratic interpretation of the external standard chosen, or by the employment of some ethical principle that is personal which lies at the base of the standard chosen. The outsider cannot predict the outcome even of seemingly like cases.

Weber tells us that the jury decision is an exemplary case. After the prosecutor and defense have presented their cases in a trial, the judge instructs the jurors as to the points of law that should be the basis of their decision (formal rationality). This is called the "charge to the jury." For example, the judge might instruct the jurors that: "you will find the defendant guilty in the first degree of homicide if premeditation existed; second degree, if premeditation did not exist but gross negligence did; third degree, if mere negligence existed," etc. Even though the judge instructs the jury on the points of law that should be the basis of the verdict (consistent with the ideal type of formal rationality), in actuality the decision may be based on some other (substantive) standard(s) invoked in the jurors' minds or by some idiosyncratic interpretation of the charge. During jury deliberation, then, it remains unclear what standard(s) and/or interpretation would be invoked as the actual working standard(s) in the determination of the verdict.

Instructive were the trials surrounding the Rodney King episode (1991, police beatings of an African American where four police officers were acquitted of excessive force, but in a subsequent civil trial awarded $3.8 million in damages to Rodney King), and the O.J. Simpson trials (criminal trial, ending in acquittal, 1994 and civil trial where he was found liable and assessed $33.5 million in damages). Some have argued that an "equalizing principle" (external standard) was at play for the jurors.

We also note "jury nullifications" (jurors might not return a guilty verdict while even believing the defendant factually guilty) as well as "runaway grand juries" (jurors go beyond what the prosecutor lays out as the basis of the case) indicating the relatively independent actions by jurors. And instructive was a long, sordid history of acquittals in the South delivered by all-white jurors where a white person was charged for committing a crime against an African American, until the Civil Rights Act (1964) was employed in these cases in retrying the defendant.

In the context of pretrial proceedings, one might make the argument that during jury selection, where the prosecutor and defense interview and quiz prospective jurors *(voir dire)*—ostensibly in order to "stack the deck," with jurors that are potentially favorable to each's respective side—what is being investigated by the lawyers is the underlying framework, standard or principle (substantive rationality) that might be the possible basis of the prospective juror's future decision. But even if discovered, there is no accurate way of predicting how it would be interrupted (substantive irrationality).

In sum, for the substantive irrational form of law, different external criteria invoked will assure different treatment (outcomes). And even where the same external criteria are applied to similarly situated persons, different results occur. This ideal type would be the least predictable of the four.

Formal Rationality

Sometimes also referred to as "logically formal rational" (we employ, for simplification, formal rationality henceforth), is where rules are applied to all similarly situated cases in an identical manner. Here the rules themselves are clearly stated and followed. In other words, there exists a "high" degree of rationality and a "high" degree of formality. High predictability in decision making exists here. This ideal finds expression, for example, in the "equal protection clause" of the Fourteenth Amendment to the U.S. Constitution and its idealization of "formal equality." This is the standard that is taught in most U.S. law schools. In examining case law, the question for students is why law-making and law-finding may have varied from formal rationality.

In this model, no external criteria are applied. All decision making depends on the rules themselves. The rules are abstract and general. According to Weber, "only unambiguous general characteristics of the facts of the case are taken into account" (1978: 656–657). For example, the elements of a crime are written into the penal codes of the state: e.g., the elements of the crime of shoplifting might include leaving the premise with merchandise without payment (last point of possible purchase). In other cases, perhaps there are multiple elements defining the crime; absent one, it is no longer that particular crime. Thus, only these specified elements are relevant in law-finding. Hence, abstract interpretations of meaning, aided by the use of given rules, are generalized in law, establishing precedents *(stare decisis)* for future cases. Legal cases, in other words, are supposed to draw from past resolutions of similar controversies.

The notion of "logically formal rationality," a cumbersome term, can be broken down into its elements. Law is *rational* to the extent that decisions are based on existing, unambiguous rules. It is *formal* to the degree that the criteria, the standards used for arriving at a decision, are totally internal (intrinsic) to the legal system. And it is *logical* to the degree that rules are the product of conscious construction by specific ways of reasoning (i.e., syllogistic reasoning). This reasoning, this form of legal thought, is based on deductive logic, logical deductions based on a previously established rule or principle (see below). Weber states the purest form of this law in five postulates (1978: 658):

> [F]irst, that every concrete legal decision be the "application" of an abstract legal proposition to a concrete "fact situation"; second, that it must be possible in every concrete case to derive the decision from abstract legal propositions by means of legal logic; third, that the law must actually or virtually constitute a "gapless" system of legal propositions, or must, at least, be treated as if it were such a gapless system; fourth, that whatever cannot be "construed" ra-

> tionally in legal terms is also legally irrelevant; and fifth, that every social action of human beings must be visualized as either an "application" or "execution" of legal propositions, or as an "infringement" thereof, since the "gaplessness" of the legal system must result in a gapless "legal ordering" of all social conduct.

Let us return to the form of reasoning that is at the heart of formal rationality. Here, the claim is, that law-making and law-finding is accomplished by *syllogistic reasoning* and *deductive logic.* Take an Aristotelian example:

All desire is good. (major premise)

Ambition is desire. (minor premise)

Therefore, ambition is good. (conclusion)

Here we begin with a major premise and then apply it to the minor premise. In law, we begin with some legal principle (the major premise), such as the "equal protection clause" incorporated in the 14th Amendment to the U.S. Constitution, and apply it to the "facts" (the "what happened?"). By deductive logic, it is claimed, *one* decision will ultimately be reached. The law student learns quickly how to identify the applicable and relevant major premise (i.e., some constitutional right, some statutory rule, some state or Federal regulatory norm, etc.) and how to apply it to some "factual" situation. By syllogistic reasoning, they learn how to arrive, step by step, to the correct decision in law. One learns, for example, how to do an "equal protection argument," a "due process argument," etc. When the student researches statutory and case law, they summarize each respective case in the form of a "legal brief." Here summarized are the "facts," the "issue" and the decision/rationale. It is in the latter that the student attempts to identify the formal steps in the syllogism used by the justice(s) in arriving at the decision in law.

Let's use the "equal protection clause" of the Fourteenth Amendment as an example of the major premise. Paraphrased it states that equally situated should be equally treated (formal equality). Picture a defense attorney attempting to apply this constitutional right to an incarcerated inmate who has just been deprived of two years of their "good time" credit (good time is awarded and accumulated for good behavior in the prison). The defense attorney makes the following comparison (see Figure 2).

Here, legal right A may be the right to be heard; B, the right to know the charges; C, the right to counsel; D, the right to cross-examination; E, the right to confront the accuser. Now applying deductive logic and syllogistic reasoning by the defense counsel: first, they state the major premise, "equally situated should be equally treated" (the notion of formal equality embedded in the Fourteenth Amendment). Then they state that the inmate and the free citizen are equally situated vis-a-vis the potential deprivation that each faces—the loss of two years liberty. They then apply syllogistic reasoning and claims that the free citizen had rights A,B,C,D,E, whereas the inmate had only A,B. And thus the conclusion: this is a deprivation of the equal protection clause of the U.S. Constitution since rights C,D,E were not provided to the inmate.

Figure 2. An Equal Protection Argument in Law

Person	Situation	Legal rights provided in case	Outcome
(1) Inmate	Infraction committed (liberty loss of 2 years possible)	A, B	2 years deprivation of liberty
(2) Free citizen	Infraction committed (liberty loss of 2 years possible)	A, B, C, D, E	2 years deprivation of liberty

Of course, they would also have to attempt to argue that the Constitution makes use of the word "persons" ("nor shall a person be deprived of....") and does not itself make a distinction between an inmate and a free citizen. The lawyer for the government, no doubt, would argue that the citizen and inmate are not equally situated, or that the Constitution does not apply to the prison system.

Referring to Figure 1 in Chapter 2, formal rationality is the basis of liberal legalism (upper right-hand corner). Those who internalize this method of reasoning are focusing on jurisprudence, rather than on the sociology of law. For jurisprudes, rationality and formality remain celebrated terms, which themselves remain unexamined. Sociologists of law, on the other hand, are much more likely to question these global forms of rationality and formality. Jurisprudes are more likely to attempt to identify biases and prejudices in legal procedures and remedy them by the appropriate syllogistic reasoning and deductive logic. Their goal is to induce a shift toward the application of a purer formal rational model of law, with the further understanding that doing so would contribute to the furtherance of the fulfillment of social values. And certainly, much reduction of suffering takes place and the realization of some social values.

Much of the activity of the student in law school deals with how to make legal forms of arguments. Students are assigned legal cases which they must examine. They fine-tune their abilities by preparing legal briefs. Here, the student states the issue (the major premise), and the "facts" (minor premise), and then attempts to trace out the syllogistic reasoning in linear fashion that was apparently involved in coming up with a conclusion in law. Through the Socratic method, by which the law professor drills the student about the case, it is said that an understanding of legal thinking develops. This exercise, it is said, prepares the law student in the mechanics of the law.

Substantively Rational Law

Substantive rationality exists where a particular *external* principle, rule or criterion is employed. By "external" we mean outside of the dominant and State-supported body of laws and procedures used in their enforcement. This includes "ethical imperatives, utilitarian and other expediential rules, and political maxims" (Weber, 1978: 657). Once chosen and applied uniformly, decisions have a higher degree of predictability. This makes them "rational" (assuming, of course, that the logic of the ethical imperative or political maxim chosen is followed precisely; if it isn't, it becomes a case of substantive irrationality). Several examples of substantive rationality are presented in Figure 3, including Marxian notions of justice (differential abilities and needs), affirmative action, comparable worth, alternative definitions of crime ("harms of reduction," "harms of repression," Henry and Milovanovic, 1996, 2020), the necessity defense, United Nation's definition of human rights or genocide, the just contract (contract of equity), ecocide (eco-justice), and mutual aid.

When activists before the U.S. courts have attempted to introduce United Nations law concerning human rights, they are summoning an external principle. As of 2020, the U.S. still had not signed on for the International Criminal Court (ICC) in the Hague, claiming, for example, that any soldier serving in other lands should only be liable in U.S. courts. Attempts by Yugoslavian officials to bring legal action against the U.S. bombing of Belgrade (1999) particularly non-combatants (TV stations, convoys, hospitals) were dismissed by U.S. courts. On the other hand, the U.S. has kidnapped and extradited criminals from other countries, even a president from another country (Manuel Noriega of Panama) and tried them in the U.S. courts (1989). Consider, for example, the appeal by Dr. Jose Solis Jordan of his conviction of setting a pipe-bomb in Chicago to bring attention to U.S. colonialization of Puerto Rico (*U.S. v. Jose Solis Jordan*, 2000). The lawyers for Professor Jordan asked the federal appeals court "whether international law, binding upon the courts of the United States, deprives the courts of the colonial power to try citizens of the nation subjected to colonialism for the offenses alleged in the indictment?" (ibid. 4; 39–50). As expected, the appeal was denied. In short, what constitutes the appropriate substantive principle and arena are political questions.

The recent second impeachment trial of former President Trump where a majority voted for conviction (57 to 43), falling short of the 2/3 necessary, is a particular example of substantive rationality at work. We previously placed many jury deliberations in the substantive irrationality form, but here, since some external principle was uniformly applied, "party loyalty" (all 50 democrat Senators voted for conviction, all but 7 republicans voted against), and since the decision was highly predictable, even before the "trial," we have an exemplary case for substantive rationality.

Debate exists in the literature about the differences between substantive irrational and substantive rational law in any particular case. Weber, for example, attributed the Chinese system of the time as "substantive irrational." Quian (2010), reviews some debates and argues that it is much more complex, suggesting there are good arguments for seeing the Chinese system of law more substantive rational since here the use of a general principle, a key factor in substantive rationality, is rooted more in Confucian philosophy.[3] It remains to be seen, however, with China's exponentially expanding its industry and overseas trade in the last decade to what extent formal rationality will become more dominant, notwithstanding socialist law.

Substantive rationality, compared to formal irrationality and substantive irrationality), is more predictable. That is, once external criteria are selected and applied (e.g., some notions of universal justice), the rules for resolution are more predictable. However, the difference between substantive rationality and formally rational law, as far as predictability of decisions in similarly situated cases is concerned, is a matter of degree.

"Insoluble Conflict": Formal versus Substantive Rationality

Clearly, much tension exists between principles of substantive rationality and formal rationality. During revolutionary changes, for example, what was previously an external principle may now become the basis of the dominant legal order, and the vanquished will now be seen as the "radical" element. But this tension often has more subtle play. Sometimes we even find that there is an incorporation—be it selectively, with often limited longevity, or confined to a historical time period—of an external substantive principle into the dominant formal ones, such as is the case with the necessity defense, the insanity defense, affirmative action, comparable worth, and the contract of equity (just contract). In other words, these "external" principles are allowed a standing in court. (Note the depiction in Figure 3 that some "external" principles are connected to the dominant ones; some, however, remain unconnected—meaning that no, or very little material from the "external" principles are allowed a standing in court). Here, an uneasy tension exists between forms of law and legal thought (i.e., between formal rationality and substantive rationality). Consider, for example, demands for fulfilling the promise of equal protection (formal rationality), but also for substantive justice (i.e., affirmative action programs to correct for systemic racism particularly focused on contributory conditions, while formal equality advocates cry, "reverse discrimination"). Ultimately, the question of which ones are indeed allowed or not in litigation is a political question and revolves on the ability to mobilize political power. Some principles, therefore, remain outside the dominant domain. Let's provide some further examples. These are portrayed in Figure 3.

When affirmative action or comparable worth principles are introduced in law-finding and law-making, an "external" principle is being applied. Note the tension here. Ever since *Brown v. Board of Education* (1954), and subsequent governmental policies and remedies that attempted to correct for past patterned forms of racial discrimination in the U.S. through the use of affirmative action, quota systems and preferential treatment, an uneasy alliance with principles of formal rationality has existed. In fact, we may conceptualize the Supreme Court's struggles in the last seven decades in terms of it first incorporating a substantive principle (suggested in *Brown*); then in a series of decisions reversing this emphasis, pushing it toward the periphery of acceptable constitutional practices in the late 1960s, 70s and 80s; and finally, with a conservative U.S. Supreme Court, expelling it as outside of the acceptable ranges ("reverse discrimination"). Here the history has been a movement from elevating substantive rational principles as pertinent in law, to a movement to formal rational principles (e.g., formal equality). More recently (chapters 6, 7) the Court in higher education admissions standards has allowed substantive/qualitative criteria (race as a "factor") for assuring a diverse student body necessary for educational goals.

Figure 3. Formal versus Substantive Rationality

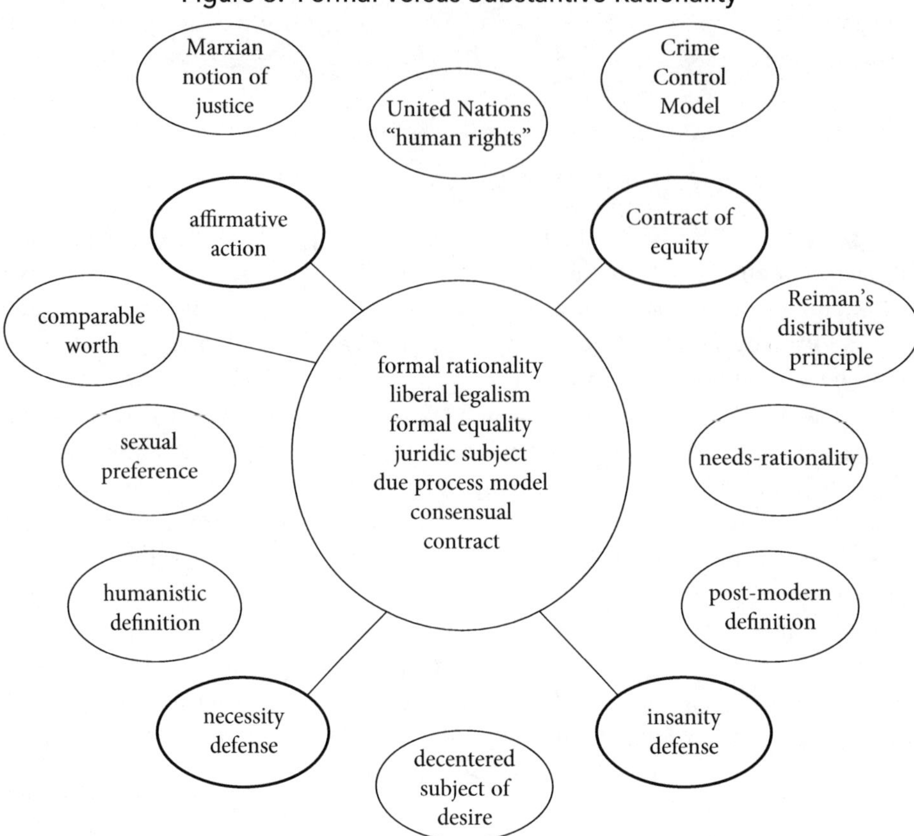

Similarly, comparable worth is the idea that if two workers do similar things at the workplace, regardless of their job title, they should be paid similarly. For example, a male and a female worker might be doing similar work and exhibiting similar skills, but the male, because of his title, might be making $75,000 whereas the female worker, because of her lesser title, only $50,000. By applying the "external" standard of comparable worth, discrimination could be shown; if the principle is not allowed, the focus on the job title itself will be enforced in formal rational law-finding.[4]

Perhaps the most open-ended use of some external criterion is in the case where the "necessity defense" is permitted by a State and allowed in a particular case by a presiding judge. Here, the defense attempts to show that the client broke some law to prevent some greater and imminent harm (see Bannister and Milovanovic, 1990). Note that in Figure 3 we indicate a connectedness and incorporation of this principle to the general body of law, formal rationality, for, in many States, this is an available defense. If the judge allows this defense in a particular case, external standards may be brought into the trial proceedings. If so, rather than merely a doctrinal legal discourse, we are much more likely to witness an oppositional discourse exercised (we shall return to this in Chapters 9, 10).

Another example of substantive rationality is Marx's ideal notion of justice (which is a substitute for bourgeois notions of formal equality): "from each according to his [their] ability, to each according to his [their] needs." Note that both "ability" and "needs" are assumed to vary for each person, a principle celebrating differences (compare this with some reactionary ideologies that claim Marx was advocating that all should be the same, automatons, walking in lock-step—hardly the case). Here "abilities" and "needs" evoke some standard, thus it is substantive; and by then applying this standard to all similarly situated (i.e., similar abilities and needs), it is rational. However, only in the rare case will there be pure substantive equality in outcome. The rule, being substantive, therefore, does not necessarily mean that all will be treated identically. This is because of different abilities and needs. In other words, because of the inherent uniqueness of being human, this moral principle would require that decision making should not produce similar outcomes. Human beings have varied interests, abilities, aptitudes, temperamental traits, drives, need, desires and so forth. It is only to the extent that one treats the individual as the "reasonable man in law"—an abstraction, a general subject and bearer of universal rights—that one removes, or disregards their unique qualities. Only here, as legal abstractions, can one talk about the logic of formally rational law. Given all the above, in Marx's notion of justice, we are left with substantive irrationality being more likely, with substantive rationality appearing as the rare case of equivalence. Note, too, that revolutionary change may witness some former external principle now being instituted as the dominant form, and the former, expelled to the outside.

Let's take another example of the tension between substantive and formal rationality. Our criminal justice system is said to be based on formal rationality as an ideal. Some years ago, a much-cited Packer (1968), in "Two Models of the Criminal Process," presented the "due process model" and the "crime control model" as competing models in our (U.S.) criminal justice system. The former placed a premium on the possibility of error always existing; an adversary process; a focus on legal guilt; a low demand for finality; a high demand for prevention and elimination of mistakes; and a presumption of innocence. Here the most important value was "due process," or fundamental fairness. The "crime control model," however, placed a premium on repression of criminal conduct, upholding "law and order," efficiency in processing (i.e., in screening, suspects, determining guilt and sentencing), factual guilt, speed and finality, and a presumption of guilt. Here the most important value is "clearance" and conviction rates. Note that the due process model (in Figure 3) is connected with formal rationality. The crime control model is connected with substantive rationality, since some external standard is at play, focusing on the bureaucratic ideal of efficiency in dealing with large numbers of defendants. And since the vagaries of plea-bargaining come into play, perhaps we could even say that substantive irrationality is the norm. Since, in large city courts, over 90% of the cases are resolved by plea bargaining, a reasonable conclusion is that we do in fact have the crime control model as the dominant operative model even though the due process model is the stated ideal and the one celebrated in the ideology of the rule of law. Those of the legal liberal persuasion, at best, attempt to fine-tune the criminal justice system in order that it progresses toward the stated ideal.

For another example of the tension between substantive and formal rational principles let's return to Durkheim's notion of the difference between the *consensual contract* and the *contract of equity* (see Chapter 3). Consensual contracts are centrally connected with formal rationality. The contract of equity, however, is based on the idea of equality in the exchange of things possessing *equal social values.* Here the contract of equity would be "low" on the formality scale, or substantive in nature (recall his three elements defining social value), and "high" on the rationality scale, since Durkheim defines a just contract as reflecting equivalence in social values in the exchange. He did note that in the "abnormal forms" the consensual contract would invariably hide substantive inequality (repressive formalism). However, he does note the increasing incorporation of fairness standards, which correct for some of the repressive potentials inherent in consensual contract (1964b: 385–386; see also how "interest balancing" has affected the delineation of rights and what constitutes fairness (Chapter 5, Karl Marx; Milovanovic, 1987). Present-day standards of "good faith" are examples. In Figure 3 we have represented this recognition by a connectedness of this external principle with the general body of law characterized as formal rationality.

Yet other substantive principles, standards, and criteria which are in tension with formal rational principles could be mentioned (see Figure 3): Reiman presented a distributive principle whereby gross inequities could gradually wither away (1990); Herman and Julia Schwendinger (1970) and Henry and Milovanovic (1996, 2020) have developed alternative definitions of harm that counter the narrowly construed legalistic definition of crime; the U.S. has devised separate standards and procedures for accused terrorists in the wake of "9/11"; eco-justice has taken seriously the question of rights of the environment (do non-human animals and even trees have rights?); and postmodernist theorists have challenged the individualistic philosophical underpinnings of the notion of the juridic subject (see below in the section on "the contract and the juridic subject") with their idea of the *decentered subject* (Lacan, 1977; Milovanovic, 1992, 2001; see also Chapter 11). All this indicates an uneasy tension between principles of formal rationality and those of substantive rationality. And, in some cases, we see that a connectedness (conduit) does exist for substantive principles to be incorporated, i.e., affirmative action, comparable worth, necessity defense, insanity defense, and the just contract (contract of equity) (see Figure 3).

A final word. These various tensions presented above between principles of formal and substantive rationality suggest that activists and rebels before the court need to generate creative strategies for developing a conduit for the incorporation of external standards into the formal system (i.e., human rights, sexual preference, comparable worth, alternative definitions of harm, redistributive principles, etc.). Otherwise, rebels and activists before the court will be faced with either accepting the formal system—arguing within a doctrinal legal discourse and hoping for acquittal because of a winning legal syllogism (by a technicality), in the process adding further legitimacy to the rule-of-law ideology—or arguing a more radical discourse replete with alternative standards which, however, will be quickly suppressed (i.e., as non-justiciable; too extensive in "scope," etc.), placing the defense team in disarray and their clients or their "cause(s)" in jeopardy. Ultimately, it remains a political question and concerns the effective mobilization of political power, as to which standard is incorporated and which is not.

Domination and Law

What motivates subjects to be obedient? Why do they orient their behavior to some order? To answer this question, Weber introduces some new terms. First, the notion of *domination.* By this he means "the probability that certain specific commands (or all commands) will be obeyed by a given group of persons" (1978: 212). In addressing the question of why people comply, the answer can range from habit to purely rational calculation. For example, individuals obey because of tradition. Or they obey because of expediency; that is, because it is self-serving, it is in their best interest. In all forms of domination, Weber tells us, some minimal degree of voluntary compliance must exist. But this still does not fully tell us why subjects comply. The missing element, for Weber, centers on the belief in the *legitimacy* of the order. Three forms of legitimate domination are presented as ideal types. The three "pure types" of legitimate domination are traditional, charismatic and legal.

"Traditional domination" stands for obedience due to the belief in the validity of the order coming from habit, custom and tradition. Commands are seen as legitimate because they have always been followed. They are age-old rules.

"Charismatic domination" is due to commands being followed because of some exceptional qualities of the leader. Subjects abandon themselves to some person who is distinguished by holiness, exemplariness or heroism. They are seen to possess superhuman, supernatural, or exceptional qualities or powers. An example would be Martin Luther King, Jr.

"Legal domination," or legal authority, stems from the belief in the legitimacy of rules themselves. Obedience is due to the belief that laws are rationally constructed. These impersonal laws are perceived as standing above subjects and leaders. Leaders selected in accordance with the law are seen as legitimate authorities. The pure type of legal authority is the bureaucracy.

All three forms of domination, then, are perceived as "legitimate" forms of domination or authority. However, in the real world, Weber tells us, these ideal types often do not appear in pure forms. He merely wishes to give us conceptually pure models. These, then, are heuristic devices for further examination of complex social phenomena.

There is an important distinction to be made. In charismatic and traditional domination, law finds its legitimation outside of itself. In other words, law has no legitimation in and of itself. Rather, it is connected with either tradition or a charismatic leader. Thus, claims to legitimacy are rooted in the special relationship between ruler and subject. For the charismatic type, the personal relationship is central. For the traditional type the leader also has the weight of tradition behind their position (see also Hunt, 1978: 114). When law becomes rational law, or where legal "domination" exists, the law itself is its own legitimizing principle. In other words, the rule of law is seen in itself as worthy of being obeyed. No necessary connection exists with a particular leader or with tradition. As a matter of fact, the slogan is: "the rule of law, not men."

Legal domination (authority) rests with the following ideas (Hunt, 1978: 217–19):

- There exist general norms established by imposition or agreement.
- The law is a consistent system, intentionally developed and made up of abstract rules.
- The "superior" is subject to the rules. They have to orient their behavior to the impersonal order.
- Obedience is directly to the rule of law itself.
- Obedience to the leader is not so much to them but to the impersonal order.

Weber indicates that there is a close relationship between a form of law, legal thought, and the type of domination. We can see this close connection by looking at the relationship between logically formal rationality and legal domination. In this case, abstractly derived rules are seen as legitimate in themselves. Obedience is toward the legal order because it is seen as rationally constructed. The claim to legitimacy rests "on a belief in the legality of enacted rules and the right of those elevated to authority under such rules to issue commands" (Weber, 1978: 215).

In fact, Weber states that the whole progress of law is toward legal authority and formal rationality (ibid., 882). Weber refers to this process as *rationalization in law.* Obedience to individuals, over time, evolves into obedience to impersonal rules. The rule of law becomes increasingly stabilized. The impersonal, hierarchical structure of the bureaucracy and its specialized rules is increasingly duplicated in the form of law. Each becomes increasingly rationalized. Both become their own legitimating principles.

The relationship between legal thought and legitimate domination can be summarized. *Traditional domination* occurs where there exists an obedience owed to individuals under the guidance of traditional practices. Law is legitimated by its continuity with historical practices. It is rooted in the sanctity of tradition. The form of legal thought that would be logically connected with this form of domination is either substantive rationality or formal irrationality (see also Figure 1). *Charismatic domination* is characterized by obedience owed to an individual who has some exceptional quality. Law is legitimated in "personal devotion." The form of legal thought prevalent is substantive irrationality or formal irrationality. Finally, in *legal domination,* authority is derived from law itself. Law is legitimated by the impersonal nature of the law. Law is the conscious use of logical, rational techniques by a staff which itself is subject to its law. This process lends further legitimacy to the rule of law. The form of legal thought here is formal rationality, or logically formal rationality.

Figure 4. Relationship between Decision-Maker, Form of Law, and Domination

Form of Law	Independence of decision-maker	Form of legitimate domination
Substantive rationality or formal irrationality	High	Traditional
Substantive irrationality or formal irrationality	High	Charismatic
Formal Rationality	Low	Legal

In the charismatic and traditional forms of domination, the person in authority (the decision maker) has a high degree of independence in decision making (see Figure 4). Here, too, the law is relatively unpredictable in its individual application. In legal domination, however, independence of the decision maker from law is low, and law is highly predictable in its application to individual cases. Again, these are ideal types. They are not meant to be statements exactly reflecting a desirable or even an actual state in society.

The question of domination and the rule of law focuses on political and ideological dimensions. We now, with Weber, turn to how economic factors interplay with the political and ideological institutions in producing the contemporary form of law and legal thought in capitalism.

Capitalism, Bureaucracy and Rationalization

The rule of law, as an ideology, arose in the West because of unique developmental conditions. For Weber, as we have seen above, attributing cause only to the economic system in explaining the evolution of a particular form of a legal system and law was a simplistic and inaccurate exercise. Instead, his multi-causal approach argued that the rise of formal rationality had its roots in a process of rationalization. Law evolved from substantive rational to formal rational systems. Political, economic, ideological as well as legal factors were influential. He stated that there was a close connection between the internal needs of the capitalist mode of production and a form of law that emphasizes logical formal rationality. But simply attributing causation of one to the other, he continued, was to overlook the complex conditions out of which each arose. And it was also to overlook the unique confluence of conditions that accounted for their mutual development.

Weber used the term *rationalization* in a number of ways (for a criticism, see Andreski, 1984: 58–82; Hunt, 1978: 101). At times he defined it as a systematic codification of rules. That is, it was characterized by the increasing development of internally pure logical interrelationships among elements. At other times, he argued that the term meant the increasing differentiation and coordination of conduct, in industry and in everyday life, on the basis of an empirical knowledge of subjects' relations with each other, toward the end of greater efficiency or productivity (See, also, Freund, 1969: 18). (This idea found expression in industrial "time and motion" studies of Taylorism during the early years of the 20th century particularly dealing with the assembly line form of production). As an example of the forces of rationalization, think in terms of traditional production where only a single layer between workers and a supervisor exists where the worker does a number of things in producing some product (or consider the lone craftsperson, building a carriage from beginning to end, the so-called "Renaissance Man"); and how, with the splitting up of workers' functions into ever more specializations also creates the need for further layers of supervisors who supervise other supervisors, etc. Production is correlatively increasing. And, once this internal logic is set free, we witness continuous differentiation of worker's functions and further growth of the bureaucracy, now with particular specializations, job titles, required formal training, pay scales, time management, production goals, formal chain of command, etc.

The rationalization of law, according to Weber, was due to "two forces operating side by side ... on the one hand, capitalism interested in strictly formal law and legal procedure ... on the other hand, the rationalism of officialdom in absolutist states led to the interest in codified systems and in homogeneous law ..." (cited in Hunt, 1978: 109). The development of modern law needed both these forces.

Several more specific factors are identified as critical in the development of the rule of law. First, the development of centers of commerce was decisive. This necessitated much interaction across time and space. Second, and along with the first, the development of the competitive marketplace characterized by commodity exchange (rather than barter relations), and the use of money, was of importance. Economic transactions needed to operate in an environment of stability. That is, whether it is the subject engaged in commodity exchange or a capitalist firm determining profit margins and investment potentials, the need for certainty and predictability are critical for rational planning or, in a word, calculability.

Weber's concept of rationality finds its counterpart in the economic sphere. "Rational economic action," he tells us, "requires instrumental rationality in this orientation, that is, deliberate planning" (1978: 63). More traditional, pre-industrial societies were marked by "communal" relationships (subjects orient themselves to each other because they feel a belongingness, a camaraderie). They exchanged for personal use (barter). This practice gave way, with the development of the competitive marketplace, to "associative" relationships (subjects orient themselves to each other because of rational calculation), and subjects now saw exchange as an opportunity for profit (ibid., 40–41, 63, 73). The competitive marketplace, then, is characterized as a domain where the calculation for profit motive is supreme.

But Weber cautions us, "economic situations do not automatically give birth to new legal forms; they merely provide the opportunity for the actual spread of a legal technique if it is invented" (ibid., 687). Furthermore, "economic conditions, have ... everywhere played an important role, but they have nowhere been decisive alone and by themselves" (ibid., 883). We must, then, look to additional factors.

A third factor was the rise of the monarchical powers and the nation state, which needed a mechanism of administration. The bureaucracy supplied the ideal form of control. It was an ideal form of efficient administration. Here specialized functions guided by some centrally stated goal were combined with functionaries with specialized training who discharged their responsibilities according to some calculable rules without any reference to people as such. The late Roman Empire was to grasp this form of administration in its dealing with its vast empire.

Bureaucracies, once created, develop a life of their own. Rules tend to become more systematized; that is, more internally coordinated in a logical way. Furthermore, the more complex a society becomes, the more depersonalized the supporting structures become. That is, the former control exerted by a lord is replaced by the control by experts who administer, not on whim, but according to established rules. "[O]nly bureaucracy," Weber explains, "has established the foundation for the administration of a rational law conceptually systematized on the basis of 'statutes' ..." (1978: 975). In other words, apart from all else, the bureaucracy offers the ideal form of control and administration.

A bureaucracy tends to continuously expand guided by its own internal dynamics. A tendency toward more specialization of functions and roles, with the need for greater coordination and control, leads to the need for specifying clearer and more rational rules defining interrelationships. For example, at an early stage, there is one supervisor with two workers each having four functions; with specialization of functions, we now have four workers each with two functions, with the addition of two new supervisors, each supervising two of the workers. At the next stage, we may have eight workers, each having one function with yet another layer of supervisors. The bureaucracy continues to expand, guided by the ideal of greater efficiency in production and control (rationalization). Difficult tasks are broken down into their simplified component elements. Simplified tasks are coordinated into the overall plan. Rules delineate responsibilities, functional roles, and competencies. Obedience is owed to this overall impersonal machine.

The interests of the nation-state and the capitalist firms and subjects, operating in a competitive marketplace oriented toward profit, coincided. In both spheres, the political and the economic, there was a need for calculability. This "alliance" between the needs of monarchical and bourgeois interests was "one of the major factors" leading toward the development of the rule of law (ibid., 847). We should not read "alliance" to mean a conspiratorial agreement, but rather a coincidental development of compatible interests. Nevertheless, this mutual interest, and its recognition, aided the further development of the rationalization of law. But yet other factors were at work.

Thus, a fourth factor was the relatively independent developments *within* the legal profession. The early Roman Law with its use of specialized, abstract, logical techniques was studied extensively in the universities of continental Europe (see also Chapter 2). It was from these universities that specialized legal notables, trained in logic and abstract techniques of reasoning within law, arose. And they were in an opportune position to verbalize and systematize the type of law needed with the development of the "alliance" mentioned above.

Thus, these four factors, or determinants, together accounted for the form of law that arose with capitalism. There was a convergence of interests, an alliance that became increasingly solidified. This is a clear reflection of Weber's multi-causal approach.

A different story emerges, Weber tells us, within England, where legal training developed as a "craft." That is, the early English attorneys were recruited from the clergy. For them, lawyering was a major source of income. Gradually the clergy was replaced by non-clergy lawyers. Legal guilds also developed. On many occasions the lawyers lived together in guild houses. It was also from them that judges were recruited. Specialized training, including apprenticeships was established. Special "guild" interests also developed. These guilds became resistant to change and attempted to maintain their own economic self-interest (see also Chapter 2). This rigidness hindered the development of rationalization in the law. During this time lawyers were predominantly interested in the immediacy of the situation (the concrete case). The development of a body of abstract, universal, or general rules was not their central interest. They held monopoly power over the development of law. New, innovative techniques that had *general* application such as formal rational law were not encouraged.

These developments were in marked contrast to developments on mainland Europe. In Germany, for example, where there were no guild organizations, legal training was performed in universities. Here, abstract rules and logic centering on Roman law was embraced. Roman law and logic entailed reducing a lawsuit with its complex issues to the most basic issues involved. It was an exercise of a highly analytical and rational dissection of parts. No theological factors were included in the legal thought itself (Weber, 1978: 793–796).

Comparing the development of law in England and mainland Europe, Weber points out that even though capitalism first appeared in England, the form of law that had close connections with it did not. Rather, it was on mainland Europe that logically formal law developed. Hence, the economic sphere itself could not be seen as the main determinant in its development (see Weber, 1978: 784–802). For Weber, then, a decisive influence in the rationalization of law was exercised by legally trained specialists (ibid., 776).

In sum, the systematization or the rationalization of law (the movement toward logically formal rationality) was due to a number of unique developments. Together these forces led to the development of a form of law that was relatively autonomous, or relatively independent from the interests or influence of specific actors. Legitimate domination now rested on the rule of law itself. Subjects oriented their behavior toward the assumed impersonal rules that created predictability, stability and an environment of calculability. Put in another way, both subjects and capitalist firms could operate within a framework that offered a range of predictability. They were assured, by the state, that obligations or expectations would be met by coercion if needed. The whim of an individual actor—be they a legislator, leader, president, capitalist, or contractor—is replaced by rules that have been consciously developed and written, thus ensuring a high probability of compliance.

Rationalization in law and the continued development of the bureaucracy go hand in hand. One supports the other. Weber saw this autonomous development in evolutionary terms. This was his "iron rule." Legitimate domination, then, is tied to the evolution and acceptance of rules that are seen as autonomously developed by legal experts who objectively and logically construct a body of laws that have general applicability. Everything falls within this "gapless" system. Everything can be litigated. New laws can be deduced from old. Previous laws now become precedents for new laws. The inherent logic of the rule of law itself determines the form of reasoning that will be respected and enforced by the state.

The Contract and the Juridic Subject

The development of the contract and juridic subject (the abstract bearer of rights, the "reasonable man" in law) finds a central place in Weber's thought. He devotes a sizable section of *Economy and Society* to this subject (1978: 666–731). Here he traces the development of the contract from its primitive to its modern form. In traditional, pre-industrial, less differentiated societies, it was the *status contract* that was the main form. In modern societies it was the purposive *contract.* It is in these pages that he questions whether with the development of "contractual freedom" more substantive freedom and less coercion develop.

He begins his analysis with the definition of a *right.* To him, it means "an increase of the probability that a certain expectation of the one to whom the law grants the right will not be disappointed" (ibid., 666–667). Every right, then, becomes the source of power. Freedom, for Weber, is intimately connected with the possession of rights (ibid., 668). The "reasonable man in law," can be conceived in terms of the totality of (1) contracts that they assume and (2) inheritance (ibid., 669). To understand contractual freedom, he points out, we must understand the development of a legal order and the agreements that it enforces. The "decisive" factor behind the development of the kind of contracts that are enforced, is "interest groups," particularly those from the marketplace, and their influence.

Weber describes the stages of development from the status contract to the purposive contract in some detail. Traditional societies were characterized by an organization based on the clan, kinship, and the household community. Any transactions affected the individual's entire status. That is, their entire standing in the community was affected. They became someone entirely different because of the transaction. These "fraternal" contracts with their attached magical rituals meant that the other would now become "somebody's child, father, wife, brother, master, slave, kin, comrade-in-arms, protector, client, follower, vassal, subject, friend, or, quite generally, comrade ..." (ibid., 672). In other words, the person's whole personality as understood and supported by the group was profoundly affected. The oath and the calling upon a divine being for recognition and enforcement was a later variation of this type of contract.

Transactions with outsiders were marked by barter. Because no enforceability existed, these transactions were originally in the form of immediate exchange of things. Central here was the notion of possession. Enforcement revolved around the idea that vengeance was appropriate where possession was violated.

The idea of an individual "obligation" by way of a contract was alien to the persons in traditional society.[5] Enforceability of the contract within the kinship structure revolved around arbitration by the elders. Neither vengeance nor litigation was the norm. At worst ostracism and boycott would take place. The entire community was the first line of defense against non-fulfillment of the contract. All members of the kinship were responsible for any contract made by any one of them. Hence, the notion of *collective responsibility* and liability was predominant. The notion of *individual liability* had not yet developed in traditional societies. Where a member of one group defaulted against a member of another group, collective reprisal against the other's whole group was only natural.[6]

When the kinship group begin to disintegrate and transform, giving rise to clusters of house communities and various political associations, new notions of responsibility, liability and enforcement arose. The coming of a money economy, the competitive marketplace and centers of commerce changed the basic traditional relationships and orientations that had assured predictability and stability. People became more involved, be it temporarily, in a variety of associations. The growing exchange economy placed much demand for transactions of all types. The solution: the development of the "juristic personality." All were now endowed with certain general and abstract rights respected and enforced in law. The "purposive contract" became dominant. It was but a "legal reflex" of the developed market orientation.

The juristic subject (or, juridic subject) as an abstract bearer of rights was now engaged in many transactions without at the same time committing their whole personality. Here, all magical and religious elements were removed. Individual responsibility, liability and obligation were now dominant concepts. Transactions agreed to were now guaranteed by the State. (One may pause here and compare the *purposive contract* with Durkheim's idea of the *contract as mutual consent,* or the *consensual contract.*)

As can be seen, the development of the purposive contract was connected with the rationalization of law. The development of the market economy, characterized by money and commodity exchange, and the clash of egotistically driven wills, needed not only a highly formal rational system of laws, but also a new entity, the juridic subject. This abstraction, the legal subject in law, now carried with it certain rights that were general. All were formally equal in the eyes of the law. This notion allowed the legal sphere to merely plug into the grand picture of the rule of law this known quantity. They were but an "organ" in the whole scheme of things. Subjects and legal firms, then, were provided with a predictable and calculable order. Predicting what the other will or should do was no longer guesswork that involved judging excessive individual variations. Rather, all were required to respect certain general rights. Mutual expectations now became enforced in law.

The overall political economic order became legitimated by the rule of law itself. Legitimate domination exists because law was seen as rationally enacted and because all were endowed with formally equal rights. The legal system, then, was perceived as autonomous from political and economic manipulation. That is, the legal system was now assumed to be independent, or autonomous. It was guided by pure rational, logical thought. A body of lawyers would, through the promulgation of laws and in litigation, decide in any instance what the applicable laws were and what they meant, but consistent with the overall internal logic of established law.

Freedom and Coercion in Law

In a scant three pages of over 1,400 pages in *Economy and Society,* Weber turns to the subject of freedom and coercion in law. But the points made are nothing short of thunderbolts. These pages deal primarily with the "insoluble conflict," the discrepancy between formal and substantive justice.

He asks: Even though contractual freedom has increased in contemporary society, does it necessarily mean that overall freedom has increased? Conversely, does it also mean that overall coercion has decreased? His answer revolves around the question of property distribution in a society.

> The exact extent to which the total amount of 'freedom' within a given legal community is actually increased depends entirely upon the concrete economic order and especially upon the property distribution (Weber, 1978: 730).

He gives an example of a worker entering a contract, and notes that the worker normally has little to say about the terms of the conditions of work. They are offered a contract, take it or leave it.

> The result of contractual freedom, then, is in the first place the opening of the opportunity to use, by the clever utilization of property ownership in the market, these resources without legal restraints as a means for the achievement of power over others. The parties interested in power in the market thus are also interested in such a legal order (ibid., 730).

Thus, for Weber, assessing the overall freedom or coercion in law cannot be simply discerned by looking at the formal qualities of law. For example, if the formal legal system stipulates that all subjects are equal in the eyes of the law (formal rationality), in no way does it mean at the substantive level, given the unequal property distribution in society, that overall coercion has decreased. Formal equality, then, does not necessarily mean greater freedom and less coercion. Anatole France's much-cited ironic quip that both the rich and the poor are equally prohibited from sleeping under the bridges of the Seine in Paris is a case in point.

The connection between the form of law and legitimate domination is not necessarily a "natural" one. Weber has noted the "need of any power ... to justify itself," and that "every highly privileged group develops the myth of its natural ... superiority" (ibid., 953). Here we are in the domain of ideology (ideological function). Normally, for Weber, a "highly privileged group" will be assured that the "negatively privileged group" (for him meaning the non-propertied group) accepts the order. But, at times, this privileged status, and the attendant legitimation principle (ideology) it has created, have become "the most passionately hated object of attack" (ibid.). As long as focused critical thought concerning an existing form of domination is lacking, legitimacy is assured. However, class struggle often followed where the created myth of superiority was openly challenged upon the observation that class position determined a person's fate, or life-chances (ibid., 953–954).

Summary

Max Weber has left us with a legacy. All theories dealing with a true sociology of law must come to terms with his writing. He has developed a systematic theory in the sociology of law, unlike Emile Durkheim or Karl Marx. Weber's emphasis on a multi-causal explanation led him to look at political, economic and ideological factors. Attributing cause to one factor alone was unthinkable. The form of law that was to develop with capitalism, logically formal rationality, even though quite compatible with its internal dynamics, was not necessarily "caused" by capitalism. For Weber, law served facilitative, repressive and ideological functions. He also implied the efficacy of the constitutive function. The rule of law, or formal rationality, assured predictability, calculability and stability. The purposive contract arose in capitalism as the exemplary expression of free exchange. A facilitative framework was developed where transactions by egotistically driven wills seeking profit would be assured. Law, in capitalism, then, served facilitative functions. And in his suggestion of recursivity, he is also advocating a form of constitutive function; that is, agents are both constituted by and constituting of the dominant legal form. But it also served repressive functions. The propertied classes because of their power, benefit from the form of law that is perceived as autonomous and general. Formal equality often disguises substantive inequality. Thus, for Weber, the facilitative function sometimes cannot be separated from the repressive functions. Calculability *and* coercion, then, could be combined even though on the face of it, the form of law and legal thought seem independent from particular interest groups.

Law also served ideological functions. The question of legitimate domination was critical for Weber. Subjects orient their behavior to the legal order because it is perceived as driven by rationally derived rules. The rule of law ideology is self-justifying. Only under certain circumstances is legitimacy withdrawn from the legal order with the possible effect of mass revolt. The relationship of the legal order to the fulfillment of social values can be summarized as follows. (Weber's position concerning greater liberty or coercion in law as we have seen was a complex one.) A form of law and legal thought that formally offers freedom in contracts or greater formal rights (for Weber, greater "empowerments") can at the same time benefit one class, the propertied, to the detriment of another, the non-propertied. This is an example of "repressive formalism" (see Chapter 2, Figure 1). Realization of social values such as equality, individuality and community does not necessarily follow a form of law that is logically formal rational. In comparing socialist and capitalist societies, Weber notes, "which system would possess more real coercion and which one more real personal freedom cannot be decided ... by the mere analysis of the actually existing or conceivable formal legal system" (1978: 731).

Review Questions

1. Strictly speaking, from Weber's definition of law, some say no law exists in traditional society. Consult his definition of law. How do you respond?

2. Weber offers a multi-causal approach to studying phenomena. Consult his methodology. Come up with an example and trace out the methodology. What would be the steps in arriving at a conclusion?

3. Weber's ideal types of law in Figure 1 include four possibilities. If instead of four categories we were to increase the possible categories to 9 (a three-by-three), or 16 (four by four), what advantages and disadvantages follow? Explain. Try and find an example to which you can apply your reasoning.

4. Research the web and/or case material and find an example of either jury nullification or runaway grand jury. Explain in terms of Weber's notion of "substantive irrationality." Bring a summary to class for discussion.

5. Learning how to employ deductive logic and syllogistic reasoning allows for a linear step by step process in arriving at a decision/conclusion. What advantages and disadvantages are there? Consider a possible conversation you are having with a recent law school graduate on a contemporary social problem dealing with racial bias or police brutality case dealing with racial bias or police brutality.

6. Think about a situation of gross injustices in court trials in the South in the 60s and 70s before the Civil Rights Act began to be employed. Was an all-white racist jury that disproportionally found a white person not guilty of a crime against an African American a case for Weber's substantive irrationality, or substantive rationality? Explain.

7. Think of teachers you had while in primary school. Some may have maintained order in the class more charismatically, traditionally, or more by legal domination. Without providing names and places, which one in your view was most effective in maintaining order for the classroom experience? Why? Explain.

8. Compare Durkheim's evolutionary model with Weber's rationalization thesis. Which is a more compelling explanation? Why?

9. Compare Weber's purposive contract with Durkheim's solemn contract. Where do they differ? Where do they agree? Explain.

10. Weber argues that arbitration (restitutive law), not corporal punishment (repressive law), was the primary response to transgressions in traditional societies, unlike Durkheim. Compare the two. Which is the more compelling argument? Explain.

Endnotes

1. As was the case with the previous chapter on Emile Durkheim, we are resisting full critical exposition of his works. We wish only to introduce Weber's work and recommend interested readers to engage further with the critical literature. For commentary and critique of Weber we recommend: Duncan (2004), Simona (2010), Lin and Tsai (2013), Qian (2010), Farmer (2013), Treiber and Matthew (2012, 2020). See also a journal devoted to Max Weber, *Max Weber Studies*, https://www.maxweberstudies.org/.

2. See also Schluchter (1985: 82–138), especially his distinctions between formal and substantive rationality and irrationality.

3. See especially the useful discussion between Marsh (2000) and Turner (2002), with Qian's (2010) further commentary on both.

4. Unlike the U.S. Federal Government, several States, Canada, Australia, and many European countries have passed comparable worth legislation.

5. Pearce (2001: 98, 101–103) criticizes both Durkheim and Weber on the notion of individual responsibility, and argues "responsibility is a universal phenomenon," and that one must make a distinction between "juridical relations" and "legal relations." This underscores the importance of definitional precision in the sociology of law.

6. Compare similarities with Durkheim.

5

Karl Marx

Law in a Socio-Political Economy

Introduction

Karl Marx stands with Durkheim and Weber as a giant in the analysis of society. Although he never attempted to develop a sociology of law, much in his work can be mined to develop a unique perspective on law. We shall see that a number of diverging perspectives have been derived from Marx's writings.

Marx was the third child (of nine) born to Henriette Pressburg Marx in 1818 in the city of Trier, Germany. His father, Heinrich, was a well-to-do lawyer, public notary and the recipient of rents from land and houses he owned. He was a well-respected community member in Trier. The young Marx developed a reputation of writing satirical verses. In 1835, Karl entered the University of Bonn to study law. His family wanted him to become a lawyer like his father. But at Bonn his behavior was already rebellious. He was arrested for drunkenness and noisiness. He was also arrested for dueling with a pistol.

Later, in 1836, he transferred to the University of Berlin. There, where Hegel had died a short five years earlier, the Hegelian philosophy was to have a marked influence on the young Marx. Marx studied law, history and philosophy. In 1838, after the death of his father, Karl Marx dropped any intention of studying law and concentrated instead on philosophy. In 1841, he finished his doctoral degree at the University of Jena. Unable to get a teaching position because of his radical politics he turned to journalism. Soon after, he became an editor of a liberal business newspaper. In 1843, he was married to Jenny von Westphalen who he had known since childhood. She was an activist and theatre critic. They had seven children; however, only three survived till adulthood. Resigning the editorship, they left for Paris where he became involved with radical literature and revolutionaries. It was there that he also met Friedrich Engels (1844), who was working as a clerk in a cotton mill, and who had just published *The Condition of the Working Class in England in 1844* highlighting the importance of the working class in struggles and the eventual revolution, which he shared with Marx. This became a life-long friendship.

In 1844, he wrote his first major piece, *The Economic and Philosophical Manuscripts*. It was a polemic in political economy. He was later to be expelled from France for his revolutionary work. He then settled in Brussels. Here he continued with economic studies and with an involvement in the working-class movement. In 1848, with Engels, he wrote the classic study, the *Manifesto of the Communist Party*. He was subsequently arrested under suspicion of supplying arms to the revolutionaries, and expelled from Brussels. He returned to Paris. But, after the numerous revolutions of 1848, he was again arrested for sedition and expelled.

In 1849, he and his family went to London where he was to spend the rest of his life. The great British Museum library was to be where he spent most of his research time. Although living in poverty, he was to continue his studies in political economy. His close friend, Friedrich Engels, whose family was well-to-do, was to give him financial support. In 1867, the first volume of his influential *Das Kapital* was published. He was drafting additional work on political economy, many working notes of which were assembled by Engels and published after Marx's death. Volume 2 and 3 were also published after his death.[1] There still remains unpublished material to be organized and published. His health had already started to give way by 1870, and by 1873 he almost had a nervous breakdown. His research and writing were irreversibly affected. In 1881, his wife died of cancer. His eldest daughter, too, died the same year. Karl Marx died at the age of 64 in London on March 14, 1883. Eleven people attended his funeral. Engels delivered the eulogy (see Eugene Kamenka's biography of Marx in *The Portable Karl Marx*, 1983, xi–xlv).

Karl Marx did not try to develop a sociology of law. Law for him was a secondary interest. He was more interested in philosophy and political economic analysis of the development of capitalism and its effects. But as early as 1837, Marx expressed his interest in law: "if feuds were settled by a and b, the courts would be swindled out of their fee" (Marx, cited in Cain and Hunt, 1979: 2). His father was to caution him about his hostility to law. However, in a letter to his father in 1837, Karl Marx stated his approach:

> exemplified by law, the state, nature, and philosophy as a whole, the object itself must be studied in its development; arbitrary divisions must not be introduced, the rational character of the object itself must develop as something imbued with contradictions in itself and find its unity in itself (cited in Cain and Hunt, 1979: 16).

This philosophical position is well worth some careful thought. It reflected his early attempts to distance himself from simply studying the independent influences of ideas in history. Rather, he was already implying that contradictions in the concrete world must be the unit of analysis (i.e., focal point of inquiry). But studying law, for him, was always subordinate to philosophy, history and economics.

Marxist Perspectives

Rather than a Marxist perspective on the sociology of law, what has developed in contemporary scholarship is a number of perspectives that draw from his voluminous writings. Interested theorists have had to gather numerous unconnected statements on his notions of law in capitalism and then systematize these in order to claim: "this is what Marx said about law." But this exercise in systematization has produced different frameworks. Thus, in the contemporary analysis of law from a Marxist perspective two major forms appear (see Figure 1).

Figure 1. Marxist Perspectives in the Sociology of Law

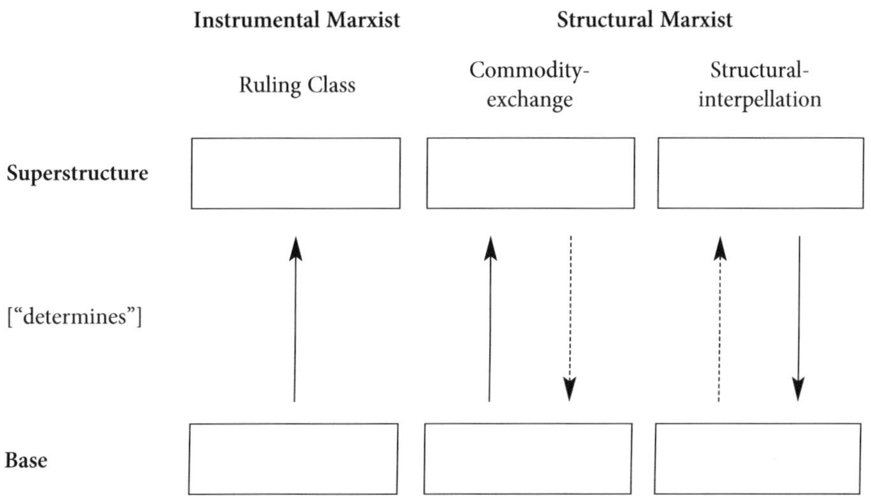

Instrumental Marxist **Structural Marxist**

Ruling Class

Commodity-exchange

Structural-interpellation

Superstructure

["determines"]

Base

The first perspective, instrumental Marxism, traces the development of law to the control exercised by the "ruling class." Law is simply class rule. The "ruling class" controls the formation of law. Law is an instrument used for maximizing ruling class interests in society and controlling the working classes. Thus, it is said that the definition of crime, laws, policy formation, and the every-day functioning of the criminal justice system are being manipulated by some conspiratorial and like-minded ruling class. From our Chapter 2, Figure 1, we recognize this framework as appearing in the lower left-hand corner.

The second major variant in a Marxist approach to law is the structural perspective. Inspired during the late 1970s by the resurrected works of Pashukanis (2002) from the 1920s and 1930s in Russia (see Beirne and Sharlet, 1980; Beirne, 1990; Milovanovic, 2011), this position seeks to explain law by focusing on the overall dynamics of the capitalist system itself. Law, in this approach, is not a direct servant or instrument of a ruling class; rather, law has a degree of independence from specific elites. This notion is known as "relative autonomy." In other words, a number of historically contingent forces produce specific effects at any point in time in a society. Both "capitalists" (bourgeois) as well as the working classes (proletariat) are subject to the effects of these forces, whether these actors are conscious or unconscious of them.

At least two variations *within* the structural perspective have been identified (Milovanovic, 1987, 1989, 1993a). The first we can identify as the commodity-exchange perspective; the second, the structural interpellation perspective (see Figure 1). We shall have more to say below.

In both the instrumental and structural perspectives, Marxist scholars have drawn from the original works of Marx in order to decipher "what he really meant." Thus, much controversy exists about the "correct" reading of Karl Marx.

In the following sections we will separate the two major perspectives in our analysis. We will first, however, present the key concepts related to the notion of a mode of production and the notion of cause. We follow with an examination of some prominent themes concerning law, the juridic subject, hegemony (domination), the contract, and property in a capitalist mode of production. We briefly consider the notion of the "dialectics of struggle." We conclude with explicating the thesis of the withering away of the state, law and the juridic subject.[2]

Mode of Production and Law

In order to understand the development of law, it is important to come to terms with Marx's theory of general social development. This he called the "materialist conception of history." Marx notes the "guiding principle of my studies":

> In the social production of their existence, people inevitably enter into definite relations, which are independent of their will, namely relations of production appropriate to a given stage in the development of their material forces of production. The totality of these relations of production constitutes the economic structure of society, the real foundations, on which arises a legal and political superstructure and to which correspond definite forms of social consciousness. The mode of production of material life conditions the general process of social, political and intellectual life. It is not the consciousness of people that determines their existence, but their social existence that determines their consciousness (1970: 20–21).

In this classic statement, Marx distinguishes two general levels of society: the base and the superstructure (see Figure 1). The economic system is the "base." The "superstructure" is the totality of beliefs, sentiments, morality, illusions, modes of thought, views of life, forms of consciousness, ideals and ideas and so forth. It also includes the political, legal and ideological spheres. The state can also be conceptualized as part of the superstructure. We should note that this base/superstructure metaphor is really more of an ideal type in the Weberian sense. It is for Marx a guiding principle. The term "social formation" will be understood to mean both base and superstructure.

The "mode of production," or the form of the economic system, may vary. In other words, every society organizes itself in some way in order to produce and distribute products or commodities. Thus, certain historical patterns do stabilize and can be conceptualized. (Weber, no doubt, would call these examples of different "orders.") Accordingly, people are offered "definite relations" that "are independent of their will." And, for Marx, one's consciousness is "determined" by one's social existence. Marx distinguishes several types of modes of production: slavery, feudalism, capitalism, and communism (yet more examples of ideal types). Socialism poses a problem as a pure type. For Marxists it is but a transitional stage to the "higher forms" (communism).

The base, in turn, can be conceptualized as having two elements. First, it includes the productive forces, or *forces of production*, which are characterized by available technology, general skills and knowledge, natural resources and so forth. Productive forces are the material means used by people to assure a livelihood. Second, we can identify the *relations of production* or the socio-economic relations. The productive forces shape how people relate to each other in producing and exchanging goods and commodities necessary for life. Thus, there are different ways of producing and exchanging goods in societies characterized, for example, by hunting and gathering, agriculture, industry, and in the current era, the internet. The productive forces are said to "determine" the socio-economic relations.

Certain forms of relations therefore begin to stabilize, for example, between master and slave, lord and serf, or capitalist (bourgeois) and worker (proletariat). Thus, in "traditional/customary" societies, barter relationships are the ideal types. Two people exchange goods without being oriented to profit motives. They exchange product for product because of the direct personal use it has for them (use-value). On the other hand, in a capitalist mode of production, two people exchange commodities generally for-profit motives (as exchange-values, more below). That is, the commodity's inherent usefulness, its "use value," is now transformed into a priced and exploitable entity (i.e., it takes on "exchange-value"). In sum, different modes of production produce different patterned relations. These, again, are independent of the will of those directly involved in these relations. These definite relations predate a newly born person. They are what they must subsequently negotiate.

Marx, in the long quote above, the base-superstructure metaphor, implied that the base "determines" the superstructure. In other words, the typical person in the feudal mode of production had a very different set of values, beliefs, aspirations, and needs than their counterpart in the capitalist society. It is also within the base that contradictions arise between the productive elements and the relations of production. That is, at a certain stage, newly developed technologies or material productive forces become incompatible with how people had normally related to each other. With the rise of commerce and trade, for example, feudal relations became obsolete. This contradiction between the new and the old sometimes led to different forms of individual resistance, at times, adaptation and compliance to the new order, at other times to revolutionary class struggle.

For Marx, "at a certain stage of development, the material productive forces of society come into conflict with existing relations of production ... The changes in the economic foundation lead sooner or later to the transformation of the whole immense superstructure" (1970: 21). This dynamic is referred to as "dialectical materialism." The notion of the "dialectic" states that the struggle of opposites, the new with the old, produces a new synthesis. This, in turn, eventually leads to contradictions, new struggles and yet a new need for synthesis. Consider, for example, the use of cave art, parchments, printing press, typewriter, computer, and more recently developments in didgimodernism (virtual realities, and the internet). Consider the assembly line of old with its reliance on manual labor versus the contemporary highly computerized state of affairs, or the office workplace prior to the computer, or the work-at-home transformation given momentum by Covid-19. Each change posed contradictions for the worker, and new adaptations followed. Thus, the historical cycle: synthesis — antithesis — new synthesis — antithesis, etc.

An examination of "causes" or "determinants" must be the initial step in understanding the different Marxist perspectives on the development of law. That is, how are we to understand that the base "determines" the superstructure? One position, we can call it the strong version of determinism, argues that a change in the base automatically produces a change in the superstructure. Given a particular economic system, specific laws, ideals and ideological systems are predicted to develop. In other words, these are reflections of the base. This position is generally referred to as economic determinism (or economic reductionism).

A second position states that the verb "determines" merely expresses the idea that the base sets limits to possible developments in the superstructure. That is, a change in the economic base will have effects in the superstructure, but other factors will come into play. These other factors could be, for example, philosophical (e.g., development of a critical consciousness), political (e.g., revolts, class struggle) and ideological (e.g., in Latin America we have seen a shift from the conventional theology of resignation to "liberation theology"; see Milovanovic, 1985). We may call the second version of "determines" the soft version. In contemporary analysis of Marxist law, it is generally referred to as "relative autonomy." The argument here is that three main spheres of influence exist, which are only relatively independent from each other: the political, economic and ideological. At times the juridic sphere has also been included. Each sphere can have an effect on each of the others and can be affected by each of the others. Understanding which sphere was the primary determinant in any period is an empirical question.

Marxist Perspectives, Instrumental and Structural

The first approach, the superstructure as reflection of the base, has its main followers in the instrumental ("determinist") Marxist perspective. They find evidence for their claim in such passages appearing in the *Manifesto of the Communist Party* as "the executive of the modern state is but a committee for managing the common affairs of the whole bourgeoisie" (1973: 110). The logic of the argument is that the state appeared because of irreconcilable conflicts that developed with the appearance of the capitalist mode of production. The state was to quickly fall under the control of the more powerful class, the dominant economic class. Economic power was thus converted into political power. The "state apparatus" — police, army, judiciary — was then "bourgeois" right from the beginning. Concomitantly, an ideological state apparatus develops as its support. The "ruling class" influences the legislative process by financing campaigns for office, by lobbying, by corruption (bribes) and so forth. Continued selective socializing, a common education, intermarriage within the capitalist class and the development of a common outlook on life (a common ideology) assures that this "class" will continue. In other words, the "definite relations" that this group of people (bourgeois) enters assures a common way of thinking to develop. This "ruling class," then, manipulates the formation of law for its own interests (see Kolko, 1962; Domhoff, 1967; Miliband, 1969; see also Beirne's critique, 1979b).

The second approach, soft determinism, or the "relative autonomy" position, is associated with the theorists from the structural Marxist perspective. They argue that, at best, the economic sphere is determinant only in the "last instance"; in other words, when all else is said and done. Reminiscent of the Weberian multi-causal perspective, they argue that three spheres—the economic, political and ideological—have collective effects in producing social phenomena. At any one instance, the unique articulation of the three produces specific results. To understand, for example, how a particular law has come into being, one has to investigate how these three factors exerted different degrees of influence at a particular historical point in time. The structural Marxists call this process "overdetermination." Althusser (1971) and Poulantzas (1973) (but Freud before them) used this term to mean that the "cause" of something is always multiple. Many factors together produce certain results.

A social scientist has the difficult task of unraveling what combination of political, economic and ideological factors were at play in producing the specific phenomena they are investigating. This combination of factors is referred to as the "articulation of instances." In other words, when examining a particular law that has been introduced, perhaps the political sphere can be shown to be the most dominant "factor," and the economic and ideological as of lesser importance. At other times, perhaps all three factors are of equal importance; at yet other times, perhaps the ideological factor is the most dominant; and so forth.

In its most strict form, the notion of a subject, a person who actively confronts and attempts to change their environment, disappears in some versions of the structuralist approach. It is replaced by the notion that subjects are only "supports" of the socio-economic system (Althusser, 1971; Poulantzas, 1973). In its less strict form, conscious rebellion, revolutionary consciousness, and class struggle are forces that become factors in explaining such developments as substantive law and social policy (see Quinney, 1977).

Within the structuralist position, we have further identified two subcategories, the commodity-exchange perspective and the structural interpellation perspective (see Figure 1). The former, we shall see below, is more economistic in orientation; that is, it still assumes that the dominant factor is the economic sphere in producing superstructural effects. It is distinguishable from the instrumental Marxist perspective in that the economic sphere is said to have effects on both the bourgeois *and* proletariat, independent of their will. The structural interpellation perspective argues that relatively independent forces within the superstructure itself—such as ideological, juridical and political factors—have affects downward; that is, they constitute economic relations and eventually forms of consciousness. In other words, here the economic sphere is a factor but not the primal determinant. (Many revolutionary leaders, or in the case of the United States, many of the early prominent radical criminologists, came, and still come from the middle classes. Apparently, using the structural interpellation argument, the development of a critical consciousness was relatively independent from the molding effects of the economic sphere.)

Structuralists, then, seek to examine the development of law not only by investigating economic factors (the base), but also certain relatively independent forces within the superstructure. Rather than seeing the state and laws as mere instruments of a particular "ruling class," the structural Marxists seek to examine the contradictory developments within a social formation that led to a particular state of affairs. The notion of a "ruling class" is replaced by the notion of a "hegemonic group." In other words, the structural Marxists do not assume that a conspiratorial elite exists. Rather, there is an assumed existence of a general interest amongst powerful segments to maintain the present socio-economic order. This can generally be maintained by a form of law that is relatively independent even from them. Block has said, for example, that "the state plays a critical role in maintaining the legitimacy of the social order, and this requires that the state appear to be neutral in the class struggle" (1977: 8). (This ironic situation will be developed below.) Nevertheless, shifting coalitions within the ruling elite (now called the hegemonic group) become dominant forces in control at that moment in history, pursuing their interests.

Domination, Form of Law and the Juridic Subject

The instrumental and structural Marxist perspectives have diverging explanations of domination — the degree of independence between the form of law and some power elite or ruling class — and the development of rights. The instrumental Marxist perspective dominated much Western thought until the discovery of Pashukanis's work in the late 1970s.

The instrumental Marxist perspective is based on much data accumulated in the analysis of state power. Works by Domhoff (1967), Milliband (1969) and Kolko (1962) described the close relationship between those with economic and political power. Consider Friedman's point: "the legal system works like a blind, insensate machine. It does the bidding of those whose hands are on the controls. The laws ... reflect the goals and policies of those who call the tune ..." (1973: 14). In the area of law formation, Quinney (1974), Chambliss (1964), Chambliss and Seidman (1971), and Mathieson (1980) provided a core of critical literature in the 1960s, 70s and 80s that would later be the subject of much critique and revision. It indicated the effects of the unequal distribution of power and instrumentality in the development of law. Quinney and Chambliss were later to develop alternative Marxist perspectives on law (see for example, Chambliss, 1988; Quinney, 1977). The instrumental perspective can be best summarized by Quinney's five propositions:

(1) The state is organized to serve the interests of the dominant economic class, the capitalist ruling class.

(2) Criminal law is an instrument of the state and ruling class to maintain and perpetuate the existing social and economic order.

(3) Crime control in capitalist society is accomplished through a variety of institutions and agencies established and administered by a governmental elite, representing ruling class interests, for the purpose of establishing domestic order.

(4) The contradictions of advanced capitalism—the disjunction between existence and essence—requires that the subordinate classes remain oppressed by whatever means necessary, especially through the coercion and violence of the legal system.

(5) Only with the collapse of capitalist society and the creation of a new society based on socialist principles, will there be a solution to the crime problem (1974: 16).

Domination, in this approach, is assured by the ruling class's control of the media and educational system (sometimes also referred to as "ideological state apparatuses," Althusser, 2014). Consciousness is said to be manipulated constantly by these institutions (see Bowles and Gintis, 1976). The family structure conveys the very values that are needed by the capitalist work place.

If these basic institutions fail to assure obedience, the legal system will provide the additional control and coercion. Law is simply an instrument to control the working classes or to curb threats made on the elite's hold on society. Formal rights given by the Constitution are said to be but mere props that mystify the basic repressive functions of law. In the end, formal procedure and processing in the criminal justice system itself "cool out the mark" by diverting attention from real problems. Those with power are "beyond incrimination" (Kennedy, 1976).

Those at risk of getting into trouble with the law are those without power. The very creation of the collective perception of crime and the need for repressive law takes place by the conspiratorial practices of elites. The concept of the "reasonable man in law," the juridic subject, serves the interests of elites in that they need predictable performances from subjects in the work force as well as citizens who are obedient to the order. In sum, the legal order, including the form of law and legal thought, are totally attributable to the ruling class's influence. No autonomy between the political and the legal order is said to exist: law is but a reflex of changing economic conditions. The primary need of the capitalist ruling class is to maintain its position of power and to assure maximization of profits.

The structural Marxists see things differently. Although drawing from the extensive works of Marx and Engels, their interpretation runs in a different direction. To begin with, the notion that the legal order is directly under the control of the "ruling class"—is not autonomous—fails to answer some deeper questions, according to the structuralist Marxists.

On the one hand, we may ask: to what degree is the legal form independent from the will of some powerful group? On the other: to what degree is the legal form independent from the capitalist system itself? These are independent questions that are often handled as if they were not (Balbus, 1977a: 571–572). Traditionally, it was the first question that was most often asked. Thus, some empirical studies investigating the relationship between powerful groups and a specific law have found that there are direct connections between the two. Conclusion: law is not autonomous. Other studies investigating this relationship generate data that indicate that no direct relationship exists between the will of a powerful group and particular laws and conclude: law is autonomous. But in neither case has the investigator asked the question about the relationship of the legal form to the mode of production itself to which the actors (powerful *and* powerless) belong. Thus, to simply show that the legal form did not respond directly to some powerful actors, and hence, to conclude that it is autonomous, "omits the possibility that the law is not autonomous from, but rather articulates with and must be explained by, the systemic requirements of capitalism ..." (ibid., 572). This conclusion has raised a host of new critical inquiries.

The structuralists focus on a different set of questions. They are interested in the internal dynamics of capitalism (often referred to as capital logic), in what makes it run as a system. And how, as a consequence, certain forms develop—including the legal form—which have their basis in the needs of the mode of production itself. (Recall Marx's guiding principle that stated, in part, "people inevitably enter definite relations, which are independent of their will.") In this perspective, the capitalist "class" may not directly control the legal form but nevertheless is benefited by its continued existence. The legal form, formal rationality, then, attains a "relative autonomy." The legal form is not merely an instrument, a tool of some class. Nor does it have a totally independent development. The state, then, must be seen as a "structure to which capitalists themselves are obliged to subordinate their wills but which nevertheless—or, rather, precisely because of this subordination—functions to secure their class interests" (Balbus, 1977b, xxi–xxii, emphasis in the original).

The unique position of the relatively autonomous legal form, formal rationality, allows two simultaneous processes to take place: repression and legitimation. The core questions for the structural Marxists, then, focus on certain processes: domination, legitimation, mystification, ideology, hegemony and reification. It is to Pashukanis that we must turn for some beginning insights on these relationships.

Pashukanis and Commodity-Exchange: Commodity and Legal Fetishism

Pashukanis (1891–1937) is a critical figure who has stimulated much Marxist analysis in law. Specializing in law and political economy at the University of Munich prior to the Russian Revolution of 1917, Pashukanis was to become the preeminent theorist in Russia in the 1920s until his demise in the 1930s. He was identified as "an enemy of the people" and executed during the Stalin purges in 1937. His developed theory of law and the state were not in accord with Stalin's desire to intensify the "dictatorship of the proletariat." But Pashukanis was to leave us with the so-called "commodity exchange" theory of law. The core ideas can be found in his treatise of 1924 entitled *The General Theory of Law and Marxism* (we will use the reprint of 1980 for citations). The rediscovery of his works led to much Marxist analysis (Beirne, 1979; Balbus, 1977a, 1977b; Milovanovic, 1981, 1989, 2011; Fraser, 1978). The legacy of this rediscovery was that the instrumental Marxist position lost the dominance it had retained throughout the 1960s and 1970s. From early 1980 onward, the structural Marxist position became the dominant position in the Marxist sociology of law in the U.S. and Europe.

The legal form, Pashukanis argued, develops directly out of the exchange of commodities in a competitive capitalist marketplace. In other words, as commodity owners exchange their commodities something else is taking place, behind their backs. Certain "appearances" (phenomenal forms) begin to materialize. The form of law, legal thought and the juridic subject (the abstract bearer of rights), are all derived from processes taking place in the economic sphere. Thus, there exists a close relationship between the economic and the legal sphere. What eventually are expressed in law are ideas generated during commodity exchange. The form of law and legal thought, then, develop somewhat independently from any wishes by the dominant class to simply control and repress. Law, as a consequence, has relative autonomy. But we are ahead of ourselves. Let us develop Pashukanis's argument and see what impact it had on the structural Marxist perspective.

Transformation, Use-Value to Exchange-Value

The starting point of analysis for Pashukanis was the beginning sections of the first volume of *Capital*, where Marx developed his pivotal idea of "commodity fetishism." To understand the logic of the legal form we must understand the logic of the commodity form. In other words, one must show how the two follow a similar logical development; that is, there exists a homology. Let us unravel this complex process and see how the two are interconnected.

We want to first indicate how commodities start as "use-value" and undergo transformation into "exchange-values." Initially, a commodity has use value. There are two elements here: commodities reflect unequal amounts of social labor used in their production; and they also correspond to the ability of fulfilling a concrete need, which also varies.[3] We have, then, inherent inequalities or differences in the first instance. Producing a thing for direct use creates use-value (and here we have products, not commodities). But, in a capitalist mode of production, when an object is produced to be transferred to another for the other's use and to gain a profit, we have commodities (Marx, 1967: 40–41).

Commodities, again, are inherently unequal. They correspond to different amounts of labor used in their production. They also reflect different abilities to fulfill some concrete need. In brief, we have inherent inequality on at least two levels at this point. But when two exchangers enter the competitive marketplace, Marx tells us, the commodity takes on exchange-value. That is, it "presents itself as a quantitative relation," as a specific "proportion in which values in use of one sort are exchanged for those of another sort" (ibid., 36). And here lies a profound transformation. The initial commodity, which was characterized as having use-value and which is inherently unequal to other commodities and their use-values, during exchange takes on an equivalent form. In other words, two commodities are brought into some mathematical or quantitative relationship (e.g., two bushels of apples = one pound of butter; the equal sign is significant). This relationship of "equivalence" hides inherent inequalities. Inherent differences are now replaced by a ratio of exchange. This is also sometimes referred to as the "law of equivalence."

Let's state this complex idea in another way. What started out as a qualitative relationship—use values and inherent differences—is now transformed, behind commodity exchanger's backs so to speak, into a quantitative relationship. We have gone from quality to quantity. It's an outcome of commodity owners coming to the competitive marketplace under capitalism to seek profit for their commodities. We must remember, too, that in actuality we have hundreds of thousands of exchanges taking place.

This ratio of exchange finds further expression in money. Two bushels of apples, for example, are worth \$2. So, too, is one pound of butter. Thus: 2 bushels of apples = \$2 = 1 pound of butter. "In the marketplace, then, qualitatively distinct commodities enter a formal relationship of equivalence, in a definite ratio, facilitated by the universal equivalent—money" (Milovanovic, 1981: 41; 2011). Put in another way, money, an abstract statement of a thing's worth, now replaces the inherent differences that existed prior to exchange. Here, \$2 represents the worth of 2 bushels of apples or one pound of butter.

A masking, however, has taken place. What has been removed from consciousness, what disappears from the scene, are the inherently unequal needs that existed and the differentiated labor used to produce a commodity. Money now replaces the value of all commodities ("universal equivalence"). Consider, for example, the toil and suffering it actually takes in the concrete world to produce, say, a car. All this disappears from the scene for the purchaser of the car. Lost from consciousness is the alienation, the monotony, exploited labor, the industrial "accidents" that have been part and parcel of the production of the car. "The memory of use-value," Marx tells us, "as distinct from exchange value, has become entirely extinguished in this incarnation of pure exchange-value" (1973: 239–240).

Certain transformations have taken place. From: quality into quantity, the concrete into the abstract, content into form. This whole process Marx calls the "fetishism of commodities." All phenomena are brought under this idea. (Note that nowhere in this analysis have we blamed the conspiratorial practices of some "ruling class.")

We may note some everyday examples. We often hear of graduating students preparing to go on the job market "to see how much they are worth." Or we hear about baseball players at contract talks squabbling over a "pittance" of a few million dollars in salary or so because they think they are worth as much as somebody else. In other words, what has happened in this process is the creation of fetishes—things are produced which we begin to worship as having sole worth, namely money. We begin to measure a person's worth in terms of money. This process extends to many diverse relations the subject now enters. Concrete human needs, differentiated labor and abilities, and genuine human value, disappear from consciousness. This whole complex process, a Marxist (and Hegelian) discovery, is duplicated in the legal form. In other words, a similar logical development occurs in the legal sphere, producing, for example, the notion of the abstraction, the "reasonable man [woman] in law." How is this possible?

It was Pashukanis who described this connection most forcefully (1980; see also, 2002). Pertinent sections concerning commodity fetishism can also be found in the following treatises by Marx: *The Critique of Hegel's Philosophy of the State*; *Capital*; *The Grundrisse*; the *Critique of the Gotha Program*; and *On the Jewish Question*. For Pashukanis, people enter ... [socioeconomic] relationships not because they have consciously chosen to do so, but because the conditions of production necessitate it. Man is transformed into a legal subject in the same way that a natural product is transformed into a commodity with its mysterious quality of value (1980: 51).

Commodification of the Legal Form

Legal rights and the notion of the juridic subject, for Pashukanis, develop in a similar (homologous) way as in commodity fetishism. The constant transfer of commodities in the capitalist marketplace creates certain appearances, certain notions of rights. Rights are defined as "the sum of benefits which the general will recognizes as belonging to a specific person" (ibid., 78). Let's follow the parallel development (homology) of the legal form and the commodity form.

The subject, analogous to the commodity and its use-value, is unique; they appear with different aptitudes, capabilities, potentials, interests, desires, wants and needs. Here we have inherent differences. But the subject who enters the market-place to exchange finds themselves in a definite relationship with another. At this exact moment three ideas begin to materialize. First, at the precise moment of exchange, the two commodity owners have entered a relationship of *equality*, of equivalence. Each recognizes the other as equal vis-a-vis the transaction. Again, there may be vast differences between the two people, but at the exact moment of the transfer of commodities we have equivalence. Second, at this precise moment, there is recognition of *free will* in each of the parties. Each recognizes the other as having willingly entered the transaction. Third, each recognizes the other as the rightful *property owner* (proprietor) of the commodity that is being exchanged.

The constant transfer of commodities—and as a logical extension, rights—in the marketplace creates the appearance of a bearer of rights. These appearances, these "phenomenal forms," reflect the notion of equality, free will, and proprietorship. Again, we must keep in mind thousands upon thousands of these exchanges taking place in a competitive, capitalist marketplace and certain appearances beginning to emerge. The notion of the "reasonable man in law," or the legal subject that emerges, is referred to as the juridic subject.

Note that this is an abstraction. In other words, quality again has been transformed into quantity: the uniqueness of being a human being (analogous to the use-value of a commodity) has been changed into a mathematical loci of certain rights (analogous to the exchange-value of a commodity). The result of this process is the juridic subject. As Pashukanis has argued, "the legal subject … assumes the significance of a mathematical point, a centre in which a certain sum of rights is concentrated" (ibid., 78). Said in another way, the subject has now taken on the qualities of exchange-value. The universal equivalent is now the juridic subject.

This constant transfer of commodities and rights produces the idea of a general and abstract bearer of rights. Lawyers subsequently give this phenomenon an "idealized expression." That is, lawyers, unaware of this underlying process, articulate rights and what a "reasonable man" in law should look like. They verbalize what is appearing during these many exchanges of commodities. In other words, such noble ideas as "freedom, equality and property" that have found their way into many national constitutions are but reflections of the underlying process of legal fetishism. They have their roots in these transactions.

Just as money became the universal equivalent for the purposes of commodity exchange, so, too, does the juridic subject. In both instances we have created a fetish, idols that we worship. These abstractions now come to dominate our lives, even as we actively produce and reproduce them (a process referred to as reification). Note, for example, the emphasis placed on the "reasonable man [woman] in law." Again, this is an abstraction, but nevertheless, when a jury of peers weighs evidence during a trial, its standard is still this abstraction: what would a reasonable man [woman] in such and-such a situation do?

In feudalism, where commodity exchange was not the norm, no conception of formal rights existed. There, one's rights, duties, and obligations were directly connected with one's standing in that particular city, town, or community. Thus, status was the key. The notion of formal equality in law, as we have seen, is but the end result of fundamental processes imperceptivity taking place in the market place. These appearances find expression in law. For example, the Fourteenth Amendment includes the "equal protection clause." It stands for the principle that equally situated people should be equally treated. This can be shown to be an outcome of legal fetishism. But if we begin with a concrete situation of inequality, followed by an application of an equal scale (equivalence, formal equality), we end by reinforcing systemic inequalities. In other words, this is a classic case of repressive formalism (see the upper left-hand corner of Figure 1 from Chapter2). For example, reconsider the speeding ticket example offered in Chapter 2, where the initial point, income differentials, vary widely.

Consider two further applications of commodification, one to criminal law and punishment, and one to eco-justice. Just as money became the universal equivalent for commodity exchanges, and the juridic subject similarly (homologously) a universal equivalent in law, so too does time, as a measure of liberty (deprivation of liberty) becomes the universal equivalent for the determination of punishment, now being proportional to the harm. Time has become a quantifiable measurement in determining punishment. So much time loss (imprisonment) for such and such harm. Similarly, in the field of environmental law, we see that pollution, water, and air have become commodified in the capitalist market place. They have developed exchange-value. Pollution credits ("cap and trade") can now be traded freely (emission trading) for profit in the competitive market ("market environmentalism"). Bottling companies, too, have commodified water (Prudham, 2016; Kosoy and Corbero, 2010; White and Heckenberg, 2014).

"Legitimate" Domination

The whole notion of legitimate domination or, in brief, legitimation, is connected with the rule of law. The rule of law, in turn, finds its determinant in commodity exchange relations. The legal form gains a relative autonomy from the political sphere. Its inherent logic merely reflects the inherent logic found in the mode of production. The centrality of such historical cries and demands for "equality before the law," and for the "rule of law," reflect the persistent orientation to these abstractions that have been created "behind people's backs." Ironically, even where obvious deviations from the rule of law occur, it is but an occasion to reinforce this ideology. How often in our reform efforts do we automatically try to seek purer adherence to formal equality in our attempts to eradicate different forms of discrimination in the criminal justice system? But our ideal end point is still "equality for all before the law." Deviation provides the very opportunity to reinforce the dominant ideology, and hence to reinforce legitimation. Put in another way, competitive, laissez-faire capitalism provides its own legitimation principles that can be traced back to commodity exchange's inherent logic (Habermas, 1975: 25).

Pashukanis's rediscovered works provided much stimulus for further refinement in the structural Marxist perspective throughout the 1980s. Many theorists from this perspective have taken his insights as a beginning point for further analysis within the Marxist tradition. There are those who simply attribute all developments in the superstructure to the unfolding of the logic of the commodity form. At the other end are those Marxist scholars who see Pashukanis's insights as a starting point for much further analysis of additional factors. We will briefly describe some current refinements in the structural Marxist perspective. We shall see that a second variant exists, which posits primacy as to the directionality of cause, to superstructural practices.

Late Capitalism

The advanced form of capitalism, many structural Marxists argue, is no longer defined by its competitive, laissez-faire characteristics of the late 19th century. The 20th and 21st century form appears as state-regulated capitalism. Consider Klare's observation that rights are:

> increasingly being transformed from one of absolute entitlements possessed by individuals as against state power to one in which the individual has a narrow claim merely to have his or her interests 'weighed' by authoritative agencies and or represented reasonably and in good faith by large, bureaucratic corporate entities over whose direction one has no real control (1979: 125).

Note, too, that:

> [t]he state sets the ground rules of most economic transactions, directly regulates many significant industries, regulates the class struggle through labor laws, through its actions determining the size of the 'social wage,' provides the infrastructure of capital accumulation, manages the tempo of business activity and economic growth, takes measures directly and indirectly to maintain effective demand, and itself participates in the market as a massive business actor and employer (ibid.).

In the more advanced form of capitalism, it is said that greater involvement by the state comes about to offset different economic crises (e.g., The Great Depression of the 1930s, the economic/financial crisis of 2008). These economic crises can often lead to legitimation crises (Habermas, 1975, 1984, 1987). That is, subjects may withdraw legitimacy from the economic system and the rule of law. Also, with the state actively intervening in the economic sphere, it can no longer rely on the inherent legitimation principles developed from commodity exchange. The state must actively formulate rules toward some specific end. The form taken by the judiciary is interest-balancing (see Milovanovic, 1986, 1987). Particularly in the judiciary, the justices must balance the interests of the subject against some other stated goal. Some ideal end point (e.g., the social good, national security, the need to run an orderly prison, crime control, etc.) guides decision making. Here, then, the form of law is changing more to a form of substantive rationality.[4] All this, the structuralist Marxists argue, necessitates a new ideology justifying existing arrangements and the obedience to them. Maine's central thesis that law progresses from status to contract can now be restated. The progression, according to this perspective, is from status, to contract, and back to status. "Status," defined by "the set of rights and duties attendant upon membership in a particular group, rather than contract, has become the paradigmatic legal relationship of the corporate state" (Fraser, 1978: 165–166; see also Reich, 1964: 785; Selznick, 1969: 61–62, 248–249; Renner, 1949: 121). In other words, individuals increasingly gain rights by way of membership in officially recognized groups (e.g., union member, prisoner, detainee, juvenile, non-management worker, welfare recipient, incarcerated mentally ill, etc.). As Renner notes:

> Formerly based upon contract, the labour relationship has now developed into a "position," just as property has developed into a public utility. If a person occupies a "position," this means that his rights and duties are closely circumscribed, the "position" has become a legal institution in character much like the fee of feudal times. The "position" comprises the claim to adequate remuneration (settled by collective agreement or works rule), the obligation to pay certain contributions (for trade unions and insurance), the

> right to special benefits (sickness, accident, old age, death) and finally certain safeguards against loss of the position or in case of its loss (1949: 121).

In sum, in the advanced form of capitalism one's status as a prisoner, welfare recipient, student, laborer, juvenile, union/non-union member, etc., becomes the key in the determination of rights honored in law. Recall that previously in a competitive, capitalist market economy, the juridic subject was more homogeneous and unitary; few distinctions, that is, were made in law. In state-regulated capitalism the notion of a global juridic subject begins to be undermined. The judiciary, then, must actively intervene in the social formation to come up with the appropriate balance in the determination of rights. But this leads to problems of legitimation. The state and its functionaries, particularly the judiciary, must increasingly create myths that justify existing exploitive socio-economic relations.[5] Hegemony (Gramsci, 1971; DuBois, 2005), the active participation of those being oppressed in their own oppression, takes on more creative and hidden forms (see Milovanovic, 1986, 2002; Bannister and Milovanovic, 1990; Henry and Milovanovic, 1991, 1996).

The notion of the state has a different significance for the instrumental Marxists than for the structural Marxists. Both base their views on Engels's classic statement that "the state arose from the need to hold class antagonisms in check" (cited in Cain and Hunt, 1979: 157). The state arose as a recognition that society "has become entangled in an insoluble contradiction with itself, that it has split into irreconcilable antagonisms which it is powerless to dispel." Thus, in order to stop society from destroying itself, a process continuously fueled by "classes with conflicting economic interests," the state arose as a power "seemingly" above society (ibid., 156). Engels further states that "the ... most powerful economically dominant class ... acquires new means of holding down and exploiting the oppressed class" (ibid., 157).

And here lies the different interpretation. The instrumental Marxists argue that the state really is a "capitalist state": that is, the state is merely an instrument by which the dominant class rules. The structuralists, on the other hand, argue that the state has a certain degree of autonomy. It should not be perceived simply as an empty shell to be filled at the whim of the ruling class. Nor is it immune from political struggles. Rather, the structure of the state is somewhat a product of the clash between elite interests and working-class movements. The particular characteristics of the state therefore reflect the class struggle between workers and capitalists. The state, the structuralist Marxists continue, also attempts to resolve contradictions in the social formation. The capitalist system itself is not fundamentally altered. Rather, the state assures that key values and structures are not changed. Oppositional groups, too, are channeled into making use of procedural formalities under the rule of law rubric in the redressing of grievances (Milovanovic, 1986, 1996; Thomas and Milovanovic, 1990; Capeheart and Milovanovic, 2020). Hence a dialectical struggle accounts for the particular form of the state (Esping-Anderson *et al.*, 1979).

The "state apparatus" (police, courts, legislators, prisons, etc.), for the structuralists, has a more difficult time of maintaining legitimation in the advanced forms of capitalism. In the early laissez-faire competitive forms, we saw that legitimation is maintained in good part by the inherent "justice" found in commodity exchange. Notions of free will, equality and proprietorships arose from the subtle processes connected with commodity exchange.

In the state-regulated forms of capitalism, the state apparatus finds itself in a more active and contradictory role in an economic system that tends toward crises. The state apparatus finds itself in the difficult position of reconciling the pressures of different interest groups. At the same time, fundamental values supporting the capitalist system must be sustained. Marxists from this school of thought point out that within this contradictory situation change occurs at a gradual pace. But, they add, the central place of such ideals as property, egotism, and the pursuit of profits will not be infringed. (For an examination of how "liberty" and "property" interests developed in the Fourteenth Amendment, see Milovanovic, 1987.)

Forces within the state apparatus may have a degree of independence from the specific interests of power elites. For example, to a great degree, lawyers are committed to the ideals of the rule of law and, specifically, formal rationality as an ideal type. To this degree, the sphere of law generates its own pressure or influence on the economic, political and ideological spheres. We are left, then, with the conclusion that phenomena are "overdetermined." That is, the "cause" of things, from the structural Marxist's perspective, is always multiple. Economic, political and ideological factors can exert pressure to produce, for instance, a particular law. It is then an empirical question as to which factors in combination are the decisive ones.

The instrumental Marxists would argue that, yes, there are a number of factors, including class struggle, that force the elite to change policies, but after all is said and done it is the economically powerful actors who have the final say. In other words, "in the final analysis," class repression will be maintained.

Property and Contract

Our next point deals with the notion of contract and property. For the structuralists, the contract as "an agreement of independent wills" is central in law. In fact, for Pashukanis, it is the ultimate expression of commodity exchange (1980: 82). It expresses, in concrete form, such notions as will and subjectivity. It disguises and denies, at the same time, the inherent inequalities existing between contracting parties. Contractual freedom disguises inequalities while at the same time giving the appearance of freely developed agreements. The "just" contract can only be defined in relation to the type of mode of production in existence. Marx has said it "is just whenever it corresponds, is appropriate, to the mode of production. It is unjust whenever it contradicts that mode. Slavery on the basis of capitalist production is unjust; likewise, fraud in the quality of commodities" (cited in Cain and Hunt, 1979: 138).

The ethical principle of equality, for example, has no standing in feudalism. Society was organized hierarchically. The serf or peasant found themselves in a hierarchy of bondage to a lord of the manor. The notion of commodity exchange between equal people had no relevance. Thus, without commodity exchange, no spontaneous notions of equality, free will or proprietorship could develop. In addition, the notion of a formal legal subject, the juridic subject, had no place. That is, the notion of a formal legal status common to all did not exist. Subjects merely had concrete rights or privileges within each estate, city, or village. The rights were not carried with them when they left for another community.

The contract, then, arose at a unique stage in the development of society. The capitalist mode of production demanded an instrument that would facilitate exchange. It was invented. Other benefits, too, were derived from it. That is, the contract served not only a facilitative function but also a repressive and ideological one. Inequality between members was disguised. Propertied classes could dictate the terms of the contract. Workers were offered a contract, "take it or leave it." But, ideologically, the notion of contractual freedom was maintained (be it in actuality merely a myth). A society, characterized by self-centered individuals meeting in the anarchy of the marketplace, where each individual strives to maximize profits, even at the expense of the other, could be stabilized by the existence of the contract. The state would be ever-present to enforce these agreements. The result: calculability and predictability—in a word, stability.

Property rights, too, are connected with the rise of capitalism. Marx recognized that "society itself ... is the root of property," and that the notion of property represents exclusion of another's will (cited in Cain and Hunt, 1979: 98, 100; see also Hegel's [1955] *Philosophy of Right* which was the basis of much of Marx's analysis of property and the contract). The right to private property stems from the state's assurance for it. With the development of the idea of exchangeability, arising from stable commodity marketplaces, exchange became increasingly regulated. Property, too, became more mobile. In addition, the notion of the right of ownership and the laws of private property developed (Pashukanis, 1980: 83–84). Feudal "property" was characterized by its immobility. "[I]t is incapable of becoming an object of mutual guarantees, moving from one hand to another ... Feudal or estate property violates the basic principle of bourgeois society—'the equal possibility of obtaining inequality'" (ibid., 83).

Property in capitalism becomes "an object of mutual guarantees." I promise to give you something, which I own, and in return I receive something of which I recognize you to be the owner. This can assure a minimum of external coercion by the state. The state, by upholding principles of formalism in law, can simply guarantee the property distributions that favor the more advantaged groups. But in times of revolt this guarantee can be dissolved.

The relationship of exchange where property is the object of mutual guarantees, once formalized, becomes a more permanent, more enduring institution. One only has to look at many challenges of the non-propertied against the powerful to find that after the revolution the former continued to meet in the marketplace to freely exchange commodities. It would be different for "proletarian" revolutions where property itself becomes the object of attack (ibid., 83–84).

Private property and rights of private property in a commodity oriented economy, then, destroy all genuine bonds between people (ibid., 85). In a society where we find peasants and the guild crafts, where the serf is directly attached to the land, we also find in existence norms limiting private property (ibid., 87; see also, Stone, 1985: 51).

On another level, with the development of the capitalist mode of production, we find a split between the owner of the means of production, the capitalist, and the worker, the seller of their own labor (Marx, 1967). Here the contractual terms reflect different and unequal relationships to property. The capitalist has more power to dictate the terms of the contract. Laws will often minimize some of the negative consequences of work conditions, but will not overly infringe upon such essential things as "management prerogatives." Namely, the question of the future of the organization, worker self-management, profit sharing, or generally, substantive issues, will not find a friendly ear in the court. The worker is given formal contractual and property freedoms, but the unequal distribution of property relationships will place the propertied in a more advantaged position in dictating the terms of the contract. The state stands ready and willing to support the unequal balance between the contracting parties.

But the worker is losing ground in a state-regulated capitalist society. More and more restrictions are placed on property owners. Many of these restrictions, from the worker's point of view, are welcomed, such as those that assure health and safety at the workplace; however, state restrictions extend to many other dimensions of all worker's property, including those less propertied. Since the domain of property is becoming more controlled, particularly for the worker, "zones of privacy" are becoming fewer (see Reich, 1964). A safe enclave where the worker can recover from the brutalizing conditions of the work place or the exploitive conditions in the economy is diminishing.

In sum, notions of property and the contract undergo transformations with the arrival of capitalism. They are intricately connected with the mode of production. Only with a change in the mode of production can notions of property and contract undergo a fundamental change.

The Withering Away of the State, Law and the Juridic Subject

Marxist analysis offers not only a critical description but also a direction for genuine change. Marxists see the state as repressive. At a minimum, the state maintains the relations and belief systems necessary for the continued exploitation of the worker. With the change to a different mode of production where class domination will not exist, namely to communism, it is argued that the necessity of the state will "wither away." Since law supports capitalist interests — either directly as in the instrumental perspective, or indirectly as in the structural Marxist perspective — then with the withering away of the state, and exploitive, predatory social relations based on profit and commodity exchange, so too the legal form will disappear. Furthermore, the notion of the formal abstract legal subject in law, which has meaning only in a commodity exchange, competitive marketplace, will also wither away. Pashukanis is quite clear here: "the problem of the withering away of law is the cornerstone by which we measure the degree of proximity of a jurist to Marxism" (1980).

Marxists note three phases in this development. The most advanced form of capitalism is said to have so many contradictions within it that it will collapse (consider, for example, the Depression in the U.S., 1930s, and near economic collapse in 2008).[6] The second phase, socialism, will be marked by the "dictatorship of the proletariat." Here there will still be class rule and domination. But instead of the capitalist class ruling, it will now be the workers who do so. Here the "narrow horizons of bourgeois thought" would still continue. In other words, vestiges of capitalist law, ideologies and consciousness would still exist for a time. But under the control of the workers, a class law, being still coercive, would be directed toward the struggle for a classless society. This, in the third phase, would be replaced by the "higher form," or communism proper. This is most clearly expressed by Marx in "The Critique of the Gotha Program" (1978; originally in 1875).

In contrast, sometimes in the literature there is specification of socialism with two phases: an earlier transitional phase and a later form (see Gilabert, 2015);[7] sometimes the latter is equated with democratic socialism (for example, the politics of U.S. Senator Bernie Sanders according to Gilabert), as a further transition to the later form; others unbashfully maintain the terminology "communism," as the "higher forms" as in Holland's (2011) free market communism.[8]

During socialism the mode of production would still have remnants of capitalism and bourgeois ideology. But, Pashukanis tells us, instead of commodity exchange, we would have a voucher system (so many hours worked can be traded in for so much produce), and the central economic policies will establish what "exchange ratios" should be. That is, these policies would establish a thing's true social value and assure that exchanged goods reflect their true value. Here, then, exchange-values will begin to disappear. We would have a return to use values. Products would have direct personal use. Thus, abstractions that emanate from commodity exchange, too, would gradually disappear.[9]

Advocates of the "withering away of the state, law, and the juridic subject" argue that people would return to appreciating the wholeness of and interconnection with the other, mutual affirmations, and recognition of differences. The other would be seen as someone who complements, not one who exploits. Competition and the profit motive would be replaced by such principles as mutual aid and community, and by the notions of need *and* ability;[10] thus, a "needs/abilities" principle rather than the often-cited but somewhat misleading "needs" principle in the singular. It states: "from each according to his [their] ability, to each according to his [their] needs" (Pashukanis, 1980: 324; Lenin, 1949: 152–163; the slogan first appeared in Marx's *Critique of the Gotha Program*, 1875). In other words, discussion often focuses exclusively on the "needs" component, whereas an equal emphasis, some argue, should be on "abilities," the variability and interconnection with needs.

These new values would be continuously fostered and cultivated. Basic guarantees for a livable income, health, and education would be assured. The legal personality would no longer be needed. That is, the abstraction, the juridic subject, would wither away. In the higher forms, Lenin tells us people will be:

> accustomed to observing the elementary rules of social intercourse that have been known for centuries ... they will become accustomed to observing them without force, without compulsion, without subordination, without the special apparatus for compulsion which is called the state (1949: 142).

Thus, habit and custom, the thesis continues, would now govern relationships. People will orient themselves to the order because they see it as consistent with enhancing human capabilities, solidaristic communities, mutual support, and equal opportunities, while cultivating sensitivity, respect and support for the other. "Excesses" will still exist because of individual variation. But these problems in living will be dealt with spontaneously. No special coercive apparatus is necessary. At most, community moots or mediation mechanisms will develop. But no need exists for specialists such as lawyers for mediating disputes.

In fact, the bureaucracy will be dismantled. Instead, Lenin tells us, accounting and control of the industries can be done by any literate person with the knowledge of the rules of arithmetic (1949: 160–161). Thus, rather than the administration by specialized bureaucrats, Lenin assures us that the average city dweller is fully capable of learning and doing these functions. "Foremen and bookkeepers," he tells us, will coordinate industrial production (ibid., 80).[11] "Collectivist organizations" will be the ideal forms of production. These will be based on orientations that focus on collective development (Rothschild-Whitt, 1979; see, also, Milovanovic, 1989, Chapter 6).[12]

Marxist analysis claims that each of the three stages has a particular form of justice. Under capitalism, formal equality is the ideal. In earlier forms of socialism, the equality principle would be more genuinely applied. But two further correlative principles would exist: (1) "he [they] who does [do] not work, neither shall he [they] eat," and (2) "an equal amount of products for an equal amount of labour" (Lenin, 1949: 150). This has been referred to as Marx's "distribution" principle (distribution according to contribution). And the equality principle will still exist: i.e., a formally equal scale will be applied to unequal persons. This, in the "higher forms," will be replaced by a standard that recognizes people as different in temperament, drives, abilities, potentialities, dexterity and so forth (see, for example, Lee, 1959: 39–52).[13] In other words, an alternative substantive standard of justice will prevail. Implying that people are basically the same and applying a form of law reflecting that notion, the Marxists tell us, are repressive practices. The standard of the "higher form" would be the abilities/needs principle.[14]

Dialectics of Struggle

We want to briefly highlight an important line of theory within sociology of law that has emerged particularly since the ascendancy of the structuralist Marxist perspective. This concerns the notion of the dialectics of struggle. Our starting point of analysis is Quinney's classic statement concerning the linear development of revolutionary consciousness in *Class, State and Crime* (1977):

> Crimes of accommodation and resistance thus range from unconscious reactions to exploitation, to conscious acts of survival within the capitalist system, to politically conscious acts of rebellion. These criminal actions … evolve or progress from unconscious reaction to political rebellion (1977: 59).

Some literature, however, has questioned this linear development. Studies of jailhouse lawyers (Milovanovic, 1988; Milovanovic and Thomas, 1989; Thomas and Milovanovic, 1999), activist lawyers before the court (Bannister and Milovanovic, 1990), and "rebels" being processed during mass arrests (Balbus, 1977b) all indicate that oppressed groups often inadvertently reconstitute the forms of domination. For example, inmates who teach themselves law and practice it while imprisoned (aiding fellow inmates with grievances not adequately attended to by the formal legal profession) buy into legal discourse in grieving their case, and thus inadvertently give further force and legitimacy to the rule-of-law ideology. Activist lawyers before the courts find themselves in a similar position. Some activist movements have inadvertently further empowered the state. Environmentalists and critics of the legal system who favor a get-tough approach to offenders, have all supported tougher and lengthier imprisonment. This position, ironically, solidifies the powers of the state. And some activists who advocate "reversing hierarchies" often do just that, maintaining the form of oppression itself (see also Cornell, 1998, and the analysis of the politics of hate, revenge politics).

Yet other activists, not well informed of theoretical and historical works, have often reverted to "us versus them" hate-politics (Groves, 1991; Milovanovic, 1991a, 1991b). Rigid political correctness is one element of this form of "schmarxism" (see Chapters 6, 7). The uncritical view that some leftists embrace concerning the situation in revolutionary and post-revolutionary governments claiming to be "humanistic," "socialistic," or "communistic" has been well-documented. Although many of the accomplishments of the Cuban regime, for example, are to be greatly admired (schooling, education, health), the critical evidence certainly raises questions in other political spheres. Some, who practice solidarity politics, would benefit from a familiarization with the critical theoretical literature, and especially with the historical literature, that has illustrated the dialectics of struggle. See, for example, Piers Beirne's book *Revolution in Law* (1990). What this indicates is that those merely practicing solidarity politics with no grounded basis in theoretical and historical analysis, or those ivory tower figures who never directly experience the barricades, are equally guilty of not developing a more fully informed transpraxis, both a critique of what is and a vision of what could be (Henry and Milovanovic, 1996; Capeheart and Milovanovic, 2020) as a basis for a humanistic transformative politics.

Summary

The Marxist approach to the sociology of law comes in two forms. The instrumental Marxists see law and legal thought as simply the product of class rule. The structural Marxists, on the other hand, argue that the form of law and legal thought as well as the state can be relatively autonomous from the wishes of particular capitalists, while at the same time maintaining an environment for the continued exploitation of the worker. Repression and legitimation can be combined. The structuralists focus on the notion of "overdetermination." Within the "superstructure" forces that have some degree of independence (relative autonomy)—such as ideology, the legal profession and political class struggles—can have an influence in the development of laws. For Marxists the question of cause, domination (hegemony), legitimation crisis, ideology, the juridic subject, the contract, private property rights, and transformation—all are central issues.

The functions of law are repressive, facilitative as well as ideological. We also see some elements of constitutive functions, particularly in the structural interpellation interpretation of Marxism. All four, in a Marxist perspective, are interrelated. Repressive functions include violence directed toward the working class. Facilitative functions include the promotion of laws that aid commodity exchange and the maximization of personal profit. Formal rationality, the contract and contractual freedoms assure this. Self-centered, calculating individuals, seeking the maximization of profits, effects of capital logic are given a framework within which to orient their conduct. Constitutive function is noted where the subject is interpolated, top-down; but is also a contributor to reproducing the superstructure, bottom-up (we will return to this in Chapter 11). Finally, the ideological function includes how law communicates a message to the exploited that they are free, equal and can gain unlimited property by abiding by the rule of law. That is, by endowing the order with legitimacy and by uncritically orienting their behaviors to it, all perpetuate the myth of the existence of equal opportunity to attain maximal fulfillment of social values. The rule of law ideology conveys the message that if personal failure exists, it is not the law, nor the economic system that is at fault. Reasons must be sought elsewhere. "Blaming the victim" of an exploitive system is the most prevalent form.

The relationship between a legal order and fulfillment of social values (self-realization, equality and community) can be summarized. Instrumental Marxists argue that the genuine fulfillment of these values in a capitalist mode of production does not develop. Rather, mystification, false consciousness and hegemony are outcomes of class rule. The structuralists, too, argue that because of repressive formalism, little genuine fulfillment of social values occurs. Workers, egoists driven by economic calculation for profits in a capitalist society, become "crippled monstrosities." They do so even as they worship its majesty.

We noted that Marx did not develop a systematic sociology of law. Rather, interested researchers have had to scrutinize his voluminous writings for scattered excerpts. Out of these, a Marxist oriented sociology of law is slowly beginning to materialize.

Review Questions

1. We have seen that there are various interpretations of Marx on law, partly because he never systematically developed his ideas on the subject. How useful, then, is consulting his work in developing a more systematic sociology of law?

2. In contemporary internet-driven society, there are many examples of how our "relation of production," our everyday activities, have been transformed from earlier epochs. Provide two examples and explain.

3. The notion of use-value in Marxist analysis can be compared with Durkheim's "social value." Explain some commonalities and differences.

4. Compare the Marxian structural interpellation view with Weber's multi-factor approach in the study of law. Where are their commonalities? Where are their differences?

5. We have seen that many prominent critical sociologists of law do not have early backgrounds in poverty nor come from deprived families. Does this limit or enhance their abilities to theorize in a sociology of law? Explain.

6. Marx, in discussing the advanced form of capitalism noted its crises tendencies and how it may affect legitimation, the belief in the rule of law. Compare with Max Weber's more critical assessment of domination. Where are their differences and commonalities? Explain. How would Durkheim chime in on this discussion, bringing up the "abnormal forms" of the division of labor?

7. Following the near financial/economic collapse in 2008 we witnessed much information disseminated about the growing disparities between the rich and the rest. What would Marx and Weber have to say about this? Explain, focusing on the question of legitimate domination and the law.

8. Marx argues that in the "higher forms" a "withering away of the state, police and law" will occur. Current democratic socialists and countries oriented around to its thesis, see things in a transitional state toward this higher form. Is this projection as an ideal useful for developing laws or does it act as a hindrance, or outright possibly leading to illegitimate forms of domination? Explain.

9. The dialectics of struggle suggests that the rule of law has positive attributes but can also disguise repressive practices. Explain.

10. Consider your personal everyday world. How often do you orient yourself to "exchange-value" rather than "use-value"? Pick two examples and explain Marx's idea of commodification and how it applies. What are the implications?

Endnotes

1. For a useful introduction, see Heinrich (2012).

2. We have been greatly aided by the excellent collection of passages dealing with law and ideology by Cain and Hunt in *Marx and Engels on Law* (1979), by Beirne and Quinney's *Marxism and Law* (1982), by Beirne and Sharlet's *Pashukanis: Selected Writings on Marxism and Law* (1980), Pashukanis's *Commodity Exchange Theory of Law* (2002), and by Beirne's *Revolution In Law* (1990). See also the anthology, *Marx and Law*, edited by Easton (2008); and analysis of Marx's needs/abilities principle by Gilabert (2015) and Spafford (2020).

3. Consider comparison with Durkheim's notion of "social value."

4. See, also, Unger, 1976: 194; Turkle, 1981; Fraser, 1978: 172; Balbus, 1977a: 586.

5. Recall, also, Weber, from previous chapter on this point.

6. In each case, an active intervention by the state (state regulated capitalism) was to save it from continuing a possible transformation. The New Deal countered the Great Depression, massive bail outs by the government countered the near financial collapse.

7. The use of the word "communism" has pejorative connotations, and capitalist generated ideology often condemns that which is its possible subversive force, pointing to historical conditions and citing cases such as post-1917 revolutionary Russia under Stalin. Nevertheless, we must always be vigilant, critical thinkers argue, for the possible co-optation of otherwise liberating struggles and social change.

8. Gilabert (2015: 2018), reviewing diverse suggestions for transitions, suggests that perhaps three phases could be productive: earlier forms of socialism governed by the "contribution principle," a middle, engaging John Rawls' (2001) "difference principle," and a later form of socialism governed by the abilities/needs principle. Rawls has offered two principles of justice: first principle, a guarantee of basic rights and liberties; the second, the difference principle, as "the idea of not wanting to have greater advantages unless this is to the benefit of others, who are less well off." Or "the greatest benefit of the least advantaged member of society (Rawls and Kelly, 2001: 42–43). Gilabert has forcefully argued for the greater engagement with libertarian philosophers advocating inclusion of greater discussion of civil and political liberties, such as in John Rawls, and other critical thinkers such as Amartya Sen (2011) and Martha Nussbaum (2011) who offer the "capability" approach to justice which has some common grounds with the abilities/needs principle. He does not explicitly engage a discussion on law, particularly the contours of socialist law; however, he does advocate formalizing human rights based on human dignity (Gilabert, 2015: 219–220; Gilabert and O'Neill, 2019).

9. We are refraining from running out all the critiques levied against this idealism due to the more expository project before us. We should mention, however, that on the point just developed, Weber would definitely have something to say about the rise of a bureaucracy that would administer this new society, which would inevitably be the basis of a new form of domination. See also the critiques by Stedman (2016). For an appraisal of Marx's methodology, see O'Connell (2018). For a reassessment, see Kandiyali (2018).

10. See, for example, Pepinsky and Quinney (1991), Tifft and Sullivan (1980), and Kropotkin (1902, 1913), Carens (2003), Gilabert (2015), Spafford (2020).

11. Some may see this as overly idealistic; however, one should keep in mind even in the most complex court cases litigating such issues as copyright law and economic transactions we find jury deliberations.

12. Holland (2011), for example, offers the notion of leaderless organizations governed by the notion of an improv jazz player metaphor where change is constantly an emergent; here, even the slightest/smallest input produces disproportional effects. Not insensitive bureaucracies, but "dissipative structures" that remain always open to change and re-ordering will be the norm.

13. Sometimes these human characteristics have been called "singular characteristics," and "native endowment," with examples offered such as "intelligence, vigor, charisma, creativity, etc. (Gilabert, 2015: 208, 210). Of course, in criticism, this brings up the question of nature v. nurture, or even co-constitutive dynamics.

14. For a critical view, see Hirst, 1986: 28–63, 85, 104–105. For further critically engaged commentary, see Gilabert (2015, 2017): Gilabert and O'Neill (2019). For an anarchist response, see Spafford (2020).

PART 2

Perspectives in the Sociology of Law

6

Sociological Jurisprudence and Critical Legal Studies

The First Wave

Introduction

In this chapter we want to survey some approaches that are focused neither purely on jurisprudence (i.e., legal science) nor on sociology of law. These are the "in-betweeners," if you will. Yet these contemporary approaches are critical in the movement toward a fully articulated theory in the sociology of law. Accordingly, in the first section we have surveyed the sociological jurisprudence and the Legal Realist schools of law. Roscoe Pound perhaps best epitomizes the former. American legal realism is best represented by Karl Llewellyn and Jerome Frank. Oliver Wendell Homes, Jr. and Benjamin Cardozo have also been associated with the development of both perspectives. Although their analysis surely went beyond merely legal dogmatics (legal science) by the introduction of sociology, psychoanalytic, economic, philosophical and anthropological literature in their critiques, it still fell short of being a more comprehensive sociology of law.

Our second section will concentrate on the Critical Legal Studies Movement ("CLS"), an outgrowth of the former two approaches. With formal beginnings in 1977, the CLS theorists, or "crits," have, in a heretical way, theorized *within* the formal legal institutions and have developed a formidable body of critical analysis that fundamentally questions the "neutrality" of the legal apparatus.[14] In the next chapter we will introduce some of the off springs of these early movements.

Sociological Jurisprudence and Legal Realism

Introduction

Although not sociologies of law in the truest sense, "sociological jurisprudence" and American Legal realism have been two major movements in law in the early 20th century. Roscoe Pound, the key inspirational figure of the former, and Karl Llewellyn and Jerome Frank, the key thinkers of the latter, will be central in the following presentation. Both movements challenged the form of law and thought (formal rationality, or formalism) that had evolved from the 19th century. Their criticisms were levied against the model of law expressed best by Christopher Langdell, Dean of Harvard Law School in 1870 (for an overview of Langdell, see Patterson, 1995; for a critique, Rubin, 2007; for a more sociological jurisprudence approach, see Cotterrell, 2017).

Law, Langdell argued, was an exact science, a legal science, much like physics, zoology, botany and chemistry. The ideal jurist used the law library as their laboratory. Not practical experience, but knowledge gained of pure, abstract law, particularly by analyzing "case law" of appellate decisions, would assure a scientific understanding of law. Through deciphering case law, and by the use of the Socratic method of recitation and quizzing by the instructor, the principles and doctrines of law could be taught to students (Langdell, 1887; Patterson, 1995).

Realists and their predecessors from sociological jurisprudence differed with this ideal. They viewed law more as a social science. Sociology, economics, psychology and philosophy would be their guide. Their laboratory was the real world. Pragmatism was their philosophy. Their focus was on judicial decision making and its non-formal (extra-legal) aspects. The law, for them, had become stagnant. It had ossified into formal procedures that did not allow equitable justice. They challenged the stated ideal of certainty and predictability in decision making (assumedly assured by abiding by the letter of the law), the strict emphasis on precedents *(stare decisis),* and the reliance on abstract and syllogistic reasoning as a basis of decision making. Their method was a socio-legal critique. They were to apply various sociological findings to the sphere of jurisprudence. They called into question the traditional methodologies and practices of law. The gap between law in theory and law in practice was torn asunder.

Important in understanding why both movements developed were the social and historical forces at work at the turn of the 20th century (Hunt, 1978: 13; Hunt, 1993: 36–57). The first few decades of the 20th century were marked by dramatic economic growth. Along with this came concentrations of power and the centralization of the state and the bureaucratic apparatus. From the 19th century to the turn of the 20th century, the legal ideology existing had, as a guiding ideal, the emphasis on the least amount of legal involvement in the economy as possible, or *laissez faire.* Intervention by the courts in the economic and social spheres was seen as undesirable. Rather, strict adherence to legal principles and the letter of the law was seen as the ideal, a path to the maximal realization of social values. But the accelerated economic and social changes in society, with their many contradictory demands, forced the courts to confront their own internal decision-making methodologies. The assault on formalism was to be centered at the prestigious law schools of Harvard, Columbia and Yale.

Sociological Jurisprudence: Roscoe Pound

Roscoe Pound, Dean of the Harvard Law School (1916–1936), is considered the "father" of sociological jurisprudence. He was a prolific writer who wrote well into his nineties. The core of his ideas was developed in the first three decades of the 20th century. It was Pound, along with the notable jurists Oliver Wendell Holmes and Benjamin Cardozo, who mounted an attack on legal formalism (formal rationality). The movement's most active period was in the years 1900 to 1920, but it continued to have some influence in the decades to come. This movement predated and in many ways set the critical groundwork for Legal realism, which had its heyday from 1920 to 1940.

Roscoe Pound was influenced by the *social control perspective,* the prevailing school of thought in sociology at the turn of the century (see also Hunt, 1993: 40). He drew heavily from the writings of sociologist Edward Ross and the philosophy of William James, a pragmatist. "Social control," Pound argued, "requires power—power to influence the behavior of men through the pressure of their fellow men" (1968: 49). His notion of social control led to his definition of law as "a highly specialized form of social control, carried on in accordance with a body of authoritative precepts, applied in a judicial and an administrative process" (ibid., 41).

Underlying his notions of social control was a vision of individuals pursuing diverse interests. Along with the inevitable conflict between individuals advancing claims, he was concerned with the stability and order of a society. Thus, his underlying sociological model was concerned with the maintenance of an equilibrium, or a status quo in society. He was less concerned with the causes of the development of the legal form. He was more interested in the *results* of law, that is, how its application affected people (Hunt, 1978: 20–22). From his very first article in 1903, Pound's rather eclectic style stressed practical problems rather than just the development of pure theory.

There were two foci in his approach. First, a re-focusing of law from analyzing legal doctrines (rules and practices) to the analysis of their social effects. That is, his approach emphasized how law affected practical, everyday life (Pound, 1907). To this end, he argued, the methods, practices and findings of the social sciences should be used. In his words, "let us look to economics and sociology and philosophy, and cease to assume that jurisprudence is self-sufficient... let us not become legal monks" (ibid., 611–612).

His second focus dealt with the application of rules. He urged that we should get away from mechanical applications of law. We should stay clear, he argued, of simply applying the letter of the law in all cases (formal rationality). The idea that decision making should follow the letter of the law, and that mechanical deductions from previous decisions in law *(stare decisis)* should be the rule, was contrary to his law-in-action framework. Legal rules, rather, should be "general guides" for the judge. The judge should be given a degree of discretion in determining justice in individual cases. It is only with respect to property and commercial law that there should be a "mechanical application of law." The reason for this, he argued, is because these transactions were very similar and repetitive in nature. But when the question of the morality of the individual or corporate behavior was concerned, the standard should be one of "equitable application." Equity was established by the judge based on individual circumstances. Formal logic, then, should be merely an "instrument" employed in arriving at a fair decision. In brief, his sociological jurisprudence was hostile to formalism. In a classic statement he said: "Legal monks who pass their lives in an atmosphere of pure law, from which every worldly and human element is excluded, cannot shape practical principles to be applied to a restless world of flesh and blood" (1907: 611–612; 1908).

Pound's theory of *interests* (1943) is central to his writings. Interests, he argued, could be individual, social or public (arguably, public interests could be subsumed under social interests). An interest is "a demand or desire which human beings, either individually or through groups or associations or in relations, seek to satisfy ..." (1968: 66). Law does not create these. Conflict occurs because of competition amongst these interests in a society where no assurance exists for total satisfaction, ibid.). For Pound, "there has never been a society in which there has been such a surplus of the means of satisfying these claims ..." (ibid.). A legal system gives legitimacy to certain of these interests in law (ibid., 65). That is, it recognizes some and assures their protection in law.

The law, for Pound, should function so as to assure the maximum amount of fulfillment of interests in a society. And it should do so by minimizing sacrifices, waste and senseless friction. This would occur through *interest balancing* by the courts. They would, for example, balance a social interest, like the "general safety" or the "general health," against an individual's interest from being free from some governmental intrusion into their privacy and effects. Hence, he has called his model of law "social engineering" (see also comments by McManaman, 1958).

Along with his notion of interests and social engineering, Pound explicated his principle of ethics, his "jural postulates of civilized society" (1968: 113–115): in the application of interest-balancing certain ethical postulates should be guiding principles. Put in another way, these postulates are the ends, the goals and objectives of substantive law. They include the more general idea that in a civilized society one should be able to depend on certain general expectations; the expectations that others will not intentionally inflict harm; that one can control what one has legally discovered, acquired or created through one's labors; that the other will act with due care and create no unreasonable risk; that the other will act with good faith in their contractual dealings; and that, where the other owns a potentially dangerous thing they will not let it get out of hand. In his later writings he added the expectations of security of a job and of compensation for injuries suffered at the workplace (ibid., 115–116). As perhaps a part of the second, he also suggested a social security system in which the whole society should assume responsibility for the misfortunes of its citizens (ibid.).

Finally, Pound outlined certain stages in the development of law. His stages went from their primitive forms towards the "socialization" of the law. The goal in this latter ideal type would be the maximal fulfillment of wants and desires. Law would attempt to recognize the maximum number of interests and allow their fulfillment *within* the framework of law. In the higher forms, greater weight would be attached to public and social over private interests (see Hunt's typology, 1978: 30). One only has to look at the evolution of property rights to see how increased restrictions have developed in the name of "the public good." This, of course, has been the end result of interest-balancing.

To conclude, Pound was an important force in reconceptualizing how law should be understood. He was interested in law in practice. He did not develop a systematic sociology of law, but he did argue that the social sciences should be applied in the field of jurisprudence. It was not until after 1920, when a new movement—legal realism—was well under way, that the differences between sociological jurisprudence and it were brought out in some sharp debates (see, generally, Rumble, 1968).

Legal Realism: Realistic Jurisprudence

The development of legal realism, or "realistic jurisprudence," owes much to the groundwork set by sociological jurisprudence. It has more continuity than differences with it. The differences perhaps are more of degree.

Legal realism must be seen more as a movement rather than as a perspective or a school. There were various positions within the movement, from the more politically centralist Karl Llewellyn, to the more leftist Jerome Frank. Frank was influenced by the sociologist William Graham Sumner and psychological theory, particularly the work of Sigmund Freud. Llewellyn was also influenced by the sociological work of Sumner. The most active period of the movement was between 1920 to 1940.

Contrary to those who argued that this was a "radical" polemic, this movement, like its predecessor, was not concerned with a critique of capitalism itself. Rather, the underlying sociological framework placed high value on the idea of pluralism. That is, it assumed a society in which individuals with varying interests compete for scarce resources. Capitalism, individualism, the Constitution, and the desirability of the existing form of the legal system (formal rationality) were taken as a given, although, at various times some elements of substantive rationality were advocated. Perhaps not sufficiently recognized was that the door which now opened for substantive rationality could both enhance and restrict the fulfillment of social values. The realists were reformers interested in progressive change in an age of increasing social complexity and state intervention.

Given the depression of the 1930s and the increasing intensity of conflict in society, the need for change and the regulation of diverse conflicts was even more compelling than that recognized during the previous critical Sociological Jurisprudence movement in law. This had its effects on the sharpness of the realists' attack. The realists attacked the notion that law in practice is an exact science. The whole emphasis of "realism," generally, was to present and engage with things "as they really were." Their concern with the practical led to much direct involvement by key theorists in the New Deal Administration of Franklin Roosevelt responding to the great Depression of the 1930s.

The underlying philosophical assumptions of the realists rested on pragmatism (Rumble, 1968; Hunt, 1978: 41–42; Hunt, 1993: 180). In the 1920s and 1930s in the United States, pragmatism was a dominant school in philosophy. Not abstractions, nor elaborate theories, but concrete human conditions and how humans cope with various demands of living must be understood, according to this philosophy. Theorists like William James and John Dewey were highly respected. This carried over to the legal arena. Pragmatists were hostile to formalism, the use of abstractions, and exclusive reliance on strict deductive types of reasoning. For James (1955: 45), such ideals as fixed rules and principles, closed systems, dogma, and finality in truth should be discarded. For Dewey, the "problem is not to draw a conclusion from given premises; that can best be done by a piece of inanimate machinery by fingering a keyboard. The problem is to find statements of general principle and of particular fact which are worthy to serve as premises" (1931: 134). Thus, rather than relying on mechanical deductive reasoning from given rules, decision makers should be result-oriented; that is, concerned with probable consequences of their decision. (Of course, recalling the discussion from Chapter 4, we see here the tension between the principles of formal rationality and substantive rationality.)

The realists attacked, even more vehemently than their predecessors, formal judicial decision making. The *classical view* in arriving at a judicial decision had it that justices merely apply specific rules in a mechanical way to the "facts" of the case. Rules structure decisions. Judges, it was felt, have little independence in interpreting these rules. The Constitution, statutes, and/or precedents *(stare decisis)* dictate decision-making processes. The manner in which a decision is reached, therefore, is formal, mechanical and predictable. Extra-legal factors — that is, factors outside of law — such as the particular feelings, or biases of a particular judge, it was argued in the classic view, do not have, and should not have an influence in decision-making processes.

In the *classical view,* justices engage in syllogistic reasoning and deductive logic. Particular (major) premises are established that are rooted in the U.S. and state constitutions, rules and precedents. Then, logical and formal reasoning is applied to the "facts" (minor premise), which leads to a conclusion (recall Chapter 4, Figure 2). Thus, the judge has only to look at the "facts," decide on the doctrine or principle at play, search for the appropriate rule or precedent(s), and apply it, by deductive logic and syllogistic reasoning, to the case. This, then, will lead to the correct decision. Because of the assumption that uniformity, formality, value neutrality and impersonality in the application of this method existed, predictability, certainty, and even-handedness of the decision is said to be realizable. In a word, law is an exact science. And this represents the ideal of formal rationality, the rule of law (formalism).

The realists, in particular Llewellyn and Frank, attacked these notions of the classic view in law on two levels (Rumble, 1968). First, on the level of "rule-skepticism," and second "fact-skepticism."

As to the first level, rule-skepticism, the realists, with varying degrees of vehemence, argued that there is a difference between "paper" rules and "real" rules. That is, there is a difference between what the justices are supposed to do (and the appearance of what they are doing) and what they actually do. Earlier jurists such as Holmes had already argued that "I will admit any general proposition you like and decide the case either way" (cited in Rumble, 1968: 40).

In rule-skepticism, the assumed linearity of syllogistic reasoning was questioned. In other words, the deciding of a case is based more on hunches, feelings, intuition, flashes, instinct, conviction or unconscious processes (e.g., extra-legal factors). After the fact *(ex post facto)* justifications or rationalizations can always be provided, based on some theory, doctrine, formula, rule or precedent, which justifies the decision. Consider, for example, a police officer testifying before the court that they made an arrest based on the "plain view doctrine"—a judicially established doctrine that stipulates that a police officer in their normal duties, when witnessing a crime or contraband, does not have to obtain an arrest or search warrant. At times, it could be unclear whether, in fact, the police officer engaged within the latitude allowable by the plain view doctrine or if they engaged in unlawful activity and only later justified the arrest or search based on this doctrine.

Even the same "factual" situation, the realists argued, could be interpreted in different ways. Jerome Frank has been the most forceful on this point. In *Law and the Modern Mind* (1963) he argued:

> The process of judging, so the psychologists tell us, seldom begins with a premise from which a conclusion is subsequently worked out. Judging begins rather the other way around—with a conclusion more or less vaguely formed; a man ordinarily starts with such a conclusion and afterwards tries to find premises, which will substantiate it (1963: 108).

Thus, rather than accepting the idea that the existence of formal, deductive-type syllogistic reasoning structures the decision-making process, the realists argue that it works the other way around. Conclusions are first made based on some extra-legal factor, and then the judge works backward in providing a justification. "The court," Frank tells us, "can decide one way or the other and in either case can make it's reasoning appear equally flawless" (1963: 72).

Similar attitudes and values of judges (extra-legal factors) are said to account for uniformities in decision making. Llewellyn has said that the search for certainty in law is an illusion and "you must turn, for purposes of prediction, to the reactions of the judges to the facts and to the life around them" (1960: 68). Therefore, for Llewellyn, it is not the rule of law that is central but "law through men" (1962: 62). Frank, much more extreme and perhaps representing the most left-leaning in the Realist movement, has argued that the reasoning one finds in case opinions is more of a "window dressing," or "formal clothes in which he [the justice] dresses up his thoughts" (1963: 140–141). Again, the tension between principles of formal and substantive rationality is quite apparent in these critiques. And these criticisms, it might be added, went well beyond any formulations by those from the Sociological Jurisprudence movement.

The second level of attack against the classical notions of judicial decision making involves "fact-skepticism" (Rumble, 1968). What, in other words, constitutes a "fact" of a case? The traditional method stated that R (a rule) × F (the "facts") = D (the decision). But establishing the "facts," the realists argued, is the product of a multitude of factors, some of the most important of which are hidden. Frank has argued that the main source of uncertainty or unpredictability in law is "fact-uncertainty." That is, the "facts" that are established in trial proceedings are always disputable. They are constructs or the end result of definitional and constructional processes. Only through oral testimony by witnesses with vastly different capacities, recollection abilities, and motivations for describing "what happened," are the "facts" established.

A pervasive obsession for certainty, however, permeates the decision making process according to the realists. For example, Frank tells us, a form of "Cadi [Khadi] justice" exists in law in action. "Courts," he argues, "often decide first and then arrange their 'facts' and 'rules' so as to justify the decision previously arrived at" (1931a: 29). In other words, substantive rationality, substantive irrationality, or formal irrationality could in fact have been the decisive factor in the decision-making process. Frank has stated bluntly that "our judicial system is permeated through and through with Cadi justice ... Ours is a system where it [Cadi Justice] is active but concealed" (ibid., 31). Thus, the formula R × F = D must be restated as S (the stimulus that is affecting the judge) × P (the personality of the particular judge) = D (the decision) (1931b: 242). Again, here we are a far cry from principles of formal rationality, even though an *ex post facto* application of linear logic (syllogistic reasoning) may make the decision appear as having been "logically" developed within the terms of law.

Frank has also criticized other realists for simply overlooking the importance of how a "frozen record" from below is established. By a "frozen record" it is meant that "facts" become "frozen" in trial courts and are often taken for granted by the appellate courts. Frank criticizes Pound, Cardozo, as well as Llewellyn for their emphasis on upper-court decision making processes to the neglect of the lower trial court. It is within the trial court proceedings that "facts" are established, and it is here that much uncertainty exists. Recall, court decisions are published as case books and stored in law libraries for reference. Each case is organized in three steps: the facts of the case are summarized at the beginning of the published decision, followed by the relevant issue in law, which then is followed by articulating each step in the syllogism leading to the decision (the issue is the major premise and the principle involved is applied to the factual situation by the use of a linear deductive logic whereby a decision is rendered). But, clearly, the writing of the decision that appears in published form is created after the fact, after the apparent process has taken place. It is here where the "facts" are selectively summarized by the justice(s); realists would argue, arranged to fit the decision already decided in an extra-judicial manner ("substantive rationality,"? "substantive irrationality"?). Articulated facts, then, become frozen in their published form, and it is these facts that are legally relevant at subsequent appeals. Dissenting views, however, often construct a different picture of the facts of the case that lead to their particular application of a legal principle.

The realists, generally, with the major exception of Frank, argued that predictability could be re-established if better adherence existed to the scientific method in the study of law (Rumble, 1968: 140). Llewellyn, for example, presented 14 "major steadying factors in our appellate courts." These points ranged from advocating the use of experienced lawyers, to better understandings of the use of a "frozen record from below," to life tenure for the justices to, finally, the establishment of a "professional judicial office" (1962: 19–51). On the other hand, Frank's (1949) recommendations included:

(1) advocating the development and the institutionalization of a "constructive skepticism" concerning how courts actually operate;

(2) altering legal education so as to include more practical internships and examinations of cases in law school that included the complete record;

(3) improving the adversarial trial processes (i.e., allowing greater pretrial discovery practices where each side would know all the relevant facts of a case, and appointing an impartial government official to independently research facts);

(4) allowing the trial court judge to attend appeal court's review of the case;

(5) abandoning the ritualistic robes worn by judges;

(6) advocating something akin to self-analysis by judges so they could understand their own biases; and

(7) greatly improving the trial-by-jury method.

It is illuminating to briefly compare the two major theorists' views as to the desirable end in law. For Frank, judges should take as fiction the notion that rules alone make the decision. The judge should be concerned with delivering equitable justice. "The law," he tells us, "is not a machine and the judges not machine-tenders" and "there never was and there never will be a body of fixed and predetermined rules alike for all" (1949: 129). In delivering justice, then, abstract rules have to be adaptable and adjustable. The sense of justice of a keen, non-biased judge will produce an equitable decision. Yet Frank also admits that law, with his proposal, could become even more unpredictable (ibid., 143–144, 169).

Llewellyn, on the other hand, first notes the distinction between the "grand" and "formal" style in decision making. The formal style represents the classical, formal method in arriving at conclusions in law. The grand style, on the other hand, is an approach in which "every current decision is to be tested against life-wisdom." Here, "'precedent' is carefully regarded, but if it does not make sense it is ordinarily re-explored ... [An] alleged 'principle' must make for wisdom as well as for order if it is to qualify as such" (cited in Rumble; 1968: 201). By 1940, he informs us, the trend in law had moved away from the exclusive formal to include more of the grand style. In Llewellyn's model, more certainty and predictability is of a greater value and is seen as more attainable, than in Frank's. For Frank, however, the search for predictability and certainty is illusory. These ideals can never be attained because of the uniqueness of the human condition.

Summary

The first four decades of the 20th century saw the development of a frontal attack on formalism, or formal rationality in law. The Sociological Jurisprudence movement, spearheaded by Pound, questioned the very methods that had devolved in the 19th century. The Legal realists in the 1920s and 1930s continued the attack but in a more critical way. The emphasis in both movements was on judicial decision making. The notion that decisions by justices are formal, impersonal, value-free, and derived logically by a method of syllogistic reasoning was questioned with differing degrees of vehemence.

The appearance and sanctity of formalism in law was never the same. But, by the early 1940s, Legal Realism was to wane abruptly from its point-position. No major scholar seemed to have picked up the banner after this time. It was not until some 35 years later that yet another eruption, the Critical Legal Studies movement, was once again to pick up the work that was begun by Holmes, Pound and Cardozo and sharpened by Frank and Llewellyn. But the attack was to be much more vehement and expansive in its scope. It was to be centered in one of the bastions of law—Harvard Law School.

Critical Legal Studies

Introduction

Just as legal realism was a logical heir to Sociological Jurisprudence, Critical Legal Studies, or, more often calls CLS, or "cls") was an outgrowth of the critical developments within the legal realist's initiatives (Tushnet, 1986, 1991; Freeman, 1988; Hunt, 1993: 13, 9–181, 211–226; Kennedy, 1997; Kairys, 2007; Unger, 2015). It was focused on ideology, indeterminacy in law, extra-legal basis of decision-making, political nature of law, hierarchical preparation in law school, and repressive functions. Early founding figures for CLS movement experienced the various oppositional movements (anti-Vietnam war, civil right, women's rights) and support for alternative forms of society of the 1960s. They brought their experiences to law school to find that similar forms of hierarchy and alienation existed. Upon graduating with law degrees and now faculty in some of the most prestigious law schools such as Harvard Law school, they synthesized their experiences and research and began to challenge law practices from inside the bastion. CLS's formal beginnings can be traced to the First Conference on Critical Legal Studies in 1977, held at the University of Wisconsin at Madison. By 1982, its annual meeting had almost a thousand in attendance.[15]

For over 30 years after the most active days of legal realism the critical perspective on law had become more subdued. But things changed quickly. Due to the different social movements and struggles of the 1960s and early 1970s, and to the perception that law as it was practiced, formalism, was out of accord with the realities that existed, a group of critical lawyers surfaced to carry on the critique begun by the realists (Gordon, 1992). Their critique was to be much more vehement and extensive. Semblance of a systematic sociology of law was in the making, but never fully realized such as the Weberian model; nor was it apparently the intent. Theirs were primarily challenges, critique, and deconstruction.[16] Roberto Unger, a key figure in the movement was to offer a reconstruction agenda (1984, 1987, 1996, 2015). But those within the ivory towers responded with their own attack on CLS and its adherents (see generally, Russell, 1986).

By the latter part of the 80s, the CLS movement had waned, due more to internal critiques, the call for more group-specific foci of disenfranchised (e.g., Fem-crits, Lat-crits, CRT, Asian-American, Queer-Crits), and perhaps lack of new energies and theoretical direction, but spawning a multitude of critical law perspective, with differentiation of perspectives ongoing. The CLS movement was the catalyst for movements that had not yet taken off; those that followed drew inspiration for what they accomplished and set in motion.

A similar movement, BritCrits, began in United Kingdom in the early 1980s building to the first conference held at Kent in 1986, the Critical Legal Conference. They drew inspiration from the legal realists and the CLS movement in the U.S. (see Thomson, 1987; Goodrich, 1992; Fitzpatrick and Hunt, 1987). However, before even the formal beginnings, there were lively debates between proponents of different perspectives.

Key journals reflecting the themes of CLS include *Law and Critique* in the UK; and in the U.S., *Unbound: Harvard Journal of the Legal Left*, and *The Crit: A Critical Legal Studies Journal*. Other journals are also regularly outlets: *The Australian Feminist Law Journal*, *The Harvard Civil Rights-Civil Liberties Law Review*, and the international journal, *Social and Legal Studies*.

Theoretical Orientation

The CLS movement has developed in roughly four stages, with its base established in the 1970s to mid-1980s. The first stage, the initial foray, extended from the early to mid-1970s. Theorists spearheaded by Duncan Kennedy[17] led a mixed bag of criticisms against formalism and the teaching of law (1970, 1973).[18] The second stage extended from the late-1970s to the early 1980s. This was marked by case studies and internal critiques of formalism. This period was highlighted by the publication of a collection of case studies edited by David Kairys, entitled *The Politics* of *Law* (first edition, 1982; the greatly expanded third edition was published in 1998).[19] The third stage, from the mid-1980s to the early 1990s, can be conceptualized as a search for theory. This change has been expressed best by the publication of a special issue on the CLS in the *Stanford Law Review* in January, 1984. Pivotal, too, was the change signified by the 1987 Conference on Critical Legal Studies (CCLS), with the theme, "Sounds of Silence: Racism and Legal Scholarship." This third stage was an internal "critical" phase. Although CLS had lost some of its appeal, as witnessed by the decline in attendance at its annual meetings, it continues to provide internal critiques of formal rationality. Since the 1990s to the present, arguably the fourth stage, we are witnessing the continuing differentiation of CLS into distinct perspectives, but all of which build from the momentum established by CLS. The next chapter will move to these various perspectives.[20]

Common Focal Points

Several foci unite those within CLS. First, rule- and fact-skepticism carry over from the realists' polemic. The traditional baggage of formalism—the reliance on "neutral" and linear syllogistic reasoning, and the belief in value-neutrality, objectivity, predictability, certainty, and the stability in law based on *stare decisis* (precedents) in law—all are said to be a Big Lie. No distinction, they argue, exists between law and politics. In fact, politics is seen as the ultimate determinant of decisions. Case opinions are but rationalizations or justifications hiding value choices (for a connection between legal reasoning and politics, see Kennedy, 1997 and comments by Klare, 2001).

Second, the notion of legitimacy is central in their critiques. One of law's functions, they argue, is the legitimization of domination by power elites. People in society are led to believe that they are governed by the "rule of law, not of men." The CLS theorists are, however, interested in how belief-systems—that is consciousness and ideologies—are shaped with the help of law. In fact, they argue, law is ideology (Kerruish, 1991; see also Litowitz, 2000). Two components of the legitimacy function are reification and hegemony. Reification stands for the process in which people together, consciously and/or unconsciously, contribute to creating the very structures and institutions that dominate them. These structures take on objective-like qualities and are, to various degrees, worshiped. Hegemony stands for the process by which ruling elites govern by the active consent of those who are oppressed (see Chapter 4).

In the next chapter, we shall have occasion to note that some critical race theorists ("CRT") have argued that giving up on a "rights-discourse," even though it is understood that this discourse does have a hegemonic function, may relinquish too much and leave oppressed peoples without any possible redress (see for example, Crenshaw, 1988). Consider Crenshaw's point: "The subordinate position of Blacks in this society makes it unlikely that African-Americans will realize gains through the kind of direct challenge to the legitimacy of American liberal ideology that is now being waged by Critical scholars" (ibid., 1385; see also West, 1989).

Third, CLS theorists question the Langdellian teaching method that had been solidified in the major law schools in the last quarter of the 19th century. Law schools, they argue, prepare the lawyer for hierarchy. The good lawyer is the "cheerful robot" who functions as an automaton.

Fourth, CLS, by the late 1980s early 1990s, was in search of theory. The movement appeared in the U.S. just at the time that major reexaminations of Marxian theory were taking place in social thought. CLS theorists in search of a socio-political theory to adopt in their critical examinations of law found, then, competing perspectives with unresolved contradictions. (See also Hunt, 1986b: 9; Hunt, 1993: 211–248). Hence, Weberian, Marxist, Anarchist, Foucaldian, Derridarian, Freudian, Lacanian, postmodern, and pluralistic theories have been variously applied (see, generally, Boyle, 1985). Central to much of their investigation is the work of Gramsci on hegemony (1971; for a good introduction and application to law, see Litowitz, 2000), and the critical social theory of the Frankfurt School (Habermas, 1975). What has brought CLS into sharp relief in the 1990s and the new millennium is the extensive internal critiques by fem-crits, crit-race theorists, lat-crits, Asian-American crits, queer-crits, "global critical race feminism," and emerging perspectives from LGBTQ and beyond. Critical legal studies has undergone qualitative internal differentiation, but has contributed, and continues to contribute profoundly to critical analysis in law.

Fifth, the CLS scholars generally discount instrumental versions of Marxism. They see law as being relatively autonomous (see Hunt, 1993: 165–169). Law is neither the direct servant of a power elite, nor is it totally independent of the dynamics of capitalism. Law is an arena where contradictions are faced and struggles fought. Here interpretive processes unfold. The propertied and non-propertied classes seek to establish their view of the world and give it legitimacy. Unique coalition of power-interests at particular historical junctures, however, are determinative of the form and substance of law.

Sixth, the CLS scholars' methodology in examining existing case law and opinions is one of "trashing." The more refined terminology is "deconstruction," which is based on Derrida (1992; see also Balkin, 1987). The approach consists of a critical examination of underlying, unstated assumptions that inhere in case opinion. These are made visible and traced to particular interest groups.

Seventh, and finally, the "crits," partially in response to criticism, particularly from "fem-crits" and "critical race theorists," began to offer more comprehensive visions of a more desirable form of society and law. Roberto Unger (1987) remained the most prominent visionary for the early Critical Legal Studies movement. However, little further systematic analysis has followed his profound visions of an "empowered democracy" and a "transformative politics." Feminist jurisprudence, which we will develop below and in the next chapter, has taken the lead in offering not only a philosophy of deconstruction but also visions for possible reconstruction. Critical Race Theory has provided new challenges for both the "crits" and "fem-crits" (Delgado and Stefancic, 2015). They have also introduced the notion of "intersections"; that is, race, gender, ethnicity, and class are often intersecting, and the combinations produce greater be it at times more subtle forms of discrimination. Thus, arising from Critical Race Theory have been variants such as "critical race feminism" (Wing, 1995). A "global critical race feminism" (Wing, 2000) was developed, which focuses on women of color in a global context. And currently, in the early days of the new millennium we see further splintering in the development of a Latina/o-critical ("LatCrit") group (Carrasco, 1996; Valdes, 1996), a queer-crit group (Stockdill, 1999), an Asian American jurisprudence (Matsuda, 1996) (see Delgado and Stefancic, 2015: 6), and a critical legal geography (Braverman, 2014).

Substantive Issues

In the following section we have chosen nine substantive issues that represent some of the CLS positions (for a good early overview see Kairys, 1992, 2007; see also the collection by Caudill and Stone, 1995). These have been chosen to illuminate the form of critique that had evolved. We are specifically focusing on developed works of the early years of CLS. It established the base from which other variations sprung. Accordingly, visiting this history is essential in establishing continuity and discontinuities that followed. This section is more a situated historical-ideological study much as if we were visiting ancient Rome or Athens in 100BC for a ten-year period examination of what views prevailed at the time. We thus summarize but do not try to extensively bring the selected fields up-to-date. We can learn what the basis of this movement was, and from there build on the present. (For a useful summary of the internal and external critiques, see Boyle, 1985; Harper, 1987; Hunt, 1993: 139–181, 211–226; Kramer, 1995; Kennedy, 1994, 1997, 1998; we shall briefly return to some highlights in the last section.)[21] Let us provide some of the examples from Kairys' (1992, 2007) edited book.

Law school as preparation for hierarchy. Several theorists have argued that law school prepares the student for their future position in hierarchical structures (see especially Kennedy, 1970, 1992, 1994; Litowitz, 2005; see also a feminist critique by Menkel-Meadow, 1988; Penther, 1999; for interviews of Kennedy, see Clark, 1994; Trever, 2015). Students, it is said, are taught such topics as contracts, torts, property, criminal law and civil procedure within the time frame of late 19th-century capitalism. They are taught that legal reasoning is a distinct and an objective method in arriving at a correct decision in law. They gradually internalize the distinct language of law. Students learn doctrines, rules, principles, procedures and reasoning techniques that remove them from the real world and other possible employment or outlook *(verstehen)*. Putting it another way, the "crits" claim that the ideology of the rule of law and formal rationality are internalized rather quickly by law students and become central to future practice (see especially the case studies by Granfield and Koenig, 1990a, 1990b).

In addition, a more subtle process entails disempowerment. Law school teaches "students that they are weak, lazy, incompetent, and insecure. And it also teaches them that if they are willing to accept dependency, large institutions will take care of them almost no matter what. The terms of the bargain are relatively clear" (Kennedy, 1992: 52). The educational orientation itself teaches the student to be dependent, to fit into the slots, to be a team player (Alberstein, 1999; Hooks, 1994; Guinier *et al.*, 1997). The anticipated financial rewards, particularly after the personal sacrifices and efforts made pursuing the law degree and passing the bar exam, assure this compliance.

Labor relation law. CLS theorists have looked at labor relations law and have argued that, ever since the passage of the National Labor Relations Act (NLRA) in 1935, workers have been coopted into believing that procedural justice resolves conflicts fairly in the workplace (Klare, 1978, 1992; see also Barenberg, 1993; Kennedy, 1997: 249–251). Thus, Klare has focused on three areas: how the U.S. courts have "deradicalized" the progressive intent behind the Wagner Act of 1935, how collective bargaining contracts favor management, and how grievance proceedings "cool out" the laborer.

The Wagner Act was potentially one of the most radical pieces of legislation in U.S. history. The higher courts, however, according to Klare, interpreted the act rather narrowly. Not only that, but in their interpretations (which then established precedents), the higher courts framed the acceptable ideology of worker-management interactions (acceptable labor relations) in a conservative way, heavily favoring management. The "free" labor contract, Klare argues, is but a tool for economically privileged classes to dictate the terms of work and to maintain domination. The courts' opinions had it that workers are purely sellers of labor with no interests in production.[22] Hence, the wage was central and the structure of the workplace was seen as out of bounds for union grievances. Such things as worker self-management, profit sharing, and fulfilling work roles were defined as non-arguable, non-litigable points (i.e., they were "management prerogatives"). The courts thereby restricted the vision of workers. Finally, the courts emphasized procedural justice over substantive justice. In other words, the courts reinforced the idea that conflicts with management could be fairly resolved by arbitration, that the machinery of grievance-submission and resolution could handle conflicts. Klare argues, however, that because of power differentials between the worker and management, equitable justice is not necessarily assured. Workers, because they work within the framework established by the courts' rulings, willingly and actively give up challenging oppressive practices at the workplace. Workers are led to believe that procedural justice translates into substantive justice.

Swidorski (1995) has also looked into U.S. Supreme Court decisions in labor law and finds that the dialectics of freedom and oppression plays itself out in this arena. He informs us: "The Court has fulfilled two principle functions since the New Deal era: (1) legitimating the transformation of property that has occurred in the modern capitalist economy; and (2) managing social conflict by ensuring formal, but limited, representation for select groups, primarily before the administrative agencies of the modern state" (ibid., 163; see also Barenberg, 1993).

Anti-discrimination law. This is an active topic that the CLS scholars have investigated (Freeman, 1992; for a different emphasis, see Crenshaw, 1988; see also Russell, 1998). Freeman, examining the court rulings on discrimination since the famous *Brown v.*

Board of Education case in 1954, has concluded that law has not eradicated race discrimination but "it has served more to rationalize the continued presence of racial discrimination in our society ..." (1992: 97; see also Freeman, 1988).

Underlying a court decision, whether a judge recognizes it or not, is an emphasis on either a *victim* or *perpetrator perspective.* The victim perspective sees racial discrimination in terms of particular *conditions*—lack of adequate employment, housing, education, health facilities, recreational, etc. The perpetrator perspective, on the other hand, assumes the problem is with "bad apples." The villain is the unscrupulous, racist bigot. In the perpetrator perspective, to effectively deal with discrimination the emphasis is in rooting out these villains. The overall political economic system is not seen as contributing to racist practices. Freeman argues that particularly since 1974, the courts have established case law, that effectively curtails the scrutiny and improvement of *conditions.* In other words, the "bad apples" approach has been central. Proof of intent to discriminate, not merely the showing of statistical disparities, must now be conclusively proven in law ("beyond a reasonable doubt"), a standard that is extremely difficult to attain. Strict standards of causation and responsibility also apply. Consider, too, the U.S Supreme Court decision *McCleskey v. Kemp* (1987) where, despite the well-documented empirical evidence (The Baldus Study) that African-American men are disproportionally sentenced to death for killing a white than compared to when the roles were reversed, the Court nevertheless said establishing just a pattern is not good enough: intent to discriminate must be proven ("perpetrator perspective"). All these effectively work against the improvement of *conditions,* which contribute to racial inequities. Consider, for example, the extreme differences on the average money spent per child for schooling or health facilities in poorer versus well-to-do communities. And the ideological message being created is that if failure occurs it is not because of the law or because of political economic institutions. Rather the fault lies with the individual. This has generally been referred to as the "blaming the victim" ideology.

For example, the U.S. Supreme Court, in *Johnson v. Transportation Agency* (1987), ruled that the standard to be applied in "reverse discrimination" cases[23] is a comparison of the firm's work force with that of the general area labor market. Thus, if the firm has 99% white and 1% black in a job category at a firm, but in the area labor force the requisite skills are divided say 60% and 40% respectively between white and black, then an affirmative action program instituted to equalize the firm's labor force is *not* deemed equivalent to "reverse discrimination." In other words, even though there was a significant number of qualified black workers with requisite skills (40%), only 1% were being employed at the firm. Thus, in this scenario, hiring policies that tried to correct the imbalances were not seen as reverse discrimination.

However, if the firm employs 99% white with 1% black, and the labor force *with the requisite skills* is of the same percentage (even though the labor *force generally* is 60% white and 40% black), then no affirmative action program will be held to be constitutional. But the Court says nothing about the economic *conditions* contributing to the development of these unequal skills, and merely leaves it to the "invisible hand" of capitalism to do its thing. This avoids, or glosses over the fundamental problem. Formalism again results in substantive injustice. (Later, U.S. Supreme court decisions backtracked and reasoned affirmative action was contrary to the "equal protection" clause of the 14th Amendment of the U.S. Constitution.)

Contract law. The law of contract has been central in the CLS scholars' critique (Gabel, 1977, 2018; Gabel and Feinman, 1992; Dalton, 1985; Ingram, 1995). In some rather dense but insightful analysis, Gabel has shown how, often, the jurist's thought is imprisoned within the functional requirements of capitalism itself. In other words, the very dynamics and structure of the economic sphere are often reproduced within the legal sphere.[24] What underlies case decisions and opinions, particularly as they deal with the contract, is a nexus between the requirements of capitalism and the form of contract. Contract law in the 18th century society, for example, was more focused on customary and traditional practices, where a person's *status* within given hierarchies determined their standing in the community. Decision making reflected and reinforced these relations in society. Contract law, as central to property law, simply reflected individuals' exchange of things, possessions, in the immediate here and now. Thus, litigation over agreements and promises were relatively few compared to subsequent eras. In disputes, the jury would apply community standards of fairness. However, in the 19th century, where laissez-faire capitalism was at its height, a person was assumed to be a calculating, profit-seeking egoist. Free competition meant that those who gained more property were in a more advantageous position in society. The moral and traditional bonds of the previous era were torn asunder. Legal decisions and opinions were but a "reflex" of the "logic" of the competitive marketplace. Citizens were seen as formally free and equal. This freedom extended to contracts made. The courts' function was to articulate an ideology that would assure that contracts made were kept. "Contractual freedom" was central. Contract law, however, did not include the scrutiny of the substantive fairness of the transactions. (Recall, again, Durkheim, Weber, and Marx on this point.)

This changed in the 20th century. With the development of monopolies, increased centralization and increased government intervention in the social order, law was concerned with balancing interests so as to assure the overall coordination of society toward some desirable end. Courts were guided by the ideals of coordination, integration, and the overall maintenance of stability in society. The state became active in intervening in the economy and society to balance various interests for the "general welfare." "Good faith" dealing in transactions was the standard that emerged. The courts decided what constitutes good faith by way of interest-balancing. Formalism was tempered by the incorporation of some standards of substantive justice. In sum, the courts reflected the changing conditions within the economic sphere. Principles, doctrines, standards, and case law—are all the product of the internal needs and the dynamics of the evolving political economic order.

Ingram's (1995: 141) analysis of contract law, agreeing with other "crits," starts with the assumption that capitalism "does not resolve social conflict," but tries to "suppress and contain it." He goes on to argue that, contrary to Weber's view that rationality underlies orderly contractual relations, it is rather moral considerations that lie beneath these undertakings (ibid., 152). Following Unger, and echoing perhaps Durkheim, Ingram argues that "equity in bargaining power" (ibid., 153) is required for contractual relations to be fair. Only in this way would substantive justice become a reality.

Criminal law. Criminal law is yet another area the CLS scholars have "trashed" (Kelman, 1981; Peller, 1993; Reiman, 2016). Kelman has argued that underlying criminal law doctrine and decision making are "interpretive constructions" that are often unconscious. An interpretive construction is the "process by which concrete situations are reduced to substantive legal controversies: it refers both to the way we construe a factual situation and to the way we frame the possible rules to handle the situation" (ibid., 592). Thus, in deciding a case, justices often "frame" the situation outside of law, as was also argued by legal realists.

Framing as a practice, in other words, is not a precise science. Often, in an actual court room proceeding, the prosecutor may "object" to the line of questioning from a defense counselor saying it is too broad, or sometimes abbreviated, "objection your Honor ... scope." The judge must exercise judgement to either sustain or overrule. For example, in establishing the facts, a time frame can be either broad or narrow. If the time frame is narrow this means the immediate, concrete act, say assault, is the focus. A broad frame may include the relationship of the specific act to other contributing factors in society. Hence, in the broad framework, many factors in combination may be seen to have additive effects as to behavioral developments such as crime. Likewise, "intent" might be construed narrowly or broadly. So, too, in situating the defendant within the framework of society, one can use a narrow or broad frame. That is, the defendant or the act could be placed in context or taken out of an overall context.[12] Thus, specifying the appropriate space and time dimension is critical to how an infraction may appear.

In each of the above situations, the justice is framing time, intent, the defendant and the act either more narrowly or broadly in an unconscious or semi-conscious way. The point is, if one frames these factors broadly (focusing, for a moment, on the crimes of those from the lower socio-economic class), then, more "understandability" results, and hence less legal culpability can be construed. In other words, more excusability attaches as the frames expand, and less excusability as the frames narrow. More understandability is often connected with greater plausibility and hence is connected with excusability, or lowering the attributable degree of intent involved. Of course, this pushed to its logical conclusion, confronts the issue of the wherewithal of responsibility, which classical law and critical thought all too often avoided.[13]

As we progress upward in the class structure (from the lower to the higher), frames applied become broader. Consider a firm that is accused of polluting the environment. Lawyers bring in a mountain of evidence for allowing the continued pollution (jobs, producing scarce and needed material, taxes paid, helping the community, etc.), in short benefiting the majority. In the use of injunction proceedings law only asks "why is it not the case that you should be stopped in doing what you are doing?" Imagine asking this of a poor person who has just stolen some food in a store for their family. And the resolution in law, a "consent decree," would simply allow the culprit to agree to cease doing what they are doing, but not acknowledging they were doing what they were accused of. Double talk?

Conversely, as we go downward, frames applied become more narrowly construed, i.e., strict reliance on the act (*actus reas*) and specific intent (*mens rea*) of the moment. Hence, the result: greater excusability in an upward direction; and, conversely, less excusability and more culpability as we go downward. Some upper-class subjects, then, are "beyond incrimination" (Kennedy, 1976). Note, too, the constitutive function of law at play: created is a population to be policed, and the policed population comes to represent the dangerous classes, which provides justification for given practices of legal enforcement such as profiling (Henry and Milovanovic, 1999; Henry and Milovanovic, 2020). This becomes a social reality of crime (Quinney, 1970).

Reiman's (2016) more openly Marxist critique of criminal justice explains how distinctions in law—such as civil versus criminal law—are constructs favoring the well-to-do. As he (ibid., 129) tells us, "there is considerable overlap in the content of criminal and civil law; criminal acts, such as theft or battery, can also be causes of civil action. But this overlay is largely asymmetrical: virtually any criminal act can be a cause of civil action, but only some civil causes are subject to criminal prosecution."

Along the same directions, Peller (1993) has indicated how an emphasis on procedural law, as opposed to substantive law in criminal proceedings, has undermined the effectiveness of those attempting to deal with race biases in law. We have previously seen this in Chapter 4 with Weber's analysis of the difference between formal and substantive rationality. Durkheim (see Chapter 3), too, had indicated this form of "repressive formalism."

To counter discriminatory practice, Russell (1998: 25) reviewing the 350-year history of slave codes, has offered a "fairness principle" by which our criminal justice system can be judged. This includes, at a minimum:

(1) Criminal penalties apply to everyone equally, regardless of the race of the *offender*.

(2) Criminal penalties apply to everyone equally, regardless of the race of the *victim*.

(3) The race of the offender is not relevant in determining whether his actions constitute a crime. The offender's actions would have been considered criminal, even if the person were another race.

(4) The race of the victim is not relevant in determining whether the offenders' action constitutes a crime.

(5) The offender's race ("degree of Blackness") is not used to determine punishment.

(6) Checks and balances should be included that mitigate against racial bias within the legal system.

Tort law. The area of "tort" law has been investigated by Abel (1982) and Brion (1995). A tort can be defined as a harm done by one person to another, where law gives a remedy. For Abel, the evolving notion of a tort is intimately connected with the rise of capitalism. Although formalism includes as an ideal, that individuals harmed in society, regardless of their standing in the class structure, should have available an equal remedy, in practice, substantively, gross inequality exists.

First, Abel notes that the blue-collar as opposed to the white-collar worker is subject to qualitatively and quantitatively different kinds of risks, harms and illnesses, both at the workplace and within residential areas. Inequality in the risk of harm is a function of differences in socio-economic standing (see also Beck, 1992; Curran, 2016; O'Malley, 2016). Consider, for example, the unskilled worker living next to a polluting company, as compared to the highly paid technician who lives in a well-to-do area away from the pollution. Second, race, class, ethnicity, and gender will affect whether and to what extent the injured party will pursue an injury claim. In other words, certain groups, perhaps based on experience with the courts, have given up the court as an avenue of redress. Third, the law discriminates as to the remedies available. Although workers' compensation pays for some of the injuries of the blue-collar worker, many other individuals—women, children, the elderly, ethnic minorities, the poor—have difficulty in successful tort recovery. Although victims of harm, including violent crime, they have great difficulty recovering for damages.[14]

In sum, not only are there vast differences in risk, but also in the remedies available to those harmed. The law simply situates all in a position of formal equality both as to risk and as to remedy available. The majesty of formal rationality, it is claimed, hides the repressive, formalistic dimensions.

Abel's recommendation to overcome this state of affairs, his "socialist approach to risk," would hinge on two guiding ideals (1982). First, he offers the ideal of the equalization of risk. That is, all should share equally in the risk of potential harm. Second, he claims, we should empower each person with the knowledge and some real control concerning the risk to which they will be exposed. For these two ideals to be possible, he argues, capitalism must be replaced by decentralized, democratic socialism.

Brion's (1991, 1995) analysis of tort law employs chaos theory (see also Chapter 11). Brion posits decision making based on two processes: first is *heresy*, by which he means the forces of pluralism playing out their effects. The second process he calls *heritage*, by which he means the pressures of *stare decisis* (decision making based on precedents set in law). Conflict takes place between these two poles in decision making. Oscillation continues until one pole gains dominance in the decision. Thus, chance plays a large factor in any particular decision. Schulman (1997) has taken this same approach in a more detailed analysis, by applying the various "attractors" that are said to exist in chaos theory. She shows how the oscillation between the two poles produces a far-from-equilibrium state within which a very slight perturbation may throw it in support of one or the other of the poles. Things are therefore somewhat indeterminate.

Women's subordination. The role of law in women's subordination has become increasingly central in the CLS "trashing." One prominent argument made by the CLS scholars is that law has separated the sphere of "men's work" from "women's work"

(Taub and Schneider, 1992). "[W]omen have been consigned to a private realm to carry on their primary responsibilities, i.e., bearing and rearing children, and providing men with a refuge from the pressures of the capitalist world" ibid., 118). Male dominance has been given legitimacy in legal decisions. For example, well known statistics show that in the last 30 or 40 years, females, given the same position as males, a statistically significant gender gap still exists. In the private sphere, tort law has not provided sufficient remedies for women abused, physically and/or psychologically, by their spouses. We should add that only recently has a substantial body of literature developed on a feminist jurisprudence that goes beyond the earlier critiques. We shall return to this in the next chapter.

The areas of gay rights (Colker, 1995), same-sexed marriage (Hunter, 1995), sexual preferences, and sexual freedom (Fineman, 2000; Cornell, 1998) had, in the late 80s and 90s become central issues in Critical Legal Studies and particularly with its offspring. Cornell (1998), for example, has argued that family law should be rewritten to reflect three ideas: (1) "regulation of the family should protect all lovers who choose to register in civil marriage"; (2) "the government must provide a structure for custodial responsibility for children" (see also Davis and Williams, 2000). In other words, if one partner does not wish to become a parent, they could still choose to stay married to the partner and choose not to have full responsibility for the child, but allow the partner to choose someone else to take the full custodial responsibility (ibid., 125). And (3), the government should provide for health care for children (ibid., 128). That is, the government should provide "some kind of publicly funded child-care as part of parental entitlement" (ibid.). According to Cornell, these provisions would provide (1) sexual freedom, and (2) stability in raising children.

Judges' decision making. Finally, crits have theorized how judges go about making their decisions. We provide a brief summary of Duncan Kennedy's (1997) much cited and discussed book, *A Critique* of *Adjudication (fin de siecle).* A special issue of *Cardoza Law Review* (volume 22, 2001) was devoted to discussion of his book. Kennedy's self-professed perspective is from a "leftist and a modernist/postmodernist point of view" (ibid., 207). In this book, Kennedy presents the role of ideology in judges' decision making. Do judges simply vote their political and ideological leanings? If they are conservative or liberal, do they blindly decide in this direction? However, he rejects the Marxist notion that they are merely acting in "false consciousness," the notion that judges are simply tools of elites, and the idea that judges always impose their particular ideological positions in law. Rather, judges act in "bad faith" and "denial." The former concept he draws from the phenomenologist Jean Paul Sartre's (1980) work, the latter from psychoanalyst Anna Freud's (1992) analysis of the unconscious and its "defense mechanisms."

To begin with, a judge is faced with gaps, conflicts and ambiguities which they must resolve by rendering a legal decision. A number of constraints limit the judge's ability to simply act out their political leanings.

For the first constraint, the judge may find themselves bound by the law in either of two ways. The judge could be exposed to a given set of facts and posed with two contradictory stories explaining them. If alternative interpretations of what rule to apply were not relevant, the judge might "unselfconsciously" apply the appropriate rule in the method of deductive logic. Another situation could be where the facts are known but the interpretation of the rule is in question. The judge may dislike the outcome that will result if they apply a particular rule, tries as hard as they can to develop an alternative interpretation, fails to do so, and so applies the given distasteful rule, once again in deductive fashion (ibid., 161). The duty of "fidelity" to the facts in hand constrain the judge; they do "what the law requires."

In the second constraint, the judges "are also constrained by the reactions they anticipate from their audience" (ibid.). Judges want to look like they are following the rule-of-law. They are constrained by "internal" factors (e.g., the judge looks for legal arguments that are personally acceptable) and "external" factors (e.g., the judge looks for arguments that will appear good to the audience, their "interpretive community") (ibid., 161).

Given, then, ambiguities, conflicts, and gaps in a particular case, how is a judge to decide? Kennedy argues that there are three types of judges:

(1) The "constrained activist judge." This judge attempts to develop legal interpretations that fit their activist agenda, but has no intention of going against the law. After numerous attempts to devise alternatives (in either the liberal or conservative direction), they succumb to writing an opinion that is formalistic (guided by deductive logic) and argue that the law requires this outcome;

(2) The "difference-splitting judge." This judge spends much time figuring out what the two opposing positions may be and chooses the middle position. Between the liberal and conservative there lies a "moderate" position towards which they strive;

(3) The "bipolar judge." This judge alternates between working hard in either the liberal or conservative direction. In some cases, they work hard to develop a liberal ruling (the "constrained activist"); in others, a conservative. However, they are always vigilante to be sure, that in the long run, decisions even themselves out. They make a career of difference splitting; they alternate between the two ideologies over their career and strive for the appearance of objectivity and neutrality.

How do the judges actually proceed? For Kennedy (ibid., 191), their activity in law finding must be described as "half-conscious." They are neither fully conscious nor fully unconscious of their decision making. They also act in "denial" and "bad faith." For Kennedy (ibid., 192), the "big secret" the judges collectively maintain is that what they do limits possibilities of real impartiality and neutrality. But, at the more unconscious level, this contributes to quite a bit of cognitive dissonance: it is disturbing and unsettling. This "secret" of seemingly abiding by the law while at the same time knowing that law finding is otherwise, can only be maintained by the unconscious defense mechanism of "denial" that Anna Freud developed. As Kennedy (ibid., 193) says, "the motive for denial is to prevent or get rid of this anxiety." And thus, in their insistence that they are non-ideological, they are acting in "bad faith." The constrained activist, difference splitter and bipolar judge who experience cognitive dissonance and role conflict make use of denial in order to maintain the appearance of neutrality in law finding and to be able to reconcile their various, often distasteful decisions to themselves. They act in bad faith because, with conscious reflection, they know exactly what is taking place.

Kennedy (ibid., 203) also argues that not all judges fall within the three types he presents. Some have nothing to deny. Apparently, they entertain the facts of the case, establish the appropriate rule, and follow deductive reasoning to its logical conclusion.[15]

In sum, judges are neither controlled by elites, nor are they entirely independent, nor do they simply apply their political/ideological position in all cases. More often, they are in denial and act in bad faith.

CLS and Deconstruction

Earlier we had said that the "crits" offered a "trashing" technique. A more refined terminology situates it in the framework of *deconstruction,* which is based on the inspirational but rather dense (almost inaccessible) works of Jacques Derrida (1992, 1997).[16] Balkin, on the other hand, has probably given the most accessible rendition of Derrida's thoughts on law. He develops this exposition in his article entitled "Deconstructive Practice and Legal Theory" (1987; see also 1998a, 1998b). There are three reasons, he tells us, to be interested in the deconstructive technique in law. First, it provides a methodology for in-depth critiquing of legal doctrines. Second, deconstruction can illuminate how legal arguments disguise ideological positions. And third, it offers a new method of interpretation of legal texts (Balkin, 1987: 744).

Two particular practices are embedded in the deconstruction practice: the reversal of hierarchies, and the liberation of the legal text from the original author.

The notion of reversal of hierarchies has been a cornerstone in the deconstruction approach (see Balkin, 1998b: 2–4). Any value position, it is argued, takes on its particular valuation in opposition to some other value: one becomes dominant, the other repressed. In his language, this brings out the "metaphysics of presence." What this means is that in every opposition one value dominates and is privileged as presence; the other is repressed and is rendered an absence. Consider the dominance of the male's voice, for example, over the female's. Consider, too, statements of good, which always imply the bad; sanity, which always implies insanity, etc. See also Arrigo and Williams's (1999: 400) notion of receiving treatment and refusing treatment in prison. Activating one course always implies the possibility of the other. Similarly, with competence to be executed and incompetence to be executed (ibid., 407–408). Each, however, implies a location in a hierarchy where one is privileged. These hierarchies are basic to all phenomena. A text, however, can always be turned on its head (reversal of hierarchies) to illuminate this opposition, and to reveal how the two are, at core, interdependent (Balkin, 1987: 746–751).

This notion of a fundamental interdependence is further explained by Derrida's notion of différance (with an "a") (see Balkin, 1998b: 4–9). This neologism implies both to differ and to defer. In any hierarchy (say of two terms where one is seemingly superior to the other), the two terms are different from each other, each defers to the other in the sense of implying the other term, and each of the two terms defers to the other in terms of its dependence on the other.

Différance also implies the *trace*. Within each term of a hierarchy, one term contains the hidden trace of the other. This is what maintains a relation between the two terms. Hence, in deconstructive strategies, one must start with the idea that any term (presence) always implies a hidden one (absence); both are essential to any meaning of each. The *trace* is that part that exists in each and maintains the relation. In many ways, it is the "glue." For those practicing deconstruction, the challenge is to identify the absent term which maintains the term that is felt as present. Thus, the history of ideas can be seen as the privileging of one term over another, which nevertheless exists in relation to it. The privileging of male discourse, for example, always comes at the cost of de-privileging female discourse. A central tenet for later fem-crits was advocating "counter-narratives" that resurrected denied voices.

To take this argument one step further, every stage of human development has a core of privileged terms (presence) and a periphery of deprivileged terms (e.g., well-to-do, poor; male, female; white, black). Thus, the strategy of deconstructive reversal attempts to make visible the hidden, the deprivileged term.[17] As Balkin has said:

> [a]ny social theory must emphasize some human values over others. Such categorizing necessarily involves a privileging, which in turn can be deconstructed. But the goal of deconstruction is not the destruction of all possible social visions. By recalling the elements of human life relegated to the margin in a given social theory, deconstructive readings challenge us to *remake* the dominant conceptions of our society (ibid., 763; emphasis added).

The second major contribution of deconstruction is the idea of the "free play of the text." Any constructed text, including a legal decision or legal doctrine, is "liberated" once it is constructed. A text always says more than is intended. In other words, once constructed, the text takes a life of its own. Consider, for example, an ongoing debate in law concerning the "founding fathers'" *intent* in the language of the Constitution. Conservatives claim it can be clearly spelled out through consulting the original philosophical statements of its founding authors. Liberals and radicals, however, claim that the intent can never be reconstructed, particularly in conditions over 200 years later. The meaning of the text for those making use of deconstructive strategies, is always situated historically. It means something different in different contexts. This is the idea of "iterability." The search for original meaning, much like peeling the layers of an onion to find its core, is a search for foundations for interpretations that in actuality do not exist.

Of course, all this leads to one of the central dilemmas that the "crits" have been facing since the turn of the 1990s. This is the dilemma of *foundational positions.* In other words, *if* indeed some truth claim can be supported by some foundational position (i.e., some ethical principle, some reliance on conclusions drawn from data, or some body of knowledge that has assumed the character of conventional wisdom), but nevertheless, a position which can be deconstructed by some other foundational position, and this position in turn can be deconstructed by yet another position, *ad infinitum,* then there is no such thing as some cross-cultural and historical position which can substantiate for all time any claim to "truth" (the latter called "anti-foundationalism"). And this is the dilemma. Stanley Fish has been most persuasive, and a thorn in the side of the CLS Movement with this critique (see Fish, 1980, 1984; Rosenfeld, 1991: 170–179). In other words, the dilemma is of profound consequence: on the one hand, one conclusion might be "why bother about anything, all is relevant and relative," a rather conservative stance, lending itself to passivity and nihilism; on the other, for political activists, what possibly can an adequate support for their position be? What foundational position can support their grievances? This dilemma is difficult to overcome. Spivak (2008) in a much-cited article, for example, has asked from what position, from where can the subaltern speak?

Feminist and other identity-groups are grappling with this question in constructing an alternative jurisprudence, and constantly pursue ways of maintaining a deconstructive strategy without falling into the trappings of nihilism or the conservative agenda. We shall return to this in the next chapter, but first we want to examine Roberto Unger's reconstructive agenda.

CLS and Reconstruction

In this final section, we would like to present some key recommendations in the sociology of law made by Roberto Unger, one of the most respected members of the CLS movement. This highlights the situated historical-ideological understanding of major thought on a subject during a specific historical time period. Unger has been a prolific writer in the early years of the CLS movement (Unger, 1975, 1976, 1984, 1986, 1987). A substantial discussion and critique of his analysis has evolved.[18] Here we will focus on his books, *The Critical Legal Studies Movement* (1986, 2015) and *False Necessity* (1987), where he lays out his reconstructive agenda that includes a call for an "empowered democracy" and the development of "transformative politics."

But first a few words on a preceding text, *Passion* (1984), where he offers us an ethical theory that underlies his reconstructive strategies. By passion he means all "non-instrumental" dealings with other people. He situates the individual in society as a person with strivings, despairs, weaknesses, faith, hope, love and desires. The basic contradiction that they face is twofold. First, the recognition that one needs the other while at the same time fearing the other. Second, the constraints of conformity and the longing for transcendence. The development of the self and the potential for solidarity revolves around this double dialectic (see also Gabel, 2018).

In *The Critical Legal Studies Movement,* first presented at the Sixth Annual Conference of Critical Legal Studies in 1982, and in his more developed *False Necessity*

(1987), Unger presents several change strategies for a transformative politics. He characterizes his philosophy as "super liberalism." He advocates the development of an "empowered democracy." As far back as 1975, Unger was attempting to develop a non-Marxist alternative in the sociology of law.

His change strategy, what he calls "transformative activity," would entail a "deviationist doctrine." Since society tends toward stagnant, non-responsive hierarchies (i.e., insensitive bureaucracies), the solution, for Unger, is to prevent their ossification. That is to say, he is concerned with ways of preventing a social order from becoming resistant to change. This can come about, he claims, if certain "destabilizing rights" are granted which, taken together, will disrupt any ossifying tendencies while assuring the protection of the individual's rights in society. These rights both support deconstructive challenges as well as provide economic and political resources for well-being and reconstructive practices. Stability, in other words, will be constantly established anew, taking into consideration new factors or conditions as they develop in a society.

To this end, he offers us four core rights. First, "immunity rights" would assure the individual zones of privacy much like existing civil liberties. Second, "destabilization rights" would give the individuals the right to challenge developing hierarchies (e.g., later developed "whistleblowing" statutes). These rights would be guaranteed by (a) the present form of the judiciary and (b) a separate broadly based public agency established for their protection. Third, "market rights" would be derived from his two economic principles: (a) a rotating capital fund would be made available to teams of workers for temporary use; and (b) the low interest charged would be used for governmental administration and for encouraging "risk-oriented or socially responsive investment" (ibid., 35). And fourth, "solidarity rights" would develop out of a two-stage career. Standards such as "good faith loyalty or responsibility" would be established with a degree of openness. Subsequent refinements would come about when individuals themselves in practice resolve conflicts in society (ibid., 40). Unger does not give us substantial details on how this is to occur. Perhaps this anticipated later developments of restorative justice.

Ideally, his deviationist doctrine and his transformative activity would undermine hierarchical, non-responsive structures in society. A gradual movement toward a responsive, participatory democratic and humane society would result. The state, in this view, is necessary and inevitable. It must, however, be made responsive and held accountable.

Criticism of CLS: Setting the Seeds for the New

The CLS movement, as we saw, was very active during the 70s to late 1980s. In the mid- to latter part of the 1980s it began to be increasingly criticized, while the same critics acknowledged the important groundwork that had been established by its founders. These criticisms include: intersectional analysis was not sufficiently addressed as the new basis of understanding overt and more covert forms of disenfranchisement;

minority scholars were infrequently referenced; that the early developers were white males, with fewer female as well as people of colors' voice being heard; giving up the pursuit of rights gives up too much since it is one of the few concrete weapons available for social change; there was a plethora of deconstruction talk but little outside of Unger's work offered new possibilities; that no new possible normative system was suggested as a replacement to the said repressive order; that false consciousness assumes a privileged location from which to pass judgement, and who holds that position if it exists at all?; that little critical self-analysis by movement members were articulated; that some progressive change through law does take place and should be welcomed; the same research paradigm employed by liberal legalists was being employed with no alternative suggested; indeterminacy is not as all-encompassing as assumed; minimal attempts at outreach to engage the non-converted; and comprehensive theories of law and their respective connectedness with variously inflicted harms were not fully developed even with the move toward embracing postmodernism and other emergent philosophies of the 1990s (see Munger and Seron, 1984; William, 1987, 1991; Matsuda, 1987; Delgado, 1987; West, 1988; Cornel, 1988; MacKinnon, 1989; Price, 1989; Altman, 1990; Whitehead, 1999; Russell, 1994; Stewart, 2019; Trever *et al.*, 2015).

Although on its surface seemingly insurmountable challenges, CLS movement members nevertheless had the courage to challenge hierarchies and dominant institutions, and the legal apparatus that was its support. Theirs was a useful beginning. The legacy of the critical spirit and plethora of insight remain and has had major influences in progressive legal thought.

Summary

The CLS movement, picking up from, but going beyond the legal realists in scope, emphasis and vehemence of attack, was in the center of a storm in the development of a sociology of law. Its legacy continues to have an impact in contemporary critical legal scholarship.

Although some of the crits sought guidance from Marx, others did not. Scholars were rather eclectic in their approach particularly in the 90s. The fourth stage of the CLS movement, one in which the search for theory and more differentiated perspectives which was to become dominant, was a creative period for the development of a sociology of law. By the mid-1980s, much external and internal critique had already taken place setting the seeds for the new.

In the 1990s, CLS scholars began to develop a unified approach in the sociology of law by drawing primarily from the critical thoughts of the Frankfurt School, especially focusing on the whole question of legitimation. The work of Gramsci and his notion of hegemony was critical. The works of Max Weber and Karl Marx continue to exert an influence on the critical thought being developed. A foray into linguistics and semiotics led to some valuable insights. And most notably, "crits" turned their attention specifically to the question of race and gender and their intersections with class, sexual preference, ethnicity, and legal repression. However, new perspectives began to emerge, a movement that has continued into the 21st Century. The next chapter will develop some of the key writings.

CLS scholars have concentrated on the facilitative, repressive and ideological functions of law. The relationship between the legal order and fulfillment of social values is central in their critique of what is and in their projection of what could be. Although most CLS scholars agree that the current legal form is repressive *(repressive formalism)*, there is disagreement as to the purpose, scope and desirable form of law in a more humane society. Even the vision of the "good" society is unclear. Nevertheless, although quite controversial, the CLS movement was and continues to be on the cutting edge in the development of the sociology of law in the United States. The Trojan Horse has made major inroads into the legal Bastion.

Review Questions

1. Should more sociological information be allowed to be introduced in trial proceedings? Why? Why not? Perhaps separate the class into those who say "yes" and those who say "no." Summarize each student's position on the board under the appropriate heading. Follow with class discussion.

2. Roscoe Pound advocated a "social engineering" model in law. Assess its viability and usefulness. Perhaps half the class argue for social engineering, the other the benefits of exclusive reliance on formal rationality and the Langdellian methodology.

3. Legal realists have brought up the notions of "rule-skepticism" and "fact-skepticism. Explain each. Then, provide an example of each not already used in the book.

4. If, as Duncan Kennedy (and Litowitz) argues, law schools are preparation for hierarchy, how would a student with an activist agenda navigate the terrain? Compliance first, and when employed, showing who you "really are?" Or is it too late then? How, following Kennedy, would you endure the experience?

5. If law allowed greater "scope" in criminal trials, both time and space, would this substantially contribute to more equitable substantive justice practices? Explain.

6. The victim and perpetrator perspectives are two different foci in confronting systematic racism and other biases. What are the advantages of looking at "conditions" associated with the victim perspective? And how far or extensive do we search? Should there be limits even with the expansion of allowable "conditions?"

7. The U.S. Supreme Court decision in *McCleskey* (1987) has often been discussed. If the justices had accepted the Baldus study that was introduced to show disproportional death sentences of African Americans compared to their white counterparts charged with murder, how might it have impacted (a) subsequent law practices, since it establishes precedents, and (2) correcting systematic racism?

8. Kennedy discusses judge's decision making. How relevant is this when Supreme Court Justices are in the process of being picked? Is their previous record sufficient

in determining what kind of justice they would be?

9. Roberto Unger has offered a reconstruction agenda that builds on previous deconstruction. Consider each of the four suggestions he makes. How, together, would more just practices develop? And, how would a more "intersectional" analysis qualify each of his points?

10. CLS proponents advocate deconstruction and "trashing" of legal institutions while offering few alternatives. Can one do one without the other? Are they connected? Explain your position.

Endnotes

1. A recent google search witnessed 963,000,0000 results on March 4, 2021.

2. My own experience at attending the 1982 conference in Boston, indicated an amazing display of energy, excitement, hope, and talk of change. Lively discussions extended to every sector of the building. When Duncan Kennedy and other key founding figures made their appearance it generated the excitement of a rock star. Meeting rooms filled to the brim, with audiences spilling out into the hallways, hoping to hear some inspirational words from their idols. Animated discussions existed everywhere. Discussions on the possibilities of change permeated the whole meeting. It felt like we were on the cusp of fundamental change. It was hard not to be swept up in the excitement.

3. For a bibliography of publications of the formative years, see Kennedy and Klare, 1984.

4. See interview of Duncan Kennedy (Clark, 1994; Trever, 2015). For further personal recollections of the movement and Duncan Kennedy, see Schlegal (1984), Goodrich, (2001c).

5. Among the most prominent early crits were Roberto Unger, Robert Gordon, Morton Horwitz, Duncan Kennedy, Katherine MacKinnon, and Peter Gabel.

6. This was considered the key collection of works by CLS at the time. It has expanded to over 700 pages in the third edition.

7. For a useful research guide to critical legal studies, see Allison (2021) at Harvard School Library.

8. Matthew Kramer, in *Critical Theory and the Challenge of Feminism* (1995), perhaps offers one of the more comprehensive critiques of critical legal theory. He organizes his critique around five issues: contradictions, contingency, patterning, perspective, and ideology. He points out the various paradoxes at play in critical legal theory, and thus paves the way for constructive change.

9. In Marxian terms, the focus was on the sphere of circulation where commodity-exchange ruled rather than on the sphere of production where structures and institutions of formal capitalist enterprises ruled.

10. Here proponents argued that the "equal protection clause" of the U.S. Constitution does not allow preferential treatment regardless of how noble the supporting ideals. In other words, substantial rational principles need not apply.

11. See also Chapter 5 and Pashukanis' thesis, that there is a homology of the commodity and legal form.

12. Delgado (1985), working within a broadened view advocates a new defense, in addition to the traditional "diminished capacity" or "duress" that recognizes that "unremitting, long-term exposure to situations of threats, stress, and neglect indelibly marks the minds and bodies of those exposed," which he calls "socioeconomic deprivation" (ibid., 9, 90). "The jury would be instructed as they are in negligence cases in some jurisdictions, to determine the proportion of individual and societal fault" (ibid., 89). The defense would be allowed to bring up failing social institutions that are claimed to contribute to the criminal offense.

13. Consider the Hopi Indian of Southwest America. In their world view and language, everything is interconnected. Attributing a distinct and separate agent that "causes" phenomena is alien (see Chapter 11).

14. Note also how business has responded with the proliferation of "risk management" and "legal risk management" programs (see for example, Whalley and Guzelian, 2016).

15. Of course, devising a scientific study establishing the percentage of judges within each category, and to more fully quantify denial and bad faith would take some imaginative methodology, but a challenge for critical legal scholars to pursue.

16. See, also, Cornell *et al.*, 1992; Balkin, 1987; 1998a, 1992b; Landau, 1993; Arrigo, 2000; Goodrich, 2001; see also the special issue of the *Cardozo Law Review* devoted to deconstruction and law, December, 1991; for a general introduction to Derrida, see Culler, 1981; for an accessible introduction, Reynolds, 2021; for an illuminating example of an application to legally defined rape, see Scheppele, 1987; for a critical reading, see Lloyd, 2017.

17. Consider the parody by Randal (2002), *The Wind Done Gone: A Novel*, which reverses the privileged terms (plantation owners) and deprivileged terms (black slave workers) found in *Gone With the Wind*.

18. See particularly, Cornell, 1985; Boyle, 1985; Milovanovic, 1988c, 1992a: 243–256; 1997: 195–209; Henry and Milovanovic, 1996: 235–241.

7

Critical Approaches in Law

Spawnings, Second Wave

Introduction

If CLS can be considered first wave critical law theorizing, notwithstanding sociological jurisprudence and legal realism, then the second wave begins with the solidification of feminist and critical race theory in law in the mid-1980s to early 1990s. Whether considered off springs or spawnings of CLS or results of their own internal development, the CLS movement had an impact on their development, if for no other reason polemical differences that sharpened the contours of their respective fields. In this chapter we want to first provide a summary of the evolution of feminist jurisprudence. Perhaps two wings can be established. The liberal feminists remain in the jurisprudence tradition of legal dogmatism (Chapter 1) and will be the topic in the first section of the chapter. The "fem-crits," Critical Race Theorists (CRT, race-crits), along with the further differentiations in the field (Queer-crits, Lat-crits, Asian-crits, Tribal-crits, etc.) engaged cross-disciplinary sources as well as commenting on traditional jurisprudential practices, bringing this initiative closer to the discipline of the sociology of law. The second section of the chapter will delve into CRT a bit deeper. The final section will explicate the various further developments many of which reached take-off in the 1990s, with continuous engagement with CLS.

Feminist Jurisprudence

Introduction

Feminist jurisprudence is not a homogeneous field. Feminist legal theory, or alternatively, feminist jurisprudence, having sources in the 1960s, took considerable shape in the late 1980s in the U.S.[1] Some of this movement was aided by greater amounts of women entering and graduating from law school in the 1970s and 80s. Some had its basis or was brought into sharper relief with its engagement with Critical Legal Studies movement, but much lies outside of this tradition, especially liberal feminist of the jurisprudence school and in fact developed as a critical response to it.[2] The more critical wing of feminist jurisprudence, "fem-crits" was particularly critically engaged with the "crits" in the mid to late 80s. "Feminists believe that history was written from a male point of view and does not reflect women's role in making history and society. Male-written history has created a bias in the concepts of human nature, gender potential, and social arrangements. The language, logic, and structure of the law are male created and reinforce male values" (*Feminist Jurisprudence*, 2021: 1).

This movement fundamentally challenged some key assumptions in conventional legal theory, as well as some conventional wisdom within Critical Legal Studies. Consider, for example, Goldfarb's point: "Many feminists have identified patriarchy as an ideology more threatening to their lives than legal ideology, and have directed their efforts at undermining the former even through the use of the latter" (1992: 704). Traditional liberal feminist remained within the jurisprudence tradition (see Chapter 1) and advocated equality with men. The "fem-crits," on the other hand, ventured outside legal dogmatics and were heavily influenced by feminist work in philosophy, psychoanalysis, semiotics, history, anthropology, postmodernism, literary criticism, and political theory (see Menkel-Meadow, 1988; West, 2018). But, more basically, they drew heavily from experiences of women (West *et al.*, 2019; Disch and Hawkesworth, 2016).

Three key years for establishing a critical mass within the CLS movement were 1985, 1987, and 1992. They added substantial momentum in the development of various versions of feminist jurisprudence. In 1985 the Annual Meeting of Critical Legal Studies had as its theme feminism and law. In 1987, the theme was racism and law. And in the 1992 Annual Conference, the CLS constituency was made up of several sponsors (other sponsors being race theorists and feminist theorists). The movement's further development in the 1990s has led to far ranging challenges to contemporary law and legal institutions (see also Goldfarb, 1992; West, 2018). In a later chapter on the postmodern perspective, we shall have further occasion to develop yet another feminist approach in law, one based on the works of Jacques Lacan, as well some post postmodern developments.

Journals and law reviews on feminist jurisprudence have proliferated.[3] Useful reference guides have also been published (see Disch and Hawkesworth, 2021; West and Grant, 2019; *Feminist Jurisprudence*, 2021; *Feminist Legal Research*, 2021).

Perspectives in Feminist Jurisprudence

The literature has conceptualized various "camps," sometimes referred to as "schools," or perspectives in feminist jurisprudence. These are more generally seen as paradigms which offer core assumptions from which particular views spring. Often, in the literature, theorists lose sight of these core assumptions and they remain uncritically examined by respective advocates. An earlier model was presented by Jaggar (1983) which includes liberal, radical, Marxist, and socialist feminism. Others have called for seven foci: liberal, radical, socialist and Marxist, care, poststructuralist, decolonial, and performative feminism (McAfee and Howard, 2018).

Consolidating from the literature, a useful conceptualization could include liberal, radical, Marxist, socialist, postmodernist, and post postmodernists. Liberal feminist in law argue that women are just as rational as men and advocate formal equality. Radicals see the core issue with power and domination. Law reflects men's views. Marxists focus on the relations found in capitalism. Capital logic drives class relations and female subordination is a reflection of the logic of ownership of property. Socialist draw from both radical and Marxists to insist domination existed prior to capital relations, and thus both domination and class relations should be studied as an integral model in studying law. Postmodernists take issue with the previous camps and question the core assumption developed from the Enlightenment. They argue for the emergent nature of agency, its situational, contextual, relational, and constructed expression, and thus no essentialist position can be articulated. Post postmodernist, a term for a number of emerging approaches at the turn of the 21st Century, references posthumanism, new materialism, sociomaterialism, digimodernism, among the more developed[4] (we shall return to the postmodernist and post postmodernist in Chapter 11 and 12).

Another more basic split has been articulated by Robin West (2018), feminist jurisprudence and feminist legal theory. Feminist jurisprudence is a broad category, perhaps the umbrella terms, for scholarship applicable to gender inequality. The more dominant form is jurisprudence analysis (see Chapter 1), or legal dogmatics. Feminist legal theory, on the other hand, is "an attempt to fashion a broad-based theoretical account of the relationship of law in liberal legal regimes to women's subordination, patriarchy, and gender and sexual inequality ..." (West, 980–981). This direction of thought can be associated with developing a sociology of law, although adherents expanded to other disciplines. For West, feminist legal theory was a development of the 1970s with a maturation in the 1990s (ibid. 981). At the turn of the millennium, however, West argues it has begun to decline and in "retreat," with feminist jurisprudence asserting itself (ibid., 995). West argued that feminist legal theory, as critical theory, was beginning to develop interconnections between law and justice, but since its decline, doctrinal analysis and pragmatism stripped the latter's theoretical underpinnings from the former.

Yet others argue for a basic split in feminist jurisprudence between reformist feminists and radical feminists (Burchard, 2021). Reformist feminists maintain a liberal base and argue change can take place within the given legal system as it exists. The emphasis would be more on formal equality. The radical feminists argue that the legal apparatus has been dominated by patriarchy and must, in part or whole, be changed. Burchard (ibid.) argues that the two approaches can also be reconciled: rights, for example, can be retained as Williams (1991) has argued, but that systemic racism that permeates the legal apparatus must also be recognized and the focus of change. And drawing from Baer (1990: 55), both sides can be drawn together: "women can have it both ways" in treating women and men similarly where they are similar, and differently where differences exist.

Women's Rights Movements

Five overlapping stages can be distinguished in the women's rights movement in the U.S. First, during the 19th century to the early 20th century a number of efforts were organized in order to gain the right to vote, to gain access to private property, and to legal rights to birth control. Early pioneers of the women's suffrage movement include Susan Brownell Anthony (1820–1906) and Elizabeth Cady Stanton (1815–1902). The 19th Amendment to the U.S. Constitution that gave women the right to vote was ratified in 1920. The "Equal Rights Amendment" was first formulated in 1923 and introduced for possible ratification (3/4s of the State needed) in 1972, but was to face numerous obstacles (Cohen and Codrington, 2020). The second movement began in the 1960s and was characterized by a greater number of women entering law schools and legal practice. This increased in momentum in the 1970s and 80s.[5] Here a number of legal victories resulted from the greater access to power. The third movement took place in the 1970s, where the focal point included a critical analysis of employment, family law and legal definitions of rape. A number of successful litigated cases resulted. The fourth movement that began, perhaps, in the late 1980s and was carried over to the 1990s, witnessed a number of setbacks in its early stages (e.g., the defeat of the Equal Rights Amendment, restrictions placed on abortion rights in spite of *Roe v. Wade*, 1973). It also witnessed critical developments connected with but going beyond the The Critical Legal Studies Movement. There was a re-centering of emphasis to the women question. Just as critical feminist jurisprudence started to question its male-centered nature, others pointed out it equally applies to the question of color. Harris (1990: 588), for example noted that "white, straight, and socioeconomically privileged people" were for too long represented the dominant position in CLS as well as in earlier developments of feminist jurisprudence, until the emergence of "fem-crits." We saw in the late 1990s a renewed drive that was informed by critical findings in other fields—political theory, literary criticism, philosophy, and psychoanalysis. The fifth movement, beginning with the new millennium, not only has seen further diversification in perspectives, but extensive intra- and inter-perspective dialogue and ever more sophisticated and keen critique amongst the various perspectives. There now exists an active, diverse, and critical field, while still witnessing more dogmatic forms of feminism (feminist jurisprudence).

Law, critical feminist theorists have discovered, presents a number of limitations to the realization of social values (Bartlett and Kennedy, 1991: 2–5; Fineman, 2005; Baer, 1999; Williams, 1991; McAfee and Howard, 2021; West, 2018). First, due to the reliance on precedents *(stare decisis),* feminists have noted that the established body of law is overly phallocentric (male dominated), so that any issue brought before the court that substantially deviates from this body of knowledge is less likely to attain a hearing and a favorable resolution. It is a male-centered framework and standard that acts as the basis of decision-making in law, hidden with the "objectively" and "neutrality" of formal rational thought. This is constantly reinforced in traditional legal decision-making (formal rationality). Thus, the status quo is more likely to predominate. Substantive rational principles, however, always exist as a potential de-stabilizing force.

Second, the very work-context for activist feminist lawyers within the legal structure poses problems for feminists attempting to defend clients and to simultaneously contribute to larger feminist movements. Consider Bartlett and Kennedy's point

(1991: 3) that mounting a successful defense of "battered woman's syndrome" (Hoeffer, 2001; Coker, 2001) is difficult, and hence a legal defense is often instituted claiming "diminished capacity." The latter is a more "acceptable" defense in law, and consequently has a greater chance for a successful resolution for the defense. But consider, too, the disempowering that has taken place, not only in the particular instance but also in the sense of a larger contextual understanding of the motive that was involved.

A third limitation concerns the court's focus on the rational and coherent. Feminists' claims often arise from a multitude of sources, and these claims may appear to be contradictory at times. Consider a woman objecting to work conditions and a hostile work environment, whose claims are countered by the recitation of the ideology of contractual freedom. The "choice" remains of taking it (the job), or leaving it; but, given unemployment rates and the inability to counter power inequality inherent in worker contractual relations, "choice" becomes an illusory conception. Feminist analysis has shown that even where women work within the legal discursive categories themselves to oppose, they often inadvertently reinforce the legal structures that they wish to change (ibid.).

Case Material: Landmark Decisions Concerning Gender

Several prominent U.S. Supreme Court decisions are associated with attaining increased rights to women.[6] We include several to highlight the potential use of the legal avenue for social change. Here, change in law brought about by social activism has led to change in behavior. *Roe v. Wade* (1973) was a class action sought challenging the constitutionality of Texas law on abortion. The statute had made abortion illegal except for the purpose of saving the mother's life. The U.S. Supreme Court held that up to the first trimester of pregnancy, the decision was up to the mother in consultation with her physician. This decision and its underlying logic spelled out expanded rights to privacy. An earlier case, *Griswold v. Connecticut* (1965), allowing contraceptives to be used by married couples, was a precursor establishing the logic. Justice Douglas said a right to privacy could be inferred or is implied by the First, Third, Fourth, Fifth and Ninth Amendments to the U.S. Constitution. "Zones of privacy" are imbedded, creating a "penumbra" of rights (Henly, 1987; Dee, 2009).

These two cases are under constant attack by more conservative sectors, arguing the courts went beyond merely applying principles in law that existed: the rights were, they argued, inventions of the justices. Some critics have argued that the cases could also be understood dialectically. Although a victory, it becomes a loss in terms of the further subjecting the body to the "disciplinary mechanisms" of political-economic determinants and standards of usefulness. Thus, on the one hand privacy issues are given force, but yet on the other, further regulating structures become established for various enforcements. In other words, the legal apparatus as a disciplinary mechanism furthers the development of a body of "docility" and "utility" (Foucault, 1997a; see also Milovanovic, 2002: Chapter 9).

There have been several other landmark decisions. The workplace in particular has seen important litigation. Let us summarize and comment on a few cases.

An especially illuminating legal case concerning the ideological and repressive functions of law involved female workers in a much-discussed case, *EEOC v. Sears, Roebuck and Co.* (1988). According to Williams's analysis (1991), Sears won this suit because it was successful with its argument that women were disproportionately underrepresented in the higher paying sales positions at Sears not because they were discriminated against, but rather because they lacked "interest" in working in commission sales. The women bringing the suit had to prove not only statistical disparities, but also that women and men had "equal interest." Sears, in its defense, presented an essentialist case, arguing that men were historically competitive and self-interested, whereas women were "humane and nurturing." Accordingly, the court ruled that the sex segregation that did exist was an expression of women's own choice. The court was unwilling to entertain the view that locates women's work aspirations in the historical context of labor market discrimination (Schultz, 1991: 126).

In *Burlington Industries, Inc. v. Ellerth* (1998), the issue revolved around allegations of sexual harassment by petitioner' s (Ellerth's) supervisor (Slowik). In spite of this, the "facts" showed that the petitioner was not subject to any retaliation for challenging, and even was promoted one time. However, Ellerth also argued that these challenges forced her subsequent "constructive discharge." The larger question of a "hostile work environment" was also suggested. In other words, to what degree does a "vicarious liability" exist when the employer (Burlington industries) does not take corrective action against their supervisors (here Slowik)?

In another related landmark decision (actually delivered on the same date as the previous case) — *Faragher v. City of Boca Raton* (1998) — the court stipulated that "an employer is subject to vicarious liability to a victimized employee for an actionable hostile environment created by a supervisor with immediate (or successive higher) authority over the employee." (In *Faragher* the "sexually hostile atmosphere" involved "uninvited and offensive touching," lewd remarks, and by offensive terms directed toward women.) When no "tangible employment action" results (e.g., when no negative actions follow the sexual harassment), the Court stipulated, the employer may raise an "affirmative defense." In other words, the employer is given an opportunity to counter the claim that their inaction created a hostile work environment. The employer is subject to the standard of "preponderance of the evidence" (one must show more evidence for than against).

The Court stipulated two necessary elements that would clear the employer from vicarious liability: (1) "that the employer exercised reasonable care to prevent and correct promptly any sexually harassing behavior," and (2) "that the plaintiff employee unreasonably failed to take advantage of any preventive or corrective opportunities provided by the employer or to avoid harm otherwise." Again, where there exists a "tangible employment action" (i.e., demotion, firing, etc.) this defense would not be allowed in law. The Court decided that Burlington (the employer) should be given an opportunity to prove the affirmative defense concerning his supervisor, Slowik.

In an earlier U.S. Supreme Court case, *Oncale v. Sundower Offshore Services, Inc.* (1998), the Court stated that workplace harassment can violate the law (Title V11 of the Civil Rights Act of 1964) even when the harasser and the harassed employees are of the same sex. The Court, of course, defined "work environment" narrowly, focusing on individual action; however, "hostile work environments" may be more difficult to attribute to the creation of one person, and in fact sexual harassment may be much more subtle and pervasive. Another case, *Harris v. Forklift Systems, Inc.* (1993) has three criteria: frequency of the harassment, its severity, and whether it unreasonably interferes with the person's performance. The court further ruled that "the standard requires an objectively hostile or abusive environment—one that a reasonable person would find hostile or abusive—as well as the victim's subjective perception that the environment is abusive." In determining a hostile environment, the courts have argued, one must consider the "totality of the circumstances."[7] Note, even so, ultimately it comes down to individual intent that must be established, often overlooking the subtleties, cumulative effects, symbolisms used, innuendos, etc.

The question of comparable worth, sometimes referred to as "pay equity," has been an important concern in feminist jurisprudence. One direction has to do with noting that many jobs are more likely to find women employed (nurses, teachers, clerical workers) which are often underpaid. Another direction concerns equal pay for equal work. Advocates argue that jobs with equal skill requirements should be equally compensated. The title alone should not be justification for different compensation. If, "administrative secretary" (often relegated as a "female job") has the same skill level as "administrative assistant" for example, but the latter is compensated at a higher pay level, then this should be corrected for equal pay (Kuperstein, 2007). The Ninth Circuit Court of Appeals, in *AFSCME v. Washington* (1985), greatly limited any claims on the basis of comparable worth even as a state-commissioned body clearly indicated that a twenty percent disparity between women and men workers existed (Kuperstein, 380). The court, drawing from its reading of Title V11, ruled "reliance on a free market system in which employees in male-dominated jobs are compensated at a higher rate than employees in dissimilar female-dominated jobs is not in and of itself a violation of Title VII ..." (*AFSCME*, 1403, 1408; quoted in Kuperstein, ibid., 380). Rather, intent to discriminate must be shown. This was also the outcome of an earlier case, *Washington v. Gunther* (1981), which ruled for the requirement of showing "intent to discriminate." Showing patterns alone would not be decisive.

These cases indicate the difference between a focus on conditions v. a perpetrator perspective. Situating decision-making in wider contextual settings, conditions, as sociologists of law would argue, provides a better understanding of the issues, and pathways to social justice. Presently, "conditions" fall more in the "substantive rational" arena, outside of formal rational decision-making (recall Weber's distinctions in Chapter 4). On the other hand, California, in 2015, passed the California Fair Pay Act. This was a major victory for comparable worth advocates, since it required equal pay for similar work. Minnesota has had a comparable worth in action since the

1980s. However, a backlash has been that fewer women have been hired (Kuperstein, ibid., 387). Senators in the U.S. House of Representatives witnessed the eleventh defeat in introducing the "Paycheck Fairness Act" in 2019. These onerous restrictions and understandings are not shared in Canada nor Europe (Kuperstein, 380).

Turning to same-sexed marriages, the U.S. Supreme Court decision, *Obergefell v. Hodges* (2015) established the right for same-sexed marriages, based on the Fourteenth Amendment to the U.S. Constitution. It was a 5–4 decision. It was a pivotal historical occasion. The Court dismissed the claim by States that voters should determine the issue, stipulating "fundamental rights may not be submitted to a vote."

Court cases such as these have placed feminist jurisprudence front stage, and particularly require dilemmas to be addressed. We have not been exhaustive in this exposition, merely highlighting some of the prominent cases that have been litigated (for a more detailed chronology of key cases, see "Timeline of Major Supreme Court Decisions on Women's Rights," 2020). What we find is that on the one hand, law contributes to empowerment — having access to law to combat various instances of abuse and restrictions on the realization of social values does produce some change (see for example, Williams, 1987; Cook, 1990; Crenshaw, 1988; Delgado, 1987). On the other, working within the legal categories often reinforces the legitimacy of the legal apparatus, the rule-of law ideology, and, in the end, the rule of men (phallocentricism, or androcentricism).

Equality Theory and Sexual Difference

One of the pillars of Western democracy has been the notion of formal equality, or "equal rights" (see our discussion of formal rationality, Chapter 4). This had and has serious implications in the feminist movement. Consider Bartlett and Kennedy's comment: "Equality doctrine requires comparisons, and the standard for comparison tends strongly to reflect existing societal norms. Thus, equality for women has come to mean equality with men — usually white, middle-class men" (1991: 5; Frug, 1992: 665–682; Naffine, 1990; Roach-Anleu, 1992; Burchard, 2021). Accordingly, should women want to be like men? Or are there other comparisons to make to indicate "essential" differences? An affirmative answer to the former question can find an ally in the "equal protection" clause of the Fourteenth Amendment of the Constitution. If, on the other hand, the first question is rendered essentially counterproductive and the second question is taken seriously, what existing legal doctrine could be applied in situations of existing biases and restraints on the realization of various social values? Is substantive rationality being invoked here? And doesn't it go against the "equal rights" doctrine? The tension between formal and substantive rationality (see Chapter 4) is quite apparent.

Since the 1990s a key question in feminist legal analysis has to do with the subject of the category "woman." A clear distinction has been established between those who advocate a universal subject, sameness, the other, arguing for differences (Dietz, 2003; Fineman, 2005; McAfee and Howard, 2018; Burchard, 2021). The sameness-feminists argue that women are as rational, the same as men, and thus should have formal equality protected by the "equal protection clause" of the U.S. Constitution. Treatment, protections, privileges, and rights should be the same for men and women. Sexual differences were being employed too often as a basis of subordination. For this school, talk of diversity waters down possible gains in equal opportunities; it would disadvantage women. They challenged any preferences given to men in law. Along with the 14th Amendment they employed Title V11 of the Civil Rights Act (1964).

Difference-feminists, on the other hand, argue that women are uniquely different from men (e.g., sexual differences, sexual orientation).[8] Catharine McKinnon (1991a, 1991b) was a key early architect for articulating their position. They draw specifically from the classic studies by the psychological developmental theory of Carol Gilligan (1982). Women, it is argued, are more likely to place a premium on substantive rationality, on relationships, contexts and care, whereas men, more on abstract rights and formal rationality. Thus, differences demand different treatment in law to respect the uniqueness of what it is that constitutes being a woman. But, in traditional practices, the differences were being used to subordinate women. Rather, differences should be seen as a cause of celebration of diversity and respected in law. Courts should and did begin to see that women's reactions to situation are not similar to men's, and thus the "reasonable man in law" must be rethought to include "the reasonable women in law" or, later, the "reasonable person in law." Women's reactions at the workplace (e.g., "flirtation"), or threats and violence at home are "typically" not the same as men's (Fineman, 2005: 18).

Not fitting neatly in either, is postmodern feminism which questions fixed gender identities, or binaries, and rather focuses on performances and constitutive processes (Butler, 1990; Cornell, 1993, 2003; McAfee and Howard, 2018: 5, 9–12). We shall return to this in later chapters.

But this only begins the questioning. What, as Crenshaw argues (1991: 57–73; 2019; 2022; see also Milovanovic and Schwartz, 1999), does one then do with the issue of the intersection of sex, sexual orientation, ethnicity, and race? Of class, gender, sexual orientation, and race? In other words, should a lower economic scale African-American woman use the standard of white upper economic scale woman in arguing her defense? Some, such as MacKinnon (1991b: 81–91) have argued that this debate is misinformed, and the issue boils down to *domination:* how do males gain institutionalized domination and how, as a consequence, are females rendered subordinate?

These questions have led to one of the most debated issues in feminist jurisprudence concerning the underlying basis of the legal subject (the "reasonable person in law"). This concerns the issue of *essentialism*. This is an outgrowth of our just discussed sameness-feminism v. difference-feminism. Are women essentially different from men or should they be considered the same in law? Harris (1991: 242), for example, in critiquing MacKinnon for being an essentialist has argued that she

> assumes, as does the dominant culture, that there is an essential 'woman' beneath the realities of differences between women — that in describing the experiences of 'women' issues of race, class, and sexual orientation can therefore be safely ignored, or relegated to footnotes.

For Harris, black women offer a "post-essentialist" alternative for feminist jurisprudence that includes: the assumption of a self that is multifaceted, not unitary; the idea that "differences are always relational rather than inherent"; and the belief in "the recognition that wholeness and commonality are acts of will and creativity, rather than passive discovery" (Harris, 1991: 250; see also Collins, 1991; Matsuda, 1987; McAfee and Howard, 2018: 9–12). Minorities' experiences of oppression can be the basis of the development of a distinct political consciousness, which could, in turn, be the basis of a deconstructive practice and a transformative political agenda (Matsuda, 1987; Cook, 1990; Goldfarb, 1991, 1992; Cornell, 1991, 1998, 2003, 2007).

Feminist Legal Methods

What is to be done? Needed within feminist jurisprudence is a feminist legal method. Bartlett perhaps has presented one agenda rooted in a standpoint epistemology still of weight in the contemporary field (1991; Bartlett, 2000; Collins, 2009). Feminists doing law should focus on at least three factors. First, "asking the woman question." That is, what needs to be articulated is the often silenced voice, the voice of the excluded (see also Coombe, 1989, 1991a, 1991b, 1992; Howe, 1994; Derrida, 1992). According to Bartlett, this entails "looking beneath the surface of law to identify the gender implications of rules and assumptions underlying them and insisting upon applications of rules that do not perpetuate women's subordination" (1991: 373–374).

Second, this method privileges a "feminist practical reasoning," which may encompass some aspects of deductive logic, but takes into consideration the experiential — the unique, concrete experiences of the repressed. This approach does not assume a one-dimensional picture of phenomena, but sees them "as dilemmas with multiple perspectives, contradictions, and inconsistencies." This orientation opposes the dichotomizations imposed by the court, e.g., yes-no answers in court proceedings. It is contextual: new situations pose yet more opportunities for understanding, and "imaginative integrations and reconciliations."

The third aspect is consciousness-raising. The goal is for individual and collective empowerment, not for personal vendettas, nor for the celebration of "hate politics," "revenge politics," or political correctness (see Cornell, 1999, on this point). Again, it is gained by the integration of concrete experiences of the oppressed, self-reflection and theorizing (see also Schneider, 1986; Cook, 1990; Cornell, 1998, 1999; Collins, 2009; Burchard, 2021; Fineman, 2005: 20–23). It is always sensitive to the multiple forms of consciousness in existence. In sum, Bartlett's offering of a feminist legal method is focused both on deconstruction and reconstruction, consistent with CLS theorist Unger's (2015) update of his earlier statement underscoring the importance of both.

The literature on feminist legal method has presented, among other strategies, three distinct forms. First, *reversal of hierarchies*, a derivation from Derrida's deconstructive strategy (Reynolds, 2021; in the Australian context, see Papedelos, 2006), that argues action must be directed toward liberating women from their subordination by reversing their position in various hierarchies (see particularly MacKinnon, 1987, 1989; Allen, 2016).

Second, standpoint epistemology, a position that argues that we must privilege the position ("standpoint") of the disenfranchised and help create an understanding ("epistemology") from these concrete, pragmatic-based occurrences of repression or domination (see Barlett, 1991; Howe, 1994; Collins, 2009; Hartsock, 2003; Harding, 1991, 2004; Smith, 1981, 1987, 2009; Bowell, 2021).

> Feminist standpoint epistemology identifies woman's status as that of victim, and then privileges that status by claiming that it gives access to understanding about oppression that others cannot have (Bartlett, 1991: 385).

Hence, this approach argues that knowledge is based upon experience of the oppressed (Matsuda, 1987; Cook, 1990), but it rejects objectivity and any possibility of an essential truth. Rather, truth is always situated, contingent and partial (Bartlett, 1991: 389). Thus, while some basis can be established for concrete political action (i.e., some historically situated "truth" based on empirical evidence), commitments are always provisional and are always subject to further critique and revision (ibid., Cook, 1990 Schneider, 1986; Collins, 2009; West, 2018: 998–999).

Thus, knowledge gained by experience by women is unique and cannot be necessarily universalized. Standpoint epistemology has built on a Marxist basis, the proletariat standpoint (Hartsock, 2003). According to Bowell (2021: 1):

> Feminist standpoint theorists make three principal claims: (1) Knowledge is socially situated. (2) Marginalized groups are socially situated in ways that make it more possible for them to be aware of things and ask questions than it is for the non-marginalized. (3) Research, particularly that focused on power relations, should begin with the lives of the marginalized.

Feminist standpoint theorists argue that knowledge gained in individual experiences as well as concerted activism based on collective experiences are necessary for change in social policies and laws. Traditional methodology as well as an on-going self-critique should be the basis for assessing truth claims (Harding, 2004, 2008; Walby, 2001; Bowell, 2021; Kourany, 2009).

Although, this is a general orientation, we actually see various standpoints. Critical Race Theory, for example, argues for the unique experience of African Americans (Collins, 2009) and thus advocates a Black feminist standpoint. We shall develop this in the next part of this chapter. Standpoint epistemology is not without its critics.[9] Some proponents of postmodern theory, as we shall see later, question any foundational positions as a basis for constructing a more genuine knowledge. Advocates of intersectionality argue that multiple forms of domination exist (Crenshaw, 2019, 2022). It has also been referred to as "kyriarchy" (Zinn and Thornton, 1996; Fiorenza, 2001). This will be brought into focus in our section on critical race theory below (CRT). (We shall return to a feminist postmodernist view of standpoint epistemology in Chapter 11.)

And third, *contingent universalities*, a perspective that argues that neither the search for objective nor relative "truths" can contribute to the ideal foundations for building political agendas, but rather a mid-course position. This perspective argues that at historical moments certain positions that are "contingent" can be temporarily forged, which become, for a time, "universalities" by which focused action can follow. Perhaps Harris's "post-essentialist" alternative can be assimilable here; or, perhaps with more, could be developed into a clear-standing alternative. These contingent universalities (dissipative foundations), however, are always subject to reflection, debate, qualification, redefinition and deletion as historical contingencies emerge (see Butler, 1991; see also Laclau's notion of "historical dislocations," "structural undecidability," and "historical articulations," 1996: 87–104; 2000; for a debate between Laclau, Butler and Zizek, see Laclau *et al.*, 2000). Critical race theory would find itself situated between the latter two strategies: from standpoint epistemology it focuses on resurrecting repressed voices and pragmatism in legal challenges, and from contingent universalities it points out the plurality of overlapping and intersecting forms of consciousness and identifications that change over time.

Each of the three strategies have been debated: the first may easily turn into "revenge politics" (Cornell, 1999) and forms of rigid political correctness; the second, some argue, especially the postmodernists, overlooks how the existing discourse (i.e., legal discourse, dominant discourse, academic discourse, even some oppositional discourses) itself limits what can be said in narrative constructions (See, for example Spivak's (2008) question, from where can the subaltern speak?); and the third, dissenters say, may quickly slip back into the negative forms of either or both of the first two.

Critical Race Theory

Introduction

Critical Race Theory (CRT) had its beginnings in the 1960s. It "questions the very foundations of the liberal order, including equality theory, legal reasoning, Enlightenment rationalism, and neutral principles of constitutional law" (Delgado and Stefancic, 2017, 2018). Some considered it a spawning or "spin-off" of the CLS Movement, with the caveat that a critical internal engagement with CLS led to clarifications and further development. Inspirational were early autobiographic accounts of struggle and activism. Three particularly clear and concise books are foundational to understanding the perspective: Richard Delgado and Jean Stefancic's *Critical Race Theory* (2017); Kimberle Crenshaw *et al.*'s, *Critical Race Theory: The Key Writings That Formed the Movement* (1995); and Mari Matsuda *et al*'s, *Words That Wound* (1993).[10] Derrick Bell has often been cited as one of the founders of CRT. See his works (1980, 1994, 2005).

Many African-American legal scholars from a CRT perspective sometimes referred to as "race-crits," have rejected the CLS's critique of rights litigation as repressive ideology, noting that this "project ... relinquishes too much, since appeals to legal ideology represents one of the only strategies that has effectively elicited a response to the desperate needs of subordinate people" (Goldfarb, 1992: 696). As Crenshaw has poignantly stated: "The most troubling aspect of the Critical program, therefore, is that 'trashing' rights consciousness may have the unintended consequence of disempowering the racially oppressed while leaving white supremacy basically untouched ..." (1988: 1357–1358). In other words, the recognition of this dialectics of struggle has necessitated a more comprehensive approach for a critical race jurisprudence where both the concrete experiences of people of color as well as more comprehensive theorizing in law need to be integrated.

Historical Development

Critical race theory[11] underwent an evolutionary development. Prior to listing the more formal stages, we must pay homage to those enslaved and their struggles, whose voices were denied, whose stories were infrequently circulated, but whose experiences were inspirational for social movements to follow.[12] The first stage[13] of its development can be traced to various civil rights movements of the 1960s. The second stage, the 1970s, could be seen as a time of retrenchment by the legal apparatus, when many rights gained during the 1960s were being undermined. *Brown v. the Board of Education* (1954), which can be read as attacking "conditions" behind the creation of discrimination, was now being undermined in law by the reliance on standards that focused on "intent" of a particular individual to engage in racist practices. This "bad apples" approach effectively undermined the broad perspective that looked at political economy, systematic and unconscious racism. Nevertheless, the 1970s saw the rise of activists, legal scholars and a number of lawyers, who actively confronted these rollbacks. The early 1980s saw some significant activist social movements in prestigious law schools. In 1981, for example, students organized protests against Harvard Law School to increase the number of faculty of color (Matsuda *et al.*, 1993: 3–4). When the administration was not responsive, the students organized their own course. Practitioners and leading scholars were invited for weekly discussions on chapters from Derrick Bell's publications (Bell had just left Harvard Law School). Kimberle Crenshaw, Mari Matsuda, Richard Delgado, and Charles Lawrence were all participants in this new course. Some in this group were also connected with the Critical Legal Studies group, although with some reservations about its predominantly white makeup and scholarly orientation. Nevertheless, by the end of the 1980s a new identity was being forged, critical race theory (CRT).

The third stage could be envisioned as beginning in the mid to late 1980s. Several formal conferences emerged. In 1988, at the Yale Law School, the First Annual Women of Color and Law Conference took place. In 1987, the Tenth National Critical Legal Studies Conference, had its theme as "The Sound of Silence: Racism and the Law" (for commentary about the conference, see Haines, 1987; Hardwick, 1991). From 1987 on, the Annual Critical Legal Studies conference saw significant presentations by women of color. The CRTs encouraged the predominantly white activist of the Critical Legal Studies to reflect on their own relations to possible racism, be it at more unconscious levels. There were also questions about white activists representing Black women in legal theory. For Harris (1990: 588) the concern was with "white, straight, and socioeconomically privileged people who claim to speak for all of us."

The fourth stage, perhaps beginning in the early to middle of the 1990s extending into the new millennium, can be characterized as a time for additional differentiation and splintering. Thus, in the 1990s we saw the development of: Lat-Crits, global critical race feminism, critical Asian writers, queer-crit studies, and others (see also the "multiracial category movement," Robinson [2000]). The internal critical discussions amongst the various perspectives brought into sharp relief the various forms of racism at play and often its intersectional nature.

There is a long history of the U.S. Supreme Court responding to cases on racial segregation.[14] U.S. Supreme Court decisions have responded to racism in *U.S. Plessy v. Ferguson* (1896), interpreting the 14th Amendment equal protection standards. It stipulated the infamous and outlandish "separate but equal" standard, essentially allowing segregation in public places. *Brown v. Board of Education* (1954) overturned it — separate but equal "is inherently unequal." In the educational arena, several decisions have defined the contours of legal thought particularly in providing access and in maintaining diverse student bodies: *California v. Bakke* (1978) overturning any use of quota systems in affirmative action; *Grutter v. Bollinger* (2003), affirming admission policy of Michigan Law School, ruled tailored use of race is part of a compelling state interest in maintaining diversity; *Gratz v. Bollinger* (2003) overturned University of Michigan's admission practices in awarding points automatically to different groups (African-Americans, Hispanics, Native Americans) noting it was not sufficiently tailored to consider race; and *Fisher v. University of Texas* 11 (2016) ruled that the admissions policy at University of Texas sufficiently considered individuals and race as *a factor* in order to maintain a diverse student body complies with Constitutional concerns.

We have also witnessed formal attacks on CRT, particularly highlighted by former President Trump's (2020) wholesale effort to dismantle any influence of, specifically, critical race theory in governmental agencies such as in sensitivity training (by Executive Order, September 22, 2020), and in establishing a "1776 Commission," an advisory committee, to ostensibly re-write history (instilling a "patriotic education") in response to the *New York Times* initiated "1619 Project" (Silverstein, 2019) which focused on slavery and how the legacy has continued as well as highlighting African-American accomplishments. Both of Trump's executive orders were subsequently rescinded by incoming President Biden (January, 2021).

We also are seeing the emergents of "critical white studies." Delgado and Stefancic (2017: 85; see also Feagin, 2013; Lopez, 2006) ask: "If ... race is not objective or biologically significant but constructed by social sentiment and power struggle, how did the white race in America come to exist, that is, how did it come to define itself?" In popular media and culture, whiteness is often connected with the good and superiority, black, the evil. Whiteness establishes the standard of measurement (Delgado and Stefancic, 2017: 86). We have also witnessed the ascendancy of advocates of "white supremacy" under the Trump Presidency, much literature of which suggests with his blessings.

Basic Tenets

Critical race theorists have drawn from a broad body of literature: critical legal studies, pragmatism, Marxism, literature, poetry, fiction, law and society movement, personal histories, revisionist history, feminism, and postmodernism. Key figures who were influential include: W.E.B Du Bois, Martin Luther King, Jr., Frederick Douglas. The Black Power movement and Chicano movements during the 1960s and 1970s were also inspirational (Delgado and Stefancic, 2017: 5). The works of Gramsci and Derrida were often consulted (Matsuda *et al.*, 1993: 5). "Our work presented racism not as isolated instances of conscious bigoted decision making or prejudiced practice, but as larger, systemic, structural, and cultural, as deeply psychological and socially ingrained" (ibid.). A classic and enduring pre-amble to CRT has been developed by Matsuda *et al.* (1993: 6). Its core tenets:

(1) recognizes that racism is endemic to American life.

(2) expresses skepticism toward dominant legal claims of neutrality, objectivity, color blindness and meritocracy ...

(3) challenges ahistoricism and insists on a contextual/historical analysis of the law ...

(4) insists on recognition of the experiential knowledge of people of color and our communities of origin in analyzing law and society ...

(5) is interdisciplinary and eclectic ...

(6) works toward the end of eliminating racial oppression as part of the broader goal of ending all forms of oppression ... This recognition of intersecting forms of subordination requires multiple consciousness and political practices that address the varied ways in which people experience subordination.

Delgado and Stefancic (2017: 8–11; numbers added) provide additional themes:

(1) that racism is ordinary, not aberrational ... the usual way society does its business ... the common, everyday experience of most people of color in this country ...

(2) our system of white-over-color ... serves important purposes [functions], both psychical and material ...

(3) race and races are product of social thought and relations ... races are categories that society invents, manipulates, or retires when convenient.

They also add: "differential racialization"—how more powerful groups create racial categories responding to changing political economic conditions; intersectionality—how identities are multiple; the uniqueness of voices of color, standpoints, and legal storytelling; social construction — how identities are constructed; and interest-convergence — how convergence of self-interest of whites and the aspirations of disenfranchised are often the basis of social change (ibid., 10–11). We shall return to each below.

Method: Jurisprudence of (in) Color

CRTs often refer to their method as "outsider jurisprudence," or jurisprudence of/in color" (Matsudo *et al.*, 1993: 18–20). At the outset, law is said to be inescapably political. Law should be used pragmatically, as a tool for social change. "Legalism," it is argued, "is a tool of necessity" (Matsuda, 1996: 6). Along with this, CRT recognizes contradictions, ambiguity, and duality (ibid., 18), which lead CRTs to an uneasy alliance with some forms of postmodern analysis. This alliance is uneasy because postmodernists, it is said by CRTs, argue for the "disutility of law as a tool of progressive social change" (Matsuda, 1996: 48), while "people of color cannot afford to indulge in deconstruction for its own sake" (ibid., 24). Although CRTs also recognize some merits in postmodern analysis,[15] critical race theorists, rather, focus on pragmatism: i.e., law as a tool, a resource, even an available weapon for social change. (In Chapter 11 we will indicate that some in the postmodernist perspective see pragmatism and postmodern insights as reconcilable, even a very useful direction for future research, but bathed in the notion of the dialectics of struggle.)

There are several key components of the jurisprudence of/in color. To this we now turn.

Race and racialization. Defining race has generated considerable discussion (Cornell and Hartmann, 1998; James and Burgos, 2020). First, race and ethnicity should be distinguished. In popular media, race is often associated with appearance (e.g., white, black, brown) and something perceived as inherent in biological makeup. Ethnicity, on the other hand, is described more in terms of ancestry and sense of belongingness to a similar cultural group (e.g., language, religion, nationality, etc.). Others, however, bring out the complexities involved. The social construction approach defines race as "a human group defined by itself or others as distinct by virtue of perceived common physical characteristics that are held to be inherent … [it] is a choice human beings make" (Cornell and Hartmann, ibid., 24) and is not determined by biology. Ethnicity "is defined as a sense of common ancestry based on cultural attachments, past linguistic heritage, religious affiliation, claimed kinship, or some physical trait" (ibid., 19). Thus, those categorized as Black may have several ethnic affiliations and identities (Cornell and Hartmann, 10). For example, Asian-Americans may embrace the racial category in response to discrimination or violence against them (Espiritu, 1992); similarly with embracing an Hispanic ethnic identity as a response to exercise of white privilege (Alcoff, 2006; both examples cited in James and Burgos, ibid., 10–11). There is also a "pragmatic black nationalism" based on more pragmatic, instrumental concerns in responding to racism (Shelby, 2005; cited in James and Burgos, ibid., 10–11).

Similarly, we have clarifications needed as to what constitutes gender. Most often, gender is perceived as a social construction, whereas sex is difference according to anatomy and biology (see for example, Butler, 1991). There are many gender orientations; whereas contemporary social views and bureaucratic practices see binaries. When we engage "class" we also have various definitions available. Gender, race and class are most often used as markers in society. Here we can see that they do not really exist, but are social constructs. Nevertheless, as markers and points for political mobilization as well as the focus of discriminatory practices these categories find reification tendencies. They are re-invented in discursive dialogue and performative practice.

We also observe "differential racialization," "ways the dominant society racializes different minority groups at different times, in response to shifting needs such as the labor market" (Delgado and Stefancic, 2017: 11; 2018, 6; Gans, 2017). "In one era," they continue, "Muslims are somewhat exotic neighbors who go to mosques and pray several times of day—harmless but odd. A few years later, they emerge as security threats" (Delgado and Stefancic, 2017: ibid.). Consider the rounding up of Japanese-Americans during WW2 and being placed in concentration camps ("internment" camps), further legitimatized by a U.S. Supreme Court decision, *Korematsu v. United States* (1944). We have also observed this racialization with its deleterious consequences for African-Americans in the mass incarceration movement (Wacquant, 2009, 2001; Alexander, 2012).

Micro-aggressions. Yet another theme is the notion of "petit apartheid" (Georges-Abeyie, 1990; Milovanovic and Russell, 2001) or "microaggressions" (Russell, 1998; Nadal, 2014; Nadal *et al.*, 2015). It has been the basis of considerable literature since the inception of the concept. This represents the more hidden and subtle dimension of racism in the criminal justice system, at the moments just prior to its formal mobilization. It is also at work outside of the formal criminal justice arena. It can range from: the more covert/informal, such as in the nonverbal form (gestures, postures, other mannerisms, non-person status, etc.); to more verbal but unofficial action (put downs, fighting words, expletives, hate/race speech, etc.); to informal action (informal racial profiling such as directed against DWB (driving while black), RWB (running while black), and SWB (standing while black); to race as a proxy for dangerousness; to official verbal behavior (invocation of selective discourse of law, *ex post facto* discursive constructions, etc.); to, finally, overt/formal verbal action (formal racial profiling,[16] open-ended loitering laws, gang profiles, etc.) (Milovanovic and Russell, 2001: xx).

Other descriptions of forms of micro-aggression have been offered. Sue *et al.* (2007; see also Nadal, 2014; Nadal *et al.*, 2015) reports three forms:

> *Microassaults* consists of overt and verbal discriminatory behavior, verbal and nonverbal;
>
> *Microinsults*, the unconscious or unintentional forms of communication that has a discriminatory negative effect;

Microinvalidations, verbal, overt statements that don't recognize (exclude, negate) the targeted person's unique standpoint.

Microaggressions have been shown to be extensively prevalent in the legal system (Ruan, 2020; Isom, 2015; Parks *et al.,* 2008; Fujii-Doe, 2017; Dejusus-Torres, 2000) at different stages in criminal justice processing where degrees of discretion exist, and within this, microaggressions directed toward people of color (Dejusus-Torres, ibid.). We witnessed active stop-and-frisk policies in New York City that were ruled as not only violation of the Fourth Amendment that guarantees protection against "unreasonable searches and seizures" but also, in practice, represented a "policy of indirect racial profiling" in so much as people of color were disproportionally impacted (Goldstein, 2013; see also Gelman *et al.,* 2013). A recent report by the ACLU on border patrols along the Canadian border by the Customs and Border Protection (CBP) indicated 96% of those arrested at the border were designated by their codes as one of the following: "Black," "Dark Brown," "Dark," "Light Brown," "Medium Brown," "Medium" or "Yellow" (The Border's Long Shadow, 2021). And evidence for their negative impact on mental health has been reported (Nadal, *et al.,* 2014b; Nadal *et al.,* 2014b; Williams, 2020).[17]

There have also been strategies suggested for responding to microaggressions (Nadal, 2014: 73–74; Limbong, 2020). Nadal has a three-step process as a prelude to responding to microaggressions, asking: (1) Did this microaggression really occur? (2) Should I respond to this microaggression?; and (3) How should I respond to this microaggression? Included, too, is *how* to respond if I commit a microaggression? (ibid., 74). There are cases where one could be totally unaware of one's actions, other occasions where someone points it out to you, and others when one realizes their actions. For the first, not much can be said, unless confronted and engaged. For the second, try to listen to what is being said and not become defensive and admit your slight with a meaningful apology. For the third, "own up to it!", admit with an apology (ibid., 74–75).

Rule- and fact-skepticism. CRTs, borrowing from "crits" and legal realists before them, embrace the idea of rule- and fact-skepticism. Rule-skepticism, we have previously shown in our section on the legal realists (Chapter 6), means that "not every legal case has one outcome ... [i]nstead, one can decide most cases either way" (Delgado and Stefanie, 2017: 5). It often involves *ex post facto* constructions that clothe racist practices in acceptable constitutional language. As to fact-skepticism, we mean "interpreting one fact differently from the way one's adversary does" (ibid.). Thus, the "facts" are always social constructs. It is in the exercise of unequal power that determines why one version is dominant over another version. Both forms of skepticism, when practiced in law, often privilege the world-views and underlying assumptions of whites and subordinates those of people of color.

Narratives, legal storytelling, counter-storytelling. "Language can construct understanding, language can assault, and language can exclude. Words have power ... words are part of the struggle" (Matsuda, 1996: xiii). CRT advocates argue for storytelling and narrative analysis as a key component in their critical methodology (Delgado and Stefancic, 2017: Chapter 3; 2018; Ross, 1996). Thus, autobiographies, anecdotes, parables, and fiction become part of legal storytelling. CRTs make use of "everyday experiences with perspective, view-point, and the power of stories and persuasion to come to a better understanding of how Americans see race" (Delgado and Stefancic, 2017: 38). Dominant storytelling elevates some voices and experiences, and represses others. CRTs see alternative stories as being deconstructive as well as having components of possible reconstruction. "Stories can name a type of discrimination; once named, it can be combated" (ibid., 49; see also Matsuda *et al.*, 1993: 13). "When ideology is deconstructed and injury is named, subordinated victims find their voices" (Matsuda *et al.*, 1993: 13). Thus, storytelling according to such theorists as Derrick Bell and Patricia Williams has resurrected otherwise denied voices (Lopez, 1992; Alfieri, 2016; Miller, 1994; White, 1990).

The dynamics of courtroom trials is a "battle of narratives ... and the relationship between an attorney and a client may be seen as an effort to impose a narrative, or understanding, on their mutual journey" (Delgado and Stefancic, 2018: 10). Not only is storytelling important that develops between the client and lawyer, but also the combat between prosecutor and defense counselor is about whose story will count in the jury's mind. The latter is about narrative coherence (Jackson, 1988; we will return in Chapter 9). It is also involved in developing an appeal for the court to listen ("legal standing"). It has been pointed out that "the traditional concept of case theory, however, ignores the reality of client life experience and provides no role for clients in developing and shaping case theory" (Miller, 1994: 576).

Storytelling in the genre of music can have contradictory effects and has come under sharp internal criticism. See, for example, Crenshaw's (1993: 120–132) critique of "2 Live Crew." 2 Live Crew's lyrics, particularly their subordinate depiction of women, appeared quite controversial within the African-American community. Crenshaw takes issue with the idea that 2 Live Crew were merely trying to "explode" various stereotypes (images of sexual subordination); rather than "exploding" these stereotypes, she argues, they more often "reinforce and entrench the image" (ibid., 128; see also Adam and Fuller, 2006; Weitzer and Kubrin, 2009). Racist humor, too, is problematic.

Matsuda (1996: 124–129) provides one way to deal with this issue in suggesting consciousness raising and "learning to talk." A constructive strategy, a counter-storytelling (see also Feagin, 2013: 163–198), can be one in which space is opened up for people "to talk nonconfrontationally about race, gender, and sexuality," which can turn the learners into teachers (ibid., 125). She mentions how students in her seminar were encouraged to present both funny and damaging stories of mistaken identities (ibid.). This "space" provides moments for new narratives to develop and for new understandings. It is a space, which encourages not political correctness, but the development of narratives based on Paulo Freire's (1973, 1985) dialogical pedagogy (in law, see Lopez, 1992; Alfieri, 2016).

Consider the rendition of *Gone with the Wind* by Alice Randall (2001), in her book, *The Wind Done Gone: A Novel,* which was subject to much litigation (Reardon, 2001: 9). Randall's book was a retelling of the classic book but from an African-American perspective. The issue was whether the new book was a "sequel" to the original, and thus covered by copyright laws, and here, an infringement, or whether it was a parody. In the book, many of the roles of white plantation owners and families as superordinate and African-Americans as subordinate figures are reversed. As Randall says, "In my parody the black characters are multidimensional, and the white characters are stereotypes — flat would be the word" (ibid.). She continues: "I wanted to ridicule *Gone With the Wind.* I wanted to ridicule it forcefully. I intended ... to ridicule the racism in that book. I intended my book to give solace to African-American men and women, especially women, who have been injured by the stereotypes in [Mitchell's] book" (ibid.). Thus, retelling stories, counter-storytelling, from an African-American perspective, particularly a women's perspective, frontally confronts an entrenched establishment, which was willing to battle long and hard with the weapons of law to maintain hegemony. "Critical writers use counter-stories to challenge, displace, or mock these pernicious narratives and beliefs" (Delgado and Stefancic, 2017: 50).

There has been lively debate about the usefulness of storytelling (a useful summary appears in Ross, 2020; Bowell, 2021; Delgado and Stefanci, 2017: 53–54, Chapter 6; Reynolds, 2002). Some critics claim story-telling is too subjective, stifles debate by arguing for a superior position of understanding, and lacks scientific vigor. Others respond that this misses the point and that storytelling highlights the importance of lived experiences and racial realism (Ladson-Billing, 2005: vi–vii); that self-critique by adherents of standpoint knowledge is ongoing and recognizes contingency (Harding, 2004); that dominant knowledge used as a basis of comparing in establishing "objectivity" is already ideological (Harding, ibid.); that no universal standard is being proposed, rather acknowledged are multiple standpoints; that presenting coherent and substantive issues via legal storytelling by activist lawyers aids getting a case fuller hearing; and that "the traditional epistemic view that knowledge is only achieved by adopting a disinterested, impartial view from nowhere — is unachievable, for knowledge is always from somewhere" (Harding, 2004: 93, cited in Lee, 2020).

Standpoint epistemology. Returning to standpoint epistemology previously discussed, we find its applicability as central to CRT (Collins, 2009; Harris, 1991; Matsuda, 1987; Cook, 1990). Equally, we see compatibility with other outgrowths of the CLS Movement, each with unique contextual understandings in political economic and historical evolving times. CRT, however, cites the legacy of slavery and its continuous effects and manifestations: old Jim Crow Laws have seen contemporary evolution to new Jim Crow Laws, often more insidious, pervasive, and deleterious (Alexander, 2012; Wacquant, 2009); microaggressions, as we saw previously continue to have their effects.

Storytelling and counter storytelling are based on knowledge gained from this contextualized location. Standpoint theory is rooted in Marx's analysis of the proletariat and its privileged position as a generator for social change.

Black Lives Matter, a social movement begun in 2013, has been a much-publicized voice of African-Americans, bringing much attention to the standpoints of people of color as recipients of police brutality and violence (see https://blacklivesmatter.com/). Police killings of Trayvon Martin, Michael Brown, Eric Garner and George

Floyd were the basis of large demonstrations across the U.S. with demands for criminal justice reform. Some legal reforms are afoot, including greater police accountability, use of body mounted cameras, reducing or eliminating bail, reforming "no nock rules," rethinking the strategy of active "stop and frisk," reconsidering "stand your ground" defenses, eliminating citizens arrests, and reducing prison populations. It remains to be seen whether legal reforms will remain piecemeal or will move to serious consideration of such things as reparation for slavery, greater distribution of resources in minority communities, reduction of income inequalities, genuine reintegration programs, greater use of restorative and transformative practices than the criminal justice model, etc.

Standpoint theory. Standpoint theory has generated an ongoing body of substantial discussion and constructive critiques, internal and external (see Lee, 2021; Bowell, 2021: 11–14; Delgado and Stefancic, 2017: Chapter 6; see also debate between Hekman, Harstock, Harding, and Collins in Harding, 2004). Like critics of story-telling, questions of objectivity, scientific vigor, proclaimed universality and superior position of knowledge are each lively debated in the literature (Ladson-Billing, 2005; Harding, 2004; Lee, 2020; see above). CRT counters that knowledge gained in standpoints is multiply constructed in evolving historical conditions and political economies: diversity is valued in their constructions (Reynolds, 2002). Direct experiences of African-American women, it is argued, because recipients of oppression, can reflect more clearly than those who desire to speak for them, and because of this, can also offer insights to other oppressed groups. And that because they are often both insiders *and* outsiders (professors in academic settings, women of color experiencing everyday world), they can develop a "bifurcated consciousness" having a "dual perspective" or "double vision," and understand both realities more clearly (Bowell, 2021; Collins, 2009; Smith, cited in Harding, 2004: 27). Because of living in the intersections, a "third space" is created from which more genuine understandings can develop (Mirza and Reay, 2001; Mirza, 2009; 2013). We now turn to the intersectionality issue, often advocated by difference-feminists.

Intersectionality. CRTs look at how race, ethnicity, gender, class, sexual orientation, and national origins often appear in combination and, in that state, how more insidious and ubiquitous discriminatory practices take place (Delgado and Stefancic, 2017: Chapter 4; Crenshaw, 1989, 1993, 2019, 2022; Milovanovic and Schwartz, 1999). Not only are these separate categories often sources of discrimination, but in various combination they can have even greater damaging effects. Intersectionality is a recognition of multiple consciousnesses, of multiple identifications and outlooks in life (Frank, 2014; Whisnant, 2016; Snyder, 2008; McAfee and Howard, 2018).

Intersectionality can be illustrated in the George Zimmerman trial (Franks, 2014: 1061–1067). He was charged with second degree murder for shooting Trayvon Martin. Zimmerman was a Hispanic adult male (voter registration form listing), Martin was a black teenager, and the jury was all female, parents, with one person of color. Zimmerman claimed self-defense. Martin was not in the act of committing a crime, merely walking through a neighborhood where Zimmerman was a security agent. Who would the jurors more likely identify with? Franks (ibid.) asks: would the hooded sweatshirt as a basis of Zimmerman's suspicions be equated with women's clothing sometimes cited for sexual attacks? Is the increased surveillance and stereotyping the key? In possible identifications, the question of who the jurors would more likely identify, the "unarmed young black man or the armed Hispanic would-be enforcer" brought into play race, class, gender. Was Martin stereotypically viewed, according to Natalie Jackson, co-counsel for Martin, as "the black boogeyman everybody is afraid of" (Jackson reported in Frank, 1063), and stereotypically did the jurors then view Zimmerman as "a flawed hero, regrettably but understandably overreacting to a perceived threat to the neighborhood." The play of "multiple consciousnesses" and profiling was ostensibly at play. Nor should it be compelling that Martin may have had some troubles in school, for many teenagers do without subsequently engaging in violent acts.

The social movement that this case generated included diverse hooded demonstrators who proclaimed "I am Trayvon Martin," and President Obama declaring "Trayvon Martin could have been me 35 years ago. There are very few African American men in this country who haven't had the experience of being followed when they were shopping at a department store, and that includes me" (Obama reported in Franks, 1064). The jury returned a verdict of not guilty, and juror B29 was later to proclaim, although reluctant, she was bound by the particular instructions to the jurors concerning "intent."

"Intersectional individuals" (Delgado and Stefancic, 2017: 55) may experience diverse forms of identity constructions applied to them. Delgado and Stefancic provide the example of black responses to black criminality. Two possible responses are the "politics of distinction," and the "politics of identification." In the former, the black law-breaker is seen as evil and the black community reverts to a get-tough approach—more police, harsher punishments, tougher gang laws, etc. In the latter, the black community sees the law-breaker as a "race rebel," and thus receives some support by the community. Here, the black community wants the police to stay out of the business of their neighborhood so that they can respond to it in their own way.

A variant of this has been analyzed by Russell (1998) in her notion of "black protectionism" (ibid., 56–65). "The Black community builds a fortress around its fallen hero and begins to offer explanations and defenses" (ibid., 57). Thus, "whenever colorless [e.g., "crossover status" had been achieved] Blacks fall into national disgrace and scandal, they are picked up and brushed off by the Black community. Like a good wife, Black people 'stand by their man'" (ibid.). Russell presents the example of O.J. Simpson. Russell also presents the example of U.S. Supreme Court nominee Clarence Thomas in 1991, who, attacked by an all-white Senate Judiciary Committee, invoked the symbols and metaphor of a disgraceful period in American history by referencing the hearings as a "high tech lynching." At that point he became black. However, Russell continues, black protectionism often does not extend to women of color (ibid., 63). She provides two examples. In the nomination of Lani Guinier, a professor of law, to become the assistant attorney general, President Clinton (1993) dropped his support after a large conservative opposition was mounted. But there was a low black protest. Similarly, with a former Surgeon General Dr. Joycelyn Elders. After coming under attack for statements about sex education, she was fired by President Clinton in 1994. But again, no large protest followed in the Black community (ibid., 64–65). Both women were denied black protectionism.

For Delgado and Stefancic (2017), by the notion of "perspectivism," intersectional individuals are likely to have their identities framed in various ways. The key, for the authors, is how to frame in such a way as to respect human complexity and minimize oversimplifying the human condition. This leads to the dilemmas of essentialism (Harris, 1990; Franks, 2014). Is there a common element for people in struggle, or does perspectivism doom social movements to being incapable of providing a common position ("foundations") from which to establish focused change strategies? Should, therefore, various disenfranchised people compromise their uniqueness for the sake of developing a united front? (Delgado and Stefancic, ibid., 58).

A related question here is the question of assimilation (ibid., 59–63). The authors present the example of two African Americans, William and Jamal, both successful and graduates of top universities. Whereas Jamal lives in a black community and consciously does as much business as possible with other African Americans, Williams assimilates into a white business community and integrated suburb with 90% white, but occasionally does *pro bono* work on behalf of prison inmates. Williams believes that he can break down various racial barriers. There are three middle positions that are discussed also. The question, then, revolves around "nationalism" versus "assimilation." Which could offer a better direction for social change? Although the authors go no further than posing the question and suggesting robust discussion, they have provided some key contrasts that demand devising clear-headed strategies for social change.

For sociology of law, both intersectional analysis and standpoint theory are cause to rethink responsibility and liability in law, the so called "reasonable man in law" (formal rationality, legal formalism), the latter based on a universalism, an abstract bearer of rights and obligations independent of context, and is at basis a gender- and race-biased term privileging what a white man would do under particular circumstance. Both intersectional analysis and standpoint theory suggest that if "conditions" are sufficiently expanded and greater understandability results, given the circumstances, then attributing blame solely on the abstract individual misses the point for considering responsibility. What then would be the determinants? Should, as some suggest, we use a "reasonable woman in law," "reasonable person in law," or perhaps a "reasonable intersectional person in law?" CRT already makes the case that responsibility is judged differently for white and people of color in the discriminatory practices in law that are well-documented. If people are situated differently, and if they experience these realities differently, then to what extent should this be considered in any conceptualization of a reasonable person in law? Baer, for example, argues: "Women can have it both ways. Law can treat men and women alike where they are alike and differently where they are different" (Burchard, 2021: 13, citing Baer, 1999: 55).

Interest-convergence. Derrick Bell (1980) articulated the interest-convergence concept in examining the *Brown v. Board of Education* (1954). The concept stands for the idea that no significant or substantive legal change will take place unless in the self-interest of whites. The *Brown* decision was a direct refutation of the U.S. Supreme Court decision, *Plessy v. Ferguson* (1996) that established the principle of "separate but equal," essentially justifying segregation in public places. In *Brown*, separate but equal was proclaimed as inherently unequal. On its face, it could be construed as inspired by humanitarian, enlightened, rational thought. Bell, however, argued that two forces were at work: the returning African-American soldiers from the Korean War and the active communist recruitment of disenfranchised peoples during the 1950s in the Cold War era. The African-American soldier was hardly likely to accept sitting in the back of the bus. Although accused of cynicism (noted in Delgado and Stefancic, 2017: 23–24), an historical study by Mary Dudziak (2011) of various U.S. ambassadors and foreign press reports substantiated Bell's thesis in that the U.S. was seriously concerned about improving its image in the Third World (ibid).

More recently, it could be argued that the U.S. bombing in Yugoslavia (1999), ostensibly to curtail killings (claimed ethnic cleansing) by Serbs in Kosovo, reflected other not so obvious motivations: not only geopolitical concerns to establish a foothold in the area, but siding with Muslims in showing empathy and symbolizing a moving away from the strong pro-Israel support over the years as it continues, for many, to engage in ethnical cleansing of the Palestine people, as well as perhaps responding to a deep collective unconscious guilt for its extermination of Indigenous peoples of the U.S., along with its continued ethnic cleansing of African Americans, a "black genocide" (for the latter, Johnson and Leighton, 1995). In short, an interest-convergence (in the Latinx context, see Delgado, 2006; for granting Puerto Ricans U.S. citizenship, see Venator-Santiago, 2019; on black health issues, Crossley, 2016). Bell (2005) was to reconfirm the validity of his thesis of 1980 as applied to *Brown*. It was also applied to the election of President Obama (Delgado, 2015). There have been some critical responses, see, for example, Driver (2011) and Weeden (2016). Delgado dismisses two other possible explanations for election of President Obama, one that "he arrived because he was a brilliant and charismatic figure and that many brave souls before him prepared the way by forcing the country to come to terms with its own longstanding racism" (ibid., 369), the other that the country has become colorblind," in opting for Bell's interest convergence. Certainly, there will be a range of lively responses evoked in the reader by each of these three possible explanations.

Further Spawnings of New Identity Groups

Introduction

The CLS movement has been an inspirational force for critical legal studies. Feminist jurisprudence, fem-crits, and race-crits, through their critical engagement as well as independent developments have pushed the field considerably in furthering a sociology of law. Yet a new wave, spawnings if you will, a third wave, of identity groups has taken place and continues further differentiation.[18] Lat-crits, Asian American crits, Queer Crits, Tribal-crits, Decolonial-crits, Eco-crits, Critical legal geography, and the continued developing of LGBTQIA (lesbian, gay, bisexual, transgender, queer or questioning, intersex, and asexual or allied), sometimes LGBTQ+ (with the + representing inclusivity; for a timeline, see LGBTQ Rights Milestones Fast Fact, 2021), variations of which include LGBTQQIP2SAA (lesbian, gay, bisexual, transgender, questioning, queer, intersex, pansexual, two-spirit (2S)), androgynous and asexual (with two-spirit referencing indigenous North Americans).[19] In Chapter 11 we will move to the postmodern approach as well as variants of the post postmodern approach, Chapter 12 (for the latter, see for example, Leong, 2016).

These will certainly pose challenges for bureaucratic categorization by legislative bodies and law. How will legal formalism (formal rationality) incorporate substantive rational principles? What constitutes the reasonable person in law, given standpoint and intersectional analysis? Will interest convergence be a key engine for change? How will different identity groups accommodate to diversity outside their group of identification and nuances within? What constitutes a "jury of your peers?" Does legal formalism have enough elasticity to accommodate to ongoing change? Will formal rationality be relegated to relic status? If so, what would be its replacement?

Some countries resist official recognition of emerging identity groups arguing for universalism, such as the French experience, dismissing these as "subjective data" (Onishi, 2021; Simon, 2010). It is ironic in so much as French intellectuals have been influential theorizes for advocates of diversity in identities, and that the French have a long history of colonization (Onishi, ibid). "The French State does not compile racial statistics, which is illegal, describing it as part of its commitment to universalism and treating all citizens equally under the law" (ibid., 3). It remains to be seen what effects the continuous unrest responding to racial and ethnic violence that France has experienced as well as to the mass immigration ("refugee crisis") that took place particularly 2014–2015, will have on this model (Beaud and Noiriel, 2021).

Lat-crits, Asian-American crits, Queer-crits and Tribal-crits are illustrative of some of the emerging critical legal theorists. Let us briefly explore each.

Lat-Crits

Lat-crits' central issues include immigration, bilingual schooling, farm workers, and language rights. Valencia *et al.* (2004) and Montoya (2013) have reviewed a long history of involvement with the law, criticizing the stated race-neutrality in law. The formal beginnings of the Lat-crit movement can be traced to the Hispanic National Bar Association Law Professor's meeting in 1995 in San Juan, Puerto Rico (Lee, 2021). An early rallying cry was in response to the so-called "Sleepy Lagoon" trials (1944) where U.S. servicemen attacked Mexican Americans after some rumors of insults circulated which initiated riots. Twelve Mexicans were charged for their involvement and subsequently wrongly convicted of murder (appeals court overturned; see Valencia *et al.*, 2014). The California Court of Appeals, however, ruled the claim of "racial prejudice" was "without foundations and ... [had] no support in the record" (cited in Valencia, ibid.). All this was during a tense time with racial conflict in Los Angeles near the end of WW2.

Latinx people continue to be recipients of microaggression (Nadal *et al.*, 2014). The key tenets of Lat-crits include (Solórzano and Villapando, 1995; reported in Lee, 2021; see also Solórzano and Bernal, 2001; Montoya, 2013):

1. An emphasis on experiential knowledge;
2. A challenge to dominant ideologies;
3. The centrality of race and racism and their intersectionality with other forms of subordination; and
4. A commitment to social justice

Asian-Crits

Asian-crits arose building on CRT and the CLS Movement. It responds to the discrimination that begins with stereotypes. Asian Americans are often depicted as "model minorities," "quiet and industrious, with intact families and high educational aspiration and achievement," but also "soulless, humorless drones whose home countries are at fault for the United States periodic economic troubles" (Delgado and Stefancic, 2017, 94; see also Osajima, 2005; Museus, 2013; Chou and Feagin, 2015). This has been brought out during the Pandemic where Asians are depicted at fault and subject to violent attacks as well as micro-aggressions in their different form (Nadal *et al.*, 2014, 2015; Sue *et al.*, 2007). The killing of Vincent Chin in 1982 has been a rallying beacon for the present (Choy and Tajima, 1989). Chin was beaten to death by two white men who were angry with the declining U.S. auto industry. One uttered "It's because of you little m-f-s that we're out of work" (ibid.). After a plea-bargaining arrangement the two offenders were sentenced to three years of probation. The sentencing judge, Kaufman, said "These weren't the kind of men you send to jail."

More recently, the brutal attacks on a 91-year-old man in Oakland's Chinatown, an 89-year-old woman in Brooklyn, New York, and a Thai man in San Francisco have been rallying cries for change (Weiyi *et al.*, 2021). And we have previously noted the U.S. Supreme Court decision, *Korematsu v. United States* (1944) that justified the internment of over 100,000 Japanese Americans. No espionage cases were ever established. This case appeared shortly after the surprise attack by Japan on Pearl Harbor after which hostility was high toward those of Japanese descent. Iftikar and Museus (2018; see summary by Lee, 2021) have offered seven foci for the movement: Asianization (racialization of Asians); transnational context; (re)constructive history; strategic (anti)essentialism; intersectionality; counter stories; and commitment to social justice.

Queer-Crits

Queer-crits, perhaps finding foundational the work by Judith Butler, *Gender Trouble* (1993) and by Teresa Lauretis, *Queer Theory* (1991), argue against binaries/dualities in gender (male, female) and for a much more intersectional and nuanced identity of sexual orientation (see for example, "Black Queer Studies"; Johnson and Henderson, 2005). For Butler, gender identities are constructions.

Queer theory grew out of the gay and lesbian movements, particularly in the 1990s. Teresa de Lauretis organized the first formal conference in 1990. Queer-crits have been active in law reforms (Adler, 2018). Two U.S. Supreme Court cases have established key sexual rights. *Obergefell v. Hodges* (2015) established right to marry for same-sex couples. *Bostock v. Clayton County* (2020) established employment rights based on sexual-orientation. It drew from Tittle V11 of the Civil Rights Act (1964) that prohibited discrimination "against any individual ... because of such individual's race, color, religion, sex, or national origin." The focus in this case was on the definition of "sex." It was a 6–3 decision. Justice Alito, in dissent argued for the original intent of the 1964 Civil Rights Act. Justice Kavanaugh, in dissent, argued that the definition of sex should rely on the "ordinary meaning" rather than any "literal meaning." He thus concluded that gender identity or sexual orientation is not the understanding within the Civil Rights Act. Of course, the counter was that definitions have an evolving nature, not a stagnant one.

Tribal-Crits

Tribal-crits have evolved as an outgrowth of CRT and the momentum established by the Critical Legal Studies Movement. It concerns both the legacy of colonization and racism in contemporary society. The U.S., Canada, Australia, and New Zealand have a legacy of discrimination against indigenous peoples.[20] Land claims, oral traditions and "native title" have been central in legal actions: for example, in Australia, *Mabo v. Queensland* (1992) established "native title," deference to the oral history tradition and understandings of Aboriginal peoples (Jessup, 1992; Christensen and Tatum, 2019); in Canada, *Delgamuukw v. British Columbia* (1997) did similarly; see also *Tsilhqot'In Nation v. British Columbia* (2014).[21] In the U.S. the decisions have been dispersed at various levels of courts. Overturned in the Australian and Canadian context was the colonizer's justification for subjugating indigenous people under "terra nullius" (empty land).

History will show that the Australian experience of the "lost generation" ("stolen children") whereby the government and church forcefully, between 1910–1970, removed indigenous children from their families—by some estimates over 100,000 were affected, between 10% to 33% of all indigenous families—and placed in non-indigenous families for assimilation, and the U.S. experience of removal to boarding schools to "civilize the savages" are despicable commentaries of practices of "civilized societies." In 2021, Australia established reparation of 280 million dollars for the lost generation.

Key Tribal-Crit's tenets include (Brayboy, 2005: 429; see also "What is TribalCrit?," 2021):

1. Colonization is endemic to society.
2. U.S. policies toward Indigenous peoples are rooted in imperialism, White supremacy, and a desire for material gain.
3. Indigenous peoples occupy a liminal space that accounts for both the political and racialized natures of our identities.
4. Indigenous peoples have a desire to obtain and forge tribal sovereignty, tribal autonomy, self-determination, and self-identification.
5. The concepts of culture, knowledge, and power take on new meaning when examined through an Indigenous lens.
6. Governmental policies and educational policies toward Indigenous peoples are intimately linked around the problematic goal of assimilation.
7. Tribal philosophies, beliefs, customs, traditions, and visions for the future are central to understanding the lived realities of Indigenous peoples, but they also illustrate the differences and adaptability among individuals and groups.
8. Stories are not separate from theory; they make up theory and are, therefore, real and legitimate sources of data and ways of being.
9. Theory and practice are connected in deep and explicit ways such that scholars must work towards social change.

A sociology of law approach in the literature that investigates how a Native American legal system (see also Richland and Deer, 2015) interfaces with Anglo-American law was conducted by Richland (2008). His anthropological case study of law-in-practice was with the Hopi Tribal Court system of Southwestern United States based on Hopi tradition. He shows how the tension of the two legal systems play themselves out. Focusing on a narrative and a semiotic approach of C.S. Peirce, he shows how conflicts can be translated into either legal system, and each can be used strategically to enhance one's case. However, the tension with vestiges of colonial law remains, a question of basing law on authentic traditional practice or the abstract formalism of Anglo-American law. One also must be reminded, that the Hopi Tribal Council, Hopi Constitution and Hopi Tribal Court were not indigenously developed but are traced to the U.S. Congress. In 1934, the United States Congress established the Indian Reorganization Act (the Wheeler-Howard Act) that was a major force that established its contours (Sekaquaptewa, no date), even as the Hopi subsequently voted for a Hopi Tribal Court in 1972, ostensibly to retain power in the Hopi Tribe (Richland, 2008: 148).

Richland notes particularly how the judge in the Hopi Tribal Court frames issues, attempting to gain legitimacy by adhering to Anglo-American law focusing the issues on generalities, while allowing for traditional views built on specificities (singularities). A similar finding was by Walsh (2008) in the context of Australian Aboriginal land claims. The evolving tribal jurisprudence remains in this state of tension between the adversarial and traditional approaches, a tension that is exemplified by Weber's notion of the "insoluble conflict" between substantive and formal rationality.

Intersectionality and the Law: Defining "Diverse Student Bodies"

These developments from CRT, Critical Legal Studies Movement and their outgrowths have also led to some controversies between the various identity groups. In the U.S., intersectional analysis and identity politics (for an introduction, see Heyes, 2020) have been poignantly brought out in legal cases. Two court cases in point illuminate some of the parameters of the issue, one dealing with admission standards at Harvard University, the other admission standards at the elite high schools in New York City.

Asian-Americans filed a suit against Harvard University claiming discriminatory practices in its admission policies (for an introduction, Millhiser, 2021). Graduating from the highest universities has often been shown to be a ticket for lucrative and prestigious employment. Well-established case law has it that use of race must further a "compelling interest" and undergo strict scrutiny, here the importance of a diverse student body necessary for an educational experience acknowledged by major American businesses. The initial Federal Court decision sided with Harvard, the appeals court also did so, and it has currently, at this writing, been appealed to the U.S. Supreme Court, in *Students for Fair Admissions v. President and Fellows of Harvard College*. For the class of 2022 there were over forty thousand applicants for 2,015 seats. The initial six criteria for admission decision-making include: "academic ratings, extracurricular ratings, athletic ratings, school support ratings, personal ratings, and overall ratings." This has been also referred to as the "whole person review." Personal ratings might include "a particularly compelling story about how they [student applicant] overcame racism to succeed academically" (Millhiser, ibid., 6). Ever since Bakke (1978) race could be considered *a* factor but not *the* factor (a "plus" factor) in decision making. In Harvard's system "tips are plus factors that might tip an applicant into Harvard's admitted class" (cited in Millhiser, ibid., 6). These might include "outstanding and unusual intellectual ability, unusually appealing personal qualities, outstanding capacity for leadership, creative ability, athletic ability, legacy status, and geographic, ethnic, or economic factors." The Federal District Court found that if this criterion was not used it would "reduce African American representation at Harvard from 14% to 6% and Hispanic representation from 14% to 9%." Harvard showed that in 2018, Asian-Americans had 22% admitted while being 6% of the population.

The plaintiffs, SFFA, argued that Asian-Americans had significantly higher academic scores, grades, and extracurricular activities, but their "personal ratings" were lower and hence brought down the overall score. The plaintiffs argued that stereotyping was at work, negatively describing Asian-Americans (e.g., on the indices of likability, kindness, respectability) that lowered their scores. Peter Arcidiacona an economics professor from Duke University testified that omitting the personal scores would have the effect of a 16% increase in admitted Asian-Americans. Harvard's expert empiricist, David Card, from UC Berkeley in his study did not report substantial race effects in the personal ratings (see *Students for Fair Admissions v. Harvard*, 2021: 3). Harvard offered a response and the Court agreed to hear a consolidated case in early 2022.

At the first level, Federal district court, Judge Allison D. Burroughs ruled (2019) in favor of Harvard. It was appealed, and the Federal Appeals court ruled (2020) for Harvard and that the District Court was not in error. There has been much critical literature on these cases. Jeena Shah (2020: 143), for example, has argued that the articulated issue misses the point, and the outcomes essentially support "the inherent value of whiteness in the racial caste system of the United States." Whiteness, in other words, remained an unstated standard of comparison in the lower and appeals court decisions. This case also underscores divisions and conflict being created between identity groups, here, African-Americans, Asian Americans, Hispanics, and retrenchment by whites. Under the standard of "diverse student bodies" as a compelling interest, it remains to be seen how diversity issues will appear in coming days with ascending identity identifications. Will, for example, an exclusionary identity politics reign with increasing competition among groups for seats available? Could a standard upholding both differences and sameness emerge in a climate of limited seats available?

Another instructive case concerns the admissions policies at eight elite New York City High schools, *McAuliffe PTO v. de Blasio* (2018; see also Hirsch, 2020). Graduating from one of the elite high schools provided excellent opportunity to be admitted in top universities in the country, and provided a base for future successful and lucrative employment in high positions. During 2018–2019, Black and Latinx students constituted 66% of all students in New York high schools but only 10% at the elite schools (Kim, 2020). Asian American and white students were 31% of New York city's students but were 86% at the elite high schools. At one of the elite schools, Stuyvesant, only 7 African-American students were admitted out of 895 spots (see Shapiro, 2019). Ten were admitted the previous year, and 13 prior to that year. Hispanic students had 33 admissions, Asian-Americans 587, and white students 194 (ibid.). At Bronx science, admitted Hispanic students dropped from 65 the previous year to 43 (ibid.). 190 African-Americans of a total of 4,800 students were admitted to the elite schools. Mayor Blasio called this a "monumental injustice." Some have called this as yet another facet of the New Jim Crow Laws.

Blasio first, unsuccessfully tried to phase out the admissions tests based on raw scores. He then pushed for the "Discovery" program catered to disadvantaged backgrounds. Its criteria: "a student must come from a 'disadvantaged' background and show good SHSAT scores [admission test scores], high potential, and the ability to cope with a rigorous high school program" (reported in Kim, 2020: 2). Asian Americans responded that the Discovery program would place them at a disadvantage and violated the equal protection clause of the 14th Amendment in that it discriminated against Asian Americans (*McAuliffe PTO v. de Blasio*).

The Federal District court ruled in favor of Blasio's Discovery plan,[22] and ruled it was "rationally related to a legitimate interest in helping more economically disadvantaged students receive a high-quality education" (reported in Kim, 2020; see also Shapiro, 2021; Hirsch, 2020). How will higher courts rule on these scenarios?[23] Once again, we see conflict between identity groups, here Asian-Americans, African-Americans, Latinx, and whites. As in admissions tests at the college and university level, it remains to be seen, under the rubric of the necessity for diversity in the student population for the education process, protected as a "compelling state interest," how it will unfold as other identity groups seek redress for their under representation, and what effects this will have on inter-identity group conflict. Or, will there be a greater recognition of the conditions from which disparities develop in the first instance?

Intersectionality, Identity Groups and Alternative Conceptualization: Seeking Commonalities

The above diversity of identity groups and particularly given the court cases reviewed underscores more basic questions about identity groups and identity politics. A sociology of law would look beyond the legalistic resolutions based on legal formalism (formal rationality) and to the nature of historically and politically economically situated solidarity and identity formations and how these are incorporated in legal identities and resolutions. West (2018), we recall, was lamenting the decline of feminist theory and the ascendancy of feminist jurisprudence in confronting repressive practices, even as we witness the courts struggling with the increasing conflicts between ascending identity groups and what should be adequate representation (diverse student bodies) in schools and universities. We have witnessed a plurality of emergent and emerging identity groups, noting differences. Intersectionality, identity groups, and standpoint epistemology have become increasingly problematized (for an insightful critical constructive commentary, see Heyes, 2020).[24]

Can we come full circle and look at what constitutes similarities as a basis of solidarity? We get a hint from Durkheim's notion of organic solidarity, and some philosophers who argue for the inherently unbreakable connection between self and other, an "I-thou" identity. Three particular approaches provide possible directions for a fuller development of sociology of law that provides a balance between theory and jurisprudence: Hardt and Negri, the multitude; Gloria Anzaldúa, Chicana Third Space feminism; and David McNally and Sue Ferguson, social reproduction feminism.

Michael Hardt, more postmodernist, and Antoni Negri, more revisionist Marxist have offered the notion of the "multitude" (Hardt and Negri, 2004). They characterize human beings as singularities, "multiplicities," unique in every way; but it is a multitude, raising the often-expressed image of a "rainbow coalition," that is a nonessentialist "multiplicity of singularities" (ibid., 106). A multitude is more what chaos theory calls "dissipative structures," temporary organizations that with even the slightest perturbation, constantly dissipate, evolving into new responsive forms, each of which can be the basis for political mobilization for social change (see Chapter 11).

Gloria Anzaldúa (2009) offers the idea of a "third space feminism," responding to Chicana's experiences. Her central idea is building metaphorical "bridges," which acknowledge a plurality of identities, always in movement, always contingent, always a becoming connected to active practices that "foster dialog across categories" (Merla-Watson, 2012: 504). With the intensity that often arise, she also advocates incorporating "breaks," "the temporary need to temporarily withdraw from this work and to reenergize" (ibid., 505; Anzaldúa, 2009: 141, 147–148). This active involvement makes use of "mediating, being able to go beyond binaries, to help locate commonality through differences ... a working toward the common" (Merla-Watson, 506, 508). Merla-Watson criticizes Hardt and Negri as being unduly static and unhistorical.

The third idea is "social reproduction feminism" drawing from a Marxist historical materialist analysis with emphasis on dialectical development (Ferguson, 2016, 2020; McNally, 2017; McNally and Ferguson, 2015). This approach argues that intersectional analysis sometimes overlooks historical and political economic development of identity groups, particularly their reproduction, and their shifting coalitions and differences. An active critical engagement with Crenshaw's and Collin's groundbreaking work on intersectionality is advocated for a more integrative position concerning the complexities that are involved. For example, in an interview, McNally and Ferguson (2015: 2) say intersexuality has "not developed any coherent explanation of how and why, for instance, heterosexualized relations intersect with patriarchal relations in some ways and not others (why the family, though its form changes over time to accommodate, for instance, same-sex marriage, nonetheless remains a private institution through which heteronormativity and patriarchy are routinely if not always affirmed)." In other words, social totality is not comprehensively theorized, particularly historically and political economically, "*why* these multiple oppressions exist and are reproduced throughout late capitalism" (ibid., 8).

One suggestion for an alternative conceptualization for the development of bonds of solidarity based on sameness is the use of metaphor, a call to "stand in the river of life, where multiple creeks and streams have converged into a complex pulsating system" (McNally, 107; Capeheart and Milovanovic, 2020: 265). They advocate, then, a contingent holistic approach that builds on the findings of anti-racist and anti-colonial theory.

A sociology of law would build on the struggles of disenfranchised groups, Critical Legal Studies Movement and CRT and its spawnings, integrating theory with practice (jurisprudence) into possible unitary frameworks that respects difference *and* commonalities. A necessary strategy is recruiting and sensitizing activist lawyers, often limited in theory because of their more formal legal training in formal rationality, as co-developers of new strategies for social change.

Summary

Early second wave critical approaches in law include feminist jurisprudence ("fem-crits") and "race-crits" (CRT) which continue to grow in scope and intensity. Key insights concerning the repressive and ideological functions of law have been, and continue to be articulated. Fem-crits and race-crits not only advocate dismantling repressive legal institutions and their legitimizing ideological structures, but are approaches that are offering tangible policy recommendations in its reconstructive agenda. Critical race theory in law reached a take-off point in the late 1980s. It continues to have a significant impact in social movements. Doing a sociology of law is much connected with greater societal conditions and practices. They are interconnected. Advocates of CRTs offer insightful analysis as to how law is politically mobilized and sustained. They go further than other critical legal theorists in so much as theirs is a much more encompassing methodology, from how people form identifications to how societal structures sustain racist practices in law. Particular concepts include racialization, microaggressions, rule- and fact-skepticism, narratives, legal storytelling, counter storytelling, standpoint epistemology, intersectionality, and interest-convergence. We have also examined two illustrative legal cases that highlights intersectional identities and conflicts between them. Although CRT and the CLS Movement reside at the intersections of jurisprudence and the sociology of law, their program tends towards a fully developed and comprehensive sociology of law. We have also witnessed "spawnings" or "spin-offs" of the Critical Legal Studies Movement. Given the proliferation of identity-groups, we returned to the question of commonalities. How will liberal legalism (dogmatic law, jurisprudence, formal rationality) accommodate to the continuous growth of identity groups and conflicts that emerge? How will substantive rational principles be incorporated in law? What constitutes a "reasonable person in law" (replacing the "reasonable man" standard)? Can formal rationality accommodate to a possible "reasonable intersectional person" standard? How will the tension between universalism and difference develop?

Review Questions

1. Feminist jurisprudence has predominantly argued *within* the legal system (legal dogmatics, formal rationality), whereas "fem-crits" were to engage various disciplines in formulating platforms for social change. What are the benefits of each approach? What drawbacks are there for each approach?

2. West (2018) has argued that there is a decline of feminist legal theory and an ascendancy of feminist jurisprudence. Why is this significant? Explain.

3. Some feminists have argued for equal rights as protected by the "equal protection clause" of the 14th Amendment to the U.S. Constitution. Some have seen this as a problem. And some, particularly race-crits, see it as a necessary step. Explain each.

4. Some, faced with problems with basing political agendas on objective truths versus subjective truths opt, instead, for "contingent universalities." Does this overcome the dilemma in formulating a political agenda from which to launch social movements?

5. Search newspapers and find a case of "differential racialization." Bring to class. Be prepared to summarize and show how it is an example. How does CRT explain it?

6. Profiling takes different forms. Bring to class for discussion an example where you were profiled, or inaccurately stereotyped. Explain how you felt. What did you do about it? How did the attributors respond? How did you respond? How was it resolved, or how did the incident eventually conclude, if at all? Alternatively, given an example of someone you know (keep identity anonymous).

7. Bring to class a situation where several people in your group were talking about a particular member of some ethnic group and you had some disagreements as to how they were portrayed, and offered a "counter story." How did the encounter go?

8. Standpoint theory and intersectionality imply the need for a replacement to the "reasonable man," now, "reasonable person in law," with a possible "reasonable intersectional person." What is its viability? Can it adequately respond to the universal legal subject of law?

9. Brings to class an example of what CRT calls "interest convergence" that you have seen on the media. Explain how it is so.

10. We have seen a number of new developments from the initial momentum established by the Critical Legal Studies Movement. Should identity groups also seek commonalities? Explain why or why not. Then, in the legal system we are now seeing more cases where different identity groups are in conflict for admission to prestigious high schools and colleges, even with the call for a "diverse student body" as a "compelling state interest." Can this genuinely be resolved in the legal arena, or must we also go outside of it incorporating a sociology of law?

Endnotes

1. For good introductions to the field, see the website, *Feminist Jurisprudence: An Overview*, 2021; Burchard, 2021; West, 2018; Fineman, 2005; McAfee and Howard, 2018;

2. See Goldfarb, 1992; Bartlett and Kennedy, 1991; see also the two-volume special issue of the *New England Law Review* (vol. 26, nos. 3 and 4, 1992) devoted to feminist critical legal studies, and also Kramer, 1995.

3. For one ranking system of various feminist journals, see *Scimago Journal and Country Ranking* (2021).

4. There are some affinities and differences with "performative feminism" offered by McAfee and Howard (2018) with the post postmodern perspective.

5. Enrollment of women in law school increased from nine percent in 1971 to thirty-four percent in 1981 (see Fineman, 2005: note 4).

6. See, for example, "Timeline of Major Supreme Court Decisions on Women's Rights," 2020.

7. Note the question concerning the threshold is outstanding. In *Abdel-Ghani v. Target Corp.* 686 F. 377 (2017), even where the plaintiff was called by coworkers a "camel jockey," "terrorist," and that "people like him should be rounded up in one place and nuked," and was informed to "go back home, go to [his] country," the court ruled in favor of the employer.

8. Diertz (2003) and McAfee and Howard (2018) argue that there are two subcategories of difference-feminists: one rooted in the caring tradition, the other, French psychoanalytic feminist tradition which includes Irigaray, Cixous, and Kristeva.

9. For an illuminating critical debate on feminist standpoint theory between Susan Hekman (1997), a postmodernist and critic, and responders Sandra Harding, Nancy Hartsock, Hill Collins

and Dorothy Smith, see Harding's anthology (2004). See also comments on these debates by Bowell (2021: 11–14).

10. Other introductory contributions are by Mari Matsuda, *Where is Your Body?* (1996) and Katheryn Russell's *The Color of Crime* (1998). (See also two early special issues of journals: *International Journal of Qualitative Studies* [1998], and *California Law Review* [1994].)

11. Some of the key figures in the development of Critical Race Theory have been Derrick Bell, Alan Freeman, Kimberle Crenshaw, Angela Harris, Charles Lawrence, Mari Matsuda, and Patricia Williams. Latinos/as include Richard Delgado, Kevin Johnson, Margaret Montoya, Juan Perea, and Francisco Valdes. Asian scholars include Eric Yamamoto, Mari Matsuda, and Neil Gotanda (see Delgado and Stefancic, 2017: 4).

12. See autobiographical writings of those who experienced slavery and struggled for abolition, which include Mary Prince (1788–1833; see Pringle, 2020); Frederick Douglas (1818–1895; see Douglas, 2016); and Sojourner Truth (1797–1883; see Painter, 1997; Truth, 2008).

13. For a useful reference time-line, 1940s to 1960s, see "Civil Rights Movement Timeline," (2021).

14. See *Wikipedia* "List of Landmark Court Decisions in the United States," section entitled "Discrimination Based on Race and Ethnicity," for a collection of key cases, 2021.

15. See Lawrence's (1987) oft-cited notion of "unconscious racism"; see also Crenshaw's favorable nod to postmodern analysis as contributing to an understanding of the notion of "intersectionality" (1993: 114).

16. See the recent cases in New York City and Newark on aggressive stop and frisk that disproportionally impacts people of color (Goldstein, 2013; Gelman *et al.*, 2013).

17. For useful, general research beginning, see Wikipedia, "Microaggression," section on "criticism," accessed on 3/27/2021, https://en.wikipedia.org/w/index.php?title=Special:CiteThisPage&page=Microaggression&id=1012037271&wpFormIdentifier=titleform.

18. There is considerable research material readily available on the topic. Due to space limitation we cannot do justice in any attempt to canvas all the identity groups that have emerged.

19. See Hand (2018). For a resource center and glossary of terms, see "LGBTQIA Resource Center at University of California Davis (2021).

20. This included the forceful removal of Native Americans to attend special boarding schools in the U.S. where the focus was to "civilize the savage," see R. Callimachi, "Lost Lives, Lost Culture: The Forgotten History of Indigenous Boarding Schools," *New York Times*, July 19, 2021, accessed, 8/30/2021, https://www.nytimes.com/2021/07/19/us/us-canada-indigenous-boarding-residential-schools.html?action=click&module=Top%20Stories&pgtype=Homepage.

21. For key Indigenous Canadian Court cases, see Simon Fraser University library's depository, "Supreme Court of Canada Cases Involving Indigenous Peoples," accessed 8/30/2021, ib.sfu.ca/help/research-assistance/subject/criminology/legal-information/indigenous-scc-cases.

22. See https://casetext.com/case/christa-mcauliffe-intermediate-sch-pto-inc-v-de-blasio-3.

23. See recent case, *Integrate NYC, Inc. v. New York*, filed March 9, 2021, claiming New York City public schools perpetuate racial hierarchies (Cruz, 2021), that the curriculum teaches "civilization is equated with whiteness."

24. Not the least of which is that identity politics creates its own internal disciplinary mechanism normalizing its members to the appropriate understanding, and sometime creating the very barriers to engage other groups that they seek to overcome, and in its opposition with dominant powers and identities, creates dependence on these others in the creation of their own identity and hence inadvertently reconstitutes oppressive hierarchies (Heyes, 2020: 3–6).

8

Structural Functionalism, Autopoiesis and the Behavior of Law

---

Introduction

A number of perspectives in the sociology of law have concentrated on the overall dynamics of a socio-political system and have asked how law is related to it; that is, how law functions in relation to the core structures of a particular society. In this approach, the question of agency, or, in other words, the question of the subject, is directly connected with system-created needs. Another perspective has taken the view that law "behaves" in patterned ways and is related to various structural aspects of a society such as differences in income levels and degrees of integration of two people in dispute.

Sociological jurisprudence, we have seen, is predominantly focused on discussions and critiques of the logic of legal formalism, although social sources are sometimes applied such as with Roscoe Pound. Sociology of law draws primarily from social sources in questioning the wherewithal of the legal system in place for the purpose of developing more comprehensive understandings especially drawing from sociology. Jurisprudence, legal dogmatics, is legal formalism where critique remains predominantly internal to the legal system (formal rationality). Sociological jurisprudence, as suggested by the modifier, begins external critique but remains imbedded primarily within the legal arena. Sociology of law, we have found out, is more an external critique, although sociological jurisprudence, unlike jurisprudence of the more dogmatic form (legal pluralism) begins to move toward the former. This chapter is exemplary of a sociology of law approach.

This chapter is divided into three sections. The first section will provide an overview of structural functionalism. Talcott Parsons is a key sociological figure to have laid out the groundwork for this sociological view. So, too, Adam Podgorecki. Niklas Luhmann is perhaps one of the most recognized theorists in the sociology of law in this tradition. We will pay particular attention to his views.

In the second section, we shall develop the autopoiesis perspective and structural coupling in law. A derivative of structural functionalism, the key theorists here are

Guenther Teubner and Niklas Luhmann. Its main concern is with a self-regulating legal system. That is, law is seen as developing a relatively independent existence that then provides the elements out of which it continuously reconstructs itself with the willing help of subjects. Put another way, there is a circularity that produces regularity, predictability and homeostasis in law and society.

In the third section, we will focus on a behavioristic theory of law as developed by Donald Black. Black argues that law "behaves" in predictable ways. In other words, it is patterned in its everyday functioning. He identifies these patterns in a number of summary propositions, provides some implications of these findings, and then argues for a new approach in the sociology of law—the sociology of the case. He points out "how" law behaves and leaves the reader to answer the "why" it behaves as it does.

Structural Functionalism and the Sociology of Law

Introduction

Structural functionalism is one of the main schools of thought in sociology. The 1940s and 1950s witnessed much development. Emile Durkheim, it has often been argued, was most influential in its development. Theorists from this approach generally look at the overall functioning of a social system and ask what purpose a particular institution ("subsystem"), including law, serves within the overall scheme of things. We will briefly present the key themes of this approach and then point out their impact on a sociology of law.

The structural-functional approach places much emphasis on the socialization process by which shared values and outlook are acquired. It assumes a certain conception of the human subject. Human nature is connected with the idea of *tabula rasa* (a person is assumed to be born a clean slate and society writes its program on it). The notion of *homo duplex* is also closely connected with this approach. People, by nature, are assumed to be half egoistic (self-oriented) and half altruistic (social). Durkheim's position reflects this view. External forces such as the family, school, religion, media, and the legal and political structures are said to produce a particular, and a necessary, balance between the two. When out of balance, deviance and conflict are outcomes; where balanced, order, stability, and predictability.

According to this approach, people perform many *social roles* (repetitive patterned behavior, e.g., mother, father, police officer, teacher, lawyer and so forth). These roles are learned in early childhood experiences and are subsequently reinforced in everyday behavior. A social role has two components. Occupiers of a role are expected to behave in certain ways. And the person within the role senses an obligation to perform certain acts that are consistent with the role assumed. Roles, in turn, are always situated in some context which provides background relevancies. That is, certain community standards provide the relevant background within which social roles are performed. Thus, roles in combination with some community standard structure every-day behavior. Roles and different institutions within a society must be coordinated by some mechanism to assure that smooth interactions take place.

A smooth running, well-oiled machine is the ideal society for the structural functionalists. In other words, to make use of an analogy with a biological organism, different organs have to be integrated in one whole for smooth functioning of the organism. Any malfunctioning in one organ will have effects on others. Deviance and pathology in this framework mean anything that disturbs the overall balance or equilibrium. Excessive strain or inadequate socialization are said to be the prime determinants of deviance. The deviant is seen as out of adjustment and harmony, or in a state of *anomie* (Durkheim). Well-adjusted individuals are those who have been socialized into accepting the obligatory character of roles in society. This ideal is also referred to as homeostasis. Talcott Parsons, the key theorist, has noted that "health may be defined as the state of optimum capacity of an individual for the effective performance of the roles and tasks for which he has been socialized" (1963: 176). The family, educational institutions and the media are said to be the main forces for socialization. Internal (psychological) and external (societal) constraints assure that deviation will not be the dominant expression. Norms (recurring behavior) and the normative order (generally accepted behavioral norms, particularly dealing with expectations and obligations) are established and stabilized over time.

The central purpose or function of law in this framework is to integrate various roles and institutions for the smooth functioning of the whole society. Parsons, for example, has stated that the "primary function of a legal system is integrative" (1962: 58).

Laws are not necessarily written. For example, Malinowski, an anthropologist, has shown how rules stand out because they are felt to be obligatory. Sanctioning forces—those forces that assure compliance to norms (i.e., claims made on another and readily respected by the other as obligatory)—are rooted in "mutual dependence" and "reciprocal services" in a society where one finds oneself in many interconnected relationships (Malinowski, 1976: 55). Put in another way, the glue, the bond of each to the other in traditional society, was based on a web of relationships that were sustained over time (see also Durkheim, Chapter 3). Each person depended on the other. Each found themselves in many reciprocal relationships, which further cemented solidarity and the normative order in the group.

Talcott Parsons: Integrated Systems and the Sociology of Law

Talcott Parsons (1902–1979), a prominent thinker in sociology, was influenced by Max Weber and Emile Durkheim in developing a structural functionalist view of society and law (1937; 1951). Law, however, was not his central concern (for a useful collection of his key works on law, see Trevino, 2008; see also Thomas, 2006). Parson (2008: 99) laments: "After the brilliant start by Durkheim and Max Weber ... it is something of a mystery why the social sciences and particularly, perhaps, sociology have shown so little interest in the study of law and the legal system."

Law is a subsystem that serves as a mechanism of social control but has a primarily integrative function. As social control, it regulates people's actions to assure smooth functioning and avoidance of deviance and conflict. According to Parsons (2008: 307), "law ... consists in body of norms or rules governing human conduct in social situations...." Law, in its social integrative function, regulates the various subsystems toward mutual adjustments to assure smooth coordination, social equilibrium, social harmony, sometimes referred to as homeostasis. It functions to maintain, metaphorically speaking, a well-oiled machine. It seeks to prevent disintegration, conflict and disharmony. Members, through socialization, primarily by way of the educational, familial, and religious subsystem, are encouraged to conform to the dominant values in society. Consensus in expectations and internalization of the normatively defined pathways to established ideals produces the ideal equilibrium point. It is realizable by way of functional integration and coordination of all subsystems.

The legal system is a facilitator. "The primary function of a legal system," Parsons tells us, once again, "is integrative" (2008: 292). It is also seen as relatively independent from the executive and legislative branches of government due to the professionalization of law (Parsons, 1960: 144; 2008: 295–296; Trevino, 2009: 321). In another sense, however, the legal system is closely associated with the political system: "If the enforcement of law through physical coercion is monopolized by the political system..., then the legal system must have a close association with it" (Trevino, ibid., 320–321). Both must be highly integrated for the well-oiled machine to function smoothly. Rewards and sanctions are further inducements for compliance by the citizenry. His more formal definition of law (1960: 264) states:

> ... law may be said to be any relatively formalized and integrated body of rules which impose obligations on persons playing particular roles in particular collectivities ... that there is a machinery of authoritative interpretations, i.e., something analogous to a system of courts, and a machinery of the definition and implementation of sanctions, and relatively clear focus on legitimation.

The practicing lawyer's role is both a public servant and "private advisor" (Parsons, 2008: 296). In the latter capacity, the lawyer functions to smooth over conflicts (ibid.). Lawyers take input from their clients and translate this into the appropriate, acceptable language of law, and thereby integrate client's issues with system rules in tending toward smooth resolutions. In more sober moments, he acknowledges strains that exist in the lawyer role (ibid., 297–302):

> The legal profession, then has to maintain difficult balances in a tradition that is in itself exceedingly complex, that is applied to a very complex and changing conditions, subject to severe pressures from interest groups, authoritatively based only on very general and partly ambiguous documents, and subject to change within considerable limits by the more or less arbitrary and unpredictable 'will of the people' (ibid., 297).

The legal profession is a "mechanism of social control," predominantly in its interpretive function: it socializes neophytes, brings them in accord with societal expectations, and back where they deviate—"by advising the client in ways that will keep him better in line, and also by 'cooling him off'" (ibid.). All facilitates greater integration in society. Legal procedures, he tells us, in its "cooling off" function, reduces passions. The attorney often helps the client to "face reality," encourage only claims that have probabilities of "stand[ing] up," and "to realize and emotionally to accept the fact that the other fellow may have a case too" (ibid., 300). The long delays in court proceedings, he says, further aid this cooling off function. Those under strain, he argues, must also have opportunities for "tension release" (ibid.). Lawyers contribute to system integration, stability, and homeostasis.

Niklas Luhmann: Structural Functionalism and the Sociology of Law

Niklas Luhmann (1927–1998) is a central figure in the contemporary structural functional approach in the sociology of law. He was born in Luneburg, Germany in 1929. His early training was in law, which he practiced for a short while. In 1960–61, he taught at Harvard, where he was influenced by the noted structural functionalist Talcott Parsons. Luhmann has authored over 30 books and numerous articles. Luhmann's clearest rendition of sociology of law was developed in *A Sociological Theory of Law* (1985; see also 1988, 1990, 1995). It is extremely dense in its analysis. Little disagreement, if any, exists that his approach is one of the best examples of a structural-functional analysis in the sociology of law. We will outline components of Luhmann's structural functionalism in law; in the next section we will elaborate more specifically on two key components, autopoiesis and structural coupling.

For Luhmann, the function of law is not primarily repressive. It is facilitative. Its function is that of providing a predictable environment in which subjects can plan and carry out their everyday activities and be assured that disappointments will be few; and if they do occur, that remedies will be readily available to put things back into order.

The essence of law is "congruently generalized normative behavioural expectations." This rather cumbersome phrase, central to an understanding of Luhmann, can be clarified. "Behavioral expectations" stands for the idea that each person in interaction with others has certain expectations of the other as to what might take place. People in society find themselves orienting themselves to each other. I expect that the other will act predictably, according to the role they are occupying in a certain context. On the other hand, once I find myself in a social role, I feel a sense of obligation to conform to it, or at a minimum, a necessity to orient myself to it, even if only to the extent of using it to sensitize myself to what is commonly done. As long as the other and I mutually orient ourselves in this way, smooth interactions can be assured. By "normative," he means the extent to which a *pattern* of expectations develops and becomes stabilized over time. It is "congruently generalized" to the extent that both the self and the other acquire and assume *similar* expectations of each other (and understand that each understands this) in interactions. This expectational structure, social philosophers tell us, is often taken for granted and becomes a set of background relevancies in social encounters.

These normative behavioral expectations may be conscious. But many times, they are semiconscious or unconscious. Subjects are not always aware of the structural influences on their decision making and behavior. Consider the following test. You are in a general conversation with somebody and deliberately begin to move closer to them during the conversation. You will note at some point that a reaction of confusion and some anxiety by the other will be forthcoming. Sometimes the other will simply back off to an appropriate distance, sometimes they will begin to question your motives. What has occurred is that you have offended an unstated or unwritten rule (behavioral expectations) as far as the appropriate distance (normative) two interactors should stand from each other. Normally, both understand the given rule or norm (= congruently generalized). And each understands the other as understanding this. One need not state what the rule is; this is unnecessary. Both assume that each is planning in accordance with the accepted, taken-for-granted rule. It is only in its infraction that the rule becomes clear by the reaction that it generates. (We may recall Durkheim's notion of the "social fact.")

Take a more complicated example, which brings out the central problem for Luhmann. In R.D. Laing's remarkable book entitled *Knots,* there are many examples of the potential problems in interpersonal interaction (1970: 21). Consider the following:

> JILL: I'm upset you are upset.
>
> JACK: I'm not upset.
>
> JILL: I'm upset that you're not upset that I'm upset you're upset.
>
> JACK: I'm upset that you're upset that I'm not upset that you're upset that I'm upset, when I'm not.

And so on. This guessing what the other is thinking and vice-versa, then, can continue to no end (an infinite regress) creating problems in interpersonal interactions. At what point can I be assured that I am "in sync" (congruence) with the other? And at what point can the other be assured that they are "in sync" with me? At what point, in other words, are we communicating at the same level (congruent generalizations)? If we are not at the same level, are we even communicating? These are not trivial questions. Law, for Luhmann, helps to stabilize mutual expectations. It produces order. That is, it establishes a rule that both interactors take as a given, as a premise for further action. Having established a rule, the interaction can continue coherently with minimal friction. Laing's potentially destabilizing infinite spiral will be minimized.

At times, we are performers who attempt to assure the smooth flow of events, even when we occasionally glimpse the role-playing that is taking place. Consider, for a moment, how on an informal level, the strength of unwritten rules assure that roles are performed correctly. Laing (1970: 1): "They are playing a game. They are playing at not playing a game. If I show them I see they are, I shall break the rule and they will punish me. I must play their game, of not seeing I see the game."

Differences exist in expectational structures (expectations that become general in a society) in traditional and modern societies (recall Durkheim). In traditional societies, marked by relatively low complexity, predictability is high. Tradition assures that a set of behavioral expectations is internalized by all. In other words, a "normative order" has gained stability. All understand the rule. They need not be written. In more complex societies, however, establishing common premises for action becomes a problem. Because of "contingencies" (unplanned, chance happenings), and hence the ever-present potential for conflict in interpersonal interaction, subjects need some relatively stable order and a degree of predictability for their orientation. This poses the fundamental problem. Is the stranger first to ask the other for an inventory of the core assumptions upon which they rely on before the interaction can continue? Clearly not. Law, however, fulfills this function according to Luhmann: it acts as a background set of assumptions, expectations and premises for action.

Thus, the social system needs a specific form of law that reflects its degree of complexity. Rigid, concrete norms rooted in traditional practices of traditional societies would not serve a function in a relatively highly complex society, where much flexibility is demanded. Norms, in a more complex society, become separated from their original, concrete context and become applicable to many contexts. They become more abstract and less contextual (i.e., less tied to concrete situations). Law has to be more elastic, and hence more abstract, to be able to cover diverse possibilities. On the other hand, in a society marked by kinship structures or by the feudal order, rights and duties are concretely defined. For example, law states who "may marry whom, who may hunt, who may start a business, who must serve on foot or on horseback, etc." (Luhmann, 1985: 12).

In a more complex society, particularly those that developed after the dissolution of the feudal society, an individual becomes an abstraction in law, the so-called "reasonable man" or juridic subject. An individual becomes the bearer of general abstract rights (recall Pashukanis, Chapter 5). After the 18th century, it is the abstraction that is infused with rights and duties. Even though people vary, psychologically and in terms of social class, gender, race, ethnicity, etc., the law subsumes all within this category, giving all universal rights. In traditional societies as well as in feudalism this would be unheard of. One's rights, duties and obligations attach to one's position in a hierarchy, or one's status in a particular village, clan, kinship or household community.

Sir Henry Sumner Maine's evolutionary thesis of the development of law from "status to contract" is given support in Luhmann's analysis. In traditional societies, contingencies—and hence uncertainties—were fewer. Or at least, stable patterns emerged as a response to commonly faced situations over time. The normative order was stable and predictable. All knew what to expect of the other. All knew the obligations and duties that existed. All participated very concretely and intimately with each other in society. In a more complex society, contingency in interactions increases. Hence, certainty in expectations decreases. Stability is more precarious. Disappointments are greater. There is, to use Luhmann's phrase, "an overproduction of possibilities." This is twofold. First, expectations of the other's behavior become more problematic. And, second, knowing what one's own behavior means to the other is also unclear. In other words, in both situations an accurate judgment, and hence planning and smooth interaction, become much more difficult. Law, here, serves to reestablish predictability. It assures that each person in an interaction orients their behavior to the same premises. The risk of error, therefore, decreases. As Luhmann tells us,

> the orientation toward the rule makes the orientation toward expectations unnecessary. It further absorbs the risk of error arising from expectation or at least reduces it ... rules thus unload complexity and contingency from consciousness (1985: 30).

The individual is relieved of testing the other. Thus, potential anxieties or disappointments are reduced. Law functions so as to secure these expectations. It produces a stable framework (normative order) within which planning and decision making can occur.

Evolution of law. Luhmann has an evolutionary theory of law. The "motor" of this evolutionary process is the increasing complexity of society (ibid., 106). With increasing complexity, and with it contingency, more demands are placed on law to be more effective in establishing "congruent generalizations" (ibid., 83). Put in another way, as society evolves toward greater complexity, particularly due to the development of more differentiated roles, and with the prevalence of greater stress because of greater unpredictability, something is needed to coordinate these roles so that constant disappointments are not experienced. This "something," again, is law.

Luhmann notes three stages in the development of law. The first stage is characterized by "archaic laws." Society is based on kinship; that is, the family is of central importance. Complexity is low. Alternatives are few. The degree of abstraction, too, is low. Rather, the concrete world, the here and now, is the relevant world in which people orient their behavior. Expectations of the other are stable. Where major disappointments do arise, they are often handled by "violent self-help" (ibid., 117). In other words, when someone intentionally or unintentionally goes beyond the acceptable understandings, they are met by anger, sometimes in a collective form. Blood revenge, the curse, and the oath are all mechanisms available, if necessary, for restoring the expectations that had existed. Since all participate in a similar environment, and all internalize the normative order, there is no need to develop relatively sophisticated, abstract rules that exist separate from the immediate context of life in the kinship group or clan. Finally, the time perception of archaic society is in the present. A future time orientation is of less value. Laws are not constituted in such a way as to promote a future good. Rather, they are simply reactive. Their main focus is on the attempt to right a wrong, here and now.

"Pre-modern high culture" is the second stage. Here, differentiation has begun. "Economic developments," particularly the change from an agricultural to a trading society, are said to be the critical determinants (ibid., 125). A rigid hierarchy characterized the early stage of this period. That is, there was a specific rank ordering of individuals in society. And here, too, society was very stable and lacked many alternatives. But procedures began to develop to take the place of blood revenge for violation of expectations. The judge is now vested with the power to decide the correct expectations that exist or should have existed. Law becomes more complex. It is now made up of an increasing body of procedural rules. Law, too, becomes more independent of the immediate, concrete context. Decision making becomes more and more dependent on the legal procedure itself. It is as if a critical mass had been reached and law took on a life of its own. But law also became more and more abstract in order to take into consideration more situations separated out of their concrete contexts. Decision making itself becomes more predictable as it is based on procedural rules. Little choice is left for the judge but to abide by the previously created law.

The final stage is the "positivisation of law." In the most complex societies where many differentiated roles exist and where new ones continue to develop due to the demands of the economy, law must be consciously developed. Decision-making processes demand the application of consciously examined and determined law. Technical and economic arguments now determine the law's make-up (ibid., 157). The vastly increased "over production of possibilities" demands deliberate law-making to offset destabilizing conflicts. Laws are more and more selectively made (positive law). In other words, many kinds of laws could develop. But certain laws are selected out of the many possible. The goal is to reduce uncertainty in interactions. The ideal end is homeostasis.

Underlying the development of law is a changing conception of time. In traditional society, one marked by archaic law, the here and now or the concrete situation was of most importance. In other words, law was not focused on some future good, or some conception of a desirable future state. The present was just a continuation of the past. The past, or tradition, reinforced the present. The person who deviated from accepted norms called into question the group's whole way of life. They brought confusion to the group. And their entire status or standing in the community was called into question. The immediate focused response to the more serious transgressions—that of revenge—restored traditionally accepted practices, and thus expectations.

But a problem always existed, or its potential was always there, that the person punished might have their kin retaliate in turn. For Luhmann, only in society marked by the Judea-Christian tradition, with its notion of individual guilt, can one effectively isolate these disappointments and thus their correction (ibid., 93). As he argues, "guilt permits *absolution*—i.e., it provides for an end in the temporal dimension to the consequences arising from deviant behavior" (ibid., emphasis in the original). Thus, when society has developed to the point where the pervasive ethic of individual guilt exists, it can then isolate particular deviants and punish them without having continuous challenges to the "correction" inflicted (i.e., by the punished person's supporters). Guilt implies that some feelings have been aroused and can be reduced by some action. Equilibrium is seen as restorable. If one feels guilty, the argument goes, and is punished, then there is absolution; guilt feelings wither away.

In modern society, the past loses its hold; it no longer dictates the formation of law. Rather, law is based more on future possibilities, future consequences. It is consciously made with an eye toward future effects (ibid., 268), i.e., positive law. Thus, subjects orient their behavior within a system of law in which their consequences must be thought through. Luhmann is poignant: "The central concern of law is what may happen in the future" (ibid., 264).

An important problem in law is to determine how far in the future one should contemplate and what expectations should be stabilized as normative expectations.[1] For Luhmann, for social stability to exist, law must function to stabilize, by selecting certain expectations that should be entertained. The task for justices, then, would be to consciously select certain expectations that generally have been considered as appropriate in planning. These become the basis of evaluating the behavior of defendants, for example, before the court. The jury would decide if a "reasonable man [woman, person]" had relied on these expectations in doing or reacting the way they did. The task for this *positive law* is to create "expectancy structures" which, most of the time, would lead to desirable results for society as a whole. Luhmann does not give us a blueprint as to how this actually takes place.

In sum, modern law focuses more upon future consequences. The orientation of subjects is to these expected results. The past is said only to provide the basis for change to an open future. According to Luhmann, law's orientation to the open future should leave us "prepared for surprises" (ibid., 101). Even deviant behavior of the past, Luhmann tells us, is an opportunity for discovering new and more adaptive mechanisms to be used in the future.

Law and its functions. For the structural functionalist, law serves certain purposes (functions). Luhmann's central integrative function of law states that law stabilizes expectations and it establishes expectational structures, a framework within which subjects can work in a predictable manner.

Other functions have been specified. Aubert (1983), while cautioning us about developing classifications, nevertheless offers us five functions of law. In the real world, these overlaps. The functions of law include:

1. *Governance:* law shapes, influences or steers behavior into desirable directions by way of negative or positive sanctions.
2. *Distribution:* law helps in the distribution of resources such as retirement pensions, social security, employment compensation and so forth. Resources are distributed to reduce burdens in society.
3. *Safeguarding expectations:* law promotes predictability between subjects by securing expectations.
4. *Conflict regulation:* law helps to resolve disputes between subjects.
5. *Expression of values and ideals:* law functions so as to promote certain ideals in a society. Tax exemptions, for example, can be a positive incentive for subjects to contribute to some overall ideal.

Even though Aubert recognizes the repressive (coercive) function of law (ibid., 30–31), he argues that this has now "receded into the background" (ibid., 161). In the modern state, he argues, the emphasis has been more on the "promotional functions" of law; that is, law is primarily a mechanism by which the modern state promotes certain ideals by positive incentives.

Adam Podgorecki: Empiricism, Social Engineering and Sociology of Law

Adam Podgorecki (1925–1998) was a noted Polish authority on the sociology of law. Podgorecki's main works include *Law and Society* (1974) and *A Sociological Theory of Law* (1991). For a brief biography, see Wicenty (2018; Czarota, 2007). He was influenced by Leon Petrazycki (1867–1931) who wrote *Law and Morality* (Petrazycki and Trevino, 2017). Petrazycki has also been recognized as one of the key ("unrecognized") developers of sociology of law (Podgorecki, 1980; Kojder, 1994).

A key component of Podgorecki's sociology of law concerns social engineering. "The main objective of sociological investigation into the functioning of law," he tells us, "is to provide expert advice for social engineering, allowing for rational and effective remodeling of the human condition" (1974: 8). Thus, it has a pragmatic usefulness for social change (Podgorecki, 1962; Podgorecki *et al.*, 1996; Ziegert, 1977).

He has offered five functions of law, which he calls the "tetrad" (1974: 274–278). They include [numbers added]:

1. *Integration:* law stabilizes mutual expectations. That is, duties and rights are specified and brought into accord with the overall values of a given social system.
2. *Petrification:* law selects, through trial and error, those patterns of behavior that are functional in satisfying social needs. Those behaviors that have been tested and found useful, acceptable and just between parties are given legal recognition. Non adaptive patterns are not given force in law.
3. *Reduction:* law selects out of the many diverse behaviors in a complex society those that are acceptable. Thus, law simplifies. It reduces complexity. It makes decision making manageable. It provides a framework within a complex society in which subjects may plan within a predictable, stable order.
4. *Motivation:* law regulates individual's attitudes so that they will select behaviors that are in accord with the values of a society.
5. *Educational:* law not only punishes and motivates but also educates and socializes. This is done by rewards, which reinforce desirable performances. The goal is to instill habitual performance.

Podgorecki (1974) also informs us that the actual practice of law — that is, living law — should not be seen as a simple communication process. He suggests a "three-step hypothesis" that explains the actual communication and functioning of law. In other words, different prisms refract the laws established by lawmakers.

First, the letter of the law can be interpreted differently over time even though the actual law does not change. The social and economic system, then, will determine the meaning of law in practice.

Second, different subcultures—groups that are part of the greater society and share its general cultural ideals, yet have distinctive values, ideals and a way of life—will interpret the same law differently. In other words, students, soldiers, artists, scholars, lawyers, activists, and the homeless interpret the law differently. The law (or the legal message) is filtered through the particular culture of the group. The law, as it moves from the lawmaker to the targeted group, is refracted through subcultural prisms. These cultural forces influence its "correct" reading.

The third prism consists of personality differences. Since different psycho-social, political and economic forces produce different types of personalities, various attitudes toward the law will develop. For example, older folks more than younger folks are likely to respect the law. The civil rights workers of the 1960s, the anti-war demonstrators of the late 60s and early 70s, conscientious objectors, draft resisters, and other oppositional groups had and continue to have different interpretations of the law and its functioning particularly as to the connections to power elites and their ideological manipulation than the conventional law-abider. The point is that the personality prism produces different readings of the meaning of the law.

Podgorecki tells us that if we apply a "social engineering" perspective, laws made will be effective and efficient to the degree that all three of the above factors are considered. The least efficient law would be one operating in an unpopular social and economic system, opposed by subcultures and by rebellious personalities (ibid., 236). He adds two caveats. First, additional factors to the three mentioned above are formal procedures and semantic frameworks (i.e., structures such as those conveyed by a particular discourse such as "legalize"). These can have an influence on the transmission of the content of laws. For example, formal contractual freedom may produce substantive injustices when power differentials of the parties come into play (as we saw with Max Weber's analysis in Chapter 4); the propertied are in a better position to dictate the terms of the contract. Different semantic frameworks, too, can frame issues differently. But these are, for Podgorecki, of "minor importance" (ibid., 235).

Second, he cautions us that even if the social system is in a state of equilibrium where these three factors are functioning smoothly, it does not necessarily mean that the "law resembles the just distribution of rewards and punishments" (ibid., 276). He notes only in passing the effects of power, pointing out that it should be considered in the determination of what constitutes just laws.

Autopoiesis and Law

Introduction

Niklas Luhmann (1988, 1990, 1992, 1995) and Guenther Teubner (1983, 1989, 1992, 1993) have been the central figures in developing the autopoiesis perspective in law. A special issue of *Cardozo Law Review* (vol. 13, no 5, March 1992) was an earlier dedication in scholarly journals devoted to the subject (see also Rogowski, 2015; Baxter, 2013; Sinclair, 1992; Jacobson, 1989; Baxter, 1998; Lempert,1998; Teubner *et al.*, 2003; Mingers, 2002).

The autopoietic perspective in law has been developed from drawing on an analogy to living biological systems. The work of Humberto Maturana (1970, 1987) has been a key (Luhmann,1985, 1992). Biological systems, it is argued, are always controlled by the properties of previous generations. Systems, too, tend toward closure. An autopoietic system is therefore one in which self-reproduction continues by the use of given elements *within* the system. Similarly with law: as Teubner puts it, "Law is defined as an autopoietic social system, that is, a network of elementary operations that recursively reproduces elementary operations" (1989: 739). A system, such as law, in other words, once reaching stability, provides its own internal elements that reproduce this system. Said yet in another way, it becomes a self-generating system.

The autopoietic view has it that the legal system is a closed system (Luhmann, 1985: 282), or in Luhmann's precise words it is a "normatively closed system." Thus, any element within it has a distinct life and unity only within that system. This includes forms of consciousness and communication (for a useful comparison, see Bourdieu's notion of the *legal habitus,* 1987; Mautner, 2011). Consider, for example, the notion of the "reasonable man in law," "intent," including such defenses as "insanity," "negligent," "entrapment," etc., as well as the form of law talk. Each is an element in an overall coherent, rational, self-supporting system. Each element is related to each of the other in some overall rational framework.

Paradoxically, the legal system is also a "cognitively open system" (ibid., 283). It remains oriented to its particular environment; it is precisely this that allows the legal system to have a learning capacity. In other words, law attains a degree of relative autonomy. It takes on qualities of being objective, and thus retains a resistance to direct manipulation. The immediate environment is but a factor, which further fuels the relatively independent factors within the legal system itself. A form of self-justifying circularity thus reigns. As Luhmann would have it, "all hierarchies are circular structures: legal decisions are valid on the basis of legal rules, although (even because!) rules are valid on the basis of decisions" (ibid., 285). This rather abstract analysis produces a different line of inquiry into the character of law. Consider Luhmann's point about legal theorizing by practitioners (as opposed to a sociological examination):

> legal theory for its part participates in the autopoietic process and has to reflect on its contribution to the normative qualification of rules and decisions; thus far it goes beyond the sociological analysis of law. This at the same time

> restricts its radius of insight and the formulations, which can be propounded in that analysis (ibid., 287).

We read this quote as meaning that legal practitioners who engage in theorizing in law, or those who are law makers and decision makers in legal proceedings, find themselves imprisoned within the categories that are of the legal system's own (self) making. In other words, legal practitioners or academics from law schools, because of their training and immersion in the categories of law, will necessarily reconstruct these same categories by their use, and consequently further support and help sustain the legal system as is (jurisprudence).

Structural Coupling

But how is a legal system both normatively closed and cognitively open? In other words, how does a legal system respond to the environment within which it is situated? Is there a causal direction? Is there an identifiable causal priority? In Luhmann's lead article in the 1992 special issue of *Cardozo Law Review* (mentioned above) on autopoietic law, the answer is given in the idea of "structural coupling."[2] He tells us: "It [structural coupling] removes the idea of an over arching causality (admitting it, of course, as a construct of an observer interested in causal attribution), but retains the idea of highly selective connections between systems and environments" (Luhmann, 1992: 1432). This is the process by which the extra-legal elements from the environment (i.e., factors outside of the direct legal sphere, including substantive rational principles) are channeled into the legal environment and, in turn, back into the extra-legal environment (see also Nobles and Schiff, 2013b; Harste and Febbrajo, 2013; Nobles and Schiff, 2013).

For Luhmann, "structural couplings provide a continuous influx of disorder against which the system maintains or changes its structure" (ibid.). In other words, ideas, formulations, conceptualizations, and other data from the non-legal environment will undergo translation within the machinery of the legal order, and this translated material, in turn, will have an effect on the non-legal environment. In this sense, there are affinities with the constitutive approach in law. Luhmann makes problematic the question of causality: "[s]tructural couplings are forms of simultaneous (and therefore, not causal) relations" (Luhmann cited in Cornell, 1992: 77). Consider Jessop's explanation of structural coupling (1990: 358). According to him, it consists of four "features":

> first, the structures ... are neither hierarchically controlled nor functionally subordinate to other structures; secondly, they are not autarkic or self-sufficient but depend on inputs from their environment for their own operation; thirdly, they are not hermetically sealed off from their environments but experience changes therein as perturbations or disturbances which affect their own operation; and, fourthly, in reacting to changes in their environment, they do so in terms of their own rules for reducing the complexity of that environment and thus environmental influences are always mediated through the system's own procedures.

Examples of "structural coupling" are provided by: Nobles and Schiff (2013b) in their analysis of criminal convictions, criminal appeals and the media; Jessop (1990: 358–359) in his integration of this idea with Marxian analysis of relative autonomy in explaining how the State operates; Hunt (1993: 296–297) in his analysis of how information moves between the courts and the police; Cornell (1992: 77) in her explanation of how a dualistic gender system and hierarchy is maintained and remains a dominant point of reference for subjects; and, in a more critical way, by Sinclair (1992: 88–98) in his application of the autopoietic theory to the development of statutory law. Structural coupling could also be applied to court cases focused on admission policies in high schools, universities and law schools that have laid the groundwork for assuring diverse student bodies as a compelling state interest. Once established, self-referencing (stare decisis) in future litigation supports the initial notion of the importance of diverse student bodies for educational attainment even as refinement takes place cognizant of various identity groups' litigation. Newly formulated procedures and rights by the courts in turn structure the character of future activities in educational settings, and set the parameters for further possible litigation.[3] And procedures established in the legal arena can be coupled with other subsystems, such as in the employment arena, where, for example, a diverse employee environment should be coupled with the variations in existence in society or particular areas. But, variations exist in requisite abilities producing its own issues.

The vehicle for the autopoietic theory and structural coupling, Luhmann tells us, is communication (1992; see also Teubner, 1992; Teubner *et al.*, 2003; Harste and Febbrajo, 2013; and the critiques by Fletcher, 1992; Haverkamp, 1992; Munch, 1992). Thus, the causative arrow, from say the legal to non-legal order, goes both ways simultaneously. Law, therefore, becomes somewhat autonomous from general social communication. It has its own existence, and outside data is continuously reformulated within its categories. Structural coupling is, then, offered as the dynamic by which relatively autonomous structures such as law nevertheless have effects on other structures and are affected by them.

Teubner (1989) has examined the communicative aspects in some detail. His point is that human actors have several identities; each is located within particular domains of society. Within law, one identity will be at the forefront, or if you prefer, one mask *(persona)* will be worn. But by donning the mask, one is then subject to the discourse that is attached to it.[4] The subject is, according to Teubner, "decentered" (ibid., 741). Cognition, or thought processes, as well as forms of consciousness, are specific to a particular communicative network (i.e., particular discourses such as the legal, scientific, revolutionary, etc.). In fact, "Society is seen as fragmented into a multiplicity of closed communicative networks" or, borrowing from Foucault, into *epistemes* (ibid., 738–741). Thus, law represents a sphere or an arena where a certain form of consciousness is at play subject to the discursive elements that are unique to law (i.e., legal discourse and categories).

In sum, Luhmann's theory of autopoiesis is biologically based. Much of its persuasiveness stands and falls with this basic analogy. But this biological analogy is very consistent with structural functionalism generally, and continues to have a strong persuasive force in theorizing in law in the Western world.

The Behavior of Law and the Sociology of the Case

Introduction

Donald Black provides a behavioral model of law and propositions informing us to how law behaves in patterned ways. His sociology of law (1976, 1989, 1993, 1995, 2010; see also interview by Abramowitz, 2010) has initiated much debate. Some works have expanded on his analysis (Horwitz, 1990). Other works have attempted to subject it to empirical investigation (see for example, Kuo *et al.*, 2012; Dai and Gao, 2021; Wong, 2010; Rojek and Rosenfeld, 2012; Graham *et al.*, 2013).[5] There have also been international studies: in Canada, (Wong, 2010); China, (Kuo *et al.*, 2012); and in Canada, (Golladay, 2017), to name a few.

Empirical investigations have indicated both support and contrary findings. Some have even questioned its standing as a theory (Greenberg, 1983; Golladay, 2017; Dai and Gao, 2021). Be that as it may, Black has offered us a conceptualization of law as patterned behavior. Law behaves in a predictable manner, he tells us. In other words, if we were to take the hundreds of thousands of interactions over the course of the year at various levels of criminal justice processing, the pattern that would emerge would take the direction of the propositions that Black provides. He also draws out his implications and tells us that law is not primarily concerned with rules and that discriminatory practices are not merely aberrations, but rather that bias is inherent in the very way law behaves. One implication of his study is that the "sociology of the case" better explains law and offers various strategies for lawyers to improve their practice, and for reformers to become more aware of how to minimize biases within the courtroom.

The Behavior of Law

To understand his propositions of how law behaves, Black first provides some definitions. First, he defines law as "governmental social control" (1976: 2; 1989: 8). Then he tells us law is a quantitative variable. The amount of law mobilized can increase or decrease even in a similar situation. In other words, law is measured in terms of how much mobilization of social control takes place in a particular instance. In his words, "the quantity of law is known by the number and scope of prohibitions, obligations, and other standards to which people are subject, and by the rate of legislation, litigation, and adjudication" (ibid., 3). The more response that is mobilized, the more law that has taken place.

The peculiar thing about this is that law can vary in time and space. That is, different amounts of law can be mobilized given a similar harm at different times and at different locations. Law therefore varies "across the centuries, decades and years, months and days, even the hours of the day" (ibid.). Consider for example, the amount of law that would probably be mobilized against a 14-year-old youth if the infraction took place at 2 o'clock in the afternoon as opposed to 2 o'clock in the morning.

Styles of law. Apart from the law having a quantitative dimension, there also exist different *styles of law* (a qualitative dimension). Black identifies four specific styles of social control (1976: 5; see Figure 1).

Figure 1. Four Styles of Social Control

	Penal	Compensatory	Therapeutic	Conciliatory
Standard	prohibition	Obligation	Normality	Harmony
Problem	Guilt	Debt	Need	Conflict
Initiation of case	Group	Victim	Deviant	Disputants
Identity of deviant	Offender	Debtor	Victim	Disputant
Solution	Punishment	Payment	Help	Resolution

Briefly, the *penal style* is the criminal model. The standard is a prohibition of certain behavior; the problem, to determine guilt or innocence; the initiator of the case is the group (e.g., "The People of the State of Illinois vs. John Doe"); the identity of the deviant is that of an offender; and the solution to the case is punishment. Note that for each style, or ideal type, language differs with consequence (e.g., how we construct social reality and how we perceive the deviant). The *compensatory style* is somewhat analogous to the civil model. Here the standard is obligation; the problem is debt owed; the initiator of the case, the victim; the identity of the deviant, the debtor; and the solution, payment. The *therapeutic style* is similar to the rehabilitation model. The standard is some notion of normality; the problem is need; the initiator of the case the deviant; the identity of the deviant, the victim; and the solution, help. In the *conciliatory style,* the standard is harmony; the problem is identified as conflict; the initiator of the case is the disputant(s); the identity of the deviant, a disputant; and the solution of the problem is identified as resolution (the notion of "conflict management" is also consistent with "resolution").

A particular conflict in society may have any of the four styles of social control applied to it, but with profound difference as to how problematic situations are conceptualized and handled. Consider, for example, how at the turn of the 20th century, labor activists were dealt with by way of the penal model. Since the late 1930s in Western societies, the conciliatory model has been seen as the appropriate model (e.g., binding arbitration, mediation, etc.). In the late 1990s, the "restorative justice model" based on the conciliatory model has become more prevalent (Van Ness and Strong, 2014).

Black also tells us that the penal and compensatory model can be placed together in the category of *accusatory styles* in so much as "both have contestants, a complainant and a defendant, a winner and a loser" (ibid., 4). In this combined model, there is a "zero-sum" game at work: "it is all or nothing—punishment or nothing, payment or nothing" (ibid.). In contrast, the therapeutic model and the conciliatory model can be categorized together as *remedial styles:* they are "methods of social repair and maintenance, assistance for people in trouble ... [i]t is not a question of winning or losing, all or nothing. Rather, ... the question is what is necessary to ameliorate a bad situation" (ibid.). In other words, the remedial style is a "variable sum" game.

Black goes on to tell us that just as law varies quantitatively, so too the styles of law vary across time and space. In other words, even in the same situation of conflict a different style of social control could be mobilized.[6] Consider for example, the discretion police officers normally have to invoke one style of social control over another. And these have consequences as to how the situation is defined and handled. In fact, the history of the criminal justice system's response to the law-breaker can be seen in terms of the dominant model employed.

The theory of the behavior of law, according to Black, predicts how law will behave without any consideration whatsoever as to any assumption of human nature (ibid., 7): "[i]t neither assumes nor implies that he is, for instance, rational, goal directed, pleasure seeking, or pain avoiding" (ibid.). In this model, deviant behavior is defined as "conduct that is subject to social control" (ibid., 9). Thus, the seriousness of a crime is defined in terms of how much social control is mobilized against some behavior. It is also defined by the type of model of social control applied. The greater the quantity of social control mobilized, the more serious is the behavior perceived. Invocation of the "penal" produces different definitions of action than the other styles. Thus, as we shall see shortly, Black's propositions of the behavior of law predict: (1) the definition of crime, (2) the crime rate, (3) who the offenders are, and (4) the seriousness of the crime.[7]

Black offers us two possible dimensions in viewing a society: the vertical dimension, which stands for inequality of wealth he calls "stratification"; and the horizontal dimension, which stands for the relation of people to each other, including the degree of intimacy and integration, which he calls "morphology." Given these two dimensions, he presents his propositions that predict how law will behave.[8] These are probabilistic statements: they predict the likelihood that law will behave in a particular manner. Of course, with prediction comes deviation from the norm. We will have occasion to choose only some of his propositions to exemplify how his theory predicts the behavior of law and to draw out some consequences.

We should point out some further definitions here. By "varies directly," sociologists mean that two variables increase or decrease at similar rates (e.g., the more one studies for an exam, one variable, the higher the grade one expects, the second variable). By "varies inversely" they mean the situation where one variable increases while the other decreases at a similar rate (e.g., the warmer the weather, the fewer the clothes one wears; and the converse, colder the weather, the more the clothes one wears). In each of his propositions, there are two people (dyad) in a conflict situation. Black also assumes "all else constant" for each variable: here he means the harm inflicted in each dyad is similar, either by the way it is formally constructed in law, or by a more abstract analysis of equivalent harm.[9] In each proposition, he tells us "how" law behaves, not "why." To answer the "why" we need to do some additional application of relevant theories.

Propositions, behavior of law: stratification. His first proposition states: "law varies directly with stratification." Here the two variables are "stratification" and "quantity of law." Each variable can range from high to low. The more stratified a society, the greater the quantity of law that is mobilized. As he explains, "as traditional modes of production and distribution disappear, inequality proliferates across the world and law increases in every way" (ibid., 14–15). If, in fact, the movement of society is toward greater stratification, and if more law is proportionally mobilized, then it would seem to follow that more "crime" will be discovered. Note that he does not explain "why" this is so (i.e., law proliferating). In answering the "why" question, we must integrate additional theoretical models. We may, for example, draw from Durkheim, Weber, Marx and others.

The second proposition states: "law varies directly with rank." Law, again, is a quantitative variable and can range as to how much law is mobilized. Thus, the higher the rank, the more likelihood of law employed. With "all else constant" (meaning, two situations are similar without any undue variation in external force), "if a poor man commits a crime against another poor man, for example, this is less serious than if both are wealthy. Less happens." (ibid., 17). Lower ranks are less likely to invoke law. Note, again, he is pointing out the general pattern, the *how* law behaves. We are left to answer *why* it behaves that way.

The third proposition is: "downward law is greater than upward law." This can be pictured for clarification (see Figure 2). Here: "all else constant"; meaning, situation A = situation B as to the harm inflicted and income differences. What varies is the direction (upward? downward? in the stratified system) of the deviance and law applied.

Notice that the only difference in the two situations is with which direction the harm is inflicted. Thus, in situation A there is "upward" deviance (i.e., harm inflicted by a lower income person against a higher income person) and, as a consequence, downward law (i.e., law being applied against the lower ranking person who is committed the harm). In situation B, this is reversed. The prediction in the model is that there exists greater overall downward law than upward law. More law is likely to be applied (mobilized) downward than upward. Notice that if this is indeed the case, and if we multiply this schema several hundred thousand times in the course of the year in the U.S., the model is then predicting who the most likely offenders are, the seriousness of their offenses, the crime rate, and the very definition of crime. Each is a result of how law behaves. This will be further supported in the propositions to follow. And these predictions are borne out by *official* (governmental) crime statistics (the Uniform Crime Reports),[10] which indicate the lower classes commit disproportionally more crime than the upper classes.

Figure 2. Downward Law Is Greater Than Upward Law

Situation A (Harm inflicted in each case is similar) *Situation B*

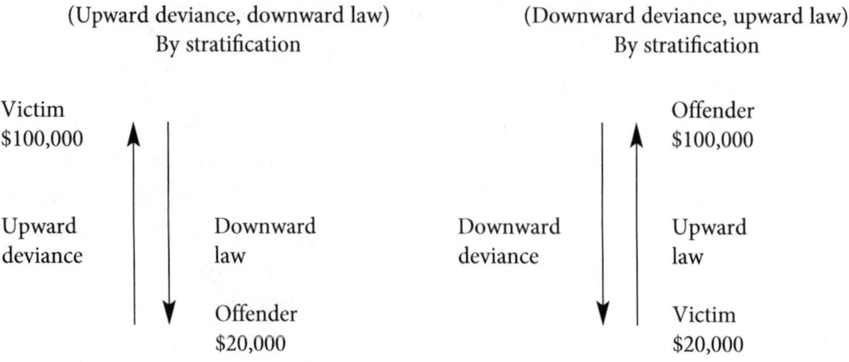

But this may be a perception created by the behavior of law. The model is not arguing that the lower class is necessarily committing more crimes; rather, it is predicting who will more likely be recipients of law. If law is indeed mobilized at a greater rate against the lower socio-economic end of the stratification schema, then this group will be perceived as the dangerous class. If the penal style is more likely to be applied in a downward direction, the net societal perception is that the lower socio-economic classes are committing more serious crimes. Self-report studies—a random sample is asked to anonymously confess to crimes they have committed—often show that the middle- and lower-class rates of self-reported crimes are not that far apart; if this so, then, what accounts for the official crime rates that indicate as we move downward in the income scale that the crime rates increase? Black would respond that it is an artifact of how law behaves. Lower classes are more likely to be recipients of the penal style of social control, and the social perceptions of the criminal class are molded accordingly.

Again, the "why" question is not being answered. CRT, fem-crits, race-crits and others would be quick to respond by pointing to growing inequalities, systemic biases, and discriminatory legal practices. Note again, Black is separating the "how" from the "why" law is behaving the way it is. For the latter, we are left to provide explanations.

A fourth proposition is: "downward law varies directly with vertical distance"; and the converse, "upward law varies inversely with vertical distance" (see Figure 3). The two variables are: "law" and "vertical distance." Again, all else is constant (situation A = B = C). Harm inflicted in each case is similar (see Note 9). The former part can be illustrated. Note that the "vertical distance"—the difference in income levels—increases, respectively, from A to B to C. For situation A, the difference is $5,000; for B, $80,000; for C, 480,000. In each situation, the lower income person inflicts some harm against a higher income person ("upward deviance"), and, as a consequence, law is mobilized "downward," against the offender ("downward law").

What the model is predicting is that in situation A less law will be applied than in situations B and C. Said differently, situation B more law, and in C even more law will be applied (in a downward direction). As we go from A to B to C we see progressively more law being applied (mobilized). A poor offender who commits a harm against victims who are progressively more well-to-do would be subject to progressively more law. More happens, more law is mobilized. Or, restated, consider a person whose income is $20,000 who commits a harm against a person making $25,000: less law is mobilized than the $20,000 person committing harm against someone making $100,000 than $500,000. At each step more law is mobilized with increased vertical distance. Conversely, a harm inflicted by the well-to-do against the very poor (diagram not included) is likely to see less happening: less law will be mobilized, or the quantity of law will be less ("upward law varies inversely with vertical distance").

Figure 3. Downward Law Varies Directly with Vertical Distance

A B C

(In each case: upward deviance, downward law)

(Harm inflicted in each case is similar)

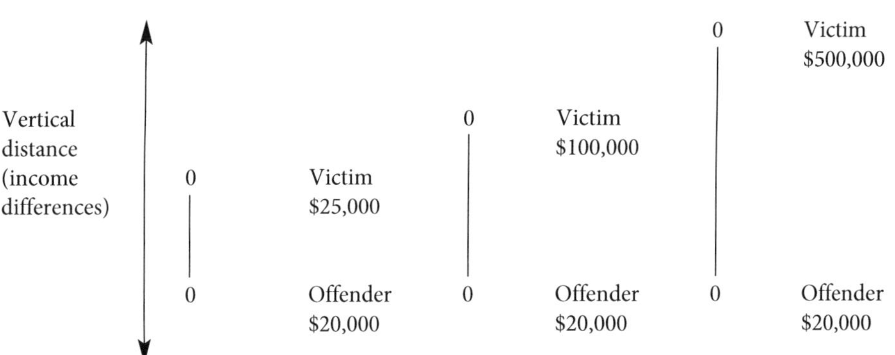

Propositions, behavior of law: styles of law. Black's propositions also explain the behavior of the *styles* of law (note again the four styles in Figure 1). For example, our fifth selected proposition is that: "downward law is more penal than upward law." And the sixth proposition: "upward law is more compensatory [or more therapeutic] than downward law." The fifth proposition considers a situation where the less wealthy person commits harm against the wealthier person. Here, law is mobilized in a "downward" direction. Here, too, we are not looking so much at how much law is mobilized (the quantitative variable), and from a previous proposition, more law will be applied, but the type (style) of law mobilized (qualitative aspect), and here, more penal law in a downward direction.

The proposition predicts that in a downward direction, law, when it is mobilized, is more likely to be the penal style (the criminal model); in an upward direction, all else constant, it is likely to be the compensatory (the civil model) or therapeutic style (the rehabilitation model). In fact, it is proportionally so (seventh proposition): "in a downward direction, penal law varies directly with vertical distance, and in an upward direction it varies inversely with vertical distance." (Recall, here "inversely" means the greater the vertical distance, the less the imposition of law.) What this means is that, with all else constant, and the only differentiating factor being the direction of the harm committed and vertical distance, the style of social control will be qualitatively different (i.e., different styles will be more likely to be mobilized). The higher income person, having committed a harm against a lower, will less likely have penal law inflicted against them. In fact, as the differences in wealth increase, this becomes increasingly the more likely event. More likely, too, in an upward direction, non-penal styles of law will be inflicted.

If this pattern appears in hundreds of thousands of interactions between agents of social control and the law-breaker, then the societal *perception* that will develop is that the lower classes are committing disproportionally more crimes, and more serious ones at that. Said in another way, if the penal style is consistently more likely to be applied against lower income persons, and the compensatory and therapeutic styles against higher income persons — with lower income persons put behind bars, higher income persons paying fines, or diverted to some non-institutionalized treatment — the perception created is that the lower classes are doing more serious crimes. In. other words, by observing how law behaves in a predictable way, we predict the seriousness of the event, who the offenders are, the crime rate, and the definition of the crime. For example, a person behind bars (penal model) is *perceived* as a more dangerous offender than one who is at liberty and is paying a fine (compensatory model). We are implying something about how "harms" are categorized by looking at what "style" of law is being mobilized. Black does not engage the political dimensions that possibly interface with the economic. He explains "how" the law behaves, not "why." To explain the "why", again, we would need to integrate or consult some other theorist or theory.

Black also tells us that (eighth proposition): "conciliatory law varies inversely with stratification." In other words, the greater the stratification in a society, the less the use of the conciliatory style. Or to approach it from the other direction, the less the stratification, the greater the use of the conciliatory style. That is, for the latter, crime begins to "disappear." Conflicts are handled by way of mediation, arbitration, community moots, and other informal proceedings.

With more stratification, more penal law and more crime results as we previously stated. In answering the "why," we would need to consult various relevant theorists. For example, we could draw from Durkheim, Weber and Marx and note: the significance of greater social density, the rise of individualism, the development of contrasting styles of life, increased amounts of conflict and alienation, depersonalization, hierarchical class differences, and growing power differentials — all could be offered as possible explanatory theories or hypotheses as to why crimes increase as stratification increases.

Propositions, behavior of law: morphology. We now move briefly to some propositions that exemplify the relationship between *morphology* (the horizontal aspects of social life) and the behavior of law. Previously we were examining stratification, the vertical dimension, indicating the difference in wealth and how law behaves. Morphology has to do with degrees of integration, participation and involvement in society, with a center (better integrated) and a periphery (less integrated extending to the margins of society).

Before continuing, we offer further clarification on terminology. In Black's conceptualization concerning morphology, there are two forms of deviance: one is committed by a more socially integrated person against a more marginal[11] person—this is *centrifugal deviance* (and consequently, we have *centripetal law*); the second is where the marginal member commits a harm against a well-integrated member—this is *centripetal deviance* (and consequently, we have *centrifugal law*).

The ninth proposition is: "centrifugal law is greater than centripetal law." The proposition, then, predicts that "all else constant," more law will be mobilized against those who commit centripetal deviance (i.e., a marginal person who commits a harm against a well-integrated person) than against those who commit centrifugal deviance. And there are degrees of this (tenth proposition): "centrifugal law varies directly with radial distance" and "centripetal law varies inversely with radial distance."

In this model of morphology, Black assumes a social organization where there are different degrees of social involvement among people. "Every kind of social life," he tells us, "has a center, periphery, and rings of participation ... Each [person] is more or less integrated" (ibid., 48). Thus, based on one's integration, the implication is that there exist degrees of vulnerability to law. As Black states: "At every stage of the legal process, a marginal person is more vulnerable to law" (ibid., 55). In fact, he continues,

> Since law varies inversely with the integration of the offender ... so do criminality and delinquency ... a person without work, a family, or other involvements is more likely to get into trouble with the law. Indeed, the authorities may even justify their severity by invoking the marginality theory of deviant behavior (ibid.).

Let's briefly provide two examples of this invocation of a "marginality theory of deviant behavior."[12] Take bail decisions as well as presentence investigations (PSIs). The former, ostensibly justified to assure the appearance of the defendant for trial, is based to a considerable extent on the status of the defendant (i.e., community ties/roots; employment, residential stability). The PSI takes place after conviction and before sentencing, and leads eventually to a recommendation (presentence report, PSR) to the judge concerning probation or prison (essentially, "in" or "out"). And once again, it too relies heavily on community ties/roots, employment and residential stability. It should be noted that structural factors that may be at the base of the defendant's situation are not being entertained to any considerable degree. In other words, the "conditions" behind different degrees of attaining stability are not scrutinized (recall the focus on "conditions" behind racism in *Brown v. Board* of Education, 1954; recall, also, the critique by "crits" of how excusability in criminal law can expand or contract as a function of socio-economic class location.

Certainly, then, some segments of the population (the poor, minorities, disenfranchised, non-propertied, etc.) are at risk as to: (1) being denied bail, i.e., on claimed poor employment history, residential instability, history of continuous family problems. And there exists much evidence for a positive correlation between being denied bail and the likelihood of conviction, even holding constant the seriousness of the crime. And (2) being deemed, after conviction, a "poor risk" for probation, with the consequence that this person is more likely to be sentenced to prison by the judge. Marginal people (the less integrated) are at greater risk before the law. The "marginality theory of law" predicts, once again, the particular "social reality of crime" (Quinney, 1970, 2000).

In sum, Black's "behavior of law" has offered us an entirely novel conceptualization in the sociology of law. Whether it is in fact a full-blown theory is still subject to debate. But nevertheless, there exist some profound consequences to sociology of law. Again, his theory does not explain *why* law behaves as it does. It is simply descriptive, explaining *how* it behaves. In other words, Black settles for informing us how certain patterns exist, not why they have *emerged.* The latter question would entail the application of a more holistic theory to account for these emergent patterns. Interested theorists must be willing to integrate his findings with some larger schema to explain the *why*.

Black's thesis is not without its critical engagement (for example, see empirical studies by Dai and Gao, 2021; Kuo *et al.*, 2012; Gottfredson and Hindelang, 1997a, 1997b; Clay-Warner and McMahon-Howard, 2009; Golladay, 2017). These empirical studies indicate support, qualified support, and non-support. Qualitative examinations have also appeared (early critique, but still most poignant, see Hunt, 1983; Greenberg, 1983). Unfortunately, empiricists rarely engage theoretical critiques such as Hunt's and Greenberg's, more often focused on methodological issues. Critical concerns about the propositions include: his use of a legalistic definition of crime (law as "governmental control"),[13] that association is being implied to mean causation, that behavioral aspects of his proposition do not constitute a theory in the traditional understanding of the term, that human agency is rendered obsolete, and, we can add from our earlier discussion, that intersectional identities problematize location. Each can be seen as a call for refinement or rethinking. The utility of the propositions, however, is validated by its long history of research applications and critical engagement. It does point out vulnerable peoples in law, even given the same harm committed. It shows that law is not a static concept but can vary in time, place, and manner (style). It encourages critically constructive dialog and further development of how law behaves, which also demands responding to the why question.[14]

The Sociology of the Case

We now turn to some of the implications of Black's theory. He offers the notion of the "sociology of the case." He tells us that it is rooted in the tradition of legal realism (1989: 5). It is offered as a direct challenge to legal formalism, which sees law primarily as an affair of formal rules and their application. Consider, for example, the importance attached to the notion of precedents *(stare decisis)* in the legal ideal type of formal rationality. In Black's approach, a lawyer searching for precedents should go beyond cases that are similar in terms of legal technicalities; they should also search for cases in which similarity exists as to their "social structure," even if the cases themselves are *technically* dissimilar (ibid., 30). Black argues that the lawyer should also investigate such things as differences in stratification and morphology (see Borg, 1998, 2001). In fact, Black goes so far as to say that a lawyer who does not take into consideration legal sociology is incompetent (ibid., 39).

Black contrasts the *jurisprudential model* (formal rationality, or the classical view of law) with the *sociological model* (ibid., 19–22). The former "regards law as a logical process. The facts of each case are assessed in light of the applicable rules, and logic determines the result." For the latter, on the other hand, "law is not assumed to be logical. Law is how people actually behave, and that is all" (ibid., 20). In the sociological model, the emphasis is on the social structure of the case, whereas in the jurisprudential model social characteristics are supposed to be irrelevant, they are extra-legal. Of course, law school emphasizes the jurisprudential. The sociological model is seen as an extra-legal affair.

Recall, from Chapters 4 and 6, the "classical view," following the principle of formal rationality, claims to make use of syllogistic reasoning and deductive logic and follows the dictates of the "rule of law not men."

Black argues that the outcome of any litigation is based not so much on formal rationality but rather on the sociology of the case. The emphasis is on social structure of the case. What he means is that the social status of the parties, the degree of intimacy, speech organization between conflictual parties, as well as the perceived authoritativeness of actors before the court, and other factors will all influence: (1) whether a complaint will be filed in court, (2) who will win, who will lose, and (3) what the outcome will be (punishment, fine, etc.). Let's summarize some of his examples.

Let's take the example of social status. Conventional and everyday wisdom has it that social status (usually defined in terms of such things as wealth, education, position, etc.) has a direct effect on how a case will be handled before the courts. For Black, however, "we must consider simultaneously each adversary's social status in relation to the other's" (ibid., 9).

The degree of intimacy, or relational distance is also a factor. Black tells us that "the closer people's relationships are, the less law enters into their affairs" (ibid., 11). Thus, in handling a case involving intimates, "the police are less likely to regard it as a crime or to make an arrest. If an arrest is made, the prosecutor will be less likely to bring formal charges; and if the case goes to court, a conviction and a prison sentence will be less likely" (ibid., 12). We may note, however, that "spouse abuse" has undergone a change in social perception, and, in fact, police departments now often require their officers, faced with evidence that assault has taken place between spouses, make use of the penal code (penal model), not the conciliatory model as was often the previous case. Here, all else is not constant; rather, a political and ideological dimension has been introduced affecting how law currently "behaves."

Black goes on to tell us that his sociology of the case also predicts how "third-parties" to the case affect it. Lawyers, for example, can produce diverging effects on litigants who are strangers to each other as opposed to litigants who are more intimate. Lawyers, because of their continued involvement and sharing of a bond, may make the litigants much closer than they were at the outset of the case. In other words, the lawyers, perhaps inadvertently, narrow the social distance. On the other hand, in cases where the litigants are more intimate, the entrance of lawyers could produce greater social distance, as witnessed in conflicts in marriage, within family and business operations, or within the same organization.

The authoritativeness of third parties (i.e., judges, jurors) also affects how the case will be handled. More authoritative judges (and jurors), for example, are more likely to see a winner and loser (i.e., zero-sum games) without prospects for a compromise, whereas less authoritative judges (and jurors) are likely to be more lenient and more likely to seek some variable sum resolution (ibid., 15).

Speech forms also have an effect on the outcome of the case, Black tells us. Two forms of speech can be distinguished: "powerful" and "powerless." "Powerful speech," Black informs us, "involves fewer hedges such as 'sort of' and 'kind of'... fewer fillers such as 'uh,' 'um,' and 'let's see,' fewer questions directed at the examiner by the witness, fewer deferential expressions such as 'sir,' and fewer intensifiers such as 'very' and 'surely'" (ibid., 18). Those testifying in a court in the "powerful speech" mode are perceived as more credible. Thus, since higher status people are more likely to speak in this mode, they are perceived as more believable and competent. On the other hand, manual laborers more than professionals, blacks more than whites, and other disenfranchised and marginalized people generally, are more likely to employ "powerless speech," and hence are more at risk in court proceedings (ibid., 18–19). Their story-telling is perceived as less credible.

In addition, those who give short answers are more at risk as to believability and credibility than are those who present longer narratives or verbose styles (ibid.). Higher status people are more prone to talk at will and at some length, and lawyers are more likely to yield to their interjections and lengthy prose. Thus, again, higher status people before the court are more likely to be seen as credible. Conversely, lower status people are at risk before the court. We recall in earlier chapters how legal discourse is a form of storytelling, and how some voices are denied expression in law (for example, see Jackson's narrative coherence model, Chapter 9, and CRTs' critique of dominant story forms, Chapter 7). The challenge: how to make counter storytelling more credible.

All this suggests some profound reconsideration of what law-finding is in fact about. Black tells us that doing "sociological litigation" (ibid., 25) — that is, taking into consideration all these extra-legal factors — should be a central component of the legal practice. Therefore, sociological analysis should be brought to bear on: screening cases; scheduling fees; choosing particular participants in the proceedings; deciding whether to settle out of court; preparing a case for trial; selecting judges, jurors, etc.; devising trial tactics; and, choosing whether to appeal. (For his specific suggestions see 1989: 25–38.) Black, in other words, is arguing that lawyers should familiarize themselves with what are often seen as extra-legal factors so as to fully understand their consequences.

Law professors, it needs to be added, most often present these factors to their students only in anecdotal form, even while acknowledging their importance in particular cases. But no systematic "sociological litigation" is taught in law school. Black, in passing, does qualify his suggestions for sociological litigation by saying that he is not at this time questioning its social desirability (ibid., 25). He only tells us how it may be done and why it should be understood given the widespread misinformed nature as to factors contributing to formal decision making in law.

For reformers, understanding the dimensions of sociological litigation better prepares them to fight different forms of biases entering court proceedings. Discrimination can enter law-finding practices, as Black has indicated, in many subtle ways that formal rationality and conventional wisdom have overlooked. And we are led to some provocative implications worthy of exploration.[15] As Black suggests (1976: x), the reader will be able to better imagine how "to engineer a legal outcome in or out of the courtroom, to reform a legal system, or even to design a community with little or no law at all."

Summary

For Parsons, Luhmann, Podgorecki, and structural functionalists generally, law is primarily facilitative. Repressive and ideological dimensions are secondary. The relationship of the legal order to the fulfillment of social values is such that law functions to provide an optimal framework within which people can accurately plan their activities. With increased complexity in society, increased contingencies develop. It is the law that provides security and assurance in expectational structures. In this waltz, societal development leads and the form of law follows.

In modern societies, however, a greater demand is placed on consciously selecting laws, which contribute positively to system stability. Law tends to become more abstract and more removed from the immediate context. It becomes general in its application. The structural functionalists emphasize the *form* of law over its *content*. That is, such things as procedural or substantive injustice (due, for example, to power differences), although recognized, are less important than specifying how the form of law is functional for the society as a whole.

Black's thesis of the behavior of law and the sociology of the case provides, once again, an understanding of the tension between formal rationality and substantive rationality (or, for that matter, even substantive irrationality and formal irrationality). The notion that law is preoccupied exclusively with rules must be abandoned as incomplete, Black has argued. Sociological litigation, the sociology of the case, and the behavior of law—all indicate that formal rationality exists in an uneasy alliance with other forms of decision making.

Review Questions

1. Parson's structural functionalist view of law sees one of the functions of professional lawyers to "cool off" the client. If so, how does counter storytelling by the client resolve itself faced with this function? How does it survive?

2. Luhmann's sociology of law is primarily focused on the facilitative function. Can this alone further understanding in law?

3. Possible class exercise or individual assignment. For class exercise, summaries can be listed on the board for and against social engineering, followed by discussion. Podgorecki's notion of social engineering seems to be also shared by Roscoe Pound (Chapter 6). But conventional jurisprudence argues that lawyers should be out of politics, out of any possible social engineering and just follow the letter of the law. Is this tension resolvable? Or does one have to choose one or the other?

4. Possible class exercise or individual assignment. Summaries on board followed by discussion. Can a social engineering perspective in law be a useful orientation in fighting against system-wide racism? What are some of the impediments?

5. The autopoiesis perspective in law suggests that jurisprudence orientation and its practitioners reconstruct the legal order and categories in their repetitive practice and thus provide legitimacy to the conventional order. But those from CRT argue a tool for social change is the use of law. Are these reconcilable? Can one do one without reconstructing the other? Explain.

6. Teubner's structural coupling thesis, it was said, can be applied in court decisions dealing with admissions policy assuring diverse student bodies, which in turn affect other areas (workplace, recreational, etc.). Explain how.

7. Black's behavior of law focuses on the "how" not the "why." Should we be quick to criticize Black for not being complete, or does he provide a useful guide for further discussions that address the "why."

8. Choose one of Black's propositions of the behavior of law dealing with stratification and one for morphology. Briefly explain in your own words. Then, provide an example for each. Then, use either Marx, Weber, Durkheim or the "crits" to address the "why" Explain.

9. Black's behavior of law dealing with morphology suggests a "marginality theory of deviance." Explain in your own words. Then, is crime merely a label? Explain.

10. Should law school build into their curriculum Black's approach of the "sociology of the case" and "sociological litigation?" In other words, should future lawyers be made aware of the possible sociological principles at play behind legal decision-making? Would this enhance legal decision-making toward social justice? (Perhaps a class discussion? Face-to-face class could have summaries on board, discussion, and responses listed.)

Endnotes

1. Analogously, consider law of liability in which a new product introduced has negative health consequences many years later. The law generally states that the corporation introducing a new product in the environment will be held responsible for any consequences. For example, asbestos cases, as we have seen, sometimes did not develop until 20–30 years later.

2. This term has also been employed by early critical legal theorists: see Cornell, 1992: 76–78, 81–83; Hunt, 1993: 295–297; Jessop, 1990: 331–335, 358–360; see also Sinclair's critique, 1992; Baxter, 1998; Lempert, 1998; Mingers, 2002.

3. Consider, too, the right of privacy. In the U.S., the United States Supreme Court, in *Griswold v. Connecticut* (1965) established the "right to privacy." Once established it becomes an element within the legal habitus that is continuously regenerated. It should also be mentioned that the United Nations Universal Declaration of Human Rights, Article 12 (1948) declares: "No one shall be subjected to arbitrary interference with his privacy, family, home or correspondence, nor to attacks upon his honour and reputation. Everyone has the right to the protection of the law against such interference or attacks." This, as we showed in Chapter 4, is an "external" substantive rational principle that continuously perturbs State's stated rights.

4. See also some parallels with the idea of "intersectional identities" raised by CRT, Chapter 7.

5. See also: Doyle and Luckenbill, 1991; Gottfredson and Hindelang, 1979a; Braithwaite and Biles, 1980; Hembroff, 1987; Meyers, 1980; Stables, 1987; Borg, 1998, 1999, 2001; Cooney, 1994, 1997, 1998. For a good summary of the literature in the application and test of Black's propositions of the behavior of law, as well as some critical commentary, see Dai and Gao (2021).

6. For example, during the middle of a shift or "tour," a police officer might invoke the penal style to an infraction; however, a few minutes before their shift is over, in haste to "punch out," they might invoke the conciliatory style for the very same infraction. A number of years ago, the New York City Police Department was plagued with "courtesy arrests." With upcoming holidays such as Christmas, a number of police were invoking the penal style near the end of their shift in order to collect overtime pay for the 3 to 5 hours extra time needed to book a suspect in the crowded New York City courts.

7. For a quantitative critique of the behavior of law thesis, a response by Black, and a counter, see Gottfredson and Hindelang, 1997a, 1979b; Black,1979. See also Kuo *et al.*, 2012; Hunt, 1983; Clay-Warner and J. McMahon-Howard, 2009.

8. He also informs us that the behavior of law is associated with culture, organization, and social control. For our introduction to his work we will focus on stratification and morphology.

9. For example, Henry and Milovanovic, 1996, 2020, have developed an alternative notion of crime/harm: "harms of reduction"—a reduction from a position one has, and "harms of repression," a denial from a position one seeks. Theoretically, we conceivably can establish degree of harm and/or repression, beyond how they are normally defined and punished in law (e.g., legalistic definition of crime). This is, of course, only a starting point; for, human complexity is greater than its possible categorization. Given this, and applying to Black's propositions, we can establish equivalence and compare and contrast dyads in conflict situations. In other words, constructively, one particular white collar crime could be shown to have the same degree of harm as a blue collar crime, thus an equivalence.

10. The Uniform Crime Report is a summary of "crimes known to the police," sometimes referred to as official crimes. "Unofficial crime rates reported by Victimization Surveys (random sample of households, responders are asked which crimes have occurred against them in the last year) and self-reports (subjects are asked to respond to crimes they have committed in the last year, anonymously, but with questions locating them in the stratification system), differ with the UCR suggesting a substantial "dark figure of crime."

11. By "marginal" it is meant being situated toward the periphery. In other words, there are degrees of integration in a society with the well-integrated at the center, and then moving outward toward the periphery where we find less-integrated members.

12. In criminology, marginality theory appears in the form of strain, opportunity structure, anomie, bond, and social control theory among others (see Lanier *et al.*, 2018).

13. The legalistic definition of crime is a political construct. It has come under serious questioning as to covering the scope and to the selectivity of what constitutes social harms. Crimes known to the police are what are included in the official statistics, the Uniform Crime Report. Non-reported crimes, the dark figure of crime, question many of the distributive patterns of the UCR (see note 10). Alternatively, for example, we have offered a constitutive definition of harm (Henry and Milovanovic, 2020) that sees crime as harm, either crimes of reduction (reducing a person from a position they have), or crimes of repression (denying a person further development and fulfilment).

14. For example, applying the structural functional logic, especially the notion of structural coupling—here the subsystems made up of the legal system, media, politics, economics, etc., as well as the accepted definition of crime (legalistic) and prevalence of fears, insecurities and hostilities, expression of which is often targeted toward particular populations—collectively constitutes through its configurations, integrated dynamic, and recursivity a social reality of crime (our collective perception of crime and who the offenders are, Quinney, 1970). This places some (disproportionally disenfranchised, non-propertied, people of color, other diverse peoples) at greater risk of criminalization (particularly, because of greater amount of law mobilized in a downward and outward direction, and where applied, the penal style); and, conversely, for crimes committed downward and outward (upward law, centripetal law, and more likely, compensatory model), which the propositions reflect in probabilistic statements. Of course, as crits have well argued the case, due to systemic racism, injustices also go beyond just location in stratification and morphology. Consider, on the other hand, realities having constructions where perpetrators remain "beyond incrimination," committed particularly by the state (Kennedy, 1976): black genocide, ethnic cleansing of aboriginal peoples, supporting governments engaging in ethnic cleansing (Palestinian situation), destroying the environment (ecocide), a President (Trump) instigating sedition and the sacking of the Capital Building in the U.S., assassination of foreign leaders and invasions under the name of democracy, to name a few. An alternative set of propositions of the behavior of law would be at play in a different structurally coupled social system, which in turn would demand responding to the why issue.

15. Just as there has been a call for the greater engagement of a "sociological imagination" (C.Wright Mills, 1959) and the "criminological imagination" (Young, 2011), an equal call is for a greater "legal imagination," already in its incipient stages with sociological jurisprudence, CLS, and the crits.

9

Semiotics and Law

Introduction

Since the middle to late 1980s, a growing body of theory has been developing on a semiotic perspective in law. There is a growing realization that in doing law one is drawing from some unstated semiotic understanding, and that legal language is structured allowing some things more readily to be said, others, more difficult. "The lawyer, though he knows it not," Marriott (2015: 379) informs us, "is a semiotic practitioner ..." and further "the legal discourse, although complex and willful in the pursuit of its chosen ends, remains largely blind to the nature of semiosis, which gives it life." Semiotics is "the science of signs" (Morris, 1938; for a concise and accessible introduction, see Chandler, 2007; see also his online version, 1995). It is the study of signs, sign-processes (production) and their usage that relays a particular meaning to a receiver who interprets it. It is distinguishable from linguistics.. Linguistics is generally seen as the study of spoken language as a communicative media, incorporating syntax (sentence structure), semantics (word meaning), phonetics (sound system), morphology (structure of words), and pragmatics (context).

Semiotics is generally seen as encompassing linguistics; it is more the umbrella term, although there is some dissent. It studies any sign system that constructs and communicates meaning. It incorporates, for example, audio and visual semiotics, biosemiotics, and more recently, the language of nature. The two founding figures are Ferdinand de Saussure (1857–1913) and Charles Sanders Peirce (1839–1914). See a brief useful comparison by Yakin and Totu (2014). Saussure is generally recognized as a founder of both semiotics and linguistics. Noam Chomsky is also sometimes mentioned as a founding figure of linguistics, even though Saussure's name is more often referenced. Saussure (cited in Chandler, 2007: 4) provided a key early statement:

> It is ... possible to conceive of a science which studies the role of signs as part of social life. It would form part of social psychology, and hence of general psychology. We shall call it semiology (from the Greek *semeîon*, 'sign'). It would investigate the nature of signs and the laws governing them ... Linguistics is only one branch of this general science. The laws which semiology will discover will be laws applicable in linguistics, and linguistics will thus be assigned to a clearly defined place in the field of human knowledge.

Charles C. Morris, in his book *Foundations of the Theory of Signs*, has suggested semiotics of signs encompasses three dimensions: *semantics* (interpretations of signs, word and sentence meanings), *syntax* (rules governing how signs are configured in sentence structures to convey meaning), and *pragmatics* (application in particular contexts and their meaning therein). Law school, for example, prepares the student for correct understandings of: legal words employed such as those included in *Black's Law Dictionary* (semantics); methods of constructing narratives and syllogistic type reasoning (syntax); and the context for their use and interpretation, initially the class room setting and the Socratic method of teaching, and subsequently the court house and other legal contexts (pragmatics) (see for example, Mertz, 2007; Solan and Tiersma, 2005) — together producing the ideal: "reading, talking, and thinking like a lawyer" (Mertz, ibid.). Of course, Duncan Kennedy from CLS, as we saw from Chapter 6, would remind us that this is part of the process of "law school as preparation for hierarchy."

Legal semiotics has also witnessed a number of subfields which include visual legal semiotics, visual jurisprudence, and audio legal semiotics. A socio-semiotics and a more explicit socio-legal visual semiotics will be addressed in Chapter 10. As Wagner (2010: 81) points out: "Analytical tools proposed by legal semiotics show that the legal community is confronted with written as well as visual legal representation." Interpreting signs is problematic as "they are loaded with history, emotions, and intuitions" (ibid.). To this we shall return later.

Legal semiotics, as an applied form of semiotics, is constantly in the process of defining the contours of its terrain (for an accessible introduction, see Lloyd, 2016, 2020; Wagner, 2010; Tiersma, 1999; for comments on a Saussurian and Derridarian semiotics of law, see Kennedy, 2001). Accordingly, many new and complex terms are being introduced with, at times, conflicting definitions and usages. Various perspectives have emerged and continue to emerge influenced by Saussure, Peirce, Greimas, Hjelmslev, and Lacan. There are also perspectives that derive from Jacques Derrida, Ludwig Wittgenstein, Ronald Barthes, Umberto Eco, John Austin, and C.W. Morris. Postmodern and post postmodern are included in, respectively, Chapters 11 and 12. We are witnessing integrations of semiotics with law by the jurisprudence school of thought (legal science), sociological jurisprudence, as well as by those who are attempting to integrate it into a fuller sociology of law. What underlies and distinguishes each is the explicitness of the semiotic approach employed; where jurisprudence is less explicit, sociological jurisprudence more, and sociology of law, generally the most explicit.

In Chapter 7 we had occasion to present story-telling and narrative analysis in law. This is distinguished from a semiotic perspective in terms of emphasis, scope, and depth of analysis. Whereas the former takes stories and narratives at face value, without formal analysis of constitutive elements of language itself (signifiers, signified, paradigm, syntagm, etc.; see for example, Miller, 1994 on legal storytelling), the latter delves deeper into the very structure of stories themselves. This is not to dismiss story-telling and narrative analysis; these approaches are sensitive to diverse groups and their unique representational styles in narratives. They are informative as to what they tell us about various subcultures and indigenous groups in a society. And, as we have seen, they are the basis of oppositional practices in such versions as counter storytelling. A semiotics emphasis, however, focuses on how in fact reality is being codified by the linguistic forms and how certain stories can be readily presented within the prevalent discourse available (be it an indigenous, group specific, oppositional, or dominant discourse). Discourse is not taken as a given, but is seen as placing limitations on what can and cannot be said. Below, for example, we will distinguish the Hopis' grammatical structures from standard English to show how worldviews fundamentally differ as a consequence.

The use of semiotics comes in various concentrations in legal analysis. Jurisprudential forms of analysis in law (see the elements, in Chapter 1) often make use of semiotics implicitly. An author might make use of various perspectives in semiotics and also a more everyday understanding. They usually do not delve deeper into the codification of language, its origins nor the constraining or enabling function of language; they make a minimal use of a coherent theory of semiotics. In fact, jurisprudes often argue against its abstractness. Most of the legal analysis we find in university law school journals is more jurisprudential in form. Legal language, its source, its structure, and its ability in itself of communicating ideology are topics not fully engaged (see Mertz, 2007; Marmor, 2014).

In legal semiotics, unlike jurisprudence, the author makes more explicit use of a particular perspective (Peirce, Greimas, Lacan, Hjelmslev, Derrida, Wittgenstein, Eco, Barthes, Austin, etc.; see for example, Lloyd, 2020; Bohr and Konczo, 2019). Those in legal semiotics make a priority of being true to the semiotic perspective that is in use. They often cross the boundary of doing jurisprudence versus doing a sociology of law (see, for example, Lloyd, 2016, 2020).

In the sociology of law perspective (see the key distinguishing factors in Chapter 1), embracing a more explicit legal semiotics, a particular semiotic perspective (or perspectives) is (are) integrated with a more sociological, political-economic and sometimes historical analysis in understanding law in society. Here, coherent integration is the key. Semiotics becomes a key element in the overall perspective of the author. Usually, these studies are published in social science journals as opposed to law journals. Examples of a more "sociology of law" focus with heavy integration of semiotics are the Marxist structural interpellation, postmodern feminist, constitutive perspectives, and post postmodern views.[1]

We will introduce the ideas of four key developers: Ferdinand de Saussure, Charles Sanders Peirce (pronounced like "purse"), Louis Hjelmslev, and Algiras Greimas, none of whom, however, are identified with primarily developing a legal semiotics, but who have strongly influenced the American and European traditions of legal semiotics. This is not an exhaustive list; only meant for illustration of diverse approaches. We will also survey some of the applications of their respective ideas in law. John Austin's view of language, "speech act theory," as performative will close the first part of the chapter.

The second part of the chapter will provide expressive forms of legal semiotics, to include visual legal semiotics and audio legal semiotics. There have also been some developments of a musical legal semiosis. In the next chapter we will turn to a socio-legal semiotics in the sociology of law. We include a Marxist legal semiotics, a "structural interpellationist" variant.

Postmodernist and a post postmodern approach will be a topic covered in, respectively, Chapters 11 and 12.

We can safely say that approaches that employ semiotic analysis in law vary in the degree of its incorporation: at one extreme making the claim for its autonomous existence as a paradigm, an umbrella term; or, alternatively, integrating elements of semiotic analysis with other theoretical perspectives in the analysis of law and viewing semiotics as but one component.[2] A more fully developed sociology of law would incorporate and acknowledge a particular semiotic perspective (or perspectives).

Legal Semiotics

Introduction

Although a number of semiotic perspectives in law have recently emerged, we have chosen the Peircian, Sausserian, Hjelmslevian, and Greimasian perspectives as examples in application in law in the Western world. We will also include speech-act theory of John L. Austin.

In historical review, the 1980s and 1990s witnessed two main approaches in legal semiotics, one based more in Europe, the other in America. A Peircian legal semiotics centered on Roberta Kevelson, whose incredible amount of sheer energy, commitment and precise scholarly work had thrust her into the center stage of legal semiotics. She coordinated the Roundtables for the Semiotics of Law, held annually in Reading, Pennsylvania, USA, from 1987 until her death in 1998. The Greimasian approach was developed primarily by Bernard Jackson. Eric Landowski had also been a key figure. The International Association of Semiotics of Law was held annually, coordinated by Bernard Jackson, with meetings primarily in Europe.

The European tradition of legal semiotics during this time embraced the work of Algirdas Greimas, but also Ferdinand de Saussure, and Roman Jacobson. It was more concerned with:

- Structural and semantic analysis: some "deep" structural level is said to exist which is coordinated by the paradigmatic and syntagmatic axes. Paradigm stands for the totality of dictionary meanings of words; syntagm the proper method of arranging them in linear form in order to make sense. In law, for example, a legal concept which is chosen must be placed in a particular linear narrative; in cross-examination and in deductive logic, there is a particular way of choosing only relevant legal terms and arranging them in particular sequences in narratives (consider also, for example: the allowable form in the introduction of testimony or expert witness information; the injunction against "leading the witness"; or consider the allowable "scope" for a particular line of questioning that constitutes the boundaries of discursive exchanges during the trial court proceedings);

- The binary nature of the sign: A sign, that is, a word is composed of two parts, the signifier and the signified. The former stands for the acoustic-image, the psychic imprint; the latter, to what it refers (e.g., the concept, or mental image). Say the word "tree," for example, and the image of a tree appears; in law, signifiers such as "person," "life," "liberty" and "property" have specific meanings, specific signifieds attached to them; and
- Non-referentiality: meaning is *internal* to some semiotic system, such as legal discourse. One word refers for its meaning to an other, which, in turn, refers to another, etc. Consider, for example, looking up a word in a standard dictionary; each word used in explaining can in turn be researched for their meaning, and those words in turn researched, etc. In law, one does not make use of the everyday dictionary, but *Black's Law Dictionary,* which provides particular meanings of signifiers in law.

The American tradition of legal semiotics, during the 1980s and 1990s embraced Charles Sanders Peirce but also Charles William Morris. Its focus was on:

- Pragmatism: this favors the contextual and situated nature of meaning;
- Referentiality: ultimately, sign systems and meaning refer to something outside of themselves for meaning. In other words, unlike the European tradition of non-referentiality, words refer to some particular object itself; and
- The triadic nature of meaning: the sign (or the word), interpretant (or referant), and the object (that to which the sign refers).

During the fertile, developmental stage of legal semiotics of the 80s and 90s some variations of the Peircian approach developed in the American tradition, such as those of "speech act theory." This variation looks at the intentions of the users of a discourse. Here, "'to mean something' is grammatically equivalent to the expression 'to intend something', and this intention 'imparts a purpose or point to language use'" (Jackson, 1985: 15; Brown, 1974: 118). So "referring" is equated with goal-oriented behavior; put in another way, "'action' in this tradition is firmly identified with 'intentionality'" (Jackson, 1985: 15).

In the European philosophical tradition, some variations developed that focus on unconscious motivations and forces as a basis of social action (e.g., Lacan, Kristeva, Foucault, Derrida). Eco, for example, tells us that "the subject is spoken by language" (1984: 45; Kennedy, 1997: 134). Lacan defines the subject as a *parlêtre,* or *l'être parlant* (the "speaking," or the speaking-being). Peirce, himself, is opposed to the Cartesian notion of a centered ego in control and has been identified with arguing for a subject immersed in sign usages, a "sign-using self," or "semiotic self" (Corrington, 1993: 76–115). Perhaps the most enigmatic of the definitions of the signifier has been offered by Lacan: "a signifier is that which represents the subject for another signifier" (1977: 316; for some similarities between Peirce and Lacan, see Milovanovic, 1998). Here the subject disappears in the signifier, which then comes to represent it for other signifiers within the unconscious realm. Again, meaning is non-referential; here it refers to a psychic (unconscious) reality, which has a semi-autonomous existence. Some of Lacan's work has been clearly guided by Peircian semiotics. We will return to this in Chapter 11.

In Lacan's formulation, the deep structure includes the unconscious; the binary nature of the sign, signifier and signified, always implies a third element, perhaps Peirce's interpretant (referent), which is the "*objet petit* a," the object of desire; and meaning (Lacan's "truth") is more idiosyncratic and internal to the subject. Or, alternatively, the interpretant could be conceptualized as the unconscious chain of signifiers to which the consciously applied signifier in narrative constructions is connected. In "political" trials, the state prosecutor attempts to surface the "true" meanings of the ideology professed by the defendant, attempting to show its "subversive" and "violent" intent. In Lacan's "four discourses," for example, it is connected with the effects that consciously stated signifiers have in the production of unconscious associations. Consider, for example, jury selection. The prosecutor and the defense counselor attempt to surface the prospective juror's hidden biases. We will have more to say about Lacan below.

These two broad approaches, American, European, of the 1980s and 1990s underwent a change in the early 2000s, continuing to present. What one finds, where semiotics is being made explicit and also where we see its use as implicit, that a more eclectic approach is being employed in the semiotics of law, although the work of C.S. Peirce is still heavily engaged and Greimas's work has become less central (see for example, Backer and Broekman, 2015). In part, this can be attributed to the cross fertilization[3] of the two approaches in the early 2000s and the intermingling of positions, globalization, along with internal differentiation of the field (Zirk-Sadowski *et al.*, 2009). The *International Journal for the Semiotics of Law* remains the official journal for the International Association for the Semiotics of Law. On its website it states "The ONLY journal in the world which focuses on the discipline of legal semiotics."[4]

Regardless of this recent development, two semiotic axes are generally recognized as the basic starting point in meaning production: the paradigmatic and syntagmatic axis. The paradigmatic axis stands for word choices; it is the vertical structure, if you will. It is connected with semantics or word meanings. The syntagmatic axis, the horizontal if you will, stand for grammatical rules for correct linear positioning of the words chosen from the paradigmatic axis (for an accessible explanation see Chandler, 2007). Morphology has to do with the rules that govern the structure of words, their relation to other words, and their meaning generated in context. These two axes work together in generating meaning in use.

Jakobson's (1971) study of speech disorders was a concise statement as to how the two axes interact in narrative constructions. Given a particular word-association test, for example, some subjects respond to the word by using synonyms or antonyms (paradigm axis); say the word hut, for example, and the subject says house. Others connect the word directly to some activity (syntagm); say the word horse for example, and the subject says jumps. For the subject who is more predisposed toward the paradigm axis, the subject would respond to the word horse by saying pony. There existed a range of responses in Jakobson's study, but also a polarization, from those who favor the paradigmatic to those who favor the syntagmatic axis. But, these two axes work together in producing meaning in a narrative.

Each discourse (i.e., legal, scientific, philosophic, religious, literary, etc.) is structured by particular paradigmatic and syntagmatic structures. Constructing a narrative in law, therefore, is a confined exercise, and thus the construction of "reality" in law is also limited.

C.S. Peirce (1839–1914)

The Peircian approach o semiotics had been spearheaded by Roberta Kevelson, or "Bobbie" as we affectionately called her (1987, 1988, 1990, 1991, 1992, 1993a, 1993b, 1996, 1998). She coordinated, up until her death (November 28, 1998), the Center for Semiotic Research in Law, Government and Economics at the University of Pennsylvania; organized an annual conference ("roundtable") on semiotics and law (a conference of some of the most intense discussions on semiotics and law one possibly could find); was an active contributor to the literature in the semiotics of law; and edited a yearly publication on legal semiotics, "Semiotics and the Human Sciences." Kevelson was at the center of much activity by numerous theorists debating the value of a Peircian legal semiotics. Kevelson provides a definition of her Peircian approach:

> Semiotics, a method of inquiry into the process of inquiry ... assumes that inquiry, always dialogic, is a process of communication or message exchange by means of signs and sign systems. Law is one such sign system, as are other social institutions, e.g., language, economics, politics, the family, and so on (1988: 3).

Kevelson's view is that for Charles S. Peirce "law served ... as the prototypical system for his entire theory of signs" (1991: 3). Kevelson has also argued that Peirce influenced the legal realists (1988: 50; 1991b) and Durkheim (1992). Some lively debate does exist as to the influence that Peirce supposedly has had on the legal realists and, at the minimum, it seems that an indirect influence did exist.[5] And he had an influence on Jacques Lacan (Samuels, 1993). We are unable to discuss all the complex ideas of Peirce due to space limitations, but would like to present some of his key points and then show the applicability to law.

Peirce was an American scientist and philosopher. Central to Peirce was the question of semiotics. Unlike Ferdinand de Saussure's duality of signifier and signified, which we will cover in the next section, Peirce saw it as a three-part relation. We shall review two of his critical triadic structures (Pierce, 1956: 98–119; for a good introduction, see Borch, 2021) and his three primal categories (see also application to Peircean constructed legal arguments, Verenich, 2012a).

Peirce and three relational trichotomies. The first trichotomy includes the *sign, interpretant,* and *object.* The *sign* (or *sign-vehicle,* or even *representamen*) "stands to somebody for something in some respect or capacity" (the sign might be a word).

This creates an *interpretant*—that is, "creates in the mind of that person an equivalent sign, or perhaps a more developed sign." The interpretant is the effect created in an interpreter, the receiver, by the sign. It may not always be the same as the sender's intent, thus a miscommunication or misunderstanding. A sign, too, must come to stand for something, its *object* (Pierce, 1956: 99, 275). (A later version makes use of the idea of the *referent* of the object; that which the sign interprets.) Consider, for example, in law the "insanity defense." It is a sign which communicates to another a particular legalistically defined situation, and also refers to its object, a particular person said to be engaging in irrational behavior. Consider another example, from our discussion of CRT and Asian-American crits, the notion of a "diverse student body" that was ruled to be a "compelling state interest" by the U.S. Supreme Court, with highest constitutional protection. The sign is "diverse student bodies; the interpretant, the image and understanding aroused in the person presented with the sign; and the object, a particular state of affairs in a school, university or law school setting (see also Bor and Kunczol, 2019; Verenich, 2012a, 2012b).

Peirce's second trichotomy focuses on three types of signs, and defines them as an *icon, index* or a *symbol.* In other words, he points out three ways in which the sign can refer to its object. An *icon* "is a sign which refers to the Object that it denotes merely by virtue of characters of its own, and which it possesses" (ibid., 102). An icon, then, relates to an object in terms of likeness, some resemblance. An algebraic formula, for example, is an icon. Consider a stop sign in traffic control, and the Statue of Liberty as relating to liberty, and the statue of "Lady Justice" personifying justice. An *index* resembles an icon but has additional qualities; that is, the object also modifies the icon. Some relation is established. For example, seeing a person dressed in blue with a firearm in public leads me to believe that they are a police officer. Similarly, smoke is an index, a sign of fire. Here the sign relates to the object in terms of some factual link. Finally, the *symbol* resembles an index, but has the additional quality of being a sign "which refers to the Object that it denotes by virtue of a law, usually an association of general ideas" (ibid.). Thus, they have become conventionalized (normalized) through cultural traditions. For example, words, sentences, and all conventional signs are in the category of symbols (ibid., 112). Here the relation between the sign and the object is due to some convention rather than to nature. In law, legal concepts have particular meanings that are defined in *Black's Law Dictionary.* We will show in Chapter 10, for example, in a Marxist perspective, using a dual notion of the sign, how particular signifieds are attached to particular signifiers during higher court linguistic production (e.g., how the meaning of "person," "life," "liberty," and "property" are constructed in law, and once constructed via *stare decisis*, the basis of reality construction; see also Richland, 2008, studying the Hopi of Southwestern United States and their culture of law and differences with the English-speaking community).

For Peirce, the subject is a semiotic self, immersed in the sea of signs (Corrington, 1993). Kevelson extends this to indicate how different legal actors, too, work within a specialized system of signs (1988). But the subject is more than a sign user; they are constituted by the signs being used. Doing law, is being a lawyer; being a lawyer is the act by which one immerse oneself in legalistic discourse, bounded by its terms (paradigm/syntagm), in the construction of narratives. Being a philosopher, an activist, or a revolutionary and engaging in those particular discourses while doing law, on the other hand, will bring an avalanche of "objections" by the prosecutor, which will be sustained by the judge.

All thought is *in* signs. All understanding of self is through given sign systems. In fact, a person is a sign. All this goes against the traditional conception of humans as centered, in control, determining, self-aware and the initiator of action that Cartesian philosophy celebrates. Consider Peirce's classic statement:

> the word or sign which man uses is the man himself. For, as the fact that every thought is a sign, taken in conjunction with the fact that life is a train of thought, proves that man is a sign; so, that every thought is an external sign, proves that man is an external sign. That is to say, the man and the external sign are identical, in the same sense in which the words homo and man are identical. Thus, my language is the sum total of myself; for the man is the thought (Peirce in Corrington, 1993: 91).

Peirce's semiotics, in turn, can be placed in relation to three primal categories (third trichotomy): *firstness, secondness, and thirdness. Firstness* has to do with primordial sense data: it is more a feeling state, a qualitative aspect; it is composed of "no necessary structures, only pure heterogeneous momentum" (Corrington, 1993: 127). It remains the domain of the possible. It has yet to be embodied in a formal sign system. It is in a state of pure flux and potentiality. It is pure existence. "The idea of First is predominant in the ideas of freshness, life, freedom. The free is that which has no another behind it.... If the idea of another enters, then the Firstness goes" (Peirce, 1931: 148). Everyday activity has much to do with firstness; not all is given a conscious meaning or expression.

Secondness comes into play when two elements interact. It is the sphere of "things and facts." "[T]heir being," Peirce tells us, "consists of reactions against Brute forces ..." (cited in Corrington, 1993: 69). It emerges from firstness. Consider, for example, an altercation that developed during some street-corner encounter; things took place, but the legal narrative explaining it is a construction that comes after the event. It is where one begins to connect firstness with something more specific.

Thirdness brings firstness and secondness together in some relation. Here the qualitative dimension of firstness is changed into a different form: "conscious, purposive and funded with intelligence" (Corrington, 1993: 133). It is the sphere where active and conscious connections are established between different objects. It is normatively bound by some law, informal or formal. It is also the sphere of the ethical and moral. (Kevelson, 1991b: 117, on the other hand, argues that Peircian ethics is better situated in secondness.) A sign can only take form if purpose exists; hence, it is in the domain of thirdness (ibid., 142). Only with thirdness can a sign become a symbol (ibid., 144). Consider in law how some altercation in the streets is codified in some legal category (i.e., assault) giving it meaning in legal discourse. Consider how *mens rea* is codified into various categories implying degrees of volitional behavior extending from the rational subject in law (juridic personality) to insanity (consider, too, allowable defense categories of insanity, duress, entrapment, etc.).

Thus various, often diverging narrative constructions in law explaining the "what happened?" are in the domain of thirdness. These are *ex post facto* constructions, and, as we saw from the realist school, are often motivated in a particular direction by various interested actors in the criminal justice system.

The legal order is the sphere of thirdness, of subject-produced law. (Kevelson also includes customs, promises, trusts, public opinion, etc. [1993: 59]). Implied here, of course, is a certain degree of arbitrariness of what will in fact be constituted as a body of law. It would seem that at the level of secondness many codifications of reality are at the beginning (incipient) stages of taking form, and only after the clash of alternative and budding positions will a more dominant understanding of "reality" be established at the level of thirdness, in law, for example, and in prevailing conventional wisdom. Consider, for example, trial court proceedings where there is a clash of alternative views of the "what happened?" Although a plurality of opposing positions may seek expression in signs, it would seem that Peirce is arguing that only some become part of the dominant system of signs. At the end of a trial court proceedings, for example, a "frozen record" often results, which then becomes the basis of a possible appellate review (see the section on the legal realists, Chapter 6, on this point). CLS, fem-crits, CRTs, and Lacanians would argue that understanding the connection between secondness and thirdness must be placed in the context of power differentials (i.e., power derived from class, gender, ethnic, and race differences; e.g., the "law-of-the-father") and how certain voices are denied expression. At the level of "thirdness," some understandings are more likely to be codified in law; others, those of the disenfranchised, often remain in the domain of "secondness."

Consider Verenich's (2012a) erudite discussion of Peircian logic employed in law. First, citing Peirce (ibid., 32), "logic, in its general sense, is, ... only another name for semiotics." Drawing from all the concepts above, the lawyer "starts in a mode of Firstness, gathering legal rules (legal precedents or norms), ... then proceeds into a mode of Secondness by establishing a reference between facts (evidence) and normative rules. Finally, in a mode of Thirdness the reasoners [lawyers] are able to reach a conclusion" (ibid., 37) [through deduction, syllogisms]. In other words, Firstness is more about a feeling out relevant possibilities, a more amorphous state; Secondness, connecting various possibilities; and Thirdness connecting possibilities to some rule, legal concept or principle, following linear deductive, syllogistic reasoning arriving at a conclusion in law. Moreover, "each type of Peirce's signs corresponds to a particular mode of reasoning: icons correspond to Firstness, indices correspond to Secondness, symbols correspond to Thirdness" (ibid.). All leads, in successful legal argument, to establishing a final interpretant in law, and also the basis of a new precedent.

Pure play (musement). Peirce also tells us there is a state of mind in which one occasionally enters, one of "Pure Play," where boundaries are routinely traversed. It is a form of suspending conventional associations and understandings and being open to serendipitous discoveries. "[I]t involves no purpose save that of casting aside all serious purpose ... [it] is a lively exercise of one's powers. Pure Play has no rules, except this very law of liberty" (Peirce, 1965: 313; Cooke, 2018; see also Corringston, 1993: 70; Kevelson, 1988: 122–123; 1991a: 108). This "musement," or "interpretive musement" (Peirce, 1965: 313–314; see also Corrington, 1993: 70), provides the freedom to search out possible alternative connections among the three spheres (firstness, secondness, thirdness); it allows for creative connections between the sign and that which it designates. It is imaginary play and creativity.[6] Initially it may be without purpose, no end, pure imaginings, pure wonderment, but may lead to the next stage where it is brought within rational control (Cooke, 2018). Consider Albert Einstein, unable to procure an academic position, working in an early job as a patent clerk, often daydreaming. What if I wear to catch up to the speed of light? How would time pass? Einstein thought the direction for his profound discoveries of relativity theory started with this suspended state, pure wonderment, suspending conventional physics, until, under rational control, a leap, most often irrational, to a new set of postulates that become the basis of further hypotheses. Einstein's "thought experiments" have also been advocated as a tool by others doing cutting edge work.

Cornell's (1998) advocacy of expanding the "imaginary domain" as a basis of alternative visions of society and being human can find its basis in this dynamic. It would seem that musement is what militates against entropy (ibid., 70–72), stagnation, and closure.[7] Kevelson tells us this notion of "Pure Play" is what is at the core of the indeterminacy of law advocated by legal realisms as opposed to the rigidity (determinism) of legal positivism (1991b: 108–109) and formal rationality and linear deductive logic. Contrary to legal positivists,

> [t]he main objective in Peirce's thought is for more quests, which is to say for more indeterminate situations, more problems, more chaos. The movement is not from chaos to order, but rather is from each level of a definitive and orderly arrangement of meaning thus far to a new level of disorder and meaning not yet ascertained but still vague (ibid.; see also Bryon, 1991; Schulman, 1997).

Consider, too, Cooke (2018: 10): "musement includes the initial process of opening oneself up to being surprised and to noticing strange, surprising, wonderful phenomena, and the speculation about explanations, and the generation of hypotheses."

Abduction (pragmaticism). It is here, too, that active *abduction,* as a form of legal reasoning, unfolds. The question of pragmatics (*pragmaticism*) and *abduction* (sometimes translated as "retroduction") is important to a Peircian semiotic inquiry in law (see Brion, 1997; Belluccio and Ahti-Veikko, 2020). For him, subjects draw from both conceptual experimentation and practical experiences in formulating maxims for orientating their conduct. A number of methods exist in formulating these maxims whether done for scientific explorations or for everyday behavior. Peirce outlines the two better understood and more conventional methods of logical, rational inquiry:

induction, by which we start with a case and infer some rule (more upward, we move from the "facts" to a particular rule); and *deduction*, where we start with some rule and through syllogistic reasoning and deductive logic conclude in some way (downward movement, from a rule to application to data). Abduction, therefore, draws from both inductive and deductive reasoning.

Peirce argued against the unquestioned belief in a purely Cartesian syllogistic reasoning operating in law, opting for a pragmatically-based thought process in law-finding practices (Valauri, 1991). (In Chapter 4 we had provided an example of the use of deductive logic by a lawyer doing an "equal protection" argument in law.) Peirce offers a third method: *abduction* (1956: 152). For him, *pragmaticism* is the study of the logic of abduction. It makes use of both inductive and deductive reasoning in arriving at a position.

Let's take a simple example of abduction provided by Peirce. A clock on the wall that strikes every half hour goes afoul and miss-strikes. Normally the strikes are not given conscious attention. With the error noticed, conscious attention must be given to correct the problem. New adjustments are made. Thereafter a minimal conscious level of attention once again is needed to keep track of time. In other words, both deduction (expectation of clock strike) and induction (when clock miss-strikes) are at work.

Abduction, then, is the active process of developing a hypothesis explaining some problematic event. It is a creative act, and accordingly may be connected in the most active way to "Pure Play." According to Peirce, "[i]f one's observations and reflections are allowed to specialize themselves too much, the Play will be converted into scientific study ..." (1965: 314). Explanatory hypotheses may simply come "in a flash," or through some process of fantasizing or imagination. Once formulated they compete with other hypotheses to explain the case at hand. Peirce then argues that a simplicity rule should prevail. Thus, a dialectic remains between concrete experiences and the abductive process (Corrington, 1993: 67–68). The three forms of inference—inductive, deductive, abductive—are brought to bear on problematic situations (pragmatism), resulting in a more parsimonious hypothesis that explains things, including decision making in law. A newly emergent hypothesis then becomes operative in the everyday activity of the subject until, once again, they are confronted with an anomaly.

The notion of abduction has been applied to legal semiotics (Askeland, 2020; Summers, 1991; Brion, 1991; Milovanovic, 1993d; Schum, 1994). David Schum's (1994) book, *The Evidential Foundations of Probabilistic Reasoning,* includes extensive analysis of the importance of Peirce's semiotic ideas, especially the idea of abduction as it is applied to "discovery" in law (see also Askeland, 2020; Amaya, 2015; Walton, 2005). "Discovery" is associated with the attorney's "various legally sanctioned coercive measures by which he can obtain evidence from his opponent" (Schum, ibid., 452) in law. But what is important evidence/data? Once received, how useful is it for the prosecutor's or defense's case? How does it fit into a "story" being presented as to guilt or innocence of the defendant?

Evidence is presented by lawyers for the purpose of indicating why there is on one conclusion in law. Much like a scientist, police officer, software engineer, auditor, physician and historian, the person must collect data and reach a conclusion based on this evidence (ibid.). During various stages of a court trial, these conclusions become the basis of further decision making. Schum argues, following Peirce's notion of abduction, that this process is neither entirely deductive nor inductive, but rather makes use of both until some "flash" of insight develops. As the noted philosopher Wesley Salmon argues, "our minds wander, we daydream, reveries intrude, irrelevant free associations occur, and blind alleys are followed" (cited in Schum, 1994: 453).

Salmon suggests three stages: first, we generate a hypothesis; second, we entertain its plausibility; and third, we test the hypothesis (ibid., 454). This is an imaginative type of reasoning leading up to some conclusion. "In some cases," Schum (ibid., 491) tells us, "we may be fortunate in having a datum that immediately suggests a plausible hypothesis (e.g., finding a fingerprint at the scene of a crime). In other cases, extensive inquiry and the gathering of information may be required before we can even begin to generate hypotheses." Following Peirce, this is not purely a deductive, nor inductive process. Rather, the investigator goes back and forth, creating hypotheses, checking them out, developing new ones, checking those out, drawing conclusions, making decisions at various stages of litigation, and pushing ahead in further investigation.

It matters, too, from what "standpoint" one is immersed (ibid., 459). Thus, a prosecutor and a defense counselor have very different motivations in constructing story elements leading to some type of conclusion. And even within defense work there are many frameworks or standpoints from which investigation flows.

Another noted author, Denis Brion, looking at indeterminacy in law making practices, notes that the law of tort in particular and common law in general can be better understood by abduction, whereby "the doctrinal major premises never achieve stability" (1991: 68). He also draws from chaos theory and indicates that the "strange attractor"—a figure that appears very much like butterfly wings indicating that a system perpetually oscillates between two possible outcome basins (e.g., the "wings," representing various possible and opposing resolutions)—has some affinity with this notion (see particularly, Schulman, 1997; see also Schum, 1994: 473–476; we will further develop chaos theory in the next chapter). Schum (ibid., 474), similarly, argues that it is often a "flash of insight" that develops in this state which becomes the basis of some stable meaning or a particular hypothesis. It often takes place at the intersection of two different frames of reference. Up to this point, there had been oscillation as to possible conclusions one could reach given some evidence; but, with the addition of one more small piece of information, even something appearing quite trivial, amplification in thought results, which then makes thought jump to a very different frame of reference which may bring the solution to the problem (ibid., 476).

Richard Rorty (1989), echoing noted theologian and existential philosopher Soren Kierkegrard, has offered the idea of the judge as a "good profit" who engages in a "leap of faith" in going beyond what strict linear, logical rational thought would oth-

If one reviews some break-through law cases, for example, *Brown v.* *ion,* we witness this development. Of course, the question of the pos- ively impacting possibilities always remains.

, in sum, has aroused considerable attention (for applications of Peir- tics, see Lloyd, 2016, 2020; Bor and Konczol, 2019; Verenich, 2012a, d, 2008).[8]

Ferdinand de Saussure (1857–1913)

Semiotics is often recognized as being established by the Swiss Ferdinand de Saussure along with C.S. Peirce (for a useful introduction, see Chandler, 2007, and online version, 1995). Saussure has also been recognized by many in establishing linguistics. He has had a significant influence not only on structuralists (e.g., Claude Lévi-Strauss, Jacques Lacan, and others) but a cross section of disciplines. Among others highly engaged with Saussure's work are Jacque Derrida and Julia Kristeva. In the next chapter we will see his applications by Jacques Lacan who developed a psychoanalytic semiotics. Saussure's key work was published posthumously by some of his students who collected his lecture notes from 1907–1911, the *Course in General Linguistics* (1916). For his *semiology,* as he sometimes called it, language is a system of signs and a product of society.

Unlike Peirce's triadic structure (sign, interpretant, object or referent) Saussure had a binary, two-dimensional relation of the signifier (more physical) with the signified (more mental). A sign, such as words, images, sounds, gestures, objects, etc., is composed of both signifier and signified. Meaning ("signification") is attributable to these two components in relation to other signifiers in contextual usage. The signifier, the sound-image, such as differentiated speech sounds, a sequence of sound, is what comes to represent a signified. Say the word tree (signifier) and the image of the tree appears (signified). This is an arbitrary relation. Only convention has fixed the association. The "value" of the sign is established relationally; that is, a sign takes on particular value in relation to other signs being employed; different relations and different meaning can emerge in different contexts of usage. There are some similarities of Saussure's sign with Peirce's signifier, and with the signified as interpretant and object (see for example, Yakin and Totu, 2014). Signs, for Saussure, are relational; they only make sense in relation to other signs in a sign system employed.

Take as an example the signifier "hoodie." For some, the signified is merely a form of style, a sweatshirt with a hood. For others, it represents, in negative stereotype, trouble, and Black youth. With the much publicized killings by police of Black youth in America it has been a symbol of protest, donned by both Black, White and diverse others in protest of killing of Black men by police. Take another example. The Fourteenth Amendment to the U.S. Constitution says, in part, "nor shall a person be deprived of life, liberty or property without due process of law." Note, person, life, liberty, property, due process, and law are each signifiers. It is in the courts that their signified, their meanings are legalistically established. CRT and crits generally would highlight how the conventional sign system often excludes their voice.

Another key distinction Saussure makes is between *langue* (language) and *parole* (use of language, speech). He focuses more on langue, the conventional sign system in existence. Thus, the use of a signifier, for Saussure, has an intentionality component. The applications of Saussure's notion of signifier and signified underlies many legal discourses, most often implicitly. It has been absorbed in the culture of law finding. Storytelling, for example, can be examined from a Sausserian perspective in terms of the sign system being employed and the assumed meanings attached to each of the signifieds connected to the used signifiers.

Louis Hjelmslev (1899–1965)

Hjelmselv was a Danish linguist who founded the Copenhagen School of Linguistics. He was influenced by Saussure, but considerably expanded it to include a more complex matrix constituting the sign. His most important work was *A Prolegomena to a Theory of Language* (1953).

He argued that the sign can be placed on two planes, the *expression* plane and the *content* plane (for a good introduction, see Chandler, 1995, 2007; Taverniers, 2008; Davidse and Ghesquiere, 2016). The former has similarities with the signifier, the latter with the signified. For him, "the sign is an entity generated by the connection between an expression and a content" (1953: 47). But he also added two further dimensions, *substance* and *form*. Thus, a four-part distinction: form of expression, substance of expression, form of content, substance of content.

The signifier plane includes: form of expression—language, syntactical structure; and substance of expression—the medium, the materiality, pictures, words, phonetics, sound sequence, etc. The signified plane of content includes: form of content—the semantic structure; and substance of content—the subject matter, its physical nature, phonetics, e.g., voice (Chandler, ibid., 54; Davidse, and Ghesquiere, 2016). Expression, too, has various modalities: writing, speech, gestures, pictures, sign language, etc. So, too, content: books, newspapers, radio, film, Morse code, art work, etc. (Mambrol, 2018). Take, for example, the utterance "I like apples" being an expression, its form following syntactical rules; the substance, the words employed in a given language. As an example of the content plane, both form and substance, consider again "I like apples." The utterance takes on a particular form, and the substance entail the unique voice which is doing the uttering. Or, alternatively, consider instead of uttering "I like apples," using a linear sequence of pictures: an eyeball, a heart, and apples. Expression and content by form and substance work as a composite in establishing sense or meaning ("purport").

Thus, a sign is a relation between expression and content (signifier, signified), and their respective subcategories of form or substance. In Hjelmslev's words (1953: 58), the sign is "the name for the unit consisting of content-form and expression-form and established by the solidarity that we have called the sign function." These allow application to more varied situations capturing their idiosyncrasies and complexities.

An additional concept he introduces is *purport*, one interpretation of which is sense, another, a shared meaning. In other words, the functioning of connecting expression and content, form and substance, a matrix, is to produce an effect, a gestalt, a totality sense of the phenomena in question. Purport stands external to the sign function itself. (In Chapter 12 we will show how a quantum semiotics makes use of the "collapse of the wave function" in producing a materialization of an otherwise superposed state, a composition of possibility states, in movement, and thus sense or purport.)

Foucault, for example has embraced the Hjelmslev's schema to explain the relation between prison and delinquency. Here, form of content is the prison or place of imprisonment, substance is the prisoners. Form of expression is penal law and delinquency, and substance of expression include attendant narratives and concepts. Both expression and content are interconnected establishing the meaning or sense of each and their composite meaning (purport). Deleuze and Guattari (1987), we shall see in Chapter 11, made extensive use of Hjelmslev's schema. Sociology of law can be greatly benefited by examining existing complexities: for example, of particular words that have attained a legal meaning, how this shapes an exclusive purport favoring some and disenfranchising other voices (e.g. the subaltern), and why a different purport could have developed within the same matrix, or, better, how a different matrix can better sensitize us to life-worlds of diverse peoples. Crits, for example, who advocate counter storytelling in law could benefit by creatively re-working dominant matrices and their conventional ideologically established purport in a political economy.

Algirdas Greimas (1917–1992), Greimasian Legal Semiotics

Greimasian legal semiotics focuses on the works of the Russian-born and French-educated theorist, Algirdas Greimas. He has developed his ideas in several works (1987, 1990; for a biographical sketch, see Katilius-Boydstun, 1990). His work was most prominent in legal semiotics in the 1980s and 1990s, spearheaded by Bernard Jackson (1985, 1991, 1993, 1995, 1998) and Eric Landowski (1988, 1989, 1992; see also Greimas and Landowski, 1990: 102–138). Many applications appeared in the *International Journal for the Semiotics of Law* and were presented at the Annual Meeting of the International Association for the Semiotics of Law, held mostly in Europe at the time (1980s, 1990s). (Recently, recall, this organization has been consolidated with Kevelson's Roundtables for the Semiotics for Law. This new organization of Peircian, Greimasian, Lacanian, and other persuasions is now called the International Roundtables for the Semiotics of Law. The First Annual Conference was held in Onati, Spain, in May, 2002.) Although Greimas's work has been less applied and has become less prominent since the early 2000s, we continue to see significant works published (Backer, 2015; Marriott, 2015, Verenich, 2013; Bittar, 2021). Bittar (2021), for example, has used a Greimasian approach in developing a relationship between law and justice. It is indicative that the tools Greimas offers for semiotic analysis in law are still viable and quite useful in legal semiotics. They should certainly be well worth adding and keeping in one's scholarly toolkit.

Greimas's semiotics is rooted in a structuralist tradition. He draws from a number of European semioticians: Saussure, Jakobson, Levi-Straus, Hjemlslev. His central concern is to account for the underlying structures of semiotic production; that is, how meaning is generated from these hidden (deep) structures. The conscious subject (the so-called "wide awake self") simply assumes these. They are rarely the bases of reflection, understanding or analysis, but nevertheless form a more unconscious sphere within which paradigmatic structures reside. In his semiotic perspective, language does not refer to an outside reality, but has its referent totally *within* language itself (e.g., it is non-referential). Signs refer to other signs which refer to others, etc. As Conklin (1998: 18) states, "Signs alone (the juncture of a signifier and a signified) constitute existence for Greimas." Thus, to draw from Peirce for a moment, the referent or mental image, (or here called the interpretant) which the signifier (the word) conveys is part of a discoverable underlying structure of language itself.

A lawyer's task is therefore to first give objects and lived-experiences legal representations, signifiers (ibid.). "An event does not exist until it is recognized through legal nomenclature and grammar" (ibid.). Subsequent legal discussions, then, are situated within the totality of these representative forms; real existence recedes into the background. Legal representations remain interconnected with others within a jargonistic legal discourse. Lawyers are trained in its interpretation and use.

It is the "Greimasian Square" or "semiotic square" that will uncover the hidden meaning of words (its semantic variations) as they exist within a particular discourse. It is a conceptual device used in discovering hidden connections between signs. Applied to law, Greimasian semiotics has been integrated into a narrative coherence model by Jackson (1985, 1991; Roermund, 1990; Conklin, 1998: 18–19) and has been applied to legal storytelling (Rideout, 2008; Amaya, 2013). We will return to this below. Let's first develop his semiotic square.

The semiotic square. The most elementary structure of Greimasian semiotics is the "semiotic square."[9] The semiotic square, a "discovery instrument," tells us about the process taking place in the creation of meaning; it tells us about how the paradigmatic axis operates in producing semantic variations (for a concise introduction, see Chandler, 1995, Chapter 6; 2002). It tells us all this by assuming a closed system of signification. In other words, each person retains a more hidden, more unconscious storehouse of signifiers and their relatively stabilized inter-relationships. These "deep" structures provide the basis of more conscious narrative constructions, and provide a relative stability and coherence to verbalized narratives. The semiotic square is useful because it is a discovery principle allowing us to map our thoughts and different possible interpretations. Thus, it is a pedagogical tool. It has heuristic value in experimentation and creative theorizing (Jameson, 1987: xv).

Narrative constructions (e.g., legal texts) for Greimas involve an interaction between a "deep structure," characterized by "a definable logical status," and the "superficial structure, which arranges, through a grammar, semiotic materials from the deep structure into discursive forms" (Greimas, 1987: 48; Jackson, 1985: 53–57; Landowski, 1988). The "deep structure" is essentially constituted by the paradigmatic axis, is quite logical, and is understood by the operation of the "semiotic square." The deep structure is self-referring; it has no "outside" (Conklin, 1998: 18). Each discourse, such as law, has its own deep structure. The "superficial structure" is connected with the syntagmatic axis. It is the more conscious, more deliberate organization of signifiers in particular narratives. For example, a lawyer must draw from a storehouse of acceptable legal signifiers (paradigm) — such as "intent," "duress," "responsibility," "cause," etc. — and place those signifiers in a particular ordering (syntagm) in narratives to be acceptable in a court of law.

The semiotic square (see Figure 1) is composed of binary oppositions: sl versus s2; sl versus -s1; s2 versus -s2. These symbols represent positions within the semiotic square which may be creatively occupied by various concepts, signifiers, and abstract notions. Once making the initial operative decision to arrange the words "black" versus "white" (or "reality" versus "appearance") as the dominant terms in oppositions, immediately implied are the negatives (negations) of the two dominant terms, "not-black," "not-white." Notice, too, that in this logical exercise, which is said to reveal the play of semantics, "not-black" includes more than "white," and "non-appearance" more than "reality."[10] This logical model's claim is that if we start from any corner, we can logically derive the other three by making use of the operations of contraries and contradictories. Said in another way, given one of the corners, the other three exist in a state of potentiality (Jackson, 1985: 77).

The diagonals represent the tensions that are distinct from the primary ones. S and -S (capital letters), which unite the two sides of the square, represent "synthesis," or new conceptual possibilities. Thus -S may represent: "non-black" plus "non-white" = "colorless." Whereas S may represent: "black" plus "white" = "mestizo" (Jameson, 1987: xiv). If we started with sl = day; s2 = night; -sl = not day; -s2 = not night; then, -S would represent twilight.

The "relations of implications" (in Figure 1, the vertical dotted lines) are also suggestive. Arrigo's (1997a) study of the abolition of the insanity defense is instructive (It would be useful for the reader hereafter to sketch out a representative semiotic square). The Montana legislative reform act doing away with the insanity defense can be semantically studied by the semiotic square to identify the various tensions and implications. Thus: sl = insanity defense; s2 = abolition; -s2 = non-abolition; -sl = non-insanity defense. The relations of implications could include between "abolition" and "non-insanity defense," the defense of "guilty-but-mentally-ill" (note, we could also see this as an example of "synthesis," -S); between "insanity defense" and "non-abolition" there is suggested the presence of mental illness and the use of the "insanity defense."

Jameson points out two qualifications: (1) the placement of the initial terms affects the logical possibilities, and (2) each primary term must be conceived as a site of a

Figure 1. Greimasian Semiotic Square

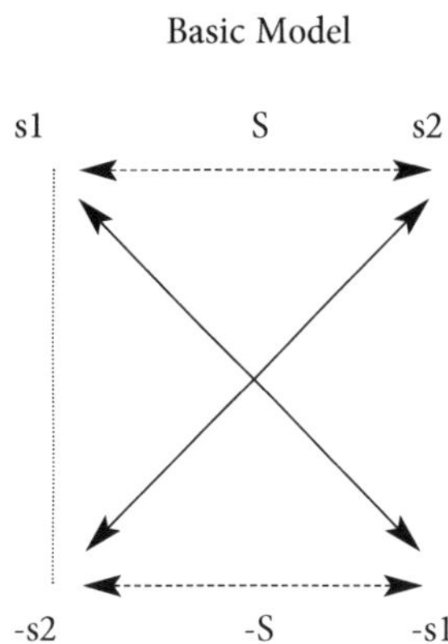

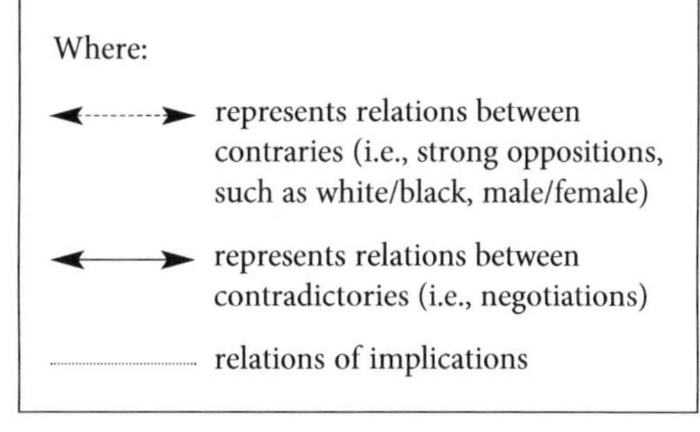

Example 1

white (s1)
black (s2)
not-black (-s2)
not-white (-s1)

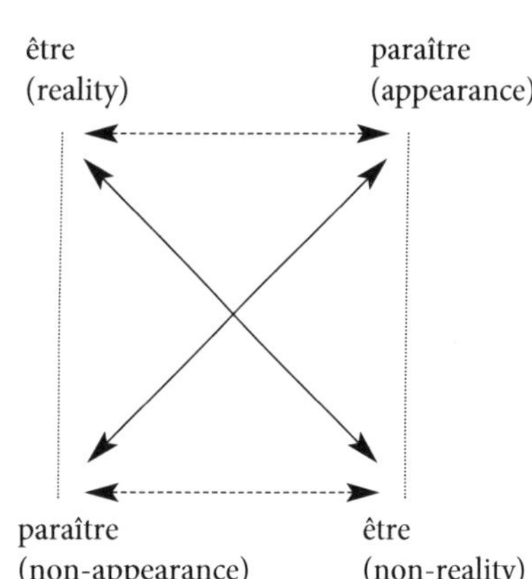

number of possible synonyms (1987: xv–xvi; see also Jackson, 1985: 102). Jackson, in the example above, argues that the binary opposition, "reality" versus "appearance," might conceivably take the form of "reality" versus "possibility" Jackson, 1985: 102). It would seem that Greimas's position is that the binary terms are derived from a concerted study and developed understanding of actual concrete discourses (e.g., legal discourse, religious discourse, philosophical discourse, etc.) wherein these oppositions are modal types (Jameson, 1987: ibid).

Jameson also points out that the lower left-hand corner, -s2, the fourth term, or the "negation of the negation," is the "place of novelty and of paradoxical emergence." He continues:

> It is always the most critical position and the one that remains open or empty for the longest time, for its identification completes the process and in that sense constitutes the most creative act of the construction ... the fourth one [term] is the place of the great leap, the great deduction, the intuition that falls from the ceiling, or from heaven (ibid.).[11]

It could then be argued that both the -s2 as well as S and -S positions are the engines for creative leaps. Richard Rorty's (1989) notion of the good profit and leap of faith in judge's decision making could profit from an application of the semiotic square in examining key court cases that have gone beyond mere linear logic in establishing new precedents.

Let's briefly look at Jackson's analysis of Greimas's French word, "être" (here translated as "reality"). Here it assumes the s1 position. It is opposed to "appearance" (s2). The other corners, then, would be "non reality" (-s1) and the fourth term would be "non-appearance" (-s2). Using the semiotic square as a means of discovery, we see that it generates a structure of meaning in the relationships offered. For example, the relationship between "reality" and "non-reality" could be defined as "immanence"; between "appearance" and "non-appearance" as "manifestation"; between "reality" and "appearance" as "truth"; between "non-appearance" and "non-reality" as "falsity"; between "appearance" and "non-reality" as "lie"; and between "reality" and "non-appearance" as "secret" Jackson, 1985: 102). Thus, the words immanence, manifestation, truth, falsity, lie, and secret all arise logically from these relationships that appear in binary opposition. These are discoveries made possible by the semiotic square. According to Greimas, these words are not randomly chosen or based on personal whim, or derived from any particular ideological persuasion; they are logically derived from the semiotic square.[12]

The semiotic square has been employed to analyze the right to refuse treatment and to competency to be executed proceedings (Arrigo and Williams, 1999: 391–400). First, as to the right to refuse treatment, they define: s1 as "receive treatment"; s2, "refuse treatment"; -s2, "not refuse treatment"; and -s1, "not receive treatment." The implications of the semiotic square are noted: between s1 and -s2, "intervention"; between s2 and -s1, isolation for criminally insane. As to synthesis: S represents "coerced treatment"; and -S, "negotiated treatment." The second semiotic square deals with competency to be executed, where the values are: s1, "competent to be executed"; s2, "incompetent to be executed"; -s2, not incompetent to be executed"; and -sl, "not competent to be executed." The implications: between s2 and -sl, "confinement for criminally insane"; between -s2 and sl, "psychological assessment ordered."

Marriott (2015) has applied the semiotic square to the "evidentiary rule" in law dealing with standards of admissibility for scientific evidence. *Frye v. United States* (1923) was the first recognized formal attempt to state the standard in law.[13] This was a response to a growing practice of lawyers introducing scientific evidence in legal cases. Thus, using the Greimasian square: s1, "admissible scientific evidence"; s2, "inadmissible scientific evidence"; -s2, "sufficiently established"; and -s1, "insufficiently established." The -S, in this case, the implications or new possibilities, is "expert representation(s)." Admissible scientific evidence as opposed to inadmissible scientific evidence remains in the legal plane; sufficiently established as opposed to insufficiently established in the scientific realm. Marriott (383), however, is quick to point out that the "battle of experts commences, but its tools are not of method or reason, but of authority," and it is the "judge who selects the victor." And we add here, the potential of Rorty's "good prophet" can assert itself engaging in a leap of faith to new law.

This evolved into new case law in *Kumbo Tire Co. v. Carmichael* (1999). Here the expert witness claimed expertise in "tire failure analysis," a field "with no peer reviewed journals of longitudinal studies," and now the semiotic square can be conceptualized as: s1, "admissible expert evidence"; s2, "inadmissible expert evidence"; -s2, "valid method"; and -s1, "invalid method." Here, -S represents "judicial science" per *Daubert* (1993, a previous court ruling on admissibility and standards for expert testimony). In other words, "judicial science" becomes a concept allowing judges to act in many ways as a social scientist to support or refute the findings of particular expert testimony.

By placing legal discourse and non-legal discourse on the semiotic square, Greimas and Landowski have shown how transformations from the latter to the former take place. In other words, Greimas's model demonstrates how the "what happened?" is translated into legal discourse. Jackson has also reviewed how syllogistic reasoning in law could be conceptualized on the semiotic square (1985: 86–99) and how the dialectics between true and false, and guilty and not guilty in criminal trials can be fruitfully studied by the semiotic square (1998). Jackson (1998: 243) demonstrates another implication of one of his semiotic squares dealing with jury verdicts, where sl = "found guilty," could lead to -S being "not proven." In other words, if -s2 is "not found not guilty" and -sl is "not found guilty," the implication is not that the person is "innocent," but rather that the case was unproven in law. This gets to the issue of legal versus factual guilt.

Narrative Coherence Model of Law (Bernard Jackson)

Derived from Greimas's work is the narrative coherence model of Bernard S. Jackson (1988; Landowski, 1988). Lawyers and judges, it is said, share a common nomenclature and grammar (Conklin, 1998: 19). "[L]awyers and judges apply the nomenclature and grammar through little stories which share narrative structures with other legal stories, thereby reinforcing the importance of the specialized nomenclature and grammar of lawyers" (ibid.; see also Verenich, 2013). Going beyond an early attempt in explaining how "reality" is semiotically constructed in the courtroom (Bennet and Feldman, 1981), Jackson indicates that decision making that seemingly follows syllogistic logic underplays the active work of the deep structure. In fact, it rests on an underlying, unverbalized narrative (deep) structure. Thus, the major premise in the syllogism hides narrative structures. The major premise of a syllogism "is informed by subconscious narrative models, of typifications of action, and our reaction to them" (Jackson, 1988: 58). The minor premise should be seen as the end result of competing narratives that claim an explanation of the event (for parole board hearings in the disadvantages of the use of inmates' narratives, see Shammas, 2019).

In other words, syllogistic reasoning in law entails the guiding use of hidden structures (deep structure) in combination with the superficial structure of legal discourse) in arriving at a decision in law. It is within the "deep" structure, for example, that biases, prejudices, and "unconscious racism" (Lawrence, 1987) may reside. These extra-legal influences, nevertheless, end up guiding decision making, producing, for example, prejudicial effects.

Consider, for example, the play of deep and superficial structure in parole board hearings (Shammas, 2019; see also Slater, 2020). Here the inmate is asked a series of questions by the parole board members who are trying to determine if the inmate has been sufficiently reformed and ready for return to society. Here, the innate must distance themselves from the prison persona, the "yard face" with its attendant lingo used for survival, and present themselves in an alternative discourse in proving the insights they have gained for their bad ways and how they have gone beyond. But, "they lack experience in performing to the standards of the law, often fail to utter sentences in an appropriately formal register, and cannot successfully manage *diglossia* — the hardened linguistic register of the prison yard *contra* the legal formalism and psychological introspection demanded in the hearing room (ibid., 156)."

The jury, to use another example, is more concerned with comparing the narratives being offered in trial proceedings with the background of conventional social knowledge that they carry with them (i.e., background assumptions, the deep structure). Thus, narrative coherence is said to account for the disposition of cases. Narratives that go against the given conventional body of knowledge are more likely to be seen as suspect by the jury.

The source of the jurors' decision, according to Jackson, "draws upon notions of unconscious rationality derived largely from structuralism — an unconscious rationality which transmits cultural values and which is expressed in cultural products, albeit in an often transformed manner" (1988: 93). This "subconscious" or "unconscious rationality" in law is manifested by, or can be seen as teased out by the logical workings of the semiotic square (ibid., 110–111). Greimas' deep structure, in other words, is materialized in the superficial structure of legal discourse and decision making. Thus, we see a play of the paradigmatic semiotic axis with the syntagmatic semiotic axis: the former provides semantic variation, the latter the appropriate linear narrative constructions. Both are constrained, to various degrees, by the pragmatics of the legal sphere. In other words, meaning construction is aided by internalized legal structures, legal rationality, discursive forms, and legally defined signifiers. But ultimately, juries decide on the basis of narrative coherence models. It is the creative strategy and tactics of lawyers, who tap into the possible deep structures in existence of the jury and make use of this knowledge that will carry the day.

During jury selection *(voir dire)*, opposing lawyers attempt to discover the "deep structure" of the prospective jurors to gain insights as to how they might decide in a case. Lawyers, by consulting jury experts, may gain an advantage by the use of the semiotic square in jury selecting proceedings.

Responding to criticism that his model overlooks how political factors come into play, privileging some narratives and repressing other voices, Jackson responds that the player must consider the given pragmatics of power structures and in making strategic decisions (1988: 171). Ultimately, Jackson tells us, t is to commit ourselves to the values of "telling the truth," "integrity,' that "we commit ourselves to honest communication of the force that which we seek to say" (ibid., 173, 189). He adds that better critical se should lead to the "demystification of the grounds of one's own thought," which, in turn, "is undoubtedly a necessary condition for demystification of the thought of others" (ibid., 189). This would lead to a person characterized by "integrity." Since "truth" is embedded in narrative constructions, and is essentially illusive, then the best one can do, according to Jackson is to depend on integrity (ibid., 193). This is not far from a Lacanian position which we will engage in Chapter 11.

Jackson ends his analysis by stating that semiotics is not in itself a transformative discourse (ibid., 190); that is, it is not a discourse that will necessarily produce social change. Semiotics is "purely descriptive." It can be either radical or conservative—all is dependent upon its use (ibid., 191). In Chapter 10, we will see others in the semiotic tradition who argue that discourse is indeed an arena of struggle, and the task of revolutionaries is to develop replacement discourses. For these theorists, in other words, we see a prescriptive dimension in studying semiotics and its relation to law and political economy.

Speech-Act Theory

Just as we can subsume linguistics under semiotics, arguably, we can also subsume speech-act theory. Accordingly, let us briefly focus on John L. Austin (1911–1960) and his highly influential, *How to do Things With Words* (1962). John Searle (1969, 1979) was to extend his theory. Austin's work is also associated with the "ordinary language philosophers" and in particular speech-acts.

One of his main contributions, extensively cited in the literature, concerns the performative dimension of language. To "say something is to do something." Consider a judge saying, "guilty!"; the priest saying "I pronounce you man and wife"; the baseball umpire saying "out!"; a lawyer in court saying "I object!"; the gambler saying "I bet." In other words, in saying something a result occurs, it produces something.

He also instructs us about other aspects. A *locutionary act* is the act of saying by using correct syntax and grammar. It is the form of the speech-act. It is about sentence construction and of phonetics. An *illocutionary act* is the performing of a locutionary act, its use in context. It "is a way of using language, and its performance is the performance of the act *in* saying something as opposed to performance of an act *of* saying something" (Berdini and Bianchi, 2021: 7). In law, for example, it is a style of rhetoric and effects intended on jurors (e.g., "if it does not fit, you must acquit" in the O.J. Simpson criminal trial uttered by the defense counsel). And a *perlocutionary act* is the resultant act, the effect, or result by the performance. It is "the effects brought about by performing an illocutionary act, to its consequences (intentional or non-intentional) on the feelings, thoughts, or actions of the participants" (ibid.). A judge pronouncing the verdict, "guilty!", for example, produces some emotional result on the person targeted. A police officer saying "hey you!" produces a reorientation of one's demeanor and senses. Note that a speech-act can have different perlocutionary force on the targeted and in different contexts. It is therefore not entirely predictable. What the person says does not necessarily translate by the receiver what they intended. Illocutionary acts are therefore more in the realm of conventionality as compared with perlocutionary acts (ibid., 8).

The importance of Austin's work in legal semiotics is apparent at the pragmatic level. The various contexts of law-finding and law-making are replete with performative dimensions as well as the three aspects of speech-acts. Austin is not without his critics. H.L.A. Hart, in *The Concept of Law* (1961), for example, among other criticism, argued against Austin's position that the very foundations of any legal system are based on obedience, but more on a sense of obligation. Others have come to Austin's defense (see Hardin, 1985).

Critical Legal Semiotics and Sociology of Law

We have presented some of the more discussed semiotics of law. Those from jurisprudence argue more dogmatically, within an unexamined language of law. Those doing more sociological jurisprudence begin to engage the makeup of language itself. The crits are concerned with the ideological function of legal language. Counter storytelling and its attempts in incorporating it into the constraints of legal language is fraught with contradiction. On the one hand, as those from CRT have noted, law and its form of usage is a tool for social change, often one of the few options to counter repressive and discriminatory practices. On the other hand, recognized too, is that the use of law and legal language, even in a rephrased counter storytelling, inadvertently reconstitutes the legal order and its ideology. And, in the process, be it inadvertently, furthers the legitimacy of the legal apparatus as a neutral forum for effectuating social change. One key obstacle, we have seen, is the necessity of converting counter storytelling into the acceptable legal frameworks of law for it to have legal "standings." In the process, many aspects of the counter story are denied full expression in the legal signifiers available, constrained form of syntax, and semantics. How then can an oppositional discourse emerge? From where, recall Spivak's cry, can the subaltern speak? Critical sociology of law examines legal semiotics from a more holistic view, integrating political economy and historically-based contexts in arguing that language is very much an integral component of the makeup of society; indeed, in some circles, constitutes it. In the next chapter, we will visit a Marxist semiotics. In the final two chapters we move to postmodern and post postmodern semiotics of law in the development of a critical sociology of law.

Expressive Forms of Legal Semiotics: Visual, Rhetoric, Audio

Introduction

We want to turn to some subcategories of legal semiotics. We will include visual legal semiotics, visual rhetoric, and audio legal semiotics. Some development has also been in musical legal semiosis. As the reader has realized by now, semiotics is a broad field with insightful applications to law. Given its recent beginnings, there is much still in the developmental stage.

Visual Legal Semiotics

Visual semiotics studies signs in the form of images of all kinds, graphs, photographs, videos, maps, etc. (Rose, 2016). It goes beyond written verbal components. It presents, in one composite, a totality which it would take many words to explain. It concerns how meaning is attributed to the image.[14] Its key development was in the late 1980s. C.S. Peirce and Ferdinand de Saussure have been, and still are the consistent theorists from which visual semioticians draw (see for example, Jappy, 2013; Danesi, 2017; Pauwels and Mannay, 2020; Aiello, 2020). Some work has drawn from a Greimasian approach (Bittar, 2021). Psychology, too, has a claim to its disciplinary boundary. Images are signifiers to which we attribute a particular signified, to use Saussure's bimodal construct. Ultimately, they are representations of the real, as, for example, René Magritte's classic picture of a pipe under which is written the caption, "This Is Not A Pipe" ("Ceci n'est pas une pipe"). Consider, too, "Lady Justice," or Justitia, the Greek "Goddess of Justice." Often evoked as an icon of justice in law, it shows a blindfolded woman, holding the scales of justice in one hand, an unsheathed sword in the other, ostensibly willing and ready to do battle to preserve justice (Knox, 2014).

Meaning construction follows visual codes that are culturally and contextually specific (Aillo, 2020). In the legal arena, we see these codes exemplified (see Wagner, 2009: 81) in coats of arms and the decorum surrounding the court building (Mohr, 2005), court clothing (Woodcock, 2003), and traffic signs (Marusek, 2006; Wagner, 2006). Consider the courthouse architecture. We approach a majestic, old style building with tall pillars, Latin inscriptions conspicuously written across the top which few comprehend, and the courtroom layout replete with architecture depicting the sanctity of law. "Yet signs," Wagner (ibid.) reminds us, "can also be visualized and difficult to verbalize, as they are loaded with history, emotions, and intuitions."

Visual legal semiotics, or sometimes referred to as visual jurisprudence or visual law, has been a relatively recent development, and gaining momentum (see Wagner and Sherwin, 2014; Sherwin, 2012, 2013; Bainbridge, 2011; Porter, 2014). We witness active application to: visual evidence introduced in court (Verenich, 2017); forms of digital media, legal framings based on popular imaginative figures, and the CSI-effect (Sherwin, 2012; Bainbridge, 2010: 201–206; Feigenson and Spiesel, 2009); the use and interpretation of emojis (Wagner and Muraskin, 2010); how popular culture has contributed to ways we perceive actors and stories in the courtroom (Baindbridge, 2010; Sherwin, 2000); and to an association of law and justice via art (Bittar, 2021) as well as music (Sykes, 2018).

Let's provide two examples of visual legal semiotics at work. Verenich (2017) analyzed visual legal evidence. Digital technology, he notes, has made it easier to not only record on the go (consider street videos of witnesses to police killings or brutality), but also in recreating reality (digital simulation, animation, graphics; see, for example, Webster and Bourn, 2106; Hoenig, 2018; Walker, 2008). Three types of evidence are generally allowable in court: direct witnesses (oral) and documents (written); real evidence (e.g., things such as a gun); and demonstrative evidence (illustrates an event, see Wex Definition Team, 2020). Increasingly, in a digital society, demonstrative evidence in the form of digital imagery is being used in law, subject to evidentiary rules (e.g., relevance, authentication, hearsay rules; see Murray, 2016a: 118). But Verenich shows that visual images never speak for themselves; they have contextual meaning. Here, "shifting signifiers of law" float awaiting the anchorage in particular contextual practices. Digital editing and digital simulation pose issues of interpreting the image, and demand authentication. But, Verenich argues, all this requires a certain competency of judges and legal practitioners as to standards of visual literacy, in interpreting the visual image for its demonstrative value, as opposed to its "argumentative" form.

Argumentative forms consist of logical arguments introduced to persuade the witness to draw a conclusion, such as a series of questions to a witness with a plan that each answer would lead to the production of certain conclusion but short of leading or badgering the witness (the lawyer cannot ask the witness to make inferences from facts introduced, this is for the jury)—all subject to cross examination and objection by the opposing lawyer ("objection, argumentative"). The demonstrative value, given Barthes' notion of connotation, however, can slip into the argumentative. Here, the judge must be versed in visual semiotic skills to make a reasoned decision as to acceptability of the image in law.

Verenich places greater value on Saussure's semiotics and one of his disciples, Ronald Barthes (1972), particularly the latter's work on denotative and connotative nature of the sign, than drawing from Peirce. Applications to law by Peirce, he claims, do not sufficiently connect all the complex terms he introduces, and thus on the whole remains undeveloped (ibid., 76–77). Denotative is the generally recognized association between a signifier and that which it signifies, the signified; connotative goes beyond to what it may also imply, particularly given subcultural practices; consider, for example the signifier "hoodie" and the many signifieds generated with real, social consequences. Denotative, such as a photograph of a gun lying at the crime scene, represents just that, a firearm. Connotative implications, however, are tied to cultural codes of interpretation (Barthes, 1974). And the connotative meaning is also a function of lighting, angles, shadings, etc., or composition from which a viewer constructs particular, culturally-informed meaning. Because of connotation, meaning is not fixed. This is brought about when opposing lawyers bring contrasting photographs of the same crime scene, and cross examination and via the use of contrasting expert testimony attempt to construct an alternative reading of the visual crime-scene image.

The second example comes from Sherwin (2012). Instructive is the U.S. Supreme Court Decision, *United States v. Yates* (2006) that addressed witness video testimony from an offsite, and whether it comported with the right to "confrontation" clause of the Sixth Amendment to the U.S. Constitution (see also Bannon and Adelstein, 2020). Confrontation seems to imply presence, actuality. This case was about mail fraud and attached other charges. The two governmental witnesses were unwilling to travel from Australia to provide evidence for the government case at the trial. At the trial court, the witnesses were allowed to present evidence based on video conferencing. In an earlier case from 1988, the Court, in *Coy v. Iowa*, stated confrontation meant face-to-face confrontations. In *Coy*, the majority said the form of confrontation allowing a screen to hide the identity of witnesses who were sexually assaulted (two thirteen-year-old girls) was constitutionally okay since other safeguard were built in. In *Yates*, the majority, using a balancing-of-interest test, said video conferencing did not violate the confrontation clause.

In dissent, Justice Scalia, argued that the "framers" of the U.S. Constitution, in their "original intent," demanded nothing short of face-to-face confrontation, and that balancing was not permissible. Here, Sherwin argues, a visual semiotic analysis of law would look at the framing of the video, the effects on the imagination that looking at a screen evokes versus face-to-face, whether eye contact and its occasionally roaming might produce undue effects in determining guilt, and so forth, compared to a live performance of speech in the courtroom. As Sherwin (152; see also 2000) argues, "viewers of screens inside the courtroom tend to see with eyes that have been conditioned by other popular images." In other words, popular characters from the media and their stock narratives might intrude on the interpretation by the viewers.

The Brennan Center for Justice has noted the potential injustices that exist in remote video conferencing proceedings in court proceedings (Bannon and Adelstein, 2020). This was especially so in bail hearings, immigration court, and witness testimony by children. When comparing in-person with remote video hearings in immigration proceedings, judges have acknowledged changing their credibility assessments (ibid.).

Visual Rhetoric

One tool available for visual legal semiotics is visual rhetorical analysis. It has been influenced considerably by the work of Barthes (1974), particularly his short and highly influential article "Rhetoric of the Image" (1964), applying the notion of denotative and connotative to an advertisement. Visual rhetoric focuses on figurative language such as metaphor, irony, metonymy, etc. (Danesi, 2017: 1) and the art of persuasion by visual images. "Visual thinking," Danesie tells us (ibid.), "is the phenomena of forming thoughts in terms of mental and real-world images, rather than words and their meanings." Thus, images in visual legal rhetoric are primary, followed by verbal explanations, highlighting the importance of both visual rhetoric and legal storytelling that shape, frame and provide further structure. This combined effort is called multimodal work/analysis.

Michael Murray has been and continues to be a key developer in the application of visual rhetoric to law (2016a, 2016b, 2019a, 2019b, 2021). He notes that judges, lawyers and law students generally are not introduced to, nor well-versed in visual literacy and thus are limited in effective use of visual rhetoric tools for possible meaning construction (2021: 1–2). Advocated (ibid., 9–10) is a seven-step methodology to overcome this limitation. It focuses on: first, the "immediate visual context" — examine the visual, outside of words, and relate these images to others employed; second, "analysis of meaning" — examine the plain meaning of the visuals and narratives together; third, "taxonomy of purpose and function" — examine the work in totality; fourth, "immediate verbal context" — examine the effectiveness of words used; fifth, "visual cultural context" — examine the community context from which meaning is framed by the denotative and connotative; sixth, "'mise en scene' and the rhetorical topic of arrangement" — examine framing, composition, perspective, etc.; and seven, "visual rhetoric and the ethical and professional propriety of the work (see also Murray, 2016a) — examine the ethics behind the work and the effect it has on communication of the message (see also, Murray, 2021, where he provides further instruction for developing skills in visual legal rhetoric).

He also cautions us that because visual rhetoric in law is "rapid, efficient, constructive, and persuasive" and because the "speed and power of visuals is seductive," they have the potential to "deceive or to overpower more deliberative forms of rational thought and analysis" (ibid: 155). Ethical considerations, in short, are essential tools in visual legal rhetoric. They should be part of the tool kit of practicing lawyers and judges. This is especially so at the opening statement and summation (closing statement) phase of a trial where lawyers are given wide latitude to introduce multimedia forms. The summation phase offers even greater latitude than at the opening statement phase. Critics have argued that the turn to visual storytelling may undermine reasoned, rational, and logical arguments in favor of the emotional response and tendency to draw from popular media and stereotype storylines and character types (Feigensen and Spiegel, 2009: 130–137; Sherwin, 2000: 41–71).

Audio Legal Semiotics

In line with multimodal forms of semiotics, audio semiotics has recently been applied to court room proceedings (see Chaemsaithong, 2018; Murray, 2016b; Oswald, 2012). Chaemsaithong, for example, shows how in "opening statements" of lawyers — an important step by which the opposing lawyer can present the bigger picture — can reanimate various voices for a desired effect favorable to their particular side of litigation. In other words, the lawyer places themselves in the character of the desired role and carries on in a fictionalized voice. This is called a "semiotic resource" (more in the next chapter). To create a more powerful opening statement, "lawyers need to arouse the interest of jurors, build rapport with them, and, at the same time, come close to being argumentative" (ibid., 3). A legal requirement for opening statement is that they are "informative" not "argumentative," the latter claiming statements of truth which must be open to cross examination and counter stories.

Murray (2016b) argues that applying Peircian semiotics is particularly useful. Firstness, for example, is initially hearing sound. Then it could progress in relation to other sounds (secondness). And then to meaning construction based on, for example, normative standards of understanding (thirdness). We could also integrate iconic (firstness, including pitch, loudness, etc.), indexical (secondness, "causal link between sound and its origin"), and symbolic aspects (thirdness, general rules, such as those appearing in spoken language connecting a particular sound with an image) (ibid., 58). Murray provides an example of a ticking clock (ibid., 60–61). The ticking is recognized as attributable to a clock; it is indexical with the recognition that it is a clock which makes this sound; it is symbolic because it is understood as passage of time. It is only in context that a particular meaning is attached to a clicking clock. Voice or films introduced in court, for example, can be effectively developed with included sound effects to suggest some state that the lawyer wants the jurors to experience.

Oswald (2012), extending on Peirce, particularly focusing on the index, icon, and symbol, has also integrated sound as a semiotic construct and has set out to "develop a theory and taxonomy of auditory signs, based on semiotics." The author introduces the notion of "polysemy," the multiple ways of interpreting a sign, including "multiple types of sign-object relations" (ibid., 41). This highlights how selected audio introduced in the courtroom can have multiple meaning effects. It highlights the importance for law school training on audio competence, along with traditional literary and visual competency. Oswald and Murray have offered a glimpse of what yet has to be done in a Peircian-driven audio legal semiotics.

Thus, to return to Chaemsaithong's article (2018), consistent with a multimodal approach to lawyering, working with sound effects in opening statements can be substantially effective to encourage jurors to favorably interpret the desired explanation of the respective lawyers in their case. The multimodal approach to litigation will put new and necessary demands for legal education.

Some have advocated an "acoustic jurisprudence" (Parker, 2015), others a "musical semiosis," that connects the "symbiotic relationship between music and law, identity politics and social justice ..." (Shaw, 2018: 302; see also special issue, "Music, Cultural Heritage, and Law," edited by Robbie Sykes, the *International Journal for the Semiotics of Law*, volume 31, issue 2, 2018; Manderson, 2000, 2014). Advocated is that doing law is analogous to doing music; both are performative (for the interconnections between law and music, see Arban, 2017). Traditional law, formal rationality, is akin to classical music, with its formalism, rationality, logic (e.g., symphony orchestra). On the other hand, non-classical law, substantive rationality/irrationality, is much like improvisational jazz. The latter is most important for case law. Advocates of jazz law value creativity, leaps, discovery, reformulations in an ever changing, diversifying, differentiating, complex society with a multiplicity of identities and subcultures (Ramshaw, 2013; Manderson, 2014; Buffo, 2018; see also special issue, edited by T. Piper, "Lex Non Scripta, Ars Non Scripta [law not written, DM]: Law, Justice and Improvisation" in the journal *Critical Studies in Improvisation,* volume 6, issue 1, 2010). Case law, in short, must be a living law that privileges emergents, much like improvisational jazz.

Summary

This chapter has focused on some key concepts and applications in legal semiotics and their contributions toward a sociology of law. We first reviewed some of the key semioticians from which legal semiotics has developed: Ferdinand de Saussure, Charles Sanders Peirce, Louis Hjelmslev, and Algirdas Greimas. We also reviewed some thoughts from John L. Austin and his performative semiotics, doing things with words, and generally, speech-act theory. We noted that during the 1980s and 1990s two general approaches in a semiotics of law were developed: one, a Peircean approach, based in America, spearheaded by Roberta Kevelson; the other, a Greimesian approach, based in Great Britain and Europe, spearheaded by Bernard Jackson. Saussure's work was applied across the Atlantic, but in law during the 80s and 90s, secondary to Peirce and Greimas. The narrative coherence model was developed, noting special applicability in storytelling and for the potential for counter storytelling advocated by crits. Subsequently, in the 2000s to present, a globalization is underway witnessing cross-fertilization and the reliance on other approaches such as the Hjelmslevian approach in law. We then moved to expressive forms of legal semiotics. These included visual legal semiotics, visual rhetoric, and audio legal semiotics. Noted, too, were developments in musical semiosis and law.

Review Questions

1. What value might the addition of legal semiotics in Law School curriculum have? Should it be required in core courses? Why?

2. You are having a discussion on a contemporary issue with your friend, a student at a law school, or a recent graduate. They insist that you respond in "yes" and "no" answers to their questions and at the end, through deductive logic, claim the logical conclusion is.... How do you insert an alternative discourse to analysis a particular issue in society?

3. Higher education introduces you to a way of speaking, a particular language style. Does it disenfranchise people of color and the poor? If so, how so? If not, why not? (Professor might consider separating the two answers and placing responses on board. Then a class discussion.)

4. Initially, those in struggle may remain in Peirce's "firstness," a general feeling of disenfranchisement or alienation. Competing groups provide different linguistic

coordinate systems within which these can be placed given more material expression. How can this be empowering, and disempowering?

5. Peirce provides the idea of "musement," or pure play as the basis of insights. Think in terms of when you came up with an important insight while in this state, perhaps an epiphany. Explain.

6. Greimas offers the idea of a semiotic square as a discovery device. Provide an example (not from those listed previously) and place it on the square. Perhaps consider recent coverage of some social movement or recent legal decision. Explain the implications.

7. Jackson's narrative coherence model and Black's sociology of the case point to important factors in constructing legal reality. How can they contribute to crits' development of a counter storytelling? How might they be useful?

8. Do some research on a recent legal case presented in the media. Briefly summarize. Then apply, in turn, a Saussurean and Peircean semiotics. Apply their concepts. What are the benefits one approach than the other? In class, the instructor might present a ledger on the board comparing the two.

9. We have seen that lawyers are often trapped in a legal language by their very training and in their everyday pragmatic concerns. Are they resigned to unintentionally or inadvertently reconstitute the dominant legal ideological apparatus, or are there ways to challenge it without repercussions? Explain.

10. Explain how a lawyer well-versed with the three expressive forms of legal semiotics we covered (visual, visual rhetoric, and audio legal semiotics) may be in a better, more advantageous position to construct stories for their respective position (defense, prosecutor).

Endnotes

1. For the relevance of legal semiotics to the legal realists and CLS, see Balkin (1990).

2. I recall attending a conference to present a paper on semiotics of law in Utrecht, Netherlands (1991), and having the pleasure of dining with Roberta Kevelson, "Bobbie" as we all affectionately called her, and Bernard Jackson. Here, Bobbie a Peircian, Jackson a Gremiasian and I at the time, a Lacanian. I asked if semiotics was the umbrella term for all of social sciences or just a component to which both responded the former.

3. With Roberta Kevelson passing away in 1998 combined with Bernard Jackson leaving the semiotics of law area of study, a vacuum developed in the following two years in which both organizations seemed on the brink of atrophying (see Wagner *et al.* (2005: 9–10). I (DM), the editor of the *International Journal for the Semiotics of Law* (*IJSL*, 1997–2007), initiated discussion for unification of the two with John Brigham associated with Kevelson's organization and Maarten Henket with Jackson's. What emerged was a new organization that combined the two previous, with an annual meeting now called The International Roundtable for the Semiotics of Law. The *IJSL* continues under the editorship of Anne Wagner, a similarly charismatic leader and doer in the organization. The journal now is issued six times a year, indicative of its standing.

4. Under its aims (https://www.springer.com/journal/11196): "We publish original and high quality papers that should ideally critique, apply or otherwise engage with semiotics or related theory and models of analyses, or with rhetoric, history of political and legal discourses, philosophy of lan-

guage, pragmatics, sociolinguistics, deconstruction and all types of semiotics analyses including visual semiotics. We also welcome submissions, which reflect on legal philosophy or legal theory, hermeneutics, the relation between psychoanalysis and language, the intersection between law and literature, as well as the relation between law and aesthetics."

5. See Whitney, 1993; Summers, 1991; Benson, 1991; Sanders, 1991; Valauri, 1991. See also Malloy's (2000: 23–39) review on theorists influenced by Peirce as well as on crits (Malloy, 2000: 24).

6. Cooke's (2018: 2) sums up: "the muser is able to notice new signs, anomalies, problems, and questions, which allow her to generate novel hypotheses by speculating about these newly notice things. Musement is about opening oneself up to new problems and anomalies, as well as opening oneself up to new explanatory hypotheses."

7. Chaos theory would see this as the inducing of far-from-equilibrium conditions within which alternative forms arise, such as novel ideas, vistas, insights, formulations, etc., and even the basis of legal decision making (see Brion, 1991, 1995; See also Chapter 11). A fully developed semiotics of law based on chaos theory awaits in the wings for creative development.

8. See also a number of applications of a Peircian semiotics to law that have been spearheaded by the efforts of Roberta Kevelson: to contract and property (Kevelson, 1988; 1993b; 1998; Brion, 1999); the idea of community (Kevelson, 1991b); legal reasoning (Valauri, 1991; Uusitalo, 1991; Whitney, 1991; 1993; Kevelson, 1998); the law of tort (Brion, 1991, 1995); legal classification schemas (Kellog, 1991); expression of feelings in law (Lachs, 1991); economic justice and economic theory (Kevelson, 1988; Whitney, 1992); law and market economy (Malloy, 1999, 2000; Ahonen, 1995); money (Klinck, 1993); international law (Kevelson, 1998; Werner, 1999); and an esthetics of freedom (Kevelson, 1993c; Brigham, 1999).

9. See Greimas, 1987: 49; Greimas and Landowski, 1990: 108–114; see also Jackson, 1985: 75–110, 117; Jackson, 1988: 137; 1998; Jameson, 1987: xiv–xxii; Arrigo, 1997a, 1998a, 1999a; Backer, 2015.

10. In Jackson's (1998) analysis of the criminal verdict, he has s1 as true, s2 as false, -s2 as not false, and -sl as not true. Another variation he analyzes is: s1 as found guilty, s2 as found not guilty, -s2 as not found not guilty, and -s1 as not found guilty. Yet another is: s1 as guilty, s2 as innocent, -s2 as not innocent, and -sl as not guilty. Each of these can be placed on the semiotic square and be analyzed for the logical implications. Again, this is a discovery tool.

For an application of the semiotic square to media analysis, see Fleming, 1996; Floch, 2000; see also Chandler, 1994: Chapter 6. Chandler's website (1994) provides a "message board" and "chatroom" where the interested student can pursue their understanding of these concepts.

11. Consider the implications of each -s2s. Of course, we are looking at the particular deep structure of law. Thus, a verdict of "not guilty" in law does not mean the same thing for a layperson, in the popular view, or even in the factual sense Jackson, 1998: 241).

12. For other examples, see Jameson, 1987: xvii–xxii, where he examines Hayden White's book *Metahistory;* for application of the semiotic square to various novels, see Jameson, 1981: 166–167, 253–280; for situating Nietzsche, Hegel and Marx, see Jameson, 1987: xx–xxii.

13. It has evolved into Rule 702: "If scientific, technical or otherwise specialized knowledge will assist the trier of fact to understand the evidence or to determine a fact in issue, a witness qualified as an expert by knowledge, skill, experience, training or education, may testify thereto in the form of an opinion or otherwise" (cited in Bracker, 385).

14. It has been pointed out that mental images do not arise just from visual perception, but can have other sources (Danesi, 2017): "by imagining such phenomena as the sound of thunder (auditory image), the feel of wet grass (tactile image), the smell of fish (olfactory image), the taste of toothpaste (gustatory image), the sensation of extreme happiness (emotional image), and so on."

10

Socio-Legal Semiotics in Sociology of Law

Introduction

This chapter turns to a more sociological examination of legal semiotics in furthering a sociology of law. We first introduce social semiotics. Then, turn to socio-legal semiotics which applies many of these tools to the legal arena. We follow with an introduction to critical discourse studies (CDS). Returning to socio-legal semiotics, a more comprehensive approach is suggested in a critical socio-legal semiotics that incorporates social semiotics, visual, audio, rhetoric semiotics, CDS, and narrative studies. We will finish with presenting the resurgence of materialist Marxist semiotics and one particular example, a structural interpellation variant.

A critical socio-legal semiotic approach to law is in its infancy in the U.S. For many years it has been recognized that the language of law and lawyers is unique and has effects, yet until the 1990s little in the way of a systematic analysis had taken place. This emerging perspective was more likely to be situated in an overly legal analysis and critique (e.g., jurisprudence/legal science), which drew from various perspectives without an overall plan for developing a coherent theory. A critical socio-legal semiotic/discourse approach to law integrates the insights from social semiotics, critical discourse analysis/studies, visual and audio semiotics. Legal semiotics, in short, can be broadened in scope to encompass semiotic resources advocated by these approaches. A comprehensive approach that recognizes the multimodal nature of semiosis is in store in future integrative work. Let's first turn to some foundational work in social semiotics.

Social Semiotics, Socio-Legal Semiotics

Social semiotics is a subcategory of semiotics. It extends semiotic analysis to more explicit theorizing and application to culturally and socially based codes, incorporating, to a certain extent, discussion of power and ideology. It is more about how texts are constructed and the consequent meaning produced. Text can take many forms, but some code is at work in their construction. Rather than privileging only codes, as is often the case in semiotic analysis alone, it incorporates both language and *modes* of communication (i.e., images, written, music, gestures, speech, etc.), especially their multimodal expression in context (Kress, 2010: 79). This approach is sometimes referred to as "multimodal discourse analysis" (Jewitt, 2014). These joint practices constitute semiotic work in making meaning. Visual and audio semiotics are constitutive element of social semiotics.

The key journal, established in 1991, that welcomes articles in social semiotics is entitled *Social Semiotics*. In its "aims and scope" it provides the contours of the journal, and by implications, the field. It focuses on:

> ... the study of semiotic resources and practices including words, images, behaviours, settings, sounds, design, etc., and the way these are connected to the organization of societies and everyday life ... the ways in which semiotics resources/practices may perpetuate biases, imbalances or legitimize and maintain kinds of power interests ... [it] might draw on linguistic analysis, visual analysis, content analysis, ethnography, interviews, as well as production studies, and can be tied to political economy ... [and includes] sociopolitical significance of representations.

Social semiotics had its origins in a structuralist orientation. Key early contributors include Bob Hodge and Gunther Kress (1988) and Michael Halliday (1978). It has been significantly modified in recent years (Kress, 2010), especially building on Halliday, by van Leeuwen (2005) and his co-author (Kress and van Leeuwen, 2006; see also Gualberto and Kress, 2018). Hodges and Kress draw from Peirce and Saussure as well as Marx. They highlight pragmatic semiotic work that takes place beyond that merely driven by the analysis of given linguistic codes.

Key elements include a focus on:

(1) "Semiotic resources" (visual, verbal, auditory), "the actions, materials and artifacts we use for communication purposes" (van Leeuwen, 2005: 285);

(2) Fields of meaning potentials (Halliday, 1978: 39) associated with often used semiotic resources or sets of resources which shape possible meaning construction in particular contexts, and thus provide semiotic potential material to be used in the construction and interpretation of meaning (e.g., the "modes," especially multimodal forms of possible expression in meaning production and interpretation, i.e., images, written forms, music, gesture, speech, etc.) (Kress, 2010: 79);

(3) "Fields," to be read as context-bounded fields, loci or domains of activity offering affordances that enable or limit certain productions and interpretations (e.g., consider the courthouse, police station houses, prisons, court room, etc.);

(4) as well as the effects of power differentials of senders and receivers of messages and their ideological underpinnings (Aiello, 2020).

Social semiotics thus focuses on both existing language and particular modes of communication (Caldas-Coulthard and van Leeuwen, 2003) in context. It highlights social processes in production and interpretations shaped by conventions, rules, or normative structures ("genre"), a particular way of speaking and writing ("style"), and populated discourses with histories ("discourse") (van Leeuwen, 2005; see Rose's clear exposition, 2016: 139–142). Gesture, too, as a mode, is a semiotic resource, be it a non-verbal form with distinct effects. See, for example, the use of hand gestures in closing arguments of trials (Matoesian and Gilbert, 2016, 2018). Highlighted in social semiotics, therefore, are genre, style, discourse, and gesture.

Text construction, or "semiotic work," for those in social semiotics, examines multimodal forms of text production, the material semiotic tools or semiotic resources used in meaning making; that is, we often make use of more than one mode in actualizing signs. Modes both shape what can be communicated, and in turn are shaped in everyday social practices. Users of semiotic resources make use of both their historically and subculturally shaped meanings which in turn reinforce and shape the conventional meanings in their use, a co-constitutive process. Consider, for example, police culture maintaining the ideology of the thin-blue-line and how it is continuously reconstituted in practice. But these constructions of texts are constantly tested by social activists demanding police reform and accountability. Wearing body-mounted cameras, a semiotic resource, for example, shows how the otherwise invisible practices are now subject to regulatory concerns and the public gaze.

Working against tendencies of ossification driven by power-driven dynamics alone, Rose (ibid., 142), following Kress (2010: 21), notes that the world wide web and rise of neo-liberalism with its attendant focus on individualism has produced increasing participatory practices whereby power's influence is somewhat flattened, particularly finding expression in the form of social networking in the form of blogs, Myspace, wikis, twitter, Facebook, etc. And semiotic modes do not remain static: they "are constantly modified," and "as every occasion of sign-making differs from ever other, social semiotics asserts that signs are always newly made. In every sign-making action, the already designed world is constantly re-designed" (Gualberto and Kress, 2019: 5).

Law-in-action, for example, is shaped by its semiotic resources, that is, acceptable semiotic modes employed in textual production in law (i.e., forms of legal reasoning, deductive logic, particular language, semantic and syntactical constructions, electronic technologies, and case law), as well as architecture of courts, emblems, formal robes, and other symbolic visual displays. They, in their totality, contribute to a field of meaning potential. Reality construction follows the shaping effects of the semiotic resources ("modes," e.g., those based on visual, audio, and written forms) employed in doing law (e.g., correct law-talk, acceptable visual animations, simulations, and remote video conferencing in court proceedings, etc.); anything else is nonjusticiable, has no "legal standing." Thus, constructing the "what happened" in trial court is greatly circumscribed, limiting forms of storytelling, notwithstanding "crits" advocating counter storytelling and the limited forms it may take. But the legal arena also draws from popular media and its depiction of changing types of characters, plots, and storylines. Bainbridge (2010), for example, provides an application of these social processes in the shifting nature of signifiers and their signified (below).

Socio-legal semiotics builds on social semiotics and visual legal semiotics in theorizing and application to the legal arena. Within socio-legal semiotics, as is with social semiotics, a range of approaches exist incorporating political economic and ideological aspects. The perspective, by definition, is at least liberally oriented; however, we can also distinguish a wing with a more explicit focus on power and an equal concern for social change which can be identified as *critical socio-legal semiotics*. Whereas a good part of social semiotics has implicit critical theoretical frameworks, in many cases, they are not fully made manifest, unlike the critical socio-legal semiotic version. The last part of the chapter will provide one example of a Marxist-driven approach. In the next chapter we will look at the postmodern and in the following, post postmodern variations. Only recently are those in the sociology of law approach incorporating more of the above dimensions. A convergence of fields is underfoot in some sectors. Let's provide some examples of applying socio-legal semiotics.

Bainbridge (2011) has applied Saussurian semiotics to the connection between popular visual media and how the representations shape an understanding of law's functioning (see also Sherwin, 2000). He argues that a good part of understanding of law and how it functions is gained by viewing virtual reality shows dealing with law and enforcement, as well as key jury trials that are often broadcasted live. Here, visual semiotics begins to be integrated with a more social legal semiotics. Changing times produce, he argues, a change in the particular signifier of law employed and the mental concept of law (signified). He examines: the father as signifier of law, the lawyer as signifier of law, the policeman as signifier of law, the vigilante as signifier of law, and the female signifiers of law. He also addresses the relationship of law to justice.

The "father as signifier of law" traces the authority of the paternal figure represented in both popular media accounts in virtual programing as well as in real life to Sigmund Freud's classic development of the Oedipus conflict as a basis of social order. This is claimed to be the primordial point in which two sons slay their father for authority, but, finding themselves in conflict with each other, form a social contract (Bainbridge, 196). Hereafter, the father as signifier stands for the signified: authority, order, stability, and predictability, both present in popular media and played out in real courtroom dramas. The "lawyer as signifier of law" in popular media portrays, most often an "older, wiser and male agent." We do see, more recently, a movement away from merely male figures. The lawyer as signifier appears generally in three forms: heroic figure in legal dramas; heroic protagonist in legal thrillers; and part of a supporting cast where law itself is often seen as restricting substantive justice (ibid., 197). The lawyer as signifier has as associated signified: order, the rule-of-law, certainty, predictability, and procedural forms of justice. Thus, the lawyer representation in popular media most often reflects the key ideological functions of formal rationality. However, there are some scripts where the lawyer is seen as the impediment to justice with their rigid formal rational thinking and action (e.g., due process model, Packer, 1969), and hence the appearance of the contrary figure using extra-legal methods associati[ng] the signified with a fighter for substantive justice, often by whatever means.

The policeman [policeperson] as signifier of law can represent either the protector of order, or, as in the more common case in popular mass media, a circumventer of due process in law, in taking on a working philosophy of what Packer (1969) calls the "crime control model," as a protector of "the thin blue line," where rules are created, and so too justice, in the streets. The vigilante as signifier of law is often represented as doing extra-legal justice, perceived as doing society's wishes, rather than adhering to the rigidities and hindrances of the due process model and formal rationality. As in the TV serial, *Dexter*, the vigilante only does-in bad people. The signified here is a superhero, a person working outside of the formal law to establish justice. Finally, the female signifier of law is often associated with the signified of representing the Other, the subaltern, the invisible, the disenfranchised, as well as substantive justice of care. This in marked contrast of the paternal figure of the father and strict rationality, order, authority. We will have more to say in the next chapter on postmodern feminist law. Baindbridge (ibid., 212) concludes with the merits for pursuing this form of examination: "using semiotics to unpack how law is defined in popular visual culture is therefore a vitally important part of understanding how fluid law is and how very different law can become, in different contexts and for different institutions."

Sherwin (2012: 139) has well-highlighted the importance of popular media images in doing law. "Effective prosecutors and defense lawyers often mine the popular imagination for well-known characters ("she-devil," "femme fatale,") and stock scripts ("sex games gone wrong") to help frame their story in court. Once a narrative frame is set, so, too, is the belief system that it embodies." And he (ibid.) continues, "with recognizable story frame and a cast of familiar characters in hand, advocates can coax their audience (jurors and judges alike) to fill in missing details." Thus, this resource contributes to strategic story-telling, particularly as to how to position actors in narratives (Chaemsaithong, 2019a, 2019b). Distinct discursive practices and narrative constructions by opposing lawyers position identities in particular story-lines in hopes of creating realities that benefit their respective side in litigation (see also Rosulek, 2009). Sherwin's insights can be applied to Chaemsaithong's study in highlighting the "intersemiotic operation between discourse, law and society" to include popular images and their use in trial court proceedings (Cheng and Danesi, 2019: 279).

Chaemsaithong's (2019a) empirical case study highlights how the prosecutor and defense counselor differ in their use of semiotic resources. The prosecutor "individualizes and personalizes the victims by their names, age, and details of what happened to their bodies. For depicting the offender, they attempt to depersonalize them "by seldom referring to him by name, but as 'the defendant.'" The prosecutor attempts to show that the defendant had full capacity in choosing in the commission of the crime; whereas the victim is depicted with little agency, "who does nothing wrong and lives his or her life and yet is affected by the defendant's action." On the other is mainly silent about casualties, and avoid[s] referencing the vic- izes the defendant ... by principally using his first name, and by ood experiences and his internal feelings and thoughts" (ibid., s to rationalize the actions of the defendant "so that his actions m another agent's influence, or so that he appears as being ...ers, rather than affecting others." The victim's experience is hardly ...t up (ibid.). Chaemsaithong (2019b) has also shown how identity constructions are differentially constructed by prosecutor and defense in opening statements of trial court proceedings.

A special issue of the journal, *Social Semiotics,* entitled "Exploring Legal Discourse" and edited by Le Cheng and Marcel Danesi (volume 29, issue 3, 2019), was devoted to legal social semiotics and brings out the call for applying social semiotics to the legal arena. The special issue focuses on "an intersemiotic operation between discourse, law and society." Articles included application of social semiotics to cyber bullying, cyber security laws, "e-victimization," internet fraud, reform in Chinese laws, amongst others.

Critical Discourse Studies

Critical discourse studies (CDS) focuses on narratives, textual production, and speech in meaning making, in constructions of social reality. It is more "parole" of Saussure; that is, the actual *use* of language, speech acts, rather than "langue," the latter characterized by particular rules and codes (e.g., consider the difference between English and German language). Storytelling, for example, is a narrative. It is some ordering of action and/or events, generally with a linear development from beginning to middle to an end that is often framed in a typical way (genre), such as tragedy, irony, comedy, romance (Forchtner, 2021a: 305, 308; 2021b). And we would include legal narratives as a genre. Recall from a previous chapter, "crits" have made storytelling and counter storytelling a key strategy for socio-legal change. Critical discourse studies is related to critical discourse analysis (CDA). The main journal for its researchers and writers is the journal of *Critical Discourse Studies.* In its "aims and scope" it states:

> Its primary aim is to publish critical research that advances our understanding of how discourse figures in social processes, social structures, and social change ... the relationship between discourse and social dynamics ... [and it] also welcome[s] papers which connect critical academic research with practical concerns and agendas, including those of activist and grassroots political movements.

Literature on "critical discourse analysis" continues to grow (Fairclough, 2014, 2018; Fairclough and Graham, 2002; Borrelli, 2018; Ashgar, 2014; Beltramini, 2007) with applications that include environmental policy (Leipold *et al.,* 2019), environmental disputes (Smith, 2006) and intellectual property (Hollis, 2017). In a Latin American context, see Gandler (2018). Integrative work also continues to grow. Borrelli (2018), for example shows some compatibility, a "convergence," of a materialistic-semiotic approach, particularly a Marxist semiotics of Rossi-Landi (below) with CDA offered by Fairclough, in *Language and Power* (1989; see also Fairclough and Graham, 2002).

Fairclough informs us (emphasis in original, 2018) "CDA combines *critique* of discourse and *explanation* of how discourse figures in existing social reality as a basis for *action* to change reality." He continues (ibid.), "[W]ithout explanation and understanding of social reality, including causal and dialectical relations.... between discourse and other elements of social life, we cannot know what needs to be changed, what can be changed, and how." He insists that CDA considers simultaneously both semiotics and material analysis (Fairclough, 2008). Fairclough (2002) draws considerably from Karl Marx, who he claims was involved in critical discourse analysis. Key objectives of CDA include (Ashgar, 2014: 226; Bloor and Bloor, 2007): "to investigate how ideologies can become frozen in language and find ways to break the ice," "to increase awareness of how to apply these to specific cases of injustice, prejudice, and misuse of power," "to demonstrate the significance of language in social relations of power," and "to investigate how meaning is created in context."

Forchtner (2021b) argues that CDA and CDS are interchangeable, and extends this analysis to a "discourse-historical approach" (DHA). He proposes to apply how "narrative genres" (romance, tragedy, comedy, and irony), as semiotic modes, create historically-situated/contextualized meaning complexes. We could extend his analysis via CDA to include law-talk as a narrative genre and show how law-talk changes with changing societal conditions, and how changing identity structures, media portrayals, and shifting power structures implicate constructions of legal narratives. Crits, for example, in criticizing conventional, dominant framing in storytelling, narratives of exclusion, can constructively draw from struggles, and consequently revised societal thinking, in constructing counter storytelling.

Critical Socio-Legal Semiotics

Although it may seem that a critical approach is already a wing in social semiotics, it is worth underscoring the more explicit centering in a sociology of law and more comprehensive analysis of structures of domination, as was the early emphasis of the originators, Halliday, Hodge, and Kress. Fairclough, too, in his CDA furthers this enterprise. Here, concern about domination, power, ideology, hegemony, and inequalities become much more salient, and the underlying socio-political and economic-based theory more explicit. Along with critical analysis, what distinguishes the critical version of socio-legal semiotics from the non-critical is an equal concern for social change, particularly highlighted by the various crits whom we addressed in a previous chapter. Accordingly, a critical socio-legal semiotics would integrate social semiotics; visual, rhetoric, and audio semiotics; CDA/CDS; and narrative studies—all in a comprehensive whole, specifying the interconnections and feedback loops between different foci of analysis: that is, micro (face-to-face), intermediary (community), and macro (social structural/institutional).

Caldas-Coulthard and Van Leeuwen's introduction to the special issue of *Social Semiotics* (volume 13, issue 1, 2003) clearly state the critical emphasis: "The 'critical' in 'critical social semiotics'... indicates that social semiotics takes part in the enterprise of critical discourse analysis. It does not stop at description, but analyses multimodal texts as playing a vital role in the production, reproduction and transformation of the social practices that constitute the society in which we live." We add, that "critical" also means an equal concern for social and socio-legal change.

Critical socio-legal semiotics provides critical tools that can be constructively applied in investigating the traditional legal order, particularly the failing criminal justice system and its restrictive semiotic resources (e.g., legal discursive constructions, rational logical reasoning belied by an otherwise crime control model in practice, architectural and dress symbolism that signify distance and hierarchy, images of crime and its causes that are often created elsewhere, etc.). In short, the criminal justice system can be viewed as constituting a restrictive field of meaning potentials. Realities constructed by the allowable semiotic resources, in short, are but sterile, virtualized renditions of the real struggles and suffering by the many in a political economy where survival is not assured and where Darwinian competition for survival is acute. Mertz (2007: 62–64, 220) has also highlighted the effects of "legal-linguistic filters" that obfuscate the telling of real stories of humans in struggles and overcomings, and disguises hierarchical powers that dominate our lives. Consider the associated representative signifiers and signifieds that have crystallized, often narrowly construed categories of victim, offender, community. Criminal justice reifies these categories; law-in-practice, particularly via precedents, reconstitutes identity positions in fixed ways leaving little for transformation.

Semiotic resources and their modes of expression are greatly restricted in storytelling in the legal arena. Restorative justice begins to reconstitute signifiers and their signifieds in an alternative discourse of reconciliation and discourses sensitive to diversity, change, struggle, emergents, and different reality constructions that may lead to conflict. Transformative justice goes beyond with its ethics of care, solidarity, and concern for emerging identities, subcultural variations, real struggles, an approach tempered by real, materialist commitments for social justice, redistribution of resources, and a more egalitarian society. Black, as we have seen in his "styles of social control," has sensitized us to how each style of social control, a potential stand-alone, has contrasting signifiers and signified. Consider, for example, how the signifier, "domestic disputes," more situated in a conciliatory style, has undergone revision in the penal style of social control, particularly how identities have changed from "disputants" to criminal. Woolford (2019), too, has advocated alternative identity formations in the legal order connected to a transformative justice and legal order.

Consider, as an illuminating exercise, applying a critical socio-legal semiotics to the following signifiers, and how employing various conceptual tools (semiotic resources, modes) to existing hegemonic narratives and effects of power, economics, ideology, and media depictions might illuminate the respective areas (how differently can we construct the associated signified?): "ghetto" (particularly how the meaning changed over time); "colonists" (early American arrivals);[1] "homesteaders" (U.S. Homestead Act of 1862 providing "free land" in the West);[2] "settlers" (Israel's term for those moving into occupied [Palestinian] lands); "squatters" (those taking over abandoned buildings on the Lower East Side in the 1970s, New York City);[3] "subversives," "rioters," "criminals," "patriot," "rebel," and "hoodie" (denotative, sweatshirt with hood; but also with connotative implications). Similarly, consider the signifiers, "life," "liberty," and "property" mentioned in the 14th Amendment to the U.S. Constitution.

Resurgence of a Materialist Marxist Semiotics

The first two decades of the 21st millennium have witnessed a renewed interest in a material Marxist semiotics. This responds to the developments of the 1990s that downplayed the economic and elevated the primal importance of a free-floating discursive formation (Laclau and Mouffe, 1985). A resurgence of a material Marxism semiotics, be it a "post Marxism discourse," is highlighted by three special issues of the journal, *Critical Discourse Studies*: "Class and Discourse," 2008, issue 5(4); "Post-Marxist Discourse," 2014, issue 11(3); and "Marx and Discourse," 2018, issue 15(4). A return to a materialist Marxism has also been highlighted by "social reproduction theory" that focuses on social relations of production and the reproduction of social structures and its constituent institutions (Giménez, 2019; Bhattacharya, 2017; Cammack, 2020; Ferguson, 2016).

"Materialist" implies objective structure to which a post-Marxism substitutes "material-discursive" to suggest that all phenomena to have social meaning must be brought into some contextualized signifier-signified relation be it a radically contingent form whereby hegemony is a major shaping factor as to what is included, what is excluded. It is contingency that resists closure and opens up the possibilities of new articulations. By contingency it is meant a resistance to closure, the openness, contextual variations, and changing nature of all phenomena. Nor does this view profess an anti-realism, only that objects obtain meaning in particular systems of semiosis; that is, constituted as meaningful objects of discourse (Laclau and Mouffe, 2014: 94).

Let's first briefly review the key critiques of the 1990s to be followed by the resurgent forms of a materialist-discursive post-Marxist semiotics. We suggest the latter's contribution to a critical socio-legal semiotics and provide one possibility in the application by a materialist Marxist approach in law by Rossi-Landi (1977, 1983).

The turn to a semiotic Marxism (1980s, 1990s). A useful beginning in understanding the turn to a Marxist semiotics begins in a discussion of the traditional interpretation of the base-superstructure thesis, by which, recall (Chapter 5), the economic base was said to determine the superstructure (ideological, juridical, and political). Recall, in this view, the legal structure is but a reflex of the economic, so too consciousness, ideology, language, etc. The lively discussions in the 1980s and 1990s, however, led to revisionist understandings, including reversal of the causal direction of base-superstructure. The key players for a semiotic Marxism were Gramsci, Althusser, Poulantzas, and Laclau and Mouffe. According to a very useful summary by Bergesen (1993), the end result of this debate was turning the traditional understanding of base-superstructure "on its head." Four stages to this conversion were delimitated by Bergesen.

The first stage is associated with the work of Gramsci (1971). Hegemony is the key idea by which Gramsci means the working class (proletariat) increasingly incorporating the working logic of the propertied classes (bourgeoisie), so that blatant power dynamics are no longer necessary since the working class reproduces the dominant hierarchical order ("consent of the governed"). Now, the state leads in educating the working class in incorporating its ideology. The second stage applies Althusser (1971). Here, in Bergesen's interpretation, the heightened influence of the state (superstructure) is directed downward by the disseminating institutions called "ideological state apparatuses" (ISAs), e.g., education system, media, church, family, and law. The ideological and political are now combined into one. Subjects are now "interpellated"[4] into specific (identity) subject positions conducive to continuous class rule by the bourgeoisie. Here, Sausserian structural semiotics is closely tied with the ISA. The "logic of language becomes the Althusserian logic of ideology" (ibid., 7). We are in the domain of Saussurian "langue" (language). Here, interpellated subjects with their constituted identities and incorporated language of the bourgeoisie construct reality that reifies dominant hierarchical powers. Everyday speech acts, the domain of Saussure's "parole," co-constitute hierarchical, exploitive practices.

The parallel between Althusser and Saussure is as follows. Recall, for Saussure, the sign has two parts, the signifier (acoustic image/sound) and the signified (the concept/idea represented). Thus, for Bergesen (ibid.): "In Althusser the subject is similar to the Saussurian sign, representing a concrete individual (like the concrete acoustic sound) plus a social position in a division of labor, which is similar to a sign position in a system of rules and linguistic sign relations." Thus, hegemonic ideology is connected with *langue* which makes speech possible (*parole*); in short, ideology as encoded in ISAs is the engine, the "deep structural logic of language" (ibid., 8). Speech (parole), as a "linguistic logic," is now intimately connected with a social logic of reproduction. Interpellated subjects now follow the logic of their interpellated identities/subject positions. "Define someone as a worker, and he will act as one; define him as a boss and he will act as one; define a mode of production as capitalist and it will act as one" (ibid., 9).

The third stage continues with this process. Enter Poulantzas (1973, 1978). Here, the base and superstructure have solidified into one. The various spheres, political, ideological, juridical, and economic are now a composite, and particular "articulation of instances," the actual historical configuration, is now the causal agent in social development. Now (ibid., 11), "Ideology is not to be left in the superstructure as ideas, culture, belief, or values, but merged with material social relations." In other words, "relations of production" (recall Chapter 5) now embody hegemonic ideology necessary for reproduction of the capitalist hierarchical-based, exploitive system. Thus now, the social formation has become "free-floating," now determined by the historically informed/shaped work of configuration of instances. It is no longer, as in traditional Marxist analysis, that the base determines the superstructure.

The fourth stage is a "post-structuralist inversion," with a free-floating social formation, where cause and determination lose any particular directionality. Social relations via discursive relations are now ideological/cultural. Laclau and Mouffe (1985) are the key promulgators of the change from the primacy of social formation to "discursive formation," a semiotic formation. Social relations are now discursive relations, associated with Saussure's logic of signs (ibid.,14). Now, relations between subject-identities replace social class relations. Here, "the concept of discourse describes the ultimate nonfixity of anything existing in society" (Laclau cited in Bergesen, ibid., 14). In this post-structuralist view, Laclau and Mouffe tell us, the thesis that only "in the last instance" does the base "determine" the superstructure must be abandoned. "Everything is set adrift," nothing is fixed (Bergesen, ibid.). Everything is contingent, there is no "unified totality." It is the discursive formation embedded with Saussurian linguistic logic that is the overall determining force for everything spoken (parole). In other words, social construction of reality is now always contingent. Interests, Mouffe informs us (cited in Bergesen, 17), "never exist prior to the discourses in which they are articulated and constituted; they cannot be the expression of already existing positions on the economic level."

Thus, an overall determining logic, cause, must be abandoned, and replaced by the notion of "contingencies." Contingencies are only "resolved in struggle, alliances, bonding, agreement, consensus and articulations, between different and infinitely plural social subjects" (Bergesen, 17). In this semiotic Marxism, associated with the logic of Saussure, social identities are only established by differences in relation, but never in final form. They are constantly being deferred in a world of contingencies. Class relations disappear into sign relations of Saussure. It is "the complete triumph of the semiotic over the material" (ibid.). All values are now constituted and defined by differences and in their opposition to other differences (Laclau and Mouffe, 1985: 106). Again, classic Saussure. For Bergesen, observing the development of a semiotic Marxism in the 80s and 90s, there only remains, at the time of his writing, a split that emerged between semiotic Marxism that sees all as semiotic entities, and those who advocate a form of "rational choice Marxism." Social structure, and particularly up to then Marxist notion of "social relations" of production, have disappeared into Saussurian semiotic logic, a logic of differences, contingencies, deferral.

In this view, the legal sphere, too, is part of the discursive/semiotic formation. Identity politics, for example, are outcomes of differences and opposition in a continuous state of deferral. Legal rulings concerning different identity groups follow. Applying Laclau and Mouffe's view, continuous differentiation of identity groups is expected, as in the proliferation of identity affiliations, particularly in the 1990s to the present, with more vocal voices of articulation manifested in the different offshoots of Critical Legal Studies we have previously studied.

Lamenting, Bergesen notes the decline of grand theorizing in the tradition of Marx, Durkheim, and Weber, with no successor in sight, for lively sociological investigation of social issues. The focus on structure has been abandoned, he claims, with a move to idealism embodied in discursive/linguistic/semiotic models and rational choice theory, the latter prevalent, for example, in criminology in the late 1990s to present. Further lamenting in 1993, he asks "why wasn't a new materialism formulated?" (ibid., 20). To this we turn in the next section.

Post-Marxist legal discourse. But things have changed. In the early 2000s new formulations of semiotic Marxism developed. The three special issues of the journal, *Critical Discourse Studies* (2008, 2014, 2018), provide some clear exposition of this movement. Laclau (2005, 2006) continues to be an influential voice.

At the outset, a reductionist economic theory (e.g., base determines superstructure) is reformulated by the use of discourse language. It is "not a self-contained entity operating as an infrastructure; that the coherence it reaches is, as with everything else, hegemonically constructed" (Laclau, in Glynos and Stavrakakis, 2010: 242). So, posited is an association between hegemony, ideology and existing discursive formations. For some, Marx made a contribution to semiotics, partly due to his early studies in philology and rhetoric and manifested in some of his key texts (Jessop and Sum 2018; Borelli, 2018).

A critical sociology of law builds on post-Marxist discourse theory. "Post" is somewhat misleading in so much as it continues to rely on a revisionist understanding of Marx. "Post-Marxism" has been popularized by Laclau who wants to suggest that Marx is neither totally rejected nor totally accepted. In this view, discourse is characterized by a "radical contingency," meaning it remains always resistant to closure, representing some views, denying others', and thus always open to reformulation including oppositional perspectives and understandings (see particularly Laclau, 2005, 2006; Dahlberg, 2014; Phelan and Dahlberg, 2014; see also work in critical media studies, Schou, 2016). It concerns hegemony defined now as a discourse of exclusion but again, one that is "always lacking, incomplete, and failed" (Dahlberg, 2014: 258).

The capitalist system is now conceived as driven by different logics: "social logic" "political logic" and "fantasmatic logic" (Laclau, 2005; Glynos and Howarth, 2007; Howarth, 2018). With social logic, Dahlberg (2014: 258) asserts a new understanding of cause-effect. Political logics concern the working of hegemony, the origination of discourses and their continuation. It is driven by capital logic. It is about articulation of various elements, "a complex array of elements" (i.e., those contributing institutions that are part of the machinery of capitalism, including subject identities, ibid., 258), somewhat reminiscent of Althusser's "articulation of instances" or historical configurations of various elements of capital-driven logic. Struggle produces a particular articulation, a more dominant discourse of exclusion; in short, hegemony. The associated ideology functions to "naturalize" the relatively stable system (make it seem normal, natural, common sense).

Social logics, on the other hand, are "principles or rules that inform and organize social practices and institutions" (Dahlberg, 263). It is about the logic shaped by existing relations of production. It is about the interactional processes and practices between agents and objects and how coherent wholes, be they contingent and contextual, are created, a certain logic for discursive practices to take place in meaning constructions.

It is about rules, rule-following, grammar—"which make some combinations and substitutions [i.e., some hegemonic articulations] possible and exclude others" (Laclau cited by Dahlberg, 264; his bracketing added). These rules are "historical and mutable" (Howarth, 2018: 385). "Social and political logics," Dahlbert (2014: 264) informs us, "intertwine, mutually affecting each other." Thus, a co-constitutive relationship.

Howarth (2018: 386) also notes a third logic, "fantasmatic logic." It is more the unconscious realm of desire, fantasy, imaginary identifications, objects of desire, and imaginary gratifications. Lacan (1977) and Zizek (1989) offer one understanding of unconscious desire, Deleuze and Guattari (1987) offer a differing view (see Chapter 11). Thus, the conscious levels of political and social logics intertwine with the unconscious. We shall return to this for further elaboration in the next chapter. Thus, political, social and fantasmatic logics work together ("quilting") in everyday meaning production in historically shaped contexts.

We add the existence of a multiplicity of social logics associated with emerging identity formations and collectivities. In other words, within each, distinct grammar and rules mark their formations. We have noted this, for example, with the proliferation of "crit" groups.

Social logics can respond to the call for offering a better understanding of cause-effect. Rather than a linear, predictive model, Dahlberg offers a "radically contingent cause-effect relations" model. In other words, understanding social logics expressed discursively, is to be able to develop "contingent mappings of cause-effect relations," a prognosis not prediction (2014: 265). "Through social logics," Dahlberg (ibid., 267) informs us, "we can get an idea of a range of possible consequences resulting from instituting particular discursive systems and practices." In other words, Marxist's use of "determines" in the base-superstructure metaphor of socio-political development can be better conceptualized as contingent mappings that allow us to map possible developments, but not necessary ones—all subject to the forces of contingency, social change, struggle. Since all is contingent and with discourse resisting closure, there remains always the possible development of a counter discourse. For Dahlberg, the periodic economic crises faced by capitalism, echoing a Marxist principle, are particularly ripe for the relative stabilization of counter discourses (ibid., 267; we might also recall Max Weber on this point, Chapter 5).

Building on the co-constitutive nature of political, social, and fantasmatic logics—the formation of relatively stable, be they radically contingent discourses and their hegemonic expressions—this thesis could expand to include a similar logic, legal logic, particularly formal logical rationality that has gripped Western capitalist societies. It too must be similarly articulated. Legal language (semantic and syntactic constructions, paradigm and syntagm, syllogistic reasoning, deductive logic, etc.) is co-constitutively articulated with political, social and fantasmatic logics with a relative hegemonic stability periodically established, with ideology naturalizing the way things are, and in particular historical articulations, displaying ability for generating order and stability in society. In doing a critical sociology of law, then, this direction would integrate a simultaneous concern for *langue* and *parole*, language and speech. It would encompass a historically-based integration of political logic, social logic, fantasmatic logic, and legal logic particularly their co-constituted articulations and dialectical play. It is also cognizant of diverse social logics, not unitary, homogenous and stable forms. "Crits," as we have previously read, have brought light on alternative identity formations, often in intersectional forms, embodying group-specific social logics.

As we have previously seen, the proliferation of identities within a capitalist economy has generated dialectical forms of struggle, oftentimes inadvertently reconstituting the hegemony of legal logic. "Rainbow coalitions," and Hardt and Negri's (2011) advocacy of a "multitude" are calls for new forms of collective struggles replacing "class struggle." Advocates of social change by way of law would need to theorize how to create commonalities for mobilization purposes, but particularly cognizant on how to overcome divisive forms of legal challenges to denial of voice and representation. How can, for example, we both bring to legal challenge under-represented diverse disenfranchised groups and render justice for the particular group as well as for the totality of groups? Can it be done in a formal rational system of law?

Post-Marxist legal discourse could, in anticipating a more explicit materialist Marxist semiotics (see below), usefully expand political, social, fantasmatic and legal logics to an additional form: material logic (e.g., commodification, and pursuit of surplus value — capital logic and associated semiotic forms). We could, analytically disentangle legal logic and material logic from the previous three logics identified by Howarth and posit each as relatively autonomous forms. Thus, to return to insights generated by Althusser, Poulantzas and Gramsci (see Marx, Chapter 5), we could study discourse as situated in emerging and contingent configurations of the five logics, with perhaps the ascendance of a more dominant form offering the coordinates for meaning production. (In the final section, we will refer to a dominant linguistic coordinate system). This articulation of the five logics is a modification of Althusser's and Poulantzas's notion of "articulation of instances" (see Marx, Chapter 5) where "instances" are now seen as coproduced; each constituting the others, and in turn being constituted by the others. Thus, to borrow an additional idea from Althusser and Poulantzas, "overdetermination" now replaces "cause": the cause of something is always multiple and contingent.[5]

Althusser's earlier structuralist account, attributing little to an active subject and arguing for the influence of the economic "in the last instance," can be modified (see critique by Ranciere, 2011; Grant, 2005; McGee, 2012, 2013). His later work (2006) focused on the contingencies of "encounters" where things are always in-process, an approach he called "aleatory materialism," a materialism of the encounter (Grant, 2005; Buonamano, 2014). His later work highlights political logic which supports the reproduction of relations of production within which people locate themselves, and hence by which they are shaped. With repetition in reconstructions of relations of production dominant powers maintain their hegemonic hold. In this view, law reflects and reproduces relations of production. But since everyday encounters are always in the singular, always in process, open to contestation and conflict, there remains space for a possible development of alternative discourses, including oppositional forms (see also Grant, 2005).

Thus, spaces are produced from which resistance and alternative discourses potentially emerge (ibid.). In this view, interpellation of the subject by way of a particular hegemonic ideology is tempered by a plurality of ideologies in degrees of manifestation, particularly as constantly being developed in the singularities of the encounter. Dialectics returns as agents find themselves in the singularity of encounters in particular contextual spaces with their opportunity of disruption, and the ever present repetition by which relations of productions are willingly reproduced.[6] Althusser never developed a full statement on the legal subject, but integrating other works, such as Max Weber's notion of the "insoluble conflict" between formal and substantive rationality, perhaps offer additional force for how singular spaces are encountered where substantive justice may take form.

Thus, struggles and dialectical development undermine stable totalities, and social logics are ever present in offering alternative understandings. Let us further develop the material logic.

Materialist-discursive Marxist semiotics. A materialist-discursive Marxist semiotics makes socioeconomic relations more explicit. "Materialist" implies objective structure. A Post-Marxism substitutes "material-discursive" to suggest that all phenomena, to have meaning, must be brought into some signifier-signified relation in contrast to other signifiers in narrative constructions, be it a radically contingent form whereby hegemony is a major shaping factor as to what is included, what is excluded (Beetz and Schwab, 2017a; 2017b). Materialist Marxism brings into sharper relief more enduring structures and insists it is not merely language or discourse that creates reality, but more how relations of production rooted in historical political economic conditions provide a backdrop in which discourse and material conditions are co-constructed in recurrent patterns. (Recall Marx's notions of relations of production, and means of production, Chapter 5.) As Beltramini (2007) explains, "signs and codes are not seen as standing outside of time, place, and socioeconomic relationships." Two Russian authors are being revisited for their insights, Valentin Voloshinov (1983) and Ferrrucio Rossi-Landi (1977). Let's first briefly turn to Voloshinov. We will address Rossi-Landi and have some additional commentary on Voloshinov in more detail in the following section of the chapter. Social reproductive feminism has also resurrected the importance of socio-economic relations within capitalist social formations.

Voloshinov attempted to integrate subjective and objective structures. Identities reside not in some vacuum of rational thought, but are rooted in historical struggle. "His study of language and signs," Beltramini (2007) summarizes, are "the sites where subjects and objects meet or interpenetrate each other" (see also Beetz and Schwab, 2017b). To understand ideology as semiotic work (semiosis) one must begin at this point. For Voloshinov, the sign is equated with ideology: "everything ideological possesses semiotic value" (Voloshinov, 1973; web version, p. 3). A particular class does not have an exclusive use of a particular language. Others can use the same language and sign system (ibid.): "language and signs become sites of struggle." Signs emerge in struggle, in historical and material contexts. "Human beings," Beltramini (ibid.) continues, "are seen as active cocreators of meaning as they use, make, modify, and struggle over signs." Beltramini comments that those in this tradition, including some in cultural studies, underuse and could make more explicit use of Peirce. Others, however, have argued for the use of Saussure, since both Marx and Saussure pay much attention to the way values are created, respectively, in commodities and signs, in opposition and in relation (see for example, Gandler, 2018).

An alternative more traditional Marxist approach, one that builds on Lukács's work in *History and Class Consciousness* (1972), makes a direct connection between class, language and specifically class-based ideology (ibid.). People are "thingified," objectified, rendered as commodities that leads to alienation, a "linguistic alienation" (Beltramini, ibid.). Beltramini argues that the work of Rossi-Landi (1977) arises from this tradition. Rossi-Landi's material semiotic Marxist begins with Marx's idea of commodification extended by a homology to sign fetishism, and the rise of legal principles imbedded in commodity exchange relations (we will return to this in the next section for fuller development). In this view, people are the active creators of signs, "but cannot understand the meaning of the sign which they have created. From the moment of its creation, the meaning of that sign is independent from the language that the social actors adopt to interpret what they have originated" (Borrelli, 2018: 361). And more forcefully still, "it is not the language of the social subjects which *shapes* the language of real exchange, but the language of commodities which shapes the language of the social subjects" (ibid., 361; italics in original).

A related resurgence of a material Marxist position, one that focuses on "social reproduction" argues that both conditions of productions and relations of production must be equally studied as to how they are continuously reproduced (Althusser, 2014; Cammack, 2020; Battacharya, 2017). A "social reproductive feminism" is especially poignant about the significance of social relations and their ongoing reproduction (Ferguson, 2017). Hence, we must speak of a material-discursive construction (Beetz and Schwarb, 2018; 2017a, 2017b; Beetz, 2016). It highlights that discourses are produced within material conditions. It highlights how social systems, institutions, structures, ideology, and we add, the form of law under capitalism, formal rationality, as described by Max Weber, are continuously reproduced. Marxist-feminists have articulated this position and its significance for intersectional analysis, particularly noting the dialectical developments in social reproduction (Ferguson, 2016).

Ferguson, for example, uses the language of parts and wholes to show how they are co-constituted. Each "part," such as intersectional identities, collectively, under capital logic, a logic that emphasizes accumulation and profit over needs, contributes to co-constructing a social totality, be it a contradictory totality and driven by dialectics. Nevertheless, the social totality produces a logic greater than the sum of its parts, and sets limits or exerts pressure on the parts. Ferguson asserts that a capitalist system needs to reproduce itself, and that intersectional feminism often lets this requirement fade into the background. She returns to materialist Marx's insight concerning the difference between relations of production (socio-economic relations) and forces of production (productive forces) and their dialectical play (see Chapter

5, Marx). Each person does not emerge from a vacuum, but is located in certain geographical spaces with each both enabling and limiting possibilities.[7] It is within these contexts that labour, or "practical human activity" takes place. It is within these contexts, too, as intersectional feminism has argued, that various injustices flourish, and within which indigenous social movements begin. We add, as we have witnessed in previous chapters, that litigation in law often finds different identity groups in opposition. Ferguson would argue that we need to keep cognizant the larger whole within which struggle is taking place. In short, it is capital logic that offers the context whereby parts and wholes are integrated (ibid., 55). (Note, we have come full circle in our journey above that began with Bergesen's tracing the stages of Marxism from the disappearance of the materialist dimension, substituting "discursive formations" as primary, and extending this to a renewed interest in materialism.)

Ferguson does not explicitly relate social reproductive feminism to law, but we can begin, consistent with this approach, to seek a link by consulting Engel's insight: "in a modern state, law must not only correspond to the general economic condition and be its expression, but must also be an internally coherent expression which does not, owing to internal conflicts, contradict itself" (Engels cited in Cain and Hunt, 1979: 57). This, by itself, can be read as an economic reductionism, but with Ferguson's insight, suggests that law responds ultimately to capital logic, somewhat mitigated by dialectical development, "cross-movement political solidarity" (ibid., 42),[8] social struggles, and newly created "geographic locations" within which identities are co-constructed.[9] Here, too, as we saw with Max Weber (Chapter 4), capital logic and formal rationality have a logical fit and thus mutually re-constitute each other in reproducing capitalist social formations. A critical socio-legal semiotics could be productively integrated in showing how relations of production correlate with a semiotic production, distinct narrative forms of expression, and representation and transformation into legal forms of expression. And how social reproduction is furthered, co-constitutively, by these associated and ever-emerging changing forms, responding to dialectical development and social struggle.

Toward Critical Methodologies in Legal Semiotics

Useful offerings of a critical methodology have appeared in the literature (see, for example, Salter, 2010; Fairclough, 2008, 2018; Howarth, 2018: 385–388). We will focus on Salter's and Fairclough's suggestions.

Salter's (2010: 138–139) six stages of a semiotically-informed critique in legal semiotics include:

(1) The "rejection of criteria for critical assessment that are not indigenous to the [legal] topic in question";

(2) "Critics need to distance themselves, as far as possible, from the grip and closure devices of prevailing ideologies which misrepresent legal topics ...";

(3) "Identifying relevant internal norms expressed in discourses that our society officially endorses";

(4) "Critical semiotics research [needs] to develop from within an analysis of the practical implications of these norms, a vision of how the status quo would need to operate before we could reasonably conclude that their key legitimating norms have been fully realized in practice";

(5) "[I]nvestigate evidence of *discrepancies* between these normative implications and the record of accomplishment of institutions responsible for the realisation of these legally relevant norms in practices"; and

(6) "Identifying those aspects of the *status quo* that need to be changed to remove, or at least minimize, discrepancies between ideological rhetoric of justification, and the practical outcomes of their institutional practices."

Commentary. In reference to the first point, Salter advocates not privileging universalization, gross generalizations posed as if applicable to all, but to focus on contextual criteria that are indigenous to what is being studied. American Indian's claim to an "oral history," for example, was dismissed for too long in legal circles. Researchers should be especially critical of dominant ideologies and legitimizing principles that seem on their face self-justifying, such as the "rule of law" and "equal rights," and be cognizant of their often justifications for the status quo (second point). As to point three, we must embrace legal signifiers that already highlight the possibilities for human emancipation, possibilities to fulfillment of needs and more genuine justice. Such ideals as "justice for all" and "equality," as linguistic categories, can be scrutinized in their conventionally established associations with particular signifieds and be springboards for new associations, e.g., substantive justice rather than merely formal rational justice. As Voloshinov (1983) has informed us, these are sites of struggle. The fourth point looks to practical possibilities, imaginary constructions that might replace given status quo practices. Not blueprints, but visions of the possible, "ideal-type models," are needed that can be tested against existing models for their efficacy. These "counter factual models" can offer comparative value in scrutinizing where we are and the benefits and pitfalls that might develop with our alternative. A call for anarchy, for example, or a call for a replacement discourse and/or a transformative justice model, or a substantive rational system of law must also scrutinize possible inadvertent developments.

The fifth point is the flip side of point four: a return to empirical research that compares the status quo with the designed alternative model. It can start, for example, in a search of discrepancies that often appears in people's use of linguistic categories and accepted standards compared to their actual lived experiences. Are there contradictions? Why are the conventional linguistic categories and signified still maintained? If for example, one maintains, honors and justifies the notion of formal equality and the rule of law, and their very position as say laborer, an underpaid, underutilized and alienated worker is not meaningfully confronted, then the researcher can mark this discrepancy for possible change. Why does the discrepancy or contradiction remain? What forces, internal and external keep the discrepancy ongoing? Perhaps instructive is returning to Max Weber's positing an "insoluble conflict" between principles of formal and substantive rationality. Why, faced with this conflict does formal rationality in law prevail?

Finally, point six, given the working through of points one through five, addresses identifying what specific components of institutional practices are in need of change. This step is particularly cognizant of the discrepancies identified in point five. How do we go about changing the particular discrepancy? For example, in everyday conversation concerning people who do not attain greater fulfilment we often witness discourses such as "anyone can make it if they work hard enough," "it's up to the individual," or, in the other direction, "it's genetics." Given substantial evidence that locates one's life chances tied to socio-economic status, why does this discrepancy persist? How is it being sustained? How do everyday conversations that make use of the signifiers "equal rights" and the "rule of law" maintain the status quo? Why do they nevertheless continue? How do we present counter-factual evidence that penetrates defense mechanism of those who profess these statements? Do we focus on changing the content of signifiers, or must we invent new signifiers with alternative content (signified)? Existing rights, for example, focus on the linguistic category, human rights, as "negative rights" (restrictions on the State as well as restrictions of what one can do); social and economic rights, on the other hand, are more "positive rights," focusing their linguistic content on enhancing capabilities, rights to be sure, yet to be developed (Salter, 136). Can we affect change by purely legal and institutional reforms, or must we address, ultimately, structure?

Fairclough (2008: 7; 2018) offers four steps or stages in a "dialectical-relation approach to critical discourse analysis." He looks at what is prevalent, and practices to overcome forms of oppression. He uses "dialectical" to mean how social processes are co-constituted where each "element" is not totally separable from the others, and are both contributory but not reducible to any other. He defines discourse as "the language associated with a particular social field of practice" (ibid., 1) such as political discourse. Though targeting social sciences generally, we could apply specifically to critical legal semiotics. Fairclough's four steps include:

(1) "Focus upon a social wrong, in its semiotic aspects";

(2) "Identify obstacles [including forms of texts and semiosis (ibid., 10)] to addressing the social wrong";

(3) "Consider whether the social order 'needs' the social wrong"; and

(4) "Identify possible ways past the obstacles."

Commentary. By "social wrong," stage one, he means what is "detrimental to human well-being" and what can be changed, citing "poverty, forms of inequality, lack of freedom, or racism." The focus is on the semiotic features of a defined social wrong. He advocates a trans-disciplinary methodology, by which he means drawing from a number of disciplines including theories of discourse and semiosis. The relationship between reality and discourse employed will be most relevant. In the legal arena, consider inequalities and how law responds. For example, consider capitalist's hierarchical order and its association with how formal equality has been semiotically formulated in legal cases, particularly in formal rational law.

In stage two, the researcher can focus on texts and integrate a linguistic analysis to include other forms such as visual images, as well as an interdiscursive analysis of genres, discourses, and styles and how they work together. Recall social semiotics and their advocacy of "semiotic resources" (written, visual, auditory) and "modes" (particular forms and genre employed), especially multimodal forms of expression.

Stage three investigates how the social wrong may be intricately connected with a social order. "Discourse," for Fairclough (ibid., 11), is "ideology in so far as it contributes to sustaining particular relations of power and domination." For example, one might begin with the latent functions of law and seek discursive constructions that sustain the status quo, particularly those that are inadvertent (dialectics of struggle). The latent function, recall, stands for the unverbalized, more invisible and/or unconscious factors that are hidden when discussing manifest functions, the more dominant discursively articulated texts. How are the two connected? Can we change one without changing the other?

In the last stage (four), the research moves from critique to possible positive contributions. The researcher provides insights as to possible ways of overcoming obstacles to social wrongs. How are these obstacles "actually tested, challenged and resisted" in people's everyday lives? What are the ways the "dominant discourse is reacted to, contested, criticized and opposed" (ibid., 11)? We add, we can return to social semiotics earlier presented in the chapter, in looking at contextually applied semiotic resources and their particular mode/genre of expression. How are these forms beneficial or constraining? Do they reconstitute power, hierarchy, and domination, be it inadvertently? In the politics of identity, for example, are there also negative consequences, such as "the reversal of hierarchies" (Cornell, 1985,1993) or possibly reducing inter-group relations and communication, or in downplaying commonalities? In counter storytelling—useful strategy, we previously saw to make visible otherwise repressed voices,—can there also be inadvertent negative consequences, such as privileging one story over another establishing hierarchies of privileged stories? Can a more inclusive counter storytelling be developed acknowledging differences *and* sameness? Will this semiotic form water down the particular concerns of a disenfranchised group?

Hypothetical: employing critical methodology in legal semiotics. Let's consider an example in applying Fairclough's four stages in critical discourse studies. (Alternatively, one could apply Salter's six stages of a semiotically-informed critique in socio-legal semiotics. And perhaps a creative synthesis of the two can be produced and then applied.)

You are researching for a progressive law firm in a class action suit (or defense of an accused) which seeks to extend allowable legal defenses to include "severe environmental deprivation," SED (Delgado, 1985; see also Judge Bazelon's dissenting opinion in an appeals court ruling, *United States v. Alexander*, 1973).[10] This in the spirit of other allowable defenses such as duress, diminished capacity, as well as court recognized potential coercive contexts such as entrapment and police station house interrogations. Your firm hopes to overturn *McCleskey v. Kemp*'s (1987) bad apple approach (individual intent) even faced with overwhelming evidence suggesting the necessity of a system's analysis and return to the standard in *Brown v. Board of*

Education focusing on conditions or systems analysis. Your research leads you to investigation the relationship between ghettos identifiable as harbingers of SED, noting that contrary to popular views, not all ghettos, even though impoverished, are harbingers of crimes. You would like to draw from the tools of a critical socio-legal semiotics.

First, you address semiotic usages and find that signifiers such as ghetto and crime have alternative constructions for the appropriate signified. The signifier, urban ghetto, for example has both denotative and connotative meaning, and has changed over time from being a place of seclusion and impoverishment to one that is equated with violent crime. Crime can be defined officially by the Uniform Crime Reports in the U.S., as crimes known to the police. You find that this signifier is misleading in that many crimes are unreported and/or defined and rationalized away. And you find that a political process defines what is crime; thus, crime is created in this sense. You conclude that crime as a signifier is a site of struggle for appropriate meaning (signified). You then find that in law-finding practices the defendant has a narrow scope (semiotic resources and allowable mode of expression) in which to make a discursive construction of "what happened," denying the nuanced lifestyles, values, understandings, and language of heterogeneous groups (social logics). You then recall from Donald Black's propositions of the behavior of law that downward law is greater and more likely accusatory and penal than upward law. The very behavior of law produces a narrow perception of the dangerous classes. Thus, you conclude, these pose obstacles in fuller understanding of heterogeneous lifestyles and identity groups. You also come across empirical literature that clearly shows a connection between life chances and socio-economic status. Your investigations of semiotics and discourse analysis leads to the question of ideology and you find that the latter is relayed in everyday usage by such clichés as "anyone can make it if they work hard enough," "it's up to the individual," "all have free choice," etc.

You then move to the question of whether the social order "needs" the social wrong and are immediately drawn to your reading of Emile Durkheim on social solidarity. You find that society can create deviance by where it sets the boundaries of acceptable versus nonacceptable behavior, identified in people's reactions to an event. This leads you to Lois Wacquant's (2001) article on "Deadly Symbiosis," which states that the prison is but another form of social control of poor African-Americans, much in the spirit of new Jim Crow laws. You find that the ghetto can be traced to the early movement of African Americans to the industrial city centers where they found themselves confined in geographic spaces increasingly with limited basic services (e.g., educational, medical, housing, employment, leisure, etc.) — notwithstanding indigenous resources such as self-help, extended family support, the church — but like Marxists would say, sufficient to force people into more menial, low paying jobs of the industrializing order. You find that many of those in prison come from these areas and return to these same areas. So, with Wacquant, you see that there is a pipeline from the urban ghetto to prison and back to the ghetto. A population is now defined as the "real" criminals in our society, and social control resources are allocated according to this image. Discursive constructions, semiosis, and everyday constructions are now codified in a language of a criminal class, the "dangerous classes." You revisit the thesis of the reproduction of relations of production for a specification for cultural transmission. You surmise that the manifest functions of prisons (to control crime) cannot be adequately understood unless we look seriously at the latent functions. Thus, you conclude, that the criminal justice system and penal system do more than just respond to harm: they contribute to and even create the very harm they ostensibly say they are policing in the name of public safety.

You find that ghetto life is not without incipient oppositional discourses, such as in rap music, uprising, and other expressive forms, and that in fact some inmates undergo a political conversion while incarcerated, such as was the case with Malcolm X. And you find that apart from the most salient negative outcomes of ghetto conditions that a resiliency persists and a human commonality that cuts across socio-economic standing, not to mention the many accomplishments and crime-free lifestyles irrespective of heavy odds against realization.

You also find in your investigation that corporate crime, occupational crime, and environmental crime have far greater impact although the discourse is only recently developing to reflect this state of affairs. You find that there is an inverse relationship between understandability and hence excusability and socio-economic standing: as you go upward in the socio-economic scale the latitude for allowing stories increases, as you go downward, it decreases. With greater latitude in storytelling, greater understandability, greater excusability, and the converse. As a case in point, you note how a lower socio-economic defendant finds that they may relate very little of the conditions (lack of resources — housing, jobs, education, medical, leisure, etc.) in which they are situated and the nuanced understandings that exist; rather, the focus in court is on individual intent (*mens reas*) and whether the act took place (*actus reus*). For the higher socio-economic defendant, you find a plethora of injunction proceedings, cease and desist orders, pleas of *nolo contendere* and consent decrees where the corporation is basically saying "I will stop doing what you claim I'm doing but do not admit I'm doing it." For the latter group, the conditions are widened to include discursive constructions of providing jobs, needed medicines, tax money to the community, etc. The corporation hires the very best lawyers from the most prestigious firms, lawyers well committed to a refined, sophisticated, and abstract legal discourse. Poor defendants have state assigned lawyers that are heavily overcommitted with little time for adequate preparation. And you find that well-off lawyers speak a different abstract language with which the poor defendant knows little. For the disenfranchised, their stories are never fully told; rather, they are redefined in the narratives of law in attaining legal standing. And where you do find a defense counselor sympathetic or well in-tune with alternative lifestyles, that they confront the dialectics of legal repression. How then, you ask, can an alternative relatively stable discourse develop that is truer to the diverse lifestyles of struggling people? The echo from Spivak (2008) begins to beckon: "from where can the subaltern speak?"

Not to be missed, your investigation comes across much literature on institutional racism in housing, policing, medical services, school admissions, etc., as well as more hidden forms of micro-aggressions including profiling—all of which contribute substantially to "keeping people in their place."

You now move to the fourth stage of your investigation and find that intervention must take place at multiple levels, including, most importantly, at the structural level. You begin to sense that rigid formal rational law upholds the dominant ideology. You now see a connection to institutional racism and how dominant discourse has not sufficiently made this apparent.[11]

Your report to the law firm recommends pursuing the establishment of a new legal defense, "severe environmental deprivation," that builds on a qualified "societal fault" model (Delgado, 1985) whereby responsibility can be proportionally distributed within the context of production.[12] But you also point out that nothing less than a system-wide socio-economic and material change will address system-generated forces that lead to social harms. Just as in pivotal cases in law that manifested a leap going beyond mere dogmatic legal analysis, the law firm hopes that this will follow herein.

In sum, we have seen that social semiotics, CDS, CDA, and a resurgence of a materialistic semiotic Marxism have ushered in a critical social legal semiotics, a call for a material-discursive analysis in law. But readers of critical analysis must also be critical of critical works. Accordingly, critical readings must extend downward, upward, and horizontally: "downward," in the sense of more explicitly tracing the given critical works to their roots, particularly engaging not only the various revisionists Marxist theorizing, but to include Durkheimian and Weberian interrogation and beyond. Fairclough's (2002, 2008, 2018) critical discourse analysis, for example, explicitly refers to the necessity of both material and discursive integrations that are particularly cognizant of power, ideology, hegemony, and dialectics. We also need to look "upward," in the sense of generating new oppositional material-discursive articulations that pave the way for social change. Recall Fairclough's (2018) call for "*critique* of discourse and *explanation* of how discourse figures in existing social reality as a basis for *action* to change reality." And "horizontally," to be more inclusive of diverse identity groups and ways of life, including integrating an informed "cause lawyering."

In the final section of this chapter we want to return to Rossi-Landi's material-discursive legal semiotics inspired by Marx's study of the commodification process, extended to the homology with sign systems.

Material Marxist Semiotics in Sociology of Law: Toward a Revisionist Structural Interpellationist Variant

Introduction

In the following we offer a possible development and possible applications of a materialist-discursive Marxist semiotics in the sociology of law. It can also be considered as a specification of one version of a materialist Marxism, structural interpellation but modified along the lines of articulating five logics (social, political, fantasmatic, material, and legal logics previously developed) developed in the last section. We noted a movement away from Marxism in the 1990s, particularly the economistic form, and its replacement with the notion of the autonomy of a "discursive formation"—both seemed to abandon the material (Bergesen, 1993). However, we also noted the resurrection of a materialist form of Marxism in the early decades of the 21st century. It had many forms of expression. In Chapter 5 on Marx, we suggested several possible interpretations of the relationship between base and superstructure, one of which was the structural interpellation perspective. Given recent developments focusing on *relations of production* and semiosis it would be reasonable to revisit Althusser, Poulantzas, Gramsci, as well as those who actively and critically engaged them in developing new understandings of Marx (Laclau and Mouffe, 1985, 2015; Laclau, 2005, 2006). Althusser's late work (Althusser, 2006), for example, has been interpreted by some to bring the material back into discussion (what earlier seemed to be left out (Buonamano, 2014; de Sutter, 2013; Grant, 2005; McGee, 2012, 2013), particularly with his notion of "aleatory materialism," the materialism of the encounter whereby encounters are contingent singularities, sites of possible disruption, contestation and struggle.

Materialism and Hegemonic Practices

In previous sections we noted a significant emerging development, a post-Marxist approach, that neither abandons nor wholly embraces Marxism. This focuses on material-discursivity, especially in the works of Beltramini (2007), Bianchi (2015), Borrelli (2018), Beetz and Schwab (2007); Beetz (2007a, 2007b), Coratelli *et al.* (2015), Howarth (2007, 2019), Glynos and Howarth (2007), and Faiclough (2014, 2018). In this spirit we want to provide, if for no other reason than pedagogical purposes, a Marxist view that sees the relationship of base to superstructure in terms of contingency, hegemony, dialectics, and struggle in the semiotic and materialist-discursive production of law. Here, a renewed interest, too, exists on the relations of production along with forces of production, and the sphere of circulation and production. Thus, relations of production and their reproduction are material-discursive (Beetz and Schwab, 2018) and in their ongoing reproduction are hegemonic formations, privileging certain states of affairs in the social formation. In the previous section we noted how Howarth's (2018; Glynos and Howarth, 2007) notion of three logics (political, social, fantasmatic) can be extended to five, with the addition of material and legal logic, showing how all five find themselves articulated in particular historical configurations and the source of a material-discursive production. Accordingly, we revisit the work of Rossi-Landi who centers relations of production and materialism as essential to semiotics in law. The linguistic relativity principle of Benjamin Whorf will also be integrated in developing the notion of linguistic coordinate systems. But, unlike the "commodity exchange" perspective, we further show how the causal arrow runs not only upward, but with shaping effects of hegemonic practices, downward (Howarth, 2018). We conclude the chapter with some examples of applying a critical semiotics in the sociology of law.

Let's first consider some vignettes on linguistic usage/narrative constructions:

- A U.S. infantryman in Vietnam: "We have to hump five clicks today and I've got point. Yesterday, five grunts got sent home in body bags after a firefight. We had puff-the-magic Dragon rolling hot, 155s, foo gas, quad-fifties and a cobra around but the VC were able to over-run the perimeter. Wish I was on the freedom bird for the states."
- Skydivers preparing for a jump: "Okay, let's figure out who are in the base and who are going to be floaters and stingers. We'll exit at fifteen thousand on the second pass of the DC, do a slot-perfect round, an opposed diamond, then fly wedges, then a cat, then a horny gorilla. We'll first do a dirt-dive and a door jam. At three five we break off, track away, big wave off and dump. We don't want anyone to go in, and no mals. Do a good throw out; we don't want a pilot-in-tow, or a line-over. If you do have a mal, cut away and go for the reserve. Make sure you flair high today and no low hook turns."
- Police officer: "I caught the perpetrator on the premises who was in plain view. It was a B-and-E. Since I had probable cause, I arrested him and conducted a search incidental to the arrest. He had a concealed weapon and resisted arrest. I gave him the Miranda, but he willingly confessed. I took him into custody and booked him."
- Prosecuting attorney in court: "And is it not true that on the 13th you were at the Shopwell supermarket at two o'clock?" Defendant: "Yes." Prosecutor: "And isn't it true that when you were there you took several steaks, placed them under your clothing and then walked out of the store without paying for them?" Defendant: "Yes, but I can't get a job, my family is starving, they closed down my plant after I worked there for twenty years ..." Prosecutor: "Objection, 'scope,' your honor, the witness wasn't asked to explain why they did it." Judge: "Sustained, the witness will answer the question asked. The jury will disregard those answers. They have nothing to do with the commission of the crime."

In each of the above situations a unique linguistic form is being used. To understand the full meaning of what is taking place, one must situate oneself within the respective linguistic coordinate systems. To be a skydiver is to not only do the activity, but to internalize the verbal constructions of the activity and to frame activity in terms of it. To do law is to internalize legal language and to construct "reality" according to its linguistic forms.

A revisionist structural interpellation can be summed up in several tentative propositions that will be further explored in the pages to follow. We offer this as a guide to building more holistic approaches that integrates the key post-Marxist writers we have presented above.

(1) Language is not neutral. It is value-laden. Notions of space, time, and subjectivity are embedded within linguistic forms and grammatical/syntactical structures. Language is a product of dialectical material practices in which overdetermination, historical-specific hegemonic formations, contingent encounters, struggle, social relations, and co-construction are integral elements.

(2) Language structures thought. The world "out there" does not appear in a random flux. The users of a language and its grammar are, to a considerable degree, predisposed to making certain observations.

(3) Language can be more usefully conceptualized as a linguistic coordinate system. Each is characterized by boundaries of inclusion/exclusion. Reality and identity constructions are shaped within each, in particular contexts. Several prominent ones can be identified: dominant, juridic, pluralistic and oppositional. A political economy can be seen as composed of various linguistic coordinate systems (LCSs) that often pose alternative ways of "seeing the world." Accordingly, some become more dominant, some subservient, and yet others are denied the opportunity for development. Yet others are emergent, or latent, often residing at the intersections of several others.

(4) Rationality, logic and meaning are unique to a particular language in use. Reality construction is circumscribed by the language in use. Five dialectically related co-constituted logics and their articulation in historical times, a hegemonic practice, account for contingent and momentary bases for discursive activity, insertion of an "I," and reality construction. The five logics include: political, social, fantasmatic, material, and legal. Howarth (2018) theorized the first three, we added the latter two. Law reflects and shapes relations of production, and in repetition and interpellation, their reproduction, maintaining the dominant forms; but, in operating in a field of contingent encounters, it is subject to contestation and struggle and thus the site for the possible emergence of alternative discourses (e.g., substantive justice, a return of a use-value based legal agent, counter storytelling, etc.)

(5) Language may be analyzed at two levels. First, at the level of *linguistic production.* This level includes the political process by which new linguistic forms (i.e., words and utterances) develop and how they are given content (meaning). Second, once words are established and given meaning, they circulate within a particular linguistic coordinate system. This is the sphere of *linguistic circulation.* (Note, spheres of production and circulation follow Marx, see Chapter 5.) Legal language as a dominant form is especially demonstrative. Subjects situate themselves within these coordinates to construct conceptions of reality. For example, once a person situates themselves in the legal arena, they also must make use of the signifiers (paradigm) and grammatical structures (syntagm) that are an integral part of legal discourse. This is a hegemonic practice that privileges some and deprivileges others.

(6) A linguistic coordinate system can be evaluated by the ease with which things and ideas can be expressed and communicated in it. Thus, we can speak of fulfillment, ease, difficulty, or alienation in language (linguistic affordances).

(7) Linguistic coordinate systems are relatively autonomous. On one level, the form of language can be neutral. Put in another way, there is equal opportunity in the use of language: all are said to have "equal" access to language. The legal form is seen as neutral. However, the acquisition of language forms and

the skill in their usage varies as a function of socio-economic class. On another level, the content of linguistic forms (that which is established through a political process) is selectively established, often supporting dominant understandings of the world (reification, hegemony).

(8) Hegemony exists to a considerable degree by the aid of the dominant and juridic linguistic coordinate systems, neither of which is unitary, fixed, and homogenous but a radical contingency, always open to revision due to its internal dialectical development, most apparent in times of crisis. Hegemony is maintained by the transformation or by the channeling of oppositional language forms into dominant linguistic coordinate systems (i.e., by psychiatrists, lawyers, teachers, politicians, the judiciary, the media, to name a few); even disenfranchised may at times inadvertently reconstitute and hence legitimize dominant practices in their performance of dominant scripts. One understanding of the world is often replaced by another supportive of the status quo. Defendants before the court contribute to their own continued oppression by the unquestioned use of the juridical language form.

(9) Lawyers can be better conceptualized as the sellers of juridical linguistic skills. These linguistic skills are learned. They are learned in specialized institutions, law schools, which more often reflect and support the dominant political, ideological, and economic system.

(10) Authentic and open communication (non-alienating communication) can only take place within a mode of production where hierarchy, exploitation, and repression are eliminated.

Linguistic Coordinate Systems

Key contributions in semiotics for the notion of linguistic coordinate system (LCS) have come from Benjamin Whorf (1956), Valentin Voloshinov (1986), and Ferruccio Rossi-Landi (1977). The so-called Sapir-Whorf linguistic relativity principle states that "users of markedly different grammars are pointed by their grammars toward different types of observations and different evaluations of externally similar acts of observation, and hence are not equivalent as observers but must arrive at somewhat different views of the world" (Whorf, 1956: 221; see also critical engagement by Shariatmadari, 2019; Deutscher, 2011, 2010).

Benjamin Whorf, linguistic relativity. Whorf's comparison of the "Standard Average European" (SAE) languages with the Hopi Indian of Southwest United States indicated that there were vast differences in the way each language allowed its user to construct reality. He uses SAE to refer to the many European languages, such as English, French and German, which are more similarly structured (ibid., 138) in contrast to the Hopi.

The Hopi language, he argued, has no verb forms expressing the clean separations of past, present and future (see also Lee, 1959: 105–20). Rather, things are expressed as ever becoming. Furthermore, for the Hopi, the idea found in SAE, that a sentence must have a substantive and a verb, is unnecessary. We, for example, attribute an action to an agent whom we see as its author (see also Lee, 1959: 94–95, 134, 137; Benveniste, 1971: 195–204, 223–224). Take, for example, the statement: "She is roller-blading." Consider the implications: we have an agent that is responsible for some action (roller-blading). Consider, too, for a moment, how in trial proceedings the court is totally preoccupied with establishing individual responsibility—an individual connected to some willed act. Generally, the effects of larger socio-political and economic factors, for example, are pushed to the side. The Hopi, on the other hand, see action-states, verbal forms. A particular author is unnecessary. If the Hopi were asked what the person was doing, it would be simply described in terms of some action word such as "roller-blading." For the Hopi, action is interconnected (entangled) intimately and holistically with the surrounding environment. There is no separation.

Abstracting an entity—such as a self-contained subject (the self)—from the social formation, and attributing causal primacy to it, is inconsistent with the world-view of the Hopi. Compare this to the Western courts, where there is a heavy reliance in proving *mens rea* (criminal intent). The model we employ is one of individual responsibility. Compare, for example, the focus on the individual author in Western copyright laws with the notion of collective authorship and ownership of aboriginal people in their art production (Puri, 1992).

The user of SAE also splits up phenomena by the use of "form + formless." That is, we are accustomed to saying "glass of water," "piece of cake," etc. The Hopi are quite comfortable expressing these amorphous forms without the aid of a quantity term. No boundaries need exist. Note again how our language, including legal discourse, imposes bounded terms. We operate as if the world is divided into clear-cut categories, that at best are only partly connected. For the Hopi, anticipating quantum mechanic's notion of "non-locality," a trace of each "part" of existence appears in various other sites, *all at once.*

Finally, we make heavy use of metaphors. We place phenomena in an imaginary space in our mind when communicating or thinking. We say, for example, "spring into action," "coiled for action," "she's a real dynamo," etc. Consider, too, the various metaphors inspired with the mass produced computer and the internet (Averbukh, 2019; Wu and Chen, 2013).[13] It's as if we have to create an image in our minds that duplicates some concrete technology in order to express ourselves. According to Whorf, the Hopi live *in* their expressions as they live *in* their experiences. They use neither the notion of "form + formless" nor an imaginary space. They are not removed but are connected to the thing they are talking about. Whorf suggests that much of the relevance of metaphors in the industrialized world can be attributed to the coming of commerce and industrialization and their needs of precise measurement and its technologies (i.e., material logic). Here, then, the "form + formless" and the use of metaphor became more prevalent, that is, part of social logic.

There are two forms of linguistic relativity. The "soft" version of linguistic relativity has it that language has some but a limited degree of independent influence in structuring thought. The "strong" version (linguistic determinism) implies that we are prisoners of the linguistic coordinate system within which we locate ourselves.

Several noted authorities have commented on the notion of linguistic *relativity*. Sapir has said that "we see and hear and otherwise experience very largely as we do because the language habits of our community predispose certain choices of interpretation" (cited in Fishman, 1960: 324). Vygotsky has noted that the development of "grammar precedes logic" (1962: 127). A child might use such words as "because," "if," "when," and so forth before they grasp their meaning. Whorf is even more direct: "every language is a vast pattern system, different from others, in which are culturally ordained the forms and categories by which the personality not only communicates, but also analyzes nature, notices or neglects types of relationships and phenomena, channels his reasoning, and builds the house of his consciousness" (1956: 252). In sum, the linguistic relativity principle points out the independent effects of language on thought processes.

Valentin Voloshinov and materialist sign production. Voloshinov, a Russian theorist, has provided a materialist grounding for signs and the plurality of sign communities. He distinguishes between the *form of signs* and *content of signs*. "Forms of signs," he continues (1986: 12), "are conditioned above all by the social organization of the participants involved and also by the immediate conditions of their interaction." In other words, the sign's form is shaped by the relational aspects of interaction in particular social organizations, and the momentary contexts in which discursive activity takes place. His emphasis, in other words, is on material conditions. He (ibid., 13) postulates three propositions: (1) "ideology may not be divorced from the materiality of the sign," (2) "the sign may not be divorced from the concrete forms of social intercourse," and (3) "communication and forms of communication may not be divorced from the material basis."

Turning to the *content of the sign*, he argues every historical stage of development witnesses "its own special and restricted circle of items which alone have access to that society's attention which are endowed with evaluative accentuation by that attention." It is only within these loci that signs develop (semiosis). Each sign, therefore, is accentuated in unique ways, contextually and within different groups. But the sign is always a site of struggle because a number of other accentuations compete for recognition. It is this intersectional form of the sign, he tells us, that contributes to its "vitality and dynamism." However, he continues, the "ruling class" attempts to accentuate the sign with its own accentuation (ibid., 14).

Ferruccio Rossi-Landi and commodity, legal and semiotic fetishism. Further materialist grounding for the sign comes from the Italian philosopher Rossi-Landi (1977). He offers the idea that we can apply the notion of "commodity fetishism" (see Chapter 5) to the sphere of language (see also Bianchi, 2015; Borrelli, 2018). He notes a similar development (homology) to commodity and linguistic forms. Recall Pashukanis who established the idea of a homology between the commodity and juridic form. Marxists, recall, have argued that a commodity has both a use-value and an exchange-value. The use-value stands for the ability of a thing to fulfill some concrete need, a qualitative aspect. It also stands for a quantity of labor used in its production. It represents the existence of differences. When commodity owners enter the marketplace and exchange their commodities, the use-value is replaced by the abstraction, exchange value. This represents a ratio of exchange. Money is the universal form. Five dollars can buy either three pounds of butter or two bushels of corn. This, the Marxists tell us, is the principle of fetishism of commodities. We create the abstraction, money, which we worship. We reduce everything to a money value. The inherent use-value of a thing loses importance. The juridic form has a parallel development: the juridic subject, recall, has undergone a movement from use-value to exchange-value. The juridic subject, in other words, is a created abstraction, but lost are the nuances and particularities of being a human.

Rossi-Landi argues that linguistic forms undergo the same process. Words and utterances have initial use-value; they correspond to the ability to express unique wants and desires. But when used in interactions they take on exchange-value. In other words, they take on more universal meaning. Their nuances, their subtle shadings of meaning, become smoothed over and are given a generally understood meaning. Thus, we can now identify three forms of fetishisms (and the homologies, or similarities in development, which tie the three together; see Figure 1).

Figure 1. Fetishism of Commodity, Juridic and Linguistic Form

Commodity Sphere	Juridic Sphere	Linguistic Sphere
Use-value	Desiring subject; unique being; multiplexities.	Signifiers embodied with unique desires of socio-historically situated subjects. Contextual meanings of signifiers (words).
Exchange-value	Juridic subject; the abstract "reasonable man [person]" in law.	Signifiers with abstract, dictionary meanings. Words with common (equivalent) meaning.

Furthermore, Rossi-Landi argues, just as the commodity is produced in the sphere of production and circulates in the marketplace, the same applies to the linguistic form. In other words, there exists a homology. A sphere of *linguistic production* exists in which linguistic forms and their content are established (i.e., given "idealized expression"). Consider, for example, how linguistic forms such *mens rea*, duress, intent, willingly, etc. are given precise content, and then how they must be used accordingly for anyone claiming to be doing law. Once established, in other words, they enter the *sphere of circulation*. These linguistic forms are then used in narrative constructions.

Thus, ideology and language are both a product of materialist conditions as well as the major shaping effects of superstructural practices. Five logics (political, social, fantasmatic, legal, material) are co-constituted in historical conditions with particular articulations or configurations shaping material-discursive practices This is a (dialectical) material semiotics (see also Beltramini, 2007). Once stabilized, a discourse offers a medium within which agents must situate themselves in order to construct texts and narratives. In other words, there is now a downward direction (superstructure → base) in effects. Agents in the social formation are interpellated, they are constituted in particular ways, their world views are shaped in particular ways, specifically by way of the relatively stabilized dominant discourse, and, in turn, the superstructure is shaped by these results; in short, a reconstruction or constitutive flow of events (↔). Material conditions, ideology, and language are intimately connected. Speech acts are performatively enacted in so much as the usage of discourse materializes it, giving it stability in repetition.

In the U.S., the higher courts (e.g., state appeal and supreme courts as well as the U.S. appeals and Supreme Court) can be envisioned as the sphere of *juridic linguistic production*. Here particular legal concepts are created and given precise meaning. To use the language of semiotics, new legal terms (the signifier) are given precise content or meaning (the signified) (see, for example, Milovanovic, 1986: 294–296). Consider how key terms of the 14th Amendment to the U.S. Constitution such as "life," "liberty," and "property," as signifiers, have been connected with particular content (signified). Recall, two perpendicular, intersecting dimensions are constitutive of narrative constructions: paradigm, the vertical structure if you will, composed of semantic variations (words and their meanings, signifiers/signifieds); and syntagm, the horizontal structure, the syntactical constructions of narratives, signifiers placed in some linear order guided by a semiotic code. Words take their precise meaning in the relations and values manifest in the end product of interaction between paradigm and syntagm. Phonetics, moreover, is the actual physical pronunciation, normatively shaped by societal conventional practices. Thus, variations exist in languages. Conventional usages within each produces distinct purport (sense), the result of a relatively stabilized signifier to signified (Saussure), sign to interpretant (Peirce), expressive form to content form (Hjelmslev). Drawing together the ideas of Whorf and Rossi-Landi, we may say that several linguistic coordinate systems (LCS) exist.[14]

Material-Based Linguistic Coordinate Systems

Generally, in modern society, one discourse, be it radically contingent and always resistant to closure, becomes more hegemonically dominant. It is continuously renewed in the mass media, formal education, law practices, as well as in everyday discursive practices. It becomes the main medium through and by which we communicate (semiotic resources); or alternatively, always present in the background as the "established" standard of logic and truth expressed in particular modes. We shall refer to it as the *dominant linguistic coordinate system*. We also have the juridic discourse, or as we characterize it, the juridic linguistic coordinate system. Training in law schools indoctrinates the developing lawyer with particular linguistic skills. A specialized vocabulary and syntax is learned. A form of deductive reasoning is internalized (Mertz, 2007; Solan and Tiersma, 2005).

The juridic linguistic coordinate system that the student learns is abstract, general and removed from concrete contexts. Here, previously established doctrines, premises, and principles (by way of precedents or *stare decisis*) guide legal reasoning. The lawyer, in litigating some "factual" situation, has only to seek the legal principle that is applicable, select the premises of their argument that are relevant, and then through logical syllogistic reasoning and deductive logic, draw the appropriate conclusion. (See also Chapter 4 concerning the ideal-type of formal rational law.) The lawyer, through their training and everyday practice, find themselves immersed in this language system (Mertz, 2007). It is a transformational process in which the student begins to think like a lawyer. To do law is to situate oneself within this framework. Anything outside of this is not acceptable law. It is likely to be judged as non-justiciable.

The *pluralistic linguistic coordinate system* consists of the language styles of the many subcultures within a society. Each offers distinct semiotic resources and modal forms of expression in meaning production. Each is characterized as boundaries of inclusion and exclusion with distinct identities and nuanced constructions of reality. Each has a particular way of expressing and communicating, differing in form and content; a plurality of "social logics" (Howarth, 2018; Dahlbert, 2014). Howarth (ibid., 385) defines social logics as "rules that govern a meaningful practice, where such rules are historically and mutable, as well as the conditions that make the operation of such rules possible." Social logic shapes material-discursive production and hence shapes how reality is constructed. Not apparent, too, but working more at the unconscious level, is a "fantasmatic logic" (ibid. 386), of identifications and desires in which enjoyment is fantasized (we shall return to this in the next chapter). Each LCS is a relatively stabilized matrix composed of expression and content, both form and substance, to draw from Hjelmselv, producing in usage, particular, nuanced sense (purport). Each communicates different relevancies of the world, with some remaining within the realm of fantasmatic logic. In other words, each accents the world differently. Bernstein (1975), for example, has shown that working classes more often use a "restrictive code" that binds its user to concrete reality. Here, gestures, intonation and the use of verbal metaphor are rooted in concrete, everyday life. The extensive use of nonverbal signs is the norm. The middle class, however, operates with an "elaborate code," which roots its user in the more abstract and less context-bound terminology. It focuses on verbalizations directed toward more general audiences removed from the concrete here-and-now. In law practices, it has been consistently shown that the use of an elaborate code has greater efficacy than a restrictive code.

Oppositional linguistic coordinate systems are defined as critical, disruptive, and politically motivated discourses. The users of this discourse make use of alternative semiotic resources by which to challenge a particular state of affairs. Consider "crits'" advocacy of counter storytelling to counter a system-wide racism. Consider, too, Rap and Reggae music (Kubrin and Nielsen, 2014; Kubrin, 2005; Daynes, 2010; Arbino, 2017; Ramshaw, 2013; Manderson, 2000, 2014). Revolutionary groups have the most explicit systematized framework within which the rebel thinks and conceptualizes the world. Take, for example, the Black Panthers, The Weathermen, Red Brigade, the Puerto Rican Nationalist group (the FALN), Basque Separatists, and others (see also Cottee and Howard, 2011). With each, a well-developed language exists (or existed) which opposes (or opposed) the given status quo. Users of this language view the world in oppositional terms.

To give a more concrete example, *liberation theology* in Central and South America developed in the mid-1960s. There is also an offshoot, the Palestinian Liberation Theology (Ateek, 2017). Its basic tenets were in marked contrast to those readings of the Bible by traditional priests (Barger, 2018; Gutiérrez, 1973). For the faithful, one resigns oneself to the way things are and looks toward being judged in their afterlife. In comparison, for those immersed in liberation theology, the here-and-now must be confronted. If oppressive structures exist, they must be challenged *now*. Liberation Theology has had, and continues to have, a significant influence in social movements. Thus, the linguistic coordinate systems convey vastly different ideologies of what is to be done. Liberation theology was a key element for many successful revolutions in Central and South America. It continues its influence in Palestinian struggles. Note, too, that liberation theology may also be appropriated for a diversity of political agendas.

Lopez, in *Rebellious Lawyering* (1992), has shown how everyday practices of lawyering minimize the genuine concerns and conflicts of everyday human beings in struggle (see also, Johnson, 2010; Capulong, 2009; Glick, 2017; for useful references, see "What is 'Rebellious Lawyering'?" 2021). He shows how a counter discourse can be established between the lawyer and client by the use of Paulo Freire's (1973, 1985) "dialogical pedagogy." This is a co-productive process by which reality can be recodified to make injustices visible. Through this method, alternative constructions of reality can be rendered. Both client and lawyer become co-producers of a new discourse more reflective of client's everyday struggles and yearnings for expression. Both consequently are further empowered. According to Johnson (2010: 1025): "The fundamental idea is for lawyers to attempt to pursue meaningful social change while at the same time employing community activism to empower the subordinated who can serve as their own advocates in future struggles when the lawyers are long gone." This has also been seen as a strategy for cause lawyering (Johnson, 2010; Capulong, 2009).

In short, linguistic coordinate systems frame construction of meaning. Meaning and rationality are specific to the linguistic coordinate system in use. Pitkin (1971), drawing from Winch's examination (1964) of rationality in more traditional societies, has concluded that "looking for experimental proof in the realm of religion is as irrational as looking for revelation in the realm of science." For example, "in science or mathematics, the rationality of an argument depends upon its leading from premises all parties accept, in steps all can follow, to an agreement upon a conclusion which all must accept." And "anyone who fails to accept the conclusion is regarded as either incompetent *in that mode or reasoning*, or irrational" (1971: 153; my emphasis).

Linguistics, Hegemony and Reality Construction

We now turn our attention to reality construction in the courtroom (Bennet and Feldman, 2014; recall, too Bernard Jackson's narrative coherence model). The typical defendant from the lower socio-economic classes must present information to a middle-class lawyer schooled well in a qualitatively different discursive framework (legalese). There is conflict between two world-views. This is resolved by the defense lawyer translating "what happened" into "legalese," or to be more precise, into the juridic linguistic coordinate system (see, for example, Milovanovic, 1988; Milovanovic and Thomas, 1989; Bannister and Milovanovic, 1990; Henry and Milovanovic, 1996).

But meaning is lost in the translation. One worldview, the one supported by the language structure of the courts, is reinforced, another is denied.

The courts have even excluded whole spheres from being argued. For example, the trial court proceedings focus on establishing *men's rea* (criminal intent) and *actus reus* (the criminal act). If both are shown, a conviction results. The defendant, however, is not allowed to present their motive. If the defendant insists, the opposing lawyer will simply "object" citing "relevance" or "scope" (abbreviations objecting to the wider parameters/conditions being presented) and the judge will "sustain," even telling the jury to disregard what was said. The point is, certain factors that are part of *why* people act the way they do are not given codification, are not entertained in a court of law (see also Goodrich, 1990: 193–201; Bourdieu, 1987: 831–832). They are non-justiciable. Thus, another reality is never made visible. "Relevant" factors for decision making are reduced to a narrow frame. "Facts" are cleansed and sterilized. They are abstracted and removed from their overall concrete, historically-specific context.

Consider, on the other hand, a corporate offender before the court. Here the traditional proceedings consist of the use of the injunction. The corporation is asked why it should not be stopped from doing what it is doing. In other words, corporations are permitted to offer articulations revolving around capitalist business practices, such as maintaining profit margins and providing "contributions" such as jobs and tax money to their community—all "safe," system-maintaining codifications. Even when a "consent decree" is arranged, the guilty party simply accepts the penalty without admitting responsibility. The reality that is reinforced is the dominant one, supportive of the status quo. What develops is a rather rich, complex understanding concerning the necessity of capitalism, all of which is rooted in and reflected by the dominant discourse. On the other hand, for the disenfranchised and marginalized, what is minimally developed is a deep understanding of their struggles for survival in a mode of production where economic survival is never assured. Some voices, in short, are denied meaningful expression. In sum, one discourse is enriched, another impoverished.

In this framework the defense lawyer can be better seen as a "social tranquilizer." The lawyer buys into the legal linguistic coordinate system and is thus bounded by the effects of this language (Arrigo, 1993b, 1994; Litowitz, 2006). During this process, the potential development of an oppositional discourse is arrested. The disenfranchised, and those victimized by the political economic system, are denied the very tools for critical thought, expression and communication. No stabilized linguistic coordinate system is established that reflects a critical reading of "reality." "Crits," of course, seek to develop alternative counter story-telling, a counter social logic.

Thus, those brutalized, exploited, and alienated, and the victims of injustices, must attempt to express themselves within the narrow framework of the dominant or juridic discourse, with its value-laden linguistic forms. Their feelings of being exploited, then, find no genuine means of expression. For example, until a 1992 high court ruling in Australia, recall from Chapter 7, aboriginal people were denied any legal claims to their land by the policy of *terra nullius* (Halpern (1993; Sartre, 1994). Indigenous "native title" claims were not accepted in the courts. We have seen similar developments in Canada and the U.S. with indigenous populations. We may define this as linguistic repression. Through this process, then, reality is constructed anew, but in the direction supportive of the status quo (Marxists call this process "reification"). Those most brutalized, as well as those aiding them are often, inadvertently, their own grave diggers. The notion of hegemony, a Gramsci insight (1971), by which we mean the willing participation by those most oppressed in their own oppression, is one of the most subtle forms of maintaining oppression.

Applications of the Semiotic Approach in the Sociology of Law: A Structural Interpellation View

Linguistic production, we have said, stands for the process by which new linguistic terms (signifiers) are created and their content given expression or meaning (signified). Meanings of words are the semantic dimension of language. Legal terms and expressions (signs) such as *mens rea* (state of mind, criminal intent), duress, product, proximate cause, reckless, willful, good faith, plain view, custodial arrest, reasonable cause, probable cause, expectations of privacy, conspiracy, attempt, voluntary, and so forth, are given precise meaning most forcefully in the higher courts. (Along with Saussure's two-part semiotics of signifier and signified, we could, alternatively make use of Hjelmslev's four-part semiotics of expression, content, either as form or substance, or Peirce's three-part system of sign, object, interpretant.) It is here that we find linguistic production. Lower courts and their lawyers must litigate within this framework—the linguistic coordinate system (the sphere of linguistic circulation) established by the higher courts. But legal logic and interpellation of subjects is never complete, always subject to contingency, contradiction, dialectical development, counter social logics (e.g., "crits," CLS), always fueling the "insoluble conflict" (Weber, Chapter 4) between principles of formal and substantive rationality. Let us present some exemplifications supporting a modified structural interpellationist view in the sociology of law.

Hegemonic balancing of interests. The Fourteenth Amendment to the U.S. Constitution includes the "equal protection clause," which reads, in part, that no state may "deprive any person of life, liberty, or property without due process of law." In litigation, two questions must be addressed. First, what constitutes a constitutionally accepted life, liberty or property interest? Second, and only if the threshold point has been reached, what is the appropriate process due before their infringement? We shall focus on the first question here, particularly the question concerning what constitutes a liberty and property interest recognized by the U.S. Constitution.

The courts in advanced, state-regulated, corporate capitalism have had to actively intervene in the economic and political spheres to offset crisis tendencies (see Chapter 5). Consider, for example, massive state intervention responding to the Great Depression of the 1930s and the economic crisis of 2008. As a means to this end, the higher courts have embraced the mechanism of interest-balancing in determining the rights of a particular group. Notions of a "liberty" or a "property" interest require the courts to balance: (1) a particular government interest (such as national security, the general welfare, the need to run an orderly prison, etc.), and (2) the interests of the particular person or group affected by the governmental policy. In the process of arriving at a liberty interest—say the liberty interest to privacy, or an inmate's interest in not being placed in solitary confinement—the courts fill in the content of the term "liberty interest" with precise meaning. This is *linguistic production.* Once the sign is given meaning, it enters the sphere of *linguistic circulation.* Lawyers, to do acceptable lawyering, must now use the precise meaning established by the higher courts.

Much critical analysis, however, indicates that many uncodified practices or phenomena (primordial sense data) are selectively given signification (codification). It has been shown, for example, that the state and state apparatuses such as the courts must be seen as filtering mechanisms (Milovanovic, 1987). Only those interests that are organizable and capable of conflict have a chance of being articulated and hence entertained in the courts (see also Laclau and Mouffe's analysis of new forms of interests that have developed beyond those of mere class interests, 1985; Laclau, 1996; Laclau, 2005, 2006). In other words, unless inmates (or welfare recipients, the homeless, and "undocumented" from Central America, and other disenfranchised people), for example, can form a class *for itself* (rather than just a class *in itself*), producing the capability of a united and conscious challenge to the dominant class, their interests will be amorphous, unarticulated and non-challenging. During interest-balancing by the courts, an inequality exists in the inputs: social protest movements and oppositional groups generally, while they do have an influence in the development of law, are, however, a poor match for the entrenched forces wishing to sustain things as they are. Often, we witness co-optation, deflection, sterile reconceptualization, and/or a watering down of initial demands for change. Thus, giving meaning—that is, giving content to the signifier, "liberty interest"—is a political process, which favors groups (hegemonic alliances) with power.[15]

Jailhouse lawyers and hegemonic practices. The second illustrative example concerns jailhouse lawyers JHLs) and their practice (Abu-Jamal, 2009; Milovanovic, 1988; see also Thomas, 1988; Milovanovic and Thomas, 1989; Thomas and Milovanovic, 1999).[16] (Since our earlier studies of jailhouse lawyers it is unfortunate that little further theoretical work has appeared in the literature beyond descriptive.) This brings out the notion of the *dialectics of struggle* (see also Chapter 5). JHLs—inmates who have taught themselves law and practice it (most often against their keepers)—find themselves in a dialectical struggle that often resolves itself in the direction of reifying legal discourse and the form of law.

The JHL find themselves within two linguistic coordinate systems. First, most inmates are from the disenfranchised class—exploited, repressed, denied access to decent resources, and subject to the worst living conditions. JHLs initially situate themselves within the linguistic coordinate system of the streets. Notions of identity, cause, responsibility, provocation, etc., and a particular relatively coherent world view on the other, are established and stabilized, revolving around much of the indignities and exploitive practices inflicted on them. Not all of these perceived exploitive practices are given precise articulation. Some escape expression but can be communicated outside of, or in combination with, the linguistic coordinate system (i.e., by way of gestures, facial expressions, as well as statements like "you know what I mean").

But JHLs, in learning the law,[17] and in situating themselves within its linguistic coordinate system, come to see the world in different terms. In other words, a different world-view develops. To do law, they quickly find out, is to situate arguments and to construct "what happened" within this linguistic coordinate system.[18] Otherwise, what is argued is judged non-justiciable. They must establish, in other words, "legal standing." Thus, the JHL, in helping a fellow inmate prepare for trial or appeal, or in filing a petition against oppressive practices by the keepers, finds themselves in two worlds, two contrasting linguistic coordinate systems.

At the trial stage, the defendant must attempt to convincingly explain "what happened." Prior to the trial, the JHL listens to the story of the client. But what the JHL does is to re-situate "what happened" into the language of law. Thus, there is a shift in linguistic coordinate systems. What is denied in the process is the articulation, the codification of the oppressive conditions under which the defendant lives. These are not codified; but even if they are, they are not allowed in court. They are seen as non-justiciable. The court is only interested in knowing whether intent existed and a proscribed act occurred; never mind the motive. And here lies the dilemma for the JHL: they know only too well how these conditions result in crime, but they also know that the court will not allow this articulation to be expressed in court. The JHL opts for the practical (pragmatism): they take the story of the defendant and re-situate bits and pieces of it within the juridic linguistic communicative market and build a legally acceptable (legal standing), and hopefully, a believable story of "what happened." Due to exclusion, reification is the result. One understanding of the world is denied, another upheld as the legitimate version. A cleansing, a sterilizing of any potential oppositional reading has taken place. The JHL becomes implicated, becomes an inadvertent co-conspirator of sorts in this hegemonic process.

Parole hearings: whose story counts? Inmates periodically participate in parole hearings that will determine "in or out." What we find is, in this third example, that a clash of two discourses prevails: those of the keepers and those of the kept (Shammas, 2019; Wattley, 2013). Parole board members are predominantly from a law enforcement background, whereas the inmate predominantly from the subaltern classes with often less than a 9th grade level formal education. The inmates find themselves at a "performative disadvantage" in these hearings. Parole commissioners make use of actuarial tables (prediction of dangerousness), incident reports, whether inmate has used programs available in prisons, as well as subjective judgements. The working philosophy, the evaluative judgement, hinges on whether the inmate has established sufficient insight as to their evil ways and whether they are ready for release. The inmates must sufficiently convince the keepers that this is so. The kept have developed a survival ethic, a "yard face" (Caputo-Levine, 2013), a discourse replete with appropriate lingo of the prison, that allows the kept to do their time with minimum conflict. The inmate's discourse contrasts with the discourse of the keepers. At the parole hearing, the inmates "fail to utter sentences in an appropriately formal register" (Shammas, 156), and have limited abilities to manage "the legal formalism and psychological introspection demanded in the hearing room." As Shammas (ibid) concludes, "the commissioners are the high priests of the parole performance and inmates are their ill-equipped neophytes. To the former, hearings are routine occurrences; to the latter, they are extraordinary ceremonies."

Activist lawyers before the law. A fourth illustrative example deals with activist lawyers defending rebels before the court, and in cause lawyering (Bannister and Milovanovic, 1990; Glick, 2017; Ela, 2017; Sarat and Scheingold, 2005; Marshall and Hale, 2014; Shdaimah, 2005; see also People's Law Office, Chicago). This example, much like the second above, brings out the notion of the dialectics of struggle. Consider the following: activists in the mid-1980s protesting against the U.S. involvement in Central America—claiming that the U.S. government had organized, trained, financed, and directed the *contras* (ex-national guardsmen under the dictator Somoza) in their killings of thousands of innocent women, children, and the elderly—were arrested and charged with crimes ranging from criminal trespass to destruction of government property, to resisting arrest, to assault on a police officer. Or consider the Black Lives Matter movement responding to police brutality in particular and the vocal demonstrations that were organized. Many were arrested. They were subject to formidable charges, and, in some cases, potentially adding up to many years spent in prison. The politically motivated activist lawyer was approached to defend these rebels. Both the defendant and the activist lawyer wished to mount a political defense, pointing out the broader picture behind their "crime." In other words, they would want to situate themselves within an oppositional linguistic coordinate system, making use of its vocabulary. But then there was the judiciary and its linguistic coordinate system that finds all these readings non-justiciable, having nothing to do with a legally acceptable defense.[19]

What is to be done? The sensitive lawyer finds themselves in two discourses. Does the defense situate itself within the juridic sphere and run out a traditional defense, citing different technical points of law? That is, do they explain "what happened" within the categories of the juridic discourse, and in the process leave aside the political issues that were behind the "crime?" Or does the defense try to mount a political trial, situating the "what happened" within the context of an oppositional discourse, knowing full well that it will not be accepted by the court and with its insistence will antagonize the judge (the result particularly made clear at sentencing time)? More often than not, the defense opts for a traditional defense. Any political arguments that surface will be objected to by the prosecutor and sustained by the judge. Whether the defense "wins" or loses, the social movement loses. That is, the broader issues are not codified, they are not given a day in court. The case has been depoliticized. A stabilized oppositional discourse, then, is denied development.[20]

Consider the following transcripts of a trial of Professor Jose Solis Jordon, accused of a pipe-bombing in Chicago, to bring attention to the U.S. colonization of Puerto Rico.[21] Keep in mind, too, that our chosen excerpts from the trial are for expository purposes of how particular narratives can be constructed or not at trial.

Question [Prosecutor's recross-examination; hereafter, Q]: You said on direct examination, though, ma'am, that your husband believes in armed struggle, right?

Answer [hereafter, A]: He believes in the right of Puerto Ricans to armed struggle according to the international law.

Q: Okay. But according to U.S. law, that would include illegal acts of terrorism, right, ma'am?

A: I don't want to call it "terrorism." Isn't international law U.S. law, also?

Q: So that would include acts of violence against the United States Government, for example?

A: Okay. Yes.

Q: Acts of violence in support of Puerto Rican independence?

A: We have to define it, because I understand that the international law protects people against colonialism.

Q: Your honor, I'm going to object and ask that the answer be stricken.

The Court [presiding judge]: The answer will be stricken as unresponsive. Listen carefully, ma'am, to the question and try to answer. If you can't answer it, let us know.

Or consider the following objections by the prosecutor to the sworn testimony being introduced by the defendant, Dr. Jose Solis Jordan, in his response to his defense counsel's questions (ibid., 1503–1504):

Q: And, Dr. Solis, I guess at this point who are the political prisoners?

A: Puerto Rico's political prisoners are persons who have been incarcerated for their engagement or alleged engagement in armed struggle recognized under the United Nations Resolution 4, 14, United Nations Resolutions 21, 26, the Geneva Convention … [Prosecutor]: Objection, irrelevant.

A: … the Algier's Declaration, and other international conventions …

[The Court]: All right. Just a moment. Just a moment, sir. [Prosecutor]: Objection to the narrative, the relevance, and move to strike the last part of that answer.

[Defense counsel]: Judge, the answer was responsive and not narrative. The relevance is that we're putting a context on the discussion of political prisoners who everybody here has been talking about for the last couple of weeks, and the jury is certainly entitled to know who they are ...

[The Court]: Knowing who they are and hearing narration from Dr. Solis about the legality of their activities are two different things. So, I will sustain the Government's objection with respect to the latter portion of the answer that went into the sections of international law that supposedly covered this area.

[Prosecutor]: And I move to strike.

[The Court]: It will be stricken, and the jury is instructed to disregard that portion of the answer.

Jordan was convicted. He lost on appeal (*United State v. Jose Solis Jordan*, 2000).[22] It is instructive in light of this chapter to see how the Federal judges constructed their narrative of the events compared to, for example, an alternative counter story (Ruiz, 1999).[23]

By arguing within the categories of the juridic linguistic coordinate system, one reifies dominant understandings of the world. Other world views, particularly of the oppositional variety, are denied articulation. And again, even politically motivated lawyers may inadvertently contribute to the very system that exploits, maintaining a hegemonic legal logic.

In sum, a critical, semiotic approach, one rooted in a post-Marxism and material-discursive theory, is just beginning to have an impact in the sociology of law. Some key concepts are beginning to emerge. We have argued that several linguistic coordinate systems exist. To meaningfully communicate, one must situate oneself within the relevant discourse. However, these discourses are not neutral. Words are value-laden. They convey an embedded ideology. Thus, users of a particular discourse are to a great extent bound by the structuring properties of linguistic forms. We have also argued that to better understand linguistic processes we can conceptualize a domain in which they are produced, the sphere of linguistic production, and a domain in which they circulate, the sphere of linguistic circulation. We noted the tension between the pluralist and oppositional discourses on the one hand, and the juridic linguistic coordinate system on, the other. We indicated that hegemony and reification could occur by the continued use of the latter discourse. Finally, we noted the dialectical quality of oppositional praxis.

Moving Forward

Given our last four examples on applications, particularly concerning the restrictions of formal rational law for more inclusive robust constructions of reality, a sociology of law beckons developments of alternatives. We continue to see that a strong link exists between capital logic and formal rational law. Can fuller realizations of social values take place in formal rational law? Can tinkering with formal rational law be the way? Moving in the other direction, is informalism the answer? Or does it potentially lead to the greatest excesses? Is law, as some argued in the 1980s, a "necessary evil?" Does Weber's "insoluble conflict" contribute to vibrancy in law, change, and necessary adaptation? Or must the prime agenda be a search for substantive rational law? For example, restorative justice as a form of dealing with conflicts of all sorts values a restorative justice encounter (meeting of disputants) during which a fuller range of emotions, issues, and discourses can take place. Althusser's late work on the "aleatory encounter," recognizing singularities in which novelty emerges, would be the highest ideal. However, a number of critics have shown how the disputants in these encounters are coaxed into accepting the bureaucratic language of negotiation; indeed, disciplinary mechanisms that begin to limit what can be said. Can an alternative problem-solving discourse be established? How so?

The recent call, instead, for a transformative justice argues that we must integrate two foci in a socio-legal semiotics, structure and the micro. Focusing on structure concerns not only redistribution of resources, but some form of substantive justice. Extending on Marx's needs/abilities principle which, some say are not sufficiently forward looking, we could include developing principles of justice that focus on needs, abilities, desires, and capabilities, as well as recognition, participation, and distribution (Capeheart and Milovanovic, 2020). As we do so, semiotic production would seem to follow as new "accentuations" emerge, following Voloshinov. If hierarchies remain, without more, would semiotic production continue to be class specific, enabling and restricting what can be said based on class location?

Structure, too, could be rethought. Holland (2011), for example, argues for a form of structure that follows the principles of improvisation jazz. Here, both order and disorder prevail, theorized more completely in dynamic systems theory (chaos theory) in the notion of "dissipative structures," whereby even the slightest input (perturbation) can produce changes in the structure (more in the next chapter). With alternative structures and sensitivity to micro dynamics, including the co-constitutive and dialectical play between the two, would there be fertile fields ushering in alternative semiotic resources and modes of expression that are more inclusive of diverse populations, their needs, abilities, desires, and capabilities? Many material-discursive oriented thinkers would suggest that semiotic production would follow in which the uniqueness of people can be better expressed. Here, signifiers and signifieds are no longer fixed but always in-process, perpetually undergoing change and always sensitive to context. If so, would or could a sufficient degree of relative stability be established for meaningful communication? Could justice-rendering (resolving disputes and harms inflicted) find a common language within which to speak? Could the logic of abduction (Peirce) sufficiently replace deductive and inductive reasoning in decision-making? How, then, would semiosis and semiotic resources be cultivated to respect differences *and* sameness? What form of law can we imagine that more closely allows for the fulfillment of social values? How can it be implemented? Could Unger's call for "destabilizing rights" be a starting point for conceptualizing rights within a structure that follows Holland's "improvisation jazz?

Summary

This chapter has covered a number of approaches in a socio-legal semiotics. As we saw, there is a lively discussion concerning the best approach. Critical discourse studies examine textual productions, more *parole* of Saussure. In the previous chapter, we examined *langue*. We saw this body of literature is usefully applicable to a sociology of law, informed by a critical socio-legal semiotics. We then presented the resurgence of a materialist semiotic Marxism. The 1980s and 1990s witnessed a number of insightful works on Marx, in particular Gramsci, Poulantzas, Althusser. All moved away from a strict economic reductionism. The mid 1980s to the 1990s saw a number of post-structuralist responses that suggested the primacy of a "discursive formation" rather than the economic, apparently jettisoning materialism. Post-Marxism that emerged in the first two decades of the 21st century brought materialism back into the picture for plausible explanations of the contributions of semiotics. We then moved onto revisiting a modified structural interpellationist Marxist approach rooted in bringing material semiotics back in. Several illustrative applications were provided. We left on a call for future imaginative thought in sociology of law inspired by critical socio-legal semiotics.

Review Questions

1. Social semiotics offers the tools of semiotic resources and modes of expression. Take a contemporary social issue appearing in mass media. Explain how these tools were applied. Were they effective? Whose stories were dominant? Who's untold?

2. Observe a reality television serial on trial courts. What stereotypes were represented? How was the intersection of race, class, sexual preference/orientation, and gender presented? How were things presented in particular narratives?

3. We have come across counter storytelling in law in a number of contexts. How can the tools of socio-legal semiotics be useful?

4. A critical socio-legal semiotics can be brought to bear on more conventionally understood signifiers. We previously encouraged the reader to apply this approach to the signifiers: ghetto, colonists, homesteaders, settlers, rebels, squatters, and hoodie. See also endnotes 1–3. Research two and report to class. In class, or a "discussion question" online, list a possible alternative signified that could be associated with each signifier. Then, explain how the tools offered in this approach can illuminate these signifiers otherwise.

5. Althusser's notion of interpellation explains how identity positions become "occupied." Explain how a police siren or lights behind you, or where an authoritative person hails you, "Hey you," places you in a particular frame from which to speak.

6. The notion of "contingencies" has often been brought up in post-Marxist analysis. How is it being used? And what is the relevance, especially in understanding law?

7. Materialist Marxists, such as social reproduction feminists, argue that we need to be more cognizant of relations of production and their reproduction. Can the dominant form of legal discourse, formal rationality, change without changing the relations of production which in turn are connected with the mode of production?

8. We developed a hypothetical application of a critical socio-legal semiotics in a sociology of law whereby a new legal defense was advocated, "severe environmental deprivation." Class exercise, or discussion question: divide the class into those who are for and those who are against. Support your respective views. Would this defense lead to a greater understanding of causes of crime, and subsequently lead to new social policies that enhance fulfillment of social values? Show how tools offered in socio-legal semiotics are useful in the debate.

9. The existence of multiple linguistic coordinate systems existing was presented. Explain how, in the course of your normal week, you have occasion to visit a number of different LCSs. How difficult or not was it for you to change your semiotic usage from one to the other? (This could be a useful class discussion.)

10. Members of oppositional groups who have been arrested experience a number of difficulties in presenting their case and in preserving the cause's integrity. Explain. Can lawyers for the defense adequately provide a defense that also preserves the social movement's claim to injustice(s)? Explain.

Endnotes

1. In the Australian context, consider the principle of "Terra Nulius," empty land, often extended to imply (connotatively) "uncivilized land," that was used by the British as a justification to colonize, a narrative that was repeated world-wide by colonizing powers.

2. The Homestead Act drove many American Indians off their lands. The "Dawes Act" of 1871 and 1887 in the U.S. was the inspiration of Senator Henry Dawes in his stated desire "to civilize Indians." It provided 160 acres allotted to each Indian. In Dawes' words, the two acts had a "civilizing effect on Indians because it forced them to cultivate land, live in European-inspired houses, ride in Studebaker wagons ... [and] own property" (see Khomina, N.D.).

3. A movement in 1970s in the Lower East Side of New York city whereby large numbers of abandoned, and/or neglected apartment buildings by landlords who saw them as unprofitable were occupied by needy people, see Starecheski, 2016. I (DM) had a meeting with Martin Sostre shortly after his release, a former inmate and jailhouse lawyer who championed the rights of fellow incarcerated inmates, who was released because of the work by Amnesty International (1973). Apart from other things, he explained his work in organizing squatters and their moral right for occupation.

4. An example of interpellation is when a police car that is following you turns on its flashing lights, or when a police officer yells to you "hey you." In each case, the person is inserted in a specific subject position in which reality is being constructed. Here, each person immediately feels the force of law.

5. We recall Weber's multi-causal approach.

6. In this revised version, Althusser states (cited in Grant, 2005: 19), "everything depends, in the last instance, not on technique but militants, on their class consciousness, on their devotion, and on their courage."

7. Ferguson (2016: 53), for example, argues "depending upon which spaces different bodies occupy within this hierarchical world-system, they have greater or lesser access or entitlement to quality education, healthcare and neighbourhoods, to safe workplaces and commutes to and from work, to

basic rights and freedoms."

8. Ferguson (2016: 57), drawing from McNally (2015: 142–44), suggests that a class consciousness could develop on the basis of recognition of the nature of oppression that is related at the micro- and macro-level, parts and wholes—"an awareness of the unity of the diverse relations that produce capitalism and society."

9. An emerging perspective, critical legal geography (Braverman *et al.*, 2014), could also augment social reproductive feminism.

10. Delgado (1985) also refers to it as signifying "rotten social background" (RSB). He summarizes: "unremitting long-term exposure to situations of threat, stress, and neglect indelibly mark the minds and bodies of those exposed. In some cases, the resulting propensity for crime is so strong as to justify the conclusion that the individual is not responsible. When this occurs, an existing criminal defense, such as diminished capacity, automatism, or duress will sometimes be available. When not, we should consider creating a new defense." For an accessible summary of Judge Bazelon's summary of the facts in *United States v. Alexander* reported in the internet, see Delgado (1985: 20).

11. The astute student, now with critical constructive tools gained from engaging the first nine chapters, may see our hypothetical as problematic, and utter: Objection! Leading the witness! Rather, as with a judge, pronouncing "Sustained!" or "Overruled!, the hypothetical was a provocation to engage in critical constructive sociology of law.

12. Delgado (1985: 89) suggests: "The jury would be instructed, as they are in negligence cases in some jurisdictions, to determine the proportion of individual and society fault ... the defense would be limited to cases in which the defendant can prove that specific social institutions, such as schools, failed to discharge a duty to the defendant, resulting in his or her commission of a criminal offense."

13. Consider Wu and Chen's (2013: 65) metaphor of the computer as a person: "A computer in our eyes has a brain (CPU), a body (motherboard), a memory, a face (interface); it has its own language. It can conduct some activities like a human being, such as sleep, wake up, eat, read, write, tell, accept, compile, create, check spelling, etc."

14. Wittgenstein has used the term "language games" (1958), Pitken, the term "language regions" or forms of discourse, i.e., moral, scientific, political, to name a few (1971).

15. Alternative to applying Saussure, we leave it to the reader to possibly apply Peirce, Hjelmslev, and/or Austin.

16. Both Jim Thomas and I had done considerable work in the prisons and jails, particularly with the John Howard Association inspecting prisons in Illinois. We made it a point to stop at the prison law library and talk with the jailhouse lawyers, and to sit in on the disciplinary hearings. My work extended to being an instructor for four years for La Guardia Community College teaching inmates at Queens House of Detention for Men, Kew Gardens, NYC. This also allowed me quite a bit of one-on-one contact in the cells, in the dayroom, and to observe jailhouse lawyer's actions in court across the street in the Courthouse.

17. *Bounds v. Smith* (1977), dealing with a right to "access," stipulated that prisons/jails should either provide adequate representation (lawyers) or provide a law library for inmate's use. Due to costs, almost all opted for the second.

18. Formal manuals are now available for jailhouse lawyering. See "A Jailhouse Lawyer's Manual," "Jailhouse Lawyer's Handbook"; see also McDonald, 2004. Correspondence courses are also available.

19. One of the few allowable, but only at the discretion of the judge, is the "necessity defense." See also Chapter 4 where Weber indicated the tension between formal and substantive rationality.

20. Of course, social movement litigation that has "won" in court will surely proclaim it as a symbolic victory and the securing of tangible social change. But the legal apparatus remains intact. Legally constructed concepts must now be applied in future activism and discursive production.

21. *U.S. vs. Jose Solis Jordan,* March 9, 1999: 1486–1487.

22. See the online version of the case, accessed on 9/4/2021, https://law.justia.com/cases/federal/appellate-courts/F3/223/676/577697/.

23. See Ruiz's article online, accessed on 9/4/2021, https://againstthecurrent.org/atc081/p1722/.

11

Postmodern Contributions to Sociology of Law

Introduction

The study of sociology of law in Western industrialized societies rest on core assumptions inherited from the Enlightenment period. It is from these core assumptions that understandings, theories, and substantive law emerges. Heretofore we have addressed approaches in the sociology of law that remain embedded in a modernist tradition, a development from the Enlightenment period. This chapter will provide new foundations, an alternate paradigm that challenge many of the assumption of the modernist tradition. The postmodern approach had its origination in the late 1960s and continued most forcefully into the 1990s. Included works are: Jacques Lacan's work on psychoanalytic semiotics, a Lacanian-based feminist law, selected postmodernist theorists in law, chaos theory, and constitutive theory. In the following chapter, our last, we will visit a post postmodern perspective that emerged most notably in the early 2000s and continues in its internal differentiation. For the latter, some continuity but many differences have emerged contrasted to the postmodern approach. Included in a post postmodern approach are: posthumanism, new materialism, eco-feminism, sociomateriality, quantum mechanics, and quantum holography.

The postmodern perspective challenges the key ontological assumptions that emerged from the Enlightenment period (17th and 18th Century). In other words, during this time some core assumptions galvanized and continue to form the basis of much Western thought in various disciplines, including law. The core assumptions were correctives to the dark ages and its turmoil, disorder, and irrationalities. Celebrated were: economic growth and private property; the liberating potentials of the newly developing sciences; new (formal) legal freedoms including formal equality and due process; the discovery of the individual as an autonomous, coherent, unified, determining, and responsible entity (the "centered subject") best expressed in *cogito ergo sum*, I think therefore I am; linear causation and hence predictability; rationalism as a force for the development of the good society; and the juridic subject, an abstract bearer of rights, the so-called "reasonable man [person] in law." This was a time of optimism.

Postmodernist thought developed a very different picture (see also Dews, 1987; Sarup, 1989). At the end of the 19th century and carrying over into the 20th century, several (non-postmodernist) writers began to portray the negative side of the coming modernist society. To name a few: Karl Marx showed how the newly developed mode of production that replaced feudalism was essentially hierarchical, exploitive and denied the fulfillment of social values for the many. This society, it was argued, produced "crippled monstrosities." Max Weber also criticized the emerging society as offering, on the one hand, new liberties (i.e., contractual freedoms), but also the "iron cage" of capitalism wherein the loss of meaning and freedom would be prevalent, particularly because of the dominance of rationality and bureaucracy. Nietzsche, perhaps even more insightfully, showed how the new person of modernism was weak and sought idols to overcome their state in being. Semiotic fictions were the salvations. These fictions included the idea that persons are centered subjects (i.e., self-determining individuals). These fictions were necessary in overcoming the inner sense of loss; accordingly, they created certainty, stability, and predictability. Fictions and idols were sought and constructed to overcome our everyday meager being. And, of course, Sigmund Freud was to change the notion of the consciously, self-determining individual forever. Most of what accounts for our behavior, Freud argued, was really unconscious. The person was more determined than determining. Finally, the critical thought of the Frankfurt school, which synthesized Marxism with psychoanalysis, was to fundamentally challenge the newly emerging "sane society."

Thus, what characterized postmodernist thought was that many of the perceived virtues of the emerging post-enlightenment society must be balanced against the new forms of manipulation and control. Human emancipation was not an inevitable development, the postmodernists argued. Recognized were: (1) the manipulative powers of the media; (2) the entrenched powers of monopolies; (3) the rigid rationalism of bureaucracies and new forms of domination and disciplining mechanisms; (4) the biases and dominance of a monolithic "global knowledge"; (5) the idea that the dominant discourse often denies other hidden voices, and only provides the medium by which conventional ideologies are constructed and reconstructed anew; (6) the unexamined reliance on "foundational truths" (i.e., positing truth claims for all times and settings), which were claimed to be objective and potentially subject to verification through the "neutral" scientific method; (7) the fallacies of the "linear development of history, as for example in the Hegelian model of the unfolding of an idea (i.e., the Absolute Spirit), in contrast to the "genealogical method," rooted more in Nietzsche, which celebrates chance, randomness, contingency, the unpredictable; (8) that the subject is not as centered and in control as prevalent ideology claimed, but instead the person should be seen as the *decentered subject*; (9) that formal rationality, the rule of law, can be the basis of repressive formalism; and (10) that struggles against different forms of hierarchies can produce unintended consequences, and even further reinforce forms of domination (i.e., the dialectics of struggle). In a few words, consciousness was the subject of new forms of manipulation and control.

Two forms of postmodern analysis emerged. One a more negative, nihilistic version that was anchored in deconstruction. The other, a more affirmative postmodernist analysis that not only criticized the injustice that existed but moved in the direction of offering insights for social change.

The more formal take-off period of postmodernist thought can be isolated as the late 1960s in France. Here, as student unrest and leftist politics dominated all aspects of society, the legacy of Hegel was giving way to the profound insights of Nietzsche. Key postmodernist thinkers, the founding figures, if you will, began to emerge from the French scene: these included Deleuze, Guattari, Lyotard, Derrida, Kristeva, Foucault, Barthes and Baudrillard. But the debate was further refined and brought sharply into focus by French postmodernist feminists: Irigaray, Moi, Cixous, and Kristeva, to name a few. By the late 1970s, a return to Freud's work was underway. The key figure in the fundamental reorientation to postmodernist thought was Jacques Lacan.

Jacques Lacan and Psychoanalytic Semiotics in Law

Just as any sound critical theory in law must work its way through a macro-structural analysis of Marx, so too, it must engage the micro-social level, with some notion of agency. Jacques Lacan continues to offer one of the few compelling comprehensive statements on the nature of agency. In spite of the considerable critiques of both, Marx and Lacan, each offers the starting point for engagement with a critical sociology of law.

Prior to Lacan, Sigmund Freud (1900) outlined the structure of the psychic apparatus in *The Interpretation of Dreams*. He established the law-of-the-father as a unifying principle of the unconscious in the Oedipus Complex. The latter was posited as a very early (4–6-year-old) attraction to the opposite sex parent and its jealously, with the resolution resulting in fixed gender roles. Henceforth, the law-of-the father reigned supreme as an organizing principle of the unconscious. Prior to this, the child is bisexual, "psychically is not yet either a man or a woman" (Zakin, 2011). There have been some discussions in the literature (see for example, Morel, 2018), however, that posit a law-of-the-mother as the very early principle due to the mother as a primal caregiver where words and feelings leave their mark as pleasure, the basis of future fantasies and symptoms. Freud posited that primordial sense date is stored in electro-chemical patterns (clusters of interconnected neurons). He showed how "word-presentations" (signifiers) residing in the pre-conscious were attached to "thing-presentations" (signifieds) embodied in the unconscious, and it was attention that "hypercathected," or charged these clusters so that they would release their energy producing a thought or idea.

Jacque Lacan (1901–1981) was a revisionist Freudian. He was influenced by: Saussure's posthumously published lectures on linguistics (1966); Kojève's lectures given in the 1930s on Hegel, especially on the nature of desire (1980); Levi-Strauss's anthropological studies on the nature of the Symbolic Order; Benveniste's examination of the nature of the personal pronouns ("I" and "you") (1971); Jakobson's analysis of the nature of aphasic (speech) disorders and how two specific axes (metaphor, metonymy) can be isolated as the determinants of semiotic production (1971); and Freud's work on the nature of the psychic apparatus, particularly the secrets of "dream work" (1965). For Lacan, Freud was doing linguistic analysis when he uncovered how desire becomes embodied in particular forms, especially verbal and imaginary. Yes, dreams were the royal road to the unconscious, as Freud said, but Lacan followed with the idea that the unconscious itself is structured like a language.

Lacan delivered a series of seminars from the early 1950s until 1980. These were attended by some of the most prominent intellectuals in the European community. Some of these figures were: Althusser, Foucault, Barthes, Guattari, Kristeva, Irigaray, Ricouer, Sartre, Levi-Strauss, Merly-Ponty. Several of these seminars have been transcribed and published in French. They are also beginning to appear in English translation. Lacan's son-in-law, Jacques-Alain Miller, has coordinated this effort. Much of his material still remains unpublished in French, and even less so in English. Even the material transcribed and published has been subject to much critique. It should be added that interested readers should be forewarned: Lacan's work is difficult prose, and it is challenging reading. Secondary sources are a must. His application to law must be read as wider than traditionally conceived law, but to include the laws of the unconscious (see Caudill, 1997; McNulty, 2020; Swiffen, 2010; Murray, 2005; Srinivasan, 2015). Lacan's earlier work builds on Freud's "law-of-the-father, whereas his later works begins to develop a "sinthome law" (Murray, 2005).

Three Primal Orders

The subject as well as speech production, for Lacan, is an outcome of the interaction of three orders: the Symbolic, Imaginary and Real. The Symbolic Order is the sphere of language and culture. In a hierarchically organized society where the male voice is dominant, the female subordinate, the Symbolic Order is said to be phallocentric (we shall pick up on this theme in our exemplifications that follow our exposition of Lacan). The Symbolic Order is also represented by the idea of the Other, which is the sphere of the unconscious. Within the Other we have unconscious and relatively independent processes taking place. The Other is a repository of signifiers (i.e., words) unique to the being. These include legal signifiers learned in law schools and practiced in doing law. The Symbolic Order predates the child; and so too, legal discourse predates the entering law student or practitioner. The child enters this order and both gains but also loses something. In other words, the child is inaugurated into the Symbolic Order and gains mastery of a discourse with which they can embody desire, but loses (is separated from) the *direct* experience itself. This is a fundamental loss creating an inherent lack-in-being. The person will forever try to compensate for this fundamental loss. The child, in other words, is castrated from being.

The child's entrance into the Symbolic Order has been described by Lacan in the "fort-da" game. An infant (Freud's grandson), playing on a bed, experiences jubilation when the mom appears and despair when she leaves. The child invents a game with a cotton real by throwing it over the bed and with its disappearance, the child feels despair. But pulling it back in it experiences jubilation. Then, it utters some of its first words, "fort" (gone), when the cotton real disappears, "da" (there) with its reappearance. This duplicates the mom's coming and going and thus creates an illusory mastery of the event by the use of words. It reduces the despair. However, it is forever separated from the real experience with language now being a substitute. This, for Lacan, represents a castration from the real. Further, the cotton real is initially an object of desire ("objet petit a") in fulfilling a felt lack, later replaced by language. Lack is forever mobilized to which desire is activated in search of objects of desire that hold the illusory capability to overcome lack.

Consider a law student finally succumbing to constructing stories by legal signifiers and in reasoning by deductive logic and syllogistic reasoning. They may want to bring in philosophical or political economic arguments to bear on the issue, but is quickly encouraged not to do so. They both deliberately construct legal narratives and yet remain alienated by this very construction, for it does not completely represent them, nor the real experience at issue.

Lacan, too, revised Freud's Oedipus complex to read the penis not as biological but as a phallus, a signifier or paternal metaphor for the potency and power of the father. Henceforth, all within the Symbolic Order will be tainted with the phallus, a basis, too, of the phallocentric symbolic order governed by the law-of-the father, Lacan's first law.

The Imaginary Order is the sphere of imaginary constructions and imagoes. These provide illusory constructions of completeness. It is developed during the *mirror stage* (6 to 18 months) of child development. Prior to the mirror stage the child perceives itself only in a fragmented state, but at a certain point it glimpses itself in the mirror (not necessarily the physical mirror) and for a moment develops the illusion of completeness. This is followed with jubilation, a *jouissance*. This is the first of the imaginary constructions of self, or the *moi*. But many others will follow.

The Real Order is the domain of lived experience. This is forever foreclosed to congruent representation in signifiers. It cannot be accurately represented in the Symbolic Order nor in the Imaginary Order, has no structure, escapes any attempts for accurate signification in signifiers, has no reference, remains unsymbolisable, and merely "ex-ists." As Zizek (2006) tells us, the Real "is a void which nonetheless functions, exerts influence, causes effects, curves the symbolic space." See for example the application of the Real to Kafka's *The Trial* and *The Castle* (Buk-Swienty, 2016). See also Kafka's short story, "Before the Law." Here, K's confrontation with law brings out the notion of an inherent void, a lack, an elusiveness, that nevertheless has effects. Consider, too, the notion of death (ibid.). These three orders work together in the production of speech and subjectivity, to which we turn.

Semiotic Axes, Embodying Desire and Anchoring Points

Lacan has built on the insights of Freud, particularly from *The Interpretation of Dreams*, in generating answers to how precisely desire is embodied in signifiers, or words, and how narratives and texts are established possessing sense. For example, for lawyers, how is it that certain narratives can be constructed and others are denied expression? How is it that certain voices do find expression, others do not? What realities can be constructed, which cannot?

The key elements in his theory are signifiers and their coordinating mechanisms. He employs Saussure's two-part semiotics, signifier and signified. However, for Lacan, the signifier does not directly address a particular signified, but other signifiers. The signifier represents the subject for another signifier. Look up a particular word in the dictionary, for example, and it refers to another signifier which refers to other words, ad infinitum. It is for Lacan, the primacy of the signifier and their movement.[1] Signifiers are not stand-alone, but always refer to other signifiers in the generation of signified and meaning.

Initially, the unconscious is populated with "letters" that "insist" (Lacan, 1977: 147–155); that is to say, psychic material (located within the unconscious) with different degrees of intensity is forever seeking expression (it "insists"). In its most formal aspect, this "letter" is transformed into the formal properties of a signifier, a word that is uttered in some social encounter, or a legal signifier expressed in a trial court proceeding.

Each subject has a unique biography and hence embodies signifiers in an idiosyncratic way. These signifiers slumber in anticipation within the locus of the Other. The Other, for Lacan, is "the treasure of signifiers." The totality of signifiers learned in law school and practiced in law resides in the "Other." The normal state of the signifiers is that they "float" within the unconscious and periodically attach themselves to certain signifieds. Lacan calls this attaching process the *point de capitonnage*. For example, the signifier "bounce" remains in an unconnected form in the unconscious—it may eventually, in context, be connected to: doing one's laundry, the image of the bouncer at a bar, a child playing with a ball, a person concerned with check writing, or, for skydivers, a person who dies on a drop zone. Some signifiers are more permanently connected to particular signifieds; this is the locus of *symptoms* (e.g., constellations of inter-connected signifiers) which produce a certain consistency in the subject's psychic apparatus and hence their speech production. A lawyer, for example, in doing law, invokes this particular sphere of their unconscious. Outside the context of work, they may invoke various other constellations of signifiers in particular contexts.

Lacan (1977) offers an original contribution to the construction of narratives, or signifying chains. In his Graphs of Desire, of which there are four, each more comprehensive and complex, he argues that in speech production there is a forward, anticipatory dimension and a backward dimension. One initially anticipates a particular signifier from the given paradigm structure (the Other), and as it takes form, the next one is "chosen," further shaped by syntactical rules. At a pause or punctuation in this construction of signifiers (signifying chain), there is a retrograde to the beginning and the utterance (signifying chain) is given meaning all at once. Each word by itself has no meaning until the pause or punctuation point. Consider: "I am going to...," or a lawyer asking "will the witness respond to..." Note, meaning is suspended until the final signifier in a chain of signifiers and some punctuation. In his final Graph he indicates how the Symbolic and Imaginary order combine with desire in speech production.

Let's give an example of this complex analysis and draw out an implication to someone doing law (see also the perceptive commentary by Naffine, 1990: 29–47; Arrigo, 1998a). What a law student actually does in law school is to internalize a number of legal signifiers that have particular content (signified). Words such as *mens rea,* intent, maliciously, negligently, and so forth, have precise meaning in law. These are internalized by the student and become the basis of understanding. Consider, for example, Asch's analysis (1992) of the word "wildlife" as it was defined in Canadian courts. The court's narrow definition stated that whereas domesticated animals are held by private individuals, wild animals are not recognized as owned until capture, leaving ownership by default to the state. This effectively denied indigenous peoples their time-honored hunting rights. Apart from learning the definitions of words employed in legal discourse, the law student learns how they are connected in linear form to produce acceptable legal discourse. In other words, the student has learned legal meanings (in conventional semiotic analysis this is usually referred to as the *paradigm* axis) and how to string these words together (conventionally defined as *syntagm*) to produce a particular text or narrative. The perpendicular intersections of the two axes are constitutive of meaningful sentences.

The available signifiers and the appropriate manner of linear construction, however, have limited the constructed text. A word such as "intent," for example, has been greatly circumscribed temporally and spatially to consider mostly the more immediate factors at play rather than including larger political economic forces that may be contributing to the event in question. Expanding the time and space dimensions included in the definition of "intent" would surely implicate a constellation of factors and certainly place a question mark to the notion of a centered subject.

Let us provide another example. Consider an incarcerated person. They find themselves in a situation of frustration, confusion, anger, bitterness and hostility. In communicating their plight, they must avail themselves of the linguistic forms derived from inmate subcultures, discourses of the numerous health professionals, discourses of the guards, legalistic jargon picked up during litigation, bureaucratic jargon as they are processed in the system, and personal biographical linguistic forms. Articulating their plight will be in terms of these linguistic forms. In other words, reality construction is a constitutive process. More often than not, an amorphous "they" or "them" are verbalized as the culprit in their situation. Note, however, that no relatively stable oppositional linguistic coordinate system exists by which to embody desire and by which to develop a more critical view of existing forms of hierarchy and oppression. Desire is merely embodied in the categories available. The dominant order may safely continue its different forms of oppression as it is faced by inarticulate and contradictory tilting at wind mills. Note, however, that incarcerated Black Panthers in the 1960s and 70s brought a more oppositional discourse but its expression was heavily censored.

Subjectivity and Discourse

Lacan explained that the subject is inherently connected to the discourse they employ. There is no separating the two. He dismisses the modernist conception of "cogito, ergo sum," as idle chatter, and offers his notion of the decentered subject: "I think where I am not, therefore I am where I do not think" (1977: 166).

There are two planes for the Lacanian desiring subject. One plane is the subject of speech. In other words, this is the grammatical subject *(le sujet de l'énoncé)*. Put in another way, when the subject is speaking and makes use of the "I" they fill in this "I," giving it content. This allows vocal or written narrative constructions. The "I" of discourse is referred to as a "shifter"; it only takes on substance on the occasion when someone uses the pronoun; otherwise, it is empty (Benveniste, 1971). It also stands for the presence of an absence. In other words, when I am speaking another plane is hidden which is the locus of the actual producer of the narrative or text. This other plane is the locus of the speaking subject *(le sujet de l' énonciation)*. It is that sphere that is responsible for producing the statements that are being uttered. It is an area that is not directly accessible; it is unconscious. This is the area that Lacan calls the Other (capital "O"). In sum, we have two subjects: the speaking subject and the subject of speech. Lacan refers to the person as the speaking-being or speaking *(l'être parlant, or parlêtre)*. Consider, for example, Lawrence's (1987) analysis of "unconscious racism" in law; here, two planes are operative, with the "deeper" often materializing in conscious discourse. That is, racism may have deeper rooting in the unconscious and it emerges in a more disguised form in legal discourse. Some forms of micro-aggression, be they more unconscious, would be another example.

The "je," the "I" is the personal pronoun that a subject "fills in" with content only in use. Otherwise, it is a shifter referring to no one (it has no content). The "I" is the grammatical subject. (Consider the legal practitioner verbally presenting their case in court.) It stands for the presence of an absence. As words are uttered, they stand for or represent the subject. As Grosz has it, "the child acquires a position from which to speak, a place where a signifier, the I, can represent the subject (for another signifier) ..." (1990: 72). The Other is the domain of the unconscious, particularly the locus of a whole constellation of signifiers that, because of biography, are unique to the being. The principle that provides constancy, or stability to the Other, is the law-of-the father (for application to law, see Voruz, 2000; Caudill, 1997). (In his later works, Lacan began to develop a second law grounded in knot theory to which we will return below.)

The law-of-the-father is traced to Freud's *Totem and Taboo* where it is posited that the jealousy of brothers of the father's control of women led to the killing of the father for supremacy, but with a forever lasting guilt complex, repressed in the unconscious. This established the law-of-the-father. Further, Freud's primacy of the penis is replaced by Lacan with the phallus, a signifier of power, potency, and supremacy, a symbol of the law-of-the-father. It is, for Lacan, what provides consistency among signifiers. This law finds continuous expression in society. See for example, our discussion of Bainbridge (2011) in Chapter 10 where the father and police are often depicted in the media as signifiers of law and order. Note, there is no inevitability or essentialism here, for another form of "law" could have appeared in historical conditions as a coordinating principle of the unconscious.

The "Other," for the law practitioner, is also the repository of legal signifiers. The "moi" is an imago, an illusory construction of self; is the conception one has of oneself that is gained through the eyes of the other person. Consider a lawyer presenting their case, mindful of how the jury may be perceiving them and the story being constructed. In Lacan's words it is "that which is reflected of his form in his objects" (1977: 194). In other words, it is the imaginary constructions one has of oneself. The *other*, small o, is that person or object of desire that reflects to the *moi* its sense of unity. Thus, in the Lacanian construct, we have an inter- and intra-subjective basis of being.

The Lacanian desiring subject, the speaking being, is conceptualized in Schema L (Lacan, 1977; see Figure 1).

Figure 1. Schema L

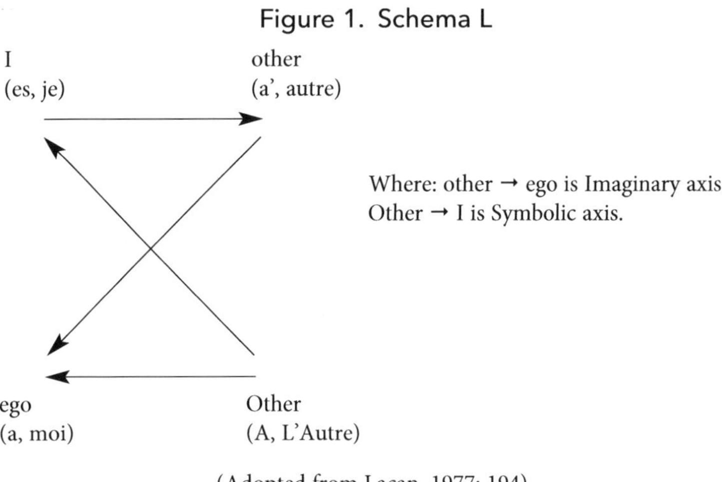

(Adopted from Lacan, 1977: 194)

Within Schema L we see two axes: the je-Other represents the unconscious axis, the Symbolic; the moi-other, the Imaginary. (In the upper left corner, Lacan has placed, alternatively, "es," "S," and "id." We shall translate as "Je" or "I.") These two axes are at work when discursive production takes place. When interactions unfold, or when narratives are being constructed, the interaction between these two axes are determinative of the particular outcome. Thus, for Lacan, the subject is drawn out over all four corners of Schema L at the same time. Put in another way, it is *decentered.* For example, think in terms of how a lawyer performs in a trial court proceeding: they must situate themselves in the discourse of law, making use of allowable signifiers in law (the je-Other axis; more unconscious), and they engage in speculations as to how their client is being perceived (moi-other axis; more imaginary). These two axes are simultaneously at work.[2]

What mobilizes the psychic apparatus, for Lacan, is desire. The person is essentially a *desiring subject.* Periodically, the subject experiences a lack-in-being, initially established in the fort-da game. There can be no escape; this is the price paid for the inauguration into the Symbolic Order. The subject is forever separated (castrated) from the Real. This lack mobilizes desire.

To return to the process by which desire mobilizes the psychic apparatus and by which it is given expressive form (embodied in signifiers). What happens is that the subject attempts to *suture* or stitch over, as in a surgical repair, the gaps in being. The subject must first find an appropriate object of desire, which Lacan refers to as the *objet petit(a).* Words can be considered one possibility (paradigm axis). For example, think in terms of lawyer's active narrative constructions in trial court proceedings. Faced with contradictions or things that are not sufficiently explained, or questions put before them, they "select" legal signifiers from their "storehouse" of signifiers residing in the Other (paradigm), and places them in the required linear ordering (syntagm) in creating a story. Here, *objet petit (a)* consists of particular signifiers (words), which provide the vehicle for the expression of the unique desire of the practicing lawyer. Keep in mind, too, that the two axes described in Schema L are simultaneously at work during this process. Thus, both the imaginary and symbolic axes are in use in the construction of legal narratives. Consider, too, how "crits'" advocacy of counter storytelling implicates the Symbolic and Imaginary Orders in their construction.

This suturing operation implicates the three Orders. The Imaginary Order provides certain illusions that are potential sources for filling in gaps in-being *(manque d'être).* The Symbolic Order provides a wealth of signifiers, or words, which can embody desire. The Real Order will also have its presence felt. What actually happens is that the subject selects appropriate objects of desire and embodies them with its unique form of desire. Lacan pictures this as:

$ <> a.

Note that the "S" has a slash that passes through it. This is Lacan's way of saying that the subject disappears in the signifiers that represent it in discourse. Again, this is the play of presence and absence. In actually uttering words, the producing entity has disappeared (absence) from the scene, replaced by a certain presence, the "I" of grammatical constructions. The < > represents a movement. The subject is disappearing into its objects of desire (a). This is a two-way process, for the objects of desire now come to reflect (mirror), be it illusory at base, the subject's being *($).*

Lacan's Four Discourses

Lacan (1991) presented the thesis of the four discourses in his 1969–1970 seminar, *L'Envers de la Psychanalyse.* He wanted to show how speaking always takes place in a structured form of discourse, which can enable and limit what can be said. These discourses—*master, university, hysteric* and *analyst*—were offered as the four main forms of discourses in existence. They accounted for how desire found, or did not find, expression in discourse. They also accounted for how in fact a body of knowledge was constituted or reconstituted. Several theorists have provided translations and/

or commentary on Lacan's work (Bracher, 1988, 1993; Lee, 1990; Melville, 1987; Milovanovic, 1993a; Schroeder, 2008; Clemens and Grigg, 2006; Bryant, 2008; Vanheule, 2016). These discourses have also been applied to law (Arrigo, 1994, 1998a, 1998b; Stacy, 1996; Schroeder, 2000, 2008; Shon, 2000). Let us first explain the four discourses and then provide illustrative examples of their applications in law. Lacan, too, has identified a discourse of the capitalist which he never fully developed (see Vanheule, 2016; Bryant, 2008).

Lacan identifies four main terms in these discourses — S1, S2, $, a; and four locations — agent, other, truth, and production. S1 represents *master signifiers.* These have been defined as key signifiers, which stem from childhood experience that have been subsequently the basis of ideologically-infused content, and reside in the sphere of the Other. In other words, these are anchored signifiers *(capitonnage).* The agent formulates these signifiers and sends this message to the other. In our application to law, key signifiers in law are master signifiers, such as intent, duress, etc. *S2* represents knowledge. For Lacan, knowledge always exists within a chain of signifiers. Meaning "insists" within these chains. Thus, within the chain, a signifier represents a subject for another signifier. The producing entity has disappeared from the scene, now represented by a signifier. For example, the narratives constructed in a trial court proceeding as well as by appeal court's decisions ("facts of the case"), take on a static meaning once they have been transcribed and published. Meanings of these narratives, however, are henceforth interpreted in various ways (i.e., the free play of the text). *$* represents the desiring subject, always inherently divided in its basic constitution. In Lacan's formulation, S stands for signifiers, and the bar adds its split, divided nature. And *a* represents the *objet petit(a),* though in the context of the four discourses, Lacan defines it as *le-plus-de jouir:* the excess in enjoyment, and what is left out. In other words, in unfolding discourse, one always says less than what one desires, and also, ironically, more (think in terms of the Freudian slip on the one hand, and, on the other, occasions of Lawrence's "unconscious racism," or more unconscious forms of micro-aggressions). It often entails an objectification.

Lacan has also identified four structured positions in the four discourses. Each of the four terms takes a different position within each of the four discourses, with pronounced different effects. These can be pictured:

$$\frac{\text{agent}}{\text{truth}} \rightarrow \frac{\text{other}}{\text{production}}$$

Here, the left side represents the sender of some message; the right side, the receiver and enactor of that message. The upper left-hand corner stands for the initiator of a message, the *agent.* The message originates in a desiring subject. The upper right corner, the *other,* represents the receiver, addressee, and enactor of the message. These locations (above the bar) exist at the more overt, manifest or conscious levels. The lower left corner represents a hidden, repressed *truth* that motivates their action and is unique to the being who initiates some message to another. In Lacan's schema it is in essence only partly knowable. Each person has their unique truth, which resides in the unconscious. It could represent, for example, core assumptions on which thinking, reasoning and writing depends. The lower right corner represents *production.* In other words, it is what is produced as an effect in the receiver's unconscious. What appears below the bar is more covert, latent, and unconscious. By a quarter turn in the model we create a different discourse which is to underscore how one can change into another quite fluidly. Having said that, we can construct the four discourses:

The discourse of the master:

$$\frac{S1}{\$} \rightarrow \frac{S2}{a}$$

Here, a sender of a message (the speaking agent who conveys master signifiers, an authoritative figure, a functionary with power, Sl), produces an enactment of knowledge by the other, S2. This builds on the master-slave dialectic of Hegel and Marx. In other words, the other produces a body of knowledge based on the implications of S1. They enact what is implicit; they make it explicit. Examples include: Althusser's theory of *interpellation;* the linguistic relativity principle; and a Marxist semiotic view from the structural interpellation framework, perhaps in combination with the discourse of the university (below). In law, formal rational law (formal rationality, see Weber) is an example. Consider colonizers, bringing some "truth," a body of knowledge (law, religion, education, politics, etc.), to a native or indigenous population.

For each example, note that something else is taking place at a more unconscious level (production): below the bar, in the lower right corner there results *le-plus-de jouir*, the little *"a."* In other words, something is left out, remains missing. This is the notion of *pas-toute* (not all, incompleteness). Consider the disenfranchised who bring their grievances to the court only to have it formulated (translated) by lawyers (S1) in the language of the courts (see, for example, Merry, 1985; Brigham, 1987; Salyer, 1989, 1991; Stacy, 1996; Bannister and Milovanovic, 1990). Also, note that the subject of desire ($) finds itself below the bar, but nevertheless supporting the master signifiers (S1) that inhere within them as their truth.

In law, Schroeder (2008), applying the discourse of the master, engages noted legal theorist H.L.A Hart (1961) seen as articulating a positivist jurisprudence (law as what is legislated as accepted practice). Here, the master signifier is positive law. Whereas Hart argues that law must be understood by its functioning, not by its content, Lacanian application would argue that content is always implicated in the form of the discourse of the university (ibid., 38) which justifies and legitimizes the form of law. In other words, we add, formal rational law practiced as a master signifier, must address justification principles for its existence to maintain legitimacy, as Weber would have it.

The discourse of the university:

$$\frac{S2}{S1} \rightarrow \frac{a}{\$}$$

Here we see some body of knowledge, S2, being enacted by the other who produces *le-plus-de jouir*. The agent proclaims, or draws from a body of dominant knowledge. The other is relegated to accepting and enacting this body of information based on unconscious, often unarticulated dogmatic truth claims (S1). For example, consider Newtonian compared to Einsteinian or quantum physics as underpinning ontological assumptions in the social sciences. Or, consider: legal knowledge that is communicated to a law student or practitioner; some overzealous revolutionaries that appear with some dogma (S2); formal education conveying more about white middle class culture and values than those of diverse segments of the population; and propaganda campaigns and brainwashing. The discourse of the university is, therefore, often conveyed by the discourse of the master. Consider a state bureaucrat or a lawyer who only recites formal rational language of their office (S2) to those serviced. Judicial opinions summarized in law books held in law libraries, that explain the verdict reached, is an example of the discourse of the university at work (see Schroeder, 2008: 54). What remains below the bar, as unconscious production, is the desiring subject. In other words, the subject is denied a full place (discursive subject-position) within which to find alternative forms of embodying desire *(a)*; they remain incomplete, *pas-toute*. They must enact S2. This continuous the discontent of the receiver *($)*, while inadvertently supporting S2. In the process, the subject reconstitutes dominant understanding and master signifiers. This clearly provides one mechanism whereby even subjects that find conditions exploitive continuously reproduce dominant ideology. And note that master signifiers exist as truth, acting as the support for S2. In other words, given some body of knowledge posing as legitimate or dominant knowledge (conventional wisdom), one can locate a number of often unarticulated, unconscious truth-claims upon which it is premised. Consider a student in law school presented with a body of knowledge (S2, legal signifiers, legal discourse) from which to construct understandings of social reality (see Arrigo, 1998a). They may find it personally objectionable given their own life experiences but must begin to think like a lawyer to advance. Ultimately, the discourse of the university rationalizes and justifies the existing order and the given rules and laws promulgated (see also Schroeder, 2008: 54).

Applying Lacanian logic, Schroeder argues that critical legal studies falls short and often: inadvertently reconstitutes the status quo in so much it fails to address the wherewithal of the split or divided subject ($): i.e., the entrance into the Symbolic Order and the primordial separation from the real; assumes that our notions of law and the legal subject could have alternative forms *but for* our conventional legal system; and that "an ideal of a complete and perfectly just law" could be realized (ibid., 58). In other words, overzealous revolutionaries could (re)create the discourse of the master and a justifying rhetoric (S2). Consider, for example, some forms of "political correctness," or reconstituted hierarchies and formal rationality in law remaining intact, now supporting and justifying the new "cause." Schroeder goes on to say "a true and sustainable critique of law comes not from within the university's discourse, but from the analyst's and hysteric's discourses" (ibid., 59).

The discourse of the hysteric:

$$\frac{\$}{a} \rightarrow \frac{S1}{S2}$$

Here the hysteric, $, (we read as not only the clinical type, but those who are alienated, in revolt, or in opposition), attempts to communicate their suffering or complaint to the other who only offers master signifiers (S1) as answers; in law, legal concepts and signifiers from which the "issue" can be constructed (i.e., articulated in law); for colonized, language they must use in addressing the courts and various state bureaucracies. For Schroeder (2008: 148), the practice of law, that is lawyer's representing clients, makes use of the discourse of the hysteric. Consider the everyday poor client before the court attempting to present their grievance. The offered master signifiers produce S2 in the receiver, or reconstitute a body of knowledge in so much as the offered categories fit into a larger body of conventionally understood knowledge. Master signifiers could be clinical diagnoses, stereotypes, clichés, deviant categories, or other linguistic categories that the media or bureaucratic organizations often provide and which are incorporated as "meaningful" summary representations of social reality. Consider, for example, a lower socio-economic client attempting to present their suffering, complaint or grievance to some bureaucratic official and the categories and discourses (S1) that will invariably be invoked (see Manning, 1988). Truth here is represented by *le-plus-de-jouir*. In other words, the subject in opposition finds themselves facing an excess, a feeling of despair, due to not having a more complete discourse within which to embody their desire. This is an inherent lack. They are denied the means of expression of truth.

The desiring subject ($) that appears above the bar can only reflect despair, alienation, or revolt to the other without the aid of precise signifiers representing their being. They are greatly limited in assuming their desire. This subject often finds themselves ultimately expressing despair in the prevailing dominant discourse in existence and hence, ironically, continuing their despairing state. Some might revert to a discourse of the master and attempt to impose their convoluted view of the world on others, as is the case in hate or revenge politics, political correctness, exorcism, and schmarxism. Here, Nietzsche's subject of *resentiment* has emerged.

The discourse of the analyst:

$$\frac{a}{S2} \rightarrow \frac{\$}{S1}$$

Here the analyst, or in our application to include revolutionaries, articulates an unsaid (a) to the other (hysteric, $, clinical and/or oppositional agents), whom, faced with new queries about their being, begins to reconstitute a new body of master signifiers (Sl). In other words, the analyst encourages the hysteric to produce alternative master signifiers that are more representative of their being and possibilities. Strategically invoked silence by the agent (analyst) is but another form of instigating the other to reformulate. In other words, what are produced in the hysteric are alternative anchorings ("capitonnage") of signifiers to signifieds as the hysteric comes to better realize their despair, or nature of revolt. These, in turn, support a body of knowledge (S2) developing in the analyst (i.e., a better understanding of what is being left out) and act as the truth that supports the mirrored information reflected in turn to the hysteric.[3] This mirrored information then becomes further information which the hysteric enacts by producing yet more master signifiers that better embody their unique and contextualized desire, and so forth. This dynamic could be seen at play in Paulo Freire's dialogical pedagogy (1973, 1985). The "analyst," or social change agent, or revolutionary, works with the "hysteric" (again more broadly defined than the clinical; to include people in struggle) as a catalyst, in producing a narrative that better reflects their unique desire (see Arrigo, 1998a).

Applications in law. Let us provide two examples in applying the four discourses to law:

(1) Stacy (1996) has explained how aboriginal women (the Ngarrindjeri) were denied a voice before the Australian courts. Their stories were not allowed expression in law; their stories were translated into legal narratives. For the courts, the aboriginal women were hysterics, did not have an identity formally recognized in law, and were provided the discourse of law (S2, Sl) from which to create their stories. In the discourse of the hysteric, the aboriginal women found themselves in the place of the sender of the message as $ (from above, the upper left corner) and were offered only master signifiers (Sl) or dominant legal signifiers with which to frame their narratives in law. This produced a body of knowledge, S2, which ultimately reflected dominant knowledges. This in turn left the aboriginal women *pas-toute* (lower left corner), incomplete, without a genuine voice. Their own unique experiences and understanding underwent transformation into the dominant linguistic coordinate system of law. The master discourse rendered them *pas-toute,* incomplete, before the law.

(2) Milovanovic (2002) comments on Lopez's (1992) Freire-driven analysis in his book, *Rebellious Lawyering,* as to how dominant legal discourse which alienates the clients before the courts can be transformed into an alternative discourse which empowers both the client and lawyers. It is furthered by applying Lacan's four discourses and chaos theory (to which we will return below) to indicate how the discourse of the hysteric in combination with the discourse of the analyst could provide moments in which an alternative discourse could emerge. That is, the everyday client before the law is often relegated to the discourse of the university (legal speak) and often becomes the recipient of the discourse of the master. A Freirean-driven approach, integrated with the four discourses and chaos theory, indicates an alternative interaction between

lawyer and client within which an alternative body of master signifiers could emerge. This becomes the basis of embodying desire in narratives that better reflect the unique desires of the client (we will return to the specific dynamics of this analysis below).

The fifth discourse, the discourse of the capitalist. Lacan in 1972 introduced a fifth discourse, the *discourse of the capitalist.* It remained undeveloped in his further work but has been the basis of much analysis (Vanheule, 2016; Bryant, 2008). It has been given a non-Marxist reading (Vanheule, 2016) as well as a Marxist reading (Bianchi, 2012; Bryant, 2008; Pavón-Cuéllar, 2011; Tomsic, 2015; Mura, 2015).[4]

$$\frac{\$}{S1} \qquad \frac{S2}{a}$$

In its Marxist version, it addresses both the logic of consumption *and* the logic of production. In its application to the logic of consumption, the capitalist injunction is "to access enjoyment at all costs ... which transforms social bonds based on desire into objectified and consumerist relations" (Mura, 2015: 162). Here: *$* represents the forever insatiated consumer, ever in search of enjoyment; S2, economic, scientific, and technological knowledge, what is often learned by the way of the media, advertising industry, experts, and talk, fashion, travel, cooking, and decorative shows (Bryant, 2008: 14); a, the surplus of enjoyment, here defined as an unbounded continuous search for illusory objects of desire that otherwise promise satisfaction that is never fully realized or never happens, much as in waiting for Godot; S1 as truth, as the answer to the agent's insatiated state, potential solutions, formulated by capital logic, with only one motif, "enjoy!," endless consumption, buying commodities and services at their exchange values in the marketplace, now cause of *$*'s motivations and actions. Capitalism exploits this circularity where the subject endlessly pursues pleasure that can never fully offer satisfaction overcoming the inherent lack.

Applicability to a sociology of law comes by way of first, revisiting Weber's stipulation of the association of capital logic with formal rational law, and thus indicating that formal rational law is but a mechanism that facilitate the operation of the discourse of capitalism. Howarth's (2018) "logics" may be recalled from the previous chapters, which included "fantasmatic logic," the work of the unconscious and its desires being interconnected with political and social logic, and we added, material (commodification) and legal logic (formal rationality). Thus, formal rational law assures the circularity of the discourse of the master; that all will continue to pursue otherwise insatiable desires, all exercising their attributed free will, but all subject to the disciplinary and normative-inducing institutions of a particular society. The "insoluble conflict" between principles of formal and substantive rationality can be traced to the inherent lack of the agent (*$*), a force that propels capital logic forward, grinding up dissidence, normalizing agent for their place in society as insatiable, but willing consumers.

We turn to the logic of production, *$* represents the worker reduced to a commodity in the marketplace selling only their labor but never attaining full realization of returns for their input; S2, know-how, technology and science that is set to work, performed, by the agent; a, profit, an incessant pursuit; S1, the owners of the means of production and their appropriation of the labor of the workers for ever more expansion and profits. In this circularity, capital logic continues its course toward ever expansion and maximization of profit. As sociologists of law, we are interested in how this fantasmatic logic is contained, shaped, and controlled by formal rational law. The insoluble conflict appears in the form of conflict, strikes, demonstrations, but capital logic responds with assimilation, deflection, punishment, and offering the avenues ever more toward illusory satisfactions. The rule of law must be maintained. Formal rational law as a logic is the grease on the axle.

Figure 2. Borromean Knot and Le Sinthome

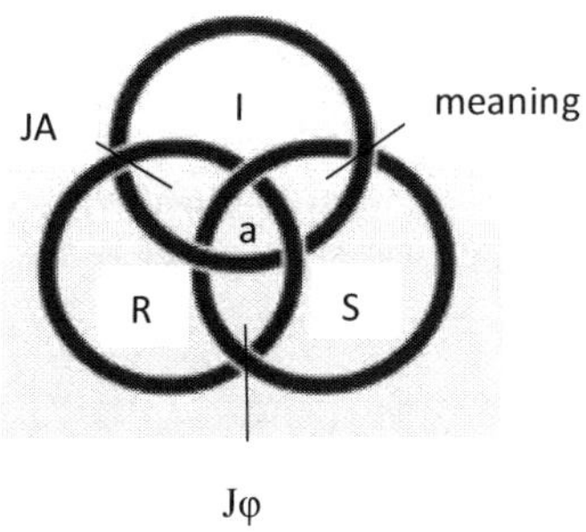

Le Sinthome

Borromean Knot

(Note how the circles, representing the Symbolic, Imaginary, and Real Orders, are intertwined where cutting one releases all of the others. Meaning exists between I and S; small a represents objects of desire; Jφ, phallicjouissance in a phallocentric order; JA, jouissance of the Other, in potentia.)

Adopted from Milovanovic (2003: 47)

Le Sinthome

(Note how le sinthome holds the three circles together. Examples of le sinthome include: name-of-the father, name-of-the-mother, juridic subject, the "reasonable intersectional person in law.")

Lacan's Late Work: Borromean Knots, Sinthome Law

Lacan was to begin to reformulate his thoughts in his late work, particularly beginning with Seminar 22 entitled *RSI* (1974–1975). He first introduces the topological construction of knot theory, the Borromean knot, to portray the three orders as joined circles, where a cut would produce their separation.[5] In their joining, relative stability is assured, that is consistency in reality for the agent; without it, madness. Mostly in Seminar 23, *Le Sinthome* (1975–76), he introduces a fourth order, *le sinthome* which acts to unify the three orders. Initially, he places the law-of-the-father, the phallus as a signifier of potency, in this role. But then he replaces the "law-of-the-father," the first law, more associated with the Symbolic Order, with Sinthome

Law where the Real Order now becomes more important (Harari, 2002; Murray, 2005; Ragland and Milovanovic, 2003). Elsewhere (Milovanovic, 2003), we have suggested that the juridic subject, the so-called "reasonable man in law," having traces to the law-of-the-father, can serve as le sinthome that ties the three Orders together, never totalizing, a formal rational logical and hence mechanistic subject, an ideology well-synchronized with capital logic. Alternatively, drawing from crits, a juridic subject could be based on the standard, "reasonable intersectional person." This recognizes intersectional identities and more complex vulnerabilities.

The fourth order is responsible for naming ("nomination"). Naming is creation. The Real, as unstructured and without law, that is chaotic, turbulent, and a sphere for emerging properties, a sphere of singularities, is populated not by signifiers, but by "letters." A letter "is how the real reveals itself ... has the status of singularity ... and ex-ists as something unique and singular that is beyond symbolic meaning but still can produce effects in meaning" (Murray, 2005: 221).[6] The mechanism for producing new signifiers out of letters is "suppletion," a naming. Further, "the real is chaos, but a chaos that can produce the sinthome that uniquely re-ties the real, symbolic and imaginary. It is, therefore, a real that should be understood not as the negative of all order, but as a productive disorder, which creates dynamic structures" (ibid., 222).

The upshot of all this for a sociology of law is that we are not imprisoned in Borromean knots that disallow innovation, creativity, new forms, but, through Sinthome Law with possible more liberating forms of law, we see new possibilities of being and becoming, leaps in which novel understandings emerge. Conventional formal rational law and its institutions can be named differently. And through alternative naming (signification) new relatively stable orders can be built. In other words, it provides a new mechanism that engenders new images of though (Murray, 223–30). Sinthome Law, for example could be an ethical law of care, commonwealth, substantive equality, etc.; see also the discussion on "the-law-of-the-mother" (Worthington, 2020; Morel, 2019). In a section below, we shall return to a dynamic systems approach and its inclusion of Sinthome Law and further indicating its implications in law. For example, Eugene Holland (2011), in *Nomad Citizenship*, has suggested an alternative image of thought in thinking in the social science based on an organization model that follows the principles of improvisation jazz, and its study, nomadology. It would suggest that formal rational law can be further rethought along the lines of substantive rational law where emergence and singularities are privileged that better reflect the diversity of human beings and their desires.

Lacanian Postmodern Feminist Law

Feminist perspectives in sociology of law, as we have seen from Chapter 7, have various forms of expression. Postmodern feminism, too, has various forms (for a lively summary, critique, and suggestions for modification, see Eichner, 2001; see also Rosenberg, 2019; for a critique by a founding and essentialist feminist, see MacKinnon, 2000). Here we want to focus on the Lacanian approach in postmodern feminism that was established in the 1970s, 80s and 90s. We are spending considerable detail in the work of Lacan justified by the significance his insights have had for postmodern analysis and feminist postmodern analysis in law in particular. Just as Karl Marx is a key thinker with whom critical scholars must come to terms particularly in understanding structure, postmodern analysis in law has Jacques Lacan, particularly with his positing the wherewithal of the agent.

Although undergoing significant critique in the 1990s (see especially, Eichner's summary, 2001), Lacanian thought still remains a source of much insight. Unlike most analysis in law that shies away from discussion of agency itself, Lacanian thought offers a rich, be it a complex and controversial engagement. To return to the literature that established much of this work, we must focus on key works during this era. Much of the early ground-breaking work was done by French feminists (see the overviews by Zakin, 2011; Grosz, 1990; Brennan, 1989). The first wave includes Luce Irigaray, Helen Cixous, Toril Moi, and Julia Kristeva. The second wave of leading figures in applying a Lacanian view for a sociology of law, from the feminist perspective, have been Drucilla Cornell (1993, 1998, 1999), Cornell and Friedman (2016), Teresa Brennan (1992, 1993), and Judith Butler (1990, 1993, 1997a, 1997b, 1999, 2015). Third wave postmodernist feminist have built on the first two waves developing nuanced perspectives such as queer theory.

A return to Lacan follows numerous critiques of the Freudian model (see for example, Beauvoir, 1989), in arguing against the law-of-the-father based on the biological differences of having (or not) the penis. Lacan's work de-biologizes Freud by focusing on the paternal metaphor, the signifier for the "law-of-the-father" that emerges more from the Symbolic Order and the initial castration from the Real experienced by all in the entrance into the Symbolic Order (see Zakin, 2011; McNulty, 2020). In this move, there is a shift to critique of the phallocentric order, its wherewithal, and possibilities for alternatives.

A person assuming the masculine discursive subject-position may experience a phallic *jouissance,* the upper limit within the phallic symbolic order. Women, on other hand, are not imprisoned within this function; they have a privileged access to a *bodily jouissance.* However, there exists no stable language that embodies this form of jouissance — it is unspeakable. Hence, Lacan's seemingly outlandish statement: "woman does not exist." She essentially "lacks" within the dominant phallic symbolic order. She is *pas-toute* (not all).

She does, however, experience another *jouissance* beyond the phallic function, a *bodily jouissance* or the *jouissance of the Other.* Whereas phallic *jouissance* is found at the confluence of the Symbolic and Real Orders; the *jouissance* of the Other is found at the intersection of the Imaginary and Real Order. Lacan gives examples of the words of the poet or mystic (see also Lecercle's notion *délire,* 1985). At best, this sense can only be half-said *(mi-dire).* He does not go further to draw out the implications for transformative politics.

Lacan's analysis concerning the nature of the phallic symbolic order, that gender roles are created in the Symbolic Order, and the fact that women are *pas-toute,* but yet have access to a different form of *jouissance,* supported the development of an *écriture féminine* (woman's writing). But this could lead to various strategies.

Essentialists support the development of an entirely new Symbolic Order that recognizes the uniqueness of being a woman. After all, the argument went, if one cannot establish some "foundational truth" then a transformative politics could not be carried through. It is claimed that only in the overthrow of the phallocentric symbolic order and its replacement by one that recognizes women's writings *(écriture féminine)* can emancipation take place. The non-essentialist theorists, however, argued that this could, without more, lead to a "reversal of hierarchies": the form of domination would still remain (Cornell, 1999: 11, 139, 185).

Accordingly, strategies for change in society and law are being developed that are sensitive to *not* reinventing hierarchy nor to fueling forms of revenge politics (as Cornell has attributed to MacKinnon, 1999: 139). And here there is much agreement by the postmodern feminists with the critical race theorists that a useful strategy to pursue is a "post-essentialist" alternative (see Harris, 1991).

Based on the considerable internal debate concerning *standpoint,* many from this perspective have now grounded their epistemology and transpraxis on the experiential dimension of oppressive feminine experiences, but with a qualification centered on the contingent and provisional nature of political commitments, which are always subject to critical evaluation and possible revision (see, for example, Bartlett, 1991; Currie, 1993; Arrigo, 1993a). In other words, rather than arguing for the existence of some "foundational" position that is somehow objective and transhistorical and trans-cultural, or rather than arguing for relativism, this position sees, at best, provisional and contingent political commitments that are rooted in historical conditions and political economies with their attendant manifest hierarchies and exploitive practices. A further qualification has to do, as we saw in Chapter 7, with the question of intersectionality, and particularly with how it has broadened understanding of diverse disenfranchised groups, but has also, be it inadvertently, reduced engagement with the key developers of the term and black feminist legal theory (Kupupika, 2021).[7]

Grant has well argued the position that if we merely rely on the experiential and supposed unique position that women find themselves in as the wherewithal of the development of a unified transformative politics, we have overlooked the critically important factor that a subject constructs a perspective by the use of certain, pregiven lenses (1993: 107, 125; Kerruish, 1991: 177–193). Indeed, this is a constitutive process (Hunt, 1993; Harrington and Yngvesson, 1990). Said in another way, agents in a society always appear on the scene with internalized perspectives and background assumptions as guides to social activity and co-produce conceptions of social reality. And this is an important limitation in transformative politics. As Grant tells us, "without a feminist interpretive lens through which to see and reinvent gender, the idea of a standpoint of women will always be essentialist" (1990: 109). Very precisely, she informs us that "the question is what possibilities are immanent in this current reality, and this cannot be based on the experiences of the oppressed woman, but on the feminist revision of what woman can be" (ibid., 116). Let us turn to two founding exponents, Drucilla Cornell and Judith Butler.

Drucilla Cornell. Given the existence of legal abstractions such as the juridic subject, linear forms of reasoning, circumscribed codifications of signifieds, dualistic conceptualizations of social reality, and forms of hate or revenge politics historically inherent in many "humanistic" movements—all of which support hierarchy—genuine change can only take place by way of a *transpraxis.* We turn to Cornell's work (1998, 1993, 1999) and with Stephen Sealy (2016) which has focused on the Imaginary Order that opens a vista as to what could be.

Accordingly, the imaginary order must also be integral to a transformative politics. Cornell (1998), for example, has suggested various strategies to expand and protect the imaginary domain. As she suggests, "the imaginary domain is the space of the 'as if' in which we imagine who we might be if we made ourselves our own end and claimed ourselves as our own person" (ibid., 8). Thus, for Cornell, metaphors are especially in need of reconceptualization, particularly those that maintain traditional forms of domination.

Cornell's (1993, 1999) extraordinary synthesis of Lacan's psychoanalysis, Luhmann's notion of autopoiesis, postmodern feminist's perspectives and Derrida's deconstructive epistemology has emphasized the imaginary elements for potential change (see also Murray, 1986; Arrigo, 1992: 24–27; Ricoeir, 1973: 111; Brennan, 1993). Media studies have also brought out how certain images are culturally derived and sustained (Silverman, 1983; Williamson, 1987; Newman, 1993; Barak, 1993, 1994). Cornell has also partly integrated Lacan's other two Orders. She has provided an insightful analysis of the wherewithal of alternative imaginary constructions (for a critique of Cornell's work, see Eichner, 2001).

Cornell builds particularly upon Irigaray's idea of *mimesis* (1999: 147–152), by which subordination is disrupted and transformed into an affirmation, and on Cixous' idea of the "retelling of the myth" (ibid., 178), in developing the wherewithal of a "utopian thinking" (ibid., 169). As she explains it: "utopian thinking demands the continual exploration and re-exploration of the possible and yet also the unrepresentable" (ibid.). In other words, the imaginary constituted by the metaphoric and metonymic functions always implies a slippage, an excess (what Lacan refers to as *le plus de jouir*) especially apparent in myths. "[I]deology," Grant tells us, "leaves some critical space" (1993: 116). Given this "space" or "slippage," consider Cornell's view: "Without the aesthetic evocation of utopian possibility of feminine difference, we are left with the politics of revenge ... the politics of feminism needs its poetry (ibid., 185]." And consider Arrigo (1992: 26):

> Precisely because the myth is a story, its beginnings are born in the imagination's capacity to conceive of and describe on-going, lived experience in intimately meaningful ways ... The work of experiential feminism through myth is to render the telling of narratives that more authentically depict the experience of women and the situations in which they find themselves.

In recreating myths, we are in the position of creating an "elsewhere." According to Cornell's read of Cixous, "[w]e re-collect the mythic figures of the past, but as we do so we reimagine them. It is the potential variability of myth that allows us to work within myth, and the significance it offers, so as to reimagine our world and by so doing, to begin to dream of a new one" (ibid., 178). In this way, an affirmative politics of the feminine can begin to emerge that is also utopian in trying to point to an elsewhere (ibid., 182, 200). As she states:

> consciousness-raising must involve creation, not just discovery. We need our poetry, our fantasies and our fables; we need the poetic evocation of the feminine body in Irigaray and in Cixous if we are to finally find a way beyond the muteness imposed by a gender hierarchy in which our desire is "unspeakable" (ibid., 201).

Cornell argues against standards based on formal equality where equality is defined by comparison with men. She (1998: 11) advocates, rather, "equivalent evaluation" which includes two foci: "a demand for women's inclusion in the moral community of persons" (e.g., establishing free and equal standing); and "a demand for fair, and thus, equitable treatment whenever our sexual difference need to be taken into account." Thus, action must be directed toward defining "what scope of rights, opportunities, and social goods would be needed to maintain freedom and equality" (ibid., 20). One's sexuality is valued without subordination (see also Rosenbury, 2019).

Cornell co-authored with Stephen Sealy in *The Spirit of Revolution* (2016), in arguing that recent thought jettisoning discussions of human agency is not productive for genuine revolutionary change. Revolutionary change must simultaneously engage two axes: a horizontal focused on transforming present variety of capitalism, and a vertical axis, focused on a political spirituality. The focus is on caring relationships that should also extend to non-human forms. Engaging with the late work of Foucault, they argue "transformation demands ... new forms of conducting ourselves individually and with others through new ways of relating to who we imagine ourselves to be" (ibid., 79). And this will be attained in struggle with no blue-print as a goal.

Judith Butler. Judith Butler is a central second wave theorist applying a feminist postmodern analysis to law. She argues that gender does not exist prior to its enactment in performative discursive practices. In other words, by assuming a gendered discursive subject-position and engaging in discourse based on it one constitutes the gender role in action. Repetition in performative discursive practice both produces and reproduces the discursive subject positions. She also has suggested a practice for subverting repetition. This entails strategies of intervention and contestation (Butler, 1993: 147; see also 1993: 187–222; 1997a: 86–95, 102; 1997b: 83–105; 1999; 2020). It also acknowledges the "contingent" nature of discursive formations (1990: 192, 202; 2000: 136–179). She argues for the development of an alternative language (2000: 179): "a language between languages will have to be found.... It will be the labour of transaction and translation which belongs to no single site, but is the movement between languages, and has it final destination in this movement itself."

Earlier, we had indicated two other strategies: reversal of hierarchies and standpoint epistemologies. Both, for postmodernist feminists in law, fall short of a bonafide strategy for change. Thus, for Butler, contingent universalities is a position that argues for the possibilities of establishing tentative "universalities," common platforms for political change, but also recognizes their contingent nature. They are continuously subject to reflection, revisions, and substitution as socio-historical conditions present novel moments.

Alternative directions. Much of this notion of social change sits well with the work of Laclau and Mouffe (Laclau, 1990, 1996; Laclau and Mouffe, 1985; Smith, 1998) with their view that traditional Marxist's reliance on "class" is outdated, for, new groupings are continuously developing, each with unique standpoints and epistemologies, that vary in their ideological positions over time. The political economy, too, can be conceived of as structurally undecidable in so much as it is in continuous change. And identities in this view are constantly in states of change: "social agents are becoming more and more 'multiple selves,' with loosely integrated and unstable identities ..." (Laclau, 1996: 99; see also Cornell, 1998: 183). Struggles, too, are multiple in form (Laclau, ibid., 101). Postmodernist feminists are beginning to look more carefully at possible integrations between the work of Irigaray and Deleuze and Guattari (to whom we shall return below), particularly as to how bodies are constituted in political economy (Grosz, 1994; Lorraine, 1999).

There have been ambivalent feelings by some postmodernist feminists in embracing the work of Michel Foucault. For example, Howe (1994: 170), citing his work favorably in the context of prison struggles, and echoing a weak position within standpoint epistemology, says "all we can do, apparently, is to help create the conditions which permit prisoners to speak for themselves," and, continuing, "appreciate the fact that only those directly concerned can speak in a practical way on their own behalf" (Foucault, cited in Howe, ibid.). Howe, however, counters this, in so much as since "Foucault's framework was masculinist, the strategies he had in mind privileged the men's prison struggle" (ibid., 209). Thus, the role of the cultural revolutionary becomes critical in various struggles in working together with the disenfranchised allowing the "subaltern" to speak.

Other suggestions have been offered. Haraway (1991) asks us to imagine a "postgender world" where the subject is constituted by "transgressed boundaries, potent fusions, and dangerous possibilities" (ibid., 150–199). It is a conceptualization of the agent as forever unfixed and contingent. In Lacan's late work we saw how le sinthome and sinthome law (Murray, 2005) suggests a movement away from the-law-of-the-father. Morel (2019; see also Worthington, 2020; Verhaeghe and Declercq, 2002), as we previously saw, suggested an engagement with the "law-of-the-mother" which in turn leads to other "fourth rings" that may unite the three orders, opening the field to queer studies, for example, and alternative forms of jouissance (Roussell, 2020; Baitinger, 2019; Cavanagh, 2019; Dean, 2006). It concerns the invention of new signifiers that knot the three orders and connects to new forms of *jouissance.*

Another suggestion is for a *relational law* (Feldman, 2017; see also Rosenbury, 2017). Feldman argues some postmodernists, in their onslaught on modernist thought, undermine the possibility of agency, struggle, and possibilities for deliberate change, on the one hand, and, on the other hand, ironically, return to the determinism which they criticize by positing overpowering social forces that account for all action, thus limiting feminist support. She argues that a relational account of agency liberates us from both constraints. A relational account moves us away from the modernist privileging of a self-centered agent, acknowledges intersectional dynamics, an emergent self, and that particular relations can either limit or enable. She draws, as an example, some literature that builds on Foucault with the metaphor of a surfer, "we can navigate power the way a surfer rides a wave," but qualifying it with the idea of surfing together, relationally, rather than alone (Feldman, 291). Given our capabilities of being able to distinguish positive enabling relations over limiting relations, real social change can develop (ibid., 292). She then, with Nedelsky (2011), argues for new forms of law: "we should stop conceiving constitutional rights as protecting atomistic individuals from state power ... we should envision rights as facilitating constructive and creative relationships and protecting against destructive or distorting relationships" (ibid., 293).

Finally, we highlight Eichner's (2001) erudite critique and suggestions for change that remains current. She has four suggestions (ibid., 64–77): (1) "[T]hat power relations reproduce themselves through, rather than apart from, social relations"; (2) the "importance of seeking more fluid notions of gender identity that are less closely linked to a particular sex"; (3) "distinguish[ing] between traits and characteristics it seeks to revalue and those it seeks to make disappear through the elimination of oppression"; (4) and a "postmodernist feminism based on differences and heterogeneity must ultimately be grounded in a politics of material equality."

Contributions to Postmodern Perspectives in Law

Introduction

In this section we want to canvass various approaches in postmodern law, more the second wave from which much engagement, critique and application builds toward a sociology of law. We find Litowitz's (1997) short book a useful beginning. It still remains an excellent foundational book on key postmodern thinkers, including Nietzsche, Foucault, Derrida, Lyotard, and Rorty. He considers these as the foundational thinkers for those who do subsequent postmodern analysis in law. We will add the work of Deleuze and Guattari. Although they did not specifically apply their work to law, we can draw out various implications. Lacan's work still remains fundamental in understanding postmodern theory. We further include chaos theory (dynamic systems theory) and constitutive theory. Litowitz stresses that many postmodern philosophers in law are doing *outsider* critique; they are looking at broader factors in law's production, compared to *insider* critique where law is generally accepted by lawyers and judges and the task is evaluation from within (formal legalism, "black letter law," analytic jurisprudence, etc.). Litowitz's goal is to evaluate each author for their possible contributions to a "positive jurisprudence," an affirmative postmodern law; that is, contributing to a normative theory as guidance for law-making, rather than just critique ("negative jurisprudence," e.g., antifoundationalism), affirmative postmodernism as opposed to the nihilistic, negative postmodernism.

Friedrich Nietzsche (1844–1900)

Nietzsche's work continues to by engaged in various disciplines. Less so in a sociology of law, although he did not develop a systematic statement on law. He critiqued both natural law and legal foundationalism (Litowitz, 1999: 42–64; see also Mootz and Goodrich, 2008; Goodrich and Valverde, 2005; Riley, 2009; Yovel, 2005). His core assumption is the "will to power," not to be confused with domination over others, although Hitler attempted to do so to justify his regime; more concerned about a life-affirming power, a quest for continuous "self-overcoming," self-exploration, and "self-mastery." Thus, existing law can be evaluated to the extent that it promotes or hinders these forces (Litowitz, ibid.), the goal, a "law of life." And "rights can only be affirmed as a human creation, as a necessary, life-affirming postulate" (ibid., 49). So, in this view, contrary to many, he is not a nihilist. In his view, law too often bases its legitimacy on natural law, a reference to God, nature, essences. These are, for Nietzsche, superstitions, fictions, myths driven by interest and power groups that hold back the full realization of human potential. Law is not discoverable, but a human creation. Creation entails interpretive processes of representation, much of which are also semiotic fictions. At best we can establish temporary postulates that are contingent, provisional, experimental. Thus, no foundations exist; law is always in movement, the ideal, a law of life that maximizes the will to power, increasing human capabilities (ibid).

As to Nietzsche's possible contributions to a positive jurisprudence, his work is more suggestive of what needs to be changed. It remains for the activist practitioners to translate his theory into affirmative legal practices.

Michel Foucault (1926–1984)

Foucault's work has been, and continues to be inspirational for a diverse group of legal scholars. He builds on Nietzsche. Although he did not write a book focused exclusively on law, extensive application by his adherents of his various dedicated sections has made his contributions center piece (see for example, Hunt and Wickham, 1994; Golder and Fitzpatrick, 2009, 2010; Golder, 2021; Litowitz, 1999; Martire, 2017; O'Malley and Valverde, 2021; Valverde, 2017; Woolhander, 2014). Remaining still as a clear exposition of his applications to law is Litowitz's essay (1999: 65–86). We draw extensively from him in the following section.

Although the Enlightenment witnessed a heightened interest in law, order, and rights as a response to the earlier dark ages, proclaiming a victory of reason, Foucault shows how a new insidious form of control has emerged that runs parallel with explicitly articulated law. The legal system emerging from the Enlightenment was based on social contract theory (Hobbes, Locke, Rousseau). But it also arose as a response to the rise of monarchical powers at the end of the Middle Ages and their need to govern (see Litowitz's summary, 1999). The Roman legal system of abstract law was also embraced as a natural fit for governance. (Recall, too, Weber's notion of a "confluence of forces" responsible for the emergence of formal rational law.) A new discourse of rights emerged. This was the focus of Foucault's study on "governmentality," the pursuit of efficient governance in society. Free will, contracts, state power, and the rule of law were now legitimizing principles in society. The ideal of the "individual" emerged: "the individual is no doubt the fictitious atom of an 'ideological' representation of society; but he is also a reality fabricated by the specific technology of power that I have called 'discipline'" (Foucault cited in Litowitz, 1999: 70).

Power is exercised in state law, but it is also exercised at the "capillaries," administrative, regulatory, work rules, etc.[8] The disciplinary mechanism of observation, correction and normalization are brought to bear in not only the military and prisons but factories, hospitals, and schools. A world of monitoring, assessing, classifying, categorizing, regulating and normalizing is upon us. Subjects are even encouraged to discipline themselves with a myriad of supports (e.g. self-help) in the media. Subjects are rendered more and more docile and agents of utility. The self that emerges is shaped at the intersection of all the power and rules to which they are subject, both in state form as well as at the capillaries. Disciplinary power is the new form of control. Hence, a new form of domination emerged that belies the newfound liberties of the Enlightenment. While at the same time jurists were busy at work articulating and systematizing formal rights of liberty, equality, proprietorship, and due process, the disciplines were undermining them in the creation of the panoptic society of surveillance, control and normalization, especially based on the new sciences that emerged at the end of the 19th century (Foucault, 1977a). In this emerging society, private spaces begin to disappear as all is brought within the disciplinary powers. It is increasingly difficult to resist power because it is everywhere.

Foucault's work identifies a historical movement away from a law that punishes the external body in penology to examining and correcting the very soul of the deviant, its internal state, a "bio-power" (1977a). Determining guilt alone no longer suffices. One is queried as to why they did it (Foucault, 2014), and the confession becomes of paramount value.

The discourse of formal rational law—neutrality, objectivity, rationality, free will, justice, equality—now is seen as self-evident in arriving at correct decisions. The question of their origination, however, recedes into the background. Now, even in struggle one must employ the discourse of formal rational law and hence continue their own domination in law. How is one to struggle? How does one resist? From where can the subaltern speak, echoing Spivak? Foucault offers only the importance of establishing "new forms of rights" and "relational rights" that are outside of disciplinary mechanisms and the discourse of formal rational law, but does not give us more. He most explicitly defines the latter as "the right to gain recognition in an institutional sense for the relations of one individual to another individual" (Foucault cited in Litowitz, 83; Golder, 2015; Golder and Fitzpatrick, 2009: 123). In his late work, he also offers the importance for an "ethics of self-mastery": "we have to create ourselves as a work of art" (Foucault cited in Litowitz, 83). For Litowitz, however, Foucault does not provide for a positive jurisprudence, but only a critical discourse of how subjects are constituted, but no grounds on which resistance can be established.

Golder and Fitzpatrick (2009: 75–76, 112), on the other hand, argue that power and resistance work together; resistance is a force that produces change, which in turn will be subject to new resistance, etc. A personal ethics can be situated in struggle and becoming (ibid., 112–130) and the self is now assumed as relational, that is, constituted in relation to another. In this struggle a person, in an ethics of self-mastery, can re-create, re-invent, and engage, echoing Nietzsche, an overcoming of self. Persons, then, in their relational struggles, enhance "relationships of differentiation, of creation, of innovation" and create "a multiplicity of relationships with others" (Foucault cited in ibid., 120). The implication being, out of this new form of rights, relational rights have opportunities to emerge along with emerging identities.

Jacques Derrida (1930-2004)

Derrida continues to be a highly influential in sociology of law. His is more an external critique. Previously (Chapter 6) we had the occasion to express some of his ideas concerning deconstruction, reversal of hierarchies, différance, free play of the text, and anti-foundationalism. Here we want to engage two of his more explicit texts on applications to law: "Declarations of Independence (1989)," and "Force of Law" (1986). There has been a considerable discussion of his application to law (Legrand, 2016; Goodrich *et al.*, 2008; Gledinning, 2016; Magalhães and Magalhães, 2017; Direk, 2014; Ville, 2007; Cornell, 1992). Litowitz (1997: 87–108) provides an accessible and useful summary and critique of his key ideas.

In "Declarations of Independence" he sets out to deconstruct often appearing self-evident declarations that found law. Consider the U.S. Declaration of Independence and referencing "laws of nature" and "nature's God" as founding principles. Consider: "all men are endowed by their Creator with certain unalienable Rights, that among these are Life, Liberty, and the pursuit of Happiness." Derrida insists these are proclamations founded on mythical foundations and based on violence in so much as some views were declared others were not. Consider, for example, the background of the "founding fathers" of the U.S. Constitution — white, male, property owners, in many cases slave owners, and upper class. Founding principles often rest on reference to God, nature, reason, and logic, but each in turn can be deconstructed as mythical, illusory. They are, nevertheless, justifications (legitimizing principles) continuously reinforced in legal practice.

In "Force of Law" Derrida makes a clear distinction between law and justice. Traditional thinking, and legal positivists, have it that if laws are followed, if similar procedures are applied, the outcome is just. Derrida separates the two. Justice, drawing from Emmanuel Levinas, is an infinite duty of care to the other. It is incalculable, irreducible, unreachable, unconditional and unrepresentable. It is "an incalculable duty to speak to the other in the other's language, to give to the other without expectation of return" (Litowitz, 1997: 107). It is an ethical duty that can never be attained but must be attempted. It is much like a gift that does not demand return. Law, on the other hand, is person-made, a concept, a fiction installed by force. Standards of legality are connected with the original mythical foundations of established law. Thus, it is deconstructable, unlike justice. Law requires some conception of justice to be incorporated into rules and procedures. It is more about calculation and economics. Justice is much like a gift; in retrying to repay in kind, one enters, however, economic utility, calculation, equity, law. It is at the moment of decision-making in law that justice and law intertwine. Sometimes the judge is mechanical, following formal rational principles, applying deductive logic, making strict use of precedents, citing "original intent"; at other times, a judge may pause to consider justice implications, not necessarily bound in the particular law in question. It is in the latter that leaps, creations, take place in which new law is founded.[9] As Litowitz (ibid., 96) sums up: "Jurisprudence requires an impossible and overwhelming task: to translate incalculable justice into calculable rules, to 'codify' an obligation that is beyond codes." This tension, as we previously have seen, has also been defined as the "insoluble conflict" by Weber, between principles of formal and substantive rationality in law.

The value of Derrida's work in sociology of law is for highlighting often neglected questions of founding positions in law. Others, such as Rawls (2001) and Habermas (1984, 1987), have attempted to ground just law with statements of, respectively, an original position or ideal speech situation, in which all are in a position of equality, from which principles can be established. Derrida would question whether justice can be embodied in *any* rule or law. It would seem that his position is better for critical investigations than for advocating concrete proposal for changing law, critiques that not only deconstruct the mythical foundations on which law rests, but offering heightened consideration of an ethics of justice that seeks better articulation and incorporation in law, even though not reachable in finished form. In so much as he does offer an ethical duty of care to the other, he cannot be considered a nihilist.[10]

Jean-Francois Lyotard (1924–1998)

Lyotard's contributions to a critical examination of the legal system were presented, be they indirectly, in three books, *The Postmodern Condition* (1984), *Just Gaming* (1999), and *The Differend* (1988). Litowitz's book (1999) remains a clear-headed and accessible initial understanding of Lyotard's work and its weaknesses and strengths. For a dictionary of Lyotard's key terms, see Sim (2011).

Lyotard attacks all forms of consensus in that they do violence to those who are not represented (*differend*). He sees "grand narratives," a dominant discourse,[11] as overlooking multiple groups and distinct discourses of each based on custom, habits, form of life, and shared understandings. The latter are "petit narratives," or small narratives, each with their own logic, each with an understanding of how the world is. We thus have a "multiplicity of narratives" and a "multiplicities of justices" where movement from one to another produces incommensurability. Identities are constructed within each of the discourses, or "phase regimes," what Wittgenstein referred to as "language games" (1958). Each phase regime is a game in the sense that indigenous rules prevail. Justice is thus local and multiple, it escapes any universalization. Consider: a worker-boss relationship game, teacher-student relationship game, bank customer-bank teller relationship game, tenant-landlord relationship game, defendant-lawyer relationship game, etc. In each context, a set of rules prevails in constructing a particular reality. Reality is constructed differently within each.

No principle can be overarching, nor a universal representation for the variety of phase regimes in existence. To attempt to do so is to do violence to differences, a "terrorism" defined as reducing a person in terms of recognition, rendering them differend. "Every one of us," Lyotard (1999: 95) argues, "belongs to several minorities, and what is important, none of these prevails. It is only then that we can say that the society is just." For Lyotard, disenfranchised peoples are rendered without voice when one narrative gains ascendancy. Thus, universal rights, or principles of formal equality would be seen as terroristic in so much as they subsume differences under sameness. They silence minorities.

As an antidote, one must always listen to otherwise silenced voices in *their* language; one must always be prepared to experiment and create new understandings particularly "at the limits of what the rules permit, in order to invent new moves" (1999: 100). One is reminded about standpoint epistemology in feminist analysis and intersectionality in critical race theory. Counter storytelling is but the yearnings of disenfranchised peoples to tell a different story. Consider, for example, aboriginal people, whom before the law were disenfranchised in not being able to cite oral history until "native title" was proclaimed as legitimate in law. Consider, also a lower socio-economic defendant or litigant before the law attempting to articulate their position, only to have it translated into a dominant legal discourse within which they remain differend, or to use Lacan, "not-all" (pas-toute).

There has been a considerable critical engagement with Lyotard's work. Litowitz (1997) remains essential initial reading (see also Dunn, 1993). Lyotard has been criticized for: not providing a criteria or standard by which we can weigh and judge differences between groups, and if so, how can judgment take place?; reducing human identities to constraints in discourse; offering no overarching principle of justice for societal stability; inadvertently justifying the continued existence of hate groups;[12] providing no guidance as to a better law and political economic systems;[13] and not providing concrete proposals for a positive jurisprudence, to name a few.

On the positive leger, Lyotard offers many critical conceptual tools in understanding: the importance of recognition and participation given the uniqueness of being human within contextualized space; how both stability and possibilities of change can exist, the latter at the limits of the boundaries with other groups where creativity, innovation and new forms of narratives and discourse may emerge; how many voices are rendered *differend*, with limited avenues of expression in dominant forms; the necessity for recognition and participation so that the "subaltern" can speak in their own voice; how social contract theory (Lock, Hobbes, Rousseau) advocacy of the social contract and consensus is not necessarily, by itself, liberatory; that his work is a useful "check" on existing law to lay the foundations for change; that legal history can be better informed in that, for example, the awareness that the male, white, middle class voice has been dominant at the expense of other histories (Litowitz, ibid., 133); in short, a "war on totality" (Lyotard, 1984: 82).

Richard Rorty (1931–2007)

Rorty has combined pragmatism with European postmodern thought. He has been described as a "postmodern pragmatist" (Allen, 2008, 2013).[14] His work has been subject to much discussion and application to law (Malachowski, 2020; Janack, 2010; Ranberg, 2009; Barreto, 2011; Litowitz, 1997). Pragmatism has a long history going back to the mid- to late-1800s (Legg and Hookway (2021) and often drawing from C.S. Peirce. Generally, pragmatism is more concerned about concrete action, use, applications, and outcomes than abstract principles, rigid rules and formal law. Rorty is inspired, amongst others, by Nietzsche, Hegel, Derrida, Lyotard, and Levinas. Major work from which a "Rortian jurisprudence" can be developed include his book length, *Contingency, Irony, and Solidarity* (1989) and from three articles (1990, 1992, 1993). Much of his pragmatism is in tune with the legal realists and the philosophers William James and John Dewey.

Similar to most postmodernists, he dismisses universal, abstract claims as the basis of law, any possibility of establishing objective standards, the ability of formal rationality to engage real human issues, and judge's decision-making based on syllogistic reasoning, precedents, rationality and reason. His approach, concerns antifoundationalism, contingency, pragmatism, human creation, experimentation, and irony. Not the past, but human practices and struggles in the present is the focus, in a world of constant change. His ideal citizen is a liberal ironist, who must act in the present but always acknowledging things can be otherwise, nothing is static, that universal applications are myths. The cultural hero is the "strong poet rather than the warrior, the priest, the sage or the truth-seeking 'logical,' 'objective' scientist" (Rorty, 1989: 53).

The ideal judge should be a "good profit," a visionary, in-tune with struggles of the age, willing to make "leaps" beyond that which is written in law, denying the static nature of law, focusing on the pragmatics of human encounters, always eager to create rather than discover, result-oriented, problem-solver, not blind follower of abstractions and deductive, linear logic, but engaged in progressive, be it piecemeal social engineering. Experimentation is valued in moving toward just, living laws. The judge as a good profit is sensitive to Weber's insoluble conflict between principles of formal and substantive rationality, but always receptive, in good faith, to incorporate substantive principles. A rigid judge is one who, to use existentialist Jean Paul-Sartre, acts in bad faith, and one who is, to borrow from Freud, in a state of denial for their actions. Such cases as *Brown v. Board of Education* (1954), *Roe v. Wade* (1973), *Griswold v. Connecticut* (1965) in the U.S., *Mabo v. Queensland* (1992) in Australia, and in Canada, *Delgamuukw v. British Columbia* (1997) and *Tsilhgot'n Nation v. British Columbia* (2014)—all represent a leap in contested areas of affirmative action, right to privacy, and indigenous rights (Native Title). But acknowledged is the danger that things can go both ways: *Dred Scott v. Sanford* (1857), *Plessy v. Ferguson* (1896), *Korematsu v. U.S.* (1944).

Rorty has also addressed the question of human rights (1993; Barreto, 2011). They should not be based on conceptions of human nature and natural law, nor rigidly entombed in law. They should be contingent, building on sympathy and solidarity, as a response to human suffering and pain, acknowledging their contingent, contextualized and historical manifestations. They are rooted in caring for the stranger, of differences as well as sameness. Human rights can be based more on visceral feelings of disgust to all forms of cruelty, every situation where pain, suffering, and humiliation is being caused (Barreto, 104). Human rights should acknowledge "emotions, imagination and fantasy" as legitimate concerns along with reason (ibid.), contrary to their expelling by Kant and his imperative of "obedience to universal rules of pure practical reason," more Hume and his concern for the sentiments as a key player (ibid., 105), an ethics of emotions. What needs to be done is to cultivate an ethos of concern, sympathy, compassion, understanding the other, including the stranger, the capability to experience the other's joys and sorrows much in line with Emmanuel Levinas, an increased capability of placing oneself "in the shoes of those despised and oppressed" (Rorty, 1993: 126–127; Barreto, 107), an ethos that would contribute to human solidarity. All this *along with* reason, defined as a "willingness to talk about things" (Rorty cited in Barreto, 107), and rationality, understood as "conversable." Barreto reads Rorty as advocating story-telling and narratives, away from theory and abstractions, where sympathy and understanding are expressed for those experiencing cruelty, humiliation, pains, abuse. Cultivating sympathy for the other both increases a person's capabilities, and contributes to furthering social solidarity. Addressing political economy, his ideal is democratic socialism, neither the far left or right will do.

As with other theorists, critical engagement with Rorty's work is abundant (as a beginning, see particularly Litowitz, 1997: 15–153; see also Weaver, 1992). Questions include defining grounds for deciding hard cases in law; their timing and direction; form of protections against bad cases; and adequacy of contextualization of oppressed groups.

Gilles Deleuze (1925–1995)

The influence of Deleuze continues to be extensive in numerous disciplines.[15] Although he would have reservations with being identified as a postmodernist, nevertheless he has been adopted as one of the key thinkers. His work has also become central in post postmodern thought. He often wrote with Felix Guattari. Their earlier work, *Anti-Oedipus* (1977) and *A Thousand Plateaus* (1987), was initiated as a polemic against the notion of a castrated subject of a symbolic order, that is driven by an inherent lack to which desire is mobilized, to posit, rather, desire as active production, a becoming, a continued differentiation toward higher form of unity and capabilities.[16] Capitalism, they argue, manipulates and induces lack to maintain capital logic and exploitation.[17] Here we will focus on Deleuze and his contributions to law, jurisprudence and human rights. Most of his statements on law took place in interviews. In an interview, he said, "I have always been fascinated about jurisprudence, about law ... If I hadn't studied philosophy, I would have studied law ..." (cited in Marneros, 2019: 1). There exist many texts applying Deleuze to law (see for example, Braidotti *et al.*, 2009; Lefebvre, 2005, 2008, 2012; Marneros, 2019; McGee, 2012; Milovanovic, 2007; Moore, 2007; Murray, 2006, 2013; Mussawir, 2011; Sutter and McGee, 2012). Deleuze's study of law begins with "images of thought," internalized images of the wherewithal of law and its supporting assumptions. His task is to develop an alternative image to dogmatic law.[18]

Deleuze, at the outset, makes a distinction between law and jurisprudence. Law concerns abstract, universal principles, often traceable to Kant, applied by practitioners who follow linear logic in reaching decisions (formal rationality). Lefebvre (2008), for example, shows how formalism is about subsuming "cases" under an appropriate law, and from there, engaging in deductive logic to decide the controversy. He demonstrates how the prominent thinkers H.L.A. Hart, Ronald Dworkin, and Jurgen Habermas — all borrowing from Kant — take as a given subsumption.

Jurisprudence is defined by Deleuze as "the philosophy of law, and deals with singularities, it advances by working out from singularities" (Deleuze and Joughin, 1995: 153). Thus, jurisprudence is more about invention, creating concepts concerning law and rights (Maneros, 2019: 6). In practical terms, it is concerned with case law and pragmatic decision-making by judges. Central are singularities of concrete encounters and the need for creativity, not discovery, for a living law, rather than universalities such as formal equal rights (Lefebvre, 2008: 56). Deleuze criticizes human rights discourse in a special sense: as valuing universalization; their axiomatic form of representation; fixing identities with essences without sensitivity to becoming and uniquely embodied agents; unresponsiveness to concrete events and encounters; and in the lack of consultation of those who are immediately affected. Rather, we start with situations, encounters, or singularities that forces law to invent the problem, which in turn leads to the creation of a right that corrects, improves, or modifies the situation (Lefebvre, 85), rather than merely trying to fit the situation under a preconceived categorical instance (subsumption), and then through the use of linear deductive logic arriving at a decision. Deleuze is not blind to conflicts. He is not advocating doing nothing; he is not, for example, against intervention in violent activity; that is, "he would not call them interventions to protect inviolable rights but interventions into problematic situations to create rights" (ibid., 87).

For some, Deleuzian jurisprudence[19] implies both a philosophy of law as well as case law. Extending on his argument, it could then be argued that C.S.Peirce's notion of abduction, a use of both induction and deduction, could respond to the singularities of encounters. Returning to Deleuze, jurisprudence places a high premium on the wherewithal of human encounters, particularly those that have gone wrong or do harm. Emphasis focuses on the appropriate question(s) to ask, and discovery or creation of new concepts reflecting the concreate encounter.

Let us apply all this to pragmatic decision-making by judges. How does a judge arrive at a decision in law? Lefebvre (2008) reads Deleuze through Henri Bergson—a critic of Kant, who advocated the primordiality of a creative, non-mechanical mind—in showing how creative law could take place, the "leaps in faith" advocated by Richard Rorty we visited in the previous section. We have already encountered Rorty's notion of the good judge as a good prophet willing to make a good faith leap in law and left realists arguing for judges to not shy away from social engineering. But, in contrast, we also have Kennedy's political judges engaged in bad faith and denial.

Bergson offers the idea that two forms of consciousness generally prevail: an inattentive recognition which is more habitual responses that make up a good part of everyday life, and an attentive recognition or judgement that is aroused in out-of-ordinary encounters. In the majority of cases a judge, according to Lefebvre, uses inattentive judgement, simply looking for the appropriate law or principle and subsuming the "case" (problematic encounter), and then through deductive logic arriving at a decision. All is linear, all is categorical, the universal lives on. In "hard cases," those that are not easily subsumed under a given principle or law, the judge's more active form of attention, attentive recognition/judgement, is aroused, often expanding the imagery of the event in its complexity, not yet identifying it as a particular "case" in law. But after a more intense review and arriving at a more sensitive definition of the situation as a singularity, a creative leap often takes place in logic, manifest in a tweaking or even entirely new law. He provides specific applications of attentive judgement and a leap in logic to: *Palsgraf v. Long Island Railroad Co.* (1928; changing the existing standard of "proximate cause" in negligence/tort law to "foreseeability"); and *Griswold v. Connecticut* (1965) (ibid., 190–195; establishing the right to privacy).

Although Deleuze does not develop an alternative to contemporary human rights discourse, some (Lefebvre, 2011, 2017, 2018: 85–103) have suggested one that could be developed based on consulting Henri Bergson's last book, *The Two Sources of Morality and Religion* (1932). Human rights could be based on the concept of love, an *élan vital*, since it suggests openness, immanence, unboundedness, connectedness with the other, singularities, ongoing creation, becoming. In short, human rights discourse becomes less important as society tends towards loving, caring relationships. Toward this end, inspired by Baxi (2012), Print *et al.* (2008), and Michel Foucault's (1997c) late work on the "care of the self," he suggests human rights education that sensitizes self to diverse others in a dynamic, complex, and continuous changing world.

Finally, Deleuze's work contributes to an understanding of social organization, law, and forces of change (see Bogue, 2003: 78–89; Bogue also comments on Deleuze's view of Kafka's confrontation with the law in *The Trial*, 2009). The natural state is a dynamic field of forces in which relatively stabilized assemblages as a unit of organization emerge, some of which are stratified in relatively stabilized hierarchical layers. A social assemblage can range from the very large to small, i.e., from a state to humans; examples include schools, prisons, the criminal justice system, the courtroom, corporations, social groups. These "structures" are composed of territorializing forces, those that compose and tend to the production of stasis, and deterritorialization, forces of disruption. Consider Weber's "insoluble conflict" between formal rationality and substantive rationality. Each assemblage can be further semiotically characterized, to use Hjelmslev's semiotics (see Chapter 9), as a form of expression and a form of content in a state of mutual presupposition. Language, "regimes of signs," for Deleuze and Guattari (1987; Holland, 2013; Milovanovic, 2007), is characterized as embedding differential power; they provide the context where agents performatively constitute speech acts that cumulatively and repetitively in their usage produce social realities in more dominant form ("major" language/literature), often denying disenfranchised peoples' understandings ("minor" language).

Each assemblage embodies an "abstract machine," a function, or logic. They produce tendencies or vector expressed as "lines of flight." A legal abstract machine in its performative function makes "cuts" in flows in a dynamic field of forces. It constitutes legal realities. Thus, formal rationality is an abstract machine tending to produce static identities in law, by way of established laws (axiomatic system), precedents, and deductive logic.[20]

Forces are always embedded; however, for dismantling assemblages ("schiz-law," Bogue, 85–86), required is a deterritorialization, a "war machine," creating new assemblages, which in turn reterritorializes in creating new assemblages. Revolutionaries hasten this dismantling while offering new images of organization and law. Consider CLS and the "crits." Law is thus not seamless, stable, coherent and enduring, but always imbued with cracks in the edifice exposing it to potential change. Others have suggested a "nomadic jurisprudence" (Newman, 2012: 327; Marneros, 2019, 2021). It is based on ethics and prioritizing becoming rather than fixed, static, and enduring laws and identities, and apposes all forms of hierarchies, dogmatism, and universalities (Marneros, 2019: 9–10).

Complexity Theory and Law

Sometimes also referred to as dynamic systems theory, or, more generally, chaos theory, this approach includes a focus on non-linearity, self-organization, emergence, dissipative structures, singularities, bifurcations, and attractors. A recent google search for "chaos theory" witnessed over 155,000,000 "hits" (DM on 7/30/2021). There is some debate whether it can be included as an example of postmodern thought (Woermann, 2016; Cilliers, 1995, 1998; Murray *et al.*, 2019), but here, our position is that since it does challenge much of conventional thinking on linear systems traced to the Enlightenment, it is arguably an approach that could be included. The literature shows both a modernist and a postmodernist variety of complexity theory. Morin (2007), for example, distinguishes between a "restricted" (modernist) and a "general" (postmodern) version, where the former prioritizes mathematical formalization, the latter, more philosophical analysis of systems theory (see also Murray *et al.*, 2019: 9–11). And, some argue for both. Another approach is quantum chaos which has more affinities with the restricted form, and which also makes use of linear equations, but introduces the notion of the "collapse of the wave function," probabilistic resolutions of a state in which a number of possible outcomes exist simultaneously (Bishop, 2015; see also next chapter). However, we do see in the developmental stages a more general version with the recently embracing of Eastern philosophy. The very definition of complexity theory is also in question, with most arguing that it provides conceptual tools and mapping devices for complex, dynamic systems.

Applications in various disciplines have occurred, but until recently, with little generally in law. There has been a recent upsurge of applying complexity theory to law (Murray, 2008; Murray *et al.*, 2019; Murray *et al.*, 2018; Webb, 2014, 2015; Carline *et al.*, 2020; Capra and Mattie, 2015; Carline *et al.*, 2018; Wheatley, 2016). Much of the recent literature goes back to the work of Ruhl (1996a, 1996b, 1997) for his ground-braking work in applying complexity theory to law (see also Hayes, 1992). In criminology and social justice, applications were developed in the 1990s (Milovanovic, 1997), extending to more recent times (Pycroft and Bartollas, 2014), and in applying a chaos-based psychoanalytic semiotics to law (Milovanovic, 1992).

Let us review some key tools offered, to be followed by some of the applications in law. Chaos theory, contrary to conventional thinking is about both disorder *and* order in complex systems. Patterns emerge out of the dynamics of complex system. Throw a rock in a pond and observe the distinct rings that appear only to disappear (dissipate) quickly. Observe a stream passing over rocks and the momentary eddies formed. Much of the literature begins with the mathematics of Henri Poincaré in the 19th and early 20th century who recognized indeterminacy in otherwise orderly systems, Edward Lorenz's work in the early 1960s predicting weather patterns and gypsy moth populations over time, and Benoit Mandelbrot's work on exotic structures with fuzzy boundaries, fractals, which produce incredibly complex patterns that repeat at every level of magnification. Nietzsche, too, had demonstrated the chaotic structure of the universe and our tendencies to attribute fictional order to them.

To begin our "magical mystery tour," complex systems are characterized by attractors (point, cyclical, torus, strange). Take a simple pendulum and let it swing side by side (dynamic system), then map it (phase map, phase portrait).[21] A phase map locates simultaneously the velocity and location. It has as many dimensions as needed, here two, velocity and location. You will note that left to itself, the swinging pendulum comes to rest at a point (point attractor). In the phase map identified as a spiraling to a point. Attach a motor and let it swing continuously, and you will have a cyclic attractor, a circle is depicted on a phase map where each point identifies both location and momentum. Add a pivot to the pendulum and you add a third degree of freedom, a wobble along the pivot, and here on the phase map you will see a torus-like structure (looks like a donut).[22]

For the strange attractor (Lorenz attractor), we go to Lorenz's work (1963). He was using differential equations to plot variables that together would allow prediction of the weather from time to time. In the old-fashioned computer of the time, he left his computer running with a set of values for pertinent variables. He returned much later and saw the plotted graph (phase map) had two wings, much like a butterfly wing, with values and predictions falling in one wing or the other, predicting either no rain or rain, for example. Increase one of the variables ever so slightly (perturbation) and after many computations (iterations), disproportion effects are realized, i.e., a jump from one wing to the other. Hence, many observers conclude the "butterfly effect": small, seemingly insignificant inputs can produce, after iteration (feedback), disproportional effects, or said in another way, this is "sensitivity to initial conditions"—a butterfly flapping its wings in Southeast Asia can produce a hurricane off the coast of the U.S. Consider the major omissions by empirically driven social scientists that round to the tenth place in their computations.[23] Chaos theory would argue that very small values, even at the .0001 level, can have significant disproportional effects after a number of iterations. This also brings out the idea of non-linearity.

Modernists assume tendencies toward equilibrium conditions, point attractors. Take, for example, socialization and how identities are said to form. Consider bureaucracies, consensus theories, gender roles, etc. Prigogine and Stengers (1984) have demonstrated that the more normal state is far-from-equilibrium conditions characterized by flux, disorder, change. In these states, emerging structures develop, attributable to the principle of self-organization. These are called relatively stable "dissipative structures" since they tend to break up even as they begin to take new forms. It has been recognized that at specific values, bifurcation takes place. They are sensitive to initial conditions and even to the very smallest perturbations, unlike, for example, bureaucracies. Consider the last time you have tried to provide suggestions for change to some governmental office! Any dynamic system tends to begin to split in possible outcomes at specific input values. Equilibrium conditions produce point attractors; far-from-equilibrium conditions produce more complex attractors at the initiation of bifurcations, first period/cyclic attractors, then with another slight increase in input values (perturbation), torus attractors, and then, with more, strange attractors. Point and cyclical attractors are favored by modernist thinkers; postmodernist look to torus and strange attractors as key factors.

Let's provide some examples in law. Law is explained as "an emergent, self-organizing system in which an interactive network of many parts—actors, institutions and 'systems'—operate with no overall guiding hand, giving rise to complex collective behaviours that can be observed in patterns of law communications" (Murray *et al.*, 2019: 3). We previously (Chapter 6) referenced Brion's study (1991, 1995) of tort law employing chaos theory. Decision-making vacillates between two poles, *heresy* (pluralistic forces) and *stare decisis* until, with a slight perturbation, one pole becomes dominant. Similar to Schulman's (1987) study which suggests decision-making oscillates between two wings of an attractor with a slight perturbation fixing it in one. Consider a jury member weighing evidence for making a decision. A perturbation, not directly related to the trial, may range from a bit of dramatic news, to the arousal of personal issues, to an informal conversation (see also Williams and Arrigo, 2002). C.S. Peirce's notion of abduction in reasoning whereby a jurist moves from deductive to inductive reasoning also suggests two wings of an attractor, a periodic/cyclic, or even a strange attractor.

It has been demonstrated (Milovanovic, 2004) how the application of the notion of bifurcation can be applied to Lopez's study, *Rebellious Lawyering* (1992) in mapping the development of an alternative to dominant legal discourse. It applies Lacan's four discourses and forms of identification along with Paulo Freire's (1972) work on dialogical pedagogy, a discourse whereby alternative more dynamic, more processual master signifiers are constructed in the legal setting between client and lawyer generating alternative constructions of reality.

Another example is Murray's (2005) development of "sinthome law" and specifically his application to electronic signatures on the Web. From a previous section, Murray reads Lacan's third order, the Real, as a realm in far-from-equilibrium conditions which is the source of immanent and emergent pockets of order expressible in terms of singularities. Whereas the Symbolic order is the realm of signifiers, the Real is populated by "letter," energetic constellations, which communicate aspects of the real, but are nevertheless not articulable but remain with effects in the Symbolic. Le sinthome, a fourth ring, as we saw, is a naming, a tying together of the three orders in producing sense. It can replace the-law-of-the-father as a unifying mechanism providing sense and stability. Consider, for example, as we previously mentioned, the law-of-the-mother, or "reasonable intersectional person" as a replacement to the legal standard, "the reasonable man." The chaotic Real can be seen as offering material for creative nomination, for conceptualizing things otherwise, a basis for new forms of organization. It is a "productive disorder." Le sinthome is more a dissipative structure offering, with slight perturbation, novel emergence, order out of disorder. (However, le sinthome can also take on more static forms in law resisting dissipation.) Murray's application to electronic signatures on the Web, showing how new digital identities (names) are created, models the notion of nomination of le sinthome.

Another example is an application of Deleuze and Guattari's (1987) assemblage theory and Delanda's (2006, 2016) more explicit complexity version applied to the courtroom as a complex, affective social assemblage, and particularly demonstrating its use in rape trials (Carline *et al.*, 2020). The courtroom is immersed in a field from which assemblages form. "Sayabilities" (expression) are flows from this field which also includes associated interacting material forms (content, including buildings, architecture, spaces, etc.) and bodies that occupy this space (lawyers, judges, various other court officials, defendant, witnesses, etc.). Expression and context are, to apply Deleuze and Guattari (1987), in "double articulation" and in a state of "reciprocal presupposition." Lawyers, for Carline *et al.* (ibid., 124), instigate affects in the given courtroom assemblage; that is, mobilize flows, suggesting connections, implying certain realities. The social assemblage, in short, becomes animated in time and space, a space of emergence. Situating the rape trial in these contexts is to show how legal realities are co-constructed. For a diverse application of complexity theory to law—

administrative law, international law, human rights, business, and legal ethics—see Murray *et al.* (2019).

Remaining useful in the literature are the early studies in applying chaos theory to law (Hayes, 1992; Ruhl, 1996a, 1996b, 1997), laying out the general applicability of chaos and showing: self-organization and adaptation in law tending toward a particular form of law such as formal logical rationality, a point attractor; the fractal dimensions of what constitutes justiciability; modeling techniques (phase space) that identify complex assemblages in far-from-equilibrium conditions, their attractors, and emergence, particularly "at the edge of chaos," the loci of the "insoluble conflict" between formal and substantive rationality; a sensitivity to the potential singularities and bifurcations embedded in complex systems; and how a law-society system can be productively conceptualized and modeled by the use of phase space (Murray *et al.*, 239–240). By visualizing law and society, Murray *et al.* argue (ibid., 241–242), as a complex adaptive assemblage, we are in a better position to visualize alternatives, particularly valuing a problem-solving approach to conflicts.

Following Ruhl, criteria of evaluation of a "good system" based on complexity theory could be developed focused on problem-solving, a bottom-up approach, that operates at the edge of chaos where singularities, bifurcations, emergence and self-organization take form. Towards this end, noteworthy is the suggestion of a "nomad jurisprudence" discussed earlier. Along these lines, to integrate law and society as an assemblage, Holland's (2011) work on a nomadology, suggesting radical jazz improvisation as a key to understanding forms of dissipative structures in society and law, could be a basis for furthering a progressive theorizing in a sociology of law. Further, works by Capra and Mattie's (2015) suggesting a return to smaller scale communities resonating with laws of ecology, Hardt and Negri's four-volume work (2000, 2004, 2009, 2017) on the commonwealth, assemblages, and multitude, and Chester and Walsh's (2007) applying complexity to social movement are illustrative of postmodern suggestions for a society-to-come where law finds an alternative basis.

Constitutive Law

Since the 1980s a number of works began to demonstrate that law did not merely originate from social realities but contributed to its construction.[24] The causal arrow, runs both ways. Each constitutes the other. Law creates frameworks within which people discursively construct realities. Agents, in turn, performatively enact law in material discursive production in their speech acts. Since law originates in contexts of inequality, it also allocates differential powers, e.g., fixing in consciousness hierarchies and inequalities in gender, race, ethnic, class and intersectional social relations (Mautner, 2011: 853). In an early chapter we indicated that one of the functions of law was constitutive (along with facilitative, ideological, repressive). Here we want to elaborate a constitutive perspective as a more formal approach.

In the 1990s, we note its development in criminology (see Henry and Milovanovic 1991, 1996, 2020). It has also been applied to cultural studies (Mautner, 2011), religion

(Moustafa, 2018), rights discourse (Mitnick, 2000; Steiner and Nielsen, 2019), critical criminology (Polizzi, 2016; Presser and Sandberg, 2015), criminal justice (Smith and Kinzel, 2021), penology (Arrigo and Milovanovic, 2009; Milovanovic and Henry, 1991) and, in an earlier form, anthropology (Geertz, 1983). A key founding book articulating a constitutive law was Alan Hunt's *Explorations in Law and Society* (1993). This approach has been incorporated by critical legal studies, legal feminism, critical race theory, law and society, amongst others. Its sources include Marxism, phenomenology, social constructionism, and semiotics. Its foundations have been inspired by Anthony Giddens' *The Constitution of Society* (1984).

Let us summarize some of the key principles of constitutive theory. We will then provide examples in application to law. Constitutive theory is a holistic approach, stressing how "parts" and "wholes" are not separate, but intricately co-produced. Constitutive law has developed considerably out of engagements with Marxist relations of the base to superstructure, Gramsci's highlighting ideology, Poulantzas' revised analysis of superstructure and interpellation effects, and Gidden's work. Let's look to early developers. Klare (1982: 135) has said: "legal discourse shapes our beliefs about the experience and capacities of the human species, our conception of justice, freedom and fulfillment, and our visions of the future." Kennedy (1997: 152; see also Ewick and Silbey, 1998: 245–250) has noted "although legal discourse is in one sense driven by the underlying opposition of ideologized interests, it may also react back on the ideologies and the interests and transform them." Geertz (1983: 232) has said law is "constructive of social realities rather than merely reflective of them." Ewick and Silbey (1998) have shown that legalities are enacted — how components are internalized in consciousness in everyday constructions of reality — within different contexts. Thus, legal discourse is said to impact, or constitute discursive formations, producing capacities and limitations on the representable and expressible. Consider, for example, juridically established case opinions such as, in the U.S. context, "plain view doctrine" or the Miranda warning. Once established they become the basis of constructing narratives of the "what happened" in law, and as legal realists have pointed out, often *ex post facto* constructions justifying initial illegal searches by police. Law, in short contributes to the shaping of consciousness. Consider, too, the considerable amount of legal terminology introduced through the media and the entertainment industry, including virtual reality programs, trial coverage, and commentaries. These contribute to shaping consciousness, frameworks of thinking ("images of thought"), and identity categories. Accordingly, "consciousness of law is reflected in both people's understandings of their rights *as well as* their efforts to enact those rights" (Steiner and Neilson, 2019: 6; emphasis in original).[25]

Causality, the directionality between law and society, can only be established in specific historical contexts (Hunt, 1993: 294; Cotterrell, 2015; Henry and Milovanovic, 2020; Gomez, 2012), between relatively autonomous spheres. Struggle and the dialectical process also impacts on the directionality (Gomez, 2012). Thus, social movements can shape the law, but in turn, what is then produced in legal categories and clarification of formal rights, shapes social struggles. Consider U.S. Supreme court decisions over specifying First Amendment rights, in establishing permissible expression. It can be regulated in "time, place, and manner," thus establishing regulated spaces within which social struggles can play themselves out.

Let us provide some examples. The police and the judiciary are two relatively autonomous spheres; but each function to co-constitute the other. Let us return to the plain view doctrine in the U.S. experience (police who are investigating a crime who come across other illicit activity need not return to a judge to obtain a search or arrest warrant, *if* all appears in plain view). Police training educates the neophyte police officer of constitutional rights and the "rule of law." Much of the activity of police is certainly guided by these principles. However, formal categories are also used, after the fact, as a way of constructing narratives that fit constitutionally permissible police operations. It is a way of avoiding dismissal of otherwise illegally obtained "evidence" during "suppression hearings" prior to a trial. Thus, both spheres, police and the courts, are implicated in the construction of narratives and in their continuance. Court established law is provided further support and legitimacy in police *ex post facto* constructions and the appearance of following the "rule of law." Police stories are, therefore, carefully constructed with the discursive elements promulgated by the courts, and by the court's acceptance of these stories, together, providing further legitimacy of law.

Mautner's (2011) focus is on constitutive effects between law and culture. Three examples are provided. Take sexual harassment law as a category. Prior to its establishment women were subject—nevertheless continue to be in more subtle ways—to numerous forms of harassment. With the law, "they will have been born into a culture that complies with the doctrine's imperative" (ibid., 854) and thus social reality can be constructed differently in accessing the courts.[26] The second example is with family law, and particularly the rights in marriage. Through the allocation of powers and duties in such things as custody rights and distribution of property in divorce, family law shapes relations between husband and wife. Consider prior to family law the unequal rights in these relationships. Same-sexed marriages pose additional requirements for new legalities, which in turn shape family practices. Mautner's third examples is labor law, arguing that it not only shapes employer-employee relationships, but also the way each begins to perceive themselves.

Gomez (2012), reviewing a number of case studies, argues that law and race are mutually constituted, along with the effects of dialectical struggle. The causal directionality runs both ways, "law not only constructs race, but race constructs law" (ibid., 47). Gomez builds on social construction theory, and particularly viewing race as a constructed category. She applies constitutive law theory to a case study of the colonial experiences in British Columbia (see alsoMawani, 2009) and explains how various racialized categories and residential segregation (by race and class) were created in law maintaining white colonial powers, diminishing the colonized. But this was not just a unilateral move. Mawani's study shows how in inter-racial encounters various conflicting ideologies played themselves out, and ultimately the perceived threat to White domination asserted itself in new laws.

Mitnick (2000; see also Brigham, 1996; Steiner and Nielsen, 2019) applies constitutive law to rights discourse. Promulgated rights are constitutive of social relations and individual identity. "Law and legally constituted relationships among persons," he argues (ibid., 186), "inform social perceptions of identity, and social perceptions inevitably influence, and at time even dominate, self-understanding ... human beings are, in part and as well, constituted by rights." Legal categories shape distinctions between and among people and groups. He argues, for example, how in *Dred Scott v. Sanford* (1857) Chief Justice Taney framed the "pertinent" issue that those of African descent, whether slave or freed slave, are different from those envisioned in the U.S. Constitution, which then justified segregation, a position that continued with *Plessey v. Ferguson* (1996), the notorious "separate but equal" standard. Mitnick also makes the case that law tends to produce essences; in its logic, it tends to attribute stereotypes to different people, even ostensibly in the hopes of being sensitive to their differences and plight. We have previously seen this in lower court and U.S. Supreme Court rulings in school and university admission standards (see for example the current pending, as of this writing, *Students for Fair Admissions v. Harvard College*). Civil rights law is a useful resource in producing social change—in providing "new discourses for reframing the meaning of social events and destabilizing existing meaning"—and resultant discourses, in turn, are useful for advocacy for further legal change (Steiner and Nielson, 2019: 6).

Our final example, is Moustafa's (2019) study of Malaysia and its attempt of reconciling differences between Muslim-Islam law and secular law. Law promises to redefine the very character of the nation. At the outset, it is stated that law does not stand apart from politics and ideological struggles. Law and the courts, it is argued "constitute political struggle over religion in at least four important ways by: delineating categories of meaning (such as "secular" and "religion"); shaping the identity of various situated actors, by providing an institutional framework that enables and even encourages legal disputes; and providing a focal point for political mobilization (ibid., 1–2). In short, law is structuring the ideological-political landscape in providing secular frameworks in the construction of reality, in, for example transactions and disputes (Kuek and Tay, 2013; Soh, 2020). There remains tension between Sharia law practiced in Syariah Courts and the civil law based on British common law tradition. See for example, the rights of women in Malaysia (Steiner, 2019). Numerous studies also focus on the tensions in the Middle East and North Africa.

A constitutive law approach is not without its critics. There have been, and continue to be, lively debates. Cotterrell (2015) has provided a qualified and supportive critique, most important of which is a pointing out that the approach overstates the unilateral power of law, insufficiently recognized the constitutive power of law in different societies, sometimes downplays law as being separate from other social forces, and may overlook the strength of tradition and cultural values. (In constitutive criminology, see the criticism and response in Henry and Milovanovic, 2020).

Summary

This chapter has provided an overview of a postmodern contribution to the sociology of law. Postmodernism was a response to the ideals of the Enlightenment. Both a nihilist, negative postmodernism as well as an affirmative postmodernism exist. Jacques Lacan who developed a psychoanalytic semiotics is a key thinker with whom postmodernists have had to come to terms. He also provided a model for the operation of the psychic apparatus. His four discourses portrayed the structured nature of discourse and the capabilities therein. A fifth discourse, the discourse of capitalist, remains underdeveloped. Lacanian postmodern feminist both criticized and provided key reformulations of Lacan's work. Several key thinkers in the postmodern perspective were addressed (Nietzsche, Foucault, Derrida, Lyotard, and Rorty), particularly for their potentials for contributing to a positive jurisprudence. The work of Gilles Deleuze was presented for possible contributions to a sociology of law, even though he did not systematically develop it. Lefebvre and others have insightfully applied his work to law. Deleuze's work has also been inspirational for providing tools for social change. Complexity theory was explicated. It challenges notions of homeostasis, linear development, proportional effects, and structure. It continues to be incorporated in applications in law. Some, using its principles, have developed a nomadic jurisprudence. Our final section was constitutive law. This concerns co-production. Realities are performatively enacted in material discursive practices.

Review Questions

1. Two versions of postmodern thought emerged, a negative, nihilist and an affirmative postmodernism. Why is it important to include both critique and suggestions for going beyond?

2. Why is it important to integrate some understanding of the psychic apparatus in doing a sociology of law?

3. Provide an example in which you found yourself in one of Lacan's four discourses. Explain how it also shifted to one of the others. Bring to class, share, and discuss the dynamics.

4. Explain how an alternative "sinthome law" could be institutionalized. What would it take? What would be its benefits? What are the possible negative outcomes?

5. Counter story-telling in law has often been offered by crits. Given Lacan's four discourses, what constructive critique can you offer to this strategy? Explain.

6. Several postmodern theorists of law were offered (choose one of the following: Nietzsche, Foucault, Derrida, Nietzsche, Rorty). Assess their possible contribution for a positive jurisprudence. Which has more persuasive power for you? Why? Explain.

7. Why does Deleuze have reservations about contemporary human rights discourse?

8. Derrida makes a distinction between law and justice. Explain in your own words. Are there possibilities for law and justice coinciding? Explain.

9. Given your reading of chaos theory, what relevance do you see for doing a sociology of law. Explain.

10. Given your reading of constitutive law, what points do you find particularly important for doing a sociology of law. Explain.

Endnotes

1. Lacan (1977) offers two algorithms for the movement of signifiers, metaphor and metonymy. Due to space consideration, we cannot further elaborate, but see Milovanovic, 2002: 143–155; Schutter, 1983. For metaphor, consider the confirmation hearings of Clarence Thomas for U.S. Supreme Court Justice who responded to intense criticism as a "high-tech lynching." Or consider the metaphor "crime as a virus," or the "prisoner as slime." For metonymy, consider the pejorative use of "single mom" or "broken homes" in the context of discussing delinquency. Their use mobilizes other conventionally associated signifiers.

2. Consider a job interview for a position as a probation officer. One prepares by reciting the language of law and order (Symbolic Order) and during the interview constantly seeks cues as to how they are being perceived by the interviewer (Imaginary Order). Both determine the use of discourse in context.

3. Vanheule's (2016) interpretation in the clinical setting has it that "to pay close attention to the singularity of the patient the analyst puts aside pre-established ideas about patients and pathologies (S2), such that key signifiers that mark the analysand's subjectivity (S1) can be formulated, which fuels the analyst's positioning qua *object a*.

4. Vectors in original have been omitted.

5. Topological constructions provide visual displays of often complex relationships, showing how a phenomenon is composed of interconnected elements. In Lacan's late years he insisted on portraying complex dynamics of the psychic apparatus by topology and knot theory. Their interpretation remains problematic, but yet sustained work by the researcher often generates deep insights. It would be useful for the reader to pause at this point and consult the figures below for further clarity.

For a visual of the Borromean knot and Le Sinthome scroll down for their representations in the following: L. Armand, "Symptom in the Machine," accessed 4/3/2022, https://www.lacan.com/sympmachf.htm; see also, L. Bryant's blog, "Notes on the Borromean Clinic," accessed 4/3/2022, https://larvalsubjects.wordpress.com/2008/12/04/notes-on-the-borromean-clinic/

6. For another explanation, see Verhaeghe and Declercq (2002: 66–67): "The signifier ... is a letter that has acquired a linguistic value ... Lacan identifies the 'letter' or object *a* with the master signifier, S1, on condition that this S1 is understood as disconnected from S2, the battery of other signifiers. The 'letter' S1 is only turned into a signifier when connected to S2."

7. Kupupika (2021: 39), for example, points out how in the "MeToo" Movement, the originator of the term, black activist Tarana Burke, witnessed its usurpation in popular discourse by reference to white actress Alyssa Milano, thus rendering it as additive.

8. Consider your new job. Immediately you are given a long list of appropriate behavior, sometimes incorporated in an ethics manual. In some cases, you also consent to constant observation by camera. Consider driving experience and the myriad of rules that need to be followed as well as the surveillance to which you are subjected (speed cameras, red light cameras, sound devices). Consider too, the various bureaucratic agencies with which you must constantly deal.

9. In Chapter 6, we noted Kennedy arguing that there were three types of judges in decision-making.

10. As with other authors, there have been critical engagements with Derrida's work. Litowitz (1997: 102–108) argues, for example, that Derrida assumes there is a core, stable subject from which to provide care for the other; that it does not provide the grounds for decision-making where there is disagreement; that he doesn't speak to the procedure that might be used in resolving differences. Other issues include: "how can one know when one has approached justice? Given two interpretations, which interpretation is more just" Who should decide which interpretation is better?" And is justice in the singular cutting across history, tradition, context? (ibid., 105). All these of course have been ripe for debate.

11. We have previously referred to the dominant discourse as the dominant linguistic coordinate system.

12. The U.S. Supreme Court's ruling on the First Amendment dealing with freedom of expression allows an extensive range of views, but subject to regulation in expression by time, place and manner.

13. For a Marxist reading of Lyotard, see Choat (2012).

14. For a non postmodernist form of pragmatism in law, focusing on eminent jurist and judge Richard Posner see Sullivan and Solove (2003).

15. Doing a google search with "Gilles Deleuze" recently witnessed over eight millions hits, DM, 7/27/2021.

16. For a general and accessible introduction to Deleuze, see Holland (1999, 2013). His notion of desire as production resonates with Nietzsche's will to power, in the sense of self questioning, self-discovery, overcoming, becoming, developing greater capabilities.

17. Recall, too, Lacan's capitalist discourse.

18. Still not fully explored on images of thought, and conspicuously missing in critical law, is Deleuze's two-volume work on the cinema, *Cinema* 1 (1986) and *Cinema* 2 (1989). Unlike his work on semiotics with Guattari in *Thousand Plateaus* (1987) that applied Hjelmslev's quadripartite notion in semiotics, in the *Cinema* texts he applied C.S.Peirce's tripartite semiotics, and in doing so, he introduces novel conceptualizations. He divided forms of cinema into two, one predominantly rooted in Newtonian ontology, characterizing it as the "movement-image," more an "organic regime," the other having affinities with quantum mechanics, the "time-image," the "crystalline regime." Elsewhere, we (Milovanovic, 2007) applied his cinema model to understanding the image of thought of criminal justice, and suggested, applying his concepts, an alternative transformative justice that centered on the "time-image." Critical Deleuzian law conceivably could make productive use of his different images of thought in understanding classical law-in-practice, and in introducing the wherewithal of alternative images of thought that capture the complexities of being human, and in so doing paving the way for alternatives signifiers that embody it.

19. Deleuze's notion of jurisprudence differs from the one we have established in this book, the latter a jurisprudence more dogmatic in form.

20. In chapter 12 we will see these lines of flight as Schrödinger waves, encoded possibilities, that undergo a collapse of the wave function in context producing the realities with which we engage.

21. In constructing a phase map of a simple pendulum, draw a circle with two perpendicular axes running through it, one representing velocity the other location. Then the movement of the pendulum can be traced as a spot on the circle simultaneously representing the distance and velocity changes. With more dimensions different phase maps are needed.

22. Take a slice of the donut, reducing it to a two-dimensional portrayal at a point in time. Within the slice we have centers of concentration, extending to less likely points as one moves outward. Take, for example, a student's schedule for a week. We can trace Tuesdays, for example, attending a class from 1–2: 45, but it is somewhat unpredictable as to the student's mental state at the class meeting, most often being at the center where they are into the lecture/discussion material, but at times wandering to the boundaries, daydreaming (or consulting smart phones). But during the semester, a pattern emerges from week to week, thus order, but disorder.

23. Consult the dominant (modernist) journal *Criminology*, for example, for endless quantitative/empirical examination with little self-critique of assumptions.

24. In contrast, consider Emile Durkheim's sociology of law where the nature of solidarity and social bonds was said to be determinative of law.

25. Constitutive law also acknowledges alternative definitions of crime. Consider Henry and Milovanovic's (2020; 1996) reconceptualization of crime as "harms of reduction" and "harms of repression," the former reducing a person (or non-humans, i.e., animal, environment) from a state they are in to a lower form, the latter, placing barriers for fuller actualization and development of capabilities. The offender is seen as an excessive investor unilaterally imposing differences without being sensitive and responsive to the other's input. This concerns inequalities in power and differential abilities to invoke change and grant recognition.

26. For example, prior to the new law, Black's "conciliatory style" was most prevalent; after, the penal style.

12

Post Postmodern Perspectives

Introduction

Responding to the "linguistic turn," representationalism, and the underplaying of material forces of postmodern analysis, the late 1990s extending into the new millennium witnessed a questioning of these turning points and focused more on bringing the material back in ("materialist turn"; for a general introduction, see Coole and Frost, 2010a, 2010b). Postmodernists, it was said, privileged the immaterial forms such as language, agency and consciousness, and downplayed the material and its effects. The New Turks questioned the exclusive focus on the human (anthropocentrism) and extended agency to non-human forms and the environment. With agency now defined as the ability to affect and be affected, a decentering of human domination was afoot. Some saw the merits of the post postmodern critique, but nevertheless resisted discarding the positive aspects of postmodern analysis, and suggested their integration (Barad, 2007). Others, however, argued for the "death of postmodernism" (Kirby, 2006, 2009). While welcomed, much of the new thought, however, prematurely in our view, jettisoned the human agent in the decentered form.

The post postmodernist view incorporated a number of diverse perspectives: new materialism, vitalism, posthumanism, eco-feminism, digimodernism, sociomateriality, eco-feminism, post-anthropocentrism, and emerging quantum holographic views. The application to law has also taken hold. See, for example, the special issue, of *Law Text Culture* (volume 23, 2019), edited by Kang and Kendall, on legal materialities. There has been a convincing argument made to include the non-human in sociology, and by extension, to a sociology of law (Peggs, 2012, 2013; Aldeia and Alves, 2019). This has been recognized in the growing discipline of environmental sociology (although questions remain as to its often reliance on a Cartesian split inherited from the Enlightenment between society and nature, Aldeia and Alves, ibid.). This development has been extended into green jurisprudence, eco-law, and rights of nature under the umbrella terms "earth jurisprudence" and "wild law."

We shall summarize some of the differences between postmodern and post postmodern views, develop one version of new materialism and application to law as illustrative (posthumanist feminism), explicate a green jurisprudence, develop quantum-based approaches, and conclude with some conjectures for a quantum holographic-informed semiotics in the sociology of law.

Retained thought from postmodernism includes: Nietzsche's critique of Rennaisance's thought and the importance of matter as "dynamic quanta" in all forms of existence; Derrida's deconstruction of binaries; Foucault's turn to "biopower" and *dispositif* (assemblage, apparatus), situating possibilities of mattering in complexes of physical arrangements; Deleuze and Guattari's assemblage theory; discursive practices as constituting realities, but not confined exclusively to the written text; Butler's performative identities; and nonlinear and contingent historical developments.

Integrated works often cited by post postmodernists, to which we shall return below, include: Bergson's vitalism, along with Deleuze's adaptation, an *élan vital,* Nietzsche's will to power and Spinoza's "joy" (see also Bennet, 2010); Latour's extension of agency (actant) to include all forms, defined as ability to affect and be affected; Barad's quantum mechanics' inspired "agential realism" and its adaptation (sociomateriality); and Hjelmslev's four-part semiotics (expression and content, by form and substance). Other ideas integrated include: performativity and its constitutive effects; the premium on material discursive practices; emphasis on overcoming binaries, often referencing indigenous knowledge; prioritizing the relational as opposed to fixed identities; decentering of the human (anthropocentrism) and rethinking the non-human; and a turn to posthumanist identities (Haraway, 1991; Hayles, 1999; Herbrechter, 2013; Braidotti, 2018). This extended to positing posthumanist or transhumanist, cyber-web-driven realities in a digital culture (Kirby, 2009) with, for example, the construction of the "digital nomad" (Makimoto and Manners, 1997; Hayes and Scott, 2021)[1] in an overflowing informational-based society.

Legal Materiality

There has been a considerable upsurge in applying the new materialism to law (Latour, 2010; Kang, 2018, 2019; Kang and Kendall, 2019, 2020; Johnson, 2018; Davies, 2017; Quiroga-Villamarin, 2020; Grear, 2018, 2020; Pottage, 2012; Vismann, 2008; Philippopoulos-Mihalopoulos, 2018). For application of new materialism to sociology, see Fox and Alldred (2016). There are several versions of legal materialism, so we shall provide only an overview (Quiroga-Villamarin, 2020; Kang and Kendal, 2020: 27–29). Doctrinal (static) analysis in law and representational theory (i.e., the independence of expressive forms) are replaced by a focus on linguistic *and* material forms in identifying how matter is transformed into recognized legal issues. The legal apparatus is conceptualized as an assemblage, a dispositif having effects. But there is no attempt to develop an overall unifying theory.

Legal materiality has been defined as: the focus "on the artefacts, practices, formats and settings in and through which law acts and is enacted" (Kang and Kendall, 2019: 3); "the conditions of possibility in and through which law arises" (Kang and Kendall, 2020, 21); and "how materials *come to matter* to law by being engaged in the production of legal meaning through interpretive and representational practices" (ibid., 21; emphasis in original). It is said that "law is a process of making and stabilizing differences, which only make sense and have an effect within a *dispositif* [assemblage, or apparatus] composed of legal enunciations" (ibid., 34). To elaborate, matter becomes a legal matter in the differences articulated and encoded (Kang and Kendall, 2019: 5). It is a linguistic or communicative act "which turns matters into arguments or claims ... matters of concern to law" (ibid., 6). It considers the conditions under which particular law is recognized representing matter. Consider colonial and indigenous laws that "crits" remind us reflected power interests. Consider *Brown v. Board of Education* in the U.S. experience and critical commentary by "crits" who saw its enactment not in some humanistic realizations, but in concerns for the returning Black soldier from the Korean War and rise of communist movements seeking recruits. The former Black soldier was hardly receptive to sitting in the back of the bus. Consider the hostilities directed to Japanese-Americans in WW2 after the bombing of Pearl Harbor, and the *Korematsu v. U.S.* (1944) case that legitimatized the imprisoning ("internment," "relocation") of over 120,000 Japanese-Americans.

In further explaining how matter becomes matter in law, new materialists enlist Foucault's (1980) notion of *dispositif*, translated as assemblage/apparatus. They also, often, enlist Deleuze and Guattari's (1987) adapted version. Recall from the previous chapter, it is characterized by territorializing and reterritorializing, and, drawing from Hjelmslev's semiotics, by expression and content, each of which can be specified in terms of form and substance. Let's look at the law assemblage (we could also look at the criminal justice system as an assemblage, the courthouse as an assemblage, etc.). Expression includes texts and signs in linguistic form (legal language, as well as protocols, standards of ethical behavior, etc.) and nonlinguistic form (e.g., images, film, sounds) on the one hand; and the material, on the other hand, including architecture, bodies in relation, files, etc. (e.g., case books in law libraries, court transcription devices, courthouse design, courtroom architecture, infrastructure for virtual, online adjudication of cases, computer technologies, appropriate courtroom dress, etc.). In short, signs and material. Matter takes on substance in naming, and expressive form, e.g., criminal, civil, administrative law and in various modalities of expression. Matter, say harms inflected, becomes formed matter as substance as it is recognized in law as justiciable, that is, having legal standing (claims and arguments now are both legally framed providing the basis of further court action). Bodies in relation (content) are differently situated in the person's habitat, in police stops, in police custody, in courtroom settings, in prison (consider a free citizen, person of interest, suspect, defendant, litigant, plaintiff, convicted offender, inmate, ex-offender). They take on substance and form as particular identities in each context. There has also been considerable critique concerning lack of sufficient attention to the diversity of bodies, particularly the intersectional forms. Wehelyie (2014; see also Spillers, 2003; Wynter, 1989), for example, highlights narratives that exclude or subordinate Black voices, a disempowering and "exclusionary logic."

But content co-depends on the expression plane to offer appropriate texts with which to formulate harms, and official identities in law. In the expressive plane, harms are codified in formal State definitions, for example the legalistic definition of crime.[2] They are further articulated as criminal or civil matters. Thus, expression and content are co-constituted and are in "reciprocal presupposition," each sphere depends on the other in the total understanding. Through repetition a common "usage," to employ

Hjelmslev's concept, is established. Legal materialism, thus, underscores the material along with expressive forms.

From our previous discussion of Deleuze and Guattari, law assemblages embed law machines, or logics with effects. Consider, for example, formal rationality and the centrality of linear deductive logic offering a distinct way at arriving at "truth" in law. Similarly, legal language — as a language game, semiotic regime, or linguistic coordinate system — could be conceived of as a "machine" in that it both enables and restricts certain construction of reality in its performative function. All, however, can undergo deterritorialization. "As the material dimensions of law have shifted," Kang and Kendall (2020: 36) argue, "with different technologies and media, a legal materialist approach takes into account how these materials affect the meaning of legal matters and processes, such as responsibility, guilt, privacy, evidence, access to justice, customs, and properties." Consider online adjudication of cases, virtual courtrooms, computer-generated simulations and animations in introducing evidence, a growing reliance on actuarial scales in legal decision-making (actuarial justice), and new cyber laws responding to new material and virtual forms of cyber-crime. In line with this, Kang and Kendall (ibid., 33–37) suggest a mode of critical inquiry in legal materiality that studies: the relations and linkages of legal assemblages; their different capabilities in creating differences; how matter comes to legally matter; their enabling and restricting functions; their re-assembling possibilities; and, perhaps going beyond Deleuze and Guattari's double articulation model, considering the investigating scholar themselves and the importance of a critical, self-reflexivity.

New materialists, and legal materialist in particular, pushed to address agency, can readily cite vitalism: Nietzsche's will to power, Spinoza's joyful relations, Bergson's *élan vital*, Freud's unadulterated libido, and Deleuze's productive desire — a continuous differentiation and development of integrated and entangled unities. They also integrate emergence dynamics, and take comfort in: assemblage theory; the notion of society organized in strata; and perhaps reproductive Marxist feminism — addressing, in short, micro-sociological (face-to-face), meso (community), and macro levels of necessary analysis. Since vitalism can be listed as a sub-micro aspect, still needed is the wherewithal of agency and a statement on the structure and functioning of the psychic apparatus, such as in Freud's id, ego, superego, or as in Lacan's graphs of desire (how the subject speaks), the four or five discourses (how desire becomes manifest), or as in his late works on the Borromean knots particularly *le sinthome*. In short, the wherewithal of human agency addresses the area between the sub-micro (vitalism) and micro-levels (face-to-face). For a more complete sociology of law, therefore, the reader can discern the importance of multiple levels that need to be integrated.

New Materialism and post postmodernism generally are witnessing considerable diversification. Quiroga-Villamarin (2020) offers a useful introduction to some trends and suggests that their boundary-crossing can enrich legal theorizing and applications. Let us include two as illustrative examples.

Posthumanist Feminism and New Materiality

Post humanist feminism, even itself not being a homogeneous field, draws from postmodern discourse analysis and adds a greater concern for the body, a material-discursive approach, and how the body is socially constituted. Matter is dynamically vibrant with emergent qualities. Decentering male privilege while resurrecting female voices in law is a central concern. There has been a considerable authorship in the area (see for example, Braidotti, 2002, 2018; Haraway, 1992; Alaimo and Hekman, 2008; Hekman, 2010; Monforte, 2018; Butler, 2011; Hein, 2016). It includes diverse approaches (for queer theory, see Jones and Otto, 2020; Otto, 2018; for postcolonial theory see Willey, 2016; for international law, see Arvidsson, 2018). There is also an ecofeminism (Jones and Otto, 2020; Bowman, 2013; Salleh, 2017; see also the outspoken and leading ecofeminist, Vandana Shiva, 2022) and an ecofeminist jurisprudence (Sahoo, 2015). Judith Butler's early work, *Volatile Bodies: Toward a Corporeal Feminism* (1994; *see also*, 1990, 1993), positing the performative function of gender identities has often been cited, along with Foucault, Derrida, and Deleuze. Haraway (1992; see also Quiroga-Villamarin, 2020: 135–136) has advocated the concept of a "material-semiotic actor." Thus, in this view, representational theory from the postmodern era needs to be supplemented with the material; they are mutually constituted. Post humanist feminist law brings to light all forms of domination. Domination of women and the exploitation and degradation of the environment are traced to patriarchy and unrestrained capitalism.

Echoing critical race theory, the call is for an alternative storytelling (Hemmings, 2011) that deconstructs dominating, hegemonic stories many of which rest on the ontologies of the Enlightenment, many echoing Eurocentric narratives, and replaces them with alternative "new materialist storytelling" (Wiley, 2016: 994, 1002). Acknowledging that feminist jurisprudence has considerable scholarship and eco-feminist jurisprudence has substantially less, Sahoo (2015) drafts some thoughts for an "eco-feminist jurisprudence." They would include: referencing a triple domination — female, nature and third world nations; recognizing voice of the silenced in law; changing law's repression of the dominated and making it more "an expression of the suppressed expressionless" (ibid., 3); promoting, recognizing, and cultivating differences; and resisting formal equality in law as it denies differences, with its authoritarianism and disciplinary impositions, without benefiting the unequally situated (substantive rational law).

Green Jurisprudence and Rights of Nature: Do Rivers, Trees, Rain Forests, Animals and Plants Have Rights?

Among the binaries inherited from the Enlightenment are human/non-human, human/animal, human/nature. They often manifest, as we learned from Derrida, as hierarchies, a privileged term with recognition, and a de-privileged term without recognition or voice. The human is placed at the center of the universe with all serving its instrumental needs (Anthropocene). Whereas animal rights (e.g., prohibition against cruelty to animals, preserving endangered species) has witnessed increased concern (Candieri, 2001; Cohen and Regan, 2001; Sunstein and Nussbaum, 2004; de Mello, 2021; Kalof, 2017), nature itself has only recently received the attention it deserves. With the greatly increased concern for global warming and degradation of the environment, recent days have witnessed much more attention.

Some time ago, Christopher Stone (1972) wrote what appeared to be a whimsical article, "Should Trees Have Standing?" Seemingly outlandish, but consider the recognition of the "legal personality" (jural person) in law, such in the granting of legal personality to corporations, governments, foundations, churches, and colleges, where each can contract and have them enforced in law. They have rights. They are persons. Why, many are asking, doesn't this extend to non-human forms? Traditionally, too, these questions were not studied in sociology, but recently strong cases have been made for their inclusion (Peggs, 2012, 2013; Ferki, 2018; Aldeia and Alves, 2019; Alger and Alger, 1997), since its focus is on the social relations between humans and non-humans. This can, by implication, be extended to a sociology of law. We are seeing work that advocates an eco-jurisprudence, sometimes referred to as "Wild Law" or "Earth Jurisprudence" (Capra and Mattei, 2015; Grear, 2015, 2018, 2020; Knaub, 2018; Rawson and Mansfield, 2018; Hillebrecht and Berds, 2017; O'Donnell and Talbot-Jones, 2018; Kersten, 2017), as well as substantial material on the politics of environmental justice and environmental social justice movements (Cole and Foster, 2001; O'Donnell and Talbot-Jones, 2018; Pecharroman, 2018; Sanders, 2018). There has also been some development of principles of eco-justice (Schlosberg, 2004, 2007; Capeheart and Milovanovic, 2020: 147–175).

Consider some recent cases on rights of nature. A Right of Nature Bill was proposed in the Philippines, legal personhood was granted to Lake Erie, USA, and legal personality was granted to the Whanganui River in New Zealand (2017) (reported in Jones and Otto, 2019). Legal decisions have been won in Columbia in protecting the Amazon river basin, and constitutional changes are appearing in Ecuador and Bolivia (Hillebrecht and Berds, 2017). In 2017, the High Court of Uttarakhand, India, in *Mohd Salin v. State of Uttarakhand and Others*, granted rights to the Yamuna and Ganges Rivers. The justices [Rorty's "good prophets" engaged in a "leap?] said that the rivers were living entities, legal persons, "with all corresponding rights, duties and liabilities of a living person ... they are accorded the rights akin to fundamental rights/legal rights." Further, it ruled "harming the river, is by law, harming the tribe, while respecting the connection between the health and wellbeing of the river and the health and wellbeing of the people means ascribing the river with rights and duties of a legal person ..." (see also Brara, 2017). And rights were further extended by the High Court of Uttarakhand (2018), in *Narayan Dutt Bhatt v. Union of India and Others*, ruling that "the entire animal kingdom including avian and aquatic" are granted legal personhood. Each entity, they ruled, has "a distinct persona with corresponding rights, duties, and liabilities of a living person." Since rivers cannot represent themselves in court, the High Court ruled, voice can be provided by guardians, *in loco parentis*, a form of *parens patriae*; in other words, someone will be assigned to speak on their behalf as advocates.

Increasingly recognized is that everything, human and non-human, is part of an entangled web, harmoniously co-existing. The centering of the human, often, the image of a Eurocentric-based white male, and the Anthropocene-based discourse of rights inherited from the Enlightenment, are witnessing a displacement to a more inclusive center, a decentering of human privilege. Recognized, too, that merely extending human rights discourse in present form to non-humans has the danger of a "hyperinflated anthropocentrism" (Greer, 2018: 139). There is also the force of capital logic that leads to the "commodification of nature," a "market environmentalism" (Prudham, 2016; Kosoy and Corbera, 2010).

New Materialist call for a re-imagination of rights. Some, in theorizing how to transcend boundaries, particularly binaries such as human/nature, have consulted indigenous views in their inseparable, co-constitutive relation with their land (Black, 2011; Rosiek *et al.*, 2019). Law is taught, and transmitted, in story-telling form (oral history) often around the campfire. Indigenous storytelling defies modernist forms of categorization and representation and are rather acts of creation situating the human in an interconnected universe (see also Garroutte and Westcott, 2013). Legal protections of the environment "should begin," suggests Quiroga-Villamarin (2020: 143), "by involving the perspectives of those who have guarded it for a millennium." This adds insights for development of an all-inclusive "earth jurisprudence" (see also Cullinan, 2011; Capra and Mattei, 2015).

Others suggest we must develop a different ontological basis of rights than that inherited from the Enlightenment and played out in modernist thought, a critique which both postmodernists and post modernists share. Ontology is about core assumptions one makes about reality and basic categories employed. Latour (2007) has made use of the concept "actant" to suggest all entities have capacities to affect and be effected; this deprivileges the centering of human agency. Greer (2018) advocate a return to Merleau-Ponty (1964), who argues for embodied perceptions and an "embodied subject," as opposed to privileging a Cartesian-based, mind/body binary. As he says, "the theory of the body is already a theory of perception," and "our own body is in the world as the heart is in the organism" (Merleau-Ponty cited in Greer, 2018: 134). Barad (2007) has argued for the intricately entangled universe where all is predicated on relationally-based intra-actions ("agential realism") and only a "cut" in this ongoing flow creates the categories we see in everyday life (we will return to Barad below). Separation into distinct categories is a constructive process of otherwise entangled states. The dynamic and entangled state is where each entity co-constitutes each other. Here, according to Greer (ibid., 138) "the human of human rights remains meaningful to speak of but becomes both contingent and productive: the human becomes a question of continuously emergent, evolutive subjectivity/ies for which the meaning of the human itself in any context is a collaborative materio-semiotic endeavor: 'we humans' are always an 'I'/'we' 'in the making.'"

Therefore, a heightened sense of vulnerability—"embracing the human being as but one vulnerable partner in a vulnerable entanglement" (Greer, 2020: 165)—must be acknowledged and this integrated into rights discourse and their formulation (ibid. 141; see also Philippopoulous-Mihalopoulos, 2011a, 2011b, 2011c). Philippopoulous-Mihalopoulos (2011a) argues vulnerability has to do with "awareness of being existentially exposed" and advocates a new middle space, not a center, where all is intertwined, a place of continuous movement, becoming, singularities, immanence, multiplicities, reconnections and dissipations. The decentering of the human releases the potentialities in the development of new holistic, entangled, co-constructed understandings of the relationships between human and the non-human and living systems, "an enriching embrace of human-nonhuman socialities," and lays open new capabilities in bodily experiences (Greer, 2020: 168; Haraway, 2008: 4). Here, new materialist notions of agency as the capacity to both effect and be affected, the "affectability of all matter," is at the basis of vulnerability and a more genuine development of human and non-human rights discourse where all problems are considered in their singularity (Philippopoulos-Mihalopoulos, 2011a: 21; Greer, 169). It is within this space that law and a discourse of rights should arise, an "earth jurisprudence."

Another beginning for establishing substantive rights for the non-human, as well as human, is to engage the literature on social justice (see, for example Loretta and Milovanovic, 2020: Chapter 7). Schlosberg's (2004, 2007) four components of justice (distribution, recognition, participation, capabilities)[3] have been applied to three components of eco-justice (White and Heckenberg, 2014): environmental justice, ecological justice, and species justice (ibid., 48–49). A sociology of law would see this arena as fertile grounds for generating concepts, including substantive rights, for an earth jurisprudence. It would require breaking out of the cells within which we conventionally think. Consider, for example recognition and participation. We have seen that some courts assume trees, forests, rivers, and non-human animals cannot speak for themselves and must have representation, *in loco parentis*. Others have argued that this is a path toward more objectification, hierarchy, separation, and distancing. Conty (2018: 86), for example, argues "forests, rivers and all other ecosystems are alive because they think and represent using semiotic signs ... they can represent themselves, and do not need human delegates to 'speak' for them." Think, for example, how we recognize healthy growing rain forests verses those that are on the decline. We must get in tune with *their* language, their forms of expression and forms of content (milieus). Anthropocentrism has restricted an open mind as to the semiotic system of the environment and non-humans. Here, again, a return to indigenous understandings could provide further insight.

But how is one to "hear" rivers, forests, diverse species, and eco-systems? How do they communicate? What semiotic system are they making use of? A growing literature is beginning to address the various creative methods for listening (Haskell, 2017, 2018; Hausheer, 2015). New understandings are developing as to how nature communicates (see for example, Toomey, 2016 on how trees "talk" to each other, through, for example, their interlocking root systems). Increasingly, we are seeing heightened engagement with such topics as *How Forests Think* (Kohn, 2013) and "Should Trees Have Standing?" (Stone, 1972).

Others have advocated a transformative eco-justice perspective (Capeheart and Milovanovic, 2020: 170–175), that would build on the preceding, and integrate critical sustainabilities studies' (Cachelin and Rose, 2018). Preston's (2011) suggestion for an "environmental court," environmental restorative justice, and emphasis on problem-solving could also be integrated in this approach.

In sum, a new materialism perspective can shed light on eco-law, an earth jurisprudence, and can be integrated in a perspective in the sociology of law.

Quantum-Informed Sociology of Law

A turn to quantum mechanics and even holography theory is beginning to be witnessed in various disciplines. This represents a paradigm shift as a quantum ontology is replacing the dominant Newtonian-based ontology inherited from the Enlightenment and privileged by modernist thinkers. There has been a spattering of articles that have appeared in legal journals (Tribe, 1989; Kelsey, 2013; Powell and Menendian, 2010; Yager, 2013; Mootz, 2013; Porter, 1991; Kuttner, 2011; see also Milovanovic, 2014: 156–165; 2019). However, Karan Barad's *Meeting the Universe* (2007) has been a game-changer. A considerable amount of cross-disciplinary work has appeared in "sociomateriality," which builds on her "agential realism." The legal arena as well as the field of criminology, as of the writing of this book, remain with few takers, while other fields are increasingly engaged.

Some works have applied quantum theory as a metaphor or analogy, some take on a more agnostic position of a quantum consciousness, but nevertheless employ quantum theory in their analysis. Many others see it as an isomorphic, physical explanation of processes that occur in everything. Let's first provide the key differences between Classical (Newtonian) ontology and quantum ontology. We will then go over the double-slit experiment, the entry point in understanding quantum mechanics. We include examples of the adaptations and applications taking place in various disciplines. Quantum decision-making is explicated. We will introduce potential modeling in a quantum informed semiotics in the sociology of law. To complete our journey, we will conjecture about the possibilities of quantum holography.

Classical v. Quantum Ontologies

Social sciences, as well as legal jurisprudence and sociology of law build on a core set of assumptions inherited from the Enlightenment. Isaac Newton's *Principia* (1687) provided key concepts which have been, and continue to be, uncritically internalized. His was a "clockwork universes," a world of ultimate predictability. It valued: linear developments (linear logic); proportionality between force and effect ("Second Law of Motion"); unfolding time; three-dimensional space; locality (causes are confined to the immediacy of the event in time and space); and objectivity, essences, clear boundaries and attributes of particles located in fixed time-space coordinates. Newton's F = ma tells us that given an observer-independent particle in 3-dimension space, with an added force, will move in a predictable, proportional way in linear time. Thus, it is said, all one has to do is to identify the forces acting on a particle/object to predict its movement in space-time. In criminology there is, for example, the focus on linear causality; in law, responsibility. These elements contribute to the classic physics paradigm. Everything is determined and it is the scientist's quest for discovering laws governing all behavior, an ideal embraced especially by empirically-driven social scientists. Albert Einstein was the first to challenge some of these assumptions, but ultimately argued for mathematical explanations, in his quip "God does not play dice," and that, like Newton, declared simple laws would eventually be discovered for all behavior, such as his classic, $E = mc^2$.

Quantum mechanics, many of the core concepts of which developed in the 1920s, and often clarified in response to Einstein's criticism, was a broadside attack on Newton's concepts. Niels Bohr's response to Einstein's quip "God does not play dice," was "Don't tell God what to do." Chance, probabilities, uncertainty, a dice throw, nonlocal effects, entanglement, dualities (particle form/wave form) — all called for a resituating science and the development of a new paradigm. Rather than F = ma, quantum mechanics offers the notion of a Schrödinger equation with the solution called the "wave function," referred to as a probability wave. It encodes various states of possibilities existing simultaneously (superposition, a "cloud of possibilities,") that evolves in time, where its "collapse" produces material forms ("mattering"); not determinacy, but probabilities rule. Said in another way, objects/phenomena are wave functions representing co-existing probability states (clouds of possibility), and the Schrödinger equation accounts for its evolution over time. In law, consider, for example, our previous discussion of an alternative standard for the legal subject, "the reasonable intersectional person" rather than the "reasonable man in law." In quantum theory, this alternative can be reconceptualized as a coherent superposition of various co-exiting possible identities (probability states). It is in context with a conscious observation that it collapses witnessing the dominance of one state.

Lawrence H. Tribe (1989), one of the leading American legal scholars, was one of the first to apply quantum mechanics and Einstein's relativity theory to law, be they more metaphorical. He chastised judges for their dogmatism, taking as a given the classic physics paradigm, pointing out, rather, "the very act of judging alters the context and relationships being judged" (ibid., 1). At the outset his criteria for engagement with this work is whether their use "promote[s] illuminating question and directions" (ibid., 2). He points out that classical-based legal language is out of date with the new social realities and sciences that have emerged. The U.S. Constitution itself, he argues, is Newtonian in structure with its inclusion of forces, checks and balances, a self-regulating machine without sensitivity to the new order. He cites Dick Howard who demonstrates the "influences of clocks, 'gadgets' and mechanical metaphors on the founding fathers" (Howard cited in Tribe, ibid., 3). Tribe, in re-reading major court decisions, provides many examples of the productive use of quantum mechanics. He stresses that observing the world alters it, much in line with the double-slit experiment (see below). He takes the U.S. Supreme Court decision, *McCleskey v. Kemp* (1987), a case in which it was clearly and overwhelmingly shown by the very best statistically obtained evidence that an African-American man who killed a white man is much more likely to be sentenced to death than a white man killing an African-American, only to see the court dismissing a system's analysis and rather arguing for prosecuting "bad apples," individual intent, a classical position. Tribe argues that the decision's message is that the government bears no responsibility and thus, the government's action are legitimized (ibid., 33). The opportunity was missed Tribe argues. If the Court ruled as the evidence indicated, "that little short of a radical overhaul in the structure of the criminal justice system, and perhaps in the structure of our society as a whole, could eliminate this tragic link between the victim's race and the system's response" (ibid., 33). A post-Newtonian perspective, he argues, would put more emphasis on patterns (waves), rather than particles (bad apples). And we must abandon a view that argues for "objective" accounts and focus on construction processes.

More specific spawning of the concepts of quantum mechanics have appeared in the sociomateriality perspective which has been applied in numerous disciplines. Law and criminology have been exceptions. Karan Barad (2007), a physicist by formal training (Ph.D.), turned philosopher, has been the inspirational force. She builds on Niels Bohr, one of the founding members of quantum mechanics (more below). There are several approaches in quantum mechanics.[4] Bohr's, that began to be called the Copenhagen school, is one of the dominant ones. All phenomena, it is argued, exist in a dualism, particle-form/wave-form, and it is observation or measurement that "collapses the wave function" whereby boundaries, properties, identities, and capabilities materialize. Let's first review the fundamental experiment on which much of this rests, the "double-slit experiment," and then we will return to Barad and a quantum-informed application to law, via sociomateriality.

Double-Slit Experiment

The double-slit experiment was originally a thought-experiment, an experiment conjured up in the mind, by Thomas Young in 1801. The 1920s and 1930s brought this into sharper relief. But it was not until the 1960s that experimental studies provided consistent support for the predictions. The experimental set up includes some barrier with two slits in it and a recording surface on the other side.[5] Light, or an electron, as an electromagnetic wave, passes through the slits and forms interference patterns on the other side, which is recorded on the receiving media in patterns of vertical white regions (the interference patterns) and dark regions (non-interference patterns) in between them. To visualize an interference pattern, think of two ships passing each other and their intersecting wakes. Fine, so far. All is predictable. But, introduce some measuring device or observation at the slits and the recording pattern changes to two vertical regions, one corresponding to each of the two slits, suggesting particle forms. Remove the measurement or observation device, and the interference pattern re-emerges (wave form). Quantum physicists theorized that the "entity/object" that passes through the slit was *both* wave and particle. The measurement or observation, later attributable to consciousness, is what collapsed the wave function into a particle-form materializing boundaries, properties, identities, and capacities/capabilities. Thus, all phenomena are characterized by this duality; or better, complementarity, a unity of mutual exclusives (Neils Bohr). The electromagnetic wave patterns can be expressed as a wave function (Schrödinger, 1925). Bohr, in his debates with Einstein, was to later clarify that the collapse of the wave function must also include the total context (e.g., experimental apparatus). We extend this to the assemblage previously reviewed.

A wave function (represented as psi, Ψ) can be conceptualized as a cloud of possibilities in movement; a probability wave that tells us how a system evolves over time; that is, all phenomena remain in a state of quantum "superposition" — numerous possibilities exist at the same time, until the collapse of the wave function and a particle-form is materialized. This directly contradicted the Newtonian model of fixed essences, located in fixed time-space dimensions following clear trajectories. In addition to the wave function, the "uncertainty principle" developed by Heisenberg (1925, published in 1927) argued one cannot measure precisely location and moment at the same time. Measure one precisely and the other one remains indeterminate. Pribram (1991, 2014) was a leading figure in applying all this to the working of the brain; Wendt (2015) to international relations; Milovanovic (2014, 2019) to criminology and law. It was also incorporated in feminist quantum thinking (see Sellberg and Hinton, 2016). An earlier popular work on a quantum self and a quantum society was by Zohar (1990, 1995).

Let us provide three examples in law. Start with a person in their everyday world that at any moment may exist in a number of possible states of expression (superposition). In the course of the day, consider the identity positions they may occupy: parent, student, worker, first baseman for their softball team, etc.[6] Let's now assume they are arrested by a police officer for an infraction, followed by an arrest, trial, conviction, imprisonment. Note how identities (and representative wave function) is collapsed along the way: free citizen, person of interest, suspect, defendant, convicted, felon, ex-felon. One identity becomes primary at each moment (collapse of the wave function). We also must include the law assemblage within which identities are collapsed. Consider a person entering the courthouse and its architecture, obscure language, decorum, legal texts, formal identities, formal procedures, etc. It is within the context of the whole apparatus of law that the wave function collapses, producing "cuts" in otherwise quantum entanglements in movement. Other nested contexts, assemblages, can include: the police stationhouse, the interrogation room, the "bullpen" (where inmates wait for trial), the prison, jail, the court trial room, etc.

Kutner (2011), applying a metaphoric account, compares two forms of negotiations in law: a particle-like orientation, and a wave-like orientation. The particle-like orientation assumes two individuals with clearly formulated self-interests in pursuit of maximum utility. Negotiations would follow linear reasoning toward rational logical conclusions. On the other hand, the wave-like orientation assumes a more dialogical, problem-solving encounter with co-constructions of interests and possible solutions. Linear logics is not always followed. He concludes with a call for both orientations.

Kelsey (2013), a Supreme Court Justice of Virginia, reviews the Newtonian-based background to classical law, particularly in the highly influential Blackstone's (2016 [1765]) *Commentaries* and noting statements such as the "Supreme Being" establishing "certain laws of motion, to which all movable bodies must conform." Kelsey introduced, in contrast, a law-equity duality. Law is more akin to particle theory and concerns formal rationality. It is based on Newtonian ontology. Equity is more quantum, more a wave approach reflecting exceptionalities and particularities. The two work together to produce law in action, although the uncertainty principle prevails between which dominates in a particular case.

Quantum Decision-Making in Law

Law in action is informed by theories of judging. Derived models of decision-making can be traced to theories and perspectives in philosophy and the social sciences shaped by their ontological underpinnings, i.e., Newtonian physics. Conventional understanding of decision-making in law is based on classical logic and probability. The core basis can be traced to Kolmogorov's (1933) axioms and Boolean logic (yes/no dichotomies). Quantum logic and probability, on the other hand, is traced to Neumann's (1932) axioms and to the notion of quantum "qubits" (superposition). Rational choice theory (utility theory whereby one freely and consciously weighs benefits and costs in making decisions) is often associated with classic logic.[7]

Rational choice theorists rely on classical probability theory in explaining decision-making, whereas quantum decision-making makes use of quantum probability and logic. However, when employing the classical model, irrational decision-making often arises. Quantum logic has been shown to account for the "irrationalities" and has been shown to be a better predictor of decision-making. Perhaps the key reference work explaining the differences between the two logics and their effects is Busemeyer and Bruza's *Quantum Models of Cognition and Decision* (2013; for a comprehensive overview, see Jaeger and Trueblood, 2019; see also Milovanovic, 2022). Those doing statistical analysis in quantum decision-making generally are agnostic as to the brain itself operating quantum mechanically, merely that decisions can be modeled, and that is all. Clearly, connective work needs to be done.

The classical approach in law, including rational choice theory, assumes fixed particles that follow predictable trajectories in space and time. At any specific moment, a person is in a definite state.[8] A person's future states can be predicted based on past and present states. Not so for the quantum model. At any particular moment a person is in a state of superposition where multiple possibilities exist at the same time. In a context, one state is instantiated (collapse of the wave function).[9] Future probabilities are influenced by the collapsed state. Rather than a trajectory we have a moving cloud of possibilities, a probability wave. In the classical approach, one is assumed to be guided in decision-making by a fixed storehouse of information which is weighed and judged, with a decision following. The quantum model differs. "[O]ur beliefs, attitudes, and intentions are not simply stored in memories as properties," state Busemeyer and Bruza (2013: 115), "instead they are constructed when needed." In the quantum model, one has various sub-spaces in which one situates oneself, some of which are conflictual, but each providing relevant information for making a decision. Sometimes this leads to the perception of an irrational decision. Consider the classic case of a priest asking the bank robber why they rob banks (Garfinkel, (1991). The priest is interested in why the robber is robbing banks and not getting a job. For the robber, the answer is "that's where the money is." The robber and priest operate within different subspaces in which decision-making is taking place. Classic probability and logic assume, rather, that one master space exists in which all relevant information is stored and from which linear reasoning leading to a decision can take place.

Let's take jury decision-making as an example. The juror, in the quantum model, finds themself in a wave form (wave function), an indefinite state which can be experienced as ambiguity, conflict, uncertainty (Busemeyer and Bruza, 2013: 3). With a decision, the juror is now in the particle state experienced as certainty and conflict resolution (collapse of the wave function, ibid.). The question posed, "Do you find the defendant guilty?" is what initiates the collapse of the wave function. "Order effects" can be experienced when the respective lawyer, prosecutor or defense, initiates a particular sequence of questions, arranging them in a particular order to elicit either damaging (for the prosecutor) or mitigating (for the defense counselor) responses. This is often the basis of an objection by the other side when it is construed as "leading the witness." In the quantum model, posing a particular question in a particular order rather than another collapses the wave function differently. Consider in this light decision-making in filling out a questionnaire. The classical researcher assumes definite states exist (i.e., opinions, attitudes) and the questionnaire merely *discovers* and records what these are. The quantum researcher sees indefinite states and asking the question initiates a *creative* act; that is, the opinion is created in the instance following the question being asked.

To return to the juror. They are faced with a decision, guilty? or not guilty? and in quantum theory this produces a coherent superposition of the two states in the context of the court. With perhaps probabilities stacked higher toward one tendency based on personal leanings, biases, experiences and memories of how things work. But, until a decision is required a non-zero probability exist for any one state to manifest.

There are many other anomalies and inconsistencies in the classical model, for example: disjunctive effects, conjunction fallacies, preference reversals, non-commutativity, etc. (see Busemeyer and Bruza: 2013; Jaeger and Trueblood, 2019: 25–36; Wendt, 2015: 154–173). Space limitations preclude a fuller examination here. Three differences between the classical and quantum model are illustrative (see Jaeger and Trueblood, 2019: 29–33). Classical probability argues that judgements arise from: definite states; a single space from which information is drawn in totality in making a decision; and commutativity (ordering is not important). Whereas, responding to each, quantum logic, argues for: indefinite states; multiple spaces in which sometimes contrasting information resides; and non-commutativity, that is ordering makes a difference. For example, if a plaintiff is litigating a trademark and a defamation case, and considers the probabilities of winning in the trademark case prior to the defamation case rather than the other way around, a different probability judgement will be made which will affect deciding on settlement (ibid., 33).

Quantum decision-making provides numerous suggestions for understanding how decisions are made in the real world. Legal realists would have an ally in quantum decision-making. Quantum game theory, for example, shows how quantum entanglement, the inherent interconnections of all entities, rather than separateness assumed by classical thought, often leads to cooperative activity than to competitive and conflict outcomes. See, for example, the numerous writings on the "prisoner's dilemma." The prisoner's dilemma is a hypothetical in which a deal is offered to two inmates in which the other can be turned in for a lenient sentence It has been demonstrated, using quantum logic, that cooperation rather than a zero-sum game often results that benefits both inmates being offered a plea-bargain (see Wendt, 2015: 168–173; Hanauske, 2010; Kim and Nho, 2019). The distinction between employing classical logic versus quantum logic is particularly valuable in understanding mediation practices in restorative justice programs where wave form dynamics are more predominant compared to traditional criminal justice practices where particle form dynamics are at play.

In short, quantum decision-making offers a fresh new way in understanding how real decisions are made by human beings in struggles and by their aspirations in their everyday world. It also provides productive hypotheses for exploration in legal decision-making settings (see for example Jaeger and Trueblood, 2019: 48–60). Their recommendations include further investigating: the influence of quantum effects on factfinder's final judgements; eyewitnesses responding to lineups for identification (sequential? simultaneous?); verdicts dealing with multiple charges and claims and/or multiple defendants; appeals court's overuse of "harmless error" principle; the ordering of evidence and their effect on legal conclusions; and police categorizing suspects in initial engagement and how it relates to force employed. In sum, these may lead to policy changes, new procedural laws and better police training.

Karan Barad and Sociomateriality

Barad's *Meeting the Universe Halfway* (2007) is a fundamental call for rethinking the conventional, classical paradigm with which we have been enthralled. She draws out the implication of the double-slit experiment and Niels Bohr's version of quantum mechanics, the Copenhagen School. She also draws from a number of postmodernists, such as Judith Butler, Michel Foucault and Jacques Derrida. She offers new conceptualizations as tools for social and philosophical inquiry. Her work has been further incorporated as the basis of the newly emerged discipline of *sociomateriality*, unhyphenated to suggest the social and the material are not separate but intrinsically interconnected and co-produced. The discipline, Informational Sciences, has taken the lead in earlier applications (see Orlikowski, 2009; Orlikowski and Scott, 2008). We witness recent entries into feminism,[10] but much more need to be done. Barad (2007) advocates a "diffractive" reading approach, a reading through different approaches in terms of each other. The clash of say a quantum informed approach with a traditional, classical approach provides opportunities for insights, revelations, clarifications, and new formulations.

A central concept includes the notion of "intra-action" as a replacement to interaction, suggesting that only *phenomena* exist—wave forms if you will, quantum entanglements, superposition—and reality is co-constituted in material discursive practices. It is performatively co-constructed in context. Quantum entanglement is ubiquitous, and only an "agential cut," a slice in the ongoing flow produces a rendition of "reality." Drawing a further lesson from the double-slit experiments, it is the total physical arrangement in relation (apparatus) to the "thing" measured that produces a "cut," whereby boundaries, properties, identities, and capabilities are created. Material discursive practices within this context produce realities. Returning to a previous discussion of the legal assemblage, represented is the total arrangement of architecture, law books, official identities (discursive subject positions—judges, jurors, prosecutors, defense counselors), legal discourse, etc. Intra-active, material discursive practices enact cuts producing various realities. By enact we mean doings, performative practices; realities are brought into being in their performative expression (recall Austin, Chapter 9; Butler, 1990). Barad draws from Judith Butler's (1990, 1993) work on how gender roles are enacted, performatively. It is with repetition that a stability is ongoingly co-constituted producing the reality we witness.

In connecting Barad's work to Deleuze and Guattari's which she does not do, we can also say, using the latter's use of Hjelmslev's semiotics focus on expression and content, material discursive practice is a co-constituted ("doubly articulated") practice of expression (language form) and content which includes phenomena (matter) as substance (formed matter)—together, co-constitutively (intra-actively) producing a composite of what is "reality" in particular contexts. The legal assemblage, in short produces a legal reality that via repetition, continuously reconstitutes itself with the appearance of being self-evident.

Let's provide some examples of the application of a Barad-informed sociomateriality. Introna (2007), applies it to police surveillance cameras (closed-circuit television, CCTV). Surveillance cameras constitute subjects and objects: the viewer is constituted as police (observer), the watched (and avoider) as suspect or deviant. "Thus, the suspect, camera, operators and the targets are co-constitutively implicated in performativity and enactments (scripts being co-created—what it means to be a suspect, what it means to be a police officer, and the relation between them)" (Milovanovic, 2022; see also Introna, 2007: 8; Bogard, 2006). In CCTV, human agents and technology are entangled, and in performative material discursive cuts we witness a co-construction of particular identities.

Another application of sociomateriality has been to recent developments in police body-warn cameras, BWCs (Guzik *et al.*, 2021; Sesay *et al.*, 2017). Similar to Introna's work, identities and affordances (capabilities) are enacted. Technology and humans co-constitutively and performatively enact identities. The identity of the police officer, for example, is transforming into a "hybrid police officer" (Sesay *et al.*, ibid., 4269), a performative act in which identities are enacted in everyday police-citizen encounters, and repetitively reconstituted as a new reality with its own affordances in doing police work. The BWC-body assemblage in action (intra-action) produces particular cuts and thus boundaries, properties, identities, and capabilities/capacities (affordances).

It may seem that Barad's model implies the eviscerating of responsibility since all is entangled. However, she offers an alternative approach. Response-ability, she argues (2010: 25), is about "our active engagement of sedimenting out the world in certain kinds of ways and not others. Being attentive to the ways in which we are re-doing, with each intra-action materially re-doing the material configurings of space-timemattering." Ethical principles must counter harms of reduction and repression and of investing in harm (Henry and Milovanovic, 2020) by cultivating response-ability that enacts greater capabilities (see also, Murris and Bozalek, 2019; Milovanovic, 2019). Murris and Bozalek (ibid., 10–12) interpret Barad's call as a: "radical openness and respect," "attentive engagement with texts," "creating new relations through mutual constitution," and a "becoming with texts and being transformed by them." "Mattering," as a process, is not in the singular, but always a co-constitutive enterprise in entangled relations, always a becoming, a doing together, experimentation, developing new capabilities and being attentive to differences that matter (ibid., see also Haraway, 2016; Taguchi, 2012; Milovanovic, 2019, 2022). All this is to say that law needs a fundamental re-orientation toward a more relational, holistic, and entangled picture of "reality." Classical notions of responsibility, adherents argue, resting on an atomistic picture of humans, cannot lead to adequately rendering justice by the continued use of an archaic model. A quantum ontology provides a new basis for such a reconsideration.

Quantum Semiotics in Sociology of Law

On a number of occasions, we have presented semiotics as an important concept to integrate into a holistic sociology of law. Indeed, we have previously noted the importance of narrative constructions and material discursive practices in the construction of "reality," particularly in legal settings. We argued that when one enters the legal assemblage one is immersed in a form of content (e.g., particular patterned physical arrangements, interacting bodies, etc.) and forms of expression (e.g., legal language). Existing entanglements and superposition (wave function) undergo a "cut" in law-in-action; that is, in material discursive practices, whereby a collapse of the wave function produces particular boundaries, properties, identities and capabilities/capacities. We now want to address quantum semiotics and particularly quantum semantic constructions.

Words remain in a superposition state (polysemy, Neuman, 2008) until they undergo a collapse whereby one signified is produced ("mattering").[11] Consider Lacan's

(1977) approach for a moment. Speech production is a process which entails both a forward and backward time direction in a construction process. The Imaginary Order provides images (consider the images and imaginary play when one enters the court house), the Symbolic Order a relevant language, here legalese, and the Real Order is always in play in the background, un-articulable, but yet with effects. Lacan's (1977) more dynamic model of speech production was presented in his "graphs of desire," four in number, the last being a composite. The short of it is that when one engages in speech production one always anticipates the next signifier which is relevant, which represents the totality of the person's desires at that point ("a signifier represents the subject for another signifier"), and while the signifier is taking form, the next signifier is being anticipated.

According to Lacan, one "chooses"[12] a signifier from the paradigm structures (word meanings, semantic structure) and places it in a linear order governed by language codes (syntagmatic structure). It is only when a pause takes place at the end of a sequence of constructed signifiers that one moves backward in time to the beginning of the sequence and grasps the meaning of what is being said all at once.[13] This is represented by Lacan as s(O), a punctuation point much like an upholstery button in old couches. (Recall, "s" represents a signified, "O," the sphere of the Other, the unconscious.) We see this as the collapse of the wave function. At that point, the quantum entangled state within the unconscious, in intra-action with available linguistic coordinate systems within which one is inserted, and discursive subject position assumed produces meaning in the instance. Lacan called the subject, a *parlêtre* (speaking) or *l'être parlant* (speaking being). Thus, entering the courthouse, an assemblage, is also entering an arena in which particular realities can be constructed. Class, race, ethnicity, gender, and intersectionalities are factors that further shape the process.

Let's explore the field of quantum semantics, the human mental lexicon structure (for an accessible introduction, see Wendt, 2015: 207–221; for mathematic modeling, see Busemeyer and Bruza, 2013: 185–210). Busemeyer and Bruza, it should be noted, do not assume a quantum brain, whereas Wendt does. Following Wendt, a person always finds themself in superposition states, not well-defined states. The brain is a quantum computer which then suggests that language is quantum (Wendt, 2015). Thus, we can speak of quantum semantics. Concepts and signifiers, are entangled and in superposition lacking definite boundaries, properties, identities and capabilities. Therefore, we have only potential meanings in probability states, represented by a semantic wave function. Wendt, following Aerts (2009, 2010), also notes that since a concept cannot be simultaneously in an abstract/potential state and an actual state, Heisenberg's uncertainty principle is implicated. It is within context and a speech act that the wave function collapses to one of the probability states finding formal expression ("eigen-state," see also Busemeyer and Bruza, 2013: 205). The speech act is equivalent to an observation or measurement in the double-slit experiment. In this view, words "are stored in memory [our lexical storehouse] as entangled superpositions and as such are not fully separable," and words "do not have distinct identities prior to their actualization" (ibid. 220). It is, again, context, "the way in which associations are measured" that specific meanings and identities are formulated. Word meanings (signified) are thus a result of quantum dynamics.

Other subspaces do exist within each person who, for example, gets involved with legal prosecution or in litigation, but word and reality constructions in these more nuanced subspaces reflecting the idiosyncratic lifestyles don't "count" in legal proceedings. Linguistic legal repression silences these constructions offering a more sterile, abstract discourse within which to speak and construct reality. Of course, as we have seen with "crits," counter story-telling will be attempted that draws from idiosyncratic subspaces and especially from class, race, ethnic, gender and intersectional nuances.

All this is highly relevant to legal semiotics and for being integrated in a more holistic sociology of law. Legal language exists in a virtual quantum coherent state, an entangled and superposed state, and legal meaning is only established with the collapse of the wave function in context. It is, following Barad (2007), collapsed in performative material discursive practices; that is, in intra-active processes that co-produce specific manifestations ("mattering") of words and realities.

Edwina Taborsky, C.S. Peirce and quantum semiotics. Let's briefly look at one model of semiosis, defined as the production of signs with specific meanings. Edwina Taborsky (2001) focuses on how energy undergoes change from a more amorphous form to information by applying quantum mechanics to C.S. Peirce's triadic semiotics. In a following section, we will follow by addressing a possible Deleuze and Guattari's employment of Hjelmslev's quadripartite semiotic model and how it can be quantized with further integration of holography theory in portraying co-constitutive, intra-active discursive practices.

Taborsky's (2000, 2001a, 2001b, 2003, 2008) work is conspicuously under-utilized in understanding the material processes of semiosis. She engages both classical mechanics and quantum mechanics in demonstrating how amorphous energy is transformed into informed mass (formed matter, or substance), usable information, allowing codification. She distinguishes two cuts, an ontological and an epistemological. The ontological cut, sometimes referred to as a "Heisenberg cut" (Atmanspacher, 1999), establishes boundaries between the "inside" and "outside," distinctions between objects and the environment. It concerns quantum mechanical rules. Amorphous energy, in other words, is transformed by the cut into particular forms, in discrete mass. Consider a person appearing in court as a litigant or defendant in their multiple feeling states. The epistemological cut, sometimes referred to as the "Cartesian cut" (Atmanspacker, 1999) is about formal codes and law. It concerns classical mechanical rules (Newtonian). Consider our defendant or litigant now being confronted with the requirements of formal rational law, with its clear distinctions, categories, identities, meaning, and form of deductive reasoning. Consider C.S. Peirce's distinction: "We call the world of fancy the internal world, the world of fact the external world" (cited in Taborsky, 2003).

Taborsky applies this to C.S. Peirce's distinction between Firstness, Secondness, and Thirdness (discussed in Chapter 9). Firstness is an amorphous, holistic, feeling state, measureless, without boundaries and distinctions and operating in an analog realm (continuous frequency waves with varying amplitudes, and contextually based). It is a "plentitude of potentialities," a "profusion of possibilities" and uncertainties (Taborsky, 2003: 5). Quantum mechanical laws are operative in this realm. Expressions are more iconic where there exists "a mere relation between the sign and the thing signified" (C.S. Peirce cited in Taborsky, 2003: 4). The process of measurement (attention), however, produces a differentiation, and boundaries. This is Secondness, things in opposition, but not yet brought within a normative order, more singular expressions, more an indexical expression based on operative relations which acknowledge separation and distinctions. Thirdness is a more stable order of universalities, normative systems, and law. It is about learned symbols, universals that take on meaning in normative systems of relationships, and shaped by semiotic codes. The tripartite structure of the sign captures the structure of dominant symbols (interpretant, object, representamen). Thirdness is characterized as operating by a digital code (binary forms, bits, zero-ones, discrete and decontextualized). It compresses the analog codes of Firstness into decontextualized, abstract, digital codes of Thirdness (Taborsky, 7). It is more about an epistemological cut establishing abstract categories, differences, universalities, and normative systems of signs.

Let's provide an example of law in action. Consider a defendant before the law, or, a person who has just been stopped, frisked, and arrested. Feeling states of despair, anxiety, and confusion, are rampant, a Firstness. Or consider driving your car and being pulled over by the police and the initial fleeting feelings and amorphous thoughts that arose. The defendant now finds themself in opposition to impinging legal forces, more Secondness, where differentiations and legal categories are beginning to emerge.[14] They obtain a lawyer. They appear in the lawyer's office for the first time in a multiplicity of feeling states. The lawyer quickly disciplines the defendant with the language of law (Thirdness), ostensibly to establish "legal standing." At the courthouse, a law assemblage — the totality of the physical arrangements, abstract legal language, and procedures — stabilizes certain constellation of signifiers, the language of law. In this context, speech acts collapse the wave function producing cuts and legal realities. Thus, the singularity of the event where energy is more amorphous undergoes various representational constructions, now cleansed of their nuanced basis.

Quantum Holographic Semiotics of Law

Along with quantum mechanics, holography theory is beginning to be applied in the social sciences. Whereas quantum mechanics is beginning to witness derivative approaches such as Barad's groundbreaking work, and in application to a third wave sociomateriality, and perhaps with the development of the quantum computer, concepts, metaphors and language that will become more reflective, holography theory remains even more of an abstraction. Although, the media is increasingly referencing and portraying holograms such as virtual concerts. Technology, too, is advancing holographic-based video displays. We have, nevertheless, seen applications in neuropsychology (Pribram, 1991, 2014), sociology (Bradley, 1999, 2006, 2007, 2010, 2011), consciousness studies (Mitchell and Staretz, 2011), criminology (Milovanovic, 2013, 2014, 2018, 2022), lexical structures (Jones and Mewhort, 2007), political science (Wendt, 2015) and some forays into law (Milovanovic, 2018) and social justice (Capeheart and Milovanovic, 2020: 232–235). Franciso Di Biase (2013, 2016) has been a prolific writer in developing an integrated model of a quantum holographic basis for consciousness. Cutting edge cosmologists and physicists have embraced holography as an essential element in any *bonafide* theorizing. Studying black holes by leading theorists Leonard Susskind, Gerard 't Hooft, Juan Maldacena and Jacob Bekenstein has led to confirmation of the principles of holography. Black holes are surrounded by an event horizon, a boundary region, on which it has been argued, holographically encoded information resides from all that falls into the center and disintegrates. The development of holography has been attributed to Dennis Gabor (1946, 1948, 1968, 1971) who, in 1971, received a Nobel Prize for his work.[15] We are particularly interested in how information is encoded, stored, accessed and decoded. In contemporary studies of law, all of this is taken for granted. Let's first review some central concepts. Then we visit applications to law and law-in-action.

Holography is about interference patterns that encode information. Think about two ships plying the seas and their intersecting wakes, or throw two stones in a pond and observe where they intersect. These intersections of waves encode information, about, for example, the tonnage of the ships, their speed, direction, etc. The creation of a holograms follows rather simple principles in which two light beams are involved: the object beam is reflected off an object and combines with a neutral laser beam producing an interference pattern that is recorded on some medium.[16] Now, shine a light (reference beam) on any location on the medium and the whole three-dimensional image re-appears. The image is spread out over the whole surface (nonlocality). This form of holography remains deterministic, for there is a one-to-one replication of the image. Quantum holography argues, instead, for the encoding of superposition, and thus implicates Heisenberg's uncertainty principle and wave collapse.[17]

Let's provide a simple example of a hologram, easily demonstrated in a class room (Pribram, 2014: 44–45; Bradley, 2011). Start with a slide projector. Insert a slide, and one sees on the recording screen, for example, a horse. Take the lens out and keep the light on. One sees "no-thing" on the screen. However, introduce a pair of reading glasses in the light's path to the screen and you will see the image of the horse re-appear on the screen. Move the eyeglasses around in the projected light cone and you will note the image still re-appears at any location on the screen which the light cone hits. Use two eyeglasses and images re-appear for each on the screen. Information is being recorded *nonlocally*. Information is encoded on the light beam from the slide projector to the recording screen. Now, here's the upshot. Your eyes represent the lens of the slide projector and can decode holographically encoded information.[18] Holography is about illuminating a recording surface for resurrecting the initial image.

All entities emit electromagnetic wave forms that encode their characteristics (information). They are constantly interfering with other wave forms producing holograms. These are stored in a sub-quantum "in-formation field" within which everything is encoded. In other words, acting much like the recording surface above (see Laszlo, 1995, 2007). We are immersed in a quantum and in-formation field. One sugar cube of space, it is said, can record all the information stored in the Library of Congress. When applying this insight, the wherewithal of information storage has several refinements. One version drawing from cosmologists and physicist's insights, has it that we can conceptualize a world of nested bounded regions in which the interior (the "bulk"), the everyday happenings in spacetime, has this information holographically encoded on the boundary surface. Another version (Pribram, 1991, 2014) has concluded that the brain is a holographic space in which memory is nonlocally stored, not, as in traditional neuroscience, stored in particular, locatable clusters. Yet another version is by Laszlo (2007) who argues memory is not stored in the brain, but "out there" in a quantum in-formation field. Consider Laszlo's position (and also suggested by such leading physicists as Leonard Susskind) in applying it to a street corner, a courtroom, an office, the courthouse, police station, workspaces—all are relatively bounded spaces. Susskind (2009), for example, asks us to consider his office, a bounded space. On his walls, he says, are holographically encoded all the conversations and interactions that have transpired within it. Consider, the much-cited study by Sykes and Matza (1957) on "techniques of neutralization"—verbalizations that rationalize impending deviant behavior. This study does not, however, explain how in fact these verbalizations are encoded. Or consider Cressey's (1957) business office where rationalizations often appear as part of the subculture which justify embezzlement. Thus, in applying to Sykes and Matza and Cressey, this information can be portrayed as holographically encoded on boundary regions, say a particularly volatile corner of the city, or at the business office, and is accessed by a process of "phase conjugation." Let's explain how this process works.

Phase Conjugation (Phase Conjugate Adaptive Resonance, PCAR)

We are interested in how all this is applied to accessing and decoding holograms in human consciousness. Offered is the notion of "phase conjugation," or, in more precise language, phase conjugate adaptive resonance" (pcar) (see Cramer, 1986, 2016; Mitchell and Staretz, 2011; Schempp, 1992; Marcer and Schempp, 1997, 1998, 1999). MRIs, as well as dolphins, bats, and whales have been shown to operate by this principle.

All entities emit wave forms encoding all their characteristics. An emitter's wave form, a wave function, is received by an absorber. After the absorber registers the wave form it sends back a wave form to the emitter without time transpiring. This establishes a "standing wave" between them along which information flows. At some point of intensity, the wave form received at the emitter collapses where one materialization insures. It is argued that the image is "out there" not in the mind. In this view, long term memory images are not in the brain, but stored out there in the information field. All entities are waves not particles. Attention by the psychic apparatus produces wave forms that access information encoded holographically. Pcar accounts for how this information is accessed and decoded.

Think now of our previous example of "techniques of neutralization." Juveniles hanging out on some street corners, a bounded region, access holographically encoded information on the surface of the boundaries.[19] Through pcar, the juvenile decodes and acts on this information.[20] Let's move to how pcar is essential understanding in the operation of the psychic apparatus. One model is Schema QD (Milovanovic, 2013; 2019; 2022; Batiz and Milovanovic, 2017).

Schema QD

Schema QD a revised, de-oedipalized adaptation of Lacan's (1977) Schema R, represents an inter- and intra-subjective human agent.[21] It is mobilized not by lack as in Lacan but production (productive desire) as in Deleuze and Guattari, a vitalism in the spirit of Bergson's *êlan vital*, Spinoza's joyful relations, Nietzsche's will to power, Schrödinger's (2012) "life force"—all suggest the fundamental force for actualizing increasing capabilities to affect and be effected.[22] Wendt's (2015: 131–147) suggestion, a "quantum vitalism," centers on superposition (coherence) and collapse (decoherence) being an ontological basis of vitalism. Matter, he says, "only becomes life when organized into quantum coherent wholes" and where it is absent you may have an actant (Latour, 2007), but not agency, "causal power yes, but not agency" (Wendt, ibid., 147).

Schema QD can be pictured as a quantum entangled four-cornered entity, each of the four in a superposition state. Let's model it (Milovanovic, 2013: 74–79; 20; 2014: 119–122). Take a rectangle, label the top left corner "ego" (imaginary constructions of self); directly to the right corner, "Other" (the person with and through whom one constitutes oneself); bottom left corner, "ego ideal" (the image of an ideal desirable person), and bottom right-hand corner, the organized other (the community standards). Now put a half twist in it, connect and glue the ends, and you have a continuous, interconnected surface (i.e., a Möbius band); here depicting the interconnected nature of the four components. Following Lacan, human agency is stretched over all four corners simultaneously. To mobilize it, trace a figure-eight on a three-dimensional topological construct called a "cross-cap" (see Milovanovic, 2013: 74–79).[23] Each figure-eight cut is equivalent to the collapse of the wave function, producing a particular matrix of the four components. With each collapse, each component takes on a particular value (eigenstate).

The cross-cap is embedded in the imaginary, symbolic and real orders including a macro-level normative system and existent discursive subject positions, an energized in-formation field of populated interference patterns. Each encounter mobilizes the psychic apparatus. Pcar is the mechanism in which incoming wave fields are absorbed and decoded in Schema QD whereby the intra-actions between the four key elements establish a unique configuration, a matrix, which generates a unique QD signature wave for each person, holographically encoding the totality of the person's being in context. It is then sent back in the reverse direction to the emitting entity or the encounter[24] where an otherwise superposed state collapses with a particular instantiation that represents "reality" in the instance. The constituted matrix generates a particular "I" that can insert itself in a discursive subject-position in a particular linguistic coordinate system from where it can speak, where it can engage in narrative constructions.[25] It takes form as a QD signature wave, encoding the collapsed state of the person's entanglements in that instance. This revises Lacan's Schema R, and one can speak of a quantum *parlêtre* (quantum speaking being).

Post posthumanism, particularly new materialism, has been too quick to jettison a notion of human agency and consciousness. In applications to sociology and law, it falls short in accounting for how consciousness emerges. Yes, it moves away from anthropocentrism in valuing an actant, but agency is a different story. Let's see how Schema QD is mobilized in assemblages. Picture assemblages being nested, meaning one can appear within an included other, which can include another, etc. Each, too, can be envisioned as a relatively stable, bounded region. We are particularly interested in the legal assemblage.

Legal Assemblage and Quantum Holography

A legal assemblage provides the context of law-in-action. Hjelmslev's quadripartite schema (expression, content, each by form and substance) provides the context of speech acts and reality construction in the legal arena where unformed matter takes on specific form (legal understanding). Law and language exist in potentiality, but must be actualized in speech acts, which collapse the wave function from a superposition state to a particular instantiation. Pcar is the mechanism by which holographically encoded information is accessed and decoded which then shapes actions to follow.

Each person who enters the legal assemblage finds themself in various encounters whereby the emitting wave form within the encounter contain encoded information which the absorber (the person) decodes, subject to the workings of Schema QD, and sends back to the emitter establishing a standing wave, until two collapses occur. One, with the quantum entangled four elements of Schema QD, each initially in states of superposition, which now undergo a transformation into a particular matrix, and then, via a representative QD signature wave is emitted back to the source, here, the totality of the encounter. At some level of intensity, the second collapse generates a particular image of "what we have here." Note, a particular "I" which can be inserted in material discursive practice is a persona of the particular matrix formed in that context.

An encounter is a context, a bounded context and can be conceptualized as generating wave forms reflective of its totality, a patterned interference pattern (holograms) transmitted by the Schrödinger holographic wave. It is in this context that action follows the collapse of the wave function and the objects (identities, realities) created. What shapes material discursive practices are enactments, performative intra-actions and speech acts which actualize the potentialities existing via pcar. The latter is further shaped by the legal abstract machine (formal rationality) which, following Deleuze and Guattari, is encoded in "lines of flight" as a function.[26] We conceptualize lines of flight as a Schrödinger holographic wave.

Let's conclude with what critical legal theorists might argue, informed by quantum holographic principles. Many who have entered and engaged the law assemblage liken it to Kafka's short story *Before the Law* (2021) or portrayed in his book *The Trial* (2009). "Kafkaesque" has become common language conjuring up experiences with a criminal justice and legal system that often defies any semblance of understanding and sense of fairness that leaves the recipients frustrated, anxious, angry, unrestored, often, with the disenfranchised recipients of unequal justice. But just as assemblages have territorializing forces that maintain stasis, the status quo, imbedded are deterritorializing forces that undermine, disrupt, and provide potential for alternatives. The Schrödinger wave, encoding superposition states, as we have seen, when collapsed in the law machine re-constructs the dominant form, leaving however, with Derrida, potential states of expression that remains repressed, (technically, having lower probability states in superposition), but nevertheless, seeking expression. The alternative "vectors and tendencies" already imbedded are counter lines of flight (Schrödinger waves). As Bogue's (2003: 84) reading of Deleuze and Guattari (1987) states, "revolutionary action proceeds through metamorphosis, change and becoming, through the transformation of a present intolerable situation toward some unforeseeable future." And further (ibid.): "The lines of metamorphosis are always present in the real in the form of virtual vectors of deterritorialization, and revolutionary action simply induces their actualization through an intensification of destabilizing, deforming and decoding forces that are being stabilized, formed and coded by the particular social system [e.g., by social movements]."

Bogue's reading of Deleuze and Guattari, not drawing from quantum holography, nevertheless can, with integration, provide some of the mechanism by which new forms can materialize. The holographic in-formation field offers a plethora of holograms representing experiences of the repressed and those denied justice. An alternative linguistic coordinate system (language game) and material discursive practices modeled by Hjelmslev's quadripartite structure, sensitive to both material conditions (content) and expressive form (legal language), co-constituted in a "double-articulation," would have an alternative basis in which speech acts that actualize potentials (collapse of wave function) emerge, better representing otherwise denied voices. Many who advocate restorative or even a transformative justice as a replacement for traditional criminal justice and formal rationality, by activating new lines of flight for social justice, would find a "diffractive reading" with quantum holographic principles offers novel concepts for their development (Loretta and Capeheart, 2020; Milovanovic, 2015, 2022). That is the theory, now we need action in transforming the potential to the actual.

Summary

In our final chapter, we have focused on a post postmodernism. Like postmodernism, it criticizes many of Enlightenment's central ideals. But it also parts ways with postmodernism on the question of representation and materiality. There are those advocating a complete break, the death of postmodernism, and those who retain some key concepts from postmodernism, but nevertheless highlight materialism. There are many expressive forms of post postmodernism. Many decenter the human agent (Anthropocene) and address nature and non-human animals. Some are pushing this to develop an "earth jurisprudence" that builds on interconnections, entanglement, and peaceful co-existence. This, too, can be encompassed in a sociology of law. We focused on new materialism in law, posthumanist feminists, green jurisprudence, sociomateriality, quantum informed, and more tentatively, quantum holographic informed sociology of law. In advancing a quantum-informed sociology of law we visited quantum decision-making and quantum semiotics in law. We concluded with a first approximation of a quantum holographic semiotics of law, recognizing the speculative nature, though quantum holography has a firm standing in the new physics. Much of post postmodernism has been quick to jettison the development and integration of human agency and the structure and function of the psychic apparatus, relegating it to the "black box." Presented to counter this tendency was an approximation of one model, Schema QD. Throughout the chapter, we have provided applications for consideration for each of the developments we have visited. As the reader surmises, much is emerging in the areas covered in this chapter.

Review Questions

1. What is new about new materialism? Why are new materialists questioning postmodernists?

2. New materialists who integrate Deleuze and Guattari's work on the assemblage stress that both material (content) and legal discourse (expression) should be considered as co-contributing to any understandings of law in action. Why is this so?

3. Consider the last time you visited some State-run office. How did the material arrangements (content) and language (expression) being employed effect how you interacted with the officials/bureaucrats?

4. Posthumanist feminists often, with "crits," argue for alternative story-telling in jurisprudence. Why do they stress materiality? Explain.

5. The question of "Should Trees have Standing?" is at the center of an earth jurisprudence (eco-jurisprudence) which counters anthropocentrism. What kind of resistance will be expected by those presented with this question in a sociology of law. (Class exercise: students will list why an earth jurisprudence should be included, or not, in a sociology of law. List on board. Discuss. Summarize.)

6. Referring to question five, would contemporary society be willing to allow a de-centering of their privilege? Why? Why not? Would it follow class, gender, sex, race, ethnic, intersectional lines? (Class exercise: students will list resistance expected. List on board. Discuss. Summarize. Given resistance based on identity groups, what needs to be done?)

7. Quantum decision-making is said to explain real world happenings. Consider eyewitness accounts/testimony and a juror that has to make a decision (guilty, not guilty). How is quantum decision-making useful in understanding each? Explain.

8. Barad's concept, "intra-action," has increasingly been employed by postmodernists and has potential in sociology of law. Why can it be useful in doing sociology of law?

9. It is said that "speech acts" collapse the wave function. Explain. Why is studying the law assemblage important in understanding this collapse?

10. Post posthumanists, it is said by critics, are too quick to jettison agency. What value does quantum mechanics and quantum holography bring to this discussion? Does sociology of law need detailed investigation of agency and consciousness along the lines developed by quantum mechanics and quantum holography? Explain.

Endnotes

1. A digital nomad works remotely using technology and communication devices and lives a nomadic lifestyle. The recent covid-19 epidemic and its variants have increased this population substantially. The increased reliance on remote learning in schools and universities is further prepping the new movement.

2. Legal mattering could take an alternative nomination by starting with the notion of harms of reduction and harms of repression, developed in the constitutive law approach (Henry and Milovanovic, 2020).

3. Distribution concerns equitable allocation of resources and burdens (often discussed in terms of need, desert, equality); participation concerns ability to engage in meaningful, representational discussion; capabilities for the unique abilities and potentials of each actant; and recognition for acknowledging differences and their voices.

4. Roger Penrose and Stuart Hameroff (2012) argued for an objective reduction model that posits that the collapse of the wave function ("decoherence") occurs objectively when a rift is created in the time-space fabric at the smallest scale scientists recognize, the Planck's scale. At some point of intensity, the collapse ensures, materializing one image amongst others that are in momentary superposition. Another model, the "multiverse," stipulates the existence of parallel universes where no collapse takes place, and all possible states unfold in their separate timelines.

5. Many You Tube presentations are available on the web, see for example the very lucid, "Professor Dave Explains: Double-Slit Experiment," accessed 8/18/2021, https://www.youtube.com/watch?v=uva6gBEpfDY.

6. Consider, too, the inattentive stream of consciousness within which we often find ourselves, until attention, however aroused, collapses the wave function and a particular thought materializes, a "cut" from the otherwise stream.

7. For an introduction in the use of rational choice theory in law, see Korobkin and Ulen (2000); and in linear (Bayesian) story construction, Bilz (2010).

8. Consider Jaeger and Trueblood's example of a classical position (2019: 29): "at any stage of litigation, the plaintiff has defined opinions of how likely she is to prevail on her trademark claim and

on her defamation claim. That opinion may change repeatedly, in light of additional information, but at any given moment the plaintiff has definite opinions." And further, "when a measurement occurs (i.e., when the plaintiff makes her settlement decision), she simply 'reads out' the probabilistic judgements that already exist in her mind at that moment and uses them to guide her decisionmaking."

9. Jaeger and Trueblood (2019: 29–30) present the example of a quantum view where judgment develops from indefinite states: "People can remain in a state of 'I don't know' about uncertain outcomes until they are prompted to make a firm judgement. When a firm judgment is prompted [guilty? not guilty?], it is *constructed* based on the interaction of the indefinite state in the decision maker's mind and the question that is posed." Our views are not always clear, "we often feel conflict, ambiguity, uncertainty" (ibid.).

10. See the special issue of *Rhizomes*, volume 30, issue 3, 2016, "Quantum Possibilities: The Work of Karan Barad," edited by K. Sellberg and P. Hinton.

11. Lacan (1977) has alluded to the signified sliding under the signifier.

12. In the Lacanian model, it is lack that mobilizes desire and a search for overcoming lack by finding appropriate objects of desire which will re-instate the (illusionary) sense of wholeness. In his formulation, this is expressed as $ ◊ a. Thus, within the legal arena, ambiguities raise the primordial castration, the cost of entrance into the Symbolic Order, to which desire is mobilized to overcome the lack experienced (here legal ambiguity). Legal signifiers are the *objet petit a*, objects of desire, that offer the illusory sense of overcoming the lack.

13. Consider the unfolding sentence, "I want to ..." So far, no meaning. After the next word, say "cry," there is a pause at which point one returns to the beginning and grasps all at once providing meaning.

14. Those who have been recipients of police discrimination in profiling cases, however, because of the experience, will quickly move to more differentiated views about the nature of the process and situate themselves in narratives that are reflective (Thirdness). Those, too, who have been frequent recipients of legal proceedings may very early in the process constitute a narrative in which things are more structured. Jailhouse lawyers, we previously discussed, have undergone a self-disciplining process in identifying with the language of law as an avenue to freedom, inadvertently reconstituting the law ("dialectics of legal repression").

15. For a useful introduction, see the YouTube, "The Holographic Universe, Part 1, 2" (https://www.youtube.com/watch?v=lMBt_yfGKpU.

16. There are numerous online presentations and YouTube videos on the construction of a hologram. See for example, "Holography or How a Hologram is Made," (no author), winnersicence.com, accessed 8/20/2021, https://www.youtube.com/watch?v=WoMLI1bVSck. See also Part 1 of "The Holographic Universe."

17. Gabor (1946), for example, argues that bits of information, for us, "cuts," are "logons," quanta of information.

18. It has been argued that if it were not for the lenses of your eyes, everything "out there" would be scratchy-looking squiggly lines, nevertheless encoding information. Consider, analogously, the surface of a CD or DVD and the accessible recorded information.

19. It is not that a discursive formation causes delinquency, but Matza (1964) shows that what initiates the process toward delinquency is an act of desperation when the juvenile, because of their status, feels more a pin ball than an agent. The form of expression ("act of desperation") is shaped by the rationalizations/neutralizations accessed and the despair of experiencing a pin ball effect, pushed around without opportunity to affect change. With Cressey, it concerns engagement with a "non-shareable financial problem." A collapse of an otherwise superposition state (norm abiding, deviance) takes place after a threshold of intensity is reached.

20. Speculative in this view, all within the bulk is showered by holographically encoded waveforms emanating from the boundary to which entering agents engage in pcar.

21. We concentrate on the human form here; others such as Latour (2007) have extended agency to non-human forms, indeed panpsychism argues that all matter has a degree of consciousness. Each actant, then, would need to be examined separately for their constitution.

22. For further discussion on vitalism, see Bennet (2010).

23. For a visual portrayal and construction of the cross-cap, see Granon Lafont, Chapter 4, The Cross Cap, accessed 4/13/2022, https://www.lacanianworksexchange.net/s/19860101-Lafont-Topology-Chapter-4.pdf

24. An encounter generates a cumulative wave form expressing the totality of interference patterns that constitute it.

25. The "I" emerges, as in Lacan's (1977) dynamic model of figure-eight cuts in the cross-cap, at the "gluing point" of the half-twisted rectangle looped back on itself and reconnected at the edges, forming, a "line of intersection."

26. This is equivalent, in the formalism of quantum mechanics, to the Hamiltonian function that shapes the Schrödinger wave over time.

References

Abel, R. "A Socialist Approach to Risk," *Maryland Law Review* 41: 695–754, 1982.

________. "The Transformation of the American Legal Profession," *Law and Society Review* 20(1): 7–17, 1986.

________. *The Legal Profession in England and Wales*. London: Basil Blackwell, 1988.

Abramowitz, M. "How Law Behaves: An Interview with Donald Black," *International Journal of Law, Crime, and Justice* 38: 37–47, 2010.

Abu-Jamal, M. *Jailhouse Lawyers: Prisoners Defending Prisoners v. the USA*. San Francisco, CA: City Lights Publishers, 2009.

Adams, T. and D. Fuller. "The Words Have Changed But the Ideology Remains the Same — Misogynistic Lyrics in Rap Music," *Journal of Black Studies* 36(6): 938–957, 2006.

Adler, G. *Gay Priori: A Queer Critical Legal Studies Approach to Law Reform*, Durham, NC: Duke University Press, 2018.

Aerts, D. "Quantum Particles as Conceptual Entities: A Possible Explanatory Framework for Quantum Theory," *Foundations of Science* 1(1): 85–97, 2009.

________. "Interpreting Quantum Particles as Conceptual Entities," *International Journal of Theoretical Physics* 49(12): 2950–2970.

Affirmative Action in the United States, *Wikipedia: The Free Encyclopedia*, March 31, 2021, accessed on 4/3/2021, https://en.wikipedia.org/wiki/Affirmative_action_in_the_United_States.

Ahonen, P. "Regulating, Deregulating and Reregulating Universities," in R. Malloy and C. Braun (eds.) *Law and Economics*, pp. 127–52, 1995.

Aiello, G. "Visual Semiotics: Key Concepts and New Directions," in L. Pauwell and D. Mannay (eds.) *The Sage Handbook of Visual Research Methodology 2ed.*, 367–380, 2020.

Alcoff, L. *Visible Identities: Race, Gender, and the Self*. NY: Oxford University Press, 2006.

Aldeia, J. And F. Alves. "Against the Environment: Problems in Society/Nature Relations," *Frontiers in Sociology* 24 April 2019, accessed on 8/82021, https://www.frontiersin.org/articles/10.3389/fsoc.2019.00029/full.

Alexander, M. *The New Jim Crow: Mass Incarceration in the Age of Colorblindness*. New York: The New Press, 2012.

Alexander, J.W. "Topological Invariants of Knots and Links," *Transactions of the American Mathematical Society* 30: 275–306, 1928.

Alberstein, M. "Getting to Where? On Peace Making and Law Teaching at Harvard Law School," *Law and Critique* 10: 323–342, 1999.

Alexander-Floyd, N. "Critical Race Black Feminism: A Jurisprudence of Resistance," *Journal of Woman, Culture and Society* 35(4): 810–820, 2010.

Alfieri, A. "Rebellious Pedagogy and Practice," *Clinical Law Review* 23(5): 5–36, 2016.

Alger, J. and S. Alger "Beyond Mead: Symbolic Interaction Between Humans and Felines," *Society and Animals* 5(1): 65–81, 1997.

Allen, B. "Postmodern Pragmatism: Richard Rorty's Transformation of American Philosophy," *Philosophical Topics* 36(1): 1–15, 2008.

________. "Postmodern Pragmatism and Skeptical Hermeneutics," *Contemporary Pragmatism* 10(1): 91–11, 2013.

Allen, A. "Feminist Perspectives on Power," *Stanford Encyclopedia of Philosophy*, Edward N. Zalta (ed.), (Fall, 2016). Accessed on 3/22/2021, https://plato.stanford.edu/entries/feminist-philosophy/.

Allison, J. "Critical Legal Studies," Harvard Law School Library. Harvard, MA. Accessed on 3/8/2021, https://guides.library.harvard.edu/critical-legal-studies.

Alper, T., A. Amsterdam, T. Edelman, R. Hertz, R. Janger, J. Mcallister-Nevins, S. Rudenstine, and R. Walker-Sterling, "Stories Told and Untold: Lawyering Theory Analysis of the First Rodney King Assault Trial," *Clinical Law Review* 12: 1–202, 2005.

Althusser, L. *Lenin and Philosophy.* New York: Monthly Review Press, 1971.

________. *Philosophy of the Encounter: Later Writings, 1978–1987*, F. Matheron and L. Corpet (eds. and translators). London, UK: Verso, 2006.

________. *On the Reproduction of Capitalism: Ideology and the Ideological State Apparatus.* G.M. Goshgarian (Ed. and translator). London, UK: Verso, 2014.

Altman, A. *Critical Legal Studies: A Liberal Critique.* Princeton, NJ: Princeton University Press, 1990.

Alves, R. *Toward a Theology of Liberation.* Princeton, NJ: Princeton Theological Seminary, 1988.

Amaya, A. *A Tapestry of Reason: An Inquiry into the Nature of Coherence and Its Role in Legal Argument.* Oxford: Hart Publishing, 2015.

________. "Coherence, Evidence, and Legal Proof," *Legal Theory* 19(1): 1–43, 2013.

Andreski, S. *Max Weber's Insight's and Errors.* Boston, MA: Routledge and Kegan Paul, 1984.

Anzaldúa, G. "Bridge, Drawbridge, Sandbar, or Island: Lesbians of Color *Hacienda Alianzas*." in G. Anzaldúa and A. Keating (eds.) *The Gloria Anzaldúa Reader.* Durham, NC: Duke University Press, 2009.

Aptheker, B. *Tapestries of Lift: Women's Work, Women's Consciousness and Meaning of Daily Experience.* Amherst, MA: University of Massachusetts Press, 1989.

Arban, E. "Seeing Law in Terms of Music: A Short Essay on Affinities Between Music and Law, *Les Cahiers de Droit* 58 (1–2): 67–86, 2017.

Arbino, D. "Reggae as Subaltern Knowledge," *Mester* 45(1): 153–170, 2017.

Archard, D. *Consciousness and the Unconscious.* London: Hutchinson, 1984. Arcidiacono, P. "Expert Report of Peter S. Arcidiacono, Students for Fair Admissions, Inc. v. Harvard," No. 14-cv-14176-ADB (D. Mass).

Arrigo, B. "Deconstructing Jurisprudence: An Experiential Feminist Critique," *Journal of Human Justice* 4(1): 13–30, 1992.

________. "An Experientially–Informed Feminist Jurisprudence: Rape and the Move Toward Praxis," *Humanity and Society* 17(1): 28–47, 1993a.

________. *Madness, Language and the Law.* New York: Harrow and Heston, 1993b.

________. "Legal Decisions and the Disabled Criminal Defendant: Contributions from Psychoanalytic Semiotics and Chaos Theory," *Legal Studies Forum* 18(2): 93–112, 1994.

________. "Insanity Defense Reform and the Sign of Abolition," *International Journal for the Semiotics of Law* 10: 191–211, 1997a.

________. "Transcarceration: Notes on a Psychoanalytically-Informed Theory of Social Practice in the Criminal Justice and Mental Health System," *Crime, Law, and Social Change* 27: 31–48, 1997b.

________. "Reason and Desire in Legal Education," *International Journal for the Semiotics of Law* 11: 2–24, 1998a.

________. "Restoring Justice for Juveniles," *Justice Quarterly* 15(4): 629–66, 1998b.

________. *Social Justice/Criminal Justice* (ed.). Belmont, CA: West/Wadsworth, 1999.

________. "Law and Social Inquiry," *International Journal for the Semiotics of Law* 13(2): 127–32, 2000.

________. "Transcarceration: A Constitutive Ethnography of Mentally Ill Offenders," *The Prison Journal* 81(2): 162–186, 2001.

Arrigo, B. and D. Milovanovic. *Revolution in Penology.* New York: Rowman and Littlefield, 2009.

Arrigo, B. and C. Williams. "Law, Ideology, and Critical Inquiry: A Case of Treatment Refusal for Incompetent Prisoners Awaiting Execution," *New England Journal on Criminal and Civil Confinement* 25(2): 367–412, 1999.

________. "The (Im)Possibility of Democratic Justice and the 'Gift' of the Majority," *Journal of Contemporary Criminal Justice* 16(3): 321–343, 2000a.

________. "The Philosophy of the Gift and the Psychology of Advocacy," *International Journal for the Semiotics Law* 13: 215–242, 2000b.

Arrigo, B., D. Milovanovic and R. Schehr. "The French Connection," *Humanity and Society* 24(2): 162–203, 2000.

Asch, M. "Wildlife, Domestic Animals, and the Dene Aboriginal Rights Claim," in D. Currie and B. MacLean (eds.), *Rethinking the Administration of Justice.* Vancouver, Canada: Collective Press, pp. 115–129, 1992.

Asghar, J. "Language Power and Ideology in Commercial Discourse: A Prologue to Critical Discourse Analysis for Neophyte Analysts," *Academic Journal of Interdisciplinary Studies* 3(4): 225–232, 2014.

Askeland, B. "The Potential for Abductive Legal Reasoning," *Ratio Juris: An International Journal of Jurisprudence and Philosophy of Law* 33(1): 66–81, 2020.

Ateek, N. *A Palestinian Theology of Liberation*. Maryknoll, Michigan: Orbis Books, 2017.

Atmanspacher, H. "Cartesian Cut, Heisenberg Cut, and the Concept of Complexity," in W. Hofkirchner (ed.) *The Quest for a Unified Theory of Information*. Cambridge, MA: MIT Press, 1999.

Aubert, J. *Joyce Avec Lacan*. Paris: Navarin, 1987.

Aubert, V. *In Search of Law*. New Jersey: Barnes and Nobles Books, 1983.

Austermehl, T. "The Normalization of Exclusion Through a Revival of Whiteness in Donald Trump's 2016 Election Campaign Discourse," *Social Semiotics* 30(4): 528–546, 2020.

Austin, J. *The Province of Jurisprudence*. Cambridge; Cambridge University Press, 1995.

Austin, J.L. *How to Do Things With Words*. New York: Oxford University Press, 1962.

Averbukh, V. "Sources of Computer Metaphors for Visualization and Human-Computer Interaction, Cognitive and Intermedial Semiotics," M. Silvera-Roig and A. Azcárate (eds.), *IntechOpen*, November 22, 2019. DOI: 10.5772/intechopen.89973. Accessed 6/6/2021, https://www.intechopen.com/books/cognitive-and-intermedial-semiotics/sources-of-computer-metaphors-for-visualization-and-human-computer-interaction.

Backer, L. "A View on A.J. Greimas's Essay "The Semiotic Analysis of a Legal Discourse: Commercial Laws that Govern Companies and Groups of Companies," in Broekman, J.M. and L.C. Backer (eds.) *Signs in Law — A Sourcebook*, pp. 129–140. London, UK: Springer International Publishing, 2015.

Baer, J. *Our Lives Before the Law: Constructing a Feminist Jurisprudence*. Princeton, NJ: University Press, 1999.

Bakhtin, M. *The Dialogic Imagination*. M. Holquist (ed.). Austin, Texas: University of Texas Press, 1981.

________. *Speech Genres and Other Late Essays*. C. Emerson and M. Holquist (eds.). Austin, Texas: University of Texas Press, 1986.

Bainbridge, J. "Visual Law: The Changing Signifiers of Law in Popular Visual Culture," in A. Wagner and J. Broekman (eds.), 193–215, *Prospects of Legal Semiotics*. London: Springer, 2011.

Baitinger, F. *The Subject of Jouissance: The Late Lacan and Gender and Queer Theories*. Ph.D. Dissertation, City University of New York, 2019, accessed 7/17/2021, https://academicworks.cuny.edu/cgi/viewcontent.cgi?article=4296&context=gc_etds.

Balbus, I. "Commodity Form and Legal Form: An Essay on the Relative Autonomy of the Law," *Law and Society Review* 11: 571–87, 1977a.

________. *The Dialectics of Legal Repression*. New York: Russell Sage, 1977b.

Baldinger, K. *Semantic Theory*. Oxford: Blackwell, 1980.

Balkin, J.M. "Deconstructive Practice and Legal Theory," *Yale Law Journal* 96(4): 743–86, 1987.

________. "Law and Semiotics," *University of Miami Law Review* 44: 1119–1142, 1990.

________. Deconstruction's Legal Career: Part 1: http://www.yale.edu/lawweb/jbalkin/articles/deccar1.htm, 1–7, 1998a.

________. Deconstruction's Legal Career: Part 2: http://www.yale.edu/lawweb/jbalkin/articles/deccar2.htm, 1–5, 1998b.

________. Deconstructive Practice and Legal Theory: http://www.yale.edu/lawweb/jbalkin/articles/decprac1.htm, 1–9, 1998c.

________. "Tradition, Betrayal, and the Politics of Deconstruction," *Cardozo Law Review* 11: 1623–1651, 1990.

Bannister, S. and D. Milovanovic, "The Necessity Defense, Substantive Justice and Oppositional Linguistic Praxis," *International Journal of The Sociology of Law* 18(2): 179–198, 1990.

Bannon, A. and J. Adelstein. "The Impact of Video Proceedings on Fairness and Access to Justice in Court," Brennan Center for Justice, September 10, 2020, accessed 5/24/2021, https://www.brennancenter.org/our-work/research-reports/impact-video-proceedings-fairness-and-access-justice-court.

Barad, K. *Meeting the Universe Halfway*. Durham, NC: Duke University Press, 2007.

________. "Quantum Entanglement and Hauntological Relations of Inheritance: Discontinuities, Spacetime Enfoldings, and Justice-to-Come," *Derrida Today* 3(20): 240–268, 2010.

Barak, G. "Media, Crime, and Justice: A Case for Constitutive Criminology," *Humanity and Society* 17(3): 272–96, 1993.

________. *Media, Process, and the Social Construction of Crime: Studies in Newsmaking Criminology*. New York: Garland, 1994.

________. *Integrating Criminologies*. Boston, MA: Allyn and Bacon, 1997.

Barak, G. and S. Henry. "An Integrative-Constitutive Theory of Crime, Law, and Social Justice," in B. Arrigo (ed.) *Social Justice/Criminal Justice*. Boston: West/Wadsworth, pp. 150–175, 1999.

Barbieri, M. "A Short History of Biosemiotics," *Biosemiotics* 2: 221–234, 2009.

Barenberg, M. "The Political Economy of the Wagner Act: Power, Symbol, and Workplace Cooperation," *Harvard Law Review* 106: 1381–1460, 1993.

Barger, L. *The World Comes of Age: An Intellectual History of Liberation Theology*. Oxford, UK: Oxford University Press, 2018.

Barkum, M. *Law Without Sanctions*. New Haven, CT: Yale University Press, 1968.

Barkum, S. *Law and Society*, 2ed. Upper Saddle River, NJ: Pearson/Prentice Hall, 2018.

Barley, S. "Semiotics and the Study of Occupational and Organizational Cultures," *Administrative Science Quarterly* 28: 393–413, 1983.

Barreto, J.M. "Rorty and Human Rights: Contingency, Emotions and How to Defend Human Rights Telling Stories," *Utrech Law Review* 7(2): 93–112, 2011.

Barthes, R. *Mythologies*. New York: Hill and Wang, 1972.

________. *S/Z*. New York: Hill and Wang, 1974.

________. Barthes, R. "Rhetoric of the Image," 1964, accessed on 5/10/2021, http://williamwolff.org/wp-content/uploads/2014/08/Barthes-Rhetoric-of-the-image-ex.pdf.

Bartlett, K. "Feminist Legal Methods," in K. Bartlett and R. Kennedy (eds.), *Feminist Legal Theory*. Oxford: Westview Press, 370–403, 1991.

________. "Cracking Foundations as Feminist Method," *American University Journal of Gender, Society and Policy and Law* 8: 31, 2000.

Bartlett, K. and R. Kennedy (eds.). *Feminist Legal Theory: Readings in Law and Gender*. Oxford: Westview Press, 1991.

________. "Introduction," in K. Bartlett and R. Kennedy (eds.) *Feminist Legal Theory*. Oxford: Westview Press, 1–11, 1991.

Batiz, Z. and D. Milovanovic. "Quantum Holography and Agency: Toward a Formalism of Schema QD," *NeuroQuantology* 15(1): 45–59, 2017.

Baudrillard, J. *For a Critique of the Political Economy of the Sign*. St. Louis, MO: Telos Press, 1981.

Baxi, U. *Towards a Sociology of Indian Law*. New Delhi: Stavaha, 1986.

________. *Human Rights in a Posthuman World*. Oxford, UK: Oxford University Press, 2009.

________. *The Future of Human Rights*. New Delhi, Oxford University Press, 2012.

Baxter, H. "Autopoiesis and the 'Relative Autonomy' of Law," *Cardozo Law Review* 19: 1987–2050, 1998.

________. "Nicklas Luhmann's Theory of Autopoietic Legal System," *Annual Review of Law and Social Sciences* 9: 167–184, 2013.

Beauvoir, S. *The Second Sex*. New York: Vintage Books, 1989.

Beaud, S. and G. Noiriel. *Race et Sciences Sociales: Une Socio-Histoire de la Raison Identitaire*, Paris: Agone, 2021.

Beck, U. *Risk Society*. New York: Sage, 1992.

Beetz, J. *Materiality and Subject in Marxism, Post-Structuralism, and Material Semiotics*. Bassingstoke, UK: Palgrave Macmillan, 2016.

Beetz, J., B. Herzog and J. Maesse. "Introduction to Special Issue: Marx and Discourse," *Critical Discourse Studies* 15(4): 321–324, 2018.

Beetz, J. and V. Schwab. "Conditions and Relations of (Re)Production in Marxism and Discourse Studies," *Critical Discourse Studies* 15(4): 338–350, 2018.

________. "Material-Discursive Entanglements: Locating Materialist Discourse Studies," in J. Beetz and V. Schwab (eds.) *Material Discourse — Materialist Analysis: Approaches in Discourse Studies* (pp. ix–xxii). Lanham, MD: Lexington Books, 2017a.

________. "Materialist Discourse Analysis: Three Moments and Some Criteria," in J. Beetz and V. Schwab (eds.) *Material Discourse — Materialist Analysis: Approaches in Discourse Studies* (pp. 29–46). Lanham, MD: Lexington Books, 2017b.

Beirne, P. "Ideology and Rationality in Max Weber's Sociology of Law," in S. Spitzer (ed.), *Research in Law and Sociology* 2: 103–31. Greenwich, Conn.: JAI Press, 1979a.

________. "Empiricism and the Critique of Marxism on Law and Crime," *Social Problems* 26: 373–85, 1979b.

________. (ed.) *Revolution in Law: Contributions to the Development of Soviet Legal Theory, 1917–1938.* New York: M.E. Sharpe, 1990.

________. *Confronting Animal Abuse.* New York: Rowman and Littlefield, 2009.

Beirne, P. and A. Hunt. "Law and the Constitution of Soviet Society: The Case of Comrade Lenin," in P. Beirne (ed.) *Revolution in Law.* New York: M.E. Sharpe, 61–98, 1990a.

________. "Lenin, Crime, and Penal Politics," in P. Beirne (ed.) *Revolution in Law.* New York: M.E. Sharpe, 99–135, 1990.

Beirne, P. and R. Quinney (eds.). *Marxism and Law.* New York: John Wiley, 1982.

Beirne, P. and R. Sharlet (eds.). *Pashukanis: Selected Writings on Marxism and Law.* New York: Academic Press, 1980.

Bell, D. "*Brown v. Board of Education* and the Interest Convergence Dilemma," *Harvard Law Review* 93(3): 518–33, 1980.

________. *Confronting Authority.* Boston, MA: Beacon Press, 1994.

________. *Silent Covenants: Brown v. Board of Education and the Unfulfilled Hopes for Racial Reform.* Cambridge, MA: Oxford University Press, 2005.

Bellah, N. (ed.). *Emile Durkheim on Morality and Society.* Chicago, IL: University of Chicago Press, 1973.

Bellucci, F. and A-V. Pietarinen. "Peirce on the Justification of Abduction," *Studies in History and Philosophy of Science* 84: 12–19, 2020.

Beltramini, M. "Materialist Semiotics," In P. Bouissac (ed.), *Oxford Encyclopedia of Semiotics*, pp. 1–4. Cambridge, UK: Oxford University Press, 2017, accessed on 5/20/2021, http://www.marilenabeltramini.it/schoolwork1213/UserFiles/Admin_teacher/materialist_semiotics.pdf.

Bendix, R. *Max Weber: An Intellectual Portrait.* Berkeley, CA: University of California Press, 1977.

Bendix, R. and G. Roth. *Scholarship and Partisanship: Essays on Max Weber.* Berkeley, CA: University of California Press, 1971.

Bennet, J. *Vibrant Matter.* Durham, NC: Duke University Press, 2010.

Bennet, L and M. Feldman. *Reconstructing Reality in the Courtroom.* New Brunswick, NJ: Rutgers University Press, 1981.

Benson, R.W. "Peirce and Critical Legal Studies," in R. Kevelson (ed.), *Peirce and Law.* New York: Peter Lang, 15–43, 1991.

Benveniste, E. *Problems in General Linguistics.* Coral Gables, FL: University of Miami Press, 1971.

Berdini, F. and C. Banchi. "John Lanshaw Austin (1911–1960)," *Internet Encyclopedia of Philosophy*, accessed 3/21/2021, https://iep.utm.edu/austin/.

Bergesen, A. "The Rise of Semiotic Marxism," *Sociological Perspectives* 36(1): 1–22, 1993.

Bergson, H. *Time and Free Will.* New York: Harper and Row, 1960.

Bernstein, B. *Class, Codes and Control.* London: Routledge and Kegan Paul, 1975.

Best, B. "Speculating Without Hedging: What Marxian Political Economy Can Offer Laclauian Discourse Theory," *Critical Discourse Studies* 11(3): 272–287, 2014.

Best, S. *Postmodern Theory.* London: MacMillan, 1991.

Bhattacharya, T. (ed.). *Social Reproduction Theory: Remapping Class, Recentering Oppression.* London: Pluto Press, 2017.

Bianchi, C. "Ferrucio Rossi-Landi: Language, Society and Semiotics," in Corateli, G., F. Galofaro, and F. Montanari (eds.), *Special Issue, Semiotics of Economic Discourse, Ocula* 16: 1–28, (December), 2015, accessed 4/30/2021, https://core.ac.uk/download/pdf/54012216.pdf.

Bianchi, P. "From Representation to Class Struggle," *S. J. Jan Van Eyck Circle Lacanian Ideal. Crit.* 5: 114–126, 2012.

Bilz, K. "We Don't Want to Hear It: Psychology, Literature, and the Narrative Model of Judging," *University of Illinois Law Review* 2: 429–487, 2010.

Bishop, R. "Chaos", *The Stanford Encyclopedia of Philosophy* (Spring 2017 Edition), Edward N. Zalta (ed.), accessed, 8/1/2021, https://plato.stanford.edu/archives/spr2017/entries/chaos/.

Bittar, E. *Semiotics, Law and Art: Between Theory of Justice and Theory of Law.* Cham, Switzerland: Springer, 2021.

Black, C. *The Land is the Source of Law.* Abingdon, UK: Routledge, 2011.

Black, D. *The Behavior of Law.* New York: Academic Press, 1976.

________. "Comment: Common Sense in the Sociology of Law," *American Sociological Review* 44(1): 27–37, 1979.

________. "The Boundaries of Legal Sociology," in C. Reasons and R. Rich (eds.), *The Sociology of Law: A Conflict Perspective.* Toronto: Butterworths, 1978.

________. *Sociological Justice.* New York: Oxford University Press, 1989.

________. *The Social Structure of Right and Wrong.* San Diego, CA: Academic Press, 1993.

________. "The Epistemology of Pure Sociology," *Law and Social Inquiry* 20: 829–70, 1995.

________. *The Behavior of Law, Special Edition.* Bingley, UK: Emarald Publishing, 2010.

Blackstone, W. *The Oxford Edition of Blackstone's: Commentaries on the Laws of England.* Oxford University Press, 2016.

Blanco, E. and A. Grear. "Personhood, Jurisdiction and Injustice," *Journal of Human Rights and the Environment,* 10(1): 86–117, 2019.

Block, F. "The Ruling Class Does Not Rule: Notes on the Marxist Theory of the State," *Socialist Review* 33: 6–28, 1977.

Bloor, M. and T. Bloor. *The Practice of Critical Discourse Analysis: An Introduction.* London, UK: Hodder Arnolds, 2007.

Bogard, W. "Surveillance Assemblages and Lines of Flight," in D. Lyon (ed.). *Theorizing Surveillance,* pp. 97–122, Cullompton, UK: Willan, 2006.

Bogue, R. *Deleuze and Guattari.* New York: Routledge, 1989.

________. *Deleuze on Literature.* New York: Routledge, 2003.

Bonner, R. *Lawyers and Litigants in Ancient Athens: The Genesis of the Legal Profession.* New York: Barnes and Noble, 1969.

Bor, B. and M. Kunczol, "Toward a Semiotic Theory of Style in Law: A Peircean Approach," *International Journal of Law in Context* 15(3): 263–273, 2019.

Borch-Jacobsen, M. "What is Called Subject?: A Note on Lacan's 'Linguistery,'" Paper presented to the Annual Congress of the Society for Phenomenology and Existential Philosophy, Northwestern University, Chicago, IL, October 1988.

________. *Lacan: The Absolute Master.* Stanford, CA: Stanford University Press, 1991. Borg, M. "Effect of Vicarious Homicide Victimization on Support for Capital Punishment: A Test of Black's Theory of Law," *Criminologist* 36: 537–68, 1998.

________. "Using Violence as Social Control: Applying a Theory of Conflict Management to Juvenile Disputes," *University of Florida Journal of Law and Public Policy* 10: 313–39, 1999.

________. "Mobilizing Law in Urban Areas," *Law and Society Review* 35: 435–456, 2001.

Boréus, K. and G. Bergstrom. *Analyzing Text and Discourse.* London: Sage, 2017.

Bourdieu, P. "The Force of Law: Toward a Sociology of the Juridical Field," *Hastings Law Journal* 38: 814–853, 1987.

Borrelli, G. "Marx, a 'Semiotician'? On the (Possible) Relevance of a Materialistic-Semiotic Approach to Discourse Analysis," *Critical Discourse Studies* 15(4): 351–363, 2018.

Boyle. "The Politics of Reason: Critical Legal Studies and Local Social Thought," *University of Pennsylvania Law Review* 133: 685–780, 1985.

Bowell, T. "Feminist Standpoint Theory," *Internet Encyclopedia of Philosophy*, accessed on 3/23/2021, https://iep.utm.edu/fem-stan/.

Bowles, S. and H. Gintis. *Schooling in Capitalist Society.* New York: Basic Books, 1976.

________. *Democracy and Capitalism.* New York: Basic Books, 1986.

Bracher, M. "Lacan's Theory of the Four Discourses," *Prose Studies* 11: 32–49, 1988.

________. *Lacan, Discourse and Social Change: A Psychoanalytic Cultural Criticism.* Ithaca, NY: Cornell University Press, 1993.

Bradley, R. *Charisma and Social Organization.* New York: ToExcel Publishers, 1999.

________. "The Psychophysiology of Intuition: A Quantum Holographic Theory of Intuition," *World Futures* 63(2): 61–97, 2007.

________. "The Psychophysiology of Entrepreneurial Intuition," Proceedings of the 3rd AGSE International Entrepreneurship Research Exchange. Auckland, New Zealand, 2006.

________. "Detecting the Identity Signature of Secret Social Groups: Holographic Processes and the Communication of Member Affiliation," *World Futures* 66: 124–162, 2010.

________. "Communication of Collective Identity in Secret Social Groups," *Behavioral Sciences of Terrorism and Political Aggression* 3(3): 198–224, 2011.

Bradney, A. "United Kingdom," in D. Clark (ed.), *Encyclopedia of Law and Society: American and Global Perspectives* 1529, 2007.

Braidotti, R. "The Politics of Ontological Difference," in T. Brennan (ed.). *Between Feminism and Psychoanalysis.* New York: Routledge, 89–105, 1989.

________. "A Theoretical Framework for the Critical Posthumanities," *Theory, Culture and Society* 36(6): 31–61, 2018.

________. *Posthuman Knowledge.* Cambridge, UK: Polity Press, 2019.

Braidotte, R., C. Colebrook and P. Hanafin (eds.) *Deleuze and Law.* London, UK: Palgrave-MacMillan, 2009.

Braithwaite, J. and D. Biles. "Empirical Verification and Black's *The Behavior of Law,*" *American Sociological Review* 45: 334–38, 1980.

Brara, R. "Courting Nature: Advances in Indian Jurisprudence." in "Can Nature Have Rights? Legal and Political Insights," A. Tabios Hillebrecht and M. Berros, *RCC Perspectives: Transformations in Environment and Society* 6: 31–36, 2017. doi.org/10.5282/rcc/8212, accessed 8/12/2021, http://www.environmentandsociety.org/perspectives/2017/6/article/courting-nature-advances-indian-jurisprudence.

Braverman, I., N. Blomley, D. Delaney, and A. Kedar (eds.). *The Expanding Spaces of Law: A Timely Legal Geography.* Stanford University Press, 2014.

Brayboy, B. "Toward a Tribal CRT in Education," *The Urban Review* 37(5): 435–446, 2005.

Brennan, T. (ed.). *Between Feminism and Psychoanalysis.* New York: Routledge, 1989.

________. "Introduction," in T. Brennan (ed.) *Between Feminism and Psychoanalysis.* New York: Routledge, 1–23, 1989.

________. *The Interpretation of the Flesh.* London: Routledge, 1992.

________. *History After Lacan.* New York: Routledge, 1993.

Brigham, J. "Right, Rage, and Remedy: Forms of Law in Political Discourse," *Studies in American Political Development* 2: 303–16, 1987.

________. *The Constitution of Interests.* New York: New York University Press, 1996.

________. "Millenium Reflections," *International Journal for the Semiotics of Law* 12(3): 333–42, 1999.

Briggs, J. and D. Peat. *Turbulent Mirrors.* New York: Harper and Row, 1989.

Brion, D. "The Chaotic Law of Tort: Legal Formalism and the Problem of Indeterminacy," in R. Kevelson (ed.), *Peirce and Law.* New York: Peter Lang, 45–77, 1991.

________. "The Chaotic Indeterminacy of Tort Law," in D. Caudill and S. Gold (eds.), *Radical Philosophy of Law.* New Jersey: Humanities Press, 179–199, 1995.

________. "The Ethics of Property," *International Journal for the Semiotics of Law* 12(3): 247–283, 1999.

Brown, C.H. *Wittgensteinian Linguistics.* The Hague: Mouton, 1974.

Brown, R. *A Poetic for Sociology.* Cambridge: Cambridge University Press, 1977.

Brundage, J. *The Medieval Origins of the Legal Profession.* Chicago, IL: University of Chicago Press, 2010.

Bryant, L. "Zizek's New Universe of Discourse: Politics and the Discourse of the Capitalist," *International Journal of Zizek Studies* 2: 1–48, 2008.

Buk-Swienty, A. "The Law Ex-ists: Reading Kafka with Lacan." New York: Ark Books, accessed 7/13/2021, http://arkbooks.dk/the-law-ex-ists-reading-kafka-with-lacan/.

Buonamano, R. "The Legal Subject in Althusser's Political Theory," *Law and Critique* 25: 231–248, 2014.

Burch, R. "Charles Sanders Peirce," *Stanford Encyclopedia of Philosophy*, accessed 3/12/2021, https://plato.stanford.edu/entries/peirce/.

Burchard, M. "Feminist Jurisprudence." *Internet Encyclopedia of Philosophy*, Accessed 3/18/2021, https://iep.utm.edu/jurisfem/.

Burdon, P. "Review Essay: *Ben Golder, Foucault and the Politics of Rights*," *Adelaide Law Review* 37: 523–535, 2016.

________. *Earth Jurisprudence*. Abingdon, UK: Routledge, 2014.

Buffo, A. "Interpretation and Improvisation: The Judge and the Musician Between Text and Context," *International Journal for the Semiotics of Law* 31(2): 215–239, 2018.

Busemeyer, J. and P. Bruza. *Quantum Models of Cognition*. Cambridge, UK: Cambridge University Press, 2013.

Butler, J. *Gender Trouble*. New York: Routledge, 1990.

________. *Bodies That Matter*. New York: Routledge, 1993.

________. *Excitable Speech*. New York: Routledge, 1997a.

________. *The Psychic Life of Power*. Stanford, California: Stanford University Press, 1997b.

________. *The Subject of Desire*. New York: Columbia University Press, 1999.

________. *Undoing Gender*. New York: Routledge, 2015.

________. *The Force of Non-Violence*. London, UK: Verso, 2020.

Butler, J., E. Laclau and S. Zizek. *Contingency, Hegemony, Universality*. London: Verso, 2000.

Butz, M. "Systemic Family Therapy and Symbolic Chaos," *Humanity and Society* 17(2): 200–22, 1993.

Cachelin, A. and J. Rose. "Guiding Questions for Critical Sustainability," *Journal of Environmental Studies* 8(4): 518–425, 2018.

Cain, M. and A. Hunt (eds.). *Marx and Engels on Law*. London: Academic Press, 1979.

Cain, M. "Realism, Feminism, Methodology and Law," *International Journal of the Sociology of Law* 14: 255–67, 1986.

________. "Realist Philosophy and Standpoint Epistemologies *or* Feminist Criminology as a Successor Science," in L. Gelsthorpe and A. Morris (eds.), *Feminist Perspectives in Criminology*. Milton Keynes: Open University Press, 1990.

Cain, P. "Feminist Jurisprudence: Grounding the Theories," in K. Bartlett and R. Kennedy (eds.), *Feminist Legal Theory*. Oxford: Westview Press, 263–80, 1991.

Cain, M. and A. Hunt. *Marx and Engels on Law*. New York: Academic Press, 1979.

Caldous-Coulhard, C. and T. van Leeuwen. "Introduction," *Social Semiotics* 13(1): 3–4, 2003.

Cammack, P. "Marx and Social Reproduction," *Historical Materialism* 28(2): 76–106, 2020.

Capeheart, L. and D. Milovanovic. *Social Justice: Theories, Issues and Movements.* London: Routledge, 2020.

Capra, F. and U. Mattie. *The Ecology of Law: Towards a Legal System in Tune with Nature and Community.* Oakland, CA: Berrett-Koehler, 2015.

Capulong, E. "Client Activism in Progressive Lawyering Theory," *Clinical Law Review* 16: 109–194, 2009.

Caputo-Levine, and D. Deirdre. "The Yard Face: The Contributions of Inmate Interpersonal Violence to the Carceral Habitus," *Ethnography* 14(2): 165–85, 2013.

Cardozo, B. *The Growth of the Law.* New Haven: Yale University Press, 1924.

Carens, J. "An Interpretation of the Socialist Principle of Distribution." *Social Philosophy and Policy* 20: 145–77, 2003.

Caudill, D. and S. Gold (eds.). *Radical Philosophy of Law.* Atlantic Highlands, NJ: Humanities Press, 1995.

Carline, A. and J. Murray. "Reconceptualizing On-Street Sex Work as a Complex Affective Social Assemblage," in S. Fitzpatrick and K. McGarry (eds.) *Realising Justice for Sex Workers.* London, UK: Rowman and Littlefield, 2018.

Carline, A., C. Gunby, and J. Murray. *Rape and The Criminal Trial: Reconceptualizing the Courtroom as an Affective Assemblage.* Liverpool, UK: Palgrave-MacMillan, 2020.

Carrasco, E. "Opposition, Justice, Structuralism, and Particularity: Intersections Between LatCrit Theory and Law and Development Studies," *University of Miami Inter-American Law Review* 28: 313–328, 1996.

Carrington, K. "Essentialism and Feminist Criminologies: Relevant to All — Specific to None," *The Critical Criminologist* 5(4): 5–6, 14–15, 19–20, 1993.

Caudill, D. "Freud and Critical Legal Studies: Contours of a Radical-Legal Psychoanalysis," *Indiana Law Journal* 66(3): 651–97, 1991.

________. "Lacan and Law: Networking with the Big O[ther]," *Studies in Psychoanalytic Theory* 1(1): 25–5, 1992a.

________. "'Name-of-the-Father' and the Logic of Psychosis: Lacan's Law and Ours," *Legal Studies Forum* 16(4): 23–46, 1992b.

________. "Jacques Lacan and Our State of Affairs: Preliminary Remarks on Law as Other," in R. Kevelson (ed.) *Law and the Human Sciences.* New York: Peter Lang, 95–113, 1992c.

________. "Coming to Terms With Lacan," *International Journal for the Semiotics of Law,"* 17: 203–220, 1993.

________. "Re-Returning to Freud: Critical Legal Studies as Cultural Psychoanalysis," in D. Caudill and S. Stone (eds.) *Radical Philosophy of Law.* Humanities Press, forthcoming, 1994.

________. *Lacan and the Subject of Law.* Atlantic Highlands, NJ: Humanities Press, 1997.

Caudill, D. and S. Stone (eds.). *Radical Philosophy of Law.* Atlantic Highlands, NJ: Humanities Press, 1995.

Cavalieri, P. *The Animal Question: Why Nonhuman Animals Deserve Human Rights.* Oxford, UK: Oxford University Press, 2006.

Cavanagh, S. "Queer Theory, Psychoanalysis and the Symptom: A Lacanian Reader," *Studies in Gender and Sexuality* 20(4): 226–230, 2019.

Chaemsaithong, K. "Deconstructing Competing Courtroom Narratives: Representation of Social Actors," *Social Semiotics* 29(2): 240–260, 2019a.

________. "Names and Identities in Courtroom Narratives," *Names* 67(4): 185–198, 2019b.

________. "Use of Voices in Legal Opening Statements," *Social Semiotics* 28(1): 90–107, 2018.

Chambliss, W. *On the Take.* Bloomington, In. Indiana University Press, 1988.

________. "A Sociological Analysis of Vagrancy," *Social Problems* 12: 67–77, 1964.

Chambliss, W. and R. Seidman. *Law, Order and Power 2ed.* Boston, MA: Addison-Wesley, 1982.

Chandler, D. *Semiotics for Beginners* [www document, 1995] url: (http://www. aber.ac.uk/media/documents/s4b/semiotic.html).

________. *Semiotics: The Basics.* London, UK: Routledge, 2007.

Chang, R. *Disoriented: Asian Americans, Law, and the Nation-State.* New York: New York University Press, 1999.

Chaplin, J. "Review of David McIlroy's *The End of Law.*" London: Edward Elgar Publishers. In Theos Think Tank: Law and Justice: What's the Difference? Accessed on 2/28/21, https://medium.com/@theosintern/law-and-justice-whats-the-difference-343ed6301979.

Chase, A. "The Birth of the Modern Law School," *American Journal of Legal Philosophy* 23(4): 329–348, 1979.

Chavez, L. "Philippine Bill Seeks to Grant Nature the Same Legal Rights as Humans," *Mongabay*, August 20, 2019, accessed 8/12/2021, https://news.mongabay.com/2019/08/philippine-bill-seeks-to-grant-nature-the-same-legal-rights-as-humans/.

Cheah, P., D. Fraser and J. Grbich. *Thinking Through the Body of the Law.* New York: New York University Press, 1996.

Cheng, L. and M. Danesi. "Exploring Legal Discourse: A Socio-Semiotic (Re)construction," *Social Semiotics* 29(3): 279–285, 2019.

Chesters, G. and I. Walsh. *Complexity and Social Movements: Multitudes at the Edge of Chaos.* Abingdon, UK: Routledge, 2007.

Chou, R. and J. Feagin, *Myth of the Model Minority: Asian Americans Facing Racism.* Abingdon, UK: Routledge, 2015.

Choat, S. *Marx Through Poststructuralism: Lyotard, Derrida, Foucault, Deleuze.* London, UK: Bloomsbury Publishing, 2012.

Choy, C. and R. Tajima. "Who is Vincent Chin," accessed 4/4/2021, https://www.nbcnews.com/news/asian-america/who-vincent-chin-history-relevance-1982-killing-n771291.

Christensen, G. and M. Tatum (eds.). *Reading American Indian Law*, Cambridge, UK: Cambridge University Press, 2019.

Cilliers, P. "Postmodern Knowledge and complexity (or Why Anything Does not Go)," *South African Journal of Philosophy* 14(3): 124–132, 1995.

________. *Complexity and Postmodernism.* London, UK: Routledge, 1998.

"Civil Rights Movement Timeline," History.com editors, accessed 3/22/2021, https://www.history.com/topics/civil-rights-movement/civil-rights-movement-timeline.

Cixous, H. "The Laugh of the Medusa," *Signs* 7(1): 23–36, 1976.

________. *The Newly Born Woman.* Minneapolis, MN: University of Minnesota Press, 1986.

________. *Reading with Clarice Lispector.* Minneapolis, MN: University of Minnesota Press, 1990.

Clark, G. "A Conversation with Duncan Kennedy," *The Advocate: The Suffolk University Law School Journal* 24(2): 56–71, 1994.

Clay-Warner, J. and J. McMahon-Howard, "Rape Reporting: 'Class Rape' and the Behavior of Law," *Violence and Victims* 24(6): 723–43, 2009.

Clemens, J. and R. Grigg. *Jacques Lacan and the Other Side of Psychoanalysis.* Durham, NC: Duke University Press, 2006.

Clement, C. *The Lives and Legends of Jacques Lacan.* New York: Columbia University Press, 1983.

Cohen, S. *Visions of Social Control* Oxford: Polity Press, 1985.

Cohen, A. and W. Condrington. "The Equal Rights Amendment Explained," Brennan Center for Justice. Accessed 3/18/2021, https://www.brennancenter.org/our-work/research-reports/equal-rights-amendment-explained.

Cohen, C. and T. Regan. *The Animal Rights Debate.* London, UK: Rowman and Littlefield, 2001.

Coker, D. "Crime Control and Feminist Law Reform in Domestic Violence Law," *Buffalo Criminal Law Review* 4: 801–840, 2001.

Cole, D. *No Equal Justice.* New York: The New Press, 1999.

Cole, L. and S. Foster. *From the Ground Up: Environmental Racism and the Rise of the Environmental Justice Movement.* New York: New York University Press, 2001.

Collins, H. *Marxism and Law.* New York: Oxford University Press, 1982.

Collins, P. "Transforming the Inner Circle: Dorothy Smith's Challenge to Sociological Theory," *Sociological Theory* 78, 1992.

________. *Black Feminist Thought: Knowledge, Consciousness and the Politics of Empowerment.* New York: Routledge, 2009.

________. "Learning from the Outsider Within: The Sociological Significance of Back Feminist Thought," in S. Harding (ed.) *The Feminist Standpoint Reader*, pp. 103–126, NY: Routledge, 2004.

Collins, P. and S. Bilge. *Intersectionality (Key Concepts)*, 2ed. UK: Polity Press, 2020.

Committee to End the Marion Lockdown. *Can't Jail the Spirit: Political Prisoners in the U.S.A Collection of Biographies,* 1988.

Conklin, W. *The Phenomenology of Modern Legal Discourse.* Aldershot, UK: Ashgate, 1998.

Conley, J. and W. M. O'Barr. *Just Words: Law, Language and Power.* Chicago, IL: University of Chicago Press, 1998.

Conty, A. "The Politics of Nature," *Theory, Culture, Society* 35(7–8): 73–96, 2018.

Cook, A. "Beyond Critical Legal Studies: The Reconstructive Theology of Dr. Martin Luther King Jr.," *Harvard Law Review* 103: 985–1001, 1990.

Cooke, E. "Peirce on Musement," *European Journal of Pragmatism and American Philosophy* [online]. X-2 (2018), accessed on 4/21/2021, https://journals.openedition.org/ejpap/1370.

Coole, D. and S. Frost (eds.). *New Materialism*. Durham, NC: Duke University Press, 2010a.

________. *New Materialism: Ontology, Agency and Politics*. Durham, NC: Duke University Press, 2010b.

Coombe, R. "Room for Manoeuver: Towards a Theory of Practice in Critical Legal Studies," *Law and Social Inquiry* 14: 69–121, 1989.

________. "Contesting the Self: Negotiating Subjectivities in Nineteenth-Century Ontario Defamation Trials," *Studies in Legal Policy and Society* 11: 3, 1991a.

________. "Beyond Modernity's Meanings: Engaging the Postmodern in Cultural Anthropology," *Culture* 11: 111, 1991b.

________. "Publicity Rights and Political Aspiration: Mass, Culture, Gender Identity, and Democracy," *New England Law Review* 26(4): 1221–80, 1992.

Cooney, M. *Warriors and Peacemakers*. New York: New York University Press., 1998.

________. "The Decline of Elite Homicide," *Criminology* 35: 381–407, 1997.

________. "Evidence as Partisanship," *Law and Society Review* 28: 833–58, 1994.

Corateli, G., F. Galofaro, and F. Montanari (eds.). "Introduction: Semiotics of Economic Discourse," *Ocula* 16: 1–9, (December), 2015, accessed 4/30/2021, http://www.ocula.it/files/OCULA-16-CORATELLI-GALOFARO-MONTANARI-Introduction-on-semiotics-of-economic-discourse.pdf.

Corcos, C. (ed.). *Law and Magic: A Collection of Essays*. Durham: Carolina Academic Press, 2010.

Cornell, D. "Toward a Modern/Postmodern Reconstruction of Ethics," *University of Pennsylvania Law Review* 133: 291–380, 1985.

________. "The Philosophy of the Limit: System Theory and Feminist Legal Reform," in D. Cornell, M. Rosenfeld and D. Carlson (eds.), *Deconstruction and the Possibility of Justice*. New York: Routledge, 68–91, 1992.

________. *Transformations: Collective Imagination and Sexual Difference*. New York, NY: Routledge, 1993.

________. *At the Heart of Freedom*. Princeton, NJ: Princeton University Press, 1998.

________. *Beyond Accommodation: Ethical Feminism, Deconstruction and the Law*. New York: Rowman and Littlefield Publishers, Inc., 1999.

Cornell, D. "Autonomy Re-Imagined," *Journal of Psychoanalysis of Culture and Society* 8(1): 144–49, 2003.

________. *Moral Images of Freedom*, Lanham, MD: Rowman and Littlefield, 2007.

Cornell, D. and N. Friedman. *The Mandate of Dignity*. NY: Fordham University Press, 2016.

Cornell, S. and Hartmann, D. *Ethnicity and Race: Making Identities in a Changing World*, Thousand Oaks, CA: Pine Forge Press, 1998.

Cornell, D., M. Rosenfeld and D. Carlson (eds.). *Deconstruction and the Possibility of Justice.* New York: Routledge, 1992.

Corrington, R. *An Introduction to CS. Peirce.* Lanham, MD: Rowman and Littlefield, 1993.

Cottee, S. and K. Howard. "Terrorist (E)motives: The Existential Attraction of Terrorism," *Studies in Conflict and Terrorism* 34(12): 963–86, 2011.

Cotterell, R. "Durkheim on Legal Development and Social Solidarity," *British Journal of Law and Society* 4: 241–52, 1977.

________. *The Sociology of Law.* London: Butterworths, 1984.

________. "The Durkheimian Tradition in the Sociology of Law," *Law and Society Review* 25(4): 923–45, 1991.

________. *Emile Durkheim: Law in a Moral Domain.* Edinburgh, UK: Edinburgh University of Edinburg Press, 1999.

________. "Justice, Dignity, Torture, Headscarves: Can Durkheim's Sociology Clarify Legal Values?," *Social and Legal Studies* 20: 3–20, 2010a.

________. "Durkheim on Justice, Morals and Politics." In R. Cotterrell (ed.) *Emile Durkheim: Justice, Morality and Politics*, xi–xxiv. Farnham, UK: Ashgate, 2010b.

________. "Law as Constitutive," in J.D. Wright (ed.), *International Encyclopedia of the Social and Behavioral Sciences*, pp. 550–53. Oxford, UK: Elsevier, 2015.

________. *Sociological Jurisprudence.* New York: Routledge, 2017.

Cramer, J. "The Transactional Interpretation of Quantum Mechanics," *Review of Modern Physics* 58: 647–688, 1986.

________. *The Quantum Handshake.* London, UK: Springer, 2016.

Crawford, J. "The Recognition of Aboriginal Customary Laws: An Overview," in C. Cunneen (ed.), *Aboriginal Perspectives on Criminal Justice.* Sydney, Australia: Institute of Criminology, 53–75, 1992.

Crenshaw, K. "Race, Reform and Retrenchment: Transformation and Legitimation in Antidiscrimination," *Harvard Law Review* 101: 1356–87, 1988.

________. "Demarginalizing the Intersections of Race and Sex," *University of Chicago Law Forum* 1: 139–167, 1989.

________. "Demarginalizing the Intersection of Race and Sex," *University of Chicago Legal Forum*, 1989: 139–167; reprinted in D. Kairys (ed.), *The Politics of Law: A Progressive Critique*, 2nd edition, Pantheon, 195–217, 1990.

________. "Beyond Racism and Misogyny," in M. Matsuda, C. Lawrence, R. Delgado, and K. Crenshaw, *Words That Wound.* Oxford: Westview Press, 111–132, 1993.

________. "We Still Have Not Learned From Anita Hill's Testimony," *UCLA Woman's Law Journal 26*: 17–43, 2019.

________. Crenshaw, K. "From Private Violence to Mass Incarceration: Thinking Intersectionally About Women, Race, and Social Control," *UCLA Law Review*, 59: 1418–1472, 2012.

________. "On Intersectionality, More Than Two Decades Later," Columbia Law School (June 8, 2017), interview, accessed on 7/15/2021, https://www.law.columbia.edu/news/archive/kimberle-crenshaw-intersectionality-more-two-decades-later.

Crenshaw, K. "Intersectionality at 30," UCLA Law, accessed on 3/22/2021, https://law.ucla.edu/news/intersectionality-30-qa-kimberle-crenshaw.

________. *On Intersectionality*, New York: New Press, 2022.

Crenshaw, K., N. Gotanda, G. Peller and K. Tholmas (eds.). *Critical Race Theory: The Writings That Formed the Movement,* New York: New Press, 1995.

Cressey, D. *Other People's Money*. New York: Penguin Books, 1957.

Creutzfeld, N. "Traditions of Studying the Social and the Legal: A Short Introduction to the Institutional and Intellectual Development of Socio-Legal Studies," in N. Creutzfeld, M. Mason, and K McConnachie (eds.). *Routledge Handbook of Socio-Legal Methods.* London: Routledge, 2019.

Crook, J.A. *Law and Life of Rome, 90 B.C–A.D. 212.* Ithaca, NY: Cornell University Press, 1967.

Crossley, M. "Black Health Matters: Disparities, community Health, and Interest Convergence," *Michigan Journal of Race and Law* 22(1): 52–100, 2016.

Crownie, F. and A Bradney. "Socio-Legal Studies," D. Watkins and M. Burton (eds.), 2ed., *Research Methodology in Law*, pp. 40–61, London: Routledge, 2018.

Cruz, D. "Lawsuit Seeks to Obliterate Admission Processes of NYC Public Schools," *Gotham*, March 10, 2021, accessed 4/8/2021, https://gothamist.com/news/lawsuit-seeks-obliterate-admissions-processes-nyc-public-schools.

Culler, J. *Deconstruction.* Ithaca, NY: Cornell University Press, 1981.

________. "Demarginalizing the Intersection of Race and Sex: A Black Feminist Critique of Antidiscrimination Doctrine, Feminist Theory, and Antiracist Politics," in K. Bartlett and R. Kennedy (eds.), *Feminist Legal Theory.* Oxford: Westview Press, 57–80, 1991.

Cullinan, C. *Wild Law: A Manifesto for Earth Justice.* Devon, UK: Chelsea Green Publishing, 2011.

Cummings, S. "The Puzzle of Social Movements in American Legal Theory," *American Journal of Sociology* 4(1): 1–113, 2016.

________. "The Social Movement Turn in Law," *Law and Social Inquiry* 43(2): 360–416, 2018.

Cunneen, C. *Aboriginal Perspectives on Criminal Justice.* Sydney, Australia: Institute of Criminology, 1992.

Curran, D. *Risk, Power and Inequality in the 21st Century.* London: Palgrave MacMillan, 2016.

Curran, V. G. "The Legalization of Racism in a Constitutional State," *Hastings Law Journal* 50: 1–45, 1998a.

________. "Cultural Immersions, Difference and Categories in US Comparative Law," *American Journal of Comparative Law* 46: 43–78, 1998b.

Currie, D. "Female Criminality: A Crisis in Feminist Theory," in B. MacLean, *The Political Economy of Crime.* Scarborough, Canada: Prentice-Hall Canada, 232–246, 1986.

________. "Unhiding the Hidden: Race, Class, and Gender in the Construction of Knowledge," *Humanity and Society* 17(1): 3–27, 1993.

Currie, D. and M. Kline. "Challenging Privilege: Women, Knowledge, and Feminist Struggles," *Journal of Human Justice* 2(2): 1–36, 1991.

Currie, D., B. MacLean and D. Milovanovic. "Three Traditions of Critical Justice Inquiry: Class, Gender, and Discourse," in D. Currie and B. MacLean (eds.), *Re-Thinking the Administration of Justice*. Halifax, Nova Scotia: Fernwood Publishing, 3–44, 1992.

Czarota, A. "Adam Podgorecki (1925–1998)," in D. Clark (ed.) *Encyclopedia of Law and Society* 1118, 2007.

Dahlberg, L. "Capitalism as a Discursive System? Interrogating Discourse Theory's Contribution to Critical Political Economy," *Critical Discourse Studies* 11(3): 257–271, 2014.

Dahrendorf, R. "Out of Utopia: Toward a Reorientation of Sociological Analysis" *American Journal of Sociology* 64(2): 115–127, 1958a.

________. "Toward a Theory of Social Conflict," *Journal of Conflict Resolution* 2(2): 170–183, 1958b.

________. *Class and Class Conflict in Industrial Society*. Stanford, CA: Stanford University Press, 1959.

Dai, M. and Y. Gao. "Reporting Behavior of Bicycle Theft Victims: A Test of Black's Theory of Law," *Security Journal* 34(4): 148–164, 2021.

Daly, K. and M. Chesney-Lind. "Feminism and Criminology," *Justice Quarterly* 5: 101–143, 1988.

Dalton, H. "The Clouded Prism," *Harvard Critical Law Review* 22: 435, 1987.

Dalton, K. "An Essay in the Deconstruction of Contract Law," *Yale Law Journal* 94: 977, 1985.

Danes, S. *Time and Memory in Reggae Music: The Politics of Hope*. London, UK: Manchester University Press, 2010.

Danesi, M. "Visual Rhetoric and Semiotics," *Oxford Research Encyclopedia*, 2017, accessed 5/15/2021, https://oxfordre.com/view/10.1093/acrefore/9780190228613.001.0001/acrefore-9780190228613-e-43.

Danner, M. "Socialist Feminism: A Brief Introduction," in B. MacLean and D. Milovanovic (eds.) *New Directions in Critical Criminology*. Vancouver, Canada: Collective Press, 1991.

de Haan, W. *The Politics* of *Redress*. Boston, MA: Unwin Hyman, 1990.

Davidse, K and L. Ghesquiere, L. "Content-Purport, Content-Substance and Structure," *International Journal for the Semiotics of Law* 48(1): 85–109, 2016.

Davis, A.D. and J.C. Williams. "Gender, Work and Family Project Inaugural Feminist Legal Theory Lecture Foreword," *American University Journal of Gender, Social Policy and Law* 8: 1–12, 2000.

Davies, M. *Law Unlimited: Materialism, Pluralism, and Legal Theory*. New York: Routledge, 2017.

Dean, T. "Lacan and Queer Theory," *Cliniques Méderraneénnes* 74(2): 61–78, 2006.

Dee, J. "Shedding Light or Casting Shadows? The Penumbra Metaphor, Privacy and Privileged Communication," *Free Speech Yearbook* 44(1): 55–63, 2009.

Dejusus-Torres, M. "Microaggressions in the Criminal Justice System at Discretionary Stages and its Impact on Latino(a)/Hispanics," *The Justice Professional* 13(1): 68–89, 2000.

DeKeseredy, W.S. "Exploring the Gender, Race and Class Dimensions of Victimization: A Left Realist Critique of the Canadian Urban Victimization Survey," *International Journal of Offender Therapy and Comparative Criminology* 35: 143–61, 1991.

DeKeseredy, W.S. and R. Hinch. *Woman Abuse: Sociological Perspectives.* Toronto: Thompson, 1991.

DeKeseredy, W.D. and M. Schwartz. "British Left Realism on the Abuse of Women," in H. Pepinsky and R. Quinney (eds.), *Criminology as Peacemaking.* Bloomington, IN: Indiana University Press, 1991.

Delanda, M. *A New Philosophy of Society: Assemblage Theory and Social Complexity.* London, UK: Continuum, 2006.

________. *Assemblage Theory.* Edinburgh, UK: Edinburgh University Press, 2016.

Deleuze, G. *Proust and Signs.* New York: Braziller, Inc., 1972.

________. *Spinoza.* Paris: Minuit, 1981.

________. *Nietzsche and Philosophy.* New York: Columbia University Press, 1983.

________. *Foucault.* Minneapolis, MN: University of Minnesota Press, 1986a.

________. *Cinema 1: The Movement Image.* Minneapolis, MN: University of Minnesota Press, 1986b.

________. *Cinema 2: The Time-Image.* Minneapolis, MN: University of Minnesota Press, 1989.

Deleuze, G. and M. Joughin. *Negotiations.* New York: Columbia University Press, 1995.

Deleuze, G. and C. Parnet. "Gilles Deleuze from A to Z," DVD, produced by P.A. Boutang, 1988–1989, accessed 7/30/2021, https://www.youtube.com/playlist?list=PLiR8NqajHNPbaX2rBoA2z6IPGpU0IPlS2.

Deleuze, G. and F. Guattari. *Anti-Oedipus.* Minneapolis, MN: University of Minnesota Press, 1977.

________. *Kafka: Toward a Minor Literature.* Minneapolis, MN: University of Minnesota Press, 1986.

________. *A Thousand Plateaus.* Minneapolis, MN: University of Minnesota Press, 1987.

Delgado, D. "The Ethereal Scholar: Does Critical Legal Studies Have What Minorities Want?" *Harvard Critical Law Review* 22: 301, 1987.

Delgado, R. "Rotten Social Background: Should the Criminal Law Recognize a Defense of Severe Environmental Deprivation," *Law and Inequality* 3(1): 9–90, 1985. See also web version, accessed 9/5/2021, https://scholarship.law.umn.edu/cgi/viewcontent.cgi?article=1298&context=lawineq.

________. "The Ethereal Scholar: Does Critical Legal Studies Have What Minorities Want?", *Harvard Civil Rights/Civil Liberties Law Review* 22(2): 301–322, 1987.

________. "Rodrigo's Roundelay: Hernandez v. Texas and the Interest-Convergence Dilemma," *Harvard Civil Rights—Civil Liberties Law Review* 41: 23–65, 2006.

________. "Why Obama? An Interest Convergence Explanation of the Nation's First Black President," *Law and Inequality* 33(2): 345–69, 2015.

Delgado, R. and J. Stefancic. *Critical Race Theory, 3ed.* New York: New York University Press, 2017.

________. "Critical Race Theory," *Encyclopedia.com* (2018), accessed on 3/27/2021, https://www.encyclopedia.com/social-sciences-and-law/sociology-and-social-reform/sociology-general-terms-and-concepts/critical-race-theory.

________. *The Latino/a Condition: A Critical Reader.* New York: New York University Press, 1998.

de Man, P. *Allegories of Reading. Figural Language in Rousseau, Nietzsche, &Ike, and Proust.* New Haven, CT: Yale University Press, 1979.

________. *The Resistance to Theory.* Minneapolis, MN: University of Minnesota Press, 1986.

de Mello, M. *Animals and Society.* New York: Columbia University Press, 2021.

de Sutter, L. (ed.). *Althusser and Law.* New York: Routledge, 2013.

Derrida, J. *Speech and Other Phenomena.* Evanston: Northwestern University Press, 1973.

________. *Positions.* Chicago, IL: University of Chicago Press, 1981.

________. *Writing and Difference.* Chicago: University of Chicago Press, 1978.

________. "Force of Law: The Mystical Foundation of Authority," in D. Cornell, M. Rosenfeld and D. Carlson (eds.). *Deconstruction and the Possibility* of *Justice.* New York: Routledge, 3–67, 1992.

________. "Declarations of Independence," *New Political Science* 15: 7–17, 1986.

________. "The Villanova Roundtable," in J. Caputo (ed.), *Deconstruction in a Nutshell: A Conversation with Jacques Derrida.* New York: Fordham University Press, 1997.

Deutscher, G. *Through the Language Glass: Why the World Looks Different in Other Languages.* New York: Metropolitan Books, 2011.

________. "Does Language Shape How You Think?" *New York Times*, p. 42, August 29, 2010, accessed on 5/3/2021, https://www.nytimes.com/2010/08/29/magazine/29language-t.html.

Dewey, J. *Philosophy and Civilization.* New York: Milton-Balch, 1931.

Dews, P. *Logics of Disintegration: Post-Structuralist Thought and the Claims of Critical Theory.* New York: Verso, 1987.

Diamond, A., *The Evolution of Law and Order.* Great Britain: Richard Clay and Co., 1951.

________. "The Rule of Law Versus the Order of Custom," in R.P. Wolff (ed.). *The Rule of Law.* New York: Simon and Schuster, 1971.

Di Bias, F. "Quantum Information Self-Organization and Consciousness: A Holoinformational Model of Consciousness," *Journal of Nonlocality* 2(2): 1–15, 2013.

________. "The Holoinformational Foundations of Consciousness," in R. Poznanski, J. Tuszynski, and T. Feinberg (eds.). *Biophysics of Consciousness*, pp. 231–250. New York: World Scientific, 2016.

Dietz, M. "Current Controversies in Feminist Theory," *Annual Review of Political Science*, 6: 399–431, 2003.

Direk, Z. "Law, Justice and Politics: Derrida on Deconstruction and Democracy to Come," *The New Centennial Review* 14(2): 111–126. 2014.

Disch and Hawkesworth (eds.). *The Oxford Handbook of Feminist Theory*, Online. UK: Oxford University Press, accessed on 3/18/2021, https://www.oxfordhandbooks.com/view/10.1093/oxfordhb/9780199328581.001.0001/oxfordhb-9780199328581.

Dixon, R., W. Ramson and M. Thomas. *Australian Aboriginal Words in English: Their Origin and Meaning.* New York: Oxford University Press, 1990.

Domhoff, W. *Who Rules America?* New York: Prentice Hall, 1967.

Dor, J. *Introduction to the Reading of Lacan.* New Jersey: Jason Aronowitz, 1997.

Douzinas, C., R. Warrington and S. McVeigh. *Postmodern Jurisprudence: The Law of Text in the Texts of Law.* London: Routledge, 1991.

Doyle, D. and D. Luckenbill. "Mobilizing Law in Response to Collective Problems: A Test of Black's Theory of Law," *Law and Society Review* 25(1): 103–16, 1991.

Driver, J. "Rethinking the Interest Convergence Thesis," *Northwestern University Law Review* 105(1): 149–98, 2011.

Duan Lin and Po-fang Tsai. "Max Weber's Traditional Chinese Law Revisited," *Taiwan Journal of East Asian Studies* 10(2): 33–69, 2013. Accessed, 98/8/2021, https://www.academia.edu/5534741/2013Max_Webers_Traditional_Chinese_Law_Revisited_A_Poly_Contextuality_in_the_Sociology_of_Law.

DuBois, T.D. "Hegemony, Imperialism and the Construction of Religion in East and Southeast Asia," *History and Theory* 44(4): 113–31, 2005.

Dudziak, M. *Cold War Civil Rights: Race and the Image of American Democracy*, Princeton, NY: Princeton University Press, 2011.

Dunn, S. "A Tyranny of Justice: The Ethics of Lyotard's Differend," *Boundary* 2(20): 1993.

Durkheim, E. *Professional Ethics and Civic Morals.* Glencoe, IL: The Free Press, 1958.

________. *Montesquieu and Rousseau: Forerunners of Sociology.* Ann Arbor, MI: University of Michigan Press, 1960.

________. *Moral Education: A Study in the Theory and Application of the Sociology of Education.* New York: Free Press, 1961.

________. *Socialism.* New York: Collier Books, 1962.

________. *The Rules of Sociological Method.* New York: The Free Press, 1964a.

________. *The Division of Labor in Society.* New York: The Free Press, 1964b.

________. *Sociology and Philosophy I.* New York: The Free Press, 1974.

________. *The Evolution of Educational Thought.* London: Routledge and Kegan Paul, 1977.

________. "The Nature and Origins of the Right to Property," in S. Lukes and A. Scull (eds.), *Durkheim and the Law.* New York: St. Martin's Press, 1983a.

________. "The Nature and Evolution of Contract," in S. Lukes and A. Scull (eds.), *Durkheim and the Law.* New York: St. Martin's Press, 1983b.

________. "The Evolution of Punishment," in S. Lukes and A. Scull (eds.). *Durkheim and the Law.* New York: St. Martin's Press, 1983c.

________. *Pragmatism and Sociology.* New York: Cambridge University Press, 1983d.

Dworkin, R. *Taking Rights Seriously.* London: Duckworth, 1978.

________. *A Matter of Principle.* Cambridge, MA: Harvard University Press, 1985.

________. *Law's Empire.* London, UK: Fontana Paperbacks, 1986.

Easton, S. *Marx and Law.* London: Routledge, 2008.

Eco, U. *A Theory of Semiotics.* Bloomington, IN: University of Indiana Press, 1976.

________. *Semiotics and the Philosophy of Language.* London: MacMillan, 1984.

Edie, J. "Husserl's Conception of 'The Grammatical' and Contemporary Linguistics," in Lester Embrie (ed.). *Lift-World and Consciousness.* Evanston, IL: Northwestern University Press, 1972.

Eichner, M. "On Postmodern Feminist Legal Theory," *Harvard Civil Rights-Civil Liberties Law Review* 36(1): 1–78, 2001.

Eisenstein, S. *The Film Sense.* New York: Harcourt Brace Jovanovic, 1975.

Einstadter, W. and S. Henry. *Criminological Theory.* Fort Worth, TX: Harcourt Brace College Publishers, 1995.

Ela, N. "Litigation Dilemmas: Lessons from the Marcos Human Rights Class Action," *Law and Social Inquiry* 42(2): 473–505, 2017.

Ellis, J. *Against Deconstruction.* Princeton, NJ: Princeton University Press, 1989.

Endicott, T. "Law and Language," *Stanford Encyclopedia of Philosophy*, 2016, accessed 4/28/2021, https://plato.stanford.edu/entries/law-language/.

Esping-Anderson, G., R. Friedland and E. Ohlin. "Class Struggle and the Capitalist State," in R. Quinney (ed.), *Capitalist Society.* Homewood, IL: The Dorsey Press, 1979.

Espiritu, Y. *Asian American Panethnicity.* Philadelphia, PA: Pennsylvania State University Press, 1992.

Evans, D. *An Introductory Dictionary of Lacanian Psychoanalysis.* London: Routledge, 1996.

Evan, J. "Indigenous Australians: Language and the Law," *International Journal for the Semiotics of Law* 15(2): 127–141, 2002.

Ewick, P. and S. Silbey, *The Common Place of Law: Stories from Everyday Life.* Chicago, IL: University of Chicago Press, 1998.

Fairclough, N. *Language and Power.* Harlow: Longman, 1989.

________. "Marx as a Critical Discourse Analysist: The Genesis of a Critical Method and its Relevance to the Critique of Global Capital," *Sociolinguistic Studies* 3(1): 185–229, 2002.

________. "CDA as Dialectical Reasoning," in J. Flowerdew and J. Richardson (eds.) *The Routledge Handbook of Critical Discourse Studies*, pp. 13–25. London: Routledge, 2018.

________. "What is CDA? Language and Power Twenty-Five years on," 2014, accessed, 4/30/2021, https://www.academia.edu/8429277/What_is_CDA_Language_and_Power_twenty_five_years_on.

Fairclough, N. and P. Graham. "Marx as a Critical Discourse Analyst: The Genesis of a Critical Method and Its Relevance to the Critique of Global Capital," *Estudios de Sociolinguistica* 3(1): 185–229, 2002.

Feagin, J. *The White Racial Frame: Centuries of Racial Framing and Counter-framing*, 2ed, London: Routledge, 2013.

Feigenson, N. and C. Spiesel. *Law on Display: The Digital Transformation of Legal Persuasion and Judgement.* New York: New York University Press, 2009.

Feldstein, R. and H. Sussman (eds.). *Psychoanalysis and ...* New York: Routledge, 1990.

Felski, R. "Feminism, Postmodernism, and the Critique of Modernity," *Cultural Critique* (Fall): 33–57, 1989.

Feminist Jurisprudence: An Overview, Legal Information Institute, Cornell Law School. Accessed on 3/18/2021, https://www.law.cornell.edu/wex/feminist_jurisprudence.

Feminist Legal Research: Law Reviews and Journals, Elisabeth Haub School of Law, Pace Law Library Research Guides, accessed on 3/20, 2021, https://libraryguides.law.pace.edu/c.php?g=319316&p=2134683.

Ferguson, S. "Intersectionality and Social Reproduction in Feminism," *Historical Materialism* 24(2): 38–60, 2016.

________. "Children, Childhood and Capitalism: A Social Reproduction Perspective," in T. Bhattacharya (ed.), pp. 112–130. *Social Reproduction Theory: Remapping Class, Recentering Oppression.* London: Pluto Press, 2017.

Ferguson, M. and J. Wicke (eds.). *Feminism and Postmodernism.* Durham, NC: Duke University Press, 1994.

Ferki, A. "The Question of Non-Human Animals in Sociology," *Sloth* 4(1): 1–8, 2018.

Ferrell, J. "Anarchy Against the Discipline," *Journal of Criminal Justice and Popular Culture* 3(4): 86–91, 1995.

________. "Against the Law: Anarchist Criminology," in B. MacLean and D. Milovanovic (eds.) *Thinking Critically About Crime*, 146–54, 1997.

________. "Anarchist Criminology and Social Justice," in B. Arrigo (ed.) *Social Justice/Criminal Justice: The Maturation of Critical Theory in Law, Crime, and Deviance.* Belmont, CA: West/Wadsworth, pp. 93–108, 1999.

Fine, B. *Democracy and the "Rule of Law.* London: Pluto, 1984.

Fineman, M.A. "Cracking the Foundational Myths: Independence, Autonomy and Self-Sufficiency," *American University Journal Gender, Social Policy and Law* 8: 13–46, 2000.

________. "Feminist Legal Theory," *Journal of Gender, Social Policy and the Law* 13(1): 13–32, 2015.

Finkelman, P. *Slavery and the Founders*, 3ed. London: Routledge, 2014.

________. *Defending Slavery: Proslavery Thought in the Old South*, 2ed. New York: Bedford/St/Martin's, 2019.

Finnis, J. *Natural Law and Natural Rights.* Oxford: Clarendon Press, 1980.

________. *Fundamentals of Ethics.* Oxford: Clarendon, 1983.

Fiorenza, E. *Wisdom Ways*. NY: Orbis Books, 2001.

Fish, S. *Is There a Text in This Class?: The Authority of Interpretive Communities*. Cambridge, MA: Harvard University Press, 1980.

________. "With the Compliments of the Author: Reflections on Austin and Derrida," *Critical Inquiry* 4: 693–722, 1982.

________. "Fish v. Fiss," *Stanford Law Review* 36(6): 1325–1347, 1984.

________. *Doing What Comes Naturally: Change, Rhetoric, and the Practice of Theory, in Literary and Legal Studies*. Durham, NC: Duke University Press, 1989.

Fishman, J. *The Sociology of Language*. Rawley, MA: Newbury House, 1960.

Fitzpatrick, P. "Marxism and Legal Pluralism," *Australian Journal of Law and Society* 1: 45–59, 1983.

________. "Law and Societies," *Osgood Hall Law Journal* 22: 115–38, 1984.

________. "The Rise and Fall of Informalism," in R. Mathews (ed.), *Informal Justice*. London: Sage, 1988.

Fitzpatrick, P. and A. Hunt (eds.). *Critical Legal Studies*. Oxford: Basil Blackwell, 1987.

Flax, J. "Postmodernism and Gender Relations in Feminist Theory," in L.J. Nicholson (ed.) *Feminism/Postmodernism*. London: Routledge, 1990.

Fleming, D. *Powerplay: Toys as Popular Culture*. Manchester, UK: Manchester University Press, 1996.

Fletcher, G. "Law as Discourse," *Cardozo Law Review* 13(5): 1631–37, 1992.

Floch, J.M. *Visual Identities*. London, UK: Continuum, 2000.

Flood, S. *Mabo: A Symbol of Sharing*. Glebe, NSW, Australia: Fast Books, 1993.

Flowerdew, J. and J. Richardson (eds.). *The Routledge Handbook of Critical Discourse Studies*. London: Routledge, 2017.

Forchtner, B. "Introducing 'Narrative in Critical Discourse Studies,'" *Critical Discourse Studies* 18(3): 304–313, 2021a.

________. "Critique, Habermas and Narrative (Genre): The Discourse-Historical Approach in Critical Discourse Studies," *Critical Discourse Studies* 18(3): 314–331, 2021b.

Foucault, M. *The Archeology* of *Knowledge*. New York: Pantheon, 1972.

________. *The Order of Things*. New York: Vintage Books, 1973.

________. *Discipline and Punish*. New York: Pantheon, 1977a.

________. *Language, Counter-Memory, Practice*. New York: Cornell University Press, 1977b.

________. "Technologies of the Self," in P. Rabinow (ed.), *Ethics*, pp. 223–52, New York: New Press, 1997c.

________. *The History of Sexuality: Vol 1. An Introduction*. New York: Random House, 1978.

________. *Power/Knowledge*. C. Gordon (ed.). New York: Pantheon, 1980.

________. "The Juridical Apparatus," in W. Connolly (ed.), *Legitimacy and the State*. New York: New York University Press, 1984.

________. *Wrong-Doing, Truth Telling: The Function of Avowal in Justice*. Chicago, IL: Chicago University Press, 2014.

Fournier, M. *Emile Durkheim: A Biography*. Malden, MA: Polity Press, 2012.
Fox, N. and P. Alldred. *Sociology and the New Materialism*. London, UK: Sage, 2016.
Frank, J. "Are Judges Human?" *University of Pennsylvania Law Review* 80: 17–53, 1931a.
________. "Are Judges Human: Part Two?" *University of Pennsylvania Law Review* 80: 233–67, 1931b.
________. *Courts on Trial: Myth and Reality in American Justice*. Princeton, NJ: Princeton University Press, 1949.
________. *Law and the Modern Mind*. New York: Doubleday, 1963.
Franks, M. "I Am/I Am Not: On Angela Harris's Race and Essentialism in Feminist Legal Theory," *California Law Review* 102: 1053–1067, 2014.
Fraser, A. "The Legal Theory We Need Now," *Socialist Review* 8: 164–166, 1978.
Freeman, A. "Racism, Rights and the Quest for Equality of Opportunity: A Critical Legal Essay," *Harvard Critical Law Review* 23: 295, 1988.
________. "Antidiscrimination Law: A Critical Review," in D. Kairys (ed.), *The Politics of Law*. New York: Pantheon Books, 1992.
Freeman, A. and J. Freeman. "It's About Power, Not Policy: Movement Lawyering For Large Scale Social Change," *Clinical Law Review* 23: 147–166, 2016.
Freeman, J. "Supporting Social Movements: A Brief Guide for Lawyers and Law Students," *Hastings Race and Poverty Law Journal* 12(2): 191–204, 2015.
Freire, P. *Pedagogy of the Oppressed*. New York: Herder and Herder, 1973.
________. *The Politics of Education*. South Hadley, MA: Bergin and Garvey, 1985.
Freud, A. *The Ego and the Mechanism of Defense*. New York: Routledge, 1992.
Freud, S. *The Psychopathology of Everyday Lift*. New York: MacMillan, 1914.
________. *The Standard Edition of the Complete Psychological Works of Sigmund Freud*. J. Strachey (ed.). London: The Hogarth Press, 1956.
________. *Totem and Taboo*. London: Norton, 1950.
________. *The Interpretation of Dreams*. New York: Avon Books, 1965.
Freund, J. *The Sociology* of *Max Weber*. New York: Random House, 1969.
Friedman, L. *A History of American Law*. New York: Simon and Schuster, 1985.
________. *Law and Society: An Introduction*. Englewood Cliffs, NJ: Prentice Hall, 1984.
________. *American Law: An Introduction* 2nd ed. New York: W.W. Norton and Company, 1998.
________. *A History of American Law*, 3rd ed. New York: Simon and Schuster, 2005
Friedrichs, D. "The Legitimacy Crises in the United States: A Conceptual Analysis," *Social Problems* 27: 540–554, 1980.
________. "Critical Legal Studies and the Critique of Criminal Justice," *Criminal Justice Review* 11: 15–22, 1986.
Fruehwald, E. "Postmodern Legal Thought and Cognitive Science," *Georgia State University Law Review* 23: 375–432, 2006.
Frug, M.J. "Sexual Equality and Sexual Difference in American Law," *New England Law Review* 26(4): 665–82, 1992.
________. "Postmodern Feminist Legal Manifesto," *Harvard Law Review* 105: 1045–95, 1992.

Fujii-Doe, W. "The Effects of Microaggression on Probation." Ph.D. Dissertation, Denver University, 2017, accessed on 3/21/20021, https://digitalcommons.du.edu/cgi/viewcontent.cgi?article=2320&context=etd.

Gabel, P. "Intention and Structure in Contractual Conditions: Outline of a Method for Critical Legal Theory," *Minnesota Law Review* 61: 601–43, 1977.

________. *The Desire for Mutual Recognition.* New York: Routledge, 2018.

Gabel, P. and J. Feinman. "Contract Law as Ideology," in D. Kairys (ed.), *The Politics of Law.* New York: Pantheon Books, 1992.

Gabor, D. "Theory of Communication," *Journal of the Institute of Electrical Engineering* 93: 429–441, 1946.

________. "A New Microscopic Principle," *Nature* 161: 777–778, 1948.

________. "Holographic Model of Temporal Recall," *Nature* 217: 1288–1289, 1968.

________. "Holography, 1948–1971," Nobel Prize Lecture, December 11, 1971.

Gallop, J. *The Daughter's Seduction: Feminism and Psychoanalysis.* Ithaca, New York: Cornell University Press, 1982.

Game, A. *Undoing the Social: Towards a Deconstructive Sociology.* Milton Keynes: Open University Press, 1991.

Gandler, S. "Critical Theory and Semiotics: Contributions from Latin America to a Marxist Discussion," *Open Cultural Studies* 2(1): 136–150, 2018.

Gans, H. "Racialization and Racialized Research," *Ethnic and Racial Studies* 40(3): 341–352, 2017.

Gardiner, A. and R. Halleck. "Few Charges, Fewer Convictions: The Chauvin Trial and the History of Police Violence," *New York Times*, 4/19/2021, accessed 4/19/2021, https://www.nytimes.com/interactive/2021/04/19/us/derek-chauvin-police-killings.html?action=click&module=Spotlight&pgtype=Homepage.

Garfinkel, A. *Studies in Ethnomethodology.* London, UK: Polity, 1991.

Garroutte, E. and K. Westcott. "The Story is a Living Being: Companionship with Stories in Anishinaabe Studies," in J. Doerfler, N. Sinclair and H. Stark (eds.). *Centering Anishinaabeg Studies: Understanding the World Through Stories*, pp. 61–80. East Lansing, Michigan: Michigan University Press, 2013.

Geertz, C. *The Interpretation of Cultures.* New York: Basic Books, 1973.

________. *Local Knowledge.* New York: Basic Books, 1983.

Geidner, C. "The Court Cases that Changed LGBTQ Rights," *New York Times*, 2019, accessed, 3/21/2021, https://www.nytimes.com/2019/06/19/us/legal-history-lgbtq-rights-timeline.html.

Gelman, A., J. Fagan, and A. Kiss. "An Analysis of the New York City Police Department's Stop-and-Frisk Policy in the Context of Claims of Racial Bias," *Journal of the American Statistical Association* 102: 813–823, 2007.

Georges Abeyie, D. "The Myth of a Racist Criminal Justice System?," in B. MacLean and D. Milovanovic (eds.) *Racism, Empiricism, and Criminal Justice*, pp. 11–14. Vancouver, Canada: Collective Press, 1990.

________. "Criminal Justice Processing of Non-White Minorities," in B. MacLean and D. Milovanovic (eds.) *Racism, Empiricism, and Criminal Justice*, pp. 25–34. Vancouver, Canada: Collective Press, 1990.

Gibbs, J. "Definitions of Law and Empirical Questions," *Law and Society Review* 11: 429–46, 1967.
Giddens, A. (ed.). *Durkheim on Politics and the State.* Cambridge, UK: Polity Press, 1986.
________. *The Constitution of Society.* Berkeley, CA: University of California Press, 1984.
Gilabert, Pablo. "The Socialist Principle "From Each According to Their Abilities, Each According to Their Needs," *Journal of Social Philosophy* 46(2): 197–225, 2015.
________. "Justice and Feasibility: A Dynamic Approach," in M. Weber and K. Valier (eds.) *Political Utopias: Contemporary Debates.* Oxford: Oxford University Press, pp. 95–126, 2017.
Gilabert, P. and M. O'Neill (2019). "Socialism," in E. Zalta (ed.) *The Stanford Encyclopedia of Philosophy*, online, 2019. Accessed on 2/18/2021, https://plato.stanford.edu/archives/fall2019/entries/socialism/.
Gilligan, C. *In a Different Voice: Psychological Theory and Women's Development.* Cambridge, MA: Harvard University Press, 1982.
Gilsinan, J. *Doing Justice.* Englewood Cliffs, NJ: Prentice-Hall, 1982.
Giménez, M. *Marx, Women and Capitalist Social Reproduction.* London: Haymarket Books, 2019.
Glendinng, S. "Derrida and Philosophy of Law and Justice," *Law and Critique* 27: 187–203, 2016.
Glick, B. "Two, Three, Many Rosas! Rebellious Lawyers and Progressive Activist Organizations," *Clinical Law Review* 23: 611–634, 2017.
Gluckman, M. *Politics, Law and Ritual in Tribal Society.* New York: Mentor Books, 1965.
Glynos, J. and D. Howarth. *Logics of Critical Explanation in Social and Political Theory.* London: Routledge, 2007.
Glynos, J. and Y. Stavrakakis. "Politics and the Unconscious: An Interview with Ernesto Laclau," *Subjectivity* 3(3): 231–244, 2010.
Goffman, E. *Asylums.* New York: Anchor Books, 1961.
________. *Interaction Ritual* New York: Anchor Books, 1967.
________. *Relations in Public.* New York: Harper and Row, 1971.
Golder, B. "How to do Things with Foucault," *International Journal of Law in Context* 17(1): 44–50, 2021.
________. *Foucault and the Politics of Rights.* Stanford, CA: Stanford University Press, 2015.
Golder, B. and P. Fitzpatrick. *Foucault's Law.* London, UK: Routledge, 2009.
________. (eds.). *Foucault and Law.* London, UK: Routledge, 2010.
Goldfarb, P. "A Theory-Practice Spiral: The Ethics of Feminism and Clinical Education," *Minnesota Law Review* 75: 1599, 1991.
________. "From the Worlds of 'Others': Minority and Feminist Responses to Critical Legal Studies," *New England Law Review* 26: 683–710, 1992.
Goldstein, J. "Court Blocks Stop-and-Frisk Changes for New York Police, *New York Times*, October 31, 2013.

Goldstein, L. *The U.S. Supreme Court and Racial Minorities: Two Centuries of Judicial Review on Trial.* Cheltenham, UK: Edward Elgar Publishing, 2017.

Golladay, K. "Reporting Behaviors of Identity Theft Victims" An Empirical Test of Black's Theory of Law," *Journal of Financial Crime* 24(1): 101–117, 2017.

Gomez, L. "Understanding Law and Race as Mutually Constitutive," *Journal of Scholarly Perspectives* 8(1): 47–63, 2012.

Goodrich, P. "Law and Language: An Historical and Critical Introduction," *Journal of Law and Society* 11: 173–206, 1984.

________. "The Role of Linguistics in Legal Analysis," *Modern Law Review* 523–534, 1984.

________. *Legal Discourse: Studies in Linguistics, Rhetoric and Legal Analysis.* London: MacMillan, 1987.

________. *Languages of Law: From Logics of Memory to Nomadic Masks.* London: Weidenfeld and Nicolson, 1990.

________. "Critical Legal Studies in England: Prospective Histories," *Oxford Legal Studies* 12(2): 195–236, 1992.

________. "The Personal and the Political," *Cardozo Law Review* 22: 971–999, 2001.

________. "Europe in America: Grammatology, Legal Studies and the Politics of Transmission." *Columbia Law Review* 101: 2033, 2001.

________. "Duncan Kennedy as I Imagine Him: The Man, The Work, his Scholarship and the Polity," *Cardozo Law Review* 22: 971–990, 2001c.

Goodrich, P., F. Hoffmann, M. Rosenfeld, and C. Vismann (eds.). *Derrida and Legal Philosophy*. London, UK: Palgrave-MacMillan, 2008.

Goodrich, P. and M. Valverde (eds.). *Nietzsche and Legal Theory*. London, UK: Routledge, 2005.

Gordon, R. "New Developments in Legal Theory," in D. Kairys (ed.), *The Politics of Law.* New York: Pantheon Books, 1992.

Gottfredson, M. and M. Hindelang. "A Study of the Behavior of Law," *American Sociological Review* 44(3): 3–18, 1979a.

________. "Response: Theory and Research in the Sociology of Law," *American Sociological Review* 44(1): 27–37, 1979b.

________. *Advanced Introduction to Law and Literature.* Cheltenham, UK: Edward Elgar Publishers, 2021.

Gould, J. "Review of David McIlroy, *The End of Law: How Law's Claims Relate to Law's Aims*," *Law and Literature* 32(3): 483–86, 2020.

Graham, K., M. Borg, and B. Miller. "Mobilizing Law in Latin America: An Evaluation of Black's Theory in Brazil," *Law and Social Inquiry* 38(2): 322–341, 2013.

Gramsci, A. *Prison Notebooks.* London: Lawrence and Wishart, 1971.

Granfield, R. and T. Koenig. "From Activism to Pro Bono: The Redirecting of Working Class Altruism at Harvard Law School," *Critical Sociology* 17(1): 57–80, 1990a.

________. "Socialization into the Power Elite: Learning Collective Eminence at Harvard Law School." Unpublished manuscript, 1990b.

Grant, J. *Fundamental Feminism: Contesting the Core Concepts of Feminist Theory.* New York: Routledge, 1993.

Grant, J. "Rethinking Althusser: Ideology, Dialectics, and Critical Social Theory," Paper presented at the CPSA Annual Conference, May 31–June 3, 2005, accessed 6/18/2021, http://www.faculty.umb.edu/gary_zabel/Courses/Spinoza/Texts/Grant.pdf.

Greenberg, D. "Donald Black's Sociology of Law: A Critique," *Law and Society Review* 17(2): 337–68, 1983.

Greenhouse, C. "Durkheim and Law: Divided Reading over Division of Labor," *Annual Review of Law and Society* 7: 165–85, 2011.

Greer, A. "Deconstructing Anthropos: A Critical Legal Reflection on 'Anthropocentric' Law and Anthropocene 'Humanity,'" *Law and Critique* 26(3): 225–249, 2015.

________. "Human Rights and New Horizons?", *Science, Technology and Human Values* 43(1): 129–145, 2018.

________. "Embracing Vulnerability: Notes Towards Human Rights for a More-the-Human World," in D. Bedford and J. Herring (eds.). *Embracing Vulnerability*, pp. 153–174. New: Routledge, 2020.

Greimas, A. *Structural Semantics* Lincoln: University of Nebraska Press, 1983.

________. *On Meaning.* Minneapolis, MN: Minnesota University Press, 1987.

________. *The Social Sciences: A Semiotic View.* Minneapolis, MN: University of Minnesota Press, 1990.

Greimas, A. and E. Landowski, "The Semiotic Analysis of Legal Discourse: Commercial Laws That Govern Companies and Groups of Companies," in A. Greimas, *The Social Sciences: A Semiotic View.* Minneapolis: University of Minnesota Press, 102–38, 1990.

Grosz, E. "Feminist Theory and the Challenge to Knowledges," *Women's Studies International Forum* 10: 475–80, 1987.

________. *Jacques Lacan: A Feminist Introduction.* New York: Routledge, 1990.

________. *Volatile Bodies.* Bloomington, IN: Indiana University Press, 1994.

________. *The Nick of Time.* Durham, NC: Duke University Press, 2004.

________. *The Incorporeal.* New York: Columbia University Press, 2017.

Groves, C. "Us and Them: Reflections of the Dialectics of Moral Hate," in B. MacLean and D. Milovanovic (eds.), *New Directions in Critical Criminology.* Vancouver, Canada: Collective Press, 1991.

Gualberto, V. and G. Kress. "Social Semiotics," in R. Hobbs and P. Mihailidis (eds.) *The International Encyclopedia of Media Literacy, online,* NY: John Wiley-Blackwell, 2018, accessed on 5/20/2021, https://www.erudit.org/en/journals/cd1/2017-v58-n1-2-cd03066/1039832ar/.

Guinier, L., M. Fine and J. Balin. *Becoming Gentleman: Women, Law School, and Institutional Change,* Boston, MA: Beacon Press, 1997.

Gutierrez, G. *A Theology of Liberation.* Maryknoll, Michigan: Orbis Books, 1973.

Guzik, K., A. Sesay, O. Oh, R. Ramirez and T. Tong. "Making the Material Routine: A Sociomaterial Study of the Relationship Between Police Body Worn Cameras (BWCs) and Organizational Routines," *Policing and Society* 31(1): 100–115, 2021.

Habermas, J. *The Theory of Communicative Action. Vol. One. Reason and the "Rationalization of Society.* (Trans. T. McCarthy.) Boston, MA: Beacon Press, 1984.

________. *The Theory of Communicative Action. Vol. Two. Lifeworld and System: A Critique of Functionalist Reason.* (Trans. T. McCarthy.) Boston, MA: Beacon Press, 1987.

________. *Legitimation Crises.* Boston: Beacon Press, 1975.

Halliday, M. *Language as a Social Semiotic: The Social Interpretation of Language and Meaning.* Baltimore: University Park Press, 1978.

Hanauske, M., J. Kunz, S. Bernius, and W. Konig. "Doves and Hawkes in Economics Revisited." *Physica A* 389: 5084–5102, 2010.

Hand, J. "Lesbian, Gay, Bisexual, Transgender, Queer, Asexual, Intersexual, et al. (LGBTQAI+) Health Access Disparities in Female Identified Clients," *Columbia Social Work Review* 9(11): 1–11, 2018.

________. *An Introduction to Functional Grammar.* London: Arnold, 1994.

Harari, R. *How Joyce Made his Name.* New York: Other Press, 2002.

Haraway, D. *Simians, Cyborgs, and Women.* New York: Routledge, 1991.

________. "Situated Knowledges," in S. Harding (ed.). *The Feminist Standpoint Reader.* London: Routledge, pp. 81–102, 2004.

________. *When Species Meet.* Indianapolis, MN: University of Minnesota Press, 2008.

________. *Staying With the Trouble.* Durham, NC: Duke University Press, 2016.

Harding, S. (ed.) *The Feminist Standpoint Reader.* London: Routledge, 2004.

________. *Sciences from Below: Feminism, Postcolonialities, and Modernities,* Raleigh, N.C.: Duke University Press, 2008.

________. "Standpoint Theories: Productively Controversial," *Hypatia* 24(4): 192–200, 2009.

Hardt, M. and A. *Negri. Empire.* Cambridge, MA: Harvard University Press, 2000.

________. *Multitude: War and Democracy in the Age of Empire.* New York: Penguin Books, 2004.

________. *Commonwealth.* Cambridge, MA: Harvard University Press, 2011.

________. *Assembly.* London, UK: Oxford University Press, 2017.

Harper, C. and K. Leicht. *Exploring Social Change,* 7th ed. London: Routledge, 2018.

Harding, S. *Whose Science? Whose Knowledge? Thinking From Women's Lives.* Ithaca, NY: Cornell University Press, 1991.

Harper, W. "Review Essay: The Critical Legal Studies Movement," *American· Philosophical Association Newsletter* November 3–11, 1987.

Harrington, C. "Moving From Integrative to Constitutive Theories of Law," *Law and Society Review* 22: 963–67, 1988.

Harrington, C. and S. Merry. "Ideological Production: The Masking of Community Mediation," *Law and Society Review* 22: 709–35, 1988.

Harrington, C. and B. Yngvesson. "Interpretive Sociolegal Research," *Law and Social Inquiry* 15: 135–48, 1990.

Harris, A. "Race and Essentialism in Feminist Legal Theory," in K. Bartlett and R. Kennedy (eds.), *Feminist Legal Theory.* Oxford: Westview Press, 235–62, 1991.

________. "Foreword: The Jurisprudence of Reconstruction," *California Law Review* 82: 741, 1994.

Harris, J.W. "A Structuralist Theory of Law: An Agnostic View," in A. Podgorecki and C. Whelan (eds.) *Sociological Approaches to Law.* New York: St. Martin's Press, 1981.

Harste, G. and A. Febbrajo. *Law and Intersystemic Communication: Understanding 'Structural Coupling.'* New York: Routledge, 2013.

Hart, H.L.A. "Positivism and the Separation of Law and Morals," *Harvard Law Review* 71: 593–629, 1958.

________. *The Concept of Law.* Oxford: Clarendon Press, 1961.

________. *Essays in Jurisprudence and Philosophy.* Oxford: Clarendon Press, 1983.

Hartsock, N. *Money, Sex and Power.* Boston, MA: Longman, 1983.

Hartsock, N. "Postmodernism and Political Change: Issues for Feminist Theory," *Cultural Critique* (Winter): 15–33, 1990.

________. "The Feminist Standpoint: Developing the Grounds for a Historical Materialism," in S. Harding and M. Hintikka (eds.) *Discovering Reality*, 2ed., pp. 283–310. London: Kluwer Academic Publishing, 2003.

Harvey, I. *Derrida and the Economy* of *Difference.* Bloomington, IN: Indiana University Press, 1986.

Haskell, D. "10 Ways to Listen to Trees," *Scientific America*, May 10, 2017, accessed 8/12/2021.

________. *The Songs of Trees.* New York: Penguin Books, 2018.

Hatty, S.E. "Narratives on Crime," *The Critical Criminologist* 5(4): 3–4, 13, 1993.

Heinrich, M. *An Introduction to the Three Volumes of Karl Marx's Capital.* New York: Monthly Review Press, 2012.

Hausheer, J. "Eavesdropping on the Sounds of Rainforests," *Cool Green Science*, September 14, 2015, accessed 8/12/2021, https://blog.nature.org/science/2015/09/14/eavesdropping-on-the-sounds-of-the-rainforest/.

Haute, P.V. *Against Adaptation: Lacan's "Subversion" of the Subject.* New York: Other Press, 2002.

Haverkamp, A. "Rhetoric, Law, and the Poetics of Memory," *Cardozo Law Review* 13(5): 1639–53, 1992.

Hawdon, J. John Ryan and L. Agnich. "Crime as a Source of Solidarity," *Deviant Behavior* 31: 679–703, 2010.

Hayes, A. "An Introduction to Chaos and Law," *UMKC Law Review* 60(4): 751–773, 1990.

Hayes, A. and G. Scott. "Digital Nomads," *Investopedia*, 2021, accessed 8/6/2021, https://www.investopedia.com/terms/d/digital-nomad.asp.

Hayles, K. *How We Become Posthuman.* Chicago, IL: University of Chicago Press, 1999.

Hayman, R. "The Color of Tradition: Critical Race Theory and Postmodern Constitutional Traditionalism." *Harvard Civil Fights-Civil Liberties Law Review* 30: 57–93, 1995.

Head, M. *Evgeny Pashukanis: A Critical Reappraisal.* London: Routledge, 2007.

Heath, S. *Questions of Cinema.* Bloomington, IN: Indiana University Press, 1981.

Heckman, S. "Truth and Method: Feminist Standpoint Theory Revisited," *Signs* 22(2): 341–365, 1997.

Hegel, F. *Philosophy of Fight.* (Trans. T.M. Knox) New York: Oxford University Press, 1955.

Heilpern, D. "The Mabo Case — Black Law, White Order," *The Critical Criminologist* 5(4): 7–8, 16–17, 1993.

Heinrich, M. *An Introduction to the Three Volumes of Karl Marx's Capital.* New York: Monthly Review Press, 2012.

Heisenberg, W. "The Physical Content of Quantum Kinematics and Mechanics," *Zeitschrift fur Physic* 43: 172–198, 1927.

Hekman, S. "Weber's Concept of Causality and the Modern Critique" *Sociological Inquiry* 49(4): 67–76, 1979.

________. *Gender and Knowledge: Elements of a Postmodern Feminism.* London: Polity Press, 1990.

Hembroff, L. "The Seriousness of Acts and Social Control: A Test of Black's Theory of the Behavior of Law," *American Journal of Sociology* 93: 322–47, 1987.

Hemmings, C. *Why Stories Matter: The Political Grammar of Feminist Theory.* London, UK: Duke University Press, 2011.

Hendry, J., N. Creutzfeldt, and C. Boulanger. "Socio-Legal Studies in German and UK: Theory and Methods," *German Law Journal* 21: 1309–1317.

Henly, B. "Penumbra," *Hastings Constitutional Law Quarterly* 15(1): 81–100, 1987.

Hennis, W. *Max Weber: Essays on Reconstruction.* Boston, MA: Allen and Unwin, 1988.

Henry, S. *Private Justice.* London: Routledge and Kegan Paul, 1983.

________. "Private Justice, Capitalist Society and Human Agency: The Dialectics of Collective Law in the Cooperative," *Law and Society Review* 19: 301–25, 1985.

________. "Can the Hidden Economy be Revolutionary? Toward a Dialectic Analysis of the Relations Between Formal and Informal Economies," *Social Justice* 15: 29–60, 1988.

________. "Justice on the Margins: Can Alternative Justice Be Different?" *Howard Journal of Criminal Justice* 28: 255–71, 1989.

________. "Newsmaking Criminology as Replacement Discourse," in G. Barak (ed.), *Media, Process, and the Social Construction of Crime: Studies in Newsmaking Criminology.* New York: Garland. pp. 241–72, 1994.

Henry, S. and M. Lanier. *What is Crime?* New York: Rowman and Littlefield, 2001.

Henry, S. and D. Milovanovic "Constitutive Criminology," *Criminology* 29(2): 293–316, 1991.

________. "Back to Basics: A Postmodern Redefinition of Crime," *The Critical Criminologist* 5(2/3): 1–2, 6, 12, 1993.

________. "The Constitution of Constitutive Criminology," in D. Nelken (ed.) *The Futures of Criminology.* London: Sage, 1994.

________. *Constitutive Criminology.* London: Sage, 1996.

________. (eds.). *Constitutive Criminology at Work.* Albany, NY: SUNY Press, 1999.

________. "Constitutive Criminology," in E. McLaughlin and J. Muncie (eds.), *Sage Dictionary of Criminology*, pp. 86–90. London, UK: Sage, 2020.

Hernandez, T.K. "Multiracial Discourse: Raced Classification in an Era of Color-Blind Jurisprudence," *Maryland Law Review* 57: 97, 1998.

Heron, K. "Toying with the Law: Deleuze, Lacan and the Promise of Perversion," *European Journal of Political Theory*, forthcoming, 2020.

Herriman, N. "Sorcery, Law, and State," *Australian Journal of Asian Law* 13(2): 1–14, 2013.

Herzog, L. "Durkheim on Social Justice: The Argument From 'Organic Solidarity,'" *American Political Science Review* 112(1): 112–124, 2018.

Hillebrecht, A. and M. Berds (eds.). "Can Nature Have Rights?", *RCC Perspectives: Transformations in Environment and Society*. Environment and Society Portal, issue 6, 2017, accessed 8/12/2021, http://www.environmentandsociety.org/perspectives/2017/6/can-nature-have-rights-legal-and-political-insights.

Hirsch, C. "Constitutional Diversity in New York Specialized High Schools: The SHSAT, The Discovery Program and the 14th Amendment," *Cardozo Law Review* 41(4): 1628–1668, 2020.

Hirst, P. *Law, Socialism and Democracy*. London: Allen and Unwin, 1986.

Hirvonen, A. "A Postmodern Challenge or the Seducing Other: From the Politics of the Unfinished to the Politics of Undecidability," in B. MacLean and H. Pepinsky (eds.), *We Who Would Take No Prisoners*. Vancouver, Canada: Collective Press, 1993.

Hjelmslev, L. *Prolegomena to a Theory of Language*. Baltimore, Indiana: Indiana University Press, 1953.

Hobbes, T. *Leviathan*. Oxford: Basic Blackwell, 1946.

Hobbsbawm, E. *Bandits*. London: George Weidenfeld and Nicolson, 1969.

Hodge, R. and G. Kress. *Social Semiotics*. Cambridge: Polity Press, 1988.

Hoebel, A. *The Law of Primitive Man*. New York: Atheneum, 1974.

Hoeffer, J. "The Gender Gap: Revealing Inequities in Admission of Social Science Evidence in Criminal Cases," *University of Arkansas Law Review* 24: 41–98, 2001.

Hoenig, M. "Admissibility of Computer-Generated Animation," *New York Law Journal*, January 2018, accessed on 5/18/2021, https://www.herzfeld-rubin.com/blog/admissibility-of-computer-generated-animations/.

Hoffer, P. *Law and People of Colonial America*, 2ed. Baltimore: John Hopkins, 2019.

Hogan, P. and L. Pandit (eds.). *Criticism and Lacan*. Athens, GA: University of Georgia Press, 1990.

Holland, E. *Nomad Citizenship*. Indianapolis, MN: University of Minnesota Press, 2011.

________. *Deleuze and Guattari's A Thousand Plateaus*. New York: Bloomsbury Academic Press, 2013.

________. *Deleuze and Guattari's Anti-Oedipus*. London, UK: Routledge, 1999.

Hollis, K. "A Critical Discourse Analysis of Intellectual Property Chapter of TPP: Confirming What the Critics Fear," *Communication* 6(1): 1–39, 2017.

hooks, b. *Ain't I a Woman? Black Women and Feminism.* Boston, MA: South End, 1981.

hooks, b. *Feminist Theory: From Margin to Center*, NY: Routledge, 1984.

________. *Talking Back: Thinking Feminist, Thinking Black.* Boston, MA: South End, 1988.

________. *Teaching to Transgress.* New York: Routledge, 1994.

Horwitz, A. *The Logic of Social Control.* New York: Plenum Press, 1990.

Howard, A. "La Conception Mécaniste de la Constitution," in M. Troper and L. Jaume (eds.), *1789 et l'Invention de la Constitution* 153 (L.G.D.J. — Brussels: Bruylant, 1994.

Howe, A. *Punish and Discipline.* New York: Routledge, 1994.

Hubert, T. "On Max Weber's 'Sociology of Law,' Now Known as 'The Developmental Conditions of the Law,'" *Max Weber Studies* 12(1): 121–138, 2012.

Hunt. A. *The Sociological Movement in Law.* Philadelphia, PA: Temple University Press, 1978.

________. "Behavioral Sociology of Law: A Critique of Donald Black," *Journal of Law and Society* 19(1): 19–46, 1983.

________. "The Ideology of Law: Advances and Problems in Recent Applications of the Concept of Ideology to the Analysis of law," *Law and Society Review* 19: 11–37, 1985.

________. "Legal Positivism and Positivistic Semiotics: Old Wines in New Bottles," *Journal of Law and Society* 13(2): 271–278, 1986a.

________. "The Theory of Critical Legal Studies," *Oxford Journal of Legal Studies* 6: 1–45, 1986b.

________. "The Critique of Law: What is 'Critical' About Critical Theory?" *Journal of Law and Society* 14: 5–19, 1987.

________. "The Role and Place of Theory in Legal Education: Reflections on Foundationalism," *Legal Studies* 9: 146–64, 1988.

________. "Why Did Foucault Get Law So Wrong?: Reflections on Law, Power and Sovereignty," Unpublished manuscript, 1991.

________. *Explorations in Law and Society: Toward a Constitutive Theory of Law.* New York: Routledge, 1993.

Hunt, A. and G. Wickham. *Foucault and Law.* London, UK: Pluto Press, 1994.

Hunter, N. "Marriage, Law, and Gender," in D. Caudill and S. Gold (eds.). *Radical Philosophy of Law.* New Jersey: Humanities Press, pp. 221–233, 1995.

Husserl, E. *Ideas.* (Trans. W.R. Gibson.) New York: Collier Books, 1975.

Hutchinson, D. "Out Yet Unseen: A Racial Critique of Gay and Lesbian Legal Theory and Political Discourse," *Connecticut Law Review* 29: 561, 1997.

Iftikar, J. and S. Museus, "On the Utility of Asian Critical (AsianCrit) Theory in the Field of Education," *International Journal of Qualitative Studies in Education* 31(10): 935–949, 2018.

"Indigenous Law Resources," unauthored, Library of Congress. Washington, DC. Accessed 1/21/21, https://www.loc.gov/law/help/indigenous-law-guide/index.php.

Ingram, D. "Legitimation Crises in Contract Law: A Test Case for Critical Legal Studies and Its Critics," in Caudill, D. and S. Gold (eds.), *Radical Philosophy Law*. Atlantic Fields, NJ: Humanities Press, p. 140–161, 1995.

Integrate NYC, Inc v. State of New York, filed March 9, 2021, accessed 4/8/2021, https://iapps.courts.state.ny.us/nyscef/ViewDocument?docIndex=jHAVRjM/0VBF2bxhnEz7aA==.

International Journal of Qualitative Studies. "Special Issue on Critical Race Theory" 11(1): 1–187, 1998.

Introna, L. "Toward a Post-Humanist Intra-actional Account of Socio-Technical Agency (and Morality)," Presented at "Moral Agency and Technical Artifacts" Scientific Workshop. NIAS, Hague, 12–12 March 2007.

Irigaray, L. *Speculum of the Other Woman*. Ithaca, NY: Cornell University Press, 1985.

________. *Je, Tu, Nous: Toward a Culture of Difference*. New York: Routledge, 1993.

Isom, D. "Microaggressions, Injustice and Racial Identity: An Empirical Assessment of the Theory of African American Offending." *Journal of Contemporary Criminal Justice* 32(1): 27–59, 2015.

Jackson, B. *Semiotics and Legal Theory*. New York: Routledge and Kegan Paul, 1985.

________. *Law, Fact and Narrative Coherence*. Merseyside, UK: Deborah Charles Publications, 1991.

________. "European Convention of Human Rights Articles 6 & 12: Some Semiotic Observations," *International Journal for the Semiotics of Law* 6(16): 45–69, 1993.

________. *Making Sense in Law*. Liverpool, UK: Deborah Charles Publications, 1995.

________. "Truth or Proof?: The Criminal Verdict," *International Journal for the Semiotics of Law* 33: 227–273, 1998.

Jacobson, R. "Autopoietic Law: The New Science of Niklas Luhmann," *Michigan Law Review* 87: 1647, 1989.

Jaggar, A. *Feminist Politics and Human Nature, Philosophy and Society*. Totowa, NJ: Rowman and Allenhead, 1983.

Jaeger, C. and J. Trueblood. "Thinking Quantum: A New Perspective on Decision Making in Law," *Florida State University Law Review* 46: 4–82, 2019.

Jakobson, R., "Two Aspects of Language and Two Types of Aphasic Disorders," in R. Jakobson and M. Halle, (eds.) *Fundamentals of Language*. Paris: Mouton, 1971.

Jagger, A. *Feminist Politics and Human Nature*. Totowa, NJ: Rowman and Littlefield, 1983.

Jailhouse Lawyer's Handbook, 5th edition, Center for Constitutional Rights and the National Lawyers Guild, 2010, accessed 4/30/2021, https://www.nlg.org/jail/house-/lawyers-handbook/.

A Jailhouse Lawyer's Manual, 12th edition, NY: Columbia University, accessed 4/30/21, http://jlm.law.columbia.edu/.

James, M. and A. Burgos, "Race", *The Stanford Encyclopedia of Philosophy* (Summer 2020 Edition), Edward N. Zalta (ed.), accessed, 3/21/2021, plato.stanford.edu/archives/sum2020/entries/race/.

James, W. *Pragmatism and Four Essays From the Meaning of Truth.* New York: Meridian Books, 1955.

Jameson, F. *The Political Unconscious.* Ithaca, New York: Cornell University Press, 1981.

________. "Foreword," in A.J. Greimas, *On Meaning.* Minneapolis, MN: University of Minnesota Press, 1987.

Janack, M. (ed.). *Feminist Interpretations of Richard Rorty.* University Park, PA: Pennsylvania University Press, 2010.

Janikowski, R. and D. Milovanovic (eds.). *Legality and Illegality.* New York: Peter Lang Publishing Co., 1994.

Jappy, T. *Introduction to Peircean Visual Semiotics.* New York: Bloomsbury Academic Press, 2013.

Jessop, B. *State Theory: Putting the Capitalist State in its Place.* Cambridge, UK: Polity Press, 1990.

Jessop, B. N.L. Sum. "Language and Critique: Some Anticipations of Critical Discourse Studies in Marx," *Critical Discourse Studies* 15(4): 325–337, 2018.

Jessup, N. "Indian Claims in the Courts of the Conqueror," *American University Law Review* 41(3): 753–854, 1992.

Jewitt, C. (ed.). *The Routledge Handbook of Multimodal Analysis.* London: Routledge, 2014.

Johnson, K. "How Racial Profiling in America Became the Law of the Land," *Georgia Law Journal* 98: 1005–1030, 2010.

Johnson, P. M. Brookes, G. Woods and C. Brewster. "Legal Origins and Social Solidarity: The Continued Relevance of Durkheim to Comparative Institutional Analysis," *Sociology* 51(3): 646–665, 2017.

Johnson, P. and M. Henderson (eds.). *Black Queer Studies.* Durham, NC: Duke University Press, 2005.

Johnson, R. and P. Leighton. "Black Genocide?," *Journal of African American Men* 1(2): 3–21, 1995.

Johnson, T. "Legal History and the Material Turn," in M. Dubber and C. Tomlins (eds.), *The Oxford Handbook of Legal History*, 497–514. Oxford, UK: Oxford University Press, 2018.

Jones, A.H.M. *The Later Roman Empire 284–602.* Norman, Oklahoma: University of Oklahoma Press, 1964.

Jones, G. *Karl Marx. Greatness and Illusion.* London: Allan Lane, 2016.

Jones, M. and D. Mewhort. "Representing Word meaning and Order Information in a Composite Holographic Lexicon," *Psychological Review* 114(1): 1–37, 2007.

Jones, E. and D. Otto. "Thinking Through Anthropocentrism in International Law: Queer Theory, Feminist New Materialism and the Postcolonial — A Conversation between Emily Jones and Dianne Otto." Essex, UK: *University of Essex Research Repository*, 2020, accessed 8/11/2011.

Kafka, F. *The Trial.* New York: Dover, 2009.

________. "Before the Law," in *Franz Kaka Online*, I. Johnston (trans.), accessed 8/22/2021, https://www.kafka-online.info/before-the-law.htm.

Kairys, D. (ed.). *The Politics of Law, 3d.* New York: Pantheon, 1998.

Kalof, L. (ed.). *The Oxford Handbook of Animal Studies.* New York: Oxford University Press, 2017.

Kamenka, E. (ed.) *The Portable Marx.* New York: Penguin Books, 1983.

Kandiyali, J. (ed.). *Reassessing Marx's Social and Political Philosophy.* New York: Routledge, 2018.

Kang, H. "Law's Materiality," in A. Philoppopoulos-Mihalopoulous (ed.) *Handbook of Law and Theory*, 453–474. London, UK: Routledge, 2018.

Kang, H. and S. Kendall. "Contents, Introduction and Contributions, *Law Text Culture* 23: 1–15, 2019.

________. "Legal Materiality," in S. Stern, M. Mar, and B. Meyler (eds.) *The Oxford Handbook of Law and Humanities*, pp. 21–38. New York: Oxford University Press, 2020.

Kapur, R. "Human Rights in the 21st Century: Take a Walk on the Dark Side," *Sydney Law Review* 28(4): 665–687, 2006.

Katilius-Boydstun, M. "The Semiotics of A. J. Greimas: An Introduction," *Lithuanian Quarterly Law Journal of Arts and Sciences* 36(3): 1–7, 1990. Accessed on 3/22/2021, (http://www.lituanus.org/1990_3/90_3_02.htm).

Kehnan, M. "Interpretive Construction in the Substantive Criminal Law," *Stanford Law Review* 33: 591–74, 1981.

Kelsen, H. *General Theory of Law and State.* New York: Russell and Russell, 1970.

________. *A Guide to Critical Legal Studies.* Cambridge, MA: Harvard University Press, 1987.

Kelsey, A. "The Law of Physics and the Physics of Law," *Regent University Law Review* 25: 89–102, 2013.

Kennedy, D. "How the Law School Fails: A Polemic," *Yale Review of Law and Social Action* 1: 71–90, 1970.

________. "Legal Formality," *The Journal of Legal Studies* 2: 351–98, 1973.

________. "Legal Education as Training for Hierarchy," in D. Kairys (ed.) *The Politics of Law.* New York: Pantheon Books, 1992.

________. *A Critique of Adjudication: Fin de Siecle.* Cambridge, MA: Harvard University Press, 1997.

________. "Afterword: A Semiotics of Critique," *Cardozo Law Review* 22: 1147–1186, 2001.

________. "The Disenchantment of Logically Formal Legal Rationality, or Max Weber's Sociology in the Genealogy of the Contemporary Western Legal Thought," *Hastings Law Journal* 55(5): 1031–1076, 2004.

Kennedy, D. and K. Klare. "A Bibliography of Critical Legal Studies," *Yale Law Journal* 94: 461–90, 1984.

Kennedy, M. "Beyond Incrimination," in W. Chambliss and M. Mankoff (eds.), *Whose Law? What Order* New York: John Wiley, 1976.

Kerruish, V. *Jurisprudence as Ideology.* New York: Routledge, 1991.

Kersten, J. "Who Needs Rights of Nature?" in L. Hillebrecht and M. Berros (eds.), *RCC Perspectives: Transformations in Environment and Society—Can Nature*

Have Rights? Legal and Political Insights 6: 9–13, 2017, doi.org/10.5282/rcc/8209, accessed 8/12/2021, http://www.environmentandsociety.org/perspectives/2017/6/article/who-needs-rights-nature.

Kevelson, R. *Charles S. Peirce's Method* of *Methods.* Amsterdam: John Benjamins, 1987.

________. "Semiotics and Methods of Legal Inquiry," *Indiana Law Journal* 61: 356–371, 1986.

________. *The Law as a System* of *Signs.* New York: Plenum Publishers, 1988.

________. *Peirce, Praxis, Paradox.* Berlin: Mouton De Gruyter, 1990.

________. (ed.). *Peirce and Law: Issues in Pragmatism, Legal Realism and Semiotics.* New York: Peter Lang Publishing Co., 1991a.

________. "Peirce and Community: Public Opinion and the Legitimization of Value in Law," in R. Kevelson (ed.), *Peirce and Law.* New York: Peter Lang, pp. 99–119, 1991b.

________. "Pragmatism, Utopic Constructions and Legal Myth: A Glance at Durkheim's View of Peirce's *Method* of Semiotics as Related to Legal Norms," in R. Kevelson (ed.), *Law and the Human Sciences, Volume 3, Semiotics and the Human Sciences.* New York: Peter Lang, 193–218, 1992.

________. "Some Possible Meanings of the Idea of Human Rights," *International Journal for the Semiotics of Law* 6(16): 71–88, 1993a.

________. "Aspects of Property in Law: The Cultural, the Incorporeal, the Intellectual, the 'New,'" in R. Kevelson (ed.) *Flux, Complexity, and Illusion.* New York: Peter Lang, 209–227, 1993b.

________. *Peirce's Esthetics of Freedom.* New York: Peter Lang, 1993c.

________. *Peirce, Science, Signs.* New York: Peter Lang, 1996.

________. "Law's Revolution: Negation, and Property as Institution," in J. Levin and R. Kevelson (eds.), *"Revolution, Institutions, and Law.* New York: Peter Lang, 71–87 1998.

________. *Peirce's Pragmatism.* New York: Peter Lang, 1998.

Khomina, A. "The Homestead Act of 1862," U.S. History Scene, ND., accessed on 5/25/2021, https://ushistoryscene.com/article/1862-homestead-act/.

Kim, R. "The Legal Battle over High School Entrance Exams," *Phi Delta Kappan*, 2020, accessed on 4/3/2021, https://kappanonline.org/legal-battle-high-school-entrance-exams-kim/.

Kim, G. and E.W. Nho. "A Review of Quantum Games," *JYI* 37(2): 10–16, 2019.

Kimball, B. "'Warn Students That I Entertain Heretical Opinions, Which They are Not to Take as Law': The Inception of Case method Teaching in the Classrooms of the Early C.C. Langdell, 1870–1883" *Law and History Review* 17: 57–140, 1999.

________. *The Inception of Modern Professional Education: C.C. Langdell, 1826–1906.* Chapel Hill: University of North Carolina Press, 2009.

________. "The Proliferation of Case method Teaching in American Law Schools: Mr. Langdell's Emblematic 'Abomination,' 1890–1915," *History of Education Quarterly* 46(2): 192–240, 2006.

Kirby, A. *Digimodernism: How New Technologies Dismantle the Postmodern and Reconfigure our Culture*. New York: Continuum, 2009.

________. "The Death of Postmodernism and Beyond," *Philosophy Now* 58: 34–37, 2006.

Kirby, V. *Quantum Anthropologies*. Durham, NC: Duke University Press, 2011.

Klare, K. "Judicial Deradicalization of the Wagner Act and the Origins of Modern Legal Consciousness, 1937–1941," *Minnesota Law Review* 62: 265–339, 1978.

________. "Law-Making as Praxis," *Telos* 40: 123–35, 1979.

________. "Labor Law and the Liberal Political Imagination," *Socialist Review* 61: 45–71, 1982.

________. "Power/Dressing: Regulation of Employee Appearance," *New England Law "Review* 26(4): 1395–1451, 1992.

________. "The Politics of Duncan Kennedy's Critique," *Cardozo Law," Review* 22: 1073, 2001.

Klinck, D.R. "The Semiotics of Money and Environmental Regulation," in R. Kevelson (ed.), *Flux, Complexity and Illusion*. New York: Peter Lang, 229–50, 1993.

Kline, M. "Race, Racism and Feminist Legal Theory," *Harvard Women's Law "Review* 12: 115–50, 1989.

Knaub, S. "Conceptualizing Human Stewardship in the Anthropocene: The Rights of Nature," *Journal of Agricultural and Environmental Ethics* 37(6): 703–722, 2018.

Knopp, F. H. "On Radical Feminism and Abolition," in B. MacLean and H. Pepinsky (eds.), *We Who Would Take No Prisoners*. Vancouver, Canada: Collective Press, 1993.

Knox, B. A. "The Visual Rhetoric of Lady Justice: Understanding Jurisprudence Through 'Metonymic Tokens'," *Inquiries Journal/Student Pulse*, 6(5): 1–5, 2014, accessed on 5/10/2021, from http://inquiriesjournal.com/a?id=896.

Kohn, D. *How Forests Think*. Berkeley, CA: University of California Press, 2013.

Kojder, A. "Legal Policy: The Contribution of Leon Petrazycki," *Polish Sociological Review* 106: 155–163, 1994.

Kojeve, A. *Introduction to the "Reading of Hegel*. Ithaca, NY: Cornell University Press, 1980.

Kolko, G. *Wealth and Power in America*. New York: Praeger, 1962.

Kolmogorov, A. *Foundation of The Theory of Probability*. NY: Springer, 2013 [1933].

Korobkin, R. and T. Ulen. "Law and Behavior Science: Removing the Rationality Assumption From Law and Economics, *California Law Review* 88(4): 1051–1144, 2000.

Kosoy, N. and E. Corberra. "Payments for Eco Systems Services as Commodity Fetishistic," *Ecological Economics* 69(1): 1228–1236, 2010.

Kourany, J. "The Place of Standpoint Theory in Feminist Science Studies," *Hypatia* 24(4): 209–218. 2009.

Kramer, M. *Critical Legal Theory and the Challenge of Feminism*. London, UK: Rowman and Littlefield Publishers, 1995.

Kress, G. *Multimodality: A Social Semiotic Approach to Contemporary Communication.* London: Routledge, 2010.

Kress, G. and T. van Leeuwen. *Reading Images: The Grammar of Visual Design*, 2 ed., London: Routledge, 2006.

Kristeva, J. *Desire in Language.* New York: Columbia University Press, 1980.

________. *"Revolution in Poetic Language.* New York: Columbia University Press, 1984.

Kropotkin, P. *Mutual Aid.* Boston, MA: Extending Horizons Books, 1902.

________. *The Conquest of Bread.* New York: Benjamin Blom, 1913.

Kruttschnitt, C. "Social Status and Sentences of Female Offenders," *Law and Society Review* 15: 247–65, 1981.

Kubrin, C. "Gangsters, Thugs, and Hustlers: Identity Code of the Streets in Rap Music," *Social Problems* 52: 360–378, 2005.

Kubrin, C. and Nielson. E. "Rap on Trial," *Race and Justice* 4(3): 185–211, 2014.

Kuek, C. and E. Tay. "Religious Conversions and the Conflicts between Civil and Islamic Law of Inheritance in Malaysia," *Malayan Law Journal*, 2013, accessed 8/3/2021, https://papers.ssrn.com/sol3/papers.cfm?abstract_id=2367386.

Kuo, S., S. Cuvelier, C. Sheu, and K. Chang. "Crime Reporting Behavior and Black's Behavior of Law," *International Sociology* 27(1): 51–71, 2012.

Kupupika, T. "Shaping Our Freedom Dream: Reclaiming Intersectionality Through Black Feminist Legal Theory," *Virginia Law Review* 107: 27–47, 2021.

Kuttner, R. "The Negotiation Within: The Wave/Particle Tension in Negotiation," *Harvard Law Review* 16: 331–378, 2011.

Lacan, J. *The Seminar* of *Jacques Lacan, Book 11. The Ego in Freud's Theory and in the Technique of Psychoanalysis 1954–1955.* Cambridge, UK: Cambridge University Press, 1988.

________. *The Four Fundamental Concepts of Psychoanalysis.* New York: W.W. Norton, 1981.

________. *Ecrits: A Selection.* (Trans. A. Sheridan.) New York: Norton, 1977.

________. "Desire and the Interpretation of Desire in Hamlet," *Yale French Studies* 55/56: 11–52, 1978.

________. *Feminine Sexuality.* New York: W.W. Norton and Pantheon Books, 1985.

________. "Seminar on the 'Purloined Letter,'" in *J.* Muller and W. Richardson (eds.) *The Purloined Poe.* Baltimore, MD: Johns Hopkins University Press, 28–53, 1988.

________. *L'Envers de La Psychanalyse.* Paris, France: Editions du Seuil, 1991.

________. *The Ethics of Psychoanalysis, 1959–1960.* New York: W.W. Norton and Company, 1992.

________. "A Theoretical Introduction to the Functions of Psychoanalysis in Criminology," *Journal for the Psychoanalysis of Culture and Society* 1(2): 13–25, 1996.

Laclau, E. *New "Reflections of the "Revolution of Our Time.* London: Verso, 1990.

________. *Emancipations.* London: Verson, 1996.

________. *On Popular Reason.* London: Verso, 2005.

________. "Why Constructing a People is the Main Task of Radical Politics," *Critical Inquiry* 32(3): 646–680. 2006.

Laclau, E. and C. Mouffe. *Hegemony and Socialist Strategy.* New York: Verso, 1985.

________. *Hegemony and Socialist Strategy*, 2ed. New York: Verso, 2014.

Laclau, E., J. Butler, and S. Zizek, *Contingency, Hegemony, Universality*, NY: Verso, 2020.

Ladson-Billing, G. "The Evolving Role of CRT in Educational Scholarship," *Race, Ethnicity and Education* 8(1): 115–119, 2005.

Laing, R.D. *Knots.* New York: Pantheon Books, 1970.

Landau, I. "Early and Later Deconstruction in the Writings of Jacques Derrida," *Cardozo Law Review* 14(6): 1895–1909, 1993.

Landowski, E. "Towards a Semiotic and Narrative Approach to Law," *International Journal far the Semiotics of Law* 1/1: 101–105, 1988.

________. "Truth and Veridication in Law," *International Journal far the Semiotics of Law* 2/4: 29–47, 1989.

________. "A Note on Meaning, Interaction and Narrativity," *International Journal far the Semiotics Law* 11: 151–61, 1991.

________. "In Memoriam Algirdas Julien Greimas," *International Journal for the Semiotics of Law* 5(15): 227–28, 1992.

Langdell, C. "Harvard Celebration Speeches," *Law Quarterly Review* 3: 123–25, 1887.

Lanier, M. and S. Henry. *Essential Criminology.* Boulder, CO: Westview, 1998.

Laplanche, J. and J. Pontalis. *The Language of Psychoanalysis.* New York: Norton, 1973.

Laplanche, J. and S. Leclaire. "The Unconscious: A Psychoanalytic Study," *Yale French Studies* 48: 118–202, 1972.

Latour, B. *Reassembling the Social.* Oxford, UK: Oxford University Press, 2007.

________. *The Making of Law.* Cambridge, UK: Polity Press, 2010.

Lauretis, T. de. *Alice Doesn't.* Bloomington, IN: Indiana University Press, 1984.

Laszlo, E. *The Interconnected Universe.* London, UK: World Scientific Publishers, 1995.

________. *Science and the Akashic Field.* Rochester, Vermont: Inner Traditions, 2007.

Lecercle, J.J. *Philosophy Through the Looking Glass: Language, Nonsense, Desire.* London: Hutchinson, 1985.

________. *The Violence of Language.* New York: Routledge, 1990.

Lee, D. *Freedom and Culture.* Englewood Cliffs, NJ: Prentice-Hall, 1959.

Lee, JS. *Jacques Lacan.* Amherst, MA: University of Massachusetts Press, 1990.

Lefebvre, A. "A New Image of Law: Deleuze and Jurisprudence." *Telos* 130: 103–126, 2005.

________. *The Image of Law.* Stanford, CA: Stanford University Press, 2008.

________. "Human Rights in Deleuze and Bergson's Later Philosophy," in L. de Sutter and K. McGee (eds.) *Deleuze and Law*, pp. 48–68, Edinburgh, UK: Edinburgh University Press, 2012.

________. "Bergson, Human Rights and Joy," *Continental Philosophy Review* 50(2): 201–223, 2017.

________. *Human Rights and the Care of the Self.* Durham, NC: Duke University Press, 2018.

Legg, C. and C. Hookway. "Pragmatism," *Stanford Encyclopedia of Philosophy*," 2021, accessed 7/25/2021, https://plato.stanford.edu/cgi-bin/encyclopedia/archinfo.cgi?entry=pragmatism.

Legrand, P. (ed.). *Derrida and Law*. London: UK: Routledge, 2016.

Leipold, S., P. Feindt, G. Winkel and R. Keller. "Discourse Analysis of Environmental Policy Revisited: Tradition, Trends, Perspective," *Journal of Environmental Policy* 21(5): 445–463. 2019.

Lempert, R. "Built on Lies: Preliminary Reflection on Evidence as an Autopoietic System," *Hasting Law Journal* 49: 343, 1998.

Lenin, V. *The State and Revolution*. Moscow: Foreign Languages Publishing House, 1949.

Lemaire, A. *Jacques Lacan*. (Trans. D. Macey.) New York: Routledge and Kegan Paul, 1977.

Lanier, M., S. Henry and J. Anastasia. *Essential Criminology*. New York: Routledge, 2018.

Leong, D. "The Mattering of Black Lives," *Catalyst: Feminism, Theory, Technoscience* (2): 1–35, 2016.

Lewis, A. "Common Law," *Britannica*. Accessed on 12/5/2020, https://www.britannica.com/topic/common-law.

LGBTQIA Resource Center, University of California, Davis Campus, accessed on 3/21/2021, https://lgbtqia.ucdavis.edu/educated/glossary.

"LGBTQ Rights Milestones Fast Facts," *CNN Editorial Research*, March 16, 2021, accessed on https://www.cnn.com/2015/06/19/us/lgbt-rights-milestones-fast-facts.

Limbong, A., "Microaggressions are a Big Deal: How to Talk Them Out and When to Walk Away," NPR: Life Kit, interview of Kevin Nadal, June 9, 2020, accessed, 3/27/2021, https://www.npr.org/2020/06/08/872371063/microaggressions-are-a-big-deal-how-to-talk-them-out-and-when-to-walk-away.

Lin, D. and P. Tsai. "Max Weber's Traditional Chinese Law Revisited — A Poly Contextuality in the Sociology of Law," *Taiwan Journal of East Asian Studies* 10(2): 34–70, 2013.

Litowitz, D. *Postmodern Philosophy of Law*. Lawrence, KS: University Press of Kansas, 1997.

________. "Gramsci, Hegemony and the Law," *Brigham Young University Law Review* 20: 515–43, 2000.

________. *The Destruction of Young Lawyers*. Akron, Ohio: University of Akron Press, 2006.

Llewellyn, K. "A Realistic Jurisprudence — The Next Step," *Columbia Law Review* 30: 431, 1930.

________. "Some Realism About Realism," *Harvard Law Review* 44: 1222, 1931.

________. *The Bramble Bush: On Our Law and Its Study*. New York: Oceana, 1960.

________. *The Common Law Tradition:* Deciding Appeals. Boston: Little Brown, 1961.

________. *Jurisprudence: Realism in Theory and Practice*. Chicago: University of Chicago Press, 1962.

Llewellyn, K. and A. Hoebel. *The Cheyenne Way: Conflict and Case Law in Primitive Jurisprudence.* Norman, OK: University of Oklahoma Press, 1941.

Lloyd, C. "Law's 'Way of Words,'" *Creighton Law Review* 49: 221–290, 2016.

________. "Derrida's Law: The Socio-Historical and the Metaethical: La and Le Politique," *Social and Legal Studies* 26(2): 208–229, 2017.

________. "How to Do Things With Signs: Semiotics in Legal Theory," *University of Richmond Law Review*, forthcoming, 2020, accessed, 3/21/2021, SSRN Electronic Journal 1–57, 2020, https://papers.ssrn.com/sol3/papers.cfm?abstract_id=3516238.

Lopez, G. *Rebellious Lawyering: One Chicano's Vision of Progressive Law Practice.* Boulder, CO: Westview Press, 1992.

Lopez, I. *White by Law: The Legal Construction of Race*, 2ed. New York: NYU Press, 2006.

Lorraine, T. *Irigaray and Deleuze.* Ithaca: Cornell University Press, 1999.

Love, N. *Marx, Nietzsche, and Modernity.* New York: Columbia University Press, 1986.

Luhmann, N. *A Sociological Theory of Law.* Boston, MA: Routledge and Kegan Paul, 1985.

________. "The Third Question: The Creative Use of Paradoxes in Law and Legal History," *Journal of Law and Society* 15: 153, 1988.

________. "The Coding of a Legal System," in A. Febbrajo and G. Teubner (eds.), *State, Law, Economy as Autopoietic Systems.* Milano: Giuffre, 1990.

________. "Operational Closure and Structural Coupling: The Differentiation of the Legal System," *Cardozo Law Review* 13(5): 1419–41, 1992.

________. *Social Systems.* Stanford, CA: Stanford California University Press, 1995.

Lukács, György. *History and Class Consciousness.* Cambridge, MA: MIT press, 1972.

Lukes, S. *Emile Durkheim: His Life and Work.* New York: Harper and Row, 1972.

Lukes, S. and A. Scull (eds.). *Durkheim and the Law.* New York: St. Martin's Press, 1983.

Lukes, S. and A. Scull. *Durkheim and the Law*, 2d Edition. Hampshire, UK: Palgrave MacMillan, 2013.

Lukes, S. *Emile Durkheim, His Lift and Work: A Historical and Critical Study.* Harmondsworth, Middlesex: Penguin Books, 1975.

Lynch, M., and D. Milovanovic. "Deconstruction and Radical Criminology, Contradictions and the Problem of 'The Text,"' in R. Janikowski and D. Milovanovic (eds.) *Legality and Illegality.* New York: Peter Lang Publishing Co, 199–232, 1994.

Lynch, M. and C. Groves. *A Primer in "Radical Criminology.* New York: Harrow and Heston, 1992.

Lyotard, J.F. *The Postmodern Condition: A Report on Knowledge.* Minneapolis, MN: University of Minnesota Press, 1984.

________. *The Différend.* Minneapolis, MN: University of Minnesota Press, 1988.

________. *Just Gaming.* Minneapolis, MN: University of Minnesota Press, 1999.

MacCabe, C. *James Joyce and the Revolution of the Word.* London: MacMillan Press, 1979.

________. *Tracking the Signifier.* Minneapolis, MN: University of Minnesota Press, 1985.

MacCannell, J. F. *Figuring Lacan.* Lincoln, NE: University of Nebraska Press, 1986.

Machin, D. and J. Richardson. "Introduction: Renewing an Academic Interest in Structural Inequalities," *Critical Discourse Studies* 5(4): 281–287, 2008.

Machura, S. "The German Sociology of Law: A Case of Path Dependency," *International Journal of Law in Context* 8(4): 506–523, 2012.

________. "Milestones and Directions: Socio-Legal Studies in Germany and the United Kingdom," *German Law Journal* 21(7): 1318–1331, 2020.

MacKinnon, D. "Feminism in Legal Education," *Legal Education Review* 7: 85–89, 1989.

________. "Feminism, Marxism, Method, and the State: Toward Feminist Jurisprudence," in K. Bartlett and R. Kennedy (eds.), *Feminist Legal Theory.* Oxford: Westview Press, 181–200, 1991a.

________. "Difference and Dominance: On Sex Discrimination," in K. Bartlett and R. Kennedy (eds.), *Feminist Legal Theory.* Oxford: Westview Press, 81–94, 1991b.

________. "Points Against Postmodernism," *Chicago-Kent Law Review* 75(3): 686–712, 2000.

MacLean, B. (ed.). *The Political Economy of Crime.* Scarborough, Ontario: Prentice-Hall Canada, 1986.

MacLean, B. and D. Milovanovic (eds.). *"Racism, Empiricism and Criminal Justice.* Vancouver, Canada: Collective Press, 1990.

________. (eds.). *New Directions in Critical Criminology.* Vancouver, Canada: Collective Press, 1991.

________. (eds.). *Thinking Critically About Crime.* Vancouver, Canada: Collective Press, 1997.

Magalhães, J. and J. Magalhães. "Law, Institutions and Interpretation in Jacques Derrida," *Revista Direitogv* 13(2): 586–607, 2017.

Maine, Sir H.S. *Ancient Law.* London: J.M. Dent and Sons, 1861.

Makimoto, J. and D. Manners. *Digital Nomad.* New York: John Wiley and Sons, 1997.

Malachowski, A. (ed.). *A Companion to Rorty.* Hoboken, NJ: John Wiley and Sons, 2020.

Malinowski, B. *Crime and Custom in Savage Society.* Totowa, NJ: Littlefield, Adams and Co., 1976.

Malloy, R.P. *Law and Market Economy.* Cambridge, UK: Cambridge University Press, 2000.

________. "Law and Market Economy: The Triadic Linking of Law, Economics and Semiotics," *International Journal for the Semiotics of Law* 12: 285–307, 1999.

Mambrol, N. "Key Theories of Louis Hjelmslev," *Literary Theory and Criticism*, March 19, 2018, accessed 9/2/2021, https://literariness.org/2018/03/19/key-theories-of-louis-hjelmslev/.

Manderson, D. "Towards Law and Music," *Law and Critique* 25(3): 311–317, 2014.

________. *Songs Without Music: Aesthetic Dimensions of Law and Justice.* Berkeley, CA: University of California Press, 2000.

Manning, P. "Metaphors of the Field: Varieties of Organizational Discourse," *Administrative Science Quarterly* 24: 660–671, 1979.

________. *Symbolic Communication: Signifying Calls and the Police Response.* Cambridge, MA: MIT Press, 1988.

Marcer, P. and W. Schempp. "Model of the Neuron Working by Quantum Holography," *Informatica* 21: 519–534, 1997.

________. "The Brain as a Conscious System," *International Journal of General Systems* 27(1): 231–248, 1998.

________. "Quantum Holography: The Paradigm of Quantum Entanglement," *Computing Anticipatory Systems — Second International Conference.* D. Dubois (ed.), pp. 461–467, The American Institute of Physics, 1999.

Marcuse, H. *Eros and Civilization.* New York: Vintage Books, 1962.

Marek, Z-S., M. Golicki, and B. Wojciechowski (eds.). *Multicentrism as an Emerging Paradigm in Legal Theory.* London: Peter Lang, 2009.

Marini, M. *Jacques Lacan.* New Brunswick, NJ: Rutgers University Press, 1992.

Marmor, A. *The Language of Law.* Oxford, UK: Oxford University Press, 2014.

Marneros, C. "Gilles Deleuze: Jurisprudence," *CLT (Holding) Ltd*, 2019, accessed on 7/30/2021, https://criticallegalthinking.com/2019/11/14/gilles-deleuze-jurisprudence/.

________. "Contrasting Legacies: Deleuze and the Dogmatism of Human Rights," in R. Giappone, K.B. Collett, and I. MacKenzie (eds.), *Double Binds of Neoliberalism*, forthcoming, 2021. Lanham, MD: Rowman and Littlefield.

Marriott, R. "Signs Without Authority: The Battle of Experts, the Caricature of a Discourse and the Failure of Scientific Evidence," in Broekman, J.M. and L.C. Backer (eds.) *Signs in Law — A Sourcebook*, pp. 379–394. London, UK: Springer International Publishing, 2015.

Marsh, R. "Weber's Misunderstanding of Traditional Chinese Law," *American Journal of Sociology* 106(2): 281–302, 2000.

Marshall, A. and D. Hale. "Cause Lawyering," *Annual Review of Law and Social* 10: 301–20, 2014.

Martire, J. *A Foucauldian Interpretation of Modern Law.* Edinburgh, UK: Edinburgh University Press, 2019.

Marusek, S. "Between Disability and Terror: Handicapped Parking Space and Homeland Security at Fenway Park," *International Journal for the Semiotics of Law* 20(3): 251–261, 2006.

Marx, K. *Capital.* New York: International Publishing House, 1967.

________. *A Contribution to the Critique of Political Economy.* New York: International Publishing House, 1970.

________. *Grundrisse.* New York: Random House, 1972.

________. "The Critique of the Gotha Program." In R. Tucker (ed.) *The Marx-Engels Reader*, pp. 525–41. New York: Norton Publisher, 1978.

Marx, K. and F. Engels. “The Communist Manifesto,” in D. Femback (ed.), *Karl Marx*. New York: Random House, 1973.

Marx, K. and F. Engels. *The German Ideology*. Moscow: Progress Publishers, 1976.

Mathiesen, T. *Law, Society and Political Action: Toward a Strategy Under Late Capitalism*. New York: Academic Press, 1980.

Matoeisan, G. *Reproducing Rape: Domination Through Talk in the Courtroom*. Chicago, IL: University of Chicago Press, 1993.

________. *Law and the Language of Identity*. Cambridge, MA: Oxford University Press, 2001.

Matoeisan, G. and K. Gilbert. “Multifunctionality of Hand Gestures and Material Conduct During Closing Argument,” *Gesture* 15(1): 79–114, 2016.

________. “Let the Fingers do the Talking: Language, Gestures and Power in Closing Arguments,” in J. Leung (ed.) *Meaning and Power in the Language of Law*, pp. 137–163. Oxford, UK: Cambridge University Press, 2018.

Matsuda, M. “Liberal Jurisprudence and Abstracted Visions of Human Nature: A Feminist Critique of Rawls’ Theory of Justice,” *New Mexico Law Review* 16: 613, 1986.

________. “Looking to the Bottom: Critical Legal Studies and Reparation,” *Harvard Critical Law Review* 22: 321–300, 1987.

________. *Where is Your Body?* Boston, MA: Beacon Press, 1996.

Matsuda, M., C. Lawrence, R. Delgado and K. Crenshaw. *Words That Wound*. Oxford: Westview, 1993.

Matthews, D. and S. Veitch. “The Limits of Critique and the Force of Law,” *Law and Critique* 27: 349–361, 2016.

Maturana, H. *Biology of Cognition*. Urbana, IL: Illinois University Press, 1970.

Maturana, H. and F. Varela. *The Tree of Knowledge*, 1987.

Matza, D. *Delinquency and Drift*. New York: Wiley, 1964.

Moustafa, T. *Constituting Religion*. Cambridge, UK: Cambridge University Press, 2018.

Mautner, M. “Three Approaches to Law and Culture,” *Cornell law Review* 96(4): 839–70, 2011.

Mawani, R. *Colonial Proximities: Crossracial Encounters and Juridical Truths in British Columbia, 1871–1921*. Vancouver, CA: University of British Columbia Press, 2009.

McAfee, Noëlle and Katie B. Howard. “Feminist Political Philosophy”, *The Stanford Encyclopedia of Philosophy* (Winter 2018 Edition), Edward N. Zalta (ed.), accessed on 3/21/2021, https://plato.stanford.edu/archives/win2018/entries/feminism-political/.

McDonald, J. *Handbook for Jailhouse Lawyers*. San Francisco, CA: Warhouse Publishers, 2004.

McGee, K. “Aleatory Materialism and Speculative Jurisprudence,” *Law and Critique* 23: 141–162, 2012.

McGee, L. *Deleuze and Law*. Edinburgh, UK: Edinburgh University Press, 2012.

McIlroy, D. *The End of Law*. London: Edward Elgar Publishers, 2019.

McManaman, L. "Social Engineering: The Legal Philosophy of Roscoe Pound," *St. Johns Law Review* 33(1): 1–47, 1958.

McNally, D. "Intersections and Dialectics: Critical Reconstruction in Social Reproduction Theory," In T. Bhattacharya (ed.), *Social Reproduction Theory* pp. 94–111. London, UK: Pluto Press, 2017.

McNally, D. and S. Ferguson. "Social Reproduction Beyond Intersectionality: An Interview," *Viewpoint Magazine*, October 31, 2015, accessed on 4/4/2021, https://viewpointmag.com/2015/10/31/social-reproduction-beyond-intersectionality-an-interview-with-sue-ferguson-and-david-mcnally/.

McNulty, T. "Psychoanalysis and Law," in S. Stern, M. Del Mar and B. Meyler (eds.) *The Oxford Handbook of Law and Humanities*, 2020, online, accessed 7/6/2021, https://www.oxfordhandbooks.com/view/10.1093/oxfordhb/9780190695620.001.0001/oxfordhb-9780190695620-e-12.

Mead, G. H. *Mind, Self and Society*. Chicago, IL: Chicago University Press, 1962.

Medvedev, P. and M. Bakhtin. *The Formal Method in Literary Scholarship*. Baltimore, MD: The John Hopkins University Press, 1978.

Melville, S. "Psychoanalysis and the Place of Jouissance," *Critical Inquiry* 13: 349–70, 1987.

Menkel-Meadow, C. "Feminist Legal Theory, Critical Legal Studies, and Legal Education or 'The Fem-Crits Go to Law School,'" *Journal Legal Education* 38: 61, 1988.

Merla-Watson, C. "Bridging Common Grounds: Metaphor, Multitude, and Chicana Third Space Feminism," *ACME: An International E-Journal for Critical Geographies* 11(3): 492–511, 2012, accessed on 4/5/2021, https://www.acme-journal.org/index.php/acme/article/view/943.

Merleau-Ponty, M. "An Unpublished Text by Maurice Merleau-Ponty," in M. Merleau-Ponty and J. Edie (eds.) Evanston, IL: Northwestern University Press, 1964.

Merry, S. "Concept of Law and Justice Among Working-Class Americans: Ideology as Culture," *Legal Studies Forum* 9(1): 59–69, 1985.

Mertz, E. *The Language of Law School: Learning to "Think Like a Lawyer."* Cambridge, MA: Oxford University Press, 2007.

Metz, C. *The Imaginary Signifier*. Bloomington, IN: Indiana University Press, 1982.

Meyers, M. "Predicting the Behavior of Law: A Test of Two Models," *Law and Society Review* 14: 835–57, 1980.

Michalowski, R. *Order, Law, and Crime*. New York: Random House, 1985.

Microaggression, *Wikipedia, The Free Encyclopedia*, accessed on 3/27/2021, https://en.wikipedia.org/w/index.php?title=Special:CiteThisPage&page=Microaggression&id=1012037271&wpFormIdentifier=titleform.

Mika, H. and J. Thomas. "The Dialectics of Prisoner Litigation: Reformist Idealism or Social Praxis?," *Social Justice* 15: 48–71, 1988.

Miliband, R. *The State in Capitalist Society*. New York: Basic Books, 1969.

Miller, B. "Give Them Back Their Lives: Recognizing Client Narrative in Case Theory," *Michigan Law Review* 93(3): 485–576, 1994.

Millhiser, I. "The Supreme Court Case That Could End Affirmative Action, Explained, *Vox.com*, March 2, 2021, accessed 4/4/2021, https://www.vox.com/22301135/supreme-court-affirmative-action-harvard-college-race-students-for-fair-admission-ed-blum.

Mills, C. Wright. *The Sociological Imagination.* New York: Oxford University Press, 1959.

Mills, M. "The Opposite of Witchcraft." *Journal of Royal Anthropological Institute* 19(1): 18–33, 2013.

Milner, A. "Development of African Law," *International Lawyer* 1(2): 192–201, 1967.

Milner, R. "Critical Race Theory and Interest Convergence as Analytic Tools in Teacher's Education Policies and Practices," *Journal of Teacher Education* 59(4): 332–46, 2008.

Milovanovic, D. "The Commodity-Exchange Theory of Law: In Search of a Perspective," *Crime and Social Justice* 16: 41–49, 1981.

________. "Weber and Marx on law: Demystifying Ideology and Law — Toward an Emancipatory Political Practice," *Contemporary Crises* 7: 353–70, 1983.

________. "Autonomy of the Legal Order, Ideology and the Structure of Legal Thought," in M. Schwartz and D. Friedrichs (eds.) *Humanistic Perspectives on Crime and Justice.* Hebron, CT: Practitioner Press, 1984.

________. "Anarchism, Liberation Theology and the Decommodification of the Juridic and Linguistic Form," *Humanity and Society* 9: 182–196, 1985.

________. "Juridico-Linguistic Communicative Markets: Towards a Semiotic Analysis," *Contemporary Crises* 10: 281–304, 1986.

________. "The Political Economy of 'Liberty' and 'Property Interests'," *Legal Studies Forum* 11: 267–293, 1987.

________. *A Primer in the Sociology of Law.* Albany, NY: Harrow and Heston, 1988a.

________. "Jailhouse Lawyers and Jailhouse Lawyering," *International Journal of the Sociology of Law* 16: 455–475, 1988b.

________. "Review Essay: Critical Legal Studies and the Assault on the Bastion," *Social Justice* 15: 161–172, 1988c.

________. "Review Essay: Niklas Luhmann, A Sociological Theory of Law," *International Journal the Sociology Law* 16(3): 399–408, 1988d.

________. *Weberian and Marxian Analysis of Law: Structure and Function of Law in a Capitalist Mode of Production.* Aldershot, UK: Gower Publishers, 1989a.

________. "Critical Criminology and the Challenge of Post-Modernism," *The Critical Criminologist,* 1–3, (December, 1989b).

________. "Law and the Challenge of Semiotic Analysis: A Review Essay of Bernard Jackson's *Law, Fact and Narrative Coherence," Legal Studies Forum* 14(1); 71–84, 1990.

________. "Images of Unity and Disunity in the Juridic Subject and the Movement Toward the Peacemaking Community," in H. Pepinsky and R. Quinney (eds.), *Criminology as Peacemaking.* Bloomington, IN: Indiana University Press, 1991a.

________. "Schmarxism, Exorcism and Transpraxis," *The Critical Criminologist* 3(4): 5–6, 111–12, 1991b.

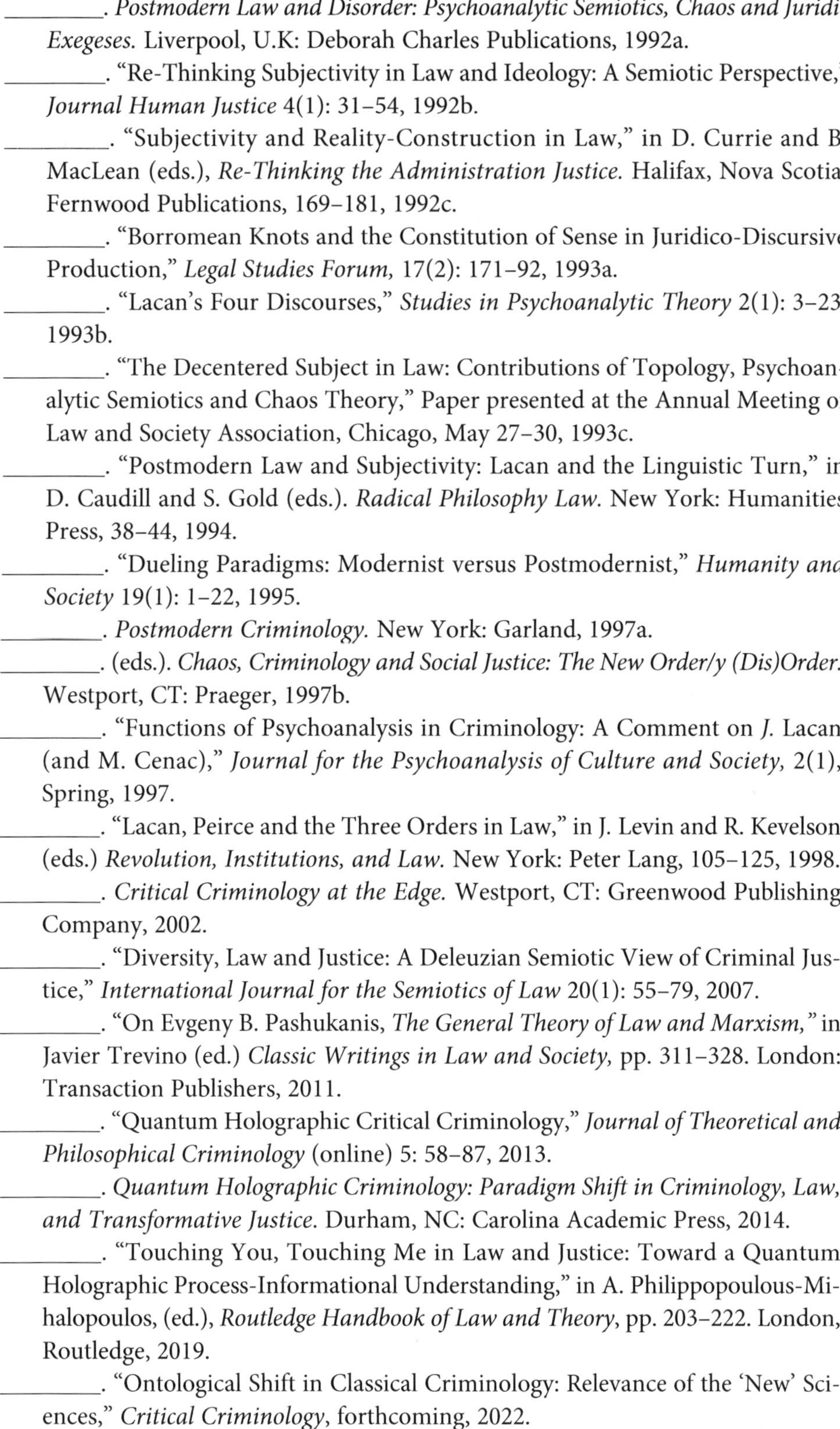

________. *Postmodern Law and Disorder: Psychoanalytic Semiotics, Chaos and Juridic Exegeses.* Liverpool, U.K: Deborah Charles Publications, 1992a.

________. "Re-Thinking Subjectivity in Law and Ideology: A Semiotic Perspective," *Journal Human Justice* 4(1): 31–54, 1992b.

________. "Subjectivity and Reality-Construction in Law," in D. Currie and B. MacLean (eds.), *Re-Thinking the Administration Justice.* Halifax, Nova Scotia: Fernwood Publications, 169–181, 1992c.

________. "Borromean Knots and the Constitution of Sense in Juridico-Discursive Production," *Legal Studies Forum,* 17(2): 171–92, 1993a.

________. "Lacan's Four Discourses," *Studies in Psychoanalytic Theory* 2(1): 3–23, 1993b.

________. "The Decentered Subject in Law: Contributions of Topology, Psychoanalytic Semiotics and Chaos Theory," Paper presented at the Annual Meeting of Law and Society Association, Chicago, May 27–30, 1993c.

________. "Postmodern Law and Subjectivity: Lacan and the Linguistic Turn," in D. Caudill and S. Gold (eds.). *Radical Philosophy Law.* New York: Humanities Press, 38–44, 1994.

________. "Dueling Paradigms: Modernist versus Postmodernist," *Humanity and Society* 19(1): 1–22, 1995.

________. *Postmodern Criminology.* New York: Garland, 1997a.

________. (eds.). *Chaos, Criminology and Social Justice: The New Order/y (Dis)Order.* Westport, CT: Praeger, 1997b.

________. "Functions of Psychoanalysis in Criminology: A Comment on *J.* Lacan (and M. Cenac)," *Journal for the Psychoanalysis of Culture and Society,* 2(1), Spring, 1997.

________. "Lacan, Peirce and the Three Orders in Law," in J. Levin and R. Kevelson (eds.) *Revolution, Institutions, and Law.* New York: Peter Lang, 105–125, 1998.

________. *Critical Criminology at the Edge.* Westport, CT: Greenwood Publishing Company, 2002.

________. "Diversity, Law and Justice: A Deleuzian Semiotic View of Criminal Justice," *International Journal for the Semiotics of Law* 20(1): 55–79, 2007.

________. "On Evgeny B. Pashukanis, *The General Theory of Law and Marxism,*" in Javier Trevino (ed.) *Classic Writings in Law and Society,* pp. 311–328. London: Transaction Publishers, 2011.

________. "Quantum Holographic Critical Criminology," *Journal of Theoretical and Philosophical Criminology* (online) 5: 58–87, 2013.

________. *Quantum Holographic Criminology: Paradigm Shift in Criminology, Law, and Transformative Justice.* Durham, NC: Carolina Academic Press, 2014.

________. "Touching You, Touching Me in Law and Justice: Toward a Quantum Holographic Process-Informational Understanding," in A. Philippopoulous-Mihalopoulos, (ed.), *Routledge Handbook of Law and Theory,* pp. 203–222. London, Routledge, 2019.

________. "Ontological Shift in Classical Criminology: Relevance of the 'New' Sciences," *Critical Criminology,* forthcoming, 2022.

Milovanovic, D. and J. Thomas. "Overcoming the Absurd: Legal Struggle as Primitive Rebellion," *Social Problems* 36(1): 48–60, 1989.

Milovanovic, D. and S. Henry. "Constitutive Penology," *Social Justice* 18(3): 204–24, 1991.

Milovanovic, D. and K. Russell (eds.). *Petit Apartheid in the U.S. Criminal Justice System*. Durham, NC: Carolina Academic Press, 2001.

Mingers, J. "Can Social Systems by Autopoietic?" *The Sociological Review* 50(2): 278–299, 2002.

Mirza, H. and D. Reay. "Redefining Citizenship: Black Women Educators and the 'Third Space,'" in M. Arnot and J.A. Dillabough (eds.), *Challenging Democracy: International Perspectives on Gender, Gender Education, and Citizenship*, pp. 58–72. London, UK: Routledge, 2001.

Mirza, H. *Race, Gender and Educational Desire: Why Black Women Succeed and Fail*, London: Routledge, 2009.

________. "'A Second Skin': Embodied Intersectionality, Transnationalism and Narratives of Identity and Belonging among Muslim Women in Britain," *Women's Studies International Forum* 36: 5–16, 2013.

Mitchell, E. and R. Staretz. "The Quantum Hologram and the Nature of Consciousness," *Journal of Cosmology* 14: 1–9, 2011.

Mitnick, E. "Constitutive Rights," *Oxford Journal of Legal Studies* 20(2): 185–204, 2000.

Moi, T. *Sexual/Textual Politics*. London: Methuen, 1985.

________. (ed.). *The Kristeva Reader*. Oxford: Blackwell Publishers, 1986.

Mohr, R. "Shifting Ground: Context and Change in Two Australian Legal Systems," *International Journal for the Semiotics of Law'* 15(1): 1–24, 2002.

Montoya, M. "Latinos and the Law," accessed 4/4/2021, https://digitalrepository.unm.edu/law_facbookdisplay/113.

Mohr, R. "Enduring Signs and Obscure Meanings: Contested Coats of Arms in Australian Jurisdictions," in A. Wagner, T. Summerfield, and F.S. Vanegas (eds.), *Contemporary Issues of the Semiotics of Law*, pp. 179–196. Onati, Spain: Hart Publishing, 2005.

Moore, N. "Icons of Control: Deleuze, Signs, Law," *International Journal for the Semiotics of Law* 20: 33–54, 2007.

Mootz, F. and P. Goodrich. *Nietzsche and Law*. London, UK: Routledge, 2008.

Mootz, F. "Is the Rule of Law Possible in a Postmodern World?", *Washington Law Review* 68: 249–285, 2013.

Morel, G. *The Law of the Mother*. London: Routledge, 2019.

Morgan, G. "Paradigms, Metaphors, and Puzzle Solving in Organizational Settings," *Administrative Science Quarter/y* 25: 605–622, 1980.

________. "More on Metaphor: Why We Cannot Control Tropes in Administrative Science," *Administrative Science Quarterly* 28: 601–607, 1983.

Morin, E. "Restricted Complexity, General Complexity," in C. Gershenson, D. Acerts, and B. Edmonds (eds.). *Worldviews, Science and Us: Philosophy and Complexity*, pp. 5–29. Singapore, IN: World Scientific.

Morland, D. "Anarchism, Human Nature, and History: Lessons for the Future," in J. Purkis and J. Bowen (eds.), *Twenty-First Century Anarchism: Unorthodox Ideas for a New Millennium.* Washington, DC: Cassell, 8–23, 1997.

Morris, C.W. *Foundations of the Theory of Signs.* Chicago, IL: Chicago University Press, 1938.

Mossman, M.J. "Feminism and the Legal Method: The Difference it Makes," *Australian Journal of Law and Society* 3: 30–52, 1986.

Moustafa, T. *Constituting Religion: Islam, Liberal rights, and the Malaysian State.* Cambridge, UK: Cambridge University Press, 2019.

Mulcahy, L. "Eyes of the Law: A visual Turn in Socio-Legal Studies?" *Journal of Law and Society* 44: 111–128, 2019.

Muller, J. and W. Richardson (eds.). *The Purloined Poe: Lacan, Derrida and Psychoanalytic Reading.* Baltimore, MD: The John Hopkins University Press, 1988.

Munch, R. "The Law as Medium of Communication," *Cardozo Law Review* 13(5): 1655–80, 1992.

Munger, F. and C. Seron. "Critical Legal Studies versus Critical Legal Theory: A Comment on Method," *Law and Policy* 6(3): 257–297, 1984.

Mura, A. "Lacan and Debt: The Discourse of the Capitalist in Times of Austerity." *Philosophy Today* 59: 154–177, 2015.

Murray, J. "Sinthome Law: Theoretical Constructions Upon Lacan's Concept of the Sinthome," *Law and Critique* 16: 201–230, 2005.

________. "Nome Law: Deleuze and Guattari on the Emergence of Law," *International Journal for the Semiotics of Law* 19: 127–151, 2006.

________. "Complexity Theory and Socio-Legal Studies," *Liverpool Law Review* 29(2): 227–246, 2008.

________. *Deleuze and Guattari: Emergent Law.* London, UK: Routledge, 2013.

Murray, J., T. Webb, and S. Wheatley (eds.). *Complexity and Law: Mapping an Emergent Jurisprudence.* London, UK: Routledge, 2019.

Murray, E. *Imaginative Thinking and Human Existence.* Pittsburgh: Duquesne University Press, 1986.

Murray, M. "New Methodology for the Analysis of Visuals in Legal Work," unpublished manuscript, 2021, accessed 5/9/2021, https://www.researchgate.net/publication/349773699_A_New_Methodology_for_the_Analysis_of_Visuals_in_Legal_Works.

________. "Mise en Scène and the Decisive Moment of Visual Legal Rhetoric," *Kansas Law Review* 68: 241–31, 2019a.

________. "The Sharpest Tool in the Toolbox: Visual Legal Rhetoric," *Journal of Legal Education* 68(1): 64–73, 2019b.

________. "The Ethics of Visual Legal Rhetoric," *Legal Communication and Rhetoric* 13: 107–129, 2016a.

________. "Adapting Peircian Semiotics to Sound Theory and Practice," *Sound Effects* 5(1): 55–72, 2016b.

Murris, K. and V. Bozalek. "Diffraction and Response-Able Reading of Texts: The Relational Ontologies of Barad and Deleuze," *International Journal of Qualitative Studies in Education* 32(7): 872–886, 2019.

Museus, S. *Asian American Students in Higher Education.* New York, NY: Routledge, 2013.

Mussawir, E. *Jurisdiction in Deleuze.* London, UK: Routledge, 2011.

Nadal, K., Y. Wong, J. Sriken, K. Griffin, and W. Fujii-Doe. "Racial Microaggressions and Asian Americans," *Asian American Journal of Psychology* 6(2): 136–144, 2015.

Nadal, K., S. Mazzula, D. Rivera, and W. Fuji-Doe. "Microaggressions and Latina/o Americans," *Journal of Latina/o Psychology* 2: 67–78, 2014.

Nadal, K. "A Guide to Responding to Microaggressions," *CUNY Forum* 2(1) 71–76, 2014.

Naffine, N. *Law and the Sexes: Explorations in Feminist Jurisprudence.* Sydney, Australia: Allen and Unwin, 1990.

Narogin, M. *Writing from the Fringe: A Study of Modern Aboriginal Literature.* Melbourne, Australia: Hyland House, 1990.

Newman, G. "Batman and Justice: The True Story," *Humanity and Society* 17(3): 297–320, 1993.

Nandan, Y. (ed.). *Emile Durkheim: Contributions to L'Annee Sociologique.* New York: Free Press, 1980.

Nasio, J.D. *Five Lessons on the Psychoanalytic Theory of Jacques Lacan.* Albany, NY: SUNY Press, 1998.

Nedelsky, J. *Law's Relations: A Relational Theory of Self, Autonomy and Law.* New York: Oxford University Press, 2011.

Nelken, D. "Beyond the Study of 'Law and Society.'" *American Bar Association Research Journal* 2: 323–38, 1986.

Newman, S. "Anarchism and Law," *Griffith Law Review* 21(2): 307–329, 2012.

Newmann, Von J. *The Mathematical Foundations of Quantum Mechanics.* Princeton, NJ: Princeton University Press, 1996 [1932].

Nicholson, L. (ed.). *Feminism/Postmodernism.* London: Routledge, 1990.

Nietzsche, F., *Beyond Good and Evil: Prelude to a Philosophy of the Future.* Random House, 1966.

________. *Twilight of the Idols and The Anti-Christ.* Penguin Books, 1968a.

________. *Basic Writings of Nietzsche,* W. Kaufmann (ed.). Random House, 1968b.

________. *The Will to Power.* Random House, 1968c.

________. *Human, All Too Human.* Cambridge University Press, 1986.

Noble, T. *Social Theory and Social Change.* New York: Palgrave, 2000.

Nobles, R. and D. Schiff. *Observing Law Through Systems Theory.* London, UK: Oxford, 2013a.

________. "Structural Coupling Between the System of Law and the Media: The Contrasting Examples of Criminal Conviction and Criminal Appeal," in G. Harste and A. Febbrajo (eds.) *Law and Intersystemic Communication: Understanding 'Structural Coupling,'* 317–327. New York: Routledge, 2016.

Norris, C. "Law, Deconstruction, and the Resistance to Theory," *Journal of Law and Society* 15(2): 166–188, 1988.

________. *The Contest of Faculties: Philosophy and Theory after Deconstruction.* New York: Methuen, 1985.

________. "Law, Deconstruction, and Resistance to Theory," *Journal of Law and Society* 15(2): 166–187, 1988.

Norval, A. *Deconstructing Apartheid Discourse.* London: Verso, 1996.

Nussbaum, M. *Frontiers of Justice: Disability, Nationality, Species Membership.* Cambridge, MA: Harvard University Press, 2006a.

________. "The Moral Status of Animals," *The Chronicles of Higher Education* 52(22): B6–B8, 2006b.

________. *Creating Capabilities.* Cambridge, MA: Harvard University Press, 2011.

Oakes, G. "The Verstehen Thesis and the Foundations of Max Weber's Methodology," *History and Theory* 16(1): 11–29, 1977.

O'Connell, P. "Law, Marxism and Method," *TripleC* 16(2): 647–655, 2018.

O'Donnell, E. and J. Talbot-Jones. "Creating Legal Rights for Rivers: Lessons from Australia, New Zealand, and India," *Ecology and Society* 23(1): 7–23, 2018.

Olsen, E. "The Slave Code in Colonial New York," *The Journal of Negro History* 29(2): 147–49, 1944.

O'Malley, P. *Risk, Uncertainty and Government.* London: Routledge: Cavendish, 2016.

O'Malley, P. and M. Valverde. "Foucault, Criminal Law, and the Governmentalization of the State," in M. Dubber (ed.) *Foundational Texts in Modern Criminal Law,* pp. 317–333. Oxford, UK: Exford University Press, 2014.

Onishi, N. "Will American Ideas Tear France Apart? Some Think So," *New York Times,* accessed on 4/3/2021, https://www.nytimes.com/2021/02/09/world/europe/france-threat-american-universities.html.

Orlikowski, W. "The Sociomateriality of Organizational Life," *Cambridge Journal of Economics* 43: 125–141, 2009.

Orlikowski, W. and S. Scott. "Sociomateriality: Challenging the Separation of Technology, Work and Organisation," *Academy of Management Annals* 2(2): 433–474, 2008.

Osajima, K. "Asian Americans as the Model Minority: An Analysis of the Popular Press Image in the 1960s and 1980s," *A Companion to Asian American Studies* 1(1): 215–225, 2005.

Osborn, G. "Dancing on the Edge of Disciplines: Law and the Interdisciplinary Turn," *Entertainment and Sports Law Journal* 8(1), 2–16, 2010. Downloaded on 3/6/2021, https://doi.org/10.16997/eslj.41.

Oswald, D. "Non-Speech Audio-Semiotics: A Review and Revision of Auditory Icon and Earcon Theory," Paper Presented at the Proceedings of the 18th International Conference of Auditory Display," Atlanta, GA, June 18–21, 2012.

Otto, D. (ed.). *Queering International Law.* Abingdon, UK: Routledge, 2018.

Oquendo, A. "Re-Imagining the Latino/a Race," *Harvard Black Letter Journal* 12: 93, 1995.

Packer, H.L. *The Limits of the Criminal Sanction.* Stanford, CA: Stanford University Press, 1968.

Papadelos, P. "Derridean Deconstruction and Feminism," Thesis Submitted for the Degree of Doctor of Philosophy, Adelaide University, accessed on 3/22/2021, https://digital.library.adelaide.edu.au/dspace/bitstream/2440/39506/10/02whole.pdf.

Parker, J. *Acoustic Jurisprudence.* Oxford, UK: Oxford University Press, 2015.

Parks, G., S. Stone, and J. Cardi (eds.). *Critical Race Realism.* New York: New Press, 2008.

Parsons, T. *Social Systems.* London: Routledge, 1951.

________. *Structure and Process in Modern Society.* New York: Free Press, 1960.

________. "The Law and Social Control," in J. Trevino (ed.) *Talcott Parsons: On Law and the Legal System.* Newcastle, UK: Cambridge Scholars, pp. 291–304, 2008.

________. "A Sociologist Looks at the Legal Profession," in J. Trevino (ed.) *Talcott Parsons: On Law and the Legal System,* pp. 305–319. Newcastle, UK: Cambridge Scholars, 2008.

________. "Law as an Intellectual Stepchild," in J. Trevino (ed.) *Talcott Parsons: On Law and the Legal System,* pp. 99–136. Newcastle, UK: Cambridge Scholars, 2008.

________. "Definitions of Health and Illness in the Light of American Values and Social Structure," in E. G. Jaco (ed.), *Patients, Physicians and Illness.* Glencoe, IL: Free Press, 1963.

________. *The Structure of Social Action.* New York: Free Press, 1968 [1937].

________. "The Life and Work of Emile Durkheim," in *Emile Durkheim, Sociology and Philosophy.* (Trans. D.F. Pocock.) New York: Free Press, xliii–lxx, 1974.

Pashukanis, E. "The General Theory of Law and Marxism," in P. Beirne and R. Sharlet (eds.), *Pashukanis: Selected Writings on Marxism and Law.* New York: Academic Press, 1980.

________. *The General Theory of Law and Marxism.* New Brunswick, NJ: Transaction Books, 2002.

Patterson, D. "Langdell's Legacy." *Northwestern University Law Review* 90: 196–203, 1995.

Powell, J. and S. Menendian. "Remaking Law: Moving Beyond Enlightenment Jurisprudence," *Saint Louis University Law Review Journal* 54: 1035–1112, 2010.

Pavlon-Cuellar, D. "Marx in Lacan," *Annual Review of Critical Psychology* 9: 70–77, 2011.

Payne, S. "Aboriginal Women and the Law," in C. Cunneen, *Aboriginal Perspectives on Criminal Justice,* pp. 31–40. Sydney, Australia: The Institute of Criminology, 1992.

Pauwels, L. and D. Mannay (eds.). *The Sage Handbook of Visual Research Methodology.* London: Sage, 2020.

Pearce, F. *The Radical Durkheim.* London: Unwin Hyman, 1989.

Pearce, Frank. *The Radical Durkheim.* 2d Edition. Toronto: Canadian Scholars' Pres, 2001.

Pecharroman, L. "Rights of Nature: Rivers That Can Stand in Court," *Resources* 7: 13–27, 2018.

Pecheux, M. *Language, Semantics and Ideology.* New York: St. Martin's Press, 1982.

Peirce, C.S. *The Collected Papers of Charles Sanders Peirce.* (C. Hartshorne and P. Weiss, eds.). Cambridge, UK: Harvard University Press, 1931.

Peggs, K. *Animals and Sociology.* Basingstoke, England: Palgrave MacMillan, 2012.

________. "The 'Animal-Advocacy Agenda": Exploring Sociology of Nonhuman Animals," *Sociological Review* 61(3): 592–606, 2013.

Peller, G. "The Metaphysics of American Law," *California Law Review* 73: 1151, 1985.

________. "Criminal Law, Race, and the Ideology of Bias," *Tulane Law Review* 67: 231–243, 1993.

Peng, H. *Law and Social Solidarity in Contemporary China.* London: Routledge, 2020.

Penrose, R. and S. Hameroff. "Consciousness in the Universe," *Journal of Cosmology* 14: 1–31, 2012.

Penther, P. "On Foreign Ground: Grand Narratives, Situated Specificities, and the Praxis of Critical Theory and Law," *Law and Critique* 10: 211–235, 1999.

Pepinsky, H. *The Geometry of Violence and Democracy.* Bloomington, IN: Indiana University Press, 1990.

Pepinsky, H. and R. Quinney (eds.). *Criminology as Peacemaking.* Bloomington, IN: Indiana University Press, 1991.

Petrazycki, L. and J. Trevino. *Law and Morality.* New York: Routledge, 2017.

Phelan, S and L. Dahlberg. "Introduction: Post-Marxist Discourse Theory and Critical Political Economy," *Critical Discourse Studies* 11(3): 255–256, 2014.

Philippopoulous-Mihalopoulos, A. *Niklas Luhmann: Law, Justice, and Society.* London: Routledge, 2009.

________. "… The Sound of a Breaking String: Critical Environmental Law and Ontological Vulnerability," *Journal of Human Rights and the Environment* 2(1): 5–22, 2011a.

________. "Towards Critical Environmental Law," in A. Philippopoulous-Mihalopoulos (ed.), *Law and Ecology: New Environmental Foundations,* pp. 18–38. Abingdon, UK: Routledge, 2011b.

________. *Law and Ecology: New Environmental Foundations.* Abingdon, UK: Routledge, 2011c.

________. (ed.). *Routledge Handbook of Law and Theory.* London, UK: Routledge, 2018.

Philippopoulous-Mihalopoulos, A. and V. Brooks (eds.). *Research Methods in Environmental Law.* London, UK: Elgar, 2017.

Phillips, D. *Toward a Just Order.* Princeton, NJ: Princeton University Press, 1986.

Pickering, W.S.F. (ed.). *Durkheim: Essays on Morals and Education.* London: Routledge and Kegan Paul, 1979.

Pintore, A. "Law as Fact?" *International Journal for the Semiotics of Law* 4(12): 233–53, 1991.

Piper, T (ed.). "Lex Non Scripta, Ars Non Scripta: Law, Justice and Improvisation," *Critical Studies in Improvisation* 6(1): [no page spread], 2010, accessed on 5/19/2021, https://www.criticalimprov.com/index.php/csieci/issue/view/102.

Pitkin, H. *Wittgenstein and Justice.* Berkeley, CA: University of California Press, 1971.

Podgorecki, A. *Law and Society.* Boston: Routledge and Kegan Paul, 1974.

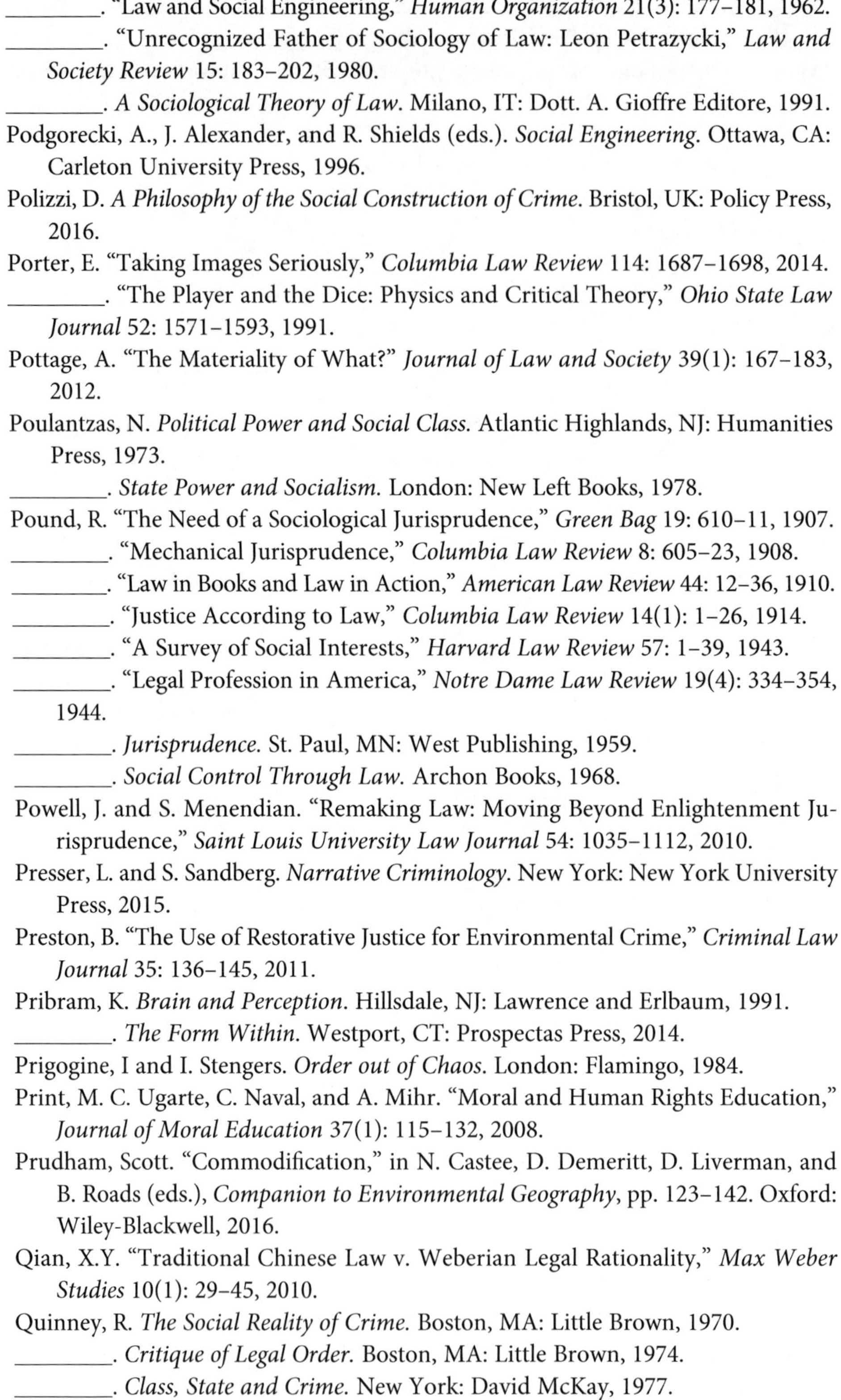

________. "Law and Social Engineering," *Human Organization* 21(3): 177–181, 1962.

________. "Unrecognized Father of Sociology of Law: Leon Petrazycki," *Law and Society Review* 15: 183–202, 1980.

________. *A Sociological Theory of Law*. Milano, IT: Dott. A. Gioffre Editore, 1991.

Podgorecki, A., J. Alexander, and R. Shields (eds.). *Social Engineering*. Ottawa, CA: Carleton University Press, 1996.

Polizzi, D. *A Philosophy of the Social Construction of Crime*. Bristol, UK: Policy Press, 2016.

Porter, E. "Taking Images Seriously," *Columbia Law Review* 114: 1687–1698, 2014.

________. "The Player and the Dice: Physics and Critical Theory," *Ohio State Law Journal* 52: 1571–1593, 1991.

Pottage, A. "The Materiality of What?" *Journal of Law and Society* 39(1): 167–183, 2012.

Poulantzas, N. *Political Power and Social Class*. Atlantic Highlands, NJ: Humanities Press, 1973.

________. *State Power and Socialism*. London: New Left Books, 1978.

Pound, R. "The Need of a Sociological Jurisprudence," *Green Bag* 19: 610–11, 1907.

________. "Mechanical Jurisprudence," *Columbia Law Review* 8: 605–23, 1908.

________. "Law in Books and Law in Action," *American Law Review* 44: 12–36, 1910.

________. "Justice According to Law," *Columbia Law Review* 14(1): 1–26, 1914.

________. "A Survey of Social Interests," *Harvard Law Review* 57: 1–39, 1943.

________. "Legal Profession in America," *Notre Dame Law Review* 19(4): 334–354, 1944.

________. *Jurisprudence*. St. Paul, MN: West Publishing, 1959.

________. *Social Control Through Law*. Archon Books, 1968.

Powell, J. and S. Menendian. "Remaking Law: Moving Beyond Enlightenment Jurisprudence," *Saint Louis University Law Journal* 54: 1035–1112, 2010.

Presser, L. and S. Sandberg. *Narrative Criminology*. New York: New York University Press, 2015.

Preston, B. "The Use of Restorative Justice for Environmental Crime," *Criminal Law Journal* 35: 136–145, 2011.

Pribram, K. *Brain and Perception*. Hillsdale, NJ: Lawrence and Erlbaum, 1991.

________. *The Form Within*. Westport, CT: Prospectas Press, 2014.

Prigogine, I and I. Stengers. *Order out of Chaos*. London: Flamingo, 1984.

Print, M. C. Ugarte, C. Naval, and A. Mihr. "Moral and Human Rights Education," *Journal of Moral Education* 37(1): 115–132, 2008.

Prudham, Scott. "Commodification," in N. Castee, D. Demeritt, D. Liverman, and B. Roads (eds.), *Companion to Environmental Geography*, pp. 123–142. Oxford: Wiley-Blackwell, 2016.

Qian, X.Y. "Traditional Chinese Law v. Weberian Legal Rationality," *Max Weber Studies* 10(1): 29–45, 2010.

Quinney, R. *The Social Reality of Crime*. Boston, MA: Little Brown, 1970.

________. *Critique of Legal Order*. Boston, MA: Little Brown, 1974.

________. *Class, State and Crime*. New York: David McKay, 1977.

________. *Bearing Witness to Crime and Social Justice.* Albany, NY: SUNY Press, 2000.

Qian, X.Y. "Traditional Chinese Law v. Weberian Legal Rationality," *Max Weber Studies* 10(1): 29–45, 2010.

Quiroga-Villamarin, D. "Domains of Objects, Rituals of Truth," *International Politics Reviews* 8: 129–151, 2020.

Ragland, E. and D. Milovanovic (eds.). *Lacan: Topological/y Speaking.* New York: Other Press, 2003.

Ragland-Sullivan, E. *Jacques Lacan and the Philosophy of Psychoanalysis.* Chicago, IL: University of Illinois Press, 1986.

________. "Counting From 0 to 6: Lacan, 'Suture', and the Imaginary Order," in P. Hogan and L. Pandit (eds.), *Criticism and Lacan.* Athens, Georgia: University of Georgia Press, 1990a.

________. "Lacan's Seminars on James Joyce: Writing as Symptom and 'Singular Solutions," in R. Feldstein and H. Sussman (eds.), *Psychoanalysis And …* New York: Routledge, 1990b.

Raiser, T. "Keynote Address: Sociology of Law in Germany," *German Law Journal* 4(1): 39–398, 2010.

Rajchman, J. *Truth and Eros: Foucault, Lacan and the Question of Ethics.* New York: Routledge, 1991.

Ramazanoglu, D. *Feminism and the Contradictions of Oppression.* London: Routledge, 1989.

Ramberg, B. "Richard Rorty" in E. Zalta (ed.) *Stanford Encyclopedia of Philosophy,* 2009, accessed on 7/25/2021, https://plato.stanford.edu/cgi-bin/encyclopedia/archinfo.cgi?entry=rorty.

Ramshaw, S. *Justice as Improvisation: The Law of the Exempore.* London: Routledge, 2013.

Ranciere, J. *Althusser's Lesson.* London, UK: Continuum, 2011.

Randall, A. *The Wind Done Gone: A Novel.* New York: Harcourt Publishers, 2001.

Rapaport, H. "Effi Briest and La Chose Freudienne," in P. Hogan and L. Pandit (eds.), *Criticism and Lacan.* Athens, GA: University of Georgia Press, 1990.

Rawls, John. *Justice as Fairness.* Harvard University Press, 2001.

Rawls, John and Erin Kelly. *Justice as Fairness: A Restatement.* Cambridge, MA: Harvard University Press, 2001.

Rawson, A and B. Mansfield. "Producing Juridical Knowledge: 'Rights of Nature' or the Naturalization of Rights? *Environment and Planning E: Nature and Space* 1(102): 99–119, 2018.

Reardon, P. "Judge 'Misunderstood' Parody, Author Asserts," *Chicago Tribune,* 9, April 24, 2001.

Redding, R. "Socialization by the Legal System: The Scientific Validity of a Lacanian Socio-Legal Psychoanalysis," *Oregon Law Review* 75: 781–802, 1996.

Reich, C. "The New Property," *Yale Law Journal* 73: 733–87, 1964.

Reiman, J. *Justice and Modern Moral Philosophy.* New Haven, CT: Yale University Press, 1990 (12th ed., 2017).

Renner, K. *The Institutions of Private Law and Their Social Functions.* London: Routledge and Kegan Paul, 1949.

Reynolds, J. "Jacques Derrida (1930–2004)." *Internet Encyclopedia of Philosophy.* Accessed on 3/8/2021. Accessed on 3/8/2021, https://iep.utm.edu/deconst/.

Reynolds, T. "Re-Thinking a Black Feminist Standpoint," *Ethnic and Racial Studies* 25(4): 591–606, 2002.

Rheinstein, M. (ed.). *Max Weber on Law in Economy and Society.* (Trans. E. Shils and M. Rheinstein.) New York: Simon and Schuster, 1967.

Rhode, D. "Feminist Critical Theories," in K. Bartlett and R. Kennedy (eds.), *Feminist Legal Theory.* Oxford: Westview Press, 333–50, 1991.

Richland, J. *Arguing With Tradition: The Language of Law in Hopi Tribal Court.* Chicago, IL: Chicago University Press, 2008.

Richland, J. and S. Deer. *Introduction to Tribal Legal Studies.* New York: Rowman and Littlefield Publishers, 2015.

Ricoeur, P. "Creativity of Language," *Philosophy Today* 17: 97–112, 1973.

________. *The Rule of Metaphor.* Toronto: University of Toronto Press, 1975.

Rident, C. "Storytelling, Narrative Rationality and Legal Persuasion," *Legal Writing* 14: 53–86, 2008.

Riley, P. "Nietzsche as a Philosopher of Law," in E. Parraro, P. Grossi, H. Hoffman, and P. Riley (eds.) *A Treatise of Legal Philosophy and General Jurisprudence.* Dordrecht: Springer, pp. 639–648, 2009.

Rio, K. "Handling Sorcery in a State System of Law: Magic, Violence and Kastom in Vanuatu." *Oceania* 80(2): 182–97, 2010.

Roach-Anleu, S.L. "Critiquing the Law: Themes and Dilemmas in Anglo-American Feminist Legal Theory," *Journal Law and Society* 19(4): 423–40, 1992.

Robinson, R. L. "The Shifting Race-Consciousness Matrix and the Multiracial Category Movement," *B.C Third World Law Journal* 20: 231–88, 2000.

Roermund, B. V. "Narrative Coherence and the Guises of Legalism," in P. Nerhot (ed.), *Law, Interpretation and Reality*, pp. 310–54. Boston, MA: Kluwer Academic Publishers, 1990.

Rogowski, R. "Autopoiesis in Law," in J. Wright (ed.) *International Encyclopedia of the Social and Behavioral Sciences*, 2d ed., 13: 554–556.

Rojek, J., A. Rosenfeld, and S. Decker. "Policing Race: The Racial Stratification of Searches in Police Traffic Stops," *Criminology* 50(4): 993–1024, 2012.

Rooney, J. "Polish Legal Semiotics," in R. Kevelson (ed.), *Flux, Complexity, and Illusion, Volume 6, Semiotics and the Human Sciences*, pp. 375–90. New York: Peter Lang, 1993.

Rorty, R. *Contingency, Irony and Solidarity*, Oxford, UK: Cambridge University Press, 1989.

________. "The Banality of Pragmatism and the Poetry of Justice," *Southern California Law Review* 63: 1811–1819, 1990.

________. "What Can You Expect from Anti-Foundationalist Philosophers?," *Virginia Law Review* 78: 717–727, 1992.

________. "Human Rights, Rationality and Sentimentality," in S. Shute and S. Hurley (eds.), *On Human Rights: The Oxford Amnesty Lectures 1993*. New York: Basic Books, 1993.

Rose, G. *Visual Methodologies*, 4th Ed. Thousand Oaks, CA: Sage, 2016.

Rosenbury, L. "Postmodern Feminist Legal Theory," in W. West and C. Bowman (eds.). *Research Handbook on Feminist Jurisprudence*, 127–137, Cheltanham, UK: 2019.

Rosenfeld, M. *Affirmative Action*. Cambridge, MA: Yale University Press, 1991.

Rosiek, J., J. Snyder and S. Pratt. "The New Materialism and Indigenous Theories of Non-Human Agency," *Qualitative Inquiry* 26 (3–4): 331–346, 2019.

Ross, L. "Frameworks of Critical Race Theory," *Oxford Research Encyclopedia of Criminology*, online, 2020, accessed on 3/29/2021, https://doi.org/10.1093/acrefore/9780190264079.013.553.

Ross, T. *Just Stories: How the Law Embodies Racism and Bias*. Boston, MA: Beacon Press, 1996.

Rossi-Landi, F. *Linguistics and Economics*. Amsterdam, Netherlands: Mouton, 1977.

________. *Language as Work and Trade: A Semiotic Homology for Linguistics and Economics*. South Hadley, MA: Bergin and Garvey, 1983.

Rosulek, F. "The Sociolinguistic Creation of Opposing Representations of Defendants and Victims," *Text and Talk* 28: 529–550, 2009.

Rothschild-Whitt, J. "The Collectivist Organization: An Alternative to Rational-Bureaucratic Modes," *American Sociology Review* 44, 1979.

Rousseau, J. *The Social Contract*. Chicago, IL: Henry Regnery, 1954.

Rousselle, D. *Gender, Sexuality and Subjectivity: A Lacanian Perspective on Identity, Language and Queer Theory*. New York: Routledge, 2020.

Ruan, N. "Papercuts: Hierarchical Microaggression in Law Schools," *Hastings Women's Law Journal* 31(1): 3–40, 2020.

Rubin, E. "What's Wrong with Langdell's Method, and What to do About it," *Vanderbilt Law Review* 60(2): 609–665, 2007.

Rudmin, F. W. "Frege's Semiotics Sampled: The Sense and Reference of the Verb 'Own,'" in R. Kevelson (ed.), *Law and the Human Sciences, Volume 3, Semiotics and the Human Sciences*. New York: Peter Lang, 357–73, 1992.

Rugemer, E. "The Development of Mastery and Race in the Comprehensive Slave Codes of the Greater Caribbean During the Seventeenth Century," *William and Mary Quarterly* 70(3): 429–458, 2013.

Ruhl, J. "The Fitness of Law: Using Complexity Theory to Describe the Evolution of Law and Society and Its Practical Meaning for Democracy," *Vanderbilt Law Review* 49: 1406–1492, 1996a.

________. "Complexity Theory as a Paradigm for the Dynamic Law-and-Society System," *Duke Law Journal* 45(5): 848–928, 1996b.

________. "Thinking of Environmental Law as a Complex Adaptive System," *Houston Law Review* 34: 933–1002, 1997.

________. "Law's Complexity: A Primer," *Georgia State University Law Review* 24(4): 885–912, 2007.

Ruhl, J. and H. Ruhl. "The Arrow of Law in Modern Administrative States," *University of California, Davis Law Review* 30: 405–482, 1997.

Ruiz, C. "The Sixteenth Puerto Rican Political Prisoner: The Case of José Solís Jordán," *Against the Current 81* July–August, 1997.

Rusche, G. and O. Kirchheimer. *Punishment and Social Structure.* New York: Russell and Russell, 1968.

Russell, S. "The Critical Legal Studies Challenge to Contemporary Mainstream Legal Philosophy," *Ottawa Law Review* 18: 1–24, 1986.

Russell, K. "A Critical View From the Inside: An Application of Critical Legal Studies to Criminal Law," *Journal of Criminal Law and Criminology* 85(5) 222–240, 1994.

________. *The Color of Crime.* New York: New York University Press, 1998.

Ryan, W. *Marxism and Deconstruction: A Critical Articulation.* Baltimore, MD: John Hopkins University Press, 1982.

Sahoo, A. "Eco-Feminist Jurisprudence: A Much Needed Change in the Perception of Law," *International Journal of Law and Legal Jurisprudence Studies* 2(6): 207–210, 2015.

Salyer, L. "Captives of Law: Judicial Enforcement of the Chinese Exclusion Law," *Journal of American History* 76: 91–117, 1989.

________. "The Constitutive Nature of Law in American History," *Legal Studies Forum* 15(1): 61–64, 1991.

Salecl, R. "Crime as a Mode of Subjectivization: Lacan and the Law," *Law and Critique* 4(1): 2–10, 1993.

Sanders, K. "Beyond Human Ownership? Property, Power and Legal Personality for Nature in Aotearoa New Zealand," *Journal of Environmental Law* 30(1): 207–234, 2018.

Salleh, A. *Ecofeminism as Politics: Nature, Marx and the Postmodern.* London, UK: Zed Books, 2007.

Samuels, R. *Between Philosophy and Psychoanalysis: Lacan's Reconstruction of Freud.* New York: Routledge, 1993.

Sarat, A and S. Scheingold. *Cause Lawyering: Political Commitments and Professional Responsibilities,* New York: Oxford University Press, 1998.

________. "Introduction: The Dynamics of Cause Lawyering—Constraints and Opportunities," in A. Sarat and S. Scheingold (eds.) *The Worlds Cause Lawyers Make: Structure and Agency in Legal Practice,* pp. 1–34. Stanford, CA: Stanford University Press, 2005.

Sarre, R. "Mabo," *Humanity and Society* 18(1). 97–104, 1994.

Sartre, J. P. *Being and Nothingness.* New York: Washington Square Press, 1980.

Sarup, M. *Post-Structuralism and Postmodernism.* Athens, GA: University of Georgia Press, 1989.

________. *Jacques Lacan.* Toronto: University of Toronto Press, 1992.

Saussure, F. de. *Course in General Linguistics.* New York: McGraw-Hill, 1966.

Sawiki, J. *Disciplining Foucault: Feminism, Power, and the Body.* London: Routledge, 1991.

Schempp, W. "Quantum Holography and Neurocomputer Architecture," *Journal of Mathematical Imagining and Vision* 2: 279–326, 1992.

Scheppele, K.L. "The Revisioning of Rape Law," *University of Chicago Law Review* 54(3): 1095–1116, 1987.

Schiff, D. and R. Nobles. *Jurisprudence.* London: Butterworth, 2003.

Schlegal, J. "Notes Toward an Intimate, Opinionated, and Affectionate History of the Conference on Critical Legal Studies," *Stanford Law Review* 36: 391–411, 1984.

Schlosberg, D. "Reconceiving Environmental Justice," *Environmental Politics* 13(3): 517–547, 2004.

________. *Defining Environmental Justice.* New York: Oxford University Press, 2007.

Schluchter, W. *The Rise of Western Rationalism: Max Weber's Developmental History.* Berkeley, CA: University of California Press, 1985.

Schneider, E. "The Dialectics of Rights and Politics: Perspectives From the Women's Movement," *New York University Law Review* 61: 589, 1986.

Schou, J. "Ernesto Laclau and Critical Media Studies: Marxism, Capitalism, and Critique," *TripleC* 14(1): 292–311, 2016.

Schroeder, J.L. "Law and the Postmodern Mind," *Cardozo Law Review* 16: 805–89, 1995.

________. "The Hysterical Attorney: The Legal Advocate Within Lacanian Discourse Theory," *International Journal for the Semiotics of Law* 13(2): 181–213, 2000.

________. *The Four Lacanian Discourses: Or Turning Law Inside Out.* New York: Routledge, 2010.

Schrödinger, E. "Quantization as an Eigenvalue Problem," *Annalen der Physik* 4: 361–376, 1926.

________. *What is Life?* Cambridge, UK: Cambridge University Press, 2012.

Schulman, C. "Chaos, Law, and Critical Legal Studies," in D. Milovanovic (ed.), *Chaos, Criminology and Social Justice.* Westport, CT: Praeger Publishers, 123–137,1997.

Schultz, E. *Dialogue at the Margins: Whorf, Bakhtin, and Linguistic Relativity.* Madison, WI: University of Wisconsin Press, 1990.

Schultz, F. *History of Roman Legal Science.* Oxford: Oxford University Press, 1946.

Schultz, V. "Telling Stories About Women and Work: Judicial Interpretations of Sex Segregation in the Workplace in Title Vl1 Cases Raising the Lack of Interest Argument," in K. Bartlett and R. Kennedy (eds.), *Feminist Legal Theory.* Oxford: Westview Press, 124–155, 1991.

Schum, D. *The Evidential Foundations of Probabilistic Reasoning.* New York: John Wiley and Sons, Inc., 1994.

Schur, E. *Law and Society: A Sociological View.* New York: Random House, 1968.

Schutz, A. "Law and the Postmodern Mind," *Cardozo Law Review* 16: 979–1002, 1995.

Schutter, D. "A Study of Metaphor and Metonymy in Lacan," *Auslegung: A Journal of Philosophy* 10(1–2): 65–74, 1983.

Schwartz, M. "The Value of Postmodern Theory to Critical Criminology: Violence Against Women and Corporate Violence," in R. Janikowski and D. Milovanovic (eds.), *Legality and Illegality*. New York: Peter Lang Publishers, 1994.

Schwartz, M. and D. Friedrichs. "Postmodern Thought and Criminological Discontents," *Criminology* 32(2): 221–246, 1994.

Schwartz, R.D. and J.C. Miller. "Legal Evolution and Societal Complexity," *American Journal of Sociology* 70: 159–69, 1964.

Schwendinger, J. and H. Schwendinger. "Defenders of Order? Or Guardians of Human Rights?" *Issues in Criminology* 5(2): 123–57, 1970.

________. *Rape and Inequality*. Beverly Hills, CA: Sage Publications, 1983.

________. *Adolescent Subcultures and Delinquency*. New York: Praeger Publishers, 1985.

Scimago Journal and Country Ranking, Scimago Institutions Rankings, accessed 3/20/2021, https://www.scimagojr.com/journalrank.php?category=3318.

Searle, J. *Speech Acts*. Cambridge: Cambridge University Press, 1969.

________. *The Philosophy of Language*. Oxford: Oxford University Press, 1971.

________. *Expression and Meaning*. Cambridge, UK: C.U. Press, 1979.

________. *Intentionality*. Cambridge: Cambridge University Press, 1983.

Sekaquaptewa, P. "Evolving the Hopi Common Law," *Tribal Court Clearninghouse*, no date, accessed 8/30/2021, http://www.tribal-institute.org/lists/sekaquaptewa.htm.

Sellberg, K. and P. Hinton. "Introduction: The Possibilities of Feminist Quantum Thinking," *Rhizomes* 30(1): 1–15, 2016.

________. "Special Issue, Quantum Possibilities: The Work of Karan Barad," *Rhizomes* 30(1), 2016.

Sellers, S. *Language and Sexual Difference: Feminist Writing in France*. New York: St. Martin's Press, 1991.

Selva, L. and R. Bohm. "Law and Liberation: Toward an Oppositional Legal Discourse," *Legal Studies Forum* 11: 243–266, 1987.

Selznick, P. *Law, Society, and Industrial Justice*. New York: Sage, 1969.

Sen, Amartya. *The Ideal of Justice*. Cambridge, MA: Harvard University Press, 2011.

Sesay, A., R. Ramirez, and O. Oh. "Digital Transformation in Police Work: A Sociomaterial Perspective on Police Body Worn Cameras (BWC)," Proceedings of the 59th Hawaii International Conference on System Sciences, 1/4/2017, accessed on 9/1/2021, https://scholarspace.manoa.hawaii.edu/bitstream/10125/41677/1/paper0528.pdf.

Shdaimah, C. "Dilemmas of 'Progressive' Lawyering: Empowerment and Hierarchy," in A. Sarat and S. Scheingold (eds.) *The Worlds Cause Lawyers Make: Structure and Agency in Legal Practice*, pp. 239–73. Stanford, CA: Stanford University Press, 2005.

Shah, J. "Affirming Affirmative Action by Affirming White Privilege: *SFFA v. Harvard*," *The Georgetown Law Journal* 108: 134–143, 2020.

Shammas, V. "The Perils of Parole Hearings: California Lifers, Performative Disadvantage, and the Ideology of Insight," *Political and Legal Anthropology Review* 42(1): 142–160, 2019.

Shapiro, E. "Only 7 Black Students Got into Stuyvesant, New York's Most Selective High School out of 895 Spots," *New York Times*, March 18, 2019, accessed on 3/30/2021, https://www.nytimes.com/2019/03/18/nyregion/black-students-nyc-high-schools.html.

________. "New York City Will Change Many Selective Schools to Address Segregation," *New York Times*, March 19, 2021.

Shariatmadari, D. *Don't Believe a Word: The Surprising Truth About Language*. NY: W.W. Norton and Company, 2019.

Shelby, T., *We Who are Dark: The Philosophical Foundations of Black Solidarity*. Cambridge, MA: Harvard University Press, 2005.

Shaw, J. "From Beethoven to Bowie: Identity Framing, Social Justice and the Sound of Law," *International Journal for the Semiotics of Law* 31(2): 301–324, 2018.

Sherwin, R. "Visual Jurisprudence," *New York Law School Law Symposium* 57: 137–165, 2012.

________. *Visualizing Law in the Age of the Digital Baroque*. New York: Routledge, 2011.

________. *When Law Goes Pop: The Vanishing Line Between Law and Popular Culture*. Chicago, Il: Chicago University Press, 2000.

Shiva, V. Aggroecology and Regenerative Agriculture. Santa Fe, N.M.: Synergetic Press.

Shon, P. "Hey You C'me Here!" *International Journal for the Semiotics of Law* 13(2): 159–79, 2000.

Shapiro, E. "New York City Will Change Many Selective Schools to Address Segregation," *New York Times*, December 18, 2021, updated March 19, 2021, accessed on 4/3/2021, https://www.nytimes.com/2020/12/18/nyregion/nyc-schools-admissions-segregation.html.

Silverman, K. *The Subject of Semiotics*. New York: Oxford University Press, 1983.

Sinclair, M.B. "Autopoiesis: Who Needs It?" *Legal Studies Forum* 16(1): 81–102, 1992.

Silverstein, J. "Why We Published the 1619 Project," *New York Times*, December 20, 2019, accessed on 4/4/2021, https://www.nytimes.com/interactive/2019/12/20/magazine/1619-intro.html.

Simmel, Georg. *Conflict and the Web of Group Affiliations*. K. Wolff and R. Bendix (trans.). New York: Free Press, 1969.

Simona, A. "Max Weber's Sociology of Law as a Turning Point of his Methodology," *International Review of Sociology* 14(2): 143–150, 2010. https://www.tandfonline.com/doi/abs/10.1080/03906700410001681257?journalCode=cirs20.

Simon, P. "Statistics, French Social Sciences and Ethnic and Racial Social Relations, *Revue Francaise de Sociologie* 51: 159–174, 2010, online, accessed 4/1/2021, https://www.cairn.info/revue-francaise-de-sociologie-1-2010-5-page-159.htm.

Sim, S. (ed.). *The Lyotard Dictionary*. Edinburgh, UK: Edinburgh University Press, 2011.

Slater, D. "Can You Talk Your Way Out of a Life Sentence?" *New York Times*, January 1, 2020, accessed 4/18/2021.

Smart, C. *Women, Crime and Criminology: A Feminist Critique.* London: Routledge and Kegan Paul, 1976.

________. *The Ties That Bind: Law, Marriage and the Reproduction of Patriarchal Relations.* London: Routledge and Kegan Paul, 1984.

________. "Feminism and Law: Some Problems of Analysis and Strategy," *International Journal of the Sociology of Law* 14: 109, 1986.

________. *Feminism and the Power of Law.* New York: Routledge, 1989.

Smith, A. *Laclau and Mouffe.* New York: Routledge, 1999.

Smith, D. "The Experienced World as Problematic: A Feminist Method," Twelfth Annual Sorokin Lecture, University of Saskatchewan, Saskatoon, January 28, 1981.

________. *The Everyday World as Problematic: A Feminist Sociology.* Toronto: University of Toronto Press, 1987.

________. "Sociology From Women's Experience: A Reaffirmation," *Sociological Theory* 10(1): 60–87, 1992.

Smith, D.A. and C.D. Uchida. "The Social Organization of Self-Help," *American Sociological Review* 53: 94–102, 1988.

Smith, J. and A. K. "Carceral Citizenship as Strength," *Critical Criminology* 29: 93–110, 2021.

Smith, P. *Discerning the Subject.* Minneapolis, MN: University of Minnesota Press, 1988.

________. "Feminist Legal Critics: The Reluctant Radicals," in D. Caudill and S. Gold (eds.), *Radical Philosophy of Law.* Atlantic Highlands, NJ: Humanities Press, 73–87, 1995.

Snyder, C. "What is Third-Wave Feminism?" *Signs* 34(1): 175–96, 2008.

Soh, V. "A Tale of Two Systems: Sharia and Civil Law in Malaysia," *Durham Asian Law Journal*, December 9, 2020, accessed on 8/3/2021, https://www.durhamasianlawjournal.com/post/a-tale-of-two-systems-sharia-and-civil-law-in-malaysia.

Solan, L and P. Tiersma. *Speaking of Crime: The Language of Criminal Justice.* Chicago: Chicago University Press, 2005.

Solórzano, D. and D. Bernal. "Examining Transformational Resistance Through a Critical Race and LatCrit Theory Framework," *Urban Education* 36(3): 308–342, 2001.

Solórzano, D. and O. Villapando. "The Chicano Educational Experience: A Proposed Framework for Effective Schools in Chicago Students in Urban Context," *Educational Policy* 9: 293–314, 1995.

Spafford, J. "An Anarchist Interpretation of Marx's 'Abilities to Needs' Principle," *The Journal of Value Inquiry* 54: 325–343, 2020.

Spivak, C.G. "Can the Subaltern Speak," in T. Sharp (ed.) *Geographies of Postcolonialism*, pp. 66–110. London: Sage, 2008.

Spillers, H. "Mama's Baby, Papa's Maybe: An American Grammar Book," *Diacritics* 17(2): 64–81, 1987.

Srinivasan, S. "What is the Psychoanalysis of Law?," *Journal of Humanities and Social Science*, 20(1): 15–23, 2015.

Stables, W. "Law and Social Control in Juvenile Justice Dispositions," *Journal of Research in Crime and Delinquency* 24: 7–23, 1987.

Stacy, H. "Lacan's Split Subjects: Raced and Gendered Transformations," *Legal Studies Forum* 20(3): 277–293, 1996.

Stanley, L. and S. Wise. *Breaking Out: Feminist Consciousness and Feminist Research.* London: Routledge and Kegan Paul, 1983.

Stareckeski, A. *Ours To Lose: When Squatters Become Home Owners in New York City.* Chicago, IL: University of Chicago Press, 2016.

Stedman J., S. *Durkheim Reconsidered*, Cambridge, UK: Polity, 2001.

Stein, P. "Roman Law," *Britannica.* Accessed 12/15, 2020. Accessed, 7/7/2021 https://www.britannica.com/topic/Roman-law.

Steiner, B. and L. Nielsen. "Introduction: A Constitutive Perspective of Rights," in Steiner and Nielsen (eds.) *The New Civil Rights Research*, pp. 1–14. London, UK: Routledge, 2019.

Steiner, K. "Islam, Law, and Human Rights of Women in Malaysia," International Human Rights of Women," in Reilly N. (ed.) *International Human Rights of Women. International Human Rights*, pp. 381–401. Singapore: Springer, 2019.

Stewart, J. "Demystifying Critical Legal Studies: A Thesis Submitted for the Degree of Doctor of Philosophy," Adelaide Law School, University of Adelaide, 2019. https://digital.library.adelaide.edu.au/dspace/bitstream/2440/120602/1/Stewart2019_PhD.pdf.

Stockdill, B. "Aids, Queers, and Criminal Justice," in B. Arrigo (ed.), *Social Justice/Criminal Justice.* Belmont, California: West/Wadsworth, 226–250, 1999.

Stockinger, P. "The Conceptual Representation of Action and its Normative Background," *International Journal far the Semiotics of Law* 1/2: 143–159, 1988.

Stone, A. "The Place of Law in the Marxian Structure-Superstructure Archetype," *Law and Society Review* 19: 39–67, 1985.

Stone, C. "Should Trees Have Standing?: Towards legal Rights for natural Objects," *Southern California Law Review* 45: 450–487.

Strawson, P.F. "On Referring," *Mind* 59: 320–44, 1950.

________. "Intention and Convention in Speech Acts, "*The Philosophical Review* 73/4: 439–60, 1964.

Strong, T. *Freidrich Nietzsche and the Politics of Transfiguration.* Berkeley, CA: University of California Press, 1975.

Sue, D., C. Capodilupo, G. Torino, J. Bucceri, A. Holder, K Nadal, and M. Esquilin. "Racial Microaggressions in Everyday Life," *American Psychologist* 62: 271–286, 2007.

Sugarman, D. "A Special Relationship? American Influences on English Legal Education, 1870–1965," *International Journal of Legal Profession* 18(1): 1–23, 2011.

Sullivan M. and D. Solove. "Can Pragmatism be Radical? Richard Posner and Legal Pragmatism," *Yale Law Journal* 113: 687–741, 2003.

Summers, R. S. "Charles Sanders Peirce and America's Dominant Theory of Law," in R. Kevelson (ed.), *Peirce and Law.* New York: Peter Lang, 153–62, 1991.

Sumner, W.G. *Folkways.* New York: Ginn and Company, 1940.

Sumner, C. *Reading Ideologies: An Investigation into the Marxist Theory of Ideology and Law.* New York: Academic Press, 1979.
Sunstein, C. and M. Nussbaum. *Animal Rights.* Oxford, UK: Oxford University Press, 2004.
Susskind, L. *The Black Hole War.* New York: Balkbay Books, 2009.
Sutter, L. *After Law.* London: Polity Press, 2021.
Sutter, L and K. McGee (eds.). *Deleuze and Law.* Edinburgh, UK: Edinburgh University Press, 2012.
Swidorski, C. "Constituting the Modern State: The Supreme Court, Labor Law, and the Contradictions of Legitimation," in Caudill, D. and S. Stone (eds.), *Radical Philosophy of Law.* Atlantic Highlands, New Jersey: Humanities Press, 162–178, 1995.
Swiffen, A. "Politics of law and the Lacanian Real," *Law and Critique* 21: 39–51, 2010.
Sykes, R. "Listening Back: Music, Cultural Heritage and Law," *International Journal for the Semiotics of Law* 31(2): 183–186, 2018.
Sykes, G. and D. Matza. "Techniques of Neutralization: A Theory of Delinquency," *American Sociological Review* 22(6): 664–670, 1957.
Symposium: Critical Race Theory, *California Law Review* 82, 1994.
Taborsky, E. "Biological Organisms as Semiosic Systems," *Signs* 2: 146–187, 2008.
________. "Energy Transformation and Semiosis," in M. Bergman & J. Queiroz (eds.), *The Commens Encyclopedia: The Digital Encyclopedia of Peirce Studies. New Edition*, 2003, Pub. 131013-1847a., accessed 8/19/2021, http://www.commens.org/encyclopedia/article/taborsky-edwina-energy-transformation-and-semiosis.
________. "The Complex Information Process," *Entropy* 2(3): 81–97, 2000.
________. "What is a Sign?, *Journal of Literary Semantics* 30: 83–94, 2001a.
________. "The Internal and the External Semiosic Properties of Reality," *Semiosis, Evolution, Energy, Developments* 1(1): 1–17, 2001b.
Takuchi, L. "A Diffractive and Deleuzian Approach to Analyzing Interview Data," *Feminist Theory* 13(3): 265–281, 2012.
Taverniers, M. "Hjelmslev's Semiotic Model of Language," *Semiotica* 171: 367–394, 2008.
Taub, N. and E. Schneider. "Perspectives on Women's Subordination and the Role of Law," in D. Kairys (ed.), *The Politics Law.* New York: Pantheon Books, 1992.
Taussig, M. *Shamanism, Colonialism, and the Wild Man.* Chicago: University of Chicago Press., 1987.
Teubner, G. "Substantive and Reflexive Elements in Modern Law," *Law and Society Review* 17(2): 239–85, 1983.
________. "The Two Faces on Janus: Rethinking Legal Pluralism," *Cardozo Law Review* 13(5): 1443–62, 1992.
________. *Law as an Autopoietic System.* Oxford, UK: Blackwell Publishers, 1993 [1989].
Teubner, G., R. Nobles and D. Schiff. "The Autonomy of Law: An Introduction to Legal Autopoiesis," in D. Schiff and D. Nobles (eds.) *Jurisprudence.* London, UK:

Butterworth, 2003, accessed 4/10/2021, https://www.jura.uni-frankfurt.de/42852943/Generic_42852943.pdf.

"The Border's Long Shadow," *ACLU Michigan*, March 21, 2021, accessed on 4/4/2021, https://www.aclumich.org/en/publications/borders-long-shadow.

Thomas, C. "Max Weber, Talcott Parsons and the Sociology of Law Reform," *Minnesota Journal of International Law* 15(2): 383–424, 2006.

Thomas, J. "Law and Social Praxis: Prisoner Civil Rights and Structural Mediations," in S. Spitzer and A. Scull (eds.), *Research in Law, Deviance and Social Control* 6: 141–170, 1984.

________. *Prisoner Litigation: The Paradox of the Jailhouse Lawyer.* Totowa, NJ: Rowman and Littlefield, 1988.

Thomas, J. and D. Milovanovic. "Revisiting Jailhouse Lawyers," in S. Henry and D. Milovanovic (eds.), *Constitutive Criminology at Work.* Albany, NY: SUNY Press, 227–46, 1999.

Thomas, J. and S. Boehlefeld. "Rethinking Abolitionism: 'What Do We Do With Henry?' Review of de Haan, *The Politics of Redress,*" in B. MacLean and H. Pepinsky (eds.), *We Who Would Take No Prisoners.* Vancouver, Canada: Collective Press, 1993.

Thomson, A. "Critical Legal Education in Britain." *Journal of Law and Society* 14(1): 183–197, 1987.

Tiersma, P. *Legal Language.* Chicago, IL: University of Chicago Press, 1999.

Tifft, L. and D. Sullivan. *The Struggle to be Human: Crime, Criminology and Anarchism.* Orkney: Cienfuego Press, 1980.

Timeline for Major Supreme Court Decision on Women's Rights. ACLU Women's Rights Project, accessed 3/21/2021, https://www.aclu.org/other/timeline-major-supreme-court-decisions-womens-rights.

Todorov, T. *Mikhail Bakhtin: The Dialogical Principle.* Minneapolis, MN: University of Minnesota Press, 1984.

Tomsic, S. *The Capitalist Unconscious: A Lacan Perspective.* London: Verso, 2011.

Toomey, D. "How Listening to Trees Can Help Reveal Nature," 2017, accessed 8/12/2021, https://e360.yale.edu/features/how-listening-to-trees-can-help-reveal-natures-connections.

________. "Exploring How and Why Trees 'Talk' to Each Other," *Yale School of the Environment, Yale Environment 360,* Sept 1, 2016, accessed 8/12/2021, https://e360.yale.edu/features/exploring_how_and_why_trees_talk_to_each_other.

Traugott, M. (ed.). *Emile Durkheim on Institutional Analysis.* Chicago, IL: University of Chicago Press, 1978.

Treiber, Hubert. "On Max Weber's Sociology of Law, now known as The Developmental Conditions of the Law," *Max Weber Studies* 12(1): 121–138, 2012.

Treiber, H. and M. Philpotts. *Reading Max Weber's Sociology of Law.* NY: Oxford University Press, 2020.

Trever, T., C. Lisberger, and M. Utzschneider. "Law on the Left: A Conversation with Duncan Kennedy, *Unbound: Harvard Journal of the Legal Left* 10(1): 1–35, 2015.

Trevino, J. A. (ed.). *Talcott Parsons: On Law and the Legal System*. Cambridge Scholars Publishing, Newcastle, UK, 2008.

________. *The Sociology of Law*. London, UK: Transaction Books, 2009.

________. *Classic Writings in Law and Society*. London: Transaction Books, 2011.

Tribe, L. "The Curvature of Constitutional Space: What Lawyers Can Learn from Modern Physics," *Harvard Law Review* 103(1): 1–19, 1989.

Trubek, D. "Max Weber on Law and the Rise of Capitalism," *Wisconsin Law Review* 3: 720–53, 1972.

________. "Complexity and Contradiction in the Legal Order: Balbus and the Challenge of Critical Social Thought About Law," *Law and Society Review* 11: 529–69, 1977.

Turk, A. "Law as a Weapon in Social Conflict," *Social Problems* 23(3): 276–291, 1975.

Turkle, G. "Rational Law and Boundary Maintenance: Legitimating the 1971 Lockhead Loan Guarantee," *Law and Society Review* 15: 41–47, 1981.

Turkle, S. *Psychoanalytic Politics*. New York: Basic Books, 1978.

Turner, Stephen. "Weber, the Chinese Legal System, and Marsh's Critique," *Comparative and Historical Sociology* 14(2): 6–26, 2002.

Tushnet, M. "Perspectives on the Development of American Law: A Critical Review of Friedman's 'A History of American Law.'" *Wisconsin Law Review* 1: 81–109, 1977.

________. "Critical Legal Studies: An Introduction to its Origins and Underpinnings," *Journal of Legal Education* 36: 505–17, 1986.

________. "Critical Legal Studies: A Political History," *Yale Law Journal 100: 1515*, 1991.

Twining, W. *Karl Llewellyn and the Realist Movement*. London: Weidenfeld and Nicolson, 1973.

Unger, R.M. *Knowledge and Politics*. New York: Free Press, 1975.

________. *Law in Modern Society*. New York: Free Press, 1976.

________. *Passion*. New York: Free Press, 1984.

________. *The Critical Legal Studies Movement*. Cambridge, MA: Harvard University Press, 1986.

________. *False Necessity*. New York: Cambridge University Press, 1987.

________. *The Critical Legal Studies Movement: Another Time, a Greater Task*. London: Verso, 2015.

United States of America v. Jose Solis Jordan, U.S. District Court, Northern District of Illinois, Eastern Division, 1999.

Urofsky, M. "Jim Crow Law." *Britannica*. Accessed on 2/21/2021, https://www.britannica.com/event/Jim-Crow-law.

Uusitalo, J. "Abduction, Legal Reasoning, and Reflexive Law," in R. Kevelson (ed.), *Peirce and Law*. New York: Peter Lang, 163–85, 1991.

Vago, S. *Law and Society*, 10th ed. New York: Prentice Hall, 2012.

________. *Social Change*, 5th ed. Upper Saddle River, NJ: Prentice Hall, 2003.

Valauri, J. "Peirce and Holmes," in R. Kevelson (ed.), *Peirce and Law*. New York: Peter Lang, 187–201, 1991.

Valencia, R., S. Garcia, H. Flores, and J. Juarez, *Mexican American and the Law*, Tucson, AR: University of Arizona Press, 2004.

Valdes, F. "Queers, Sissies, Dykes, and Tomboys," *California Law Review* 83: 1, 1995.

________. "Foreword: Latina/o Ethnicities, Critical Race Theory, and Post-Identity Politics in Postmodern Legal Culture," *La Raza Law Journal* 1: 11–35, 1996.

Valverde, M. *Michel Foucault*. London, UK: Routledge, 2017.

Vanheule, S. "Capitalist Discourse, Subjectivity and Lacanian Psychoanalysis," *Frontiers in Psychology* 7: 1–14, December 2016.

van Leeuwen, T. *Introducing Social Semiotics*. London: Routledge, 2005.

van Ness, D. and K. Strong. *Restoring Justice*, 5th ed. Cincinnati, OH: Anderson Publishing, 2021.

Verator-Santiago, C. "Interest Convergence and the Extension of U.S. Citizenship to Puerto Rico," *University of Miami Race and Social Justice Law Review* 9(1): 110–123, 2019.

Verenich, V. "The Case of Lauris Kaplinski: A Guide to a Semiotic Reading of Incitement of Hatred in Modern Criminal Justice," *Signs and Society* 1(2): 243–241, 2013.

________. "Charles Sanders Peirce, A Mastermind of (Legal) Arguments," *International Journal of the Semitics of Law* 25: 31–55, 2012a.

________. "The Semiotic Model of Legal Reasoning," *International Journal of Law, Language and Discourse* 2(3): 25–58, 2012b.

________. "Semiotics of Visual Evidence in Law," *Semiotica* 216: 63–83, 2017.

Verhaeghe, P. and F. Declercq. "Lacan's Analytical Goal: 'Le Sinthome' or the Feminine Way," in L. Thurston (ed.). *Re-Inventing the Symptom: Essays on the Final Lacan*, pp. 59–83. New York: Other Press, 2002.

Ville, J. "Deconstruction and Law: Derrida, Levinas and Cornell," *Windsor Yearbook of Access to Justice* 25(1): 31–61, 2007.

________. "Desire and Language in Derrida's *Force of Law*," *Archiv fuer Rechts—Und Sozial Philosphie* 95(4): 449–473. 2009.

Vismann, C. *Files: Law and Media Technology*. Stanford, CA: Stanford University Press, 2008.

Voloshinov, V. *Marxism and the Philosophy of Language*. Cambridge, MA: Harvard University Press, 1986. Web version, transcribed by P. Lamplugh, accessed 6/4/2021, https://www.marxists.org/archive/voloshinov/1929/marxism-language.htm.

________. *Freudianism: A Marxist Critique*. New York: Academic Press, 1976.

Voruz, V. "Psychosis and the Law: Legal Responsibility and Law of Symbolisation," *International Journal for the Semiotics of Law* 13(2): 133–58, 2000.

Vygotsky, L. *Thought and Language*. Cambridge, MA: Massachusetts Institute of Technology Press, 1962.

________. "Thought and Word," in P. Adams (ed.), *Language in Thinking*, pp. 180–213. Middlesex, UK: Penguin Books, 1972.

Wacquant, L. "Deadly Symbiosis: When Ghetto and Prison Mesh," *Punishment and Society* 3(1): 95–134, 2001.

________. "From Slavery to Mass Incarceration," *New Left Review* 12: 41–60, 2002.

________. *Punishing the Poor.* Durham, NC: Duke University Press, 2009.

Wagner, A. "Mapping Legal Semiotics," *International Journal for the Semiotics of Law* 23(1): 77–82, 2009.

________. "The Rules of the Road, a Universal Semiotic," *International Journal for the Semiotics of Law* 19(3): 311–324, 2006.

Wagner, A. and J. Broekman (eds.). *Prospects of Legal Semiotics.* London: Springer, 2011.

Wagner, A., S. Muraskin, and W. Yu. "Emojis and Law: Contextualized Flexibility of Meaning in Cyber Communication," *Social Semiotics* 30(3): 396–414, 2020.

Wagner, A. and R. Sherwin (eds.). *Law, Culture and Visual Studies.* Springer, 2014.

Wagner, A., Summerfied, T., and B. Vanegas (eds.). *Contemporary Issues of Semiotics of Law*, pp. 9–10. Portland, Oregon: Hart Publishing, 2005.

Walby, S. "Against Epistemological Chasm: The Science Question Feminism Revisited," *Signs* 26(2): 485–509, 2001.

Walker, C. "Using Computer-Generated Animations and Simulation Evidence at Trial: What You Should Know," American Bar Association, January 11, 2008, accessed on 5/18/2021, https://www.americanbar.org/groups/litigation/committees/products-liability/practice/2018/using-computer-generated-animation-simulation-evidence-at-trial/.

Walker, H. "Justice and the Dark Arts: Law and Shamanism in Amazonia," *American Anthropologist* 117(1): 47–58, 2015.

Walsh, M. "'Which Way?' Difficult Options for Vulnerable Witnesses in Australian Aboriginal Land Claim and Native Title Cases," In M. Aldridge and J. Luchenbroers (eds.) Special issue: Language and Vulnerable Witnesses Across Legal Contexts, *Journal of English Linguistics* 36(3): 239–265, 2008.

Walton, D. *Abductive Reasoning.* Juscaloosa, Alabama: University of Alabama Press, 2005.

Walton, Paul (1975), "Max Weber's Sociology of Law: A Critique." *The Sociological Review* 23(5): 7–21, 1975.

Wattley, K. "Insight into California's Life Sentence," *Federal Sentencing Reporter* 25(4): 1–5, 2013.

Weaver, W. "Richard Rorty and the Radical Left," *Virginia Law Review* 78(3): 729–57, 1992.

Webb, J. "A Progressive Critique? The Contributions of Critical Legal Scholarship to a Marxist Theory of Law," *The Law Teacher* 19: 98–102, 1985.

Webb, T. "Tracing an Outline of Legal Complexity," *Ratio Juris* 27(4): 477–495, 2014.

________. "Critical Legal Studies and a Complexity Approach," in R. Geyer and P. Cairney (eds.) *Handbook on Complexity and Public Policy*, pp. 48–64. Cheltenham, UK: Edward Elgard, 2015.

Weber, M. *The Methodology of the Social Sciences.* Glencoe, IL: Free Press, 1949.

________. *The Protestant Ethic and the Spirit of Capitalism.* New York: Charles Scribner's Books, 1958.

________. *The Critique of Stammler.* New York: The Free Press, 1977.

________. *Economy and Society,* (vols. 1 and 2). G. Roth and C. Wittich (eds.), Los Angeles, CA: University of California Press, 1978.

Weber, M. *Max Weber: A Biography.* New York: John Wiley, 1975.

Webster, V. and F. Bourn. "The Use of Computer-Generated Animation and Simulation at Trial," *Defense Counsel Journal* 83(4): 439–459, 2016.

Weeden, D. "In *Fisher v. University of Texas* Derrick Bell's Interest Convergence Theory is on a Collision Course with the Viewpoint Diversity Rationale in Higher Education," *Utah on Law: The Utah Law Review Online Supplement* 1(2): 101–119, 2020, accessed on 3/31/2021, https://dc.law.utah.edu/cgi/viewcontent.cgi?article=1027&context=onlaw.

Weheliye, A. *Habeas Viscus: Racializing Assemblages, Biopolitics, and Black Feminist Theories of the Human.* Durham, NC: Duke University Press, 2014.

Weiyi, C., A. Burch, and J. Patel. "Swelling Anti-Asian Violence: Who is Being Attacked Where," *New York Times,* April 3, 2021, accessed 4/7/2021, https://www.nytimes.com/interactive/2021/04/03/us/anti-asian-attacks.html?action=click&module=In%20Other%20News&pgtype=Homepage.

Weitzer, R. and C. Kubrin. "Misogyny in Rap Music," *Men and Masculinities* 12(1): 3–29, 2009.

Wells, C. "Langdell and the Invention of Legal Doctrine," *Buffalo Law Review* 58(3): 551–618, 2010.

Wendt, Alexander. *Quantum Mind and Social Science.* Cambridge: Cambridge University Press, 2015.

Wu, J. and R. Chen. "Metaphors Ubiquitous in Computer and Internet Terminologies," *Journal of Arts and Humanities* 2(10): 64–78, 2013.

Werner, W. "The Unnamed Third," *International Journal for the Semiotics of Law* 12(3): 309–31, 1999.

West, C. "Critical Legal Studies: A Liberal Critic," *Yale Law Journal* 97(5): 757–776, 1988.

West, R. "Feminism, Critical Social Theory and Law," *University of Chicago Legal Forum,* 59, 1989.

________. "Jurisprudence and Gender," in K. Bartlett and R. Kennedy (eds.), *Feminist Legal Theory,* pp. 201–234. Oxford: Westview Press, 1991.

________. "Women in the Legal Academy: A Brief History of Feminist Legal Theory," *Fordham Law Review* 87: 977–1003, 2018.

Westphal, M. "Derrida as a Natural Law Theorist," *International Philosophical Quarterly* 34: 250–267, 1994.

West, R. F. Haas, and C. Grant (eds.). *Research Handbook on Feminist Jurisprudence.* Edward Elgar Publication, 2019.

Wex Definition Team, "Demonstrative Evidence," Ithaca, NY: Legal Information Institute, 2020, accessed 9/5/2021, https://www.law.cornell.edu/wex/demonstrative_evidence.

Whalley, M. and C. Guzelian. *The Legal Risk Management Handbook.* UI: CPI Group, 2016.

"What is TribalCrit?," National Education Policy Center, November 26, 2020, accessed 4/4/2021, https://nepc.colorado.edu/sites/default/files/publications/Newsletter%20 tribalcrit.pdf.

"What is 'Rebellious Lawyering'?" Howard University Civil Rights Center, accessed on 5/3/2021, https://rebelliouslawyeringinstitute.org/what-is-rebellious-lawyering/.

Whisnant, R. "Our Blood: Andrea Dworkin on Race, Privilege, and Women's Common Condition," *Women's Studies International Forum* 58–76, 2016.

White, J.B. *Heracles' Bow,* Madison, WI: University of Wisconsin Press, 1985.

White, L. "Subordination, Rhetorical Survival Skills, and Sunday Shoes: Notes on the Hearing of Mrs. G.," *Buffalo Law Review* 38(1): 1–58, 1990.

White, R. "Environmental Crime and Problem-Solving Courts," *Crime, Law and Social Change* 59: 267–278, 2013.

White, R. and D. Heckenberg. *Green Criminology*. New York: Routledge, 2014.

Whitehead, J. "From Criticism to Critique: Preserving the Radical Potential of Critical Legal Studies Through a Re-examination of Frankfurt School Critical Theory," *Florida State University Law Review* 26(3): 701–741, 1999.

Whitney, G.E. "The Place of Thirdness in Legal Reasoning," in R. Kevelson (ed.), *Peirce and Law,* pp. 203–220. New York: Peter Lang, 1991.

________. "A Semiotic Model of Economic Theory," in R. Kevelson (ed.), *Law and the Human Sciences,* pp. 445–465. New York: Peter Lang, 1992.

________. "A Peircian Perspective on the Legal Philosophy of Justice Holmes," in R. Kevelson (ed.), *Flux, Complexity and Illusion,* pp. 407–429. New York: Peter Lang, 1993.

Whitt-Rothschild, J. "The Collectivist Organization: An Alternative to Rational-Bureaucratic Modes," *American Sociological Review* 44(4): 509–527, 1979.

Whorf, B. *Language, Thought, and Reality.* J. Carrol (ed.). New York: John Wiley and Sons, 1956.

Wicenti, D. "The Experience of Oppression and Price of Non-Conformity — A Brief Biography of Adam Podgoricki." *Studies in Eastern European Theory* 70(4): 61–81, 2018.

Wilden, A. *The Language of the Self: The Functions of Language in Psychoanalysis.* Baltimore, MD: The John Hopkins University Press, 1968.

Wilkinson, P. "The Potential of Functionalism for the Sociological Analysis of Law," in A. Podgorecki and C. Whelan (eds.), *Sociological Approaches to Law.* New York: St. Martin's Press, 1981.

Willey, A. "A World of Materialism: Postcolonial Feminist Science Studies and the New Natural," *Science, Technology and Human Values* 41(6): 991–1014, 2016.

Williams, M. "Microaggressions: Clarification, Evidence and Impact," *Perspectives on Psychological Science* 15(1): 3–26, 2020.

Williams, P. *The Alchemy of Race and Rights: Diary of a Law Professor.* Cambridge, MA: Harvard University Press, 1991.

Williams, R. "Taking Rights Aggressively: The Perils and Promises of Critical Legal Theory for People of Color," *Minnesota Journal of Law and Inequality* 5(1): 103–134, 1987.

Williams, C. and B. Arrigo. "Anarchaos and Order: On the Emergence of Social Justice," *Theoretical Criminology* 5(2): 223–252, 2001.

________. *Law, Psychology and Justice: Chaos Theory, and the New (Dis)Order.* Albany, NY: SUNY Press, 2002.

Williams, J. "Deconstructing Gender," in K. Bartlett and R. Kennedy (eds.) *Feminist Legal Theory.* Oxford: Westview Press, 95–123, 1991.

Williamson, J. *Decoding Advertisement: Ideology and Meaning in Advertising.* New York: Marion Boyars, 1987.

Williams, R. "Taking Rights Aggressively: The Perils and Promise of Critical Legal Theory for Peoples of Color," *Law and Inequality* 5: 103, 1987.

Williams, R. *Marxism and Literature.* New York: Oxford University Press, 1977.

Winant, T. "The Feminist Standpoint: A Matter of Language," *Hypatia* 2(1): 123–48, 1987.

Winch, P. "Understanding a Primitive Society," *American Philosophical Quarterly* 1: 307–24, 1964.

Wing, A.K. (ed.). *Global Critical Race Feminism.* New York: New York University Press, 2000.

________. (ed.). *Critical Race Feminism.* New York: New York University Press. 1997. Winner, T. G. "Prague Linguistic Circle and the Humanities," in R. Kevelson (ed.), *Law and the Human Sciences, Volume 3, Semiotics and the Human Sciences,* pp. 529–43. New York: Peter Lang, 1992.

Wittgenstein, L. *The Blue and Brown Books.* New York: Harper and Row, 1958.

Woermann, M. *Bridging Complexity and Post-Structuralism.* Berne, UK: Springer, 2016.

Wolff, K.H. (ed.). *Essays on Sociology and Philosophy by Emile Durkheim et al.* New York: Harper Torchbooks, 1964.

Wong, S. "Crime Clearance Rates in Canada Municipalities: A Test of Donald Black's Theory of Law," *International Journal of Law, Crime and Justice* 38: 17–36, 2010.

Woodcock, T. *Legal Habits: A Brief Sartorial History of Wig, Robe and Gown.* Singapore: Tien Wah Press, 2003.

Woolhander, J. "Toward a Foucauldian Legal Method," *University of Pittsburgh Law Review* 76: 131–151, 2014.

Worthington, A. "The Law of the Mother: An Essay on the Sexual Sinthome," *Psychodynamic Practice* 26(1): 68–74, 2020.

Wynter, S. "Beyond the World of Man: Glissant and the New Discourse of Antilles," *World Literature Today* 63(4): 637–648, 1989.

Young, J. *The Criminological Imagination.* New York: Polity, 2011.

Wright, E. "Thoroughly Postmodern Feminist Criticism," in T. Brennan (ed.), *Between Feminism and Psychoanalysis.* New York: Routledge, 141–152, 1989.

Yager, M. "E-Discover as Quantum Law: Clash of Cultures — What the Future Portends," *Richmond Journal of Law and Technology* 19: 10–22, 2011.

Yakin, H.S.M and T. Andreas. "The Semiotic Perspectives of Peirce and Saussure: A Brief Comparative Study," *Social and Behavioral Sciences* 155: 4–8, 2014.

Yet, S. and O. Monca. "Clothing Semiotics and Social Construction of Power Relations," *Social Semiotics* 19(2): 191–211, 2009.

Yovel, J. "Gay Science as Law: An Outline for Nietzschean Jurisprudence," in P. Goodrich and M. Valverde (eds.), pp. 23–48. *Nietzsche and Legal Theory*. London, UK: Routledge, 2005.

Young, E. *The Deleuze and Guattari Dictionary*. New York: Bloomsbury, 2013.

Young, T.R. "The ABC of Crime: Nonlinear and Fractal Forms of Crime," *The Critical Criminologist* 3(4): 3–4, 13–14, 1991.

________. "Chaos Theory and Human Agency: Humanist Sociology in a Postmodern Age," *Humanity and Society* 16(4): 441–60, 1992.

Zakin, E. "Psychoanalytic Feminism", *The Stanford Encyclopedia of Philosophy* (Summer 2011 Edition), Ed. N. Zalta (ed.), accessed on 7/13/2021, https://plato.stanford.edu/archives/sum2011/entries/feminism-psychoanalysis/.

Ziegert, K. "Adam Podgorecki's Theory of Law: The Invisible Factors of the Functioning of Law Made Visible," *Law and Society Review* 12: 151–180, 1977.

Zinn, M. and B. Thornton, "Theorizing Difference from Multiracial Feminism," *Feminist Studies* 22(2): 321–331, 1996.

Zirk-Sadowski, M., M. Golecki, and B. Wojciechowski (eds.). *Multicentrism as an Emerging Paradigm in Legal Theory*. London: Peter Lang, 2009.

Zizek, S. *The Sublime Object of Ideology*. New York: Verso, 1989.

________. "The Limits of the Semiotic Approach to Psychoanalysis," in R. Feldstein and H. Sussman (eds.), *Psychoanalysis And* … New York: Routledge, 1990.

Zohar, D. *The Quantum Self*. New York: Quill/William Morrow, 1990.

________. *The Quantum Society*. New York: Quill/William Morrow, 1995.

Cases Cited

Abdel-Ghani v. Target Corp., 686 F. 377 (2017)

AFSCME V. Washington, 578 F. Supp. 846 (1985)

Bostock v. Clayton, 590 U.S. (2020)

Bounds v. Smith, 430 U.S. 817 (1977)

Brown v. Board of Education, 347 U.S. 483 (1954)

Browne v. City University of New York, 419 F. Supp. 2d 315 (E.D.N.Y. 2005)

Burlington Industries, Inc v. Elerth, 524 U.S. 742 (1998)

California v. Bakke, 438 U.S. 265 (1978)

Coy v. Iowa, 487 U.S. 1012 (1988)

Daubert v. Merrell Dow Pharmaceuticals, Inc., 509 U.S. 589 (1993)

Delgamuukw v. British Columbia, 3 SCR 1010 (1997)

Dred Scott v. Sanford, 60 U.S. 393 (1857)

Faragher v. City of Boca Raton, 524 U.S. 775 (1998)

Fisher v. University of Texas at Austin, 579 U.S.136 (2016)

Grutter v. Bollinger, 539 U.S. 306 (2003)

Gratz v. Bollinger, 539 U.S. 244 (2003)

Griswold v. Connecticut, 381 U.S.475 (1965)

Harris v. Forklift Systems, Inc., 510 U.S. 17 (1993)

IntegrateNYC, Inc. v. State of New York, filed March 3, 2021, New York County Clerk, 3/9/2021
Korematsu v. U.S., 323 U.S. 214 (1944)
Kumho Tire Co. v. Carmichael, 526 U.S. 137 (1999)
Mabo v. Queensland (No 2), 175 CLR 1 (1992)
McCleskey v. Kemp, 481 U.S. 279 (1987)
McAuliffe PTO v. de Blasio, 364 F. Supp. 3d 253 (S.D.N.Y 2019)
Obergefell v. Hodges, 576 U.S. 644 (2015)
Oncale v. Sunflower Offshore Service, Inc., 523 U.S. 75 (1998)
Palsgraf v. Long Island Railroad Co., 248 N.Y. 339, 162 N.E. 99 (1928)
Plessy v. Ferguson, 163 U.S. 537 (1896)
Roe v. Wade, 410 U.S. 113 (1973)
Salim v. State of Uttarakhand, Writ Petition (PIL) No. 126 of 2014 (December 5, 2016, and March 20, 2017), High Court of Uttarakhand at https://www.elaw.org/salim-v-state-uttarakhand-writ-petition-pilno126-2014-december-5-2016-and-march-20-2017
Students for Fair Admissions v. President and Fellows of Harvard College, ED-MA-0002 1:14-cv-14176-DJC (Mass. 2019)
Tsilhqot'In Nation v. British Columbia, SCC 44, (2014)
Washington v. Gunther (1981)
United States v. Alexander, 471 F. 2d. 923, 957–65 (D.C. Cir. 1973) (Bazelon, C.J., dissenting)
United States v. Yates, 438 F.3d. 1307 (2006)
United States v. Jose Solis Jordan, 223 F. 3d. 676 (7th Cir. 2000)

Index

A

C

E

H

K

L

S

Y

Z